The
All England
Law Reports
Annual Review
1986

ENGLAND: Butterworth & Co (Publishers) Ltd
88 Kingsway, **London** WC2B 6AB and
61A North Castle Street, **Edinburgh** EH2 3LJ

AUSTRALIA: Butterworths Pty Ltd, **Sydney, Melbourne,
Brisbane, Adelaide, Perth, Canberra** and **Hobart**

CANADA: Butterworth & Co (Canada) Ltd, **Toronto** and **Vancouver**

NEW ZEALAND: Butterworths of New Zealand Ltd, **Wellington** and **Auckland**

SINGAPORE: Butterworth & Co (Asia) Pte Ltd, **Singapore**

SOUTH AFRICA: Butterworth & Co (Pty) Ltd, **Durban** and **Pretoria**

USA: Butterworth Legal Publishers, **St Paul**, Minnesota;
Seattle, Washington; **Boston**, Massachusetts; and
Austin, Texas
D & S Publishers, **Clearwater**, Florida

General Editor
JANE ALLEN, JP, MA

ISBN 0 406 87963 X

Printed in Great Britain by Thomson Litho Ltd, East Kilbride, Scotland

THE
ALL ENGLAND
LAW REPORTS
ANNUAL REVIEW
1986

London
BUTTERWORTHS
1987

Contributors

Administrative Law
Keith Davies, JP, MA, LLM
Barrister, Professor of Law,
University of Reading

Arbitration
J E Adams, LLB, FCIArb
Solicitor, Professor of Law,
Queen Mary College,
University of London

Commercial Law
N E Palmer, BCL, MA
Barrister, Professor of Law,
University of Essex

Company Law
D D Prentice, MA, LLB, JD
Barrister, Fellow of Pembroke College,
Oxford

Conflict of Laws
J G Collier, MA, LLB
Barrister, Fellow of Trinity Hall,
Cambridge

Consumer Law and
Contempt of Court
C J Miller, BA, LLM
Barrister, Professor of Law,
University of Warwick

Contract
Michael P Furmston, TD, BCL, MA, LLM
Barrister, Professor of Law,
University of Bristol

**Criminal Law, Criminal Procedure
and Sentencing**
G J Bennett, MA
Barrister, Lecturer in Law,
University of Leeds and
Brian Hogan, LLB
Barrister, Professor of Common Law,
University of Leeds

Employment Law
Ian Smith, MA, LLB
Barrister, Dean of the School of Law,
University of East Anglia

European Community Law
C J Greenwood, MA, LLB
Barrister, Fellow of Magdelene
College, Cambridge

Evidence and **Practice and Procedure**
Adrian A S Zuckerman, LLM, MA
Fellow of University College, Oxford

Extradition
Ian M Yeats, BCL, MA
Barrister, Lecturer in Law,
Queen Mary College,
University of London

Family Law
S Cretney, DCL, FBA
Solicitor, Professor of Law,
University of Bristol

Land Law and Trusts
P J Clarke, BCL, MA
Barrister, Fellow of Jesus College,
Oxford

Landlord and Tenant
Philip H Pettit, MA
Barrister, Professor of Equity,
University of Buckingham

Shipping
Robert P Grime, BA, BCL
Professor of Law,
University of Southampton

Solicitors
Brian Harvey, MA, LLM
Solicitor, Professor of Property Law,
University of Birmingham

Statute Law
F. Bennion, MA
Barrister, Research Associate of Oxford
Centre for Socio-Legal Studies

Succession
C H Sherrin, LLM, PHD
Barrister, Senior Lecturer in Law,
University of Bristol

Taxation
John Tiley, MA, BCL
Barrister, Fellow of Queen's College,
Cambridge

Tort
B A Hepple, MA, LLB
Barrister, Professor of English Law,
University College,
University of London

Town and Country Planning
Paul B Fairest, MA, LLM
Professor of Law,
University of Hull

Publishers' note

This is the fifth All England Law Report Annual Review and as in previous years it is designed as a companion to the All England Law Reports. A number of academic lawyers have been invited to contribute articles evaluating the decisions of the courts relevant to their particular speciality and reported in that series in 1986. Not all of the cases, of course, fall neatly into one or other of the categories of conventional legal classification. The authors have tried to avoid duplication in their discussion of cases and there are a number of cross-references to be found in the articles. Some cases, however, are examined in more than one article because different aspects are of importance in different contexts.

1986 saw the publication of another new specialist report series, Butterworths Trading Law Cases. Professor Miller has commented on some of the cases in his article on Consumer Law.

Cases from the 1986 All England Law Reports, Simon's Tax Cases, Butterworths Company Law Cases and Butterworths Trading Law Cases are printed in bold type in the Table of Cases. A bold page number indicates where discussion of the case is to be found.

This volume should be cited as All ER Rev 1986.

BUTTERWORTH LAW PUBLISHERS LTD

Contents

List of contributors   iv
Publishers' note   v
Table of cases   xv
Table of statutes   xxx
Abbreviations   xxxiv

Articles

Administration Law   1
    Availability of judicial review   1
    Legality of ministerial decisions   6
    Judicial review and immigration   9
    Judicial review and the Crown   10

Arbitration   11
    Reference to arbitration   11
    Appeals   12
    Interest   15
    Remission   15
    Transnational arbitration   16
    Right to cross-examine unrepresented party   17

Commercial Law   18
    Agency   18
    Bailments and personal property in general   21
    Banks and finance houses   27
    Carriers   38
    Copyright, patents, registered designs and trade marks   39
    Insurance   41
    Monopolies and mergers   43
    Sale of goods   44

Company Law   49
    Indemnity order as to costs   49
    The derivative action   50
    Preferential creditors   50
    Petition to wind up company being wound up voluntarily   51
    Class of shares   51
    Receivers   52
    Floating charge: automatic crystallisation   54
    Companies struck off the register   54
    Corporate opportunity   55
    Section 35 of the Companies Act 1985   56
    Winding up: debts due to a member   57
    Minority oppression: valuation of shares   57
    Minority oppression: basis on which the court's discretion
      exercised   58

Conflict of Laws 59
  Jurisdiction of the English courts: service out of the jurisdiction 59
  Jurisdiction: staying of actions and forum non conveniens 59
  Jurisdiction: restraining foreign proceedings 63
  Foreign arbitration award: recognition 64
  Contract: determination of the proper law 66
  Contract: Bretton Woods Agreement: exchange contract 67
  Movable property: foreign expropriatory laws 68
  Succession—intestate succession to immovable property 69

Consumer Law 71
  Small claims 71
  Third party provisions 72
  Extortionate credit bargains 73
  Merchantable quality and fitness for purpose 76
  Spare parts 77
  Lump sum contracts 78
  Exemption clauses and lost photographs 78
  Product liability 79

Contempt of Court 80
  Contempt and libel proceedings 80
  Substituted orders and civil contempt 82
  Procedural requirements on breach of undertakings 84

Contract 85
  1 Terms of contract 85
  2 Undue influence, economic duress, inequality of bargaining power 88
  3 Agency 90
  4 Discharge 91
  5 Contributory negligence 91
  6 Remedies 92
  7 Illegality 94

Criminal Law, Criminal Procedure and Sentencing 100
  Criminal Law 100
  General Principles 100
    1 Duress 100
    2 Parties to crime 101
    3 Force in prevention of crime 101
    4 Attempts 102
    5 Conspiracy 105
  Offences against the person 106
    1 Intention and murder 106
    2 Damage to property endangering life 108
  Offences against property 109
    1 Theft 109
    2 Forgery 110
  Miscellaneous offences 110
    1 Controlled drugs 110
    2 Public order 111

Criminal Procedure   113
Bail   113
Crown Court   114
  1 Appeal   114
  2 Changes of appeal   115
  3 Judicial review   116
  4 Variation of sentence   117
Jury   117
Magistrates   118
  1 Bail   118
  2 Civil liability   118
  3 Road traffic   119
  4 Service of Documents   119
  5 Summary trial   119
  6 Legal aid   120
Compensation   121
Sentencing   121
Appeal to Crown Court   121
Bankruptcy, fines and imprisonment   122
Forfeiture   123
Guidance for sentences   123
Rape   123
Special reasons for not disqualifying   124

Employment Law   125
Contracts of employment—contents and remedies   125
Contracts of employment—frustration by illness or imprison-
  ment   126
Continuity of employment—irregular employment   127
Continuity of employment—transfer of undertaking   128
Unfair dismissal—the relevance of internal procedures 129
Unfair dismissal—questions of fact and law   131
Sex discrimination—excluded employments   132
Sex discrimination—the EEC dimension   133
Trade union law—the problem of divorce   134
Postscript—the continuing story   135

European Community Law   136
Community legal order   136
Directives: direct effect   136
Judicial review: principal of proportionality   138
National remedies for violations of community law: competition 139
Free movement of goods   139
Restrictions imposed on grounds of public morality   139
Common commercial policy: oil exports to Israel   141
Sex discrimination   143
Retirement and pensions   143
Justification for discrimination: police officers   145
Social security: invalid care allowance   147

Evidence   148
The burden of proof in criminal cases   148
Proof of non-intoxication   151

Section 1 (f) (ii) of the Criminal Evidence Act 1898   153
Corroboration   158
Legal professional privilege   160
Public interest immunity   162

Extradition—note   165

Family Law   167
   The clean break—when does final mean final?   167
   A clean break on variation?   168
   Great expectations?   170
   The family versus the creditors   171
   Divorce and the Revenue   172
   Property—the family outside marriage   173
   Occupation rights   175
   Relevance of children's interests   176
   Children—adoption and custodianship   176
   The adoption agency's role   177
   When does a parent lose the right to retrieve his child? 177
   Custodianship or adoption?   178
   A father's rights   178
   Proof of parentage   179

Land Law and Trusts   181
    1 The wife who occupies unregistered land   181
    2 The wife and the husband's creditors   184
    3 Trustees for sale and the rights of occupiers   186
    4 The sanctity of a declared trust   190
    5 The informally created interest of the contributing cohabitant   192
    6 Tenancies in common and business leases   195
    7 Licences   196
    8 Easements   197
    9 Mortgages   199
   10 Contract and conveyance   199
   11 Land Charges Act; cautions under the Land Registration Act   201
   12 Charity   202
   13 Variation of trusts   204
   14 Perpetuities   205

Landlord and Tenant   207
   Common law   207
   Rent review clauses   213
   Business tenancies under Part II of the Landlord and the Tenant
      Act   217
   Residential tenancies   219
   Agricultural holdings   220
   Leasehold enfranchisement   221
   Local authority housing—tenant's right to buy   223

Practice and Procedure   225
   Anton Piller orders, Mareva injunctions and related relief   225
   Conclusion   231

Service outside the jurisdiction   232
Deemed service   233
Dispensing with service   237
Discovery   238
Judgment   239
Costs   241
Country court small claims arbitration   244

Shipping   247
  1 Maritime claims in Reading   247
  2 Wreck, salvage, abandonment and droits of Admiralty   249
  3 Consignees against carriers in tort: The *Aliakmon* in the House
    of Lords   252
  4 Charterer's indemnities   255
  5 Limitation, employment and multi–companies   256

Solicitors   259
Introduction   259
Right of audience in the High Court—*Abse v Smith*   259
Littaur v Steggles Palmer (a firm)   266

Statute Law   268
Introductory   268
Mandatory and directory requirements   268
The offence of contempt of Statute   269
Dynamic processing of legislation   271
Delegated legislation: parliamentary control of   271
Delegated legislation: doctrine of ultra vires   271
Finding of implications (legitimacy of)   272
Rules of interpretation laid down by statute   272
Principles of interpretation derived from legal policy: the nature
  of legal policy   274
Presumption that ancillary rules of law apply   275
Need for updating construction   275
Construction of Act or other instruments as a whole   275
Interpretation of broad terms   276
Textual amendment   276
Amendment of Act by delegated legislation   277
Generalia specialibus non derogant   277
Retrospective operation: general presumption against   277
Application of Act: foreigners and foreign matters within the
  territory   278
Application of Act: foreigners and foreign matters outside the
  territory   279
Application of Act: Briton and British matters outside the
  territory   280
Enacting history: amendments to Bill   280
Enacting history: to ascertain the mischief   280
Post-enacting history: delegated legislation made under Act   280
Post-enacting history: later Acts   281
Principle against doubtful penalisation: physical restraint of the
  person   281

Nature of purposive construction   281
Judicial acceptance of legislator's purpose   282
Construction against 'absurdity': avoiding an anomolus or
    illogical result   282
Evasion distinguished from avoidance   283
Implied application of decision-making rules of natural justice,
    etc   283
Implied application of rules of contract law   284
Implied application of rules of criminal law   284
Implied application of rules of jurisdiction, evidence and
    procedure   285
Reliance on illegality (allegans suam turpitudinem non est
    audiendus)   286
Hearing both sides (audi alteram partem)   286
Benefit from own wrong: nullus commodum capere potest de
    injuria sua propria   286
Agency: qui facit per alium facit per se   287
Ordinary meaning of words   287
Technical terms   288
Archaisms   288
Ejusdem generis principle   288
Expressio unius principle: words of extension   288
Implication where statutory condition only partly met   289

Succession   290
    Intestate succession   290
    Family provision   291

Taxation   293
    Furniss v Dawson   293
    EEC   295
    Employment income   296
    Business income   298
    Trusts   300
    Capital gains tax   300
    Corporations   303
    International   304
    VAT   305
    General   306
    Administration   307

Tort   309
    Negligence   309
        Economic loss   309
        Liability for acts of third parties   311
        Defective premises   313
        Wrongful birth   313
        Proof of medical negligence   314
    Nuisance   315
    Libel   315
    Damages for abuse of process   316

Vacarious liability 316
 Deceit 316
 Employer's liability for negligence of third party 317
Damages 318
 Exemplary or punitive damages 318
 Aggravated damages 319
 Damages for personal injuries and death 319
Town and Country Planning 321
 Injunctions in support of the planning process 321
 Demolition of listed buildings—mens rea 323

Table of Cases

A

A v Liverpool City Council [1981] 2 All ER 385 179
Abbott v The Queen [1976] 3 All ER 140 100
AB Marintrans v Comet Shipping Co [1985] 3 All ER 442 92
Abidin Daver, The [1984] 1 All ER 470 .... 59, 61
Abse v Smith [1986] 1 All ER 350 .... **264**
**Abu Dhabi Helicopters Ltd v International Aeradio plc [1986] 1 All ER
395** **234, 274**
**Aden Refinery Co Ltd v Ugland Management Co, 'The Ugland Obo One'
[1986] 3 All ER 737** 13, **277, 285**
Adoui and Cornauille v Belgian State [1982] ECR 1665 140
Aga Estate Agencies Ltd, Re [1986] BCLC 346 .... **54**
Aiden Shipping Co Ltd v Interbulk [1986] 2 All ER 409 .... **241, 272**
Aikman v White [1986] STC 1 .... **307**
Ainsbury v Millington [1986] 1 All ER 73 .... **175**
Albazero, The [1977] AC 774 .... 23, 26
Aliakmon, The. See Leigh & Sillaven Ltd v Aliakmon Shipping Co Ltd
Al Nahkel for Contracting and Trading Ltd v Lowe [1986] 1 All ER 729 .... **228**
Alphacell Ltd v Woodward [1972] AC 824 323
Alphafield Ltd v Barratt [1984] 3 All ER 795 128
Al Wahab, The. See Amin Rasheed Shipping Corpn v Kuwait Insurance Co
Amanuel v Alexandros Shipping Co [1986] 1 All ER 278 .... 59, **226, 233**
Amax International Ltd v Custodian Holdings Ltd (1986) 279 EG 759 214
American Home Assurance Co v Tjmond Properties Ltd [1986] BCLC 181 .. **56**
Amin Rasheed Shipping Corpn v Kuwait Insurance Co, The Al Wahab [1983] 2 All
ER 884 59
Amministrazione delle Finanze dello Stato v Simmenthal SpA [1978] ECR 629 138
Ampthill Peerage Case, The [1976] 2 All ER 411 167
Anderton v Ryan [1985] 2 All ER 355 103
Andrews v Partington (1791) 3 Bro CC 401 206
Anns v Merton London Borough [1977] 2 All ER 492 ....30, 253, 309
Antaios Cia Naviera SA v Salen Rederierna AB [1984] 3 All ER 229 12
Anton Piller KG v Manufacturing Processes [1976] 1 All ER 779 225
Aquila, The (1798) 1 Ch Rob 37 250
Armagas Ltd v Mundogas SA, The Ocean Frost [1985] 3 All ER 795, **[1986] 2 All
ER 385** 18, 20, 38, **90, 316**
Armory v Delamirie (1722) 1 Stra 505 252
Ashburton v Pape [1913] 2 Ch 469 160
Ashtiani v Kashi [1986] 2 All ER 970 .... **229, 238**
Aspin v Estill [1986] STC 323 .... **304**
Associated Provincial Picture Houses Ltd v Wednesbury Corpn [1947] 2 All ER
680 3
Association, The, and The Romney [1970] 2 Ll Rep 59 252
Aswan Engineering v Lupdine [1987] 1 All ER 135 77
Atlantic Star, The, Atlantic Star (owners) v Bona Spes (owners) [1973] 2 All
ER 175 .... 59, 61
Attfield v DJ Plant Hire [1986] 3 All ER 273 .... **199**
A-G v English [1982] 2 All ER 903 82
A-G v Lamplough (1878) 3 Ex D214 276
A-G v News Group Newspaper Ltd [1986] 2 All ER 833 .... **80**
A-G of the Bahamas v Royal Trust Co [1986] 3 All ER 423 .... **202**
A-G's Reference (No 1 of 1985) [1986] 2 All ER 219 .... **109, 273**
**Austin Rover Group Ltd v Crouch Butler Savage Associates [1986] 3 All ER
50** **235, 273**
Avon Finance Ltd v Bridger [1985] 2 All ER 281 .... 34, 36

B

Balogh v Crown Court at St Albans [1974] 3 All ER 283 84
Bank of Baroda v Panessar [1986] BCLC 497 .... **52**
Bank of England v Vagliano Bros [1891] AC 107 105
Bank of Tokyo Ltd v Karoon [1986] 3 All ER 468 .... **60, 64, 233**
Bankers Trust Co v Galadari [1986] 3 All ER 794 .... **240**
Barclays Bank Ltd v Quistclose Investments Ltd [1968] 3 All ER 651 203
Barder v Barder [1986] 2 All ER 918 .... **167**
Baron v Sunderland Corpn [1966] 1 All ER 349 12
Barrell Enterprises, Re [1972] 3 All ER 631 11
Bartlett v Barclays Bank Trust Co Ltd [1980] 2 All ER 92 243
Basildon DC v JE Lesser (Properties) Ltd [1985] 1 All ER 20 92
Bastow (dec'd) v Cox (1847) 11 QB 122 213
Bayer AG v Winter [1986] 1 All ER 733 .... **227**
Bayer AG v Winter (No 2) [1986] 2 All ER 43 .... **228**
Bayer AG v Winter [1986] FSR 357 229
Baylis v Gregory [1986] 1 All ER 289 .... **294, 307**
Bedford Insce Co Ltd v Instituto De Resseguros Do Brasil [1984] 3 All ER 766 94
Bedson v Bedson [1965] 3 All ER 307 .... 190, 191
Beets-Proper v F Van Lanschot Bankiers NV [1986] ICR 706 .... 133, 138
Belvoir Finance Co Ltd v Stapleton [1970] 3 All ER 664 30
**Ben Shipping Co (Pte) Ltd v An Bord Bainne, The C Joyce [1986] 2 All
    ER 177** **255**
Benarty, The [1983] 1 Lloyd's Rep 361 233
Bernard v Josephs [1982] 3 All ER 162 .... 190, 191, 192
Bernstein v Pamsons Motors (Golders Green) Ltd (1986) Times, 25 Oct 77
Bilka-Kaufhaus GmbH v Weber von Hartz [1986] 2 CMLR 701 145
Binions v Evans [1972] 2 All ER 70 190
Bird v Syme-Thompson [1978] 3 All ER 1027 182
Blacklocks v JB Developments (Godalming) Ltd [1981] 3 All ER 392 .... 188, 189
Blane SS v Minister of Transport [1951] 2 KB 965 250
Board of Inland Revenue v Suite [1986] 2 All ER 577 .... **298**
Bolton v Mahadeva [1972] 2 All ER 1322 78
Bondina v Rollaway Shower Blinds Ltd [1986] 1 All ER 564 .... **27**
Bonnard v Perryman [1891] 2 Ch 269 .... 80, 81
Boston Corpn v Fenwick and Co (1923) 28 Comm Cas 367 250
Bowen-Jones v Bowen-Jones [1986] 3 All ER 163 .... **243**
Bradley v H Newsom Sons and Co [1919] AC 16 251
Bray v Best [1986] STC 96 .... **297**
Brembridge v Latimer (1864) 4 New Rep 285 315
Briamore Manufacturing Ltd, Re [1986] 3 All ER 132 .... **162**
Brightlife Ltd, Re [1986] BCLC 418, [1986] 3 All ER 673 .... **53, 274**
Bristol and West Building Society v Henning [1985] 2 All ER 606 183
Bristow v City Petroleum Ltd [1985] 3 All ER 463 135
British Airways Board v Laker Airways Ltd [1984] 3 All ER 39 63
**British Gas Corpn v Universities' Superannuation Scheme Ltd [1986] 1 All ER
    978** **213**
**British Leyland Motor Corpn Ltd v Armstrong Patents Co Ltd [1986] 1 All ER
    850** **40, 275, 280**
British Museum (Trustees) v A-G [1984] 1 All ER 337 204
British Nylon Spinners Ltd v Imperial Chemical Industries Ltd [1952] 2 All ER 780 .. 64
British Transport Commission v Gourley [1955] 3 All ER 796 307
Brittain v Gibbs [1986] STC 418 .... **308**
Brodies Trustees v IRC (1933) 17 TC 432 300
Brooks v Richardson [1986] 1 All ER 952 .... **203**
Brumby v Milner [1976] STC 534 297
Brutus v Cozens [1972] 2 All ER 1297 111
Bryanston Leasings v Principality Finance [1977] RTR 45 24
Buchanan (Peter) Ltd and Macharg v McVey [1955] AC 516 69
Bull v Bull [1955] 1 QB 234 189

Bulk Oil (Zug) AG v Sun International Ltd (No 2) [1986] 2 All ER 744 141
Burnley Nelson Rossendale and District Textile Workers' Union v
   Amalgamated Textile Workers' Union [1986] 1 All ER 885 134
Burns v Burns [1984] 1 All ER 244 .... 173, 192, 194
Burton v British Railways Board [1982] 3 All ER 537 .... 133, 145
Butler v Egg Board (1966) 114 CLR 185 24
Bye v Coren [1986] STC 393 307

C

C Joyce, The. *See* Ben Shipping Co (Pte) Ltd v An Bord Bainne
C (a minor), Re (1986) 1 FLR 643 177
Calcraft v Guest [1898] 1 QB 759 160
Calgary and Edmonton Land Co Ltd v Dobinson [1974] 1 All ER 484 201
Canadian Aero Services Ltd v O'Malley (1973) 40 DLR (3d) 371 55
Candlewood Navigation Corp v Mitsui OSK Lines, The Mineral Transporter, The
   Iberaki Maru [1985] 2 All ER 935 .... 25, 253, 309
Cardiothoracic Institute v Shrewdcrest Ltd [1986] 3 All ER 633 212
Carr-Saunders v Dick McNeil Associates Ltd [1986] 2 All ER 888 197
Castanho v Brown and Root (UK) Ltd [1981] 1 All ER 143 .... 60, 64
Cattle v Stockton Waterworks Co (1875) LR 10 QB 453 253
Caunce v Caunce [1969] 1 All ER 722 .... 182, 189
Celsteel Ltd v Alton House Holding Ltd [1985] 2 All ER 562 .... 198, 210
Celsteel Ltd v Alton House Holdings Ltd (No 2) [1986] 1 All ER 598 .... 201, 210, 242
Chabbra Corp Pte Ltd v Jag Shakti (owners) [1986] 1 All ER 480 22
Chandris v Isbrandsten Moller Co Inc [1950] 2 All ER 618 15
Chaney v Watkiss [1986] STC 89 301
Chapman v Smethurst [1909] 1 KB 927 28
Charge Card Services Ltd, Re [1986] BCLC 316, [1986] 3 All ER 289 .... 44, 50, 54,
                                                                            75, 91
Chatters v Burke [1986] 3 All ER 168 .... 119, 124
Chebaro v Chebaro [1986] 2 All ER 897 278
Cheny (dec'd) v Batten [1775–1802] All ER Rep 594 213
Chichester Diocesan Fund and Board of Finance v Simpson [1944] AC 341 202
Chief Constable of the North Wales Police v Evans [1982] 3 All ER 141 .... 1, 5
Chilton v Saga Holidays plc [1986] 1 All ER 841 .... 17, 71, 245, 285
Chilvers v Rayner [1984] 1 All ER 843 323
Cholmondley v IRC [1986] STC 384 300
Cinderby v Cinderby (1978) SJ 436 .... 281, 282
Citadel Insurance Co v Atlantic Union Insurance Co SA [1982] 1 Lloyd's Rep 543 . 67
City of London Building Society v Flegg [1986] 1 All ER 989 .... 174, 186, 195
Clark v MacLennan [1983] 1 All ER 416 314
Clayhope Properties Ltd v Evans [1986] 2 All ER 795 201
Coca-Cola Co's Applications, Re [1986] 2 All ER 274 39
Cockle's Will Trusts, Re [1967] 1 All ER 391 206
Coldunell Ltd v Gallon [1986] 1 All ER 429 .... 34, 36, 73, 89, 174, 199
Collard v Mining and Industrial Holdings Ltd [1986] STC 230 303
Collens (dec'd), Re, Royal Bank of Canada (London) Ltd v Krogh [1986] 1 All
   ER 611 .... 70, 279, 290
Colls v Home and Colonial Stores [1904] AC 179 197
Coltman v Bibby Tankers Ltd, The Derbyshire [1986] 2 All ER 65 .... 282, 317
Columbia Picture Industries v Robinson [1986] 3 All ER 338 .... 225, 230
Commissioner of Inland Revenue v Challenge Corpn Ltd [1986] STC 548 ... 295
Conegate Ltd v Customs and Excise Commissioners [1986] 2 All ER 688 ... 140
Company, Re a [1986] BCLC 362 58
Company, Re a [1986] BCLC 376 58
Company, Re a [1986] BCLC 391 58
Conway v Rimmer [1968] 1 All ER 874 .... 162, 163
Cook v Deeks [1916] AC 554 55

Cooke v Head [1972] 2 All ER 38   192
Coombes v Smith [1986] 1 WLR 808   194
Cottee v Douglas Seaton (Used Cars) Ltd [1972] 3 All ER 750   72
Council of Civil Service Unions v Minister for the Civil Service [1984] 3 All ER
    935   2
Coupe v Guyett [1973] 2 All ER 1058   72
Cowcher v Cowcher [1972] 1 All ER 943   190
Cumana Ltd, Re [1986] BCLC 430   57
Cumbrian Newspapers Group Ltd v Cumberland & Westmoreland Herald
    Newspaper & Printing Co Ltd [1986] BCLC 286, [1986] 2 All ER 816   51
Cunningham v Harrison [1973] QB 942   319
Customs and Excise Comrs v Apple and Pear Development Council [1986]
    STC 192   295
Customs and Excise Comrs v Dearwood Ltd [1986] STC 327   305
Customs and Excise Comrs v International Language Centres Ltd [1986] STC
    279   305
Customs and Excise Comrs v J Boardmans (1980) Ltd [1986] STC 10   304
Cutsforth and Mansfield Inns Ltd [1986] 1 All ER 577   139

D

D v Meah [1986] 1 All ER 935   319
Dallal v Bank Mellat [1986] 1 All ER 239 .... 16, 64, 66
Datastream International Ltd v Oakeep Ltd [1986] 1 All ER 966   213
Davie v New Merton Board Mills Ltd [1959] 1 All ER 346   257
Davies v Davies [1986] FLR 497   171
Davies v Summer [1984] 3 All ER 831   72
Davies v Directloans Ltd [1986] 2 All ER 787 .... 74, 199, 275
Davies v Presbyterian Church of Wales [1986] 1 All ER 705   131
Daymond v South West Water Authority [1976] AC 609   271
Deeley's Settlement, Re [1973] 3 All ER 1127   206
de Lasala v de Lasala [1979] 2 All ER 1146   168
Devis (W) & Sons Ltd v Atkins [1977] 3 All ER 40   130
Dews v National Coal Board [1986] 2 All ER 769   320
DPP v Hester [1972] 3 All ER 1056   158
DPP v Kilbourne [1973] 1 All ER 440 .... 158, 159
Davis Contractors Ltd v Fareham Urban District Council [1956] 2 All ER 145   126
Dawson Line Ltd v AG Adler fur Cemische Industrie of Berlin [1931] All ER Rep .   255
Digital Equipment Corpn v Darkrest Ltd [1984] Ch 512   316
DPP for Northern Ireland v Lynch [1975] 1 All ER 913   100
Donnelly v Williamson [1982] STC 88   296
Dowse v Government of Sweden [1983] 2 All ER 123   165
Drake v Chief Adjudication Officer [1986] 3 All ER 65   147
Drew v Drew and Leburn (1855) 2 Macq 1   17
Drummond's Settlement Re [1986] 3 All ER 45   205
Dutta v Westcott [1986] 3 All ER 381 .... 117, 121
Dyce v Lady James Hay (1852) 1 Macq 305   197

E

Eades, Re [1920] 2 Ch 353   202
Eastglen International Corpn v Monpare (1986) 136 NLJ 1087, (1987) 137 NLJ 56 ..   231
Ebrahimi v Westbourne Galleries Ltd [1973] AC 360   58
Edmunds v Lloyd Italico e L'Ancona Cia Di Assicuarazioni e
    Riassicuranzionc SpA [1986] 2 All ER 249   239
Edwards v Bairstow [1956] AC 14   131
Eley v Positive Government Life Assurance Co Ltd (1875) 1 Ex D 20   51
EMI Records Ltd v Spillane [1986] 2 All ER 1016   306
EMI Records Ltd v Wallace Ltd [1982] 2 All ER 980   243
Enfield London Borough Council v McKeon [1986] 2 All ER 730   223

Engineers' and Managers' Assoc v Advisory Conciliation and Arbitration Service
(No 1) (1979) 3 All ER 223 261
Essex County Council v T (1986) Times, 15 Mar 176
Etlin (HB) Co Ltd v Asselstyne (1962) 34 DLR (2d) 191 28
Eves v Eves [1975] 3 All ER 768 .... 192, 193, 194
Eyre v Measday [1986] 1 All ER 488 .... 85, 313

F

Faccenda Chicken Ltd v Fowler [1986] 1 All ER 617 .... 98, 135
Falke v Scottish Imperial Insurance Co (1886) 34 Ch D 234 247
Fargro v Godfrey [1986] BCLC 370, [1986] 2 All ER 279 50
Featherstone v Staples [1986] 2 All ER 461 .... 220, 273
Felixstowe JJ, ex p Leigh [1987] 1 All ER 551 80
Fidelitas Shipping Co Ltd v v/o Exportchleb [1965] 2 All ER 4 12
Field v Barkworth [1986] 1 All ER 362 208
Finger's Will Trusts, Re [1971] 3 All ER 1051 203
Finlayson v James [1986] BTLC 163 78
First National Securities v Hegerty [1984] 1 All ER 139 184
Fitzgerald v Hall Russell & Co Ltd [1969] 3 All ER 1140 128
Flack v Kodak Ltd [1986] 2 All ER 1003 128
Food Corporation of India v Marastro Cia Naviera SA, 'The Trade Fortitude'
[1986] 3 All ER 500 15
Ford v Falcone [1971] 2 All ER 1138 276
Ford v Warwickshire CC [1983] 1 All ER 753 128
Forestal Mimosa Ltd v Oriental Credit Ltd [1986] 2 All ER 400 33
Forsikringsaktieselskapet Vesta v Butcher [1986] 2 All ER 488 .... 66, 91
Foster v Tyne and Wear CC [1986] 1 All ER 567 320
Frost v Feltham [1981] STC 115 301
Furniss v Dawson [1984] 1 All ER 530 293

G

GKN Centrax Gears Ltd v Matbro Ltd [1976] 2 Lloyd's Rep 555 16
GR, Re (1985) FLR 643 177
Gammon (Hong Kong) Ltd v A–G of Hong Kong [1984] 2 All ER 503 323
Gaskin v Liverpool City Council [1980] 1 WLR 1549 162
Gent (L) & Sons v Eastman Machine Co Ltd [1986] BTLC 17 77
Gidlow-Jackson v Middlegate Properties Ltd [1974] 1 All ER 830 222
Giles (CH) & Co Ltd v Maurice [1972] 1 All ER 960 93
Gissing v Gissing [1971] AC 886 .... 173, 195
Gniezno, The [1967] 2 All ER 738 234
Goad v AUEW (No 3) [1973] ICR 108 84
Goddard v Nationwide Building Society [1986] 3 All ER 264 160
Gomba Holdings v Homan [1986] BCLC 331 53
Goodman v Boycott (1826) 2 B & S 1 26
Goodman v Gallant [1986] 1 All ER 311 .... 174, 189, 190, 191
Goring, The, [1986] 1 All ER 475 247
Government of Denmark v Nielsen [1984] 2 All ER 81 166
Government of India, Ministry of Finance (Revenue Division) v Taylor [1955] 1 All
ER 292 69
Granger v Hill (1838) 4 Bing NC 212 316
Grant v Edwards [1986] 2 All ER 426 .... 173, 192, 194, 195
Greasley v Cooke [1980] 3 All ER 710 194
Greenwood v Turner [1891] 2 Ch 114 200
Grunwick Processing Laboratories Ltd v Customs and Excise Comrs [1986]
STC 441 305
Gunning v Mirror Group Newspapers Ltd [1986] 1 All ER 385 132

H

H, Re; W, Re (1982) 4 FLR 612 .... 176, 177, 178
Hagee (London) Ltd v A B Erikson & Larson [1975] 3 All ER 234   213
Hall v Brooklands Auto Racing Club [1933] 1 KB 205   20
Hall v Cotton [1986] 3 All ER 332 ....   **287**
Hamblett v Godfrey [1986] 2 All ER 513 ....   **296**
Hamlyn & Co v Talisker Distillery [1894] AC 202   66
Hare v Murphy Brothers Ltd [1974] 3 All ER 940   127
Harman v Flexible Lamps Ltd [1980] IRLR 418   126
Harman v Glencross [1984] 2 All ER 577, **[1986] 1 All ER 545** **168, 171, 184, 240**
Hart v Emelkirk Ltd [1983] 3 All ER 15   201
Harvest Lane Motor Bodies Ltd, Re [1968] 2 All ER 1012   55
Hawker v Tomalin (1969) 20 P & CR 550   198
Hewitt v Lewis [1986] 1 All ER 927 ....   **219, 278**
Hine v Hine [1962] 3 All ER 345   191
Hipwell's Settlement, Re [1945] 2 All ER 476   205
Hochstrasser v Mayes [1959] 3 All ER 817   296
Hodgson v Hart District Council [1986] 1 All ER 400 .... **235, 274**
Hodgson v Marks [1970] 2 All ER 684   188
Holden v Chief Constable of Lancashire [1986] 3 All ER 836 ....   **318**
Holland v Geogehegan [1972] 3 All ER 333   296
Holliday, Re [1980] 1 All ER 385   185
Holliday (LB) & Co Ltd, Re [1986] BCLC 227 ....   **57**
Hong Kong Fir Shipping Co Ltd v Kawasaki Kisen Kaisha Ltd [1962] 2 QB 26   287
Honig v Sarsfield [1986] STC 246 ....   **307**
Haughton v Olau Line (UK) Ltd [1986] 2 All ER 47 ....   **132**
Housecroft v Burnett [1986] 1 All ER 332 ....   **319**
Howson v Buxton [1928] All ER Rep 434   220
Hughes v McConnell [1986] 1 All ER 268 ....   **152**
Hunt v Luck [1902] 1 Ch 428 ....   183, 188
Hurd v Jones (HM Inspector of Taxes) [1986] STC 127 ....   **295**
Hussain v Hussain [1986] 1 All ER 961 ....   **84**

I

Imperial Furniture Pty Ltd v Automatic Fire Sprinkler Pty Ltd (1967) 1 NSWLR
    29   48
IRC v Berrill [1981] STC 784   300
IRC v Brackett [1986] STC 521 ....   **304**
IRC v Burmah Oil [1982] STC 30   303
IRC v Mills [1974] 1 All ER 722 ....   172, 294
IRC v Mobil North Sea Ltd [1986] STC 45 ....   **301**
**International Drilling Fluids Ltd v Louisville Investments (Uxbridge) Ltd
    [1986] 1 All ER 321** **207**
International Factors Ltd v Rodriguez [1979] 1 All ER 17 ....   23, 24
**Investors in Industry Commercial Properties Ltd v South Bedforshire DC
    (Ellison & Partners, third parties) [1986] 1 All ER 787** **313**
Irene's Success, The. *See* Schiffort und Kohlen GmbH v Chelsea Maritime Ltd.
Island Export Finance v Umunna [1986] BCLC 460 ....   **55**

J

Jackson v Jackson (1804) 7 Ves 591   196
Jacobs v Chauduri [1968] 2 All ER 124   220
Jag Shakti, The. *See* Chabbra Corp Pte Ltd v Jag Shakti (owners)
James' Trade Marks, Re, James v Soulby (1886) 33 Ch D 392   40
Jarrold v Boustead [1964] 3 All ER 76   296
Jaybird Group Ltd v Greenwood [1986] BCLC 319 ....   **49**

Jayesena v R [1970] 1 All ER 219 149
John v James [1986] STC 352 .... **306**
John v Matthews [1970] 2 All ER 643 73
Johnston v Chief Constable of the Royal Ulster Constabulary [1986] 3 All ER
135 .... **133, 137, 145**
Johnston v Duke of Westminster [1986] 2 All ER 613 .... **221**
Johnson v Moreton [1978] 3 All ER 37 221
Jones v Leeming [1930] AC 415 298
Junior Books Ltd v Veitchi Co Ltd [1982] 3 All ER 201 309

K

Kaltenbach v MacKenzie (1878) LR 3 CP 467 249
Kerr v Morris [1986] 3 All ER 217 .... **97**
Ketley (A) Ltd v Scott [1981] ICR 241 199
Keys v Boulter (No 2) [1972] 2 All ER 303 134
Khan v First East Brixton Comrs [1986] STC 331 .... **307**
Khashoggi v IPC Magazines Ltd [1986] 3 All ER 577 .... **316**
King v Liverpool City Council [1986] 3 All ER 544 .... **312**
Kingsnorth Trust Ltd v Bell [1986] 1 All ER 423 .... 34, 174, **186**
Kingsnorth Trust Ltd v Tizard [1986] 2 All ER 54 ..... 88, 174, 181, 182, 183, 190, **195**
Kingston v British Railways Board [1984] IRLR 147 127
Kirby v Thorn EMI plc [1986] STC 200 .... **302**
Knocker v Youle [1986] 2 All ER 914 .... 204, **288**
Kralj v McGrath [1986] 1 All ER 54 .... **319**
Konstantinidis v World Tanker Corp Inc, The World Harmony [1965] 2 All
ER 139 253

L

Laconia, The (1863) 2 Moo PCCNS 161 65
Lane v Esdaile [1891] AC 210 13
Layton v Martin [1986] FLR 227 174
Leake v Bruzzi [1974] 2 All ER 1196 192
Lear v Leek General Comrs [1986] STC 542 .... **307**
Leek and Moorlands Building Society v Clark [1952] 2 All ER 492 220
Leigh and Sillavan Ltd v Aliakmon Shipping Co Ltd, The Aliakmon [1983]
1 Ll Rep 203, [1985] 2 All ER 44, **[1986] 2 All ER 145** 23, 24, 25, 253, **309**
Le Marchant v Le Marchant [1977] 3 All ER 610 170
Lill Holdings Ltd v White [1979] RTR 120 73
Lim Foo Yong Sdn Bhd v Comptroller General of Inland Revenue [1986] STC
255 .... **298**
Linden v Dept of Health and Social Security [1986] 1 All ER 691 .... **217**
Linnett v Coles [1986] 3 All ER 652 .... 82, 83, 271, 281, **282**
Livesey v Jenkins [1985] 1 All ER 106 .... 167, 168
Llewellin v Llewellin [1985] CA Transcript 640 185
Lloyd v Grace-Smith & Co [1911–13] All ER Rep 51 21
Lloyd v Mostyn (1842) 10 M & W 478 160
Lloyd v Sadler [1978] 2 All ER 529 220
London Engineering and Iron Shipbuilding Co Ltd v Cowan (1867) 16 LT 573 261
Longrigg Burrough & Trounsom v Smith (1979) 251 EG 847 213
Lowerstoft Traffic Services Ltd, Re [1986] BCLC 81 .... **51**
Lowrie, Re [1981] 3 All ER 353 185
Lucas Industries plc v Welsh Development Agency [1986] 2 All ER 858 ..... **11, 12**
Lucas-Box v News Group Newspapers Ltd [1986] 1 All ER 177 .... **316**
Lusitania, The. See Pierce v Bemis
Lyster v Dolland (1792) 1 Ves Jun 431 196
Lyus v Prowse Developments [1982] 2 All ER 953 194

M

McDermid v Nash Dredging and Reclamation Co Ltd [1986] 2 All ER 676 .. 256, 317
McIlraith v Grady [1967] 3 All ER 625 83
McIlraith v Grady [1968] 1 QB 468 281
MacKinlay v Arthur Young McClelland Moores & Co [1986] STC 491 299
MacKinnon v Donaldson Lufkin & Jenrette Securities Corpn [1986] 1 All ER
  653 .... 238, 279, 280
MacShannon v Rockware Glass Ltd [1978] 1 All ER 625 .... 59, 61
MFI Properties Ltd v BICC Group Pension Trust Ltd [1986] 1 All ER 974 ... 213
Mackey v Scottish Widows Fund Life Assoc Society (1877) IR 11 Eq 541 198
Magnavox Electronics Co Ltd (in liq) v Hall [1986] STC 561 301
Maharaj v Chand [1986] 3 All ER 107 .... 175, 195, 196
Mahmoud and Ispahani, Re [1921] 2 KB 716 95
Maidstone BC v Mortimer [1980] 3 All ER 552 323
Malayan Credit Ltd v Jack Chia-MPH [1986] 1 All ER 711 195
Mancetter Development Ltd v Garmanson Ltd [1986] 1 All ER 449 209
Mancini v DPP [1941] 3 All ER 272 149
Manorlike Ltd v Le Vitas Travel Agency & Consultancy Services Ltd [1986]
  1 All ER 573 210
Manson v Duke of Westminster [1981] 2 All ER 40 222
Marfani & Co Ltd v Midland Bank Ltd [1968] 2 All ER 573 29
Mansouri v Singh [1986] 2 All ER 619 .... 67, 68, 97
Margarine Union GmbH v Cambay Prince Steamship Co Ltd, The Wear Breeze
  [1967] 3 All ER 775 .... 25, 254, 309
Marles v Philip Trant & Sons Ltd (No 2) [1954] 1 QB 29 286
Marshall v Southampton and South West Hampshire Area Health Authority
  (Teaching) [1986] 2 All ER 584 .... 133, 136, 143
Marson v Morton [1986] STC 463 298
Maskell v Ivory [1970] 1 All ER 488 200
Mason v Farbrother [1983] 2 All ER 1078 204
Masterton v Holden [1986] 3 All ER 39 111
Mauroux v Pereira [1972] 2 All ER 1085 59
Maxwell v Pressdram [1987] 1 All ER 656 80
Maynegrain Pty Ltd v Compafina Bank (1984) 58 AJLR 389 .... 24, 26
Meah v McCreamer (No 2) [1986] 1 All ER 943 319
Meah v Roberts [1978] 1 All ER 97 73
Mesher v Mesher [1980] 1 All ER 126 185
Messina v Petrococchino (1872) LR 4 PC 144 65
Metrolands Investment Ltd v JH Dewhurst Ltd [1986] 3 All ER 659 215
Michael v Michael [1986] 2 FLR 389 171
Midland Bank plc v Dobson [1986] 1 FLR 171 193
Midland Bank Ltd v Farmpride Hatcheries (1980) 260 EG 493 190
Midland Bank plc v Laker Airways [1986] 1 All ER 526 63
Millensted v Grosvenor House (Park Lane) Ltd [1937] 1 All ER 736 11
Miller (James) and Partners Ltd v Whitworth Street Estates (Manchester) Ltd [1970]
  1 All ER 796 65
Milne v Milne (1981) 2 FLR 286 170
Minton v Minton [1979] 1 All ER 79 .... 167, 170
Monarch Assurance Co Ltd v Special Commrs [1986] STC 311 301
Moncrieffe's Settlement Trusts Re [1962] 3 All ER 838 204
Montan, The. See Mutual Shipping Corp of New York v Bayshore Shipping Co of
  Monrovia
Moore v Hall (1878) 3 QBD 178 198
Moore v Thompson [1986] STC 170 300
Morris v CW Martin and Sons Ltd [1965] 2 All ER 725 .... 20, 21, 26
Muduroglu v TC Ziraat Bankasi [1986] 3 All ER 682 .... 60, 62, 233
Multiservice Bookbinding Ltd v Marden [1978] 2 All ER 489 199
Muschinski v Dodds (1986) 62 ALR 429 195
Mutual Shipping Corp of New York v Byshore Shipping Co of Monrovia, The
  Montan [1985] 1 All ER 520 15

N

Nacap Ltd v Moffatt Ltd 1986 SLT 326 27
Nanan v The State [1986] 3 All ER 248 .... **118**
NCB v Galley [1958] 1 All ER 91 126
National Provincial Bank Ltd v Ainsworth [1965] 2 All ER 472 .... 175, 188, 190
National Smokeless Fuels Ltd v IR Comrs [1986] STC 300 .... **295**
National Westminster Bank plc v Arthur Young McLelland Moores & Co (1984) 273
    EG 402 214
National Westminster Bank plc v Morgan [1985] 1 All ER 821 36
Navarro v Moregrand Ltd [1951] 2 TLR 674 .... 20, 317
Nea Tyhi, The, [1982] 1 Ll Rep 606 254
Neilson v Laugharne [1981] 1 All ER 829 163
Nethermere (St Neots) Ltd v Gardiner [1984] ICR 612 131
Nettleship v Weston [1971] 3 All ER 581 314
New Zealand Government Property Corpn v HM & S Ltd [1982] 1 All ER 624 ... 210
Newman v Keedwell (1977) 35 P & CR 393 221
Nicholson v Chapman (1793) 2 Hy Bl 254 247
Nimemia Maritime Corpn v Trav Schiffahrtsgessellschaft mbH & Co KG [1984] 1 All
    ER 398 231
Nippon Yusen Kaisha v Karageorgis [1975] 3 All ER 282 230
Niyazi Mehmet Uzun v Ramadan Ahmet (27 June 1986, unreported) 213
Norris v Southampton City Council [1982] IRLR 141 127
Northern Bank Ltd v Henry [1981] IR 1 183
Norway v Rowe (1812) 19 Ves 143 196
Norwich Pharmacal Co v Customs and Excise Comrs [1973] 2 All ER 943 238
Notcutt v Universal Equipment Co Ltd [1986] 3 All ER 582 .... **126, 284**
Nottinghamshire CC v Secretary of State for the Environment [1986] 1 All ER
    199 .... **271**

O

O'Brien v Benson's Hosiery Holdings Ltd [1979] STC 535 302
Ocean Frost, The. *See* Armagas Ltd v Mundagas SA
Oceanic v Evans (1934) 40 Comm Cas 108 250
Oinoussian Virtue, The. *See* Schiffahrtsagentur Hamburg Middle East Line GmbH v
    Virtue Shipping Corpn
O'Kelly v Trusthouse Forte plc [1983] 3 All ER 456 131
Olgeirsson v Kitching [1986] 1 All ER 746 .... **72**
O'Reilly v Mackman [1982] 3 All ER 1124 .... 1, 84
Ough v King [1969] 3 All ER 859 198

P

Paal Wilson & Co A/S v Partenreederei Hannah Blumenthal [1983] 1 All ER 34 ... 127
Palmer v Southend-on-Sea Borough Council [1984] 1 All ER 945 130
Palmer Marine Surveys Ltd, Re [1986] BCLC 106 .... **51**
Parker v British Airways Board [1982] 1 All ER 834 25
Parry v Cleaver [1969] 1 All ER 555 320
Pascoe v Turner [1979] 2 All ER 945 .... 190, 197
Passant v Jackson [1986] STC 164 .... **301**
Paterson Zonchonis & Co Ltd v Merfarken Packaging Ltd [1986] 3 All ER
    522 .... **310**
Peabody Donation Fund (Governors) v Sir Lindsay Parkinson [1984] 3 All ER 529 . 313
Peach v Commissioner of Police of the Metropolis [1986] 2 All ER 129 ..... 163, 289
Peacock v London Weekend Television [1985] CA Transcript 723 81
Peacock v Peacock [1984] 1 All ER 1069 173
Pearl Assurance plc v Shaw (1984) 274 EG 490 214
Pearlberg v May [1951] 1 All ER 1001 200
Pearlman v Keepers and Governors of Harrow School [1979] 1 All ER 365 4

Peart v Stewart [1983] 1 All ER 859   82
Penman v Parker [1986] 2 All ER 862 .... **119, 287**
Pennine Raceways v Kirklees Metroplitan Council [1982] 3 All ER 628   197
Perl (P) (Exporters) Ltd v Camden London BC [1983] 3 All ER 161   312
Pettit v Pettit [1969] 2 All ER 385 .... 173, 191, 192
**Pharmaceutical Society of Great Britain v Storkwain Ltd [1986] 2 All
     ER 635** **281**
**Phoenix General Insce Co of Greece SA v Halvanon Insce Co Ltd [1986] 1 All
     ER 908** **94, 286**
Pierce v Bemis, The Lusitania [1986] 1 All ER 1011 .... **249, 275, 280**
Pink v Lawrence (1978) 36 P & CR 98 .... 189, 191, 192
Pittalis v Sherefettin [1986] 2 All ER 227 .... **11, 239**
Platten v Brown [1986] STC 514 .... **298**
Plimmer v Wellington Corpn (1884) 9 App Cas 699   197
Pocock v Steel [1985] 1 All ER 434 .... 219, 278
Polly Peck (Holdings) plc v Trelford [1986] 2 All ER 84 .... **315**
Ponderosa International Development Inc v Pengap Securities (Bristol) Ltd [1986] 1
     EGLR 66   207
Pope v Great Eastern Rly (1866) CR 3 Eq 171   200
Portrafram Ltd, Re [1986] BCLC 376 .... **54**
Posner v Scott-Lewis [1986] 3 All ER 513 .... **93**
Powlson v Welbeck Securities Ltd [1986] STC 423 .... **302**
Practice Direction [1983] 2 All ER 679   294
Preston v IRC [1985] 2 All ER 327 .... 1, 2
Price v Hilditch [1930] 1 Ch 500   197
Priest v Priest (1980) 1 FLR 189   170
Priestley v Fowler (1837) 3 M and W 1   257
Pritchard v Arundale [1971] 3 All ER 1011   296
Puhlhofer v Hillingdon LBC [1986] 1 All ER 467 .... **276**

                                         R

R v Akan [1973] QB 491   275
R v Ayres [1984] 1 All ER 619   105
R v Billam [1986] 1 All ER 985 .... **123**
R v Birchall (1986) 82 Cr App R 208   159
R v Brentford General Comrs, ex p Chan [1986] STC 65 .... **308**
R v Burke (1986) 82 Cr App R 156   157
R v Bury Magistrates, ex p N (a minor) [1986] 3 All ER 789 .... **121**
R v Central Criminal Court, ex p Raymond [1986] 2 All ER 379 .... **116**
R v Chief Constable of Merseyside, ex p Calveley [1986] 1 All ER 257 .... **1**
R v Cooke [1986] 2 All ER 985 .... **105**
R v Courtie [1984] 1 All ER 740   104
**R v Criminal Injuries Compensation Board, ex p Warner [1986] 2 All
     ER 478** **121**
R v Crown Court at Cardiff, ex p Jones [1973] 3 All ER 1027   116
R v Crown Court at Croydon, ex p Clair [1986] 2 All ER 716 .... **114**
R v Crown Court at Maidstone, ex p Gill [1987] 1 All ER 129   117
R v Cullum (1873) LR 2 CCR 28   109
**R v Customs and Excise Comrs, ex p Hedges & Butler Ltd [1986] 2 All
     ER 164** **271**
R v Delgado [1984] 1 All ER 449   111
R v Diggines, ex p Rahmani [1985] 1 All ER 1073   286
R v Donat (1986) 82 Cr App R 173   159
R v Doukas [1978] 1 All ER 1061   106
R v Ealing LBC, ex p McBain [1986] 1 All ER 13 .... **274**
R v Edwards [1974] 2 All ER 1085   148
R v Foster [1984] 2 All ER 679   115
R v Garner [1986] 1 All ER 78 .... **122**
R v Gateshead JJ, ex p Usher [1981] Crim LR 491   114

R v Governor of Brixton Prison, ex p Thompson [1911] 2 KB 82 165
R v Governor of Pentonville Prison, ex p Goets [1986] 2 All ER 630 .... **166**
R v Governor of Pentonville Prison, ex p Singh [1981] 3 All ER 23 165
R v Hallstrom, ex p W [1985] 3 All ER 775 4
R v Hancock and Shankland [1986] 1 All ER 641 .... **106**
R v Harbax Singh [1979] 1 All ER 524 113
R v Harrow JJ, ex p Osaseri [1985] 3 All ER 185 113
R v Henn and Darby [1980] 2 All ER 166 140
R v HM Inspector of Taxes, ex p Kissane [1986] 2 All ER 37 .... **308**
R v HM Inspector of Taxes, ex p Lansing Bagnall Ltd [1986] STC 117 ...... **303**
R v Herrod, ex p Leeds City District Council [1976] 1 All ER 273 5
R v Hillingdon London Borough, ex p Royco Homes Ltd [1974] 2 All ER 643 5
R v Holinshead [1985] 2 All ER 769 119
**R v Horseferry Road Magistrates' Court, ex p Independent Broadcasting
Authority [1986] 2 All ER 666** **268**
R v Howe [1986] 1 All ER 833 .... **100**
R v Hudson [1971] 2 All ER 244 100
R v Hunt [1986] 1 All ER 184, [1987] 1 All ER 1 .... **149**
R v Hussain [1969] 2 All ER 1117 104
R v Hyam [1974] 2 All ER 41 107
R v IRC, ex p Rothschild Holdings plc [1986] STC 410 .... **306**
**R v Inner London Education Authority, ex p Westminster City Council [1986]
1 All ER 19** **289**
**R v Intervention Board for Agricultural Produce, ex p ED & F Man (Sugar)
Ltd [1986] 2 All ER 115** **138**
R v Jenner [1983] 2 All ER 46 322
R v Kray (1969) 53 Cr App Rep 125 .... 82, 100
R v Maginnis [1986] 2 All ER 110 .... **110**
R v Maloney [1985] 1 All ER 1025 106
R v Martindale [1986] 3 All ER 25 .... **111**
R v Mavji [1986] STC 508 .... **306**
R v Medway [1976] 1 All ER 527 114
R v Mental Health Review Tribunal, ex p Pickering [1986] 1 All ER 99 ..... **283**
**R v The Monopolies and Mergers Commission and the Secretary of State for
Trade and Industry, ex p Argyll Group plc [1986] 2 All ER 257** **43**
R v Navvabi [1986] 3 All ER 102 .... **109**
R v Nedrick [1986] 3 All ER 1 .... **107**
R v Newham Juvenile Court ex p F (a minor) [1986] 3 All ER 17 .... **120**
R v Olaleye (1986) 82 Cr App R 337 159
R v Owen (1986) 83 Cr App R 100 157
R v Oxford JJ, ex p D [1986] 3 All ER 129 .... **179**
R v Plymouth JJ, ex p Hart [1986] 2 All ER 452 .... **115**
R v Plymouth JJ, ex p Whitton (1980) 71 Cr App R 322 115
R v Powell [1986] 1 All ER 193 .... **154, 157**
R v Preston Crown Court, ex p Fraser [1984] LR 624 116
R v Rahmoun (1986) 82 Cr App R 217 159
R v Rankine [1986] 2 All ER 566 .... **163**
R v Renouf [1986] 2 All ER 449 .... **102, 284**
R v Richards [1973] 3 All ER 1088 101
R v Rochdale JJ, ex p Allwork [1981] 3 All ER 434 115
R v Savundranayagam and Walker [1968] 3 All ER 439 123
**R v Secretary of State for the Environment, ex p Hillingdon LBC [1986] 1 All
ER 810** **273, 288**
**R v Secretary of State for the Home Dept, ex p Bugdaycay [1986] 1 All
ER 458** **9**
R v Secretary of State for the Home Dept, ex p Herbage [1986] 3 All ER 209: **10**
R v Secretary of State for the Home Dept, ex p Swati [1986] 1 All ER 717 ... **9, 283**
**R v Secretary of State for the Home Dept, ex p Thornton [1986] 2 All
ER 641** **275**
**R v Secretary of State for Social Services, ex p Assoc of Metropolitan
Authorities [1986] 1 All ER 164** **7, 272**

R v Secretary of State for Social Services, ex p Connolly [1986] 1 All ER 998: 282, 284
R v Shivpuri [1986] 2 All ER 334 103
R v Slater [1986] 3 All ER 786 123
R v Smith [1974] 1 All ER 651 116
R v Southend JJ, ex p Wood (1986) Times, 8 Mar 120
R v Special Comr, ex p RW Forsyth Ltd [1986] STC 565 305
R v Spencer [1985] 1 All ER 673, [1986] 2 All ER 928 .... 117, 158, 159
R v Steer [1986] 3 All ER 611 108
R v Stewart (1986) 83 Cr App R 327 158
R v Tobierre [1986] 1 All ER 346 110
R v Tonner [1985] 1 All ER 807 106
R v Tyson (1978) 68 Cr App R 314 113
R v Waltham Forest JJ, ex p Solanke [1986] 2 All ER 981 118
R v Watts [1983] 1 All ER 101 153
R v Wells Street Metropolitan Stipendiary Magistrates, ex p Westminster City
    Council [1986] 3 All ER 4 323
R v White [1910] 2 KB 124 108
Ralston, Re [1906] VLR 689 .... 70, 291
Ras Behari Lal v R [1933] All ER 723 118
Ratford v Northavon District Council [1986] BCLC 397, [1986] 3 All ER 193: 52
Rea, Re, Rea v Rea [1902] Ir 451 .... 70, 290, 291
Recher's Will Trusts, Re [1971] 3 All ER 401 203
Reed v Young [1986] STC 285 293
Rees v Secretary of State for the Home Dept [1986] 2 All ER 321 165
Regan & Blackburn Ltd v Rogers [1985] 2 All ER 180 201
Rhodian River, The [1984] 1 Lloyd's Rep 373 20
Richards v Richards [1983] 2 All ER 807 175
Richardson v Richardson (1978) 9 Fam Law 86 170
Roberts v Roberts [1986] 2 All ER 483 .... 170, 277
Roberts v Tate & Lyle Industries Ltd [1986] 2 All ER 602 .... 133, 144
Robinson v Robinson (1976) 241 EG 153 191
Robinson v Robinson [1982] 2 All ER 699 168
Rogers v Parish (Scarborough) Ltd (1986) Times, 8 Nov 77
Rookes v Barnard [1964] AC 1129 318
Royal Bank of Canada (London) Ltd v Krogh [1986] 1 All ER 611 ...... 70, 290
Royle v Trafford Borough Council [1984] IRLR 184 126
Rumasa SA v Multinvest (UK) Ltd [1985] 2 All ER 208 68
Runnymede BC v Ball [1986] 1 All ER 629 321
Rustenberg Platinum Mines Ltd v South African Airways [1979] 1 Lloyd's Rep 19: 21
Ryan v Mutual Tortine Westminster Chambers Assoc [1893] 1 Ch 116 93

S

S v S [1986] 3 All ER 566 169
SCF Finance Co Ltd v Masri (No 2) [1986] 1 All ER 40 .... 31, 95
Sainsbury (J) Ltd v Savage [1981] ICR 1 130
St John Shipping Corpn v Joseph Rank Ltd [1957] 1 QB 267 32
Samuelson v National Insurance and Guarantee Corpn [1984] 3 All ER 107 41
Saunders (GL) Ltd, Re [1986] BCLC 40 50
Sayers v Harlow UDC [1958] 2 All ER 342 92
Scherer v Counting Instruments Ltd [1986] 2 All ER 529 .... 14, 241, 285
Schiavo v Anderton [1986] 3 All ER 10 .... 112, 118
Schiffahrtagentur Hamburg Middle East Line Gmbh v Virtue Shipping Corpn, The
    Oinoussion Virtue [1981] 2 All ER 887 14
Schiffart und Kohlen GmbH v Chelsea Maritime Ltd, The Irene's Success [1982] 1 All
    ER 218 254
Schofield v Church Army [1986] 3 All ER 715 240
Scottish Marine Insurance v Turner (1853) 1 Macq HL Cas 334 249
Sealand Petroleum Co Ltd v Barratt [1986] 2 All ER ER 360 135
Secretary of State for Employment v Spence [1986] 3 All ER 616 128

Selvey v DPP [1968] 2 All ER 497 156
Senhouse v Christian (1795) 19 Beav 356n 196
Serjeants at Law, Re (1840) 6 Bing NC 187 261
Sevcon Ltd v Lucas CAV Ltd [1986] 2 All ER 104 .... 41, 261
Sewell v Burdick (1884) 10 App Cas 74 22
Shamji v Johnson Matthey Bankers Ltd [1986] BCLC 278 52
Sharif v Azad [1966] 3 All ER 785 68
Shell Pensions Trust Ltd v Pell Frischmann & Partners [1986] 2 All ER 911 .. 239
Shepherd (FC) & Co Ltd v Jerrom [1985] IRLR 275, **[1986] 3 All ER 589** 126, 127
284, 286
Sherdley v Sherdley [1986] 2 All ER 202 .... 172, 283, 293
Shiloh Spinners Ltd v Harding [1973] AC 691 93
Siebe Gorman Ltd v Barclay's Bank Ltd [1979] 2 Lloyd's Rep 142 54
Sim v Robinow (1892) 19 R 265 61
Sim v Rotherham Metropolitan BC [1986] 3 All ER 387 .... 87, 92, 125
Simister v Simister [1987] 1 All ER 233 173
Simpson & Co v Thomson (1877) 3 App Cas 279 25
Singh v Immigration Appeal Tribunal [1986] 2 All ER 721 9
Smalley v Crown Court at Warwick [1985] 1 All ER 769 .... 116, 117
Smith v Croft [1986] 2 All ER 551 49
Smith Kline & French Laboratories v Bloch [1983] 2 All ER 72 60
Smith Kline and French Laboratories Ltd v Sterling-Winthrop Group Ltd [1975] 2 All
ER 578 40
Smiths Ltd v Middleton (No 2) [1986] 2 All ER 539 242
Smyth v Dublin Theatre Co [1936] IR 692 198
Société du Gaz de Paris v SA de Navigation 'Les Armateurs Francais' 1926 SC (HL)
13 61
**South Carolina Insurance Co v Assurantie Maatschappij 'de Zeven
Provincien' NV, South Carolina Insurance Co v Al Ahlia Insurance Co**
[1985] 2 All ER 1045, **[1986] 3 All ER 487** 64, 238
**Southern Pacific Insce Co (Fiji) Ltd v Comr of Inland Revenue [1986]
STC 178** 299
Southern Rly of Peru v Owen [1957] AC 334 299
Speed Seal Products Ltd v Paddington [1986] 1 All ER 91 316
Spiliada Maritime Corpn v Cansulex Ltd, The Spiliada [1986] 3 All ER 843 .. 59, 61,
232
Spindlow v Spindlow [1979] 1 All ER 169 176
Stafford BC v Elkenford Ltd [1977] 2 All ER 519 322
Stevenson v Wishart [1986] STC 74 300
Stewart v Oriental Fire & Marine Insce Co Ltd [1984] 3 All ER 777 .... 33, 94
Stoke-on-Trent CC v B & Q Retail Ltd [1984] 2 All ER 332 322
Straight v Burn (1869) LR 5 Ch App 163 198
Stream Properties Ltd v Davis [1972] 2 All ER 746 218
Street v Mountford [1985] 2 All ER 289 190
Strongman (1945) Ltd v Simcock [1955] 2 QB 525 95
Suffert's Settlement, Re [1960] 3 All ER 561 204
Sugden v Sugden [1957] 1 All ER 300 291
Sun Life Assce Co of Canada v Pearson [1986] STC 335 305
Supplementary Benefits Commission v Jull [1981] AC 1025 173
Swiss Bank Corpn v Brinks-MAT Ltd [1986] 2 Lloyd's Rep 79 21
Swiss Bank Corpn v Brinks-MAT Ltd [1986] 2 All ER 188 .... 21, 38, 288

T

T (a minor), Re [1986] 1 All ER 817 .... 177, 268
TCB v Gray [1986] BCLC 113 56
TH Knitwear (Wholesale) Ltd, Re [1986] STC 572 306
Tai Hing Cotton Mill Ltd v Liu Chong Hing Bank Ltd [1985] 2 All ER 947 20
**Tai Hing Cotton Mill Ltd v Liu Chong Hing Bank Ltd (No 2) [1986] 1 All ER
897** 244

Taly NDC International NV v Terra Nova Insurance Co Ltd [1986] 1 All
  ER 69 .... **241**
Tarleton Engineering Co Ltd v Nattrass [1973] 3 All ER 699 73
Taylor Fashions Ltd v Liverpool Friendly Society [1981] 1 All ER 897 194
Tennant v Smith [1892] AC 150 297
Tetley v Chitty [1986] 1 All ER 663 .... **315**
Thackwell v Barclays Bank plc [1986] 1 All ER 676 .... **25, 28, 96**
Thake v Maurice [1986] 1 All ER 497 .... **85, 86, 313**
Thames Guaranty v Campbell [1984] 1 All ER 144 184
Thetis, HMS, (1835) 3 Hag Adm 228 252
Third Chandris Shipping Corpn v Unimarine SA, The Pythia [1979] 2 All ER 972: 230
Thomas v Hammond-Lawrence [1986] 2 All ER 214 .... **218**
Thomas v University of Bradford [1986] 1 All ER 217 .... **135**
Thwaite v Thwaite [1981] 2 All ER 789 168
Tito v Waddell (No 2) [1977] 3 All ER 129 93
Tommey v Tommey [1982] 3 All ER 385 168
Torbell Investments Ltd v Williams [1986] STC 397 .... **299**
Tote Bookmakers Ltd v Development and Property Holdings Co Ltd [1985] 2 All ER
  555 11
Towers & Co Ltd v Gray [1961] 2 QB 351 287
Transcontainer Express Ltd v Custodian Security Ltd (9 April 1986, unreported) .. 27
**Trave Schiffahrtgesellschaft mbh & Co KG v Ninemia Maritime Corpn, The
  Niedersachen (No 2) [1986] 2 All ER 244** **14**
Trendtex Trading Corpn v Credit Suisse [1980] 3 All ER 721 .... 60, 61
Troop v Gibson [1986] 1 EGLR 1 209
Tubantia, The, [1924] P 78 252
Turner v Blunden [1986] 2 All ER 75 .... **159, 179**
29 Equities Ltd v Bank Leumi (UK) Ltd [1986] 2 All ER 873 .... **201**
Tzu-Tsai Cheng v Governor of Pentonville Prison [1973] 2 All ER 204 165

                                    U

Ugland Obo One, The. *See* Aden Refinery Co Ltd v Ugland Management Co
United City Merchants (Investments) Ltd v Royal Bank of Canada [1982] 2 All ER
  720 .... 68, 97
United Scientific Holdings Ltd v Burnley BC [1977] 2 All ER 62 215

                                    V

V (a minor), Re [1986] 1 All ER 752 .... **177, 178**
Vacwell Engineering Co Ltd v BDH Chemicals Ltd [1969] 3 All ER 1681 48
Van Duyn v Home Office [1975] 3 All ER 190 .... 136, 141
Vernon's Will Trusts, Re [1971] 3 All ER 1064 203
Vetrovec v R 136 DLR (3d) 89 159
Vimeira, The. *See* Aiden Shipping Co Ltd v Interbulk Ltd
Von Colson and Kamman v Land Nordrhein-Westfalen [1984] ECR 1891 137

                                    W

W, Re (1982) 4 FLR 612 .... 176, 177
W (an infant), Re [1971] 2 All ER 29 176
W v Meah; D v Meah [1986] 1 All ER 935 .... **319**
Wachtel v Wachtel [1973] 1 All ER 113 291
Wagg (Helbert) & Co Ltd, Re [1956] 1 All ER 129 66
Wait, Re [1927] 1 Ch 606 26
Walker v Hall (1984) 5 FLR 126 191
Wallersteiner v Moir [1974] 3 All ER 217 49
Ward v Cannock Chase DC [1985] 3 All ER 537 312

Warde v Feedex International Inc [1984] 1 Lloyds Rep 310 14
Warren v Truprint Ltd [1986] BTLC 344 79
Watteau v Fenwick [1893] 1 QB 346 20
Watts v Midland Bank plc [1986] BCLC 15 50
Weld-Blundell v Stephens [1920] AC 956 312
Wells v Wells [1980] CA Transcript 526 168
Welsh Irish Ferries Ltd, Re [1985] BCLC 327 54
Wendelboe v LJ Music Ap S [1986] 1 CMLR 476 129
West Midlands Co-operative Society Ltd v Tipton [1986] 1 All ER 513 130
Westcott v Woolcombers Ltd [1986] STC 182 302
**Westminster City Council v Government of the Islamic Republic of Iran
  [1986] 3 All ER 284** 237, 279
Whitechapel Art Gallery v Customs and Excise Comrs [1986] STC 156 305
Whyte v Ticehurst [1986] 2 All ER 158 291
Wilkinson v Ancliff (BLT) Ltd [1986] 3 All ER 427 282
Williams & Glyn's Bank Ltd v Boland [1980] 2 All ER 408 .... 181, 182, 183, 186, 195
Williams & Humbert Ltd v W & H Trade Marks (Jersey) Ltd, Rumasa SA v
  Multinvest (UK) Ltd [1985] 2 All ER 208 68
Willis v FMC Machinery and Chemicals Ltd (1976) 68 DLR (3d) 127 48
Wilsher v Essex Area Health Authority [1986] 3 All ER 801 .... 314, 318
Wilson v Alexander [1986] STC 365 296
Wilson v Brett (1843) 11 M & W 113 275
Wilson v Wilson [1963] 2 All ER 447 191
Wilson Smithett & Cope Ltd v Terruzzi [1976] 1 All ER 817 67
Wilsons and Clyde Coal Co Ltd v English [1937] 3 All ER 628 .... 257, 318
Winkfield, The [1902] P 42 22
Winson, The [1982] AC 939 27
Winward v TVR Engineering Ltd [1986] BTLC 366 79
Wood v Commissioner of Police of the Metropolis [1986] 2 All ER 570 ..... 276, 281,
                                                                        288
Woodman v Photo Trade Processing Ltd (1981), unreported 78
Woolf v Collis Removal Service [1947] 2 All ER 260 12
Woolmington v DPP [1935] AC 462 148
Wormell v RHM Agriculture (East) Ltd [1986] 1 All ER 769 .... 47, 76

Table of Statutes

Administration of Estates Act 1925
s 33 291
46 .... 70, 279, 290
Administration of Justice Act 1960
s 13(3) 15, 83, 271, 281
Adoption Act 1958
s 34(1) 178
Affiliation Proceedings Act 1957
s 4 179
Agricultural Holdings (Notice to Quit) Act 1977
s 2 220
Arbitration Act 1950
s 17 .... 12, 15
19A 15, 16
Arbitration Act 1975 65
Arbitration Act 1979 277
s 1(5) 14
(6) 14
(6A) 13
27 11
Army Act 1955
s 203 .... 170, 277
Bail Act 1976
s 6 113
(1) 112
7(1) 112
Bankers' Books Evidence Act 1879
s 7 279
Banking Act 1975
s 1(2) 95
(8) 96
Banking Act 1979 31
s 1 32
(2) 32
(4) 32
(5)(d) 32
(6)(a) 32
(8) 32
Bankruptcy Act 1914
s 42(1) 171, 185
Bills of Exchange Act 1882
s 26(1) 27
Bills of Lading Act 1855
s 1 .... 25, 253
Broadcasting Act 1981
s 4(3) 269
Capital Gains Tax Act 1979
s 20 302
27 301
32(1)(b) 302
85 302
101 301

Carriage by Air Act 1961
s 1(1) 288
Sch 1 .... 38, 288
Charging Orders Act 1979
s 3(5) 184
Charities Act 1960
s 28 203
Cheques Act 1957
s 4 .... 28, 96
Child Care Act 1980 179
Children Act 1975
s 29 178
37(2) 178
Children and Young Persons Act 1969 179
Companies Act 1948
s 94 50
293 51
Companies Act 1985
s 17(2)(b) 51
35 56
125-127 51
125(4) 51
425 51
459 58
461 57
497 53
502(2)(f) 57
653 54
Consumer Credit Act 1974
ss 137-141 199
137 74
137(1) 74
138 .... 38, 275
(1) 75, 199
(a) 74, 75
(b) 74
(2)-(4) 75
(4)(a) 199
170 270
171(7) 74, 199
Contempt of Court Act 1981
s 2(2) 81
4(1) 81
5 81
7 81
14(1) 82
Copyright Act 1956
s 3(1)(a) 40, 275
9(8) 280
48(1) 40
County Courts (Penalties for Contempt) Act 1983 82
Criminal Appeal Act 1968
s 11(2) 122
17 115

Criminal Attempts Act 1981 103
Criminal Damage Act 1971
  s 1(2) 108
Criminal Evidence Act 1898
  s 1(f)(ii) 153–158
Criminal Justice Act 1982
  s 1 124
Criminal Law Act 1967
  s 3(1) 101, 102, 284
Criminal Law Act 1977 .... 113, 270
Crown Proceedings Act 1947
  s 21(1) 10
  38 10
Customs and Excise Act 1952
  s 304 .... 104, 105
Customs and Excise Management Act 1979
  s 93(1) 271
  (2) 271
  170(1)(b) 104, 105
  Sch 1 104
Defamation Act 1952
  s 5 316
Domestic Violence and Matrimonial Proceedings Act 1976
  s 1(2) 175
Drug Trafficking Offences Act 1986 123
Employers' Liability (Defective Equipment) Act 1969
  s 1(3) 282, 317
Employment Protection (Consolidation) Act 1978
  s 57(1)(b) 127
  (3) 130
  64(1)(b) 133
  72 287
  106 129
  Sch 3 284
      para 3 126
      13, para 9 127
          (1)(b) 128
Extradition Act 1866
  s 1 165
Extradition Act 1870
  s 2 166
  7 166
  11 165
  14 165
  17 165
Fair Trading Act 1973
  s 75 43
Finance Act 1972
  s 100(6) 303
  Sch 16, para 3(1) 303
Finance Act 1973
  s 17(1) 300
  Sch 19 306
Finance Act 1974
  s 22 304
Finance Act 1975
  Sch 5, para 18 300

Finance Act 1976
  s 61 296
  64 297
Finance Act 1977
  Sch 7, para 2 298
Finance Act 1985
  s 48, Sch 2 293
Finance Act 1986
  s 49 303
Firearms Act 1968
  s 2(1) 287
Food and Drugs Act 1955 73
Forgery and Counterfeiting Act 1981
  s 3 110
Guardianship of Minors Act 1971 . 175, 179
Guardianship of Minors Acts 1971–1973 175
Hallmarking Act 1973 .... 13, 277
Housing Act 1980
  s 2(4) 223
  5 223
  10 223
  16(11) 223
  Sch 1, Part II 223
  4 223
Housing Act 1985
  s 84, Sch 2 176
Housing and Building Control Act 1984 223
Housing (Homeless Persons) Act 1977
  s 1 276
  4 276
  (5) 274
Immigration Act 1971 9
Income and Corporation Taxes Act 1970
  s 168 293
  171 293
  195 297
  196 297
  273 302
  279 303
  478 305
Inheritance (Provision for Family and Dependents) Act 1975 291
Insolvency Act 1976
  s 336(4), (5) 185
Insolvency Act 1986
  s 44 52
  46 50
  48(6) 53
  251 53
  336 172
  339 185
  341(1), Sch 14 171
Insurance Companies Act 1974
  11(1) 94, 286
Insurance Companies Act 1981
  s 36(2) 286
  Sch 5, Pt 1 286

Interpretation Act 1978
  s 6(c) 273
  7 .... 273, 274
  12(1) 274
Justices of the Peace Act 1979
  s 52 119
Land Charges Act 1925
  s 6 .... 201, 202
Land Charges Act 1972
  s 6 .... 201, 202
  17(1) 201
Land Charges Act 1975
  s 1(1)(a) 279
Land Registration Act 1925
  s 54 201
  59(1) 201
  59(5) 201
  70(1)(g) 181, 183, 186, 188
Landlord and Tenant Act 1954
  s 23 .... 217, 218
  24–28 212
  24 220
  24A 218
  (2) 218
  25 218
  38(4) 213
  41A 220
  56(3) 217
  (4) 217
  Part II 212, 217
Latent Damage Act 1986
  s 3 .... 26, 311
Law of Property Act 1922 188
Law of Property Act 1925
  s 2 188
  14 .... 187, 188
  26(1) 189
  (3) 189
  27 188
  28(1) 188
  30 .... 171, 184, 185, 189
  34 191
  36 191
  53 191
  (1)(c) 302
  (2) 194
  199 174
  (1) 181
Law of Property Act 1969 .... 218, 220
Law Reform (Contributory
  Negligence) Act 1945 91
Law Reform (Miscellaneous Provisions) Act 1934 291
Law Reform (Personal Injuries) Act
  1948
  s 2(1) 320
Leasehold Reform Act 1967
  s 4(1) 221

Limitation Act 1980
  s 2 41
  11 282
Local Government Act 1972
  s101(1)(a) 273, 288
  142(2) 289
  222 321
Local Government, Planning and
  Land Act 1980
  s 60(7), (8) 271
Magistrates' Courts Act 1952
  s 81 .... 148, 149
Magistrates' Courts Act 1980
  s 24(1) 120
  25(2) 120
  (6) 120
  101 148
  127 112
Marine Insurance Act 1906
  s 63 250
  79 250
Matrimonial Causes Act 1973 ..... 184, 291
  s 23(1)(d) 283
  25A 168
  (1)(a) 277
  (2)(a) 170
  31(5) 169
  (7) 169
  39 171
Matrimonial and Family Proceedings
  Act 1984 168
  s 12(1) 278
Matrimonial Homes Act 1983 175
Medicines Act 1968
  s 58 281
Merchant Shipping Act 1854 252
Merchant Shipping Act 1894 275
  s 510 250
  521 251
  523 252
Merchant Shipping Act 1906
  s 72 .... 252, 280
Merchant Shipping Act 1979 258
Merchant Shipping (Liability of
  Shipowners and Others) Act 1958
  s 3(2) 257
Metropolitan Police Act 1839
  s 54(13) 111
Misuse of Drugs Act 1971
  s 5(2) 111, 149
  (3) 111
  27 117
  28 104
National Health Service Act 1977
  s 87(1) 218
Occupiers' Liability Act 1957 313
Partnership Act 1890 221
Patents Act 1949
  s 13(4) 41

Patents and Designs Act 1907 39
Perpetuities & Accumulations Act 1964 206
Police Act 1964
  s 49 .... 164, 289
Prevention of Crime Act 1953
  s 1(4) 281
Rent Act 1977
  Sch 15, Pt II 278
Rent (Amendment) Act 1985
  s 1(4) 219, 278
Road Traffic Act 1972
  s 2 .... 102, 284
   6 116
   (1) 124
   (2) 116
   10 119
   (5) 287
Sale of Goods Act 1979 26
  s 14 76
   (2) 47
   (3) 47
Sex Discrimination Act 1975 125
  s 6(2) 132
   (4) 133
   10(1) 132
   52 134
   82(1) 132
Sex Discrimination Act 1986 125
  s 2 133
   3 133
Social Security Act 1975
  s 37(3)(a)(i) 147
Social Security and Housing Benefits Act 1982
  s 36(1) 7, 272
State Immunity Act 1978
  s 12 279
Supreme Court Act 1981
  s 18(1)(f) 285
   20 248
   29(3) 116, 117
   31 .... 6, 10
   35A 239
   (3)(a) 239
   (b) 239
   37 175
   48 .... 116, 122
   51(1) 272

Supreme Court of Judicature Act 1873 14
Supreme Court of Judicature (Consolidation) Act 1925
  s 22(a) 248
   31(1)(h) 285
Taxes Management Act 1970
  s 20(3), (4) 301
   79 305
   114 307
Theft Act 1968
  s 5 273
   (3) 110
   17 106
   25 106
   33(3) 276
  Sch 3, Pt I 276
Torts (Interference with Goods) Act 1977
  s 8 .... 22, 24
Town and Country Planning Act 1971
  s 55 322
   (1) 323
   (5) 323
   102 323
  Part V 321
Trade Descriptions Act 1968
  s 11 73
   23 72
Trade Marks Act 1938 39
  s 68(1) 40
Trade Unions (Amalgamations etc) Act 1964 134
Transport Act 1981
  s 19(1) 121
  Sch 8, para 25 151
Unfair Contract Terms Act 1977 ... 79
Vagrancy Act 1824
  s 4 .... 276, 281, 288
Value Added Tax Act 1983
  s 22 306
Variation of Trusts Act 1958
  s 1(1)(a) 204, 288
   (b) 204, 288
Wages Act 1986
  Part I 135

Abbreviations

BCLC	Butterworths Company Law Cases
BTLC	Butterworths Trading Law Cases
BTR	British Tax Review
CAA	Capital Allowances Act
CGT	Capital Gains Tax
CLJ	Cambridge Law Journal
CLR	Commonwealth Law Reports
Com LR	Commercial Law Reports
Conv	The Conveyancer
Cr App R	Criminal Appeal Reports
Cr LR	Criminal Law Review
ECR	European Court Reports
EG	Estate Gazette
EL Rev	European Law Review
FA	Finance Act
Fam Law	Family Law
FLR	Family Law Reports
FSR	Fleet Street Reports
ICR	Industrial Cases Reports
ILR	International Law Reports
Imm AR	Immigration Appeals Reports
IRLR	Industrial Relations Law Reports
JP	Justice of the Peace Reports
LGR	Local Government Review
LPA	Law of Property Act 1925
LQR	Law Quarterly Review
LRA	Land Registration Act 1925
LS	Legal Studies
LS Gaz	Law Society Gazette
MLR	Modern Law Review
NLJ	New Law Journal
Ox Jo LS	Oxford Journal of Legal Studies
P & CR	Property and Compensation Reports
RTR	Road Traffic Reports
SC	Session Cases
SJ	Solicitors' Journal
STC	Simon's Tax Cases
TA	Income and Corporation Taxes Act 1970
TC	Tax Cases
TMA	Taxes Management Act 1970

Administrative Law

KEITH DAVIES, MA, LLM
Barrister, Professor of Law, University of Reading

Availability of judicial review

'Judicial review is concerned, not with the decision, but with the decision-making process'. In 1986 this statement of fundamental principle made by Lord Brightman in *Chief Constable of the North Wales Police v Evans* [1982] 3 All ER 141 at 154, was itself quoted by May LJ in *R v Chief Constable of Merseyside, ex p Calveley and others* [1986] 1 All ER 257 at 265. The concept of public law over against private law, which Lord Diplock in 1982 described with such *empressement* in *O'Reilly v Mackman* [1982] 3 All ER 1124, is again being underlined and judicial review exemplifies it.

The quotation from Lord Brightman included this next sentence: 'Unless that restriction on the power of the court is observed, the court will in my view, under the guise of preventing the abuse of power, be itself guilty of usurping power'. This reminds us that the jurisdiction of the courts, even the superior courts of record up to and including the House of Lords, is not limitless, irrespective of the fact that the courts themselves have to adjudicate on their own observance of that limit. No-one in public office enjoys limitless jurisdiction, ie arbitrary power, under our present law. Public law is here the relevant area of jurisdiction; the *ultra vires* doctrine is the fundamental principle which prevails in it; judicial review is its central mechanism.

What had to be settled in the *Calveley* case was not the definition of judicial review but a derivative question, namely the extent to which judicial review is excluded by the availability of other legal redress. The ratio decidendi is expressed in the headnote of the report ([1986] 1 All ER 257) in these words: 'In exceptional circumstances the court could in its discretion grant judicial review of disciplinary proceedings to an applicant who had not exhausted or pursued his alternative rights of appeal against the decision of the disciplinary body'. But the previous authorities relied on were not confined to cases involving disciplinary bodies.

It has to be said at once that English law has *not* evolved judicial review as a mode of appeal, even though the headnote in the *Calveley* case implies that it has ('alternative rights of appeal'). The concept is not *appeal* but *challenge*. This is emphatically not a matter of splitting hairs. An appeal deals, inter alia, with the merits of the proceedings appealed against; judicial review does not. Hence the importance of the quotation from Lord Brightman in the opening sentence of this article. All three appeal judges carefully expressed their judgments so as not to call judicial review an appeal, *pace* the headnote. Sir John Donaldson MR spoke of 'the interrelationship between remedies by way of judicial review on the one hand and appeal procedures on the other' (ibid at 261). May LJ (ibid at 263) quoted Lord Scarman in *Preston v IRC* [1985] 2 All ER 327 at 330: 'Judicial review is a collateral

challenge; it is not an appeal'. Glidewell LJ ([1986] 1 All ER at 267) said:
'. . . where application is made for judicial review but an alternative remedy
is available, an applicant should normally be left to pursue that remedy.
Judicial review in such a case should only be granted in exceptional
circumstances'. Their lordships were themselves deciding an *appeal*, but it
was of course an appeal from the decision of the Divisional Court of the
Queen's Bench Division on the *application* for judicial review. It must be
proper, though perhaps pedantic, to say that the Divisional Court had
decided the case 'at first instance', even though the proceedings before it
were instituted in order to challenge a decision which was the outcome of a
hearing by a specialised tribunal.

That tribunal was, in the *Calveley* case, a disciplinary hearing held before
the Chief Constable of the respondent police authority. Five police officers
(ie the appellants) had arrested five men. The latter were charged with
offences, tried, and acquitted. They had already made formal complaints
against the police officers. An investigating officer was appointed, but was
instructed to defer action while a civil action was awaited. Two years later it
was established that a civil action would after all, not be brought. The police
investigation was then put into effect, even though relevant police records
had by then been destroyed under routine procedures. More than three
years after the making of the complaints the Chief Constable's disciplinary
hearing took place. The complaints were found proved against all five
police officers who were dismissed or compelled to resign. Under the Police
(Discipline) Regulations 1977, SI 1977/580, they then had the right to appeal
to the Home Secretary, which they exercised. They also applied to the
Divisional Court for judicial review of the Chief Constable's decision by
way of certiorari to quash it. They were given leave to proceed with this
application, but in the event judicial review was refused; whereupon they
appealed to the Court of Appeal and succeeded.

The substantive ground of the application for judicial review was breach
of the rules of natural justice. But whether there had been such a breach or
not the Chief Constable argued that the application must fail anyway on the
procedural ground that an alternative remedy to judicial review was
available. Both in the Divisional Court and in the Court of Appeal there
seems to have been a ready acceptance that the *substantive* ground was made
out. The divergence between the two decisions arose on the procedural
point about the availability of the alternative remedy. But it seems fair to
say that the substantive issue and the procedural issue were not very
precisely differentiated in the appeal judgments.

Something must be said first about the substantive issue. May LJ quoted
Lord Templeman's speech in *Preston v IRC* [1985] 2 All ER 327 at 337:
'Judicial review is available where a decision-making authority exceeds its
powers, commits an error of law, commits a breach of natural justice,
reaches a decision which no responsible tribunal could have reached, or
abuses its powers'. This seems (if exhaustive) to be a list of five grounds.
But the five matters do not on further examination seem to make up an
exhaustive or schematic list. For that it is necessary to go to Lord Diplock's
speech in *Council of Civil Service Unions v Minister for the Civil Service* [1984]
3 All ER 935 at 950, where he says:

'Judicial review has I think developed to a stage today when, without reiterating any analysis of the steps by which the development has come about, one can conveniently classify under three heads the grounds on which administrative action is subject to control by judicial review. The first ground I would call "illegality", the second "irrationality" and the third "procedural impropriety". That is not to say that further development on a case by case basis may not in course of time add further grounds.'

One speech does not necessarily make an authoritative formulation of a fundamental principle, it is true; but other judges do not seem to have produced a competing formulation of principle either to reinforce Lord Diplock's or to counter it; and perhaps therefore we can say that the formulation is acceptable even though Lord Diplock himself envisaged (ibid) that in time it may have to be re-formulated in terms not of three heads but four or even more, perhaps because of the impact of 'the administrative law of several of our fellow members of the European Economic Community' perhaps because of other developments as yet unforeseeable.

'Illegality' is explained by Lord Diplock (ibid, at 950–51) in a way that suggests he was thinking in terms of wrongfulness in principle ('the decision-maker must understand correctly the law that regulates his decision-making power and must give effect to it'). 'Procedural impropriety' is explained by him in a way which points to wrongfulness in actual procedure, embracing (as he expressly states) breach of natural justice, 'failure to act with procedural fairness', and also 'failure by an administrative tribunal to observe procedural rules that are expressly laid down in the legislative instrument in which its jurisdiction is conferred, even where such failure does not involve any denial of natural justice' (though presumably the enactment of the legislative instrument presupposed that this is what natural justice is thought to require in any case). The Police (Discipline) Regulations 1977 are clearly a 'legislative instrument'. And 'irrationality' is explained by Lord Diplock as: 'Wednesbury unreasonableness' (see *Associated Provincial Picture Houses Ltd v Wednesbury Corporation* [1947] 2 All ER 680). In other words a decision is taken on a matter which the official body is in principle entitled to decide, and by the procedure which it is required to follow, and yet in detail it is so unreasonable that no reasonable official body could have taken it. Thus 'Wednesbury unreasonableness' or 'objective unreasonableness' is wrongfulness in detail. It may be useful to express this diagrammatically:

GROUNDS FOR JUDICIAL REVIEW

Head (1) 'Illegality'	Head (2) 'Irrationality'	Head (3) 'Procedural impropriety'	Other heads to be recognised in future cases
Errors of law (ultra vires in principle) abuse of powers excess of powers bad faith, etc	'Wednesbury unreasonableness' (ultra vires in detail)	eg defaults over:— —fairness —natural justice —statutory rules (procedural ultra vires)	

All these grounds take an official decision in some manner outside the proper limits of the decision-making (ie policy) discretion conferred upon the official body making it. In the broad sense they are all ultra vires acts. As Lord Denning MR said in *Pearlman v Keepers and Governors of Harrow School* [1979] 1 All ER 365 at 372, 'The way to get things right is to hold thus: no court or tribunal has any jurisdiction to make an error of law on which the decision of the case depends. If it makes such an error, it goes outside its jurisdiction and certiorari will lie to correct it.'

In the *Calveley* case the substantive issue on which the facts justified judicial review was the delay of three years and more between the alleged offence and the disciplinary hearing. Regulation 7 of the Police (Discipline) Regulations 1977 provides that: 'The investigating officer shall, as soon as is practicable . . . inform [the accused officers] of the report, allegation or complaint . . .' The accused officers claimed that the delay of three years and more infringed reg 7, ie that the giving of the information most emphatically did not take place 'as soon as practicable'. It is true that they knew of the possibility of complaints against them, but well over two years elapsed before they were interviewed by the investigating officer and formally served with notices, and several more months before disciplinary forms specifying the charges were served on them. By that time, as May LJ pointed out ([1986] 1 All ER at 267) 'the radio log sheets and the parade states and other documents which would have shown which other officers were on duty at the relevant time have been destroyed'. He pointed out that: 'Unnecessary delay . . . does occur [but] should not tempt one to resort to judicial review where no real abuse or breach of natural justice can be shown. That said, I think that abuse can be shown in the instant case'. Sir John Donaldson MR said (ibid at 263):

> 'I think . . . counsel for the chief constable ·overlooks the fact that a police officer's submission to police disciplinary proceedings is not unconditional. He agrees to and is bound by these procedures *taking them as a whole*. Just as his right of appeal is constrained by the requirement that he give prompt notice of appeal, so he is not to be put in peril in respect of disciplinary, as contrasted with criminal, proceedings unless there is substantial compliance with the police disciplinary regulations. That has not occurred in this case' (emphasis added).

Thus the substantive claim of ultra vires conduct in the form of deficiency of natural justice was clearly and strongly made out. Sir John Donaldson MR said (ibid): 'This is so serious a departure from the police disciplinary procedure that, in my judgment, the court should, in the exercise of its discretion, grant judicial review and set aside the determination of the chief constable'. But what of the procedural point about alternative proceedings being available? Glidewell LJ referred back to his own judgment in *R v Hallstrom, ex p W* [1985] 3 All ER 775 at 789–90, where he said:

> 'Whether the alternative statutory remedy will resolve the question at issue fully and directly, whether the statutory procedure would be quicker, or slower, than procedure by way of judicial review, whether the matter depends on some particular or techincal knowledge which is more readily available to the alternative appellant body, these are amongst the matters which a court

should take into account when deciding whether to grant relief by way of judicial review when an alternative remedy is available.'

Commenting on this statement of his own he said: 'The criteria to which I there referred are amongst the matters which, in my view, a court should consider when deciding whether the circumstances are exceptional.'

In *R v Hillingdon London Borough, ex p Royco Homes Ltd* [1974] 2 All ER 643 at 648, Widgery CJ said: ' . . . certiorari will go only where there is no other equally effective and convenient remedy'. So judicial review will not be available unless there are 'special' or 'exceptional' circumstances which establish that an alternative procedure for seeking redress, though available, will *not* afford an 'equally effective and convenient remedy'. But May LJ pointed out that it is necessary to go farther than merely comparing the remedies. As Widgery CJ pointed out in the *Royco* case (ibid at 649),

> 'judicial review may well be "speedier and cheaper" than the other methods, and in a proper case, therefore, it may well be right to allow it to be used in preference to them. But I would define a proper case as being a case where the decision in question is liable to be upset as a matter of law because on its face it is clearly made without jurisdiction or made in consequence of an error of law. Given those facts I can well see that it may be more efficient, cheaper and quicker to proceed by certiorari, and in those cases when they arise it seems to me proper that remedy should be available.'

Thus in cases where rival remedies are available we have the equation: the faster and cheaper nature of judicial review, *plus* 'a proper case', *equals* rightness of allowing judicial review. It then becomes apparent that Widgery CJ's definition of a 'proper case'—the offending decision 'made without jurisdiction', 'error of law'—in effect goes straight to the basic formulation of judicial review. It is capable of reconciliation with Lord Diplock's threefold classification of the grounds for judicial review, and with other judges' less systematic formulations. It comes down to a question of ultra vires in its three manifestations: ultra vires in principle, in detail, in procedure. All of which must be understood in the light of what has been said already to the effect that judicial review, in Lord Denning MR's words, ' . . . is not an appeal at all. It is an exercise by the High Court of its power to *supervise* inferior tribunals' (*R v Herrod, ex p Leeds City District Council* [1976] 1 All ER 273 at 278). Lord Brightman's words quoted at the beginning of this article refer to the same point. Lord Hailsham LC in *Chief Constable of the North Wales Police v Evans* [1982] 3 All ER 141 at 143–144, said:

> 'The purpose of judicial review is to ensure that the individual receives fair treatment, and *not* to ensure that the authority, after according fair treatment, reaches, on a matter which it is authorised or enjoined by law to decide for itself, a conclusion which is correct in the eyes of the court.'

As far as judicial review is concerned, then, it is not what the inferior tribunal does but the way that it does it ('inferior tribunal' means any person or body acting officially, other than the superior courts themselves). The choice in the type of case under discussion, ie *Calveley, Royco, Hallstrom, Preston* and the rest, is not a choice between rival appeal procedures, it is a choice between, on the one hand, an appeal, and on the other hand an application for supervisory review. The *appeal* will be made from the official body challenged usually to a specialised tribunal. The *application* will be made to the Divisional Court of the Queen's Bench Division of the High Court for judicial review. The *appeal* will be in accordance with the provisions of one of innumerable statutes and statutory instruments. The *application* will be in accordance with the Supreme Court Act 1981, s 31, and the Rules of the Supreme Court, Order 53. The *appeal* will be decided on the merits if at all possible, though a decision on procedural grounds or some other technicality cannot be ruled out; but the *application* will be decided on the question whether the decision challenged was or was not ultra vires. In the *Calveley* case, the chief constable's decision in the disciplinary proceedings could have been challenged on the merits by an *appeal* to the Secretary of State, but was instead challenged by *application* for supervisory review (by way of certiorari) not on the merits but on the ground that the decision challenged was procedurally ultra vires.

It is important not to be unduly impressed by the fact that the practical effect of either choice of proceeding could well have been the same. A successful appeal to the Secretary of State would have cleared the police officers of the disciplinary charges proved against them in the disciplinary hearing. The actual successful application for certiorari was equally beneficial to them because it quashed the decision of the disciplinary hearing. Although in theory it would have been open to the chief constable to recommence disciplinary proceedings and conduct them on a manner which was intra vires and not ultra vires, in practice that was obviously impossible by that time. It should also be remembered that the quashing of the decision that had been reached in the disciplinary hearing precluded any appeal to the Secretary of State from that decision, and therefore avoided any possibility of failure by the officers to clear themselves if that appeal had been dismissed; whereas a decision either way by the Secretary of State could itself still have been challenged in its turn by judicial review.

To sum up, the Court of Appeal judgments in the *Calveley* case show that there may often be a very real choice lying between alternative remedies for anyone wishing to challenge the decision of an official body, But if the would-be challenger prefers judicial review he can only seek it on the substantive ground on which it must always be sought or not at all—ultra vires, in one of its threefold guises as classified by Lord Diplock—not on the merits of the claimant's case that is the subject of the official body's decision which is being challenged.

Legality of ministerial decisions

One particular arena in which judicial review has been used in countless combats recently is the political battlefield between central and local government. Anyone reading the reports of these cases is tempted to identify with Mercutio—'a plague o' both your houses'. The courts are faced by actions by local authorities seeking judicial review to challenge the legality of central government decisions where the real conflict is political, not legal. Each side believes or affects to believe that its politics and its policies should sway the legal process.

In *R v Secretary of State for Social Services, ex p Association of Metropolitan Authorities* [1986] 1 All ER 164 the dispute arose over the workings of the Social Security and Housing Benefits Act 1982, which remodelled an earlier system of payments into a housing benefits scheme embracing payments to eligible claimants in the form of rent allowances, rent rebates and rate rebates, the administration of this being placed in the hands of local authorities. The Secretary of State for Social Services was and is required by s 36(1) of the 1982 Act to consult 'organisations appearing to him to be representative of the authorities concerned' as a preliminary to making regulations; and The Association of Metropolitan Authorities was recognised as one of these organisations.

The Secretary of State proposed to amend the Housing Benefit Regulations 1982 because The Department of Health and Social Services (DHSS) had realised that certain people were claiming housing benefits who were not intended to do so when the scheme had been set up. The DHSS wrote to various bodies, including the applicant Association, asking for their views on the proposed amendment, purporting to carry out the above-mentioned requirement to consult them. Two weeks were allowed for the submission of replies. The Association claimed to be unable to meet the deadline, partly because its own membership had to be consulted, partly because the DHSS letter took nearly a week to reach it.

The Association's views comprised objections, which it sent in a week beyond the two-week deadline. By then the Department had prepared other amendments, partly disclosed to the Association and partly not. The Association protested again that the deadline for comments on these, eight days, was once more too short. The amendments were all promulgated together, as the Housing Benefits Amendment (No 4) Regulations 1984, six days after that deadline and came into effect next day. The Association sought judicial review, and succeeded; but the victory was more of a vindication of principle than a practical achievement, because the judge awarded a declaration only and not a certiorari to quash the Amendment Regulations themselves. This was because they were already in force *de facto* and being administered by local authorities generally.

How does this decision fit into the modern pattern of judicial review, and in particular Lord Diplock's categorisation illegality/irrationality/(procedural) impropriety? Webster J said ([1986] 1 All ER at 169):

> '... what is being challenged by the applicants is not the validity of a ministerial decision, but the vires of subordinate legislation, which in turn depends on the question whether s 36(1) of the 1982 Act was complied with. "Rationality", in my view, is irrelevant to that question, which is one for the court to determine [and in this case is] ... whether the substance of the requirement of consultation has been complied with ... That is not to say, however, that the Secretary of State's attitude to the making of the regulations is irrelevant.'

It is thus important to be clear at the outset about what public matter is in fact being challenged, and to distinguish it from other public matters however relevant or important they may be. In this case what the minister and his officials decided to do was very relevant and very important in itself; but still more important was the fact that their decision was not simply administrative or executive, but legislative. Their policy was to restrict the payment of benefits; but the means to the end was the enactment of the Amendment Regulations, SI 1984/1965. Policy is what public bodies are free to devise at their choice; but the steps they decide to take in furtherance of that policy are what the law looks at. Policy discretion always has its bounds set by the law. To go beyond those bounds is ultra vires. This brings the matter not under Lord Diplock's second head, 'irrationality', or third head, 'procedural impropriety', but under his first head, 'illegality'; it is a question of ultra vires in principle, 'for the court to determine yea or nay', as Webster J put it. The Amendment Regulations, being subordinate legislation, were vulnerable to challenge on the ground that they were ultra vires the primary legislation under which they purported to be made—in this case the above-mentioned Act of 1982—though probably as legislation they would not be otherwise open to attack. This means that a question of principle must be at stake, not a question of detail which can only apply to executive acts, nor a question of procedure which can only apply to 'quasi-judicial' acts so as to bring in natural justice.

The Secretary of State argued the substantive issue, asserting that the consultation required by the Act had indeed taken place but that in any case the provision in the Act was directory and not mandatory so that he had discretion whether he complied with it or not, and further that only he and not the court was competent to decide the question whether there had been proper consultation or not. The judge rejected these contentions, and reached the conclusion that the requirement of consultation had not been complied with. The duty in s 36(1) was mandatory, because the scheme of benefits is administered day to day by the local authorities, which the Association is required to represent. The Secretary of State as against the court was certainly competent to judge issues—but this applies to the governmental and policy issues not to legal issues. As to the substantive issue of adequate consultation, this means that there must be a genuine invitation to tender advice, a genuine consideration of the advice when given, and a genuine chance based on adequate information and time to give such advice. The Secretary of State, as the party required to consult, is entitled to see matters from his own point of view: urgency, desirability and so forth; but he is not entitled to disregard everyone else's point of view.

There was undoubtedly a need to move with reasonable promptness. But 'consult', like any other concept, must for legal purposes be construed reasonably and in the present case it was not reasonable to describe what happened as 'consultation' envisaged by the Act. The Association had not been given all the requisite information, and had been required to reply 'within such a short period that those views would or might be insufficiently informed or considered to be helpful'. The Secretary of State had failed to carry out the duty imposed on him by the Act of 1982 properly to consult before making Regulations under that Act. A declaration was awarded against him; but the challenged regulations survived because the judge in his discretion, bona fide exercised, concluded that the Regulations were being applied by the local authorities concerned. This amounts to upholding the Regulations in practice while invalidating them in theory. In such a way is honour satisfied, justice done, and a practical outcome achieved.

Judicial review and immigration

The distinction between appeals on the merits and applications for judicial review can be illustrated in an endless variety of cases, but in no area more sensitive than immigration. Three decisions in 1986 illustrate this.

In *Singh v Immigration Appeal Tribunal* [1986] 2 All ER 721 the House of Lords heard an appeal against the decision of the Court of Appeal to uphold an appeal against the decision at first instance of Hodgson J to grant judicial review (by certiorari and mandamus) of a decision by the respondent tribunal. The tribunal had refused the appellant, Mr Bakhtaur Singh, leave to appeal against an adjudicator's decision dismissing an appeal against the Home Secretary's decision to deport the appellant. In this case, and others like it, there are no less than six levels of decision, and one can be forgiven for thinking that even in the interests of justice it is excessive to have so many. But in this article the point to be stressed is that the three lower levels of decision (1 Home Secretary, 2 Adjudicator, 3 Immigration Appeal Tribunal) deal with such cases on the merits, whereas the three higher levels (4 Queen's Bench Divisional Court, 5 Court of Appeal, 6 House of Lords) merely review their legality under the ultra vires principle.

Mr Singh was granted temporary permission to stay in England but he remained thereafter. The Home Secretary eventually ordered his deportation. This was resisted on the ground that he was a valued member of the Sikh community because of his special religious, charitable and cultural services, which raised the issue of 'compassionate circumstances' under para 154 of the 1982 Statement of Changes in Immigration Rules made under the Immigration Act 1971.

The legal issue was whether 'compassionate circumstances' is restricted to the effect of deportation on the deportee's 'family and those intimately connected with him' so that the immigration bodies have no authority to consider a wider group of 'third parties'. The House of Lords held that the statutory provisions are not to be interpreted restrictively in that way. Because the logic of the immigration control system requires consideration to be given to effects extending beyond the particular individual there is no reason for drawing a line artificially at his family and intimate friends. Services to businesses (including partnerships), to groups and communities, to research teams and the like, are examples which, in Lord Bridge's words (ibid at 726), 'illustrate the possibility of the third party interest in avoiding deportation extending to a progressively widening circle and ultimately to the public as a whole'. He conceded that the 'third party' question is more likely to arise over immigrants who are convicted offenders than to those who merely overstay limited permissions as Mr Singh did; but that does not affect the underlying legal principle of proper interpretation. But, once again, the award of judicial review does not mean that there must eventually be a decision on the merits by the immigration bodies in the immigrant's favour. It merely means that the decision actually challenged was ultra vires.

Two other judicial review decisions which can be contrasted with this are *R v Secretary of State for the Home Department, ex p Bugdaycay* [1986] 1 All ER 458, and *ex p Swati* [1986] 1 All ER 717. In the first case the immigrant falsely told the immigration officer that he wished to enter the UK for a temporary period to study, have a holiday, and buy machinery. His real, but undisclosed, purpose was to claim asylum as a refugee, a claim which the Home Office subsequently decided was not made out. The Court of Appeal held that the real purpose was a 'material' fact, non-disclosure of which made the claimant an illegal immigrant. The further fact that disclosure of the true purpose would have meant that the claimant would be admitted but would have had his claim referred to the Home Office was irrelevant to the materiality of the main fact. In the second case the claimant was refused permission to enter at all, even for the one week which he asked for, because the immigration officer did not believe him. Was the statement 'I am not satisfied that you are genuinely seeking entry only for this limited period' a 'statement of reason for the decision' under the Immigration Appeals (Notices) Regulations 1984? The Court of Appeal held that it was. Further details could await the immigration appeal proceedings. Because there was no evidence apart from that statement 'to suggest at least an arguable case that the immigration officer's decision was irrational and flawed' there was no basis for judicial review of her decision. 'Irrational' should be noted: one of Lord Diplock's words is again being used and 'Wednesbury unreasonableness' invoked.

Judicial review and the Crown

Finally, a word may be said about *R v Secretary of State for the Home Department, ex p Herbage*, [1986] 3 All ER 209, in regard to the Crown. Section 21(1) of the Crown Proceedings Act 1947 provides that the court has 'power to make all such orders as it has power to make in proceedings between subjects', in 'any civil proceedings by or against the Crown', subject to the proviso that declarations must be substituted for injunctions and orders for specific performance. But s 38 of that Act excludes 'proceedings on the Crown side of the King's Bench Division' from 'civil proceedings'. Thus s 21(1) does not apply to judicial review, as far as prerogative orders are concerned. But the revised RSC Ord 53, r 3, confirmed by the Supreme Court Act 1981, s 31, provides that injunctions and declarations are alternative remedies to the prerogative orders in judicial review; so that they are now available in judicial review against officers of the Crown (but not the Crown itself) just as the prerogative orders are. And Ord 53, r 3(10) includes 'such interim relief as could be granted in an action begun by writ'. Therefore interim injunctions are available in judicial review against officers of the Crown, and Hodgson J so held in the *Herbage* case.

Arbitration

J E ADAMS, LLB, FCIArb
Solicitor, Professor of Law, Queen Mary College, University of London

The 1986 cases have dealt with the indicia of an arbitration agreement, aspects of appeals under the Act of 1979, the power to award interest and remission of awards. On the first, the shock of the *Tote Bookmakers* case discussed in the 1985 Review was stilled when it was overruled by the Court of Appeal in *Pittalis v Sherefettin* [1986] 2 All ER 227. Relaxation of the guidelines for appeals in rent-review cases was achieved in *Lucas Industries plc v Welsh Development Agency* [1986] 2 All ER 858 but not in the other two shipping cases discussed under Appeals below. The *Leonidas D* appeal has not yet come before the House.

On the wider scene, Canada was the first country to enact the UNCITRAL Model Law, Singapore ratified the New York Convention and the People's Republic of China decided to do so, the first 'appeal' under the Washington Convention for the Settlement of Investment Disputes, (ICSID) resulted in the reversal of the decision of the tribunal of first instance and Redfern and Hunter's *Law and Practice of International Commercial Arbitration* provided the first coverage of the topic in an English textbook (as distinct from various encyclopaedias).

Reference to arbitration

The rapid reversal of *Tote Bookmakers Ltd v Development and Property Holdings Co Ltd* [1985] 2 All ER 555, asked for in All ER Rev 1985, pp 15 and 16, duly came about in *Pittalis v Sherefettin* [1986] 2 All ER 228, which, like the earlier case, arose from a s 27 application for an extension of time to elect for arbitration. Once more, the landlord had power, under a rent review provision in a lease, to nominate a revised rent which took effect in the absence of a tenant's counter-notice requiring arbitration. The s 27 application had been made in the course of the landlord's proceedings for possession and arrears (the tenant having failed to pay the difference between the former rent of £850 pa and the notified rent of £6,000). The county court judge, at the end of a day largely concerned with the tenant's claim that he *had* served a notice, indicated that he would find against that contention. On the resumed hearing, he gave judgment to that effect, dismissing the s 27 application lodged in the meantime, and ordering possession. However, the parties were notified the next day, before the judgment had been entered, that the judge had second thoughts and proposed to allow the application. After a further hearing he did so. The Court of Appeal held that, like other judges, he was allowed a change of mind. *Millensted v Grosvenor House (Park Lane) Ltd* [1937] 1 All ER 736 was applied: *Re Barrell Enterprises* [1972] 3 All ER 631 was not followed.

On the *Tote Bookmaker's* point, the Court of Appeal found there was, in the lease, a bi-lateral agreement to refer and 'The fact that the option is exercisable by only one of the parties [is] irrelevant' (per Fox LJ at 231, see also Dillon LJ at 239 and Neill LJ at 241). *Woolf v Collis Removal Service* [1947] 2 All ER 260 was relied on, and was preferred to the relevant dicta in *Baron v Sunderland Corpn* [1966] 1 All ER 349, which were inconsistent with it, although the later decision was 'plainly right' on its, somewhat special, own facts. As all three members of the Court of Appeal pointed out, the landlord needed no right to initiate arbitration, as the rent in his 'trigger-notice' took effect in the absence of challenge by the tenant. Subsidiary arguments that the wording led not to an arbitration but to a valuation, despite an express reference to the 1950 Act, and that the absence of a timely notice meant there was no agreement to arbitration also failed.

So the court turned to the issue of discretion. They reversed the judge, holding that the tenant had not established undue hardship. The finding that the new rent was excessive, so causing 'undue hardship', was not based on any evidence of the true market rent, and the tenant's claim that he would be forced to give up his business did not establish that £6,000 was too much. The effective loss of a premium and some £25,000 spent on repairs, under a full repairing lease, did not suffice, nor did the failure to take legal advice. Perhaps most tellingly, the delay of 3½ years between the expiry of the time limit (although time was of the essence that would yield to the power to exend—see 233) and the application was so 'excessive' (Fox LJ), 'enormous' (Dillon LJ) and 'prejudical' (Neill LJ) as to make an extension unfair to the landlords. So the landlord's appeal succeeded.

The major effect is to re-establish the applicability of the Arbitration Acts to the lease allowing unilateral initiation of arbitration, but useful guidance on the nature of the case to be shown under s 27 also appears. The sighs of relief from the solicitors to countless lessors and lessees are doubtless duplicated by those of their professional negligence insurers.

Appeals

Landlord and tenant practitioners will also welcome the relaxation of the Nema/Antaios guidelines effected by the Vice-Chancellor in *Lucas Industries plc v Welsh Development Agency* [1986] 2 All ER 858. A rent-review formula left it uncertain what terms were to be ascribed to the notional letting for revalorising the rent. The standard lease used in 1978, when the lease in question was granted, was much more restricted in use and alienation clauses than the standard lease introduced in 1980 and still in use at the 1983 review date. The surveyor arbitrator, in 'a carefully reasoned award', held in favour of the latter. Leave to appeal was sought, and granted—granted moreover in a reasoned judgment a practice which had been deprecated by Lord Diplock in *The Antaios* [1984] 3 All ER 229 at 237.

Sir Nicolas Browne-Wilkinson briefly sketched in the background to the 1979 Act changes as being in commercial and shipping cases, and stressed the standard form/one-off dichotomy in the guidelines. He found (at 860) that 'approach . . . difficult, if not impossible, to apply to arbitrations on rent review clauses.' The precedents were frequently modified in practice, questions of law applied generally to clauses of a particular type, despite variations in wording, and the ruling given would apply to all subsequent reviews. He cited the 'strong dicta' in *Fidelitas Shipping Co Ltd v V/O Exportchleb* [1965] 2 All ER 4 at 10 for this last point. Accordingly he did not find the guide-lines 'capable of direct application to arbitration on rent-review clauses' (at 861).

He went on to discuss the correct approach. He concluded that if he was 'left in real doubt whether the arbitrator was right in law' that would suffice. So he gave leave to appeal, adding that the existence of other leases in like form to other tenants was an additional reason. The writer understands that the parties compromised the dispute, so the substantive issue between them will not be resolved by the court. One can only hope, however, that each feels satisfied at having provided the occasion for a firm judicial recognition of the need to temper the zeal of the House of Lords in furthering the policy of the 1979 Act in an area which received no consideration during its rapid legislative parturition, a point already urged in All ER Rev 1983, p 21. Well done, Mr Vice-Chancellor, if one may make so bold.

The background to two other decisions on appeals appears from a passage in the judgment of the Master of the Rolls in one of them, *Aden Refinery Co Ltd v Ugland Management Co, The Ugland Obo One* [1986] 3 All ER 738. After reciting, at 739, the background to the 1979 Act, viz the 1978 Report of the Commercial Court Committee, Sir John continued: '... the committee saw that there would be a need for successive amendments to the law of arbitration ... [and] recommended the establishment of an "Arbitration Rules Committee" with a view to relieving Parliament of the need frequently to consider detailed amendments to the ... Acts.' He counters the constitutional ground for rejection of that recommendation with the citation of the Hallmarking Act 1973, and ends with a plea for re-consideration of the proposal. In fact, as he then accepts, the case before the court required only construction of the Act, as amended, and the *Nema/Antaios* guidelines.

The three distinguished maritime arbitrators in the *Ugland* case split 2–1 on the point at issue, namely whether or not demurrage was payable when adverse weather prevented a vessel from berthing after arrival at the loading port. Moreover, they pointed out that judicial determination of the point, on which London arbitrators were divided, would be welcome. Leggatt J refused leave to appeal because he found a strong prima facie case that the majority was right. He also refused leave to appeal to the Court of Appeal against his refusal of leave to appeal to the High Court. The charterers sought to overturn both limbs of judgment.

The first obstacle was to overturn refusal of leave to go to the Court of Appeal, a matter governed by s 1(6A) added to the 1979 Act in 1981, making requisite such leave to appeal. Counsel had to overcome the principle established by the House of Lords in *Lane v Esdaile* [1891] AC 210 namely that, if permission for appeal is to be obtained from one body, refusal of permission cannot be overturned by the putative appeal tribunal. He sought to show that the judge below had not exercised his discretion judicially, and that those circumstances showed an exception to the *Lane v Esdaile* precept. The judge had approached the standard contract term dispute in accordance with the guidelines and, it was held, had exercised his discretion judicially in relation to both limbs of his judgment. In any event, the exception to the general principle contended for did not exist, despite an established but, it must now be conceded, anomalous exception in appeals on costs, now known as 'the *Scherer* principle' after the case of *Scherer v Counting Instruments Ltd* decided in 1977 but only reported in 1986, at [1986] 2 All ER 529, but stemming from a provision in the Supreme Court of Judicature Act 1873, as amended in 1875, and spawning various authorities which are discussed by Mustill LJ on pp 746–47.

As the Master of the Rolls pointed out, at 744b, the *Antaios* speeches had not discussed the existence of conflicts between arbitral decisions, as distinct from judicial decisions, and that state of affairs might well influence a judge to grant leave for a High Court ruling, as he states he would, or might, have done. That note of regret will be echoed, no doubt, by those engaged commercially and professionally in the shipping field.

Mustill LJ, at 749, stresses the two aspects of the *Nema* and *Antaios* decisions—the manner of approach to appeals, which is to be sparing of leave, and the guidelines which must not be treated as 'a complete and immutable code', notwithstanding the admonitions to recalcitrant courts and judges who were said to have flouted them. Does this need once more to gloss the guidance reveal continuing evidence of underground resistance?

The 1979 Act clearly distinguishes between reasoned and non-reasoned awards, but as the Master of the Rolls points out in *Trave Schiffahrtgesellschaft mbH & Co KG v Ninemia Maritime Corporation, The Niedersachsen (No 2)* [1986] 2 All ER 244 at 247, it does not define a reasoned award. In the instant case, 'privileged reasons' were given, but, in the outcome, neither party had asked for a reasoned award and the buyers in the dispute asserted that they had asked for an unreasoned one. The trial judge, Staughton J, had found that there was a reasoned award, although they were brief. He also found that it was likely that further reasons would lead to leave to appeal. He had still exercised his discretion against making the order, the neglect or refusal to ask weighing heavily with him. (There was no suggestion of 'special reasons' for not asking within s 1(6)). In this he followed his earlier decision in *Warde v Feedex International Inc* [1984] 1 Lloyds Rep 310, and not the contrary views of Robert Goff J (as he then was) in *Schiffahrtagentur Hamburg Middle East Line Gmbh v Virtue Shipping Corp, The Oinoussion Virtue* [1981] 2 All ER 887 at 892. The Court of Appeal endorsed the judge's view that the absence of a request was material, emphasising the encouragement of reasoned awards enshrined in the 1979 Act.

However, the Court of Appeal did not follow him that a reasoned award had been made; the arbitrators had merely identified which of six alternative grounds had succeeded, so as to lay the ground for the evidence and argument on quantum which was to follow their interim award on liability. So a non-reasoned award had resulted, within s 1(6) and not within the exceptions to it. The giving of the privileged reasons supported that finding, moreover (see 246). Had they upheld the judge on his analysis of a reasoned award his refusal of an order, under s 1(5), would have been sustained.

Incidentally, Sir John Donaldson's opening sentences would, for a second year running, make him a leading contender for a Booker/Whitbread Prize for Judicial Literacy Grace if only one existed:

'In my more pessimistic moments I find myself reflecting that, if angels were commonly to be found in the Commercial Court, they would be invited to mount a pin, dance and be counted. This time it is not angels, but reasons, reasons for an arbitral decision. When is a reason not a reason? ... if this appeal does nothing else, I hope that it will discourage the angelic approach.'

The process of testing, and so defining, the novel provisions of the 1979 Act has continued in 1986, as these three decisions demonstrate. This writer finds that an inevitable and not unwelcome approach, as he believes must also the practitioners and 'consumers' of arbitration. He finds little to complain of in the year's contributions to the finer details, skirmishes as they are on the battlefield so pounded by the heavy artillery from the House of Lords in earlier years.

Interest

Similarly, one of the two issues in *Food Corpn of India v Marastro Cia Naviera SA, The Trade Fortitude* [1986] 3 All ER 500 is small beer in comparison to the *La Pintada* setpiece of two years earlier. Did the power to award interest on sums paid after commencement of the arbitration but before the award, to be found in the new s 19A inserted in the 1950 Act by the Administration of Justice Act 1982, come into play for an agreement made long before the 1982 amendment came into force (in April 1983)? Leggatt J had ruled it did not; the Court of Appeal reversed him on that. Just as *Chandris v Isbrandtsen Moller Co Inc* [1950] 2 All ER 618 had held that an arbitrator had implied power to award interest on analogy with the power of the court under s 3 of the Administration of Justice Act 1934, so without s 19A, his powers would have been increased when the 1934 Act had been replaced by the wider powers given to the courts by the 1982 amendments and thus it was appropriate to give retrospective effect to s 19A. The parties must be taken moreover to have allowed the arbitrator such powers as he possessed at the date of the hearing, and the section, though silent on the point, should be so construed. Lloyd LJ prefers the *Chandris* ground to that of retrospective effect via construction of s 19A as such, Dillon LJ treats it as reinforcing his construction of the section and Nicholls LJ, in a short judgment, also points out the untoward effects of denying s 19A retrospective effect. (The charter was made in September 1974, the ship arrived off Calcutta in December, and final discharge was in January 1975. Arbitrators were appointed in March 1975; one of them, as sole arbitrator, made his award nine years later, in March 1984. The part-payment of demurrage in question had been paid in April 1982. So much for the speed of arbitration.)

Remission

Remission was also at issue in *The Trade Fortitude*. The judge had refused remission for correction of an alleged error in the arbitrator's calculations, or to declare that the arbitrator could make the correction. He was upheld in that refusal. The alleged mistake was not clearly established nor admitted, so correction by the court, under s 17 of the 1950 Act, was not possible. The use of confidential reasons to assist in the enquiry, on which differing views were expressed in *The Montan* [1985] 1 All ER 520 (see All ER Rev 1985, pp 14–15) were mentioned by Lloyd LJ at 507; however, Lloyd LJ found it unnecessary to express a decided view, for, assuming the reasons could be referred to, they did not assist. Dillon LJ took a similar line (at 502); we await a firm ruling, still. Remission for misconduct was equally ruled out as no sufficient case had been made out. It was argued that his refusal to consider exercising his s 17 powers to correct the alleged error pointed out to him was misconduct; Lloyd LJ denied he could have corrected the error under that section, and the prospect of other unproven errors was no basis. Both he and Dillon LJ cite dicta from Stevenson LJ in *GKN Centrax Gears Ltd v Matbro Ltd* [1976] 2 Lloyd's Rep 555 at 576, 'To send back an award back to enable justice which certainly has not been done to be done . . . is one thing; to send it back to make sure that justice which may possibly not have been done is done is quite another . . .'

Increased applications for remission has been seen as a possible tactic to counter the restrictions on appeal effected by the 1979 Act, so this robust approach serves a timely warning against over optimism on that score.

Transnational arbitration

'Transnational' or, as the writer would prefer, 'extra-national' arbitration not bound to any municipal system of law has attracted partisan protagonists and antagonists. Only the latter will find comfort in a dictum in *Dallal v Bank Mellat* [1986] 1 All ER 240. The plaintiff had sued the predecessor to the defendant bank, in New York, for dishonoured cheques. Following the Iranian revolution, the USA and Iran established a Joint Tribunal, sitting in the Hague, and had each forbidden continued proceedings by their nationals in their respective own jurisdictions. Mr Dallal's claim had been rejected by a 2–1 majority of the arbitrators. His fresh proceedings in England were struck out. The tribunal, and its awards, were to be afforded recognition based on international law and, secondly, acquiescence by submission. The fact that the arbitration would be void under Dutch law, for want of various formalities, was immaterial. Hobhouse J deals with these issues at length, and relies on a number of nineteenth century cases upholding the competence of the Christian Consular Courts within the Ottoman Empire. He deals firmly with the defendant's contention of there being a transnational arbitration thus (at 25):

> 'The bank sought to argue further that the proper law of the arbitration agreement might be public international law. But what I am concerned with here at this point of the argument is not an agreement between states but an agreement between private law individuals who are nationals of those states. If private law rights are to exist, they must exist as part of some municipal legal system, and public international law is not such a system. If public international law is to play a role in providing the governing law which gives an agreement between private law individuals legal force, it has to do so by having been absorbed into some system of municipal law. Therefore, the bank's argument did not provide it with an escape from the necessity to identify the municipal legal system which was the proper law of the agreement to arbitrate.'

The supporters of the concept of the 'arbitration unbound' will surely not accept this rebuff, but their task is undoubtedly made harder by it.

Right to cross-examine unrepresented party

The county court registrar in an arbitration under the County Court Rules had prevented cross-examination of a plaintiff in person by the solicitor for the defendant company. He was upheld on appeal to his judge, but not by the Court of Appeal in *Chilton v Saga Holidays plc* [1986] 1 All ER 841. In the absence of prohibition on legal representation, the procedure remained fully adversarial and so there was a right to cross-examine. The alternative offered of putting questions through the registrar himself was no substitute. The Master of the Rolls cited a quotation from Lord Cranworth LC in *Drew v Drew and Leburn* (1855) 2 Macq 1 at 3, cited in Russell in support of the proposition that, in an arbitration, natural justice requires the right to test evidence by cross-examination; the present decision reiterates that salutary principle.

Commercial Law

N E PALMER, BCL, MA
Barrister, Professor of Law, University of Essex

Agency

Ostensible authority, vicarious liability and fraud

The Court of Appeal's decision in *Armagas Ltd v Mundogas SA, The Ocean Frost* [1985] 3 All ER 795 (see All ER Rev 1985, pp 19–20) has been affirmed by the House of Lords; see [1986] 2 All ER 385. The appellants, buyers of a ship from the respondents, had sued for breach of a three-year charterparty into which the respondents (as charterers) had allegedly entered as part of the sale contract. The respondents denied the existence of any three-year chartering-back to them, contending that the only binding charterparty was a one-year transaction which had run its course.

This discrepancy in the parties' expectations arose from the duplicity of one Magelssen, who was employed as the respondents' chartering manager and vice-president for transportation. Magelssen, acting in collusion with Johannesen (a partner in the shipping brokers involved in the sale) fraudulently agreed the three-year charterparty on behalf of his employers, having been promised 'a piece of the ship'. Magelssen knew that the respondents would never have approved such a transaction, but the appellants were convinced that he possessed the necessary authority. They admittedly knew that he had no general authority to conclude transactions of this nature, because Johannesen had told them so. But they believed a representation (evidently by Johannesen) that Magelssen had persuaded the respondents to grant him specific authority to conclude this single transaction.

The truth was that the respondents would not have approved a charterparty for any period exceeding twelve months. Magelssen and Johannesen, being aware of this limitation and of the need to preserve appearances with the respondents, drew up a twelve-month charterparty and tried to get the appellants to sign it. Johannesen told them that this was required for the respondents' 'internal purposes'. The appellants did not sign, but it was on the basis of that charterparty that the ship eventually went into the respondents' service when property passed to the appellants. The appellants agreed not to divulge the real duration of the concluded charterparty (ie three years) to the respondents' chartering and operations department.

Which was the contractual period? The appellants' case proceeded on two levels. First they contended that Magelssen had ostensible authority to conclude the three-year charterparty. They conceded that Magelssen had no *general* ostensible authority to bind the respondents to contracts of that kind, but argued that he had been given *specific* ostensible authority to make his statement about the respondents' approval of the particular transaction. This specific ostensible authority was alleged to be derived, inter alia, from his appointment as the respondents' officer responsible for chartering and transportation. That appointment constituted a representation by the respondents that Magelssen was empowered to convey their approval of the three-year chartering. In short, the respondents held Magelssen out as having authority to describe his authority in the manner in which he did.

This analysis had found favour with (and may indeed have originated from) Staughton J. It had, however, been squarely rejected by the Court of Appeal, and the House of Lords confirmed that rejection. Lord Keith of Kinkel agreed with Robert Goff LJ in the Court of Appeal that a distinction between an assertion by the agent that he had already been invested with actual authority in regard to a transaction, and an assertion by the agent that he had returned to his principal and obtained such authority after the opening of negotiations, seemed to defy common sense. There was, in fact, no justifiable conceptual distinction between an agent's ostensible authority to communicate his principal's agreement to a specific transaction and his ostensible authority to conclude such a transaction on the principal's behalf. Although instances of ostensible specific authority might conceivably exist (as, for example, where a principal represents to a third party that on any occasion where the agent purports to conclude a transaction for which the agent requires specific approval, the actual conclusion of that transaction by the agent may be taken to indicate that the necessary approval has been given) such instances must inevitably be rare. The circumstances of the present case fell 'far short' of establishing such a situation.

Lord Keith of Kinkel's analysis of this aspect of the claim was accompanied by useful confirmation of certain general principles of the law of agency. First, no third party can rely upon an ostensible authority in the agent when that authority is purported to be derived from representations made by the agent himself, as opposed to representations by his principal. As Lord Keith of Kinkel observed:

> 'Ostensible authority comes about *where the principal,* by words or conduct, has represented that the agent has the requisite actual authority, and the party dealing with the agent has entered into a contract with him in reliance on that representation. The principal in these circumstances is estopped from denying that actual authority existed' (at 389: emphasis added).

Thus, even if Magelssen (as opposed to Johannesen) had represented to the appellants that the respondents had approved the transaction, this would have afforded no assistance to the appellants. Secondly, there can be no effective case of ostensible general authority where the third party, knowing of the principal's specific limitations on the agent's authority, cannot have relied upon or been misled by any impression given by the principal to the contrary effect. This would have presented an additional impediment to the appellants' argument about a specific ostensible authority in Magelssen derived from his position in the respondents' organisation; for there was no evidence to indicate that the appellants placed reliance upon this representation of his authority as distinct from the representation made by Johannesen. Finally, there is a hint in Lord Keith of Kinkel's speech that the phenomenon of usual authority may exist as something distinct from either actual or ostensible authority, apparently occupying a conceptual position somewhere between the two. Such conjectures, although tempting to those who are troubled by the ambiguous parentage of *Watteau v Fenwick* [1893] 1 QB 346 (cf *The Rhodian River* [1984] 1 Lloyd's Rep 373), are probably best left unpursued.

The second aspect of the claim involved the assertion that the respondents were vicariously liable for Magelssen's fraud, the deception being practised 'in the course of his employment'. By this assertion, the appellants sought to establish a wider category of liability for an agent's fraud than that based on ostensible authority. They relied, inter alia, upon the observation by Denning LJ in *Navarro v Moregrand Ltd* [1951] 2 TLR 674 at 680, that whereas 'the presence of actual or ostensible authority is decisive to show that [*the agent's*] conduct is within the course of his employment, ... the absence of it is not decisive the other way.' This meant, in their contention, that a defendant's tortious liability for fraud perpetrated by his representative could be more extensive than his liability in contract.

The argument was rejected. Lord Keith of Kinkel held that, short of some actual, usual or ostensible authority in the agent to perform the act in question, there could be no 'vicarious' liability for fraud, however closely related the deceit may have been to the agent's course of employment. Earlier authority which had appeared to accept concurrent bases of liability in the principal (viz, ostensible authority and course of employment) did so either on the assumption that the two foundations were congruent, or in circumstances where nothing turned upon the precise doctrinal basis of the principal's liability for fraud.

In his Lordship's view, the only circumstances in which it would be just to visit a principal with responsibility for the fraud of his agent were those where the principal had misled the plaintiff into assuming that the act was sanctioned by the principal and the plaintiff acted on the faith of that misapprehension. Nor was the appellants' claim in this case remotely improved by maintaining that the sale plus three year charterparty concluded by Magelssen was merely an unauthorised way of carrying out the task (ie the sale) which the respondents had actually entrusted to him: for the two transactions were radically distinct.

Three significant points emerge from this aspect of the decision. First, it appears to complement the modern assumption that the respective duties of parties who are contractually related should be derived solely from that contract itself and that the contract should not be disregarded in the search for some wider liability in tort: see *Tai Hing Cotton Mill Ltd v Liu Chong Hing Bank Ltd* [1985] 2 All ER 947, PC (All ER Rev 1985, pp 26–28) and cf *Hall v Brooklands Auto Racing Club* [1933] 1 KB 205 at 213, per Scrutton LJ. Secondly, there are signs that the House of Lords now regards *deliberate* wrongdoing as occupying a separate category from mere acts of negligence for the purposes of vicarious liability, and as meriting the application of peculiar principles. Admittedly, the distinction is not clear–cut, because at a later point Lord Keith of Kinkel appears to confine this peculiar category to cases of 'fraudulent misrepresentation' by the servant or agent, thereby (for example) excluding cases where a bailee's employee or delegate steals the bailed property. But in general terms a division between deliberate, malicious wrongs and other misconduct would seem to have much to commend it in this context, and might advantageously extend beyond *Ocean Frost* and *Morris v C W Martin & Sons Ltd* [1965] 2 All ER 725 types of case to cases, for instance, of deliberate assault. The accommodation of deliberate wrongdoing within the mould of conventional vicarious liability has always been an uneasy one, partly perhaps because the employee's conduct will not necessarily constitute an actionable tort against the plaintiff (cf *Swiss Bank Corporation v Brinks-MAT Ltd* [1986] 2 Lloyd's Rep 79 at 86) but largely, one suspects, because of the implausibility of characterising such misbehaviour as occurring in the course of the employee's service. It may well be preferable to judge the defendant's accountability for such conduct exclusively according to whether, in his consensual relationship with the plaintiff, he has guaranteed or undertaken that it will not occur. (Admittedly, the courts may still be obliged to decide whether certain deliberate wrongs are within the course of the wrongdoers' employment for the purposes of legislation which adopts that expression: see *Rustenburg Platinum Mines Ltd v South African Airways* [1979] 1 Lloyd's Rep 19 and cf *Swiss Bank Corporation v Brinks-MAT Ltd* [1986] 2 Lloyd's Rep 79. But this would not affect the general principle.)

Lastly, the House of Lords has unequivocally rationalised *Lloyd v Grace, Smith & Co* [1911–13] All ER Rep 51 as a case where liability depended upon the apparent authority of the clerk as represented by the defendants to the plaintiff, rather than upon some more general notion of a wrong in the course of the clerk's employment. This explanation is welcome. It is sometimes forgotten that (as Lord Denning MR observed in *Morris v C W Martin & Sons Ltd* [1965] 2 All ER 725 at 732) the House of Lord's decision was reached in two stages: first, the conclusion that the clerk's taking into possession of the plaintiff's property was, by virtue of his ostensible authority, equivalent to an assumption of possession by his employers; secondly, that having thus assumed possession of the property, the employers were answerable for the manner in which it was kept, whether by themselves or by any employee to whom they had notionally entrusted it.

Bailments and personal property in general

Burden of proof in bailment actions

Swiss Bank Corp v Brinks-MAT Ltd [1986] 2 All ER 188 has been considered elsewhere (pp 38–39, below), but deserves a mention under this rubric on the strength of Bingham J's observation (at 189) that 'The plaintiffs here have not been required to prove negligence or breach of duty of a bailee in the ordinary sense. They have been entitled to rely on the presumption of liability for which the [*Warsaw-Hague Convention*] provides.' Too much should not be made of the point, but it remains the case that a bailor is not conventionally required to adduce positive evidence of negligence on the part of his bailee in order to succeed in proceedings against him: the bailor need only establish the bailment itself and the fact of loss or damage, whereupon the bailee becomes obliged to demonstrate either that he exercised the appropriate degree of care of the goods or that any want of care on his part was causally unrelated to the ensuing misadventure. Whether the same onus of proof operates in other types of proceedings (for example, an action against the bailee for breach of some contractual promise) is, admittedly, a less settled question.

Pledges of bills of lading: damages founded on immediate right to possession

The Jag Shakti [1986] 1 All ER 480 (an appeal from the Court of Appeal of Singapore) is a significant and controversial decision which should interest all those who are concerned with the financing of international commodity sales, although its impact upon contemporary English law must be regarded as qualified by s 8 of the Torts (Interference with Goods) Act 1977 (see p 24, below). It involved a cargo of edible salt, which the sellers had shipped on the defendant shipowners' vessel. The buyers had financed the purchase by means of transferable letters of credit, and the financiers had caused the bills of lading to be indorsed over to the plaintiffs for value. At the arrival of the ship at its port of discharge, the buyers induced the shipowners to deliver up the salt to them despite their inability to produce the bills of lading, and they procured a bank indemnity in the shipowner's favour. When the plaintiffs tendered the bills to the buyers, the latter refused to take them up or to pay for them, whereupon the plaintiffs issued proceedings against the shipowners for their wrongful release of the cargo. By the time these proceedings reached the Privy Council, the plaintiffs' claim had narrowed to an action in conversion, it being conceded by the plaintiffs that their earlier action for breach of contract was misconceived. The Privy Council were of the view that this concession was properly made: when (as here) indorsement and delivery of a bill of lading is made, not with the intention of passing to the deliveree the general property in the goods represented by the bill, but merely with the intention of passing a special property by way of pledge, the Bills of Lading Act 1855 did not have the effect of transferring to the pledgee the *contractual* rights of the buyer: see *Sewell v Burdick* (1884) 10 App Cas 74.

The plaintiffs, then, were the pledgees of the bill of lading, and this pledge conferred on them an immediate right to the possession of the salt from the defendant shipowners. In these circumstances, it was clear that the release of the salt by the defendants without the consent of the plaintiffs was an act of conversion. The question in the instant appeal was as to the plaintiffs' proper measure of damages. Were they entitled to the full value of the salt at the time of conversion, or were their damages to be limited to the amount of the plaintiffs' exposure in relation to the pledge: in other words, putting it loosely, could they recover only the value of their limited interest in the cargo? The question was important, because the amount expended in the financing of the purchase was a mere $275,600 Sinapore, whereas the alleged market value of the salt was almost $390,000 Singapore.

The Privy Council held unequivocally that a plaintiff who sues for conversion relying on an immediate right of possession over the converted goods can recover the full value of those goods and not the mere value of his limited proprietary interest. The Board based its opinion on the well-established principle of *The Winkfield* [1902] P 42 (discussed in All ER Rev 1983, pp 45–46). There, a bailee who was deemed to have been in possession of the goods at the time of a wrongful act committed by the defendant was held entitled to sue for full damages based on the value of the goods, irrespective of whether that value was reflected in the actual loss suffered by the plaintiff bailee, and irrespective of whether the bailee would have been personally liable in the same amount over to his bailors by virtue of the incident whereby the goods had been lost or destroyed. It is to be noted that

Lord Diplock had recognised this decision an endorsing a special and exceptional category of 'extra-compensatory' damages under common law in *The Albazero* [1977] AC 774 at 846, HL: in short, the plaintiff under the rule in *The Winkfield* was entitled to recover more than the quantum of his personal loss. It was true that, having effected such recovery, he held the proceeds of his action (above and beyond the value of his personal interest in the goods) on trust for the parties who enjoyed the ulterior interests (viz. his bailors). But that fact alone did not preclude his original claim against the wrongdoer for the full value of the goods (in the case of wrongful loss or destruction) or for the full cost of their impairment (in the case of wrongful damage).

In *The Jag Shakti,* however, the plaintiff pledgees of the bills of lading were not (as was deemed to be the position in *The Winkfield*) in actual possession of the converted cargo at the time of its conversion; instead, they had merely an immediate right to its possession. Such a right would, admittedly, justify their suing in conversion, provided at least that it arose from some proprietary interest in the goods: see *International Factors Ltd v Rodriguez* [1979] 1 All ER 17 and cf *The Aliakmon* [1986] 2 All ER 145 at 151–2 (see p 26). But were their rights as to damages to be cast on the same generous 'extra-compensatory' scale as in *The Winkfield*; or should the lack of actual possession in the plaintiffs restrict them to the recovery of the mere value of their interest in the cargo?

The Privy Council held that the plaintiffs' position should be governed by the same quantum of damages as had been applied in *The Winkfield*. Its opinion (delivered by Lord Brandon of Oakbrook) was embodied in a lucid passage, which would reward careful consideration by any commercial lawyer ([1986] 1 All ER 480 at 484):

> 'It has . . . in their Lordships' opinion been established, by authority of long standing, that where one person, A, who has or is entitled to have possession of goods, is deprived of such possession by the tortious conduct of another person, B, whether such conduct consists in conversion or negligence, the proper measure in law of the damages recoverable by A from B is the full market value of the goods at the time when and the place where possession of them should have been given. For this purpose it is irrelevant whether A has the general property in the goods as the outright owner of them, or only a special property in them as pledgee, or only possession or a right to possession of them as a bailee. Furthermore, the circumstance that, if A recovers the full market value of the goods from B, he may be liable to account for the whole or part of what he has recovered to a third party, C, is also irrelevant, as being *res inter alios acta.*'

The only exception to this general principle arose, in Lord Brandon's view, when B had one or more cross-claims against A arising from the same or some connected transaction. But there was no question of any such cross-claim or set-off in the present case.

Can an immediate right of possession be equated with possession itself for the purpose of the rule in The Winkfield?

With respect to the Privy Council, their equation of these two forms of interest, in questions of quantum of damages, must be approached circumspectly by an English commercial lawyer. First, a number of textbooks suggest that a mere immediate right of possession to goods should entitle the interested party to recover only the value of his immediate interest in an action for conversion or negligence against an independent tortfeasor. Secondly, it seems clear that the general rule for the quantification of damages in conversion is that a plaintiff can recover only his actual loss flowing from the conversion, and this measure may be substantially less than the value of the goods themselves: see, for example, *Bryanston Leasings v Principality Finance* [1977] RTR 45 and the Australian High Court case of *Butler v Egg Board* (1966) 114 CLR 185. Now there are only two possible forms of goods-interest which can entitle a plaintiff to sue independently in conversion: actual possession, or an immediate right to possession arising (semble) from some proprietary right: cf *International Factors Ltd v Rodriguez* [1979] 1 All ER 17 and *The Aliakmon* [1986] 2 All ER 145 at 151–2. If actual possession can lead to full damages based on the market value of the goods irrespective of the plaintiff's actual loss (*The Winkfield*) and an immediate right to possession now justifies the same level of recovery (*The Jag Shakti*) what is left of the supposedly general rule of assessment that the plaintiff recovers only his actual loss? There seems to be no room for its application at all, and yet the principle is well-established. The result in *The Jag Shakti* contrasts curiously with the *dictum* of Hutley JA (of the New South Wales Court of Appeal) in another commercial pledge case, which has since been before the Privy Council: *Maynegrain Pty Ltd v Compafina Bank* (1984) 58 ALJR 389. According to Hutley JA, the rule in *The Winkfield* should not be allowed to eclipse the general principle that a plaintiff in an action for conversion can recover no more than his actual loss. Arguably, this subordination was allowed to occur in *The Jag Shakti,* and upon doctrinally questionable grounds: certainly, it is very hard to find specific authority on the issue of the quantum recoverable by the holder of a mere immediate right of possession to goods. Thirdly, it must be noted that the rule in *The Winkfield* has in any event been modified as a principle of English law by s 8(1) of the Torts (Interference with Goods) Act 1977. This states, broadly, that a defendant who is sued for wrongful interference with goods (a category of wrong which includes the tort of conversion) is now enabled to show that parties other than the plaintiff are entitled to a superior interest to the plaintiff's as regards any part of the proprietorship over those goods, and can demand that those other parties be brought before the court in order for a full and final distribution of interests to be made. If this provision operates as intended, it would seem to follow that, in cases where the defendant is willing and able to plead the interest of the *tertius,* the common law principle acknowledged (whether legitimately or not) by the Privy Council in *The Jag Shakti* has been abrogated under English law.

A postscript

In the event, the plaintiffs' victory in *The Jag Shakti* was a somewhat pyrrhic one, in so far as their success on the *principle* of assessment did not induce the Privy Council to conclude that the actual *quantum* of damages awarded by the court below was incorrect.

Possession as title: whether illegally-derived possession defensible against intruders

One observation by Hutchison J in *Thackwell v Barclay's Bank plc* [1986] 1 All ER 676 (pp 28–31, below) which is of interest in the context of possessory title is his remark (at 689) that '... public policy ... would prevent a burglar from whom the stolen goods were snatched by a third party just as the burglar left the victim's house from maintaining an action in conversion against the third party.' The judge evidently considered that such a consequence followed naturally from his acceptance of the normal principle that a claimant's knowing participation in a fraudulent venture disabled him from recovering at law the proceeds of that venture. There is, however, a considerable body of contrary authority which suggests that, in the specific case of an illegally-acquired possession, the public interest is best served by allowing the possessor to defend his possession against all dispossessors except the true owner or some prior, divested possessor, rather than by countenancing some possessory free-for-all of the sort which Hutchison J was appearing to sanction: see, most recently, *Parker v British Airways Board* [1982] 1 All ER 834 at 836–837, 843, per Donaldson LJ, and see generally Palmer, *Bailment*, (1979), p 879.

Title to sue in negligence: risk without property in goods

The facts of *Leigh & Sillivan Ltd v Aliakmon Shipping Co Ltd, The Aliakmon* [1986] 2 All ER 145, HL, are well-known (see, more fully, the title on Tort, p 309, below). The House of Lords upheld the principle that a claimant who sues for negligence in respect of the loss of or damage to goods must demonstrate either the legal ownership of, or a possessory title to, those goods at the time of the loss or damage. Mere contractual expectations or obligations, which are dependent upon the continued integrity or availability of a chattel but are unaccompanied by any such proprietary or possessory interest on the part of the claimant, are insufficient to ground an action in negligence; no duty of care is owed to a party whose relation with the impaired chattel is purely contractual in nature. In so concluding, their Lordships ratified a long series of authority, from *Simpson & Co v Thomson* (1877) 3 App Cas 279 through *Margarine Union GmbH v Cambay Prince Steamship Co Ltd, The Wear Breeze* [1967] 3 All ER 775 to *Candlewood Navigation Corp Ltd v Mitsui OSK Lines Ltd, The Mineral Transporter, The Ibaraki Maru* [1985] 2 All ER 935.

It followed that buyers under a revised c & f contract, to whom risk but not property in the goods had passed at the time of the defendant ship-owners' substantial damage to them, were unable to recover damages from the ship-owners for that impairment. Lord Brandon of Oakbrook, who delivered the leading speech, saw nothing disconcerting in this result. The transaction was an unusual one, which had been modified during its life to take account of the buyers' inability to pay for the goods upon the original presentation of the documents. In the normal course of events, a buyer would derive an adequate remedy against the ship-owner by virtue of s 1 of the Bills of Lading Act 1855. Even in the present, unusual situation, the buyers could have protected themselves against the infliction of damage upon the cargo, either by requiring the sellers to transact with the shipowners along the lines suggested by Lord Diplock in *The Albazero* [1976] 2 All ER 129, or by requiring the sellers to assign to them the sellers' rights of action against the ship-owners. Nor did Lord Brandon consider it a material distinction that in most decisions adverse to the buyers (leaving aside *The Wear Breeze*, supra, which they sought to characterise as misconceived or outmoded) the contractually-related parties had never contemplated that the claimant would become the eventual proprietor of the goods.

Lord Brandon's speech contains several observations of particular interest to commercial lawyers. First, while acknowledging that equitable interests might exist in personalty and that they might be accompanied by some 'possessory title' in the goods, his Lordship repudiated the suggestion that a mere equitable property which was unaccompanied by any possessory right could itself ground an action in negligence. In order to sue, the equitable proprietor would need to join the legal owner (but cf *Maynegrain Pty Ltd v Compafina Bank* (1984) 58 ALJR 389, PC). Moreover, Lord Brandon was sceptical about the underlying assumption that notions of equitable ownership had any function to perform within the relationship of buyer and seller of goods, and was attracted by the proposition that the Sale of Goods Act 1979 (like its predecessor) was a definitive and exclusive code on all questions of property arising in respect of contracts of sale (see also *Re Wait* [1927] 1 Ch 606 at 635–636, CA, per Atkin LJ.

Secondly, Lord Brandon rejected the argument that the ship-owners in this case could be treated as bailees of the buyers upon terms equivalent to those incorporated into the original bailment between sellers and ship-owners. In his opinion, the only relevant bailment at the time of the damage was that arising between sellers and ship-owners; and short of some attornment by the ship-owners to the buyers during the period of the latter's possession, it was impossible to discern any concurrent or succeeding bailment as between buyers and ship-owners upon the terms of the original bill of lading. No attornment had taken place in this case and accordingly no bailment on terms had resulted between the litigants.

It is extremely useful to receive authoritative endorsement of the proposition that an attornment creates a substitutional relationship of bailor and bailee upon equivalent terms to those of the original bailment. One wonders, nevertheless, whether other possible derivations of a bailment upon terms between buyers and ship-owners might not usefully be explored in future litigation. Admittedly, the type of sub-bailment envisaged by Lord Denning MR in *Morris v C W Martin & Sons Ltd* [1965] 2 All ER 725 would have been difficult to establish in *The Aliakmon*, for the simple reason that a party with no currently-recognisable proprietary or possessory interest in the goods cannot qualify as a bailor: he has no actual reversion. Greater attention might, however, have been given to the argument that the ultimate acquisition of legal property in bailed goods should confer upon the acquirer the right to sue for outstanding breaches of obligation previously committed by the bailee against the original owner: cf s 3, Latent Damage Act 1986 and Griew (1986) 136 NLJ 1201. In this context, it is perhaps regrettable that Lord Brandon did not offer any remarks upon the validity and proper analysis of cases like *Goodman v Boycott* (1826) 2 B & S 1, or upon their significance to a situation like the present. This being said, however, it does not seem likely that an argument based upon them would have succeeded.

Lastly, it is tempting to question Lord Brandon's satisfaction with the general principle confirmed in *The Aliakmon*. His Lordship said (at pp 154–155) that that general principle was both "simple to understand and easy to apply", and that it afforded certainty in commercial matters. But an instructive comparison can be made between these remarks and the complicated debate which the rule has recently produced concerning the possessory entitlements of building contractors in relation to subterranean cables, and of forwarding agents who have sub-contracted the carriage of the goods without personally acquiring any antecedent possession: see, respectively, *Nacap Ltd v Moffact Ltd* 1986 SLT 326 and *Transcontainer Express Ltd v Custodian Security Ltd* (9 April 1986, unreported) (both of them currently under appeal). Nor is the supposed certainty of the present rule appreciably fortified by a consideration of Lord Diplock's conclusion in *The Winson* [1982] AC 939, that the ship-owners' right to resume possession of the cargo for the purpose of continuing the voyage was a purely contractual entitlement, obtaining exclusively as between them and the cargo owners, and did not confer on them a sufficient title to render them answerable to the salvors as bailors, or (presumably) to render the salvors liable to them as bailees. One suspects that considerable elucidation of the expression 'possessory title' (and particularly of the question as to whether such a title may consist merely of a contractually-derived right of possession) will be needed before the rule in *The Aliakmon* will begin to possess the measure of certainty attributed to it by Lord Brandon.

Banks and finance houses

Bills of exchange

Bondina Ltd v Rollaway Shower Blinds Ltd [1986] 1 All ER 564 arose on a procedural point, but the substantive issue at stake was the construction of s 26 of the Bills of Exchange Act 1882. Sub-s (1) provides that a person who signs a bill as drawer, indorser or acceptor and adds words to his signature indicating that he signs for or on behalf of a principal, or in a representative character, is not personally liable on the bill. The sub-section goes on to qualify this general proposition, however, by adding that 'the mere addition to his signature of words describing him as an agent, or as filling a representative character, does not exempt him from personal liability.' The question for the Court of Appeal in *Bondina* was whether s 26 operated to exempt from personal liability a director of a company who had (along with a fellow-director) signed two cheques of the company's which were subsequently dishonoured. The plaintiffs (the creditor company) asserted that, since the director in question had added no qualifying or explanatory words to his signature on the cheques, he must be presumed to be personally answerable thereon. But Dillon LJ (with whom Sir George Waller concurred) held that it was not open to the court to ignore the printed writing on the form of cheque used by the director in ascertaining whether he was personally liable. An examination of the contents of the form demonstrated decisively that it was a cheque of the company and no more, and when the director signed the cheques in that form

'... he adopted all the printing and writing on it; not merely the writing designating the payee and the amount for which the cheque was drawn, if that had been written out for him ... but also the printing of the company's name and the printing of the numbers which designate the company's account. The effect ... is to show that the cheque is drawn on the company's account and not on any other account. It is not a case of a joint liability of several people (ibid at 566).'

Dillon LJ regarded the decision of the Court of Appeal in *Chapman v Smethurst* [1909] 1 KB 927 as supporting the present conclusion, while both he and Sir George Waller observed the similar conclusion reached by the Court of Appeal of Ontario in *H B Etlin Co Ltd v Asselstyne* (1962) 34 DLR (2d) 191, which Sir George Waller expressly approved.

Conversion of cheques, reasonable care and illegal transactions

In *Thackwell v Barclay's Bank plc* [1986] 1 All ER 676, a cheque drawn by Alan Jones (Plant Sales) & Co Ltd ('AJ') in favour of Thackwell was fraudulently indorsed by one Sawford, who forged Thackwell's signature. The indorsees were a company named Riva, of which Sawford was a director. The defendants were both the collecting and the paying bank. They collected the payment (some £44,200) from AJ's account and credited it to Riva (a company whose recent record had been one of substantial deficit). These events occurred in March 1980. It was not until December 1980 that Thackwell made his claim against the bank, by which time Riva had gone into receivership. Thackwell now sued in conversion.

The bank defended on two principal grounds: first, that as collecting bank they had taken reasonable care as required by s 4 of the Cheques Act 1957; secondly, that in any event the cheque in Thackwell's favour represented an integral episode in a fraudulent and illegal scheme, Thackwell's involvement in which debarred him from recovering damages for the cheque's conversion.

Both defences required a detailed examination of the history behind the £44,200 cheque and of the business relations between Thackwell and Sawford. Thackwell owned the share capital in a gold mine. Needing to raise money, he had purported to sell certain plant to AJ for the amount of the converted cheque (viz £44,200). The plant consisted of two items, one of which did not exist and the other of which was grossly over-valued. By agreement between Thackwell and Sawford, Riva then bought some £81,000 worth of equipment from AJ, including the items purportedly sold to AJ by Thackwell. Riva raised the money for this purchase by a hire-purchase agreement between themselves and Lombard North Central, who paid the £81,000 directly to AJ. The plan was for the last link in the chain to be completed by AJ's giving Thackwell its cheque for the price of the plant sold to AJ by Thackwell, viz £44,200.

What happened was somewhat different. On the same day as AJ received the £81,000 cheque, its authorised director, Jones, met Sawford at the New Bond St branch of the defendant bank. Sawford asked Mr Wadlow (the assistant manager) for permission to use a room there. Wadlow allowed them the use of the manager's office for a period which was found by the judge to amount to some 20 minutes. At the end of this period, Sawford sought out Wadlow again and told him that he wished to have two cheques credited. One of them was a cheque payable to Sawford and indorsed by him. The second was the cheque payable to Thackwell and (by virtue of Sawford's forgery) purportedly indorsed by Thackwell over to Riva.

Wadlow noticed that both cheques were post-dated, and looked quickly at the reverse of each cheque to assure himself that each bore an indorsement. He failed to observe that (as he later agreed in cross-examination) both indorsements had obviously been written by the same person. The cheques were duly paid in and collected.

In these circumstances, Hutchison J held that the bank had failed to establish that it had taken reasonable care. His Lordship's starting point was the authoritative description of the banker's obligation given by Diplock LJ in *Marfani & Co Ltd v Midland Bank Ltd* [1968] 2 All ER 573 at 579:

> 'Granted good faith in the banker . . . the usual matter with respect to which the banker must take care is to satisfy himself that his own customer's title to the cheque delivered to him for collection is not defective, ie, that no other person is the true owner of it. Where the customer is in possession of the cheque at the time of delivery for collection, and appears on the face of it to be the "holder", ie, the payee or indorsee or the bearer, the banker is, in my view, entitled to assume that the customer is the owner of the cheque unless there are facts which are known, or ought to be known, to the banker which would cause a reasonable banker to suspect that the customer is not the true owner.'

In Hutchison J's opinion, notwithstanding the apparent integrity of Sawford and the known trading associations among Thackwell, Sawford and Riva, there were sufficient peculiarities about the transaction which occurred between Jones and Sawford on the bank's premises to have put a reasonable banker in Wadlow's position upon inquiry. For example, Wadlow failed, as required by the defendant bank's rules, to 'scrutinise' the AJ–Thackwell cheque, having contented himself with a mere glance at it; such scrutiny would inevitably have led him to question the authenticity of the indorsement. Then again, there was something sufficiently unorthodox about the request to have access to a private room at the bank, and about the fact that one of the cheques with which Jones and Sawford emerged from that room was a cheque drawn in favour of but purportedly indorsed by Thackwell (who was not present), to have alerted Wadlow to the possibility of an irregularity. The combined effect of these circumstances should have been to prompt Wadlow at least to question Sawford, and very possibly to induce Wadlow to contact Thackwell directly in order to obtain his confirmation of the transaction.

Nor was Hutchison J prepared to accept the bank's alternative defence that any lack of care on its part in this respect was not materially instrumental in causing the ultimate loss, because any confrontation of Sawford by Wadlow with the apparent anomalies of the situation would simply have been met by a dishonest but entirely plausible explanation, Wadlow's inevitable acceptance of which would have advanced Thackwell's interests no further. Not only was Hutchison J unconvinced that such an explanation would have been forthcoming; he also considered (pace Diplock LJ in *Marfani & Co Ltd v Midland Bank Ltd* [1968] 2 All ER 573) that:

'as a matter of law it is no answer for a bank who have been guilty of
negligence in the collection of a cheque to prove that, even had the question
the omission of which constitutes negligence been asked, a reassuring answer
would have been given':

see [1986] 1 All ER 676 at 684, and decisions cited therein.

Much of Hutchison J's judgment on the second defence consists of a
review of the authorities concerning the recoupment of the proceeds of
illegal transactions from third parties, and of an analysis of counsel's
arguments as to the degree of intimacy which must exist between the
particular claim and some illegal activity by virtue of which, or in the course
of which, the subject-matter of the claim was generated, before that claim
will be debarred on grounds of public policy. In the event, his Lordship was
not obliged to express a conclusion on this issue. Counsel for Thackwell
had conceded that, if Thackwell had known in advance of the fraudulent
nature of the refinancing transaction in which he was participating, public
policy would debilitate his claim. As a matter of law, Hutchison J regarded
this concession as a proper one (see [1986] 1 All ER 476 at 489, and cf *Belvoir
Finance Co Ltd v Stapleton* [1970] 3 All ER 664, CA, which was not cited to
the court) and he found that Thackwell was indeed a cognisant party to the
fraudulent transaction: the action was accordingly dismissed on that
ground. Nevertheless, Hutchison J went on to express a preference for the
position taken by the bank on the more general question of a claimant's
deprivation of recovery through his involvement in illegal activity material
to his claim. The bank, relying by analogy upon Lord Wilberforce's speech
in *Anns v Merton London Borough Council* [1977] 2 All ER 492 at 498–99, had
maintained that the issue should be approached in two stages: first by
inquiring into the measure of proximity existing between the illegal
conduct and the plaintiff's claim, and secondly by examining whether other
considerations exist which as a matter of public policy ought to affect the
plaintiff's right of recovery. In their contention, there was ample modern
authority which substantially favoured this approach and, in so doing,
imposed a gloss or qualification upon the admitted conventional principle
that a party who could assert his title to property without having to rely
upon some illegal transaction could recover that property at law. That
exception required recovery to be denied whenever it would be seen as an
affront to the public conscience for it to be granted; for example, where
recovery would involve the court's assistance or encouragement of the
claimant in his illegal behaviour, or where the effect of recovery would be
to enable the claimant to benefit from the proceeds of a serious crime,
whether he was implicated in that crime or not. These propositions found
favour with Hutchison J, who proceeded to apply the suggested two-tier
criterion with consequences unfavourable to Thackwell:

'... it seems to me first that it would indeed be difficult to find a case in which
the criminal conduct relied on was more proximate, because, as counsel for
the defendants submits, the cheque alleged to have been converted constituted
in reality the very proceeds of the fraudulent conduct ... If one then considers
the second of the suggested tests, everything points in my judgment to a
denial, on grounds of public policy, of the right to recover. The underlying
crime was a serious one and there is nothing inherently unfair in a result which
deprives Mr Thackwell of the proceeds of this cheque. On the contrary, by

permitting Mr Thackwell to recover the proceeds of this cheque from the bank I should, as it seems to me, be indirectly assisting in the commission of a crime.' (at p 689).

As a final point, Hutchison J was invited by the defendants to rule that Thackwell's prolonged failure to complain to them about the absence of the cheque as a credit item on his bank statement generated some form of estoppel against Thackwell. Hutchison J found it difficult to understand how, in the absence of any implied obligation on Thackwell's part to disclose this omission, his silence over the nine-month period could be construed as an implied representation of the nature alleged by the defendants. Nor, in the light of the pending appeal to the Privy Council in the *Tai Hing Cotton Mill* proceedings, was his Lordship anxious to adjudicate upon the existence of any such obligation as a necessary incident of the banker–customer relationship, although he did suggest that the relevant representation might be harder to discover when it related to an omitted credit on the customer's statement than to a wrongfully-entered debit. In the event, however, Hutchison J's earlier conclusions had made a direct decision on this point unnecessary, and he abstained from giving an opinion. Given that the Hong Kong Court of Appeal's decision in *Tai Hing Cotton Mill* has now been reversed by the Privy Council (see All ER Rev 1985, pp 26–28), Hutchison J's reticence on this point would appear, with respect, to have been well-advised.

Deposit taking and commodity broking

SCF Finance Co Ltd v Masri and another (No 2) [1986] 1 All ER 40 concerned a claim by the plaintiffs, commodities and financial futures brokers, for a substantial sum representing the outstanding balance due in respect of liabilities incurred by the plaintiffs on behalf of the defendant, their client, in dealing in commodities and financial futures. Although the defendant had originally deposited US$50,000 with the plaintiffs he subsequently ran up an equity deficit of over $1 million; when he failed to settle his account the plaintiffs liquidated his position.

The defence proceeded on three grounds: (1) that the plaintiffs were in breach of duty in having traded on their own account, having forced the defendant to enter unwise transactions and having delayed his business; (2) that the agreement between the plaintiffs and the defendant was void under Jordanian law; (3) that the plaintiffs were carrying on a deposit taking business and had received deposits from the defendant in contravention of the Banking Act 1979, and consequently that the plaintiffs were not entitled to recover their losses and the defendant was entitled to counterclaim to recover sums already paid.

Having found that the plaintiff's business methods conformed with the standard of conduct expected of London futures brokers, that the plaintiffs had a right to liquidate the defendant's position and that English law was the proper law of the contract, Leggatt J considered the third defence.

The plaintiffs' evidence showed that at the end of each month the plaintiffs always held funds of their own in credit, which exceeded the aggregate of all moneys owing to those clients whose accounts were in 'positive equity'. Working capital was provided by the plaintiffs' parent company and a third company. Therefore, no activity of the plaintiffs' business was financed by money received from clients, although all funds received by the plaintiff were initially paid into a certain current account.

On this evidence the plaintiffs argued, first, that the sums accepted from trading clients were not 'deposits' within s 1 of the Banking Act 1979. The first payment of $50,000 and other payments while in credit were 'referable to the provision of property . . . or to the giving of security' within s 1(4)(b) and thus were not deposits. All other payments were in respect of losses or debit balances already incurred. These payments were referable to the provision of property since they were paid by way of advance or part payment for the sale or other provision of property within s 1(6)(a), and would be repayable only if such events did not take place. Proceeds returned to a client represented the onward sale of commodity contracts previously acquired. Secondly and alternatively, the plaintiffs argued that money paid by trading clients was paid as security for the provision of services provided by the plaintiff, the services being the placing of business, extension of credit and acceptance of a risk of loss. Thirdly, they argued that since none of the monies received were deposits within s 1(4) of the 1979 Act, there was no deposit taking business within s 1(2). Fourthly, they maintained that monies received from the parent company and third company were loans within s 1(5)(d), while monies occasionally received from Iraqi expatriates were not received in the course of business, and were not used to finance the business; and that the plaintiffs did not hold themselves out to accept the monies on a day-to-day basis.

The defendants argued that the plaintiffs were taking 'deposits' as the monies they received were lent to others and their activities were financed out of such monies. Consequently, the plaintiffs were carrying on a banking business, and since their own monies were not kept separately they could not contend that clients' money was not lent. Clearly, the defendants contended, the plaintiffs were taking deposits.

Leggatt J accepted that the plaintiffs' balance on its account always exceeded the sum owed to trading clients. He also found that there was much to be said for the plaintiffs' arguments, and would have been disposed to resolve the issues in the plaintiffs' favour and hold that the plaintiffs had not been in contravention of s 1 of the Banking Act 1979.

In the event, however, Leggatt J felt able to reach his decision on a simpler ground. The plaintiffs had conducted transactions for the defendants, each of which was valid and enforceable. The plaintiffs' claim was not for the repayment of a deposit but for actual loss incurred through trading for the defendant. This loss was not irrecoverable unless it was 'tainted' by the plaintiffs' intention that the defendant should pay 'deposits' within s 1(4) of the 1979 Act. Leggatt J found that the simple answer was s 1(8) of the 1979 Act, which states that 'The fact that a deposit is taken in contravention of this section shall not affect any civil liability arising in respect of the deposit or the money deposited.'

Since the main purpose of the 1979 Act was to protect depositors with unlicensed deposit-taking institutions and not to enable people such as the defendants to be absolved from payment of their losses, the principle of *St John Shipping Corporation v Joseph Rank Ltd* [1957] 1 QB 267 (recently

applied in *Stewart v Oriental Fire & Machine Insurance Co Ltd* [1984] 3 All ER
777) enabled Leggatt J to hold that, even assuming that the plaintiffs were in
contravention of s 1 of the 1979 Act, the defendants' civil liability toward
them was unaffected; consequently, judgment was awarded for the
plaintiffs.

Readers should note that an appeal in this case has been dismissed by the
Court of Appeal: see [1987] 1 All ER 210.

Documentary credits

Forestal Mimosa Ltd v Oriental Credit Ltd [1986] 2 All ER 400 was an appeal
from the decision of Bingham J, who had refused the plaintiffs' application
for summary judgment under RSC Ord 14 and had granted the defendants
unconditional leave to defend the action. The judgment of Sir John Megaw
in the Court of Appeal contains some useful observations about the proper
approach to be taken by the court in respect of the determination of an
appeal under Ord 14 where the issue is a point of law.

The main substantive issue before the Court of Appeal concerned the
obligations of the respondent confirming bank under a letter of credit issued
by the Dubai Bank. The appellants were the sellers of a quantity of five
consignments of solid wattle mimosa, the buyers being five separate
Pakistani companies, all members of the same group. Letters of credit were
opened by the Dubai Bank at the request of the five purchasers, and the
Dubai Bank in turn requested the respondent Bank to confirm the five
credits. The resultant credits were expressed on their face to be subject to
the 1984 revision of the Uniform Customs and Practice for Documentary
Credits ('UCP'). (The parties were agreed that this reference to the UCP
meant the 1983 revision which took effect on 1 October 1984.) However,
the governing effect of the UCP was stated to apply only 'Except so far as
otherwise expressly stated.' The question was whether the express terms of
the credits postponed the respondents' obligation to make payment until the
documents were accepted, notwithstanding the clear contrary provision of
Article 10(b) of the UCP. The dispute arose because the Dubai Bank had
claimed that the documents contained discrepancies and had told the
respondents that they would remit the money only when funded by the
buyers themselves (or, later, that they had accepted the appellants' drafts
indorsed 'Accepted on clear collection basis not under L/C', which,
naturally, the appellants had refused).

The respondents relied upon two particular portions of the letters of
credit as establishing that the credit was to become operative only when the
buyers actually accepted the sellers' draft upon the presentation of both it
and the documents to them. First, they pointed to the opening words of the
credit, which referred to '. . . this Irrevocable Documentary Credit which is
available by acceptance of your drafts'. Sir John Megaw concluded that,
when construed in conjunction with the explicit incorporation into the
terms of the credit of the UCP, this phrase was designed solely in order to
comply with the provision in Article 11 of the UCP that 'All credits must
clearly indicate whether they are available by sight payment, by deferred

payment, by acceptance or by negotiation.' Hence the provision in the credit that it was to be available by acceptance, which was the sole significance to be attributed to the words in question.

The second passage invoked by the respondents was the declared engagement to drawers and/or bona fide holders that 'drafts *accepted* within the terms of this credit will be duly honoured *at maturity*' (emphasis added). Again, however, there was an acceptable rationalisation of this phrase which was reconcilable with the full application of Article 10(b). As Sir John Megaw observed, the words in question must have been placed there to comply with the provision in UCP Article 10(b)(iii) that the credit should additionally be available to a bona fide holder; they did not reflect upon the generally orthodox character of the document as a 'confirmed irrevocable documentary credit'. Indeed, Sir John Megaw believed that a commitment on the terms asserted by the respondents, although admittedly of some particular benefit to the sellers ([1986] 2 All ER at 405):

> '... would not be regarded within the commercial community as being properly described as a confirmed irrevocable documentary credit... at any rate, one of the important purposes of such a credit... is that it shall not be open to the buyer by his own choice, with, it may be, no kind of legal justification whatever, when proper documents are tendered, to render the bank's obligation to the seller... a wholly useless obligation and one that has no legal effect.'

Nothing in the individual terminology of the credit was sufficiently compelling to detract from that commercial function or to usurp the normal undertaking, articulated by Art 10(b), that the confirming bank will honour the credit provided only that 'the stipulated documents are presented and... the terms and conditions of the credit... complied with.'

The decision concluded with an examination by Sir John Megaw of seven alleged discrepancies in the documents. The remarks on this point contain little of general interest, and each of the alleged discrepancies was found to be without substance.

Undue influence and agency

Avon Finance Ltd v Bridger [1985] 2 All ER 281 (discussed in All ER Rev 1985, pp 24–6) has been considered in *Kingsnorth Trust Ltd v Bell* [1986] 1 All ER 423 (where it was applied) and in *Coldunell Ltd v Gallon* [1986] 1 All ER 429 (where it was distinguished). In *Kingsnorth*, a mortgagor's wife was induced to participate in the grant of a charge over the matrimonial home, and in the release of her rights of occupation, in order to enable her husband to raise further finance for his business. She did not realise, however, that the purpose to which he proposed to put the money was not the support of an existing company of which she was secretary but the expansion of his interests into a frozen food enterprise. The wife received no independent advice prior to signing the charge and would certainly have refused to participate in the venture had she known its real purpose (which the receipt of independent advice on her part would have revealed). She was the victim of a fraudulent misrepresentation by her husband as to the objectives of the financing operation.

In these circumstances, the Court of Appeal held that the wife was entitled to relief from the mortgage. Dillon LJ conceded that the mere relationship of husband and wife does not generate a presumption of undue influence, and that there is no rule of law automatically entitling wives to avoid mortgages which they have transacted at their husbands' behest without independent advice. But here the husband could actually be shown to have exerted an improper influence. This entitled the wife to resist enforcement of the mortgage against any party on whose behalf the husband had been acting when he procured her participation in it.

The significant feature of the decision is the juristic link which the Court of Appeal felt able to make between the husband and the finance company (mortgagees) so as to render the mortgagees responsible for the influence exerted by the husband. Relying in *Avon Finance* and the older decisions cited therein, Dillon LJ expressed the position as follows ([1986] 1 All ER 423 at 428):

> '. . . where a creditor (or intending lender) desires the protection of a guarantee or charge on property from a third party other than the debtor and the circumstances are such that the debtor could be expected to have influence over that third party, the creditor ought for his own protection to insist that the third party has independent advice. That is the obvious means of avoiding the risk that the creditor will be held to have left it to the debtor to procure the execution of the relevant guarantee or security document by the third party.'

The crucial element was the entrustment by the creditor of the task of gaining the third party's participation in the security to the debtor who enjoyed and could assert the relevant influence: in other words, did the creditor leave it to the debtor to procure the execution of the charge by the third party? If such entrustment had occurred, and if the creditor should reasonably have been aware that the debtor possessed a relationship with the third party from which 'some influence' might be expected, the creditor would be equated with the debtor for the purpose of quantifying the third party's right to equitable relief.

On the present facts, such agency was held to be established. The mortgagees' solicitors had sent the mortgage deed to the husband's solicitors, with a letter requesting the latter to ensure that the deed was signed and to act as the finance company's solicitors on completion. The husband received the deed from a representative of his solicitors and agreed to arrange for the addition of his wife's signature, which in due course occurred. The effect of this series of delegations was, in Dillon LJ's opinion, to suggest two possible routes by which the mortgagees might be affixed with the husband's conduct: first, by regarding the husband's solicitors as the agents of the mortgagees' solicitors and thus as the sub-agents of the mortgagees themselves, with the result that when the husband's solicitors left it to the husband to procure his wife's signature they made themselves accountable for whatever means he adopted in order to achieve that result; or secondly, by viewing the transmission of the deed to the husband's solicitors as taking place to them as agents for the husband. It would follow from the latter analysis no less than from the former that the mortgagees had left it to the husband to obtain the wife's assent. In either event, they 'acted at their peril and are saddled with responsibility for the way in which Mr Bell in fact procured the execution of the mortgage by Mrs Bell.'

The opposite conclusion was reached in *Coldunell Ltd v Gallon* [1986] 1 All ER 429, where the participation of the dominant party in the procurement of the necessary signatures took the form of a wholly unauthorised and unadopted intervention in the transaction. In some respects the facts resembled those in *Avon Finance Ltd v Bridger* [1985] 2 All ER 281. The mortgagor and his wife were a retired couple, unversed in the ways of finance, while the villain of the piece was their son, a man in his fifties with some commercial experience. In contrast to *Avon Finance*, however, the loan in *Coldunell* was made (by arrangement between the mortgagor and his son) directly to the mortgagor, and the son was not nominally a party to the transaction. Nevertheless, he was clearly the active party in promoting the contract and was closely involved in it at every stage: the loan had been taken out purely in order to assist the son in legal proceedings in which he was involved; the signing of the mortgage and the deed of consent by his father and mother respectively had taken place in his presence, at his instigation, and in the company of a solicitor whom the son had invited to be present in order to witness the documents (and who explained the meaning of the deed of consent to the mother); the managing director of the finance company (mortgagees) had dealt solely with the son and had not met the father and mother throughout the transaction; the cheque for the amount of the loan had been handed directly to the son by the mortgagees' solicitors; the son had in some way come into possession of the relevant documents for signature prior to his parents' signing of them; and two earlier letters which the mortgagees' solicitors had written to each of his parents, warning them of the necessity for independent legal advice, had failed to reach them, thereby suggesting that the letters had been improperly intercepted by the son. Finally, the mortgagees were evidently aware that the parents' security was in relation to a loan which was to be made 'ultimately to the son' and could readily have inferred, from the age of the son, that his parents were elderly and likely to be susceptible to his influence.

The Court of Appeal had little difficulty in accepting that the parents were the victims of an improper dominance by their son, that it was through the positive exercise of that dominance that they came to sign the documents, and that the resultant transaction (adopting the requirement stated by the House of Lords in *National Westminister Bank plc v Morgan* [1985] 1 All ER 821) was manifestly disadvantageous to them. The court's reservations about relieving the parents from the security centred upon the extent, if any, to which the mortgagees themselves were responsible for the potentially vitiatory pressure exerted by the son.

In the event, these qualms proved decisive. The court held that, notwithstanding the son's extensive involvement, the mortgagees had not constituted him as their agent for the execution of the mortgage and could not be debarred from enforcing their security on the strength of his behaviour. In Purchas LJ's words, the son's conduct of matters amounted to a 'unilateral assumption' of the arrangements, which was not the product of any authorisation or consent on the part of the mortgagees and was effectively unknown to them. They had not explicitly entrusted him with the obtaining of his parents' signatures, nor had they simply 'left it to him' to procure them. The fact that the mortgagees' solicitors wrote the letters of warning to the parents demonstrated that they regarded themselves as responsible for the supervision of the transaction. At worst, the mortgagees had merely failed to take a more positive stance in forecasting and counteracting such undue influence as the son exerted over his parents; and, as Oliver LJ observed, such an omission fell far short of their adoption of him, or acquiescence in his conduct, as their agent ([1986] 1 All ER at 440):

> '... the fact is that no lender can ever be absolutely sure that a guarantor is not being subjected to pressure from the principal debtor, and to require him to do more than properly and fairly point out to the guarantor the desirability of obtaining independent advice, and to require the documents to be executed in the presence of a solicitor, is to put on commercial lenders a burden which would severely handicap the carrying out of... an extremely common transaction of everyday occurrence for banks and other commercial lenders.'

Purchas LJ felt that in order to grant the parents relief from the mortgage it would prove necessary to go beyond the principles established by earlier decisions so as to (ibid at 446):

> '... embrace a responsibility on a creditor not only to take reasonable steps to ensure that a guarantor obtains legal advice but also to guard against the fraudulent interception of the documents in which they give this advice... this would be extending the principles... to a dangerous extent and is not warranted inasmuch as it would impose on an innocent creditor the unconscionable actions of a person who was not to their knowledge acting in the transaction for the purposes of the execution of the documents.'

Although *Coldunell* turned largely on its own special facts, it suggests several points of more general interest. First, both Oliver and Purchas LJJ seem content to accept the formulation adopted in *Kingsnorth* and earlier cases, that the lender should have 'left it to' the principal debtor or other ascendant party to obtain the guarantor's or chargor's signature, in order for the lender to be affixed with the dominant person's conduct (see especially Purchas LJ at [1986] 1 All ER at 443). The recipe remains a somewhat vague and colloquial one; and one can imagine more marginal cases than *Coldunell* in which some more sophisticated description of the circumstances producing an agency relationship will prove necessary. Secondly, despite a suggestion by Purchas LJ (see preceding paragraph) that every creditor may be obliged to show that he took reasonable steps to ensure that the borrower was independently advised, it remains clear that no such necessity will arise until the transaction has given rise either to actual evidence of undue influence, or to a presumption to that effect, and until the transaction can be shown to have constituted a manifest disadvantage to the party seeking relief. When influence and disadvantageousness *are* indicated by the circumstances, however, and can be legally attributed to the creditor, it may be questioned whether it will avail the creditor merely to show that he made a gallant but unsuccessful effort to warn the guarantor or chargor about the need for independent advice: see the quotation from Oliver LJ, cited below, which requires proof not merely of the availability but of the *fact* of independent advice. Thirdly, Oliver LJ appears to accept (at 435) that proof of the availability and fact of independent advice may represent only one (albeit, perhaps, the most effective) method by which the creditor can displace evidence of undue influence:

'Once it is shown... that the party in a dominant position has achieved a
bargain in itself unconscionable, then he is saddled with the burden of
establishing affirmatively that no domination was practised to bring the
transaction about, *as for instance* by demonstrating not merely the availability
but the fact of separate and independent advice.' (ibid at 435: emphasis added)

Fourthly, it may not be unreasonable to regard both *Coldunell* and
Kingsnorth as cases of an alleged vicarious responsibility for fraudulent
misrepresentation or other deliberately wrongful conduct (such as the
application of improper pressure) on the part of the mortgagees' alleged
agents. If so, an analogy with *Armagas Ltd v Mundogas SA, The Ocean Frost*
[1986] 2 All ER 385 (and, in particular, with Lord Keith of Kinkel's
conviction that deliberate wrongs are to be treated specially for vicarious
liability purposes) may suggest that the victimised party may in future need
to show more than that the agent was simply acting in pursuance of the
entrustment to him of the task of obtaining the signature when the fraud or
other misconduct was committed. The comparison is not an exact one, of
course, because in cases like *Kingsnorth* and *Coldunell* the agent's
wrongdoing was being invoked as a defence to the enforcement of the
alleged principal's rights rather than as a positive cause of action in itself.
Whether the distinction is material (and, if not, how far the comparison can
be developed) remains to be seen.

Having dismissed the defence based on undue influence, the court in
Coldunell went on to consider whether the mortgagees could discharge the
burden of proving that the transaction was not an extortionate credit
bargain within s 138 of the Consumer Credit Act 1974. In the event, the
transaction was upheld on this point as well. This aspect of the case is
discussed (along with other recent cases on extortionate credit bargains) in
our title on Consumer Law (p 73, below).

Carriers

Air carriage: interest on damages

The litigation preceding *Swiss Bank Corp v Brinks-MAT Ltd* was lengthy
and complex, but the point reported in [1986] 2 All ER 188 is a short one.
Damages had been awarded against the second and third defendant airlines
(Swissair and KLM) under Art 22(2)(a) of the Warsaw–Hague Convention,
as incorporated into English law by the Carriage by Air Act 1961, Sch I. In
accordance with the Convention, the sums payable by these two defendants
were limited to some £267 and £579 respectively. The plaintiffs now
asserted that they were entitled to recover interest on those sums, but
Bingham J held that (despite the natural predisposition of an English judge
in favour of such an award) interest was not payable. This conclusion was
reached upon an objective construction of the text of the Convention,
Art 24(1) of which provided that actions for damages in cases covered by it
'can only be brought subject to the conditions and limits set out in this
Convention.' Bingham J's conclusion that the Convention limits were,
with a single exception, '... global and comprehensive of every expense to
which a carrier may be put as a result of any claim subject to the limits ...'
(at 191) was fortified, in his Lordship's view, by the provisions of Art 22(4),

which declares that the limits prescribed elsewhere in Art 22 are not to prevent the court 'from awarding, in accordance with its own law, in addition, the whole or part of the court costs and of the other expenses of the litigation incurred by the plaintiff.' The fact that costs were given specific inclusory treatment in Art 22(4) demonstrated clearly to Bingham J that other possible species of monetary award (such as interest) would likewise have been made the subject of a specific reference had it been intended that they should be recoverable.

Bingham J conceded that his construction of the Convention was not one which suggested itself so obviously as to make any contrary construction incapable of argument. The plaintiffs' argument that interest on damages should not be treated as part of the damages themselves, for example, was an attractive one which, had it not been contradicted by the presence of Art 22(4), might well have proved persuasive. Furthermore, had there been an 'international consensus on the construction of the Convention on this point', Bingham J indicated that he would have felt strongly persuaded to fall into line with that general opinion, even though such a construction was at variance with his own predilection. Certainly, the judge considered that it was appropriate in these circumstances to consult 'English and international authorities, authoritative writings . . . and any clear and admissible indications . . . in any travaux preparatoires or in the French text . . .' (see 191). In fact, however, he was able to detect nothing in the case-law of this or of other jurisdictions, or in the travaux preparatoires or the French text of the Convention, which remotely persuaded him to a different conclusion from that which he reached on a purely objective construction of the Convention itself. American authority was divided and of ambiguous application to the present dispute; no English decision had approached any positive consideration of the question; virtually nothing was yielded from the French text, while the travaux preparatoires were inscrutable on the point; there was little academic comment, and that which existed was not unanimous; and Bingham J did not regard a suggested analogy with English maritime practice as helpful. The survey therefore merely confirmed Bingham J in his initial opinion that he had no power to award interest in this case.

Copyright, patents, registered designs and trade marks

Intellectual property matters are not conventionally discussed within this title, but readers may find it useful to be reminded in passing of three decisions during 1986. In two of them, the House of Lords felt itself obliged to withhold the protection sought and to resist what Lord Templeman described in *Re Coca-Cola Co's Applications* [1986] 2 All ER 274 at 275, as successive attempts 'to expand on the boundaries of intellectual property and to convert a protective law into a source of monopoly.' The statute being invoked for this purpose in *Re Coca-Cola Co's Applications* was the Trade Marks Act 1938. The Coca-Cola Company had applied to the Registrar of Trade Marks for registration, as a trade mark, of the distinctively-shaped bottle under which its products had been marketed world-wide since the early 1920s. The shape of the bottle had been registered as a registered design under the Patents and Designs Act 1907, but the effect of that registration had expired in 1940. Since that time, there was no constraint upon the use of the design of the bottle by rival beverage manufacturers: hence the current proceedings.

The application failed. The quality of 'distinctiveness' alone was held to be insufficient by itself to justify registration under the Act; Coca-Cola had to go further and substantiate their 'startling proposition' that the bottle itself was a trade mark. In the House of Lords' view, this question had been answered by the decision of the Court of Appeal in *Re James's Trade Mark, James v Soulby* (1886) 33 Ch D 392, where Lindley LJ had observed (at 395) that 'A mark must be something distinct from the thing being marked. The thing itself cannot be a mark of itself . . .' Neither the normal meaning of the word 'mark', nor its statutory definition contained in s 68(1) of the 1938 Act, was capable of extending the word beyond some emblem or symbol which distinguishes goods to those very goods themselves: thus a bottle 'is a container not a mark' (per Lord Templeman at 276). Nothing in the House's decision in *Smith Kline and French Laboratories Ltd v Sterling-Winthrop Group Ltd* [1975] 2 All ER 578 warranted any contrary inference and the present conclusion was clearly regarded by Lord Templeman as a desirable one; for the prospect of a manufacturer's being able to register any distinctive container or article as a trade mark threatened to produce 'a total and perpetual monopoly in containers and articles achieved by means of the 1938 Act', irrespective of the applicability of the Patents Act, Registered Designs Act or Copyright Act. Such a result can hardly have been the intention of those drafting the 1938 Act. The policy of the law was manifestly served by allowing any rival manufacturer 'to sell any container or article of similar shape provided the container or article is labelled or packaged in a manner which avoids confusion as to the origin of the goods in the container or the origin of the article.' ([1986] 2 All ER at 276).

An earlier endeavour to synthesise a monopoly from protective legislation had been mounted by British Leyland in *British Leyland Motor Corp Ltd v Armstrong Patents Co Ltd* [1986] 1 All ER 850; here, too, the action failed. The decision of the House of Lords contains much of interest to students of intellectual property, but only the barest summary can be offered within the present confines.

The defendants had, by the process of reverse engineering, copied original spare parts of the plaintiffs' cars and sold them in competition with the plaintiffs. In so doing, the defendants had enjoyed no access to, and had made no copies of, the plaintiffs' original design drawings themselves; they simply derived their own manufactured spares from the physical shape and dimensions of the plaintiffs' original components. Taking the example of a particular exhaust system used in a model of car which they manufactured, the plaintiffs sought an injunction and damages for breach of copyright, relying on ss 3(1)(a) and 48(1) of the Copyright Act 1956. They conceded that there could be no patent in relation to the exhaust system and that the designs and drawings from which it was derived were not registrable as registered designs.

A majority of the House of Lords held that the copying of the plaintiffs' exhaust system did indeed infringe the plaintiffs' copyright in the design drawings. Even though a particular functional object might not be patentable (or its design registrable), there could nevertheless be a breach of copyright over the 'artistic work' which the design drawings for the object constituted, when an unlicensed party reproduced the object by means of a process of indirect copying of any such drawing or design. The vindication of this copyright had, however, to be regarded as subordinate to the competing entitlement of all those individuals who purchased the plaintiffs' vehicles (whether directly from the plaintiffs or at some further remove), that they should enjoy access to a free market in spare parts in order to keep their cars in good repair and working condition. To deprive such vehicle-proprietors of the necessary free market in spare parts would constitute something analogous to a derogation from grant and would not be sanctioned by the House. It followed that the plaintiffs were not entitled to enforce their copyright in such a manner as to maintain a monopoly in the supply of spare parts for their vehicles, and their action accordingly failed.

Lastly, *Sevcon Ltd v Lucas CAV Ltd* [1986] 2 All ER 104, HL, clarifies an important point concerning the time of accrual of a cause of action in respect of an infringement of patent. The House of Lords held that infringements of a patent committed between the date of publication of the complete specification and the date on which the patent was sealed were actionable because s 13(4) of the Patents Act 1949 conferred rights and privileges upon the applicant during that period, and that the rights of action in respect of such infringements accrued when the infringements were committed. Although an applicant might subsequently lose his right of action if he failed in due course to obtain his patent, or if the complete specification were retrospectively amended in such a manner that the defendant's conduct no longer amounted to an infringement, the proviso to s 13(4) of the 1949 Act merely postponed until the obtaining of the patent the time at which the applicant could take action; it did not postpone the accrual of the cause of action itself. In the present case, the result of these conclusions was that the action had become statute-barred under s 2 of the Limitation Act 1980, the alleged acts of infringement having been committed more than six years before the issue of the writ.

Insurance

Motor insurance

The decision of Esyr Lewis QC in *Samuelson v National Insurance and Guarantee Corp* [1984] 3 All ER 107 (see All ER Rev 1984, p 28) has been reversed by the Court of Appeal: [1986] 3 All ER 417. The result is an interesting exercise in the reconciliation and amplification of potentially ambiguous terms in a contract for motor insurance.

The plaintiff's De Tomaso car was stolen from Hammersmith. It had been driven and left there by a car repairer to whom he had bailed it on the previous day. The car repairer needed to take the car to Hammersmith in order to ensure that the parts which he obtained from the agents actually fitted the car. He parked it near the agents' premises and was away only for a few minutes. The car was never recovered.

In refusing to indemnify him, the insurers had relied upon the following provisions: first, exception 1(c) in the policy which purported to exclude liability whenever the car was being driven by any person other than the authorised driver, or was, for the purposes of being driven, in the charge of any person other than the authorised driver; and secondly, the statement in the motor insurance certificate, issued with the policy, which excluded the operation of the policy whenever the vehicle was being used for any purpose in connection with the motor trade. Against these provisions, the plaintiff relied inter alia upon para 1(a)(i) of the general exceptions in the policy. This stated that the exclusion from the policy of use in connection with the motor trade did not apply when the car was in the custody or control of a member of the motor trade for the purpose of its repair.

In the event, this introduction of para 1(a)(i) into the argument appears to have produced an unnecessary complication which, in the Court of Appeal's view, regrettably preoccupied the parties at the trial. The plaintiffs had contended that circumstances must exist in which para 1(a)(i) was capable of usurping exception 1(c), and that one such situation in which para 1(a)(i) would prevail would be the case where a motor trader, to whom the car had been entrusted for repair, was driving it at the time of the misadventure. The Deputy Judge's rejection of this argument was expressly approved by O'Connor and Robert Goff LJJ in the Court of Appeal, and impliedly endorsed by the third member, Nourse LJ. Para 1(a)(i) did not impose any qualification on exception 1(c) but was subject to it: the driving of the vehicle by anyone other than the authorised driver (even by a repairer to whom the latter had bailed it) remained in all circumstances an excluded risk (see Robert Goff LJ at 420).

The Court of Appeal focussed more closely upon the plaintiff's second argument, which was based simply upon the construction of exception 1(c). Here the plaintiff contended that, since the car was admittedly not being driven by the repairer at the material time, the only situation in which liability could be excluded under exception 1(c) was that in which the car was in the repairer's charge 'for the purpose of being driven.' But in this case, the plaintiff argued, such control as the repairer enjoyed over the car at Hammersmith was for purposes of repair and not for the purpose of driving it, with the result that exception 1(c) was, on its own terms, inapplicable. (Alternatively, the plaintiff contended that where the driver of the vehicle had charge of it for more than one purpose, the court should pay regard to the *primary* purpose underlying his control: which, in this case, was the purpose of repair.)

The Court of Appeal unanimously accepted the first of these arguments. In Robert Goff LJ's words:

> '... the car, while [*the repairer*] was in the agents' premises in Hammersmith, was there for a particular purpose independent of being driven; it was there to be used for seeing whether spare parts obtainable from the agents did "suit and fit the vehicle" ... once the car had arrived at the agents' premises at Hammersmith, it ceased to be "for the purpose of being driven ... in the charge of" [*the repairer*]; it was there, in his charge, for another distinct purpose, which was still operative at the time when the car was stolen' (at p 422).

The court was not persuaded to the contrary opinion by the defendant's argument that an oscillation of the policy—from being off risk, to on risk, to off risk again during a normal journey from the repairer's premises to those of the agents and back—would be contrary to the intention of the parties and would render the policy absurd. As O'Connor LJ pointed out (at 419) at least one other provision of the policy seemed to contemplate such an effect.

Of course, the Court of Appeal's interpretation still left some scope for the operation of that part of exception 1(c) which referred to the vehicle's being in the charge of an unauthorised driver for the purpose of being driven: an example would be where an unauthorised person, while driving the car, paused briefly during his journey (see per Robert Goff LJ at 421). The important point to observe, as Robert Goff LJ pointed out, was that the effect of exception 1(c) in any given situation was *not* answerable merely by posing the question 'Why is the car in the charge of the unauthorised person?' The real question was whether, at the relevant time, the car was, for the purpose of being driven, in the charge of the unauthorised person:

> 'These questions are not, I think, the same, and the answer to the second question is not dependent on ascertaining the purpose for which the insured entrusted the car to the unauthorised person or the purpose for which that person was driving the car. We are concerned here only with the question whether the car is, for the purpose of being driven, in the charge of the unauthorised person. It is the immediate situation of the car with which we are concerned. The ultimate purpose, whether of the insured or of the unauthorised person, is, I think, irrelevant' (at p 421).

Adopting this approach, the court concluded that exception 1(c) was inapplicable. The plaintiff's appeal was accordingly allowed.

Monopolies and mergers

R v The Monopolies and Mergers Commission and the Secretary of State for Trade and Industry, ex p Argyll Group plc [1986] 2 All ER 257 involved an application by Argyll for judicial review of a decision made by the Chairman of the Monopolies and Mergers Commission in the course of its takeover battle for Distillers. Argyll had made two successive offers for Distillers which were not referred by the Secretary of State to the Commission; an offer made by Guinness was, however, referred on 13 February. Argyll's delight, however, was short-lived; within the following week Guinness had so revised its takeover plans (by arranging to dispose of certain Scotch whisky brands controlled by it and Distillers from the proposed merger in order to reduce the combined group's relevant market share below 25%) that the Chairman of the Commission on 19 February was able to rule, applying s 75(5) of the Act, that 'the proposal to make arrangements such as are mentioned in the reference' had been abandoned. The Secretary of State accepted these findings, thus putting Guinness back on level terms with Argyll. Guinness then succeeded in winning the takeover battle, though in a manner which (as the world is now only too well aware) became the subject of a Department of Trade investigation.

Argyll thereupon sought judicial review of this decision by the Chairman of the Commission. The interpretation which they advanced of the phrase 'the proposal to make arrangements such as are mentioned in the reference...' was that it covered *any* merger proposal which Guinness might put forward, with the effect that the reference would have to proceed unless and until Guinness could be shown to have withdrawn all merger proposals for Distillers, of whatever kind. This interpretation failed, however, to convince McPherson J, who refused judicial review. An appeal was heard at very short notice (the judgment being given on 14 March, only eight days after the High Court decision) which confirmed his judgment on the major issues.

The leading judgment of the Court of Appeal was given by Donaldson MR who ruled, after careful analysis of the relevant provisions of the 1973 Act applying to mergers, that the interpretation put forward by Argyll was inconsistent with other provisions in the Act; these made clear that the merger proposals which the Secretary of State could refer to the Commission were those proposals *in fact* put forward by the bidder and not any or all variations upon those proposals which might subsequently be adopted. He found that it was a question of fact and degree, to be determined by the Commission (whose decision the Secretary of State should respect), as to whether in any particular case detailed alterations to takeover proposals by a bidder were of so fundamental a nature as to represent an abandonment of the original proposals or were merely an amended version of those original proposals without affecting their substantive content. The Chairman therefore had not misdirected himself on this interpretation of s 75(5) of the Act.

Whilst finding that the Chairman of the Commission had himself no statutory authority for making the decision as to 'abandonment', since technically the Act required this to be done by the group of its members appointed to conduct the reference, the Master of Rolls had no difficulty in then proceeding in the exercise of his discretion to refuse judicial review to Argyll. Pointing out that the courts had to approach such issues 'with a proper awareness of the needs of public administration', he listed the main relevant needs as concentration on substance rather than form, the proper balancing of both public and private interests involved, and the need for speed, decisiveness and finality of decision. After reviewing these issues in the context of the particular case, he found no reason to exercise his discretion in Argyll's favour.

He was, however, willing to concede that Argyll had standing to make the application, commenting that whilst 'this interest may not represent a pure and burning passion to see that public law is rightly administered ... that could be said of most applicants for judicial review'. Dillon and Neill LJJ delivered concurring decisions, differing in only minor respects from that of the Master of the Rolls.

Sale of goods

(a) Payment by credit card: nature of transaction

Re Charge Card Services Ltd [1986] 3 All ER 289 arose from the insolvency of a credit card company, and is also discussed in the title on Contract, p 91, below. The following comment is limited to certain initial conclusions reached by Millett J concerning the relationship between a supplier of goods and an acquirer who elects to pay for them by credit card.

Charge Card Services Ltd ('Charge Card') issued credit cards to selected subscribers for the acquisition of motor fuel and associated products from nominated garages within the Charge Card franchise. The arrangement was a conventional one whereby, upon the card-holder's electing to pay by credit card and signing the garage's sales voucher, the garage would collect payment minus commission from Charge Card, and Charge Card would in turn collect the full amount from the card-holder. (It may be noted in passing that certain agreed subscribers were permitted to acquire cards for use by their employees. These customers were referred to by Millett J as 'account holders', but since, in a case where the two were different, account holders would normally stand as undisclosed principals of card-holders, nothing turned on the point.)

Charge Card became insolvent, owing some £2 million to unsecured creditors. Among such creditors were a number of garages which had not yet been reimbursed by Charge Card for goods supplied by them to card-holders. The garages, anxious to maximise the fund available for distribution to unsecured creditors, fastened upon the large amount still owing to Charge Card by individual card-holders. After the liquidator had collected these 'receivables' and deducted his expenses, they produced a net amount of just over £2 million. But this fund was also claimed by a debt-factoring company (Commercial Credit Services Ltd) with which Charge Card had earlier concluded an assignment of its receivables. The garages sought to frustrate Commercial Credit's claim by contending that, in any case where the relevant debt had not been discharged by Charge Card, the garages were entitled to recover directly from account-holders the amounts outstanding under contracts for the supply of petrol and associated products.

This assertion involved Millett J in an extensive analysis of the legal anatomy of charge card transactions. His essential conclusions were as follows.

First, that the overall pattern of relationships in a case such as the present could not be rationalised as a tripartite transaction in which all of the three parties (supplier, acquirer and card company) were contractually related inter se. Rather, the situation disclosed three distinct bilateral contracts: that between acquirer and supplier, that between supplier and card company, and that between card company and acquirer. The acquirer's obligation under the first of these three contracts was primarily an obligation to pay in cash, but subject (in the case of a garage which held itself out as a member of the scheme) to a right of election on the part of the acquirer to discharge his debt by using his charge card. The resultant agreement to pay by means of the card resulted from the card-holder's acceptance of a standing offer by the supplier to receive payment by that method. It made no legal difference for this purpose whether the agreement 'is made at the pump before the contract of supply is entered into or at the till and after the contract of supply has been concluded' (at 300). In either event, the garage's agreement to accept payment by means of the card did not constitute a distinct and separate transaction but represented 'merely an agreement on the method of payment under the contract of supply' (ibid).

Secondly, payment by means of the charge card was not a mere conditional payment and was not subject to some auxiliary recourse by the supplier against the acquirer in the event of the card-company's failing to meet its own obligations under the supplier–card company transaction. Millett J rejected a proposed analogy with irrevocable letters of credit for this purpose and listed (at 303) a series of factors which served to distinguish the two species of obligation. Among these were (i) the fact that letters of credit are designed to operate within large-scale international trading contracts, where negotiation is normal and the parties are likely to be acquainted with one another, whereas charge card transactions conventionally operate in the lowlier milieu of small consumer debts, incurred without negotiation as between parties who are not previously acquainted; (ii) the fact that the issuing bank under a letter of credit will not usually be the subject of agreement between seller and buyer, but will normally be nominated exclusively by the buyer after the conclusion of the principal transaction, whereas the identity of a card-issuing company is 'necessarily a matter for agreement'; (iii) the absence in any event of any prior contract between issuing bank and seller under a letter of credit, whereas a charge card scheme was normally workable only when supplier and card company were in pre-existing legal relations; (iv) the fact that a letter of credit is employed for the 'sole purpose' of affording security to the seller, whereas the use of the credit card method of payment is advantageous to both parties, not least because it enables the supplier to consolidate his debtors; and (v) the fact that there are discrepancies under charge card transactions between (a) the amount that the card company is obliged to pay the supplier as opposed to the amount that the acquirer is obliged to pay the card company, and (b) the time at which the card company must pay the supplier as opposed to the time at which the acquirer must pay the card company. To require the acquirer to reimburse the supplier for the full amount shown on the sales voucher as soon as the card company defaulted would be to inflict on the acquirer the worst of all possible worlds: a duty to pay the larger of two possible amounts at the earlier of two possible times. The collective effect of these ingredients was, in his Lordship's opinion, 'sufficient not only to displace any presumption that payment by such means is a conditional payment only, but to support a presumption to the contrary' (at 304). The resultant analysis was seen by Millett J as conforming with public expectations, and as readily avoidable by any supplier who wished for supplementary recourse against acquirers: such a trader need do no more than insist upon the conditional form of payment by cheque, supported by a bank card.

In the course of his consideration of this point, Millett J rejected the 'general principle of law' advanced by counsel for the garages that 'whenever a method of payment is adopted which involves a risk of non-payment, there is a presumption, rebuttable by proof of special circumstances, that this is taken as conditional payment only, so that the risk of default is on the paying party.' In his Lordship's view, no such principle existed. The question had hitherto been approached by the courts pragmatically, according to the special circumstances of the particular transaction, rather than by derivation from some conceptual starting point. The rejection of the allegedly-conditional quality of the card-holders' payment by means of their charge cards in this case accorded with that pragmatic approach.

(b) C & f contract; reservation of title but transmission of risk; buyer's right to sue carrier for negligence

See the title on Tort, p 309, below and the section on Bailments and personal property in general (p 25, above).

(c) Fitness for purpose: misleading packaging

Wormell v RHM Agriculture (East) Ltd [1986] 1 All ER 769 involved the sale of some £6,500 worth of 'Commando' herbicide by the defendants to the plaintiff, a farmer. The sale followed conversations between the defendants' agricultural chemical manager and the plaintiff, who was concerned about the spread of wild oats among his winter wheat crop. On being told that Commando was the only preparation suitable for his particular conditions, the plaintiff purchased two quantities in March and April 1982. He applied it to his crop in May and June. He had been unable to spray the crop earlier than that because of unusually wet weather.

Regrettably, his use of the herbicide at those times was the result of a misunderstanding. Instructions on the label of the can in which the Commando was supplied indicated that its use outside a certain period carried the risk of injury to the crop. The plaintiff was aware of the warning but decided to take the risk of a late application of the herbicide outside that period. He interpreted the label as meaning simply that, whereas the use of Commando outside the specified time might impair the crop, it would not impair the weedkilling capacity of the product itself. The plaintiff evidently believed that the only substantial hazard of a late application was that the Commando would damage more than the weeds.

The truth was otherwise. Commando depended for its effect on the ability of the crop growth to outstrip the growth rate of the wild oats, and thus to smother the oats and deny them access to the light. Unless the Commando was applied when the crop had a further 12 inches' growth in it, this 'competitive effect' could not be achieved. The plaintiff's crop lacked the necessary remaining growth, and the result was a virtually negligible reduction in the incidence of the weeds. By August the plaintiff was complaining of a 'massive cover of seedheads' in his fields and clearly saw the spraying of his crops as a complete waste of time. He claimed under ss 14(2) and 14(3) of the Sale of Goods Act 1979 for the cost of the herbicide which he had wasted and for the cost of the wasted labour.

The deputy judge upheld the claim. His main conclusions were as follows. First, the plaintiff's interpretation of the instructions was one which a reasonable farmer or user might adopt (and was therefore, presumably, an interpretation which the defendants could reasonably have foreseen). Secondly, the defendants' representative should reasonably have foreseen that the plaintiff, in buying the Commando, was relying on the defendants to supply a herbicide which was suitable not only at the time of purchase but also, if necessary, for use several months later: in fact, as soon as the plaintiff could get on to the land to apply it. Thirdly, the instructions on the can, with their misleading indication of the continuing efficacy of the Commando, rendered the Commando unfit for its purpose within s 14(3) of the Sale of Goods Act.

It is in the third of these findings that the main interest of the decision lies. According to the deputy judge, the word 'goods' in the 1979 Act comprehended not only the herbicide itself but its packaging and accompanying instructions as well:

> 'All of these, it seems to me, are part of the goods. One must look at all of them as a whole ... [B]y selling goods with such instructions the seller is warranting that the chemical, when used in accordance with those instructions, will be reasonably fit for its purpose ... If a retailer ... sells goods (that is the chemical together with its container and instructions) and those instructions make the goods not reasonably fit for their purpose, in my view there is a breach of s 14(3) of the 1979 Act.' ([1986] 1 All ER at pp 778, 779)

In thus concluding, the deputy judge drew support from *Vacwell Engineering Co Ltd v BDH Chemicals Ltd* [1969] 3 All ER 1681 and, more particularly, from the Canadian decision in *Willis v FMC Machinery and Chemicals Ltd* (1976) 68 DLR (3d) 127. There, Nicholson J had held that the sellers' failure to supply instructions along with a certain brand of weedkiller (an omission which misled the buyer into believing that the weedkiller would operate adequately when mixed with insecticide) constituted a breach of the implied condition as to fitness for use. The deputy judge in the present case clearly saw no difference in principle between a complete lack of necessary instructions and the supply of instructions which were inadequate. In either situation, the *Willis* decision showed that the availability of proper instructions was a matter which '... at any rate can be taken into account' in considering whether or not the main product is fit for its purpose. It might be added that a similar conclusion to that in *Willis* was reached in relation to a contract for the leasing of a sprinkler system in *Imperial Furniture Pty Ltd v Automatic Fire Sprinkler Pty Ltd* (1967) 1 NSWLR 29.

The case is also discussed in the article on Consumer Law, p 76, below.

Company Law

D D PRENTICE, MA, LLB, JD
Barrister, Fellow of Pembroke College, Oxford

Indemnity order as to costs

In 1975 the Court of Appeal in *Wallersteiner v Moir* [1974] 3 All ER 217 (see now *Supreme Court Practice*, Fifth Cumulative Supplement 1985, Ord 15, r 12) formulated an imaginative procedure for the making of an indemnity order as to costs where a shareholder brings a derivative action on behalf of a company. As applications for this type of order are normally made in Chambers there has been little guidance as to the basis on which these orders are made. Recently, however, there have been a number of decisions which throw light on this area. The most important of these is the decision of Walton J in *Smith v Croft* [1986] 2 All ER 551; [1986] BCLC 207. In the course of his judgment, which evinced a less than enthusiastic reception of the procedure in *Wallersteiner* because of the unfair burden which Walton J felt that it could impose on a company, the court formulated the following propositions:

(a) An order that a company should indemnify a shareholder as to costs should normally not be made on an ex parte basis and the company should be joined as a party so that all the facts could be before the court.

(b) All relevant evidence should be made available to the company unless there are good reasons, such as legal professional privilege, for withholding the information.

(c) It was necessary for the plaintiff to show that he lacked the resources to finance the action and in dealing with this the Master should take a 'broad view' so that where the plaintiff was in reality a 'nominal plaintiff' representing a group of shareholders then the resources of these shareholders should be taken into consideration. Whereas the other aspects of the judgment in *Smith v Croft* will probably improve the efficiency of the *Wallersteiner* procedure, this limitation is more difficult to justify. The reason why an indemnity order is made in the case of a derivative action is because the plaintiff is appearing in a representative capacity and, provided he satifies the requirements for the granting of the order, then his wealth or lack of it should not be a relevant consideration. The decision of Walton J is to be contrasted with that in *Jaybird Group Ltd v Greenwood* [1986] BCLC 319 where the court considered that the wealth of the plaintiff was not a relevant consideration in deciding whether or not a *Wallersteiner* order should be made. This it is submitted is the preferable approach. As the court pointed out in *Greenwood*, making wealth a relevant factor in deciding whether or not a *Wallersteiner* order should be made could give rise to acute problems of implementation where more than one shareholder is involved in the action and it could be easily evaded by selecting an impoverished shareholder to bring the action.

(d) Normally only a percentage of the plaintiff's costs should be paid as this will provide the plaintiff with an incentive to pursue the matter diligently to recover the balance.

Also of relevance in this context is *Watts v Midland Bank plc* [1986] BCLC 15 in which Peter Gibson J was of the opinion that where a company is hopelessly insolvent then an indemnity order would normally not be made as the whole purpose of the order is to benefit the shareholders as a class who simply cannot be benefited in this situation. Of course, if the derivative action could result in the company recovering assets that would be available for the shareholders then the situation would surely be different.

Lastly, for completeness sake, some mention should be made of *Re Charge Card Services Ltd* [1986] BCLC 316 where Hoffmann J held that the court could not make a prospective order as to costs as this was a matter for the discretion of the trial judge hearing the action.

The derivative action

In the period under review, there have been two cases of interest exploring the nature of the derivative action. In the first of these, *Watts v Midland Bank plc* (mentioned in the previous section) Peter Gibson J held that a shareholder could not commence a derivative action against a receiver of a company for negligence. In this situation the board still retained a residual power to bring an action on behalf of the company and there was therefore no justification for permitting a shareholder to bring an action. Also, it is worth pointing out that in this case the action was against a third party who was not alleged to have been implicated with the directors or the majority of the shareholders in any wrong to the company and it is open to question whether a derivative action will lie in these circumstances as the wrongdoers are in no way in control of the company.

It has always been generally accepted that where a company no longer exists then it is not possible for a shareholder to bring a derivative action on its behalf; if the company no longer exists it is difficult to see how an action on its behalf would lie. *Fargro v Godfroy* [1986] BCLC 370, [1986] 2 All ER 279 is the first English case that specifically recognises this.

Preferential creditors

Re G L Saunders Ltd [1986] BCLC 40 involved a question that curiously has not been the subject of any previous authority: where a receiver appointed under a fixed and a floating charge has a surplus available after the realisation of the fixed charge, must this surplus be devoted to satisfying the claims of the preferential creditors or does it form part of the general assets of the company? Nourse J held that the fixed charge surplus was not caught by s 94 of the Companies Act 1948 (see now Insolvency Act 1986, s 46) as the section only applied to assets coming into the hands of the receiver that had been subject to the floating charge. The distribution of assets subject to a fixed charge was governed by s 105 of the Law of Property Act 1925 which provided that once the property has been paid off any surplus had to be paid to the 'person entitled to the mortgaged property', in this case the company.

Petition to wind up company being wound up voluntarily

In *Buckley on the Companies Acts* (14th edn, 1981) Vol 1, p 800 the editors state that it is rarely possible to obtain the compulsory winding up of a company already in voluntary liquidation without attacking the probity and competence of the liquidator. In *Re Palmer Marine Surveys Ltd* [1986] BCLC 106 Hoffmann J considered that this was an 'unduly reductionist' reading of the authorities and that there were other circumstances that would justify the making of a compulsory order. In the case Hoffmann J made a compulsory order with respect to a company that was being wound up voluntarily on the grounds that the petitioner would have a legitimate sense of grievance as it had not had an adequate opportunity to make its views known at the meeting of creditors summoned under s 293 of the Companies Act 1948. Hoffmann J also considered that in determining the weight to be attached to the views of the creditors all creditors were not to be treated equally; the views of creditors who were formerly shareholders or connected with the company could be appropriately discounted. Also, if there is a legitimate basis for concern as to the probity of the management of the company, this also is a factor to be taken into consideration in deciding whether a winding up order should be made (see also *Re Lowerstoft Traffic Services Ltd* [1986] BCLC 81).

Class of shares

The Companies Act 1985 on a number of occasions refers to 'class of shares' or to 'rights attached to a class of shares', but somewhat curiously it does not attempt to define these concepts (see also s 17(2)(b)). Outside the area of what constitutes a class for the purpose of s 425, there has been little judicial authority on this topic. The decision of Scott J in *Cumbrian Newspapers Group Ltd v Cumberland & Westmoreland Herald Newspaper & Printing Co Ltd* [1986] BCLC 286, [1986] 2 All ER 816 is the first case to deal with the issue of what constitutes a class of shares for the purpose of the provisions in the Companies Act 1985 dealing with the variation of class rights (s 125–127). The facts in that case were somewhat complex and arguably will occur rarely as with a more astute drafting of the defendant company's articles the problem could have been avoided. The articles of the defendant company conferred rights on the plaintiff company *eo nomine*: these included the right to appoint a director and the right to have registered in its name shares that had been transferred to it. The defendant company proposed to alter its articles of association to modify the special rights conferred on the plaintiff and the plaintiff argued that, as the alteration constituted an alteration to its class rights, the defendant because of s 125(4) had therefore to comply with the provision in the articles requiring the consent of the class in question before the alteration could be carried out.

In deciding whether rights were 'rights attached to class of shares', rights in the articles could, according to Scott J, be divided into three broad classes: (i) rights or benefits 'annexed' to a particular class of shares such as dividend rights; (ii) rights conferred on individuals but not in their capacity as 'members or shareholders of the company', for example a right conferred on a person to act as a company's solicitor (*Eley v Positive Government Life*

Assurance Co Ltd (1875) 1 Ex D 20); (iii) rights which, although not attached to a particular class of shares, were nevertheless conferred on a person in the capacity of member or shareholder of the company. It is clear that the first category is a class right (even if the right is defeasible on the transfer of the shares) and that the second category is not. It is the category (iii) right (the one involved in the *Cumbrian Newspapers* case) that causes the problem. At least as regards the variation of class rights provisions of the Companies Act 1985, the orthodox view is that the share capital of a company will only be divided into classes where the articles expressly provide for separate classes of shares. But there is no good reason why a class of shares should not be defined according to the identity of its holder. In the *Cumbrian Newspapers* case, Scott J held that the right attached to the plaintiff's shares were class rights and that therefore they could only be altered with the consent of the class in question. While this is somewhat novel it does not constitute such a dramatic departure from orthodox theory; the dividing line between category (i) and category (iii) rights may be so thin that it is not worth trying to draw it.

Receivers

The position of the receiver has rightly been considered a curious one: appointed to look after the interests of the creditors he nevertheless is the agent of the company, an agency relationship now recognised in the Insolvency Act 1986, s 44. A consequence of this is illustrated by *Ratford v Northavon District Council* [1986] BCLC 397, [1986] 3 All ER 193: joint receivers not liable for rates incurred by a company where debenture under which receivers were appointed stated that the receivers were to be the agents of the company. This dual and conflicting loyalty of a receiver is bound to create difficulties and tensions some of which have been explored in recent cases. In *Shamji v Johnson Matthey Bankers Ltd* [1986] BCLC 278 the company argued that in appointing receivers the creditor owed it a duty of care to consider all relevant matters before making any appointment. This was rejected by Hoffmann J on the grounds that where a creditor had a contractual right to appoint a receiver it owed no duty of care as regards the timing of the appointment. This is clearly supported by authority and indeed any other rule would greatly alter the nature of the security provided by a charge over a company's assets. In *Bank of Baroda v Panessar* [1986] BCLC 497 Walton J rejected another attempt to circumscribe the right of a charge holder to enforce the security. In that case it was argued that a debenture holder, where the sums secured were payable on demand, could not appoint a receiver to enforce its charge unless the notice demanding payment stated the exact amount due from the company and the company had been permitted a reasonable time in which to raise the moneys to make payment. Both of these points were rejected by the court. As regards the latter, Walton J declined to follow Commonwealth authority that a creditor was obliged to accord a debtor a reasonable time to raise the funds to make payment even where the moneys owed were due. All a debenture holder was obliged to do was to allow the debtor a reasonable time to effect the mechanics of payment and given modern methods of money transfer this would normally be hours rather than days. Both of these decisions enhance the security provided by a debenture by not circumscribing the right of the debenture holder to enforce the security once the conditions for its enforcement have arisen.

The agency of the receiver is not a completely bogus one. In *Gomba Holdings v Homan* [1986] BCLC 331 the company argued that the receiver was obliged to supply it with information relating to the disposal and proposed disposal of the assets subject to the charge under which he had been appointed. Hoffmann J considered that the receivership's agency could oblige the receiver to supply the company with information above and beyond that laid down in the Companies Act 1985, s 497. This obligation, however, had to give way to the obligation of the receiver to protect the interests of the debenture holder: 'the receiver's duty to provide... information (to the company) must be subordinated to his primary duty not to do anything which may prejudice the interests of the debenture-holder' (at 337h; cf now Insolvency Act 1986, s 48(6)). The *Gomba* case indicates that the agency of the receiver although somewhat artificial is not completely meaningless.

Floating charge: automatic crystallisation

A question that has much tantalised company lawyers is whether it is possible to insert a provision in a floating charge whereby it can be made to crystallise automatically. The answer to this was given by Hoffmann J in *Re Brightlife Ltd* [1986] BCLC 418 and it was in the affirmative. In that case the floating charge provided that it was to crystallise on the giving of a notice ('a crystallisation notice') converting it into a fixed charge. It was argued that the notice could not have this effect as the events crystallising a charge were laid down by law and the giving of a notice was not one of them. The court rejected this reading of the cases and held that the characteristics of the charge were determined by the agreement between the parties and if this provided for crystallisation on the giving of notice then the court would give effect to this as crystallising the charge.

The dispute in *Re Brightlife Ltd* was between the preferential creditors and the holder of the floating charge and in the light of the definition of floating charge in the Insolvency Act 1986, s 251, the significance of the case has been reduced as regards this contest. There remains the question as to whether the same result would obtain where the dispute is between a fixed charge holder who obtained the charge after the floating charge holder had given a crystallisation notice purportedly crystallising the charge. If the floating charge did take priority this would be unfair to the fixed charge holder as there is no way that such a charge holder could determine from the register of charges that the charge had crystallised. It has been argued that as the floating charge holder has allowed the company to deal with its assets as though they were unencumbered then he should be estopped from denying that the fixed charge holder had priority (see Goode, *Commercial Law*, at 800–803). There is much to commend this argument as there is no principled objection to the use of estoppel doctrine in this way. Where the fixed charge holder actually discovers from a search of the charges' register that the charge may be crystallised on the giving of notice then the position is more problematical as in this situation it is arguable that he should have made enquiries as to whether or not such a notice had been served (cf *Siebe Gorman Ltd v Barclay's Bank Ltd* [1979] 2 Lloyd's Rep 142).

One last point with respect to the judgment in *Re Brightlife Ltd*. The fixed charge in that case covered the company's 'book debts and other debts' and the question arose as to whether this covered a balance in the company's bank account. Hoffmann J held that it did not as a credit balance was cash at the bank and would normally not be treated as a book debt. The definition of book debt is of course one of those mysteries of company law and can lead to results that cause a considerable amount of commercial inconvenience (see, for example, *Re Welsh Irish Ferries Ltd* [1985] BCLC 327). But surely the accounting treatment of cash at the bank cannot dispose of the question as to whether a bank balance is or is not a book debt. The relationship between banker and customer is one of debtor and creditor and normally a company will record its bank balances in well kept books. On this basis credit balance would be treated as a book debt. This aspect of *Re Brightlife Ltd* may need to be re-examined. (See also *Re Charge Card Services Ltd* [1986] 3 All ER 289 at 308: '. . . a charge in favour of a debtor of his own debt is conceptually impossible').

Companies struck off the register

There have been two recent cases dealing with the nature and effects of the procedure for striking companies off the register. In *Re Portrafram Ltd* [1986] BCLC 376 a company had been struck off but nevertheless D purported to enter into a contract on its behalf with S Ltd. Proceedings were commenced to restore the company to the register and S Ltd sought to be joined in the proceedings under RSC Ord 15, r 6, on the grounds that its presence was necessary to dispose of all matters in dispute between the parties in that the restoration of the company to the register would have the effect of restoring the status quo ante with the result that an action commenced by S Ltd against D for breach of warranty of authority would collapse. Harman J held that S Ltd had no standing to be joined in the proceedings as they did not lead to the determination of any matter in dispute but were more in the way of administrative proceedings where the court on being satisfied of certain matters restored the company to the register. The outcome of the case causes no great hardship to S Ltd as when the contract was entered into it was the company to which S Ltd looked to for satisfaction and all the court order restoring the company to the register did was to deprive it of a purely adventitious claim against D.

The second case, *Re Aga Estate Agencies Ltd* [1986] BCLC 346, arguably does cause an injustice. In that case the guarantor of a company's debt had paid the debt at a time when the company had been struck off the register. Proceedings by the guarantor to restore the company to the register were unsuccessful as the guarantor was not a creditor within the terms of s 653 of the Companies Act 1985 and therefore had no standing to bring proceedings under this section. This produces a harsh result, particularly where it transpires that the company (if restored) would have sufficient assets to meet the claim of the guarantor. As a matter of principle there is no good reason why the word creditor should not be interpreted in appropriate circumstances so as to include contingent creditors. Harman J rejected this solution. His reasons for doing so were the weight of authority. While the weight of authority does support his judgment, it is far from being conclusive. Megarry J was willing to interpret the word creditor in this context so as to cover a contingent creditor in *Re Harvest Lane Motor Bodies Ltd* [1968] 2 All ER 1012 at 1015 and it is to be regretted that his lead was not followed.

Corporate opportunity

There is a considerable body of Commonwealth authority which recognises as a sub-category of a director's fiduciary obligations the corporate opportunity doctrine. Broadly this provides that a director is precluded from appropriating to himself a business opportunity with respect to which his company has formed an interest. The doctrine operates to cover opportunities in which the company has no proprietary interest as in that situation the principle in *Cook v Deeks* [1916] AC 554 would be adequate to compel a director to account for any profit made from appropriating the company's assets. *Island Export Finance v Umunna* [1986] BCLC 460 is the first English case to recognise the existence of the corporate opportunity doctrine, although the court found on the facts that there had been no breach of duty by the director. The defendant, as managing director of the plaintiff company, had been involved in obtaining on behalf of the company a contract to supply the Cameroonian postal authorities with postal boxes. The defendant resigned his position with the plaintiff and set up his own company which was successful in obtaining a contract to supply the Cameroonian postal authorities with postal boxes of roughly the same type that had been supplied by the plaintiff. The plaintiff brought an action against the defendant alleging that he had breached his duty to the company by exploiting for his own benefit an opportunity that belonged to the plaintiff. The court made two critical findings of fact: first, that when the defendant resigned his motive was not to appropriate to himself the postal box business and secondly, at the time of his resignation the company was not actively seeking orders for the supply of postal boxes. On these facts Hutchison J held that there had been no breach of duty on the part of the defendant. He recognised that a director could still be subject to fiduciary duties even though he had resigned his position and also that he could be liable for appropriating to himself an 'opportunity' (as opposed to a proprietary interest) which belonged to the company. (He cited with approval the judgment of the Supreme Court of Canada in *Canadian Aero Services Ltd v O'Malley* (1973) 40 DLR (3d) 371 which sets out the contours of the corporate opportunity doctrine.) However, before a director could be held liable for exploiting a business opportunity on resigning from office it had to be a 'maturing' business opportunity for which the company was negotiating or in which it had an express interest. It was not sufficient that the director had merely become acquainted with the opportunity because of his position as director of the company; such a principle would be far too wide and would conflict with the common law principles dealing with the permissible scope of contracts in restraint of trade. As Hutchison J found that the plaintiff company was not actively pursuing the opportunity at the time the defendant resigned, the defendant had not breached any duty to the company by exploiting it.

Section 35 of the Companies Act 1985

TCB v Gray [1986] BCLC 113 is the first reported case to deal with s 35 of the Companies Act 1985 in any great depth and it evinces a judicial disposition to interpret the section to provide the maximum protection to persons dealing with a company. (See also *American Home Assurance Co v Tjmond Properties Ltd* [1986] BCLC 181.) The facts in that case were complex, but the ultra vires point arose in the following way. A debenture was purportedly executed on behalf of a company by a person who was acting as attorney for a director of the company. Under the company's articles of association only a director had authority to enter into this type of transaction on behalf of the company and there was no provision in the articles whereby a director could act by attorney. The question arose as to the validity of the debenture. Browne-Wilkinson V-C held the debenture to be binding on the company because of the operation of s 35 of the Companies Act 1985. This section renders a transaction entered into in good faith by a third party, who was dealing with the directors of a company, binding on the company irrespective of any limitation on the capacity of the company to enter into the transaction or any limitation on the powers of the directors to bind the company. The first point raised by the defendant was that the plaintiff had not satisfied the good faith requirement: the defendant argued that although the plaintiff did not have any 'actual or imputed knowledge of any irregularity in the execution of the debenture', in the light of the abnormal nature of the transaction the plaintiff should have investigated the matter and if it had done so it would have discovered the irregularity. This was rejected by Browne Wilkinson V-C on the grounds that s 35 provided that a third party dealing with the company was not obliged to enquire as to any limitations on the powers of the directors to bind the company and it was therefore not possible for the company to establish a lack of good faith merely by showing that the plaintiff should have made enquiries that it did not have to make.

The second point raised by the plaintiff was that the person who purportedly acted for the company had no authority to do so (the company's articles not containing any provision for a director to act by attorney) and therefore there was no basis on which his acts could be treated as those of the company and binding on it because of s 35. If this argument was accepted then it would severely restrict the operation of the section as in many situations the relevant act allegedly giving rise to liability will not be that of the company in the sense that there will have been a defect with respect to the way in which it was executed on behalf of the company. On the other hand, a company needs some protection against those who purport to act on its behalf without in any way having been authorised to do so. In holding that the company was bound by the transaction in *TCB v Gray*, the court held that the effect of s 35 was to make any transaction which a company 'purports' to enter into binding on the company even though there was some defect in the way in which the transaction was carried out, and even if this defect has the effect of rendering the transaction a nullity having regard to the company's 'internal documents'. However, there is always the requirement that the company must have purported to enter into the transaction, and this will protect a company from being bound by the acts of complete strangers.

Winding up: debts due to a member

The Companies Act 1985, s 502(2)(f) (see now Insolvency Act 1986, s 74(2)(f)), provides that in a winding up any sum due to a member 'by way of dividends, profits or otherwise' shall not in a case of competition between that member and a creditor of the company be treated as a debt of the company. This section arose for consideration *Re LB Holliday & Co Ltd* [1986] BCLC 227, a case in which a subsidiary had regularly declared dividends which its parent company had regularly allowed it to retain in its business. The subsidiary went into liquidation and the question arose as to whether the claim of the parent was affected by s 502(2)(f). Mervyn Davies J held that for the parent to succeed it would have to show that the money was due to it in some capacity other than member. It could do this by proving an agreement, express or implied, that it was to be the same position as if the dividends had been declared and then lent back to the subsidiary, or alternatively after a period of time there had been some form of recognition between the parties that this was the arrangement between them. On the facts, the court was unable to find any evidence of such an arrangement. Although the parties referred to the arrangement as a loan, the arrangement bore none of the hallmarks of a loan. In particular, no interest was paid by the subsidiary, no other items appeared in the company's 'loan accounts' (which were in reality merely a record of unpaid dividends), and at the time the dividends were declared the company did not have the cash to make payment.

Minority oppression: valuation of shares

An issue of considerable importance where the court orders the shares of an oppressed minority to be purchased under s 461 of the Companies Act 1985 is the principles on which the shares have to be valued. A number of aspects of this problem were dealt with by the Court of Appeal in *Re Cumana Ltd* [1986] BCLC 430. In that case the shareholder who had been ordered to purchase the shares of another shareholder appealed against the order on the grounds that (i) the shares should have been valued as of the date of the court's order and not the date of the petition (as the trial judge had ordered) as there had been a decline in the value of the company's shares between these two dates and (ii) the court should have included an escape clause in its order to deal with the possibility that the shareholder against whom the order had been made would not be able to raise the money to purchase the shares of the petitioner. The appellant was unsuccessful. The Court of Appeal emphasised that the valuation of the shares under s 461 was a matter for the discretion of the trial judge and the court would only intervene where the trial judge had clearly erred and applied the wrong principles. In the instant case the trial judge had not erred in adopting the date of the petition rather than some other date as the time at which the shares of the petitioner were to be valued. In addition, there was no requirement that the court's order contain an escape clause to deal with the situation where the defendant lacked the funds to purchase the petitioner's shares; as Lawton LJ stated the fact that 'a wrongdoer is impecunious' is not a reason for the court not making an order against him.

Minority oppression: basis on which the court's discretion exercised

There have been a number of cases dealing with the basis on which the court will make an order under s 459 of the Companies Act 1985, and these indicate that the courts are interpreting the section in an expansive manner. These cases present rich pickings and all that can be done here is to indicate their more important points:

(i) In *Re a company* [1986] BCLC 376 Hoffmann J considered that the reasoning in *Ebrahimi v Westbourne Galleries Ltd* [1973] AC 360 was applicable to actions for relief under s 459 and that where a member of an incorporated partnership was, contrary to his legitimate expectation, excluded from the affairs of the company then this could consitute the basis of an order under s 461. This is an important and welcome development, as the point has been made that in the case of an incorporated partnership the members will expect to obtain a return on their investment in the form of salaries and s 459 should be interpreted so as to protect this aspect of their interest. However, the fact that a member of an incorporated partnership is removed from his position in the company does not necessarily entail that he will obtain some relief under s 459. His exclusion may be justified, or it may be that the relationship between the members has broken down so that one of them must leave the company. Where the latter is the case, Hoffmann J held in *Re a company* [1986] BCLC 362 that the departing member had no grounds for obtaining relief under s 459 provided the treatment of the excluded member was not unfair. It is important to emphasise with respect to this decision that although exlcusion will not ipso facto result in an order under s 459 the terms of the exclusion must be fair and if they are not then this would justify the court in making an order under the section.

(ii) To have standing to obtain relief under s 459 the petitioner must either be a member or someone to whom the shares of the company have been transferred or transmitted by operation of law (s 459(2)). To be a transferee of shares for this purpose, a petitioner must have obtained a proper instrument of transfer in his favour or one must have been lodged with the company. This means that the beneficial owner of shares will not necessarily be in a position to seek relief if such an instrument has not been executed on his behalf. Accordingly, in *Re a company* [1986] BCLC 391 the court held that a husband had no standing to obtain relief under s 459 where his wife, who was the registered holder of the shares in the company, held them allegedly as the nominee for her husband.

(iii) One of the most important features of ss 459–461 is the broad remedial jurisdiction vested in the court. In *Re a company* [1986] BCLC 376 the respondents sought to have a petition under s 459 struck out on the ground as they were no longer shareholders in the company therefore no order could be against them. Hoffmann J refused to grant the order as he was not satisfied that the chances of obtaining an order under the section against an ex-member was 'perfectly hopeless' so that the action should be struck out. This is an important decision as it entails that a shareholder cannot escape the section merely by transferring his shares.

Conflict of Laws

J G COLLIER, MA, LLB
Barrister, Fellow of Trinity Hall, Cambridge

Jurisdiction of the English courts: service out of the jurisdiction

The principle called *forum non conveniens,* which entails an inquiry into whether the English court or some particular foreign court is the more appropriate forum for the trial of an action, has always been one of those matters which guide a judge in deciding how to exercise his discretion as to whether or not to permit service out of the jurisdiction under the Rules of the Supreme Court, Ord 11, r 1 (see, for example, *Mauroux v Pereira* [1972] 2 All ER 1085.) It has recently been authoritatively discussed in a case which concerned an application for leave under RSC Ord 11, r 1(1)(f)(iii) (now (d)(iii)) on the ground that the contract was governed by English law. But in that case, *Spiliada Maritime Corpn v Cansulex Ltd, The Spiliada* [1986] 3 All ER 843, the House of Lords took the opportunity to review the whole question of *forum non conveniens* also, indeed chiefly, in relation to staying of actions brought as of right and the case is more conveniently discussed in that connection (see below).

Amanuel and others v Alexandros Shipping Co and another [1986] 1 All ER 279 needs little comment, since the head of RSC Ord 11 which fell to be interpreted has been amended and that point cannot now arise. It is sufficient to say that Webster J, having held that the defendants could be served with the writ in Ethiopia as 'necessary or proper parties' went on to hold that in the circumstances the case was not appropriate for service out of the jurisdiction because it had little to do with this country and was closely connected with Ethiopia. Also, the nature of the dispute means that the case would be tried more suitably in Ethiopia. This furnishes a clear and neat example of the application of *forum non conveniens* in RSC Ord 11 cases.

Jurisdiction: staying of actions and forum non conveniens

Since the House of Lords began to liberalise the law relating to staying of actions in *The Atlantic Star, Atlantic Star (owners) v Bona Spes (owners)* [1973] 2 All ER 175, the courts have had to face large numbers of applications for a stay and over the ensuring years some principles, though not very clear ones, began slowly to emerge. In the three leading decisions of the House of Lords itself, *MacShannon v Rockware Glass Ltd* [1978] 1 All ER 625, *Amin Rasheed Shipping Corpn v Kuwait Insurance Co, The Al Wahab* [1983] 2 All ER 884, which was in fact an Ord 11 case, and not itself concerned with staying of an action, and *The Abidin Daver* [1984] 1 All ER 470, there edged, as it were, into English law, having been previously known in the United States and in Scotland, but not in England, the doctrine of *forum non conveniens*. This doctrine means that when a court has jurisdiction to hear a case it may agree to stay the proceedings at the request of the defendant if it can be shown that there exists a court abroad which is more appropriate than itself for the trial of the action, and this is so whether or not there is a *lis alibi pendens*.

In *Castanho v Brown and Root (UK) Ltd* [1981] 1 All ER 143, the House of Lords, speaking through Lord Scarman, held that the principles which govern the exercise of the court's discretion as to whether or not to stay proceedings before it apply also in the converse situation where it is asked to restrain by injunction proceedings in a foreign country when an action is being brought concurrently in an English court.

In *Bank of Tokyo v Karoon* [1986] 3 All ER 468, which was actually decided in 1984, the Court of Appeal (Ackner and Robert Goff L JJ) when asked to restrain certain proceedings in New York on the ground of English public policy, followed, as it had to do, *Castanho v Brown and Root (UK) Ltd*, though Goff L J does not seem to have been entirely happy about doing so. This is understandable, for it is not at all clear that a principle evolved by the English court in order to deal with cases which it believes to have been inappropriately brought before itself is necessarily suitable for determining whether to restrain proceedings abroad, since the court is not in control of those proceedings. The United States courts have not made the transition from the one situation to the other and Lord Scarman gave no resason why it should be made.

It remains to be added that *forum non conveniens* has always been relevant when the court is asked to consider whether to allow service of process on an absent defendant (see p 59, above).

Several attempts have been made by courts other than the House of Lords to state and rationalise the principles upon which a judge should base his discretion about all of the types of application which has been mentioned. Perhaps the clearest was that enunciated by Robert Goff J, as he then was, in *Trendtex Trading Corpn v Credit Suisse* [1980] 3 All ER 721 at 743 (affd, by the House of Lords [1981] 3 All ER 520), a case in which there was a foreign jurisdiction clause. The judge there said that the court must consider what justice demands; that the defendant must convince it that there is a more natural or appropriate forum than the English court and that a stay would not deprive the plaintiff of a legitimate personal or juridical advantage he might have in suing in England.

But three questions have remained without any clear answer.

First, on whom lies the burden, of convincing the court and of what? Secondly, what are and are not 'legitimate personal or juridical advantages' of which the plaintiff might be deprived? Do they include such matters as whether the plaintiff would be faced with a time bar in one country but not in the other, or that he could get fuller discovery of documents from the defendant or has the prospect of the higher damages available in one country than in the other? On this last point, the House of Lords thought that the latter was such an advantage in *Castanho v Brown and Root (UK) Ltd* whereas the Court of Appeal thought that in the circumstances of the case it was not in *Smith Kline & French Laboratories Ltd v Bloch* [1983] 2 All ER 72.

Thirdly, is the test, as propounded by Robert Goff LJ and derived from speeches of members of the House of Lords in *MacShannon's* case, exclusive? The Court of Appeal has recently said it is not. In *Muduroglu v TC Ziraat Bankasi* [1986] 3 All ER 682, Mustill and Stocker LJJ and Sir John Donaldson subjected the previous case-law to considerable and minute analysis and remarked that the judges in those cases had not intended their formulation of the principle to be regarded as if the words they used were to be treated as if they were in a statute. The action before the court had clearly to be stayed. It was obviously very closely connected with Turkey and had scarcely any connection with this country. The Court of Appeal paid relatively scant attention to 'legitimate personal or juridical advantages' which the plaintiff was said to possess in suing here; it was not really convinced that he had any anyway.

The House of Lords has had the opportunity to review the present state of the law and to sort it out. It should be emphasised that what is at issue is fundamentally the exercise of a judge's discretion. The rule for appellate courts in this is that, provided that the judge exercised his discretion on correct legal principles, his decision should not be interfered with; this should only be done when he has not applied those principles. It is not for the appellate court to differ from the trial judge in his application of them to the facts of the particular case. It is disregard of this which has led to too many cases reaching the House of Lords. All this was stated clearly by Lord Brandon in *The Abidin Daver*.

In *Spiliada Maritime Corpn v Carnsulex Ltd* [1986] 3 All ER 843 Lord Goff of Chievely, as he has now become, stated the basic principles in a series of propositions of clarity and simplicity for the guidance of trial judges. If they keep to and apply these, a stop may be put to the repeated appeals from those judges and a considerable reduction may be effected in the pages of the law reports devoted to the recitation of the facts of so many cases in which the only point at issue is the exercise of the discretion by a particular judge on the facts of the actual case before him, and nothing more. In this case, an Ord 11 application, Staughton J had allowed service of a writ in British Columbia. The case arose (as in *Amin Rasheed*) out of a contract whose sole connection with this country was that it was governed by English law. The Court of Appeal had reversed Staughton J, but solely because they differed from him on the application of the law to the facts. In turn, the Court of Appeal was reversed by the House of Lords. Lord Goff's guidelines, applicable to staying of actions, leave to serve out of the jurisdiction and restraining foreign proceedings, are clear, general in their terms and easy to apply. Much is derived from Scottish decisions, in particular *Sim v Robinow* 19 R 265 and *Société du Gaz de Paris v SA de Navigation 'Les Armateurs Francais'* 1926 SC (HL) 13. They proceed thus;

1. A stay should be granted where the court is satisfied that there is another available court which has jurisdiction and which is appropriate (the correct translation of the word '*conveniens*') for the trial in that the case can be heard there more suitably for the interests of all the parties and the ends of justice.

2. The burden lies on the defendant of persuading the court to stay the proceedings, though whichever party raises a particular issue must prove it.

3. The defendant has to show not only that England is not the appropriate forum but that one other forum clearly is. This was not done in the *European Asian Bank* case, where, though the English court was not particularly appropriate, either India or Singapore was a suitable place, but neither more than the other. In *The Atlantic Star* (Belgium), *MacShannons's* case (Scotland), *Trendtex Trading Corpn v Credit Suisse* (Switzerland), *The*

Abidin Daver (Turkey) and, of course, *Muduroglu's* case (Turkey) it was easy to demonstrate this.

4. The duty of the court is to look first for the existence of such factors as the inconvenience or expense of trial including the availability of witnesses, the governing law and the parties' places of residence or business, which point to what Lord Keith, in the *Abidin Daver*, termed the court 'with which the action has its closest and most real connection.'

5. If no such court can be shown to exist, a stay will almost certainly be refused.

6. If the court thinks that such a forum does exist, then it is up to the plaintiff to show that there are circumstances, over and above those mentioned in 4, such as will deprive him of a fair trial in that court.

The significance and weight which are to be accorded to the existence of the plaintiff's 'legitimate personal or juridical advantage' are played down. Lord Goff quoted Lord Sumner in the *Societe du Gaz* case where he said:

> 'I do not see how one can guide oneself profitably by endeavouring to conciliate and promote the interests of both these antagonists, except in the ironical sense, in which one says that it is in the interests of both that that the case should be tried in the best way and in the best tribunal, and that the best man should win.'

Obviously, the plaintiff's advantage is the defendant's disadvantage. So the existence of such an advantage in England would not of itself deter the court from granting a stay or refusing leave to serve out of the jurisdiction if it was satisfied that justice would be done to all the parties in the appropriate forum. Nonetheless, it would refuse a stay or give leave if in all the circumstances England were the suitable forum. In the present case, though the action appeared to be time-barred in British Columbia but not in England, since the plaintiffs had not acted unreasonably, said Lord Goff, in not starting proceedings in British Columbia within that jurisdiction's period of limitation this would not necessarily cause the court to deprive the plaintiffs of the benefit of having complied with the English time limit if England was the natural forum.

With respect to Ord 11 applications, the views of Lord Wilberforce were said to represent the position, as he stated them in the *Amin Rasheed* case. He said there that the plaintiff has the task of showing good reasons why service of the writ should in the circumstances be permitted. In considering this, the court must take into account the nature of the dispute, the legal and practical issues involved, such as local knowledge, availability of witnesess and their evidence, and expense. This is subject to the *caveat* that Lord Wilberforce's denial that assistance can be gained from *forum non conveniens* cases is itself to be treated with caution. (Actually, it should be disregarded, one would suppose).

But there are three differences between staying of action cases and Ord 11 cases. In Ord 11 cases, the burden of proof is on the plaintiff, not on the defendant; in this sense one is the obverse of the other. In Ord 11 cases the plaintiff is seeking to persuade the court to exercise its discretion to allow service out of the jurisdiction and the Order itself requires that leave shall not be granted 'unless it shall be made to appear to the court that the case is a proper one for service out of the jurisdiction.' No such direction is given to the court in connection with applications for a stay.

Thirdly (see 858), it should be remembered that Ord 11 jurisdiction is exorbitant or extraordinary in that it allows the defendant to be sued away from his place of residence and forces him to come to England to defend himself (see Lord Diplock in the *Amin Rasheed* case). But two cautions are given by Lord Goff. The jurisdiction is not so exorbitant if the defendant's residence is one of convenience, such as a tax haven in the case of a corporation. Moreover, the alternative situations covered by Ord 11 are varied; they need not all be remotely connected with England, as is possible if the ground is that the contact is expressed to be governed by English law. The ground might be that the defendant is domiciled here, or that the harmful consequences of a tort were suffered in England.

In the *Spiliada* case it was decided that the judge had, in the circumstances, been justified in holding that the case was suitable for service of the writ out of the jurisdiction.

It is clear that the House of Lords is looking forward to some peace on this front, and *Spiliada v Cansulex* clearly discourages appeals in all these cases. For, says Lord Templeman, all that a judge had to do is to 'study the evidence and refresh his memory' of Lord Goff's speech 'in the quiet of his room without expense to the parties' and he urges that counsel's submissions will be measured in hours not days. An appeal should be rare and the appellate court should be slow to interfere.'

In conclusion, it is nice to read Lord Goff's appreciative words about the work of academic writers or, as he calls them 'jurists.' It is reassuring to know that our efforts are sometimes thus regarded.

Jurisdiction: restraining foreign proceedings

In *British Airways Board v Laker Airways* [1984] 3 All ER 39 (see All ER Rev 1984, pp 241–4), the House of Lords declined to restrain the English liquidator of Laker Airways from continuing proceedings in the United States under the anti-trust laws against, *inter alia*, two British airline companies. Lord Diplock said that the English courts should not restrain the bringing of an action which is only possible under the foreign law and not so under English law, so that no proceedings could be brought here. Exceptionally, an injunction would be granted if the plaintiff has a pre-existing cause of action against the defendant arising from an invasion of a legal or equitable right of the plaintiff or, as in the type of case in question, where the plaintiff has a legal or equitable right not to be sued, as, for example, where the defendant's conduct in suing abroad is unconscionable. In the *Laker Airways* case it was held that no such right existed.

In *Midland Bank plc and another v Laker Airways and others* [1986] 1 All ER 527, the Court of Appeal distinguished the *Laker Airways* case and granted an injunction to restrain the same liquidator from pursuing an action under the anti-trust laws against the bank, alleging that it had taken part in the same conspiracy as he alleged against the airlines and others. Unlike the airlines, who had in respect of the activities on which the anti-trust proceedings were based, submitted to United States law by carrying on those activities in that country, the Midland Bank had not done so. The allegations levelled against it (which seemed unsupported by any evidence) only arose from the bank's having lent the company large sums of money, taken part in an attempt to rescue it from collapse and then withdrawn its support and appointed a receiver. The bank's transactions with Laker Airways had taken place in England in the ordinary course of its business activities here and were intended to be governed by English law. They had no connection with the United States or the other alleged conspirators. Its separate American subsidiary was not involved.

This, it submitted, is satisfactory, for if the liquidator had been allowed to proceed, the English courts would in effect have countenanced the application of the anti-trust laws to activities in this country which they (see, for example, *British Nylon Spinners Ltd v Imperial Chemical Industries Ltd* [1952] 2 All ER 780) and Parliament, in the Protection of Trading Interests Act 1980, have been astute to guard against.

In *South Carolina Insurance Co v Assurantie Maatschappij 'de Zeven Provincien' NV, South Carolina Insurance Co v Al Ahlia Insurance Co* [1986] 3 All ER 487, on the other hand, the House of Lords reversed the Court of Appeal (see [1985] 2 All ER 1046 and All ER Rev 1985, pp 54–55), and lifted an injunction restraining the defendants, who were parties to an action in England, from continuing proceedings in the United States which were started so as to obtain pre-trial discovery, not ordinarily allowed in England, to secure evidence from third parties for use in the English action. The Court of Appeal had taken the view that to permit the defendants to do this would mean that the English court was effectively deprived of being the master of its own procedure. Lord Brandon, speaking for the majority of the House of Lords, denied that this was so. He said the conditions under which an injunction could be granted to restrain foreign proceedings as stated in the *Laker Airways* case were exclusive and were not fulfilled. Lords Mackay and Goff doubted that the power of the court to grant injunctions, being unfettered by statute (Supreme Court Act 1981, s 37(1)) is restricted to certain categories, and Lord Goff referred to his doubts about *Castanho v Brown and Root (UK) Ltd* [1981] 1 All ER 143, which he expressed in *Bank of Tokyo Ltd v Karoon* [1986] 3 All ER 468, (see p 60, above).

The House held unanimously that the above conditions had not been fulfilled. The Court of Appeal had erred, in particular, in holding that the defendant's use of pre-trial discovery was unconscionable conduct which interfered with the English court's control of its own process. The English courts do not in general exercise any control over the means by which a party obtains his evidence, which, provided they are lawful, are a matter for him.

In fact, the inconvenience which the plaintiffs alleged the American proceedings would cause them and their liability for increased costs, were self-inflicted wounds, since they had refused to co-operate in the matter. In any case these considerations were not an interference with the court's control of its own process.

Foreign arbitration award: recognition

Like a foreign judgment, a foreign arbitration award can be relied upon as a defence to an action in the English courts which is founded upon the claim which has been arbitrated. In *Dallal v Bank Mellat* [1986] 1 All ER 239 the matter arose in a unique way. The plaintiff, a US national, brought an action against the defendant, an Iranian state enterprise, in the American courts. In the Algiers Declarations of 1981, which terminated the American hostages crisis, the USA agreed with Iran to terminate all such actions then pending in the US courts. Such claims were instead to be brought before the Iran-US Claims Tribunal, created by agreement between the US and Iran, at the Hague. The Tribunal's awards were to be met from a specially created fund and would be binding. The plaintiff's American action was suspended by a Presidential decree which provided that the Tribunal's awards should be final in United States law. So the plaintiff pursued his claim for damages against the Iranian Republic and one of its state enterprises (IBI) in respect of two dishonoured cheques before the Tribunal, which rejected it.

The plaintiff then proceeded in England against the defendant, Bank Mellat, the successor to IBI. Hobhouse J struck out the action as an abuse of the process of the court on the ground that the claim had already been the subject of adjudication by a tribunal of competent jurisdiction. The novel point was that this had happened in the Netherlands and it is an essential requirement for the recognition or enforcement at common law or under the New York Convention on the Recognition and Enforcement of Foreign Arbitral Awards, enacted into law by the Arbitration Act 1975, that the award should be valid and binding by the proper law of the agreement to arbitrate (*lex arbitri*); this is normally the law of the place where the arbitration is held: *James Miller and Partners Ltd v Whitworth Street Estates (Manchester) Ltd* [1970] 1 All ER 796. It seemed to his Lordship inescapable that the proper law was Dutch and it seemed fairly clear that the award was a nullity according to Dutch arbitration law.

The bank tried to escape from this in several ways, but the only one which convinced the court was that the Tribunal's proceedings could be regarded as a 'statutory arbitration' of municipal law. Its authority could not, indeed, be derived from any legislative or other authority of Dutch municipal law, no where was this 'statutory' kind of authority to be found? Drawing on two nineteenth century Privy Council cases, *The Laconia* (1863) 2 Moo PCCNS 161 and *Messina v Petrococchino* (1872) LR 4 PC 144, Hobhouse J held that if a treaty between two governments, acting within their powers, creates a tribunal when the individual parties to the proceedings are within the jurisdiction of and subject to the law-making power of the governments and the *situs* of the property is in the territory of one of the states, then if the municipal laws of those states recognise the competence of the tribunal, it is impossible for an English court to hold that its proceedings were incompetent.

So if a tribunal is competent in international law it must be so regarded by an English court and if it is created by a state or states to sit in another state it will be competent in international law if that other state consents to its exercising its jurisdiction by treaty or by 'acquiescence in an established practice'; the Dutch government had certainly so acquiesced.

The judge also held that in any event the plaintiff had, with the consent of his own state, submitted to the jurisdiction of the Hague Tribunal and had therefore rendered it competent by his own voluntary act, which was not the less voluntary because he had been precluded from pursuing his action in the United States. He had himself argued that he could have litigated the dispute in the courts of this country.

Dallal v Bank Mellat accords with principle, though the result is reached by a roundabout route.

It should, however, be emphasised that the decision lends no support to the view, much advocated in recent years, that the parties can 'denationalise' or 'delocalise' the arbitration proceedings by their own volition and free it from the rules of any legal system at all. The protagonists of this argument would urge that had this kind of arbitration been of wholly private character the English court should have recognised its validity and not have imposed Dutch arbitration law on the parties. Hobhouse J expressly repudiates this, for he denied the validity of the defendant's argument that private individuals could make public international law the proper law of an arbitration agreement. That system, he said, could only be relevant insofar as it had been absorbed into some system of municipal law which is identifiable as such. (See further on this Schindler, 1986 102 LQR, 500–505.)

Contract: determination of the proper law

It scarely needs to be said that most of the issues which may arise in respect of a contract are governed to some extent at least by its proper law and it is now well settled that the parties are generally free to choose that law. They can expressly provide for it or the court can infer their intention from the terms of the contract and the circumstances surrounding its conclusion, failing which the contract is governed by the system of law with which it has its closest and most real connection. As a general rule, the English courts will not readily 'split' the contract, that is to say, they will apply the same proper law to determine all the contractual issues. Nonetheless, the parties may provide, or the court may decide, that they intended that the law of A is to govern the contract as a whole but that the law of B is to govern, say, its interpretation. (See dicta in *Hamlyn & Co v Talisker Distillery* [1894] AC 202 at 207, [1891–4] All ER Rep 849 at 852, per Lord Herschell and *Re Helbert Wagg & Co Ltd* [1956] 1 All ER 129 at 135, per Upjohn J).

A rare and recent example of the court deciding thus is the decision of Hobhouse J in *Forsikringsaktieselskapet Vesta v Butcher* [1986] 2 All ER 488. This case concerned a contract of reinsurance concluded by the plaintiffs, Norwegian insurers, in London with Lloyd's underwriters through brokers there on a Lloyd's slip and form. The original contract of insurance was with the owners of a Norwegian fish farm. The reinsurance policy was expressed to be on the same terms and conditions as the original insurance and provided that failure to comply with the conditions and warranties in the latter would render the insurance policy null and void. The plaintiffs settled a claim by the assured and now sought an indemnity under the reinsurance policy. The defendants repudiated liability, alleging breach of one of the conditions of insurance. By Norwegian law, breach of that condition by the assured was not a defence to liability, but by English law it was. So, if Norwegian law was the only proper law of the reinsurance policy, the defendants were liable, but if the proper law was English law, they were not. There could be no doubt that the insurance policy was governed by Norwegian law and it would seem to follow that the reference to that policy in the reinsurance policy caused the latter to be governed by

Norwegian law also. But this conclusion seemed, understandably, to the learned judge to be wholly unreal and in *Citadel Insurance Co v Atlantic Union Insurance Co SA* [1982] 2 Lloyd's Rep 543 a reinsurance contract concluded in similar circumstances was held to have its closest and most real connection with English law. So had the one in the present case. Thus the two policies appeared to be governed by two different laws which dictated opposed legal consequences, an odd state of affairs!

Hobhouse J solved the problem ingeniously by 'splitting' the contract. The reinsurance policy as a whole was governed by English law, but it should be inferred from its terms that the parties intended that a part of their contract, the interpretation and effect of the clauses which defined and limited the scope of the reinsurance cover, should be governed by that system of law which governed the contract in which those clauses appeared, the insurance contract, which was Norwegian insurance law.

The learned judge declined to categorise this conclusion as either on the one hand an application of the English substantive law of construction of an English law contract or as the application of English choice of law rules on the other. These seem curious, since the whole tenor of his judgment on this point (at 504–5) is in terms of the latter explanation. In any event, the decision, though unusual, is a common-sense solution to an unusual problem.

Contract: Bretton Woods Agreement: exchange contract

The true interpretation of Article VIII (2)(b) of the Bretton Woods Agreement, which was given effect in English law by the Order in Council of 1946 of the same name, has more than once faced the English courts with a poser. Its applicability is sometimes unclear and can produce somewhat unsatisfactory consequences. It provides that:

> 'Exchange contracts which involve the currency of any Member [of the International Monetary Fund] and which are contrary to the exchange control regulations of that member maintained or imposed consistently with the Agreement shall be unenforceable in the territories of any member.'

In *Mansouri v Singh* [1986] 2 All ER 619, the plaintiff, an Iranian who had settled in England after the Iranian revolution in 1979, could not, because of Iranian exchange control regulations, get his wealth out of Iran. So, by an arrangement with an English travel agent, the defendant, he bought airline tickets in Iran and sent them to the defendant to be exchanged for sterling at double the normal rate of exchange. The defendant drew a cheque in favour of the plaintiff as had been agreed, but stopped it before it was paid. The plaintiff sued on the cheque. The question before the court was whether, assuming the Agreement to be applicable, the arrangement was an exchange contract and therefore unenforceable. The plaintiff argued before the Court of Appeal that the obligation contained in the cheque was separate from other obligations which might exist under any underlying or associated transaction.

In *Wilson Smithett & Cope Ltd v Terruzzi* [1976] 1 All ER 817 the Court of Appeal held that an 'exchange contract' was limited to one which involved the exchange of one currency for another and did not include, for example, a contract of sale of goods where the purchase price was payable in the currency of a foreign member of the IMF, but said that such a contract could be unenforceable if it was an 'exchange contract' in disguise. The House of Lords affirmed this interpretation and held, controversially, that what was on its face a contract for the sale of machinery was, in part, a disguised attempt to circumvent the exchange control regulations of Peru. So it declined to enforce to that extent payment under a bankers' letter of credit which was opened in order to effectuate payment under the sale contract *(United City Merchants (Investments) Ltd v Royal Bank of Canada* [1982] 2 All ER 720).

It was obvious that in the present case the sale and purchase of the airline tickets was an exchange contract in disguise. Therefore it was inevitable, because of the aforementioned decision of the House of Lords, that the Court of Appeal would hold that the obligation to pay the cheque was unenforceable. Thus the defendant could get out of his obligation, which he had almost performed, by a defence which was only raised on a re-amended pleading after Hirst J had, quite properly, drawn attention to its possible relevance. The awkward and complicated case, *Sharif v Azad* [1966] 3 All ER 785, needed some explanation. There, Diplock LJ had said that where the plaintiff sues on a cheque in a case like this one, he is not suing on the exchange contract and since the latter is only unenforceable the collateral contract contained in the cheque is not 'affected by illegality.'

The trouble is that nowhere in his speech in the *United City Merchants* case did Lord Diplock refer to *Sharif v Azad* and his holding in the former appears to, and in fact does, flatly contradict what he said in the latter case. Moreover, in the *United City Merchants* case, Stephenson and Ackner LJJ in the Court of Appeal both expressly distinguished between a cheque and a banker's letter of credit. But in *Mansouri v Singh* it was held, perfectly logically, that this distinction could not be maintained since the obligation contained in a negotiable instrument and one in a banker's credit are both in law totally separate from that in the underlying contract. *Sharif v Azad* was distinguished, not very clearly, on the ground that in that case the parties to the cheque being sued on were not the same as the parties to the transaction which offended against the Pakistan currency regulations and the cheque, which was drawn in Manchester was therefore not unenforceable. This is not a wholly convincing distinction.

However, in *Mansouri v Singh* the case was remitted for retrial to see whether the whole transaction did in fact fall foul of the Bretton Woods Agreement.

Movable property: foreign expropriatory laws

A lengthy discussion appeared in All ER Rev 1985, pp 65–8 of the decisions of Nourse J and the Court of Appeal in *Williams & Humbert Ltd v W & H Trade Marks (Jersey) Ltd; Rumasa SA v Multinvest (UK) Ltd* [1985] 2 All ER 208, 619, in which it was held that the court should not strike out an action by an English subsidiary for the return of its property on the ground that the Spanish government had previously expropriated the shares in Spain of its Spanish parent company. The action was not an indirect method of enforcing the Spanish expropriatory legislation, since this had been completed in Spain and there was nothing left to enforce in England. It was pointed out in that discussion that the House of Lords had unanimously affirmed the Court of Appeal ([1986] 1 All ER 129), and there is little need to add to what was said a year ago. One or two points deserve brief mention, however.

It had been argued that the Spanish law was penal, but Lord Templeman, who delivered the leading judgment, doubted this. Nor did he consider that it would be contrary to English public policy. Compulsory acquisition legislation was neither abhorrent to English law nor to international law. This is supported by reference to foreign Declarations and Constitutions and International Conventions and to the fact of United Kingdom compulsory acquisition statutes.

His Lordship also observed that the action did not involve enforcement of the Spanish law and in doing so pointed out that if the plaintiff were to be debarred from suing on this ground, 'If English sherry clients owe Williams & Humbert £2m for sherry purchased before [the expropriation] then that sherry can now be consumed free of charge.'

To the argument first advanced by Dr F A Mann that the action could proceed but that a receiver be appointed by the court to devote any assets and debts that might be recovered to creditors and to ensure that no surplus should enure for the indirect benefit of the Spanish government, Lord Templeman's reply was that it would be unjust and inconvenient to appoint a receiver of a Spanish company or its wholly-owned subsidiary to pay the creditors and then to stand possessed of any surplus on non-existent trusts or on trust for persons who have never been shareholders of the company or former shareholders of a Spanish company who are entitled to receive and may have received compensation in Spain.

Lord Mackay of Clashfern, agreeing with all this, added an analysis of the decision of the High Court of Ireland in *Peter Buchanan Ltd and Macharg v McVey* [1955] AC 516n., which was approved by the House of Lords in *Government of India, Ministry of Finance (Revenue Division) v Taylor* [1955] 1 All ER 292 where the court declined to allow the liquidator to allow the liquidator of a Scottish company, appointed by the Scottish courts at the behest of the Inland Revenue, to recover assets of the company in Ireland. Lord Mackay pointed out that the essential feature of the liquidator's claim which disabled it from suceeding was that there was an outstanding revenue claim in Scotland which the whole proceeds of the action, expenses apart, would be used to meet. Had the claim under United Kingdom revenue law been already satisfied, no claim to enforce that law would have existed.

This, it is submitted, is a correct application of the existing law. It remains only to add that Dr F A Mann has refused, characteristically, to take the decision of the House of Lords lying down; see his typically learned and elegant criticism in 1986 102 LQR 191.

Succession—intestate succession to immovable property

Long ago the late Dr J H C Morris pointed out that nowadays little is to be said for the rule that, though intestate succession to movable property is governed by the law of the last domicile of the deceased, intestate succession to immovables is governed by the *lex situs* of the property. (See 1969 85

LQR 839, Dicey and Morris, *Conflict of Laws* (10th edn) 613–4 and Morris, *Conflict of Laws* (3rd edn) 391, where he demonstrates the anomalous results which this rule produces). His arguments can only gain force from the decision of Browne-Wilkinson V-C, arrived at 'with some regret', in *Re Collens (decd), Royal Bank of Canada (London) Ltd v Krogh* [1986] 1 All ER 611.

The intestate had died domiciled in Trinidad and Tobago in 1966, survived by a widow and by several children of a previous marriage. He left property in Trinidad and Tobago, Barbados and the United Kingdom. Part of the United Kingdom estate was immovable property in England. Not satisfied with getting $1m by a deed of satisfaction of her rights over the Trinidad and Tobago estate, the widow now claimed her £5,000 statutory legacy out of the English estate by s 46 of the Administration of Estates Act 1925, which provides that the statutory legacy shall be paid out of the 'residuary estate' of the deceased. The children argued that this was satisfied already under the deed of compromise.

However, the Vice-Chancellor, having accepted the widow's interpretation of s 46, that, even if the 'residuary estate' referred to the worldwide estate, it could only apply so as to regulate succession to immovables in England, said that it could not operate to create a charge on assets the succession to which was regulated by a foreign law to secure interests in those assets which fell only to be regulated by English law.

Since succession to the moveable property outside England was governed by the law of Trinidad and Tobago, it followed inexorably that the charge on the English immovables had not been satisfied out of the deceased's overseas assets and the widow was therefore entitled to her £5,000 of flesh. This accords with the Irish and Australian decisions in *Re Rea, Rea v Rea* [1902] IR 451 and *Re Ralston* [1906] VLR 689. It would be avoidable if intestate succession to all property were to be governed by the law of the deceased's last domicile.

Consumer Law

C J MILLER, BA, LLM
Barrister, Professor of Law, University of Warwick

There is little doubt that, in the case of consumer law, 1986 will be remembered for its activity on the legislative rather than the judicial front. In particular it was the year which saw the introduction of the Consumer Protection Bill, Part 1 of which implements the principle of strict liability contained in the EEC product liability directive. However there have been some interesting reported cases, notably in the areas of small claims, trade descriptions, consumer credit and sale of goods. These are discussed below. Reference is also made to some additional cases reported in the new specialist series, Butterworths Trading Law Cases.

Small claims

In *Chilton v Saga Holidays plc* [1986] 1 All ER 841 the plaintiffs had commenced proceedings in the Chelmsford County Court, claiming damages of £184 in respect of a holiday which the defendants had organised. The proceedings were referred to arbitration before the registrar pursuant to CCR Ord 19 and at the hearing the plaintiffs appeared in person whilst the defendants were represented by a solicitor. When the defendants sought to cross-examine the plaintiffs, the registrar refused, saying: 'In cases where one side is unrepresented, I do not allow cross-examination. All questions to the other side will be put through me.' Presumably this refusal was considered to be justified by the wording of CCR Ord 19, r 5 which both requires that the hearing be informal and permits the arbitrator to adopt 'any method of procedure which he may consider to be convenient and to afford a fair and equal opportunity to each party to present his case . . .' On appeal, however, the Court of Appeal unanimously held that the registrar had been incorrect in adopting this approach. Whilst assistance had to be provided to an unrepresented litigant (for example, in putting his points to the opposing side) it was not open to the registrar to disallow cross-examination. As Sir John Donaldson, MR, explained (at 844) the present system:

> 'is basically an adversarial system, and it is fundamental to that that each party shall be entitled to tender their own evidence and that the other party shall be entitled to ask questions designed to probe the accuracy or otherwise . . . of the evidence which has been given.'

These demands of an adversarial system are difficult to reconcile with the type of informal approach which is suited to the needs of litigants in person. Consequently it is strongly arguable that the system should be changed. It is possible that this may occur as a result of the current Civil Justice Review since the recent Consultative Paper, 'Small claims in the County Court' has suggested (para 104) that the *Chilton* decision be reversed and that a represented party be allowed to put questions only through the Registrar. It adds (para 120):

> 'If legal representation is to be retained ... new Rules of Court ... and Registrars' training will have to emphasise that the unrestricted exercise of the traditional legal skills, in particular of cross-examination, is now subordinated to the court's control of the exchanges between the parties.'

It remains to be seen whether such a proposal is considered too radical to be adopted.

Third party provisions

A common feature of consumer protection statutes is that they contain third party or by-pass provisions. Section 23 of the Trade Descriptions Act 1968 is typical in that it provides that, 'Where the commission by any person of an offence under this Act is due to the act or default of some other person that other person shall be guilty of the offence . . .' With such provisions it is clear that the second-named person may be convicted only if the first-named would have been liable under the relevant Act if charged (see eg *Cottee v Douglas Seaton (Used Cars) Ltd* [1972] 3 All ER 750) or at least would not have had a defence on the merits: cf *Coupe v Guyett* [1973] 2 All ER 1058. For the purposes of the Trades Descriptions Act 1968, the first-named person will commit an offence only if he was acting in the course of a trade or business—a limitation whose scope was considered by the House of Lords in *Davies v Sumner* [1984] 3 All ER 831; All ER Rev 1984, p 53. What has been less clear is whether this is true also of the second-named person, that is the person to whose act or default the commission of the offence is alleged to be due. The point was the subject of an appeal to a Divisional Court in *Olgeirsson v Kitching* [1986] 1 All ER 746.

The appellant in the above case was a private individual who had been the owner of a Ford Granada motor car. The car had previously been owned by the Humberside Police and had required a new odometer when it had done some 64,000 miles. It was sold by the police with the new odometer reading some 10,385 miles and later acquired by the appellant who knew that the true mileage was in excess of 74,000 miles. Subsequently when the recorded mileage was approximately 30,000 miles, the appellant sold the car to a garage which traded under the name John Roe. He represented that the true mileage was some 38,000 miles. The garage sold the car to another garage which discovered that the recorded mileage was incorrect. The appellant was then charged and convicted under the s 23 procedure. His appeal to the Divisional Court was dismissed, the court holding that a person might be guilty of an offence (as a second-named person) although acting in the capacity of a private individual.

The arguments in favour of this conclusion are finely balanced. On the one hand it is supported by a literal reading of s 23 or its 'plain and ordinary meaning'. Yet it is certainly arguable that 'the offence' of which the second-named person is guilty refers back to 'an offence *under this Act*'; and, as has been noted, such an offence can be committed only by one who acts in the course of a trade or business. So far as existing authorities were concerned, they can fairly be described as equivocal. In *John v Matthews* [1970] 2 All ER 643 a trade or business limitation was implied in respect of s 11 of the Act (false statements concerning prices), although the wording of the section does not contain such a limitation expressly. On the other hand, *Meah v Roberts* [1978] 1 All ER 97 is more directly in point and it provides some support for the Divisional Court's conclusion. Here a third party cleaner's negligence in putting caustic soda into a lemonade bottle led to a restaurant committing an offence under the Food and Drugs Act 1955. The cleaner was held liable under an equivalent third party procedure, although there was no question of his having incurred even a potential liability as a principal offender through the selling of food or drink. However he was at least cleaning in the course of his employer's business.

It must also be said that the present decision may lead to somewhat anomalous results. In particular the commission of an offence under s 23 by a private individual must be dependent on a subsequent supply (or at least an offer to supply) by a trader. Otherwise there would be no relevant offence by a first-named person. Hence a private individual (D) would not commit an offence under the Act (whether by virtue of s 23 or otherwise) by selling a 'clocked' car to a private purchaser (A). Possibly he might do so (under s 23) if A later sells the car on to a trader (B) who in turns sells it to C. This would depend, inter alia, on whether there was the necessary casual connection between B's offence and D's 'act or default': see, eg *Tarleton Engineering Co Ltd v Nattrass* [1973] 3 All ER 699. It may also depend on ones being able to describe D's act or default as being in some way 'wrongful': see *Lill Holdings Ltd v White* [1979] RTR 120. This seems problematical, or at least a bootstrap's argument. In any event one is not attracted by the idea of D's liability being dependent on subsequent conduct over which he has no control.

On balance it is submitted that the decision to extend s 23 to private individuals is to be regretted. Other offences are available to deal with the fraudulent (for example, obtaining by deception). Also, on appropriate facts, a private individual with the necessary mens rea can be charged as a secondary party aiding and abetting the commission of an offence under the 1968 Act itself.

Extortionate credit bargains

Coldunell Ltd v Gallon [1986] 1 All ER 429 was a sad case of elderly parents who had been persuaded to charge their home to licensed moneylenders so as to secure £20,000 as a loan for their son who needed funds to finance legal proceedings. Although the relationship was not one in which undue influence could be presumed, the evidence established that it was present in the circumstances. Admittedly, the initial offer of help had come from the father, imbued perhaps by the spirit of Christmas 1981, but thereafter all the running had been made by the son, an ex-grammar school boy, who was now in his mid-fifties, and who had had some insurance experience. Predictably, the parents had not received independent legal advice, although the plaintiff finance company had sought to warn them to do so. Equally predictably, the son had failed to meet the interest charges as he had agreed, so causing the finance company to claim repayment of the loan and accrued interest, and possession of the house in default.

The Court of Appeal, although clearly sympathetic to the plight of the couple, held that, in the absence of any agency or equivalent relationship, the plaintiffs were not tainted by the undue influence and unconscionable conduct of the son. Although undeniably a hard decision, it is difficult to disagree with Oliver LJ who was of the opinion that an extension of the law to provide protection would have been against the interests of ordinary commercial dealing.

In the context of consumer law the principal interest of the case perhaps lies in the alternative line of protection which it was sought to advance, namely that the bargain was an extortionate credit bargain within the meaning of ss 137 and 138 of the Consumer Credit Act 1974. The county court judge had been satisfied that the rate of interest charged (20% per annum) was not such as to render the bargain extortionate within s 138(1)(a). However, he re-opened the agreement and granted relief under s 137(1) on the ground that the creditor had not established (the onus being on him by virtue of s 171(7)) that the bargain did not otherwise grossly contravene ordinary principles of fair dealing within s 138(1)(b).

It is not surprising that the Court of Appeal should have reached a different conclusion for reasons which parallel those which were accepted in relation to undue influence. As Oliver LJ put it (at 441):

'if one once rejects the judge's conclusion that the plaintiffs fail to be tainted by the undue influence exerted by the son on his parents, the burden cast on them by s 171(7) of the 1974 Act must, I think, be sufficiently discharged by showing that the bargain was on its face a proper and not extortionate commercial bargain and that the plaintiffs acted in the way that an ordinary commercial lender would be expected to act.'

A similar conclusion was reached by Purchas, LJ. This must, with respect, be right since there was no evidence that the finance company had in any way connived at or adopted the deceitful and fraudulent behaviour of the son.

A similar 'hard-nosed' yet realistic approach is to be seen in the decision of Edward Nugee, QC, sitting as a deputy judge of the High Court, in *Davies v Directloans Ltd* [1986] 2 All ER 783. The plaintiffs in this case were both self-employed and, not having been regular savers with a building society, it was predictable that they would find it difficult to obtain a mortgage on the property in Camberwell which they were seeking to buy. They approached the defendant company which operated a complicated deferred sale arrangement. Its essential feature was to enable purchasers to occupy property over a 12 month period so as to give them time to find a building society or local authority mortgage. The defendants made a mortgage available as a fall back provision, but the interest was higher than the standard building society rate. This was made clear to the plaintiffs who also had the benefit of independent advice from the senior partner of a firm of solicitors. Having been unable to raise building society finance, the plaintiffs executed a legal charge convenanting to pay some £17,450 to the defendant over a 10 year period with interest at an annual percentage rate of

21.6 per cent. Before executing the charge the plaintiffs again consulted their solicitors who explained the nature and effect of a charge. The plaintiffs then went through a distinctly bad period, being unable either to meet the monthly instalments or to sell the house which, it transpired, had a structural fault. Eventually they were rescued by an estate agent from what was a potentially disastrous outcome. He agreed to take on the property and discharge all their liabilities to the defendant. They even had the small bonus of £500 to put towards a deposit for a furnished flat.

With the benefit of hindsight the plaintiffs would perhaps have been wise to have cut their losses and to have written the whole venture off as a thoroughly bad experience. Instead they prolonged the agony by seeking to re-open the legal charge on the ground that the loan and the terms of its repayment constituted an extortionate credit bargain within s 138 of the Consumer Credit Act. The case was argued on the grounds that the rate of interest was grossly exorbitant and that the circumstances surrounding the loan were such as to contravene ordinary principles of fair dealing. The judgment of Edward Nugee QC, dismissing the claim is, with respect, a model of its kind in the way in which it relates the evidence before the court to the factors listed in s 138(2) to (4) of the 1974 Act. It should be read in full and cannot usefully be paraphrased. It is difficult to have doubts about his overall conclusion that far from grossly contravening ordinary principles of fair dealing the scheme was in fact an entirely fair way of assisting purchasers who were not suitable candidates for building society advances.

There are other points of general interest in the judgment. One is the emphasis on the comprehensive nature of the definition of 'extortionate' contained in s 138(1) of the Act, so that 'it is neither necessary nor permissible to look outside the Act at earlier authorities in order to ascertain its meaning'. Consequently it is not necessarily in point that the creditor has or has not acted in a morally reprehensible manner. Another is the expression of a well grounded doubt whether the word 'grossly' in s 138(1)(a) carries any additional weight, since 'it is difficult to conceive of a credit bargain which required the debtor to make payments which were exorbitant but which the creditors could satisfy the court was not extortionate'. Finally, the judgment conveys a good sense of the difficulties inherent in finding and comparing true interest rates. Readers can learn of the mathematical proofs of the late Evariste Galois, killed in a duel at the age of 20, and find references to 'number crunching' and to matters which were hardly practicable before the days of computers. No doubt all this is but part of the varied life of a judge, but there is at least one semi innumerate legal academic who read this part of the judgment with a sense of admiration if not of complete understanding. The upshot was that the annual percentage rate on the charge (21.6%) did not compare badly, giving the additional risk involved, with that quoted by the leading building societies (about 17.5%). Certainly the difference was nowhere near large enough to render the defendant's rate grossly exorbitant.

For discussion of *Re Charge Card Service Ltd* [1986] 3 All ER 289 and the legal issues raised when a credit card company goes into liquidation see the article by Professor Palmer (at p 44, above).

Merchantable quality and fitness for purpose

Wormell v RHM Agriculture (East) Ltd [1986] 1 All ER 769 is an interesting case which has potentially important implications in consumer contracts. The plaintiff farmed in Abberton Essex and he had had severe problems with wild oats infesting his land. He approached the defendant suppliers of agricultural goods, asking them to recommend the best wild oat killer. Their agricultural chemical manager recommended a Shell product 'Commando' and the plaintiff bought some £6,438 worth of this herbicide from them. Since the spring of 1983 was cold and wet he could not get on his land to apply 'Commando' until early June. Before applying it he read the instructions for use carefully and quite reasonably understood them to mean that Commando would be effective to kill off wild oats at any stage (the later the better), but that there was a risk of damage to the crop if it was used after a recommended point.

The severity of the infestation was such that the plaintiff was prepared to take this risk and go ahead with a late application. Commando was duly applied and although it did not damage the winter wheat crop it was largely ineffective in controlling the wild oats. This was the message about late application which the instructions had sought unsuccessfully to convey. The ground was no worse than if it had not been sprayed but neither was it significantly better. The plaintiff had wasted the cost of the herbicide and of the labour expended in applying it.

Faced with such facts, it might be thought that the most obvious target was the Shell Chemical Company. It had, after all, been responsible for marketing Commando with misleading instructions and it was certainly arguable that it had been careless in so doing. However, Shell was not sued, presumably because it could benefit from the argument that the product had not damaged the plaintiff or his property but had only failed to confer an expected benefit. We would then have been in the unpromising area of recovery of economic loss through an action in tort. Of course, the fact that the loss is solely economic does not create a problem in contract, and presumably it was for this reason that the plaintiff sued the defendant supplier, claiming damages under the Sale of Goods Act 1979, s 14. His principal difficulty here was in running up against the argument that there was nothing wrong with the herbicide as such. It was simply that the accompanying instructions had not given a clear indication as to how it was to be used effectively. The question for Piers Ashworth, QC, was whether this was a sufficient basis on which to found a successful action. He held that it was since in the context of s 14 the 'goods' supplied under the contract meant not simply the herbicide Commando but, rather, Commando in its container with its packing and more pertinently its instructions. The defendant seller implicitly warranted that the chemical, when used in accordance with the manufacturers instructions, would be reasonably fit for its purpose.

One can agrue (see, eg Tettenborn [1986] CLJ 389) that there are potential problems in extending strict contractual liability into the area of misleading statements. The same is true of tortious liability and an attempt was made in the original version of cl 3(3) of the Consumer Protection Bill to exclude such statements from the scope of Part I of the Bill which implements the product liability directive. Certainly there is at best a very grey dividing line between liability for misleading or incorrect statements simpliciter and liability for products which are unmerchantable or defective because they incorporate such statements. It is submitted that Piers Ashworth, QC, was correct in holding that the present case was one in which liability should be imposed. Of course similar reasoning might be applied to a wide range of domestic electrical appliances. Possibly some such appliances (perhaps a toaster) may be merchantable and fit for their purposes although they have no accompanying operating instructions. However such cases must be rare. The vast majority of modern appliances (washing machines, tumble dryers, video recorders, home computers, etc) are accompanied by detailed instructions for use and it is hard to believe that they would be considered fit for their purpose without them. Shops which sell imported goods (for example, cameras) accompanied by instructions written in an incomprehensible translation from the original Japanese may find themselves subject to a wider range of liability than they had envisaged.

The attention of readers is also drawn to two further cases involving the standard of merchantable quality in relation to the sale of new cars. The first, *Bernstein v Pamsons Motors (Golders Green) Ltd* (Rougier J), *The Times*, 25 October 1986, is distinctly discouraging as suggesting that the right of rejection will be lost very rapidly indeed. The second, *Rogers v Parish (Scarborough) Ltd, The Times*, 8 November 1986, CA, is altogether more promising. A further decision of considerable interest and importance, *Aswan Engineering Co v Lupdine* [1987] 1 All ER 135, CA, will be commented on in next year's review.

As some readers will be aware, 1986 saw the publication of Butterworths Trading Law Cases (BTLC), a new series of specialist law reports in the field of consumer and trading law. In the space available it is not possible to do more than refer briefly to a small selection of the cases in the first volume of this useful series.

Spare parts

No doubt many readers will have shared the frustrations of having bought a product and then found that it had soon become unusable over a prolonged period because of the unavailability of spare parts. Some jurisdictions make provision for a statutory warranty covering spare parts and repair facilities in consumer transactions, (see Miller and Harvey, *Consumer and Trading Law: Cases and Materials*, pp 83–89) but in the United Kingdom the matter has been dealt with rather by Codes of Practice. In *L Gent & Sons v Eastman Machine Co Ltd* [1986] BTLC 17 the Court of Appeal held, in the context of a case involving an industrial sewing machine, that where there is no trade custom obliging the seller to supply spare parts a failure to have spare parts available is not of itself a ground for claiming that the goods are unmerchantable.

The commercial implications of a contrary decision would have been very far-reaching and probably such as to impose an unreasonable burden on retailers. In a future reform of the Sale of Goods Act durability will probably be explicitly recognised as an element of merchantability. However it is singularly unlikely that this will be extended to include an obligation in respect of spare parts as such. For further discussion of the difficulties involved, see the Law Commission Working Paper No 85, 'The Sale and Supply of Goods', paras 115 et seq.

Lump sum contracts

The doctrine of the lump sum contract is potentially of value to consumers, especially in relation to contract for work and materials in the home improvement area. Its effect is to enable the consumer to insist on at least a substantial performance of the contract before having to pay even a proportion of the contract price. If this is not forthcoming the benefit of the unsatisfactory work can be retained and eventually another contractor can be employed to remedy the defects at a total cost which may be significantly less than that of the original contract. A good example is *Bolton v Mahadeva* [1972] 2 All ER 1322, a case involving an unsatisfactory installation of a central heating system.

Unfortunately the potential for using this doctrine may have been reduced by the decision of the Court of Appeal in *Finlayson v James* [1986] BTLC 163. The contract here was for the removal and replacement of windows at an overall cost of some £2,304 of which £450 was paid in advance. The county court judge awarded the plaintiff contractor some £1,642 of the balance and the householder appealed to the Court of Appeal maintaining that this was a lump sum contract and that the defendant was not entitled to anything. The court dismissed the appeal for what seem to have been two related reasons. The first was that the case was not one of a lump sum contract to which *Bolton v Mahadeva* could be applied since the windows had been priced individually and there were a number of extras. Obviously itemised quotations or estimates can have their drawbacks. The second was that although the work was not well done it would not have been expensive or difficult to put it right. Since this is a matter of degree the conclusion is not really open to criticism. What is, however, more troubling is the rather clear indication that contractors will almost always be entitled to recover a proportion of the contract price even though they have not completed the work properly. Thus Sir Roger Ormrod said (at 167) that, 'to argue that the doctrine that a lump sum contract has to be completed in practically all respects in order to qualify the contractor to get any money at all is, I think, very out of date'.

Obviously many contractors are in a small way of business and some are in need of protection against over fastidious householders. Also one does not wish to have a law which encourages contractors to insist on prepayments, more especially in areas where there is a high risk of insolvency. However it would also be regrettable if the courts were to curtail one of the few effective remedies which consumers possess when they are faced with a contractor whose work is thoroughly shoddy and incomplete.

Exemption clauses and lost photographs

The judgment of Judge Clarke in *Woodman v Photo Trade Processing Ltd* (1981) is one of the better known unreported decisions at county court level.

The more recent decision of Judge Kingham in *Warren v Truprint Ltd* [1986] BTLC 344 may not achieve the same degree of prominence, but it is of interest because of its potentially general application. In another case of a lost film of special occasions, including a Silver Wedding, the limitation clauses on the defendant's envelope had again sought to limit liability to the cost of the unexposed films, plus the refund of the processing charge and postage. However it added, no doubt with *Woodman* in mind: '. . . we will undertake further liability at a supplementary charge. Written details on request.' Judge Kingham held that this was not sufficient to pass the reasonableness test of the Unfair Contract Terms Act 1977. It was at least necessary to 'plainly and clearly set out the alternative', including the cost to the consumer. The plaintiff was awarded £50 damages. Although there is a limit to the amount of small print which can be crammed on the back of an envelope, this insistence on the customer being informed of the contents (and not simply the existence) of the alternative does not seem over-demanding. It remains to be seen whether film processors will adjust the wording on their envelopes to meet the requirements of this decision. If they do not yet another unfair contract term will prove to be effective in practice.

Product liability

Of the other reported cases *Winward v TVR Engineering Ltd* [1986] BTLC 366 is of interest as indicating the high standard of care demanded of producers of specialised products. The defendants designed and assembled the TVR motor car, incorporating in it an engine marketed by Ford Motor Co, which itself incorporated a carburettor manufactured by Weber. The carburettor was defective in design, in that it was not considered good engineering practice to have a push-fit instead of a screw fit between two metals having a different coefficient of expansion. This had led to a brass ferrule being displaced, causing petrol to come into contact with the exterior of the engine. This in turn led in 1981 to a fire in which the plaintiff's wife was injured. The car in question had been manufactured in 1973.

Now it might have been thought that a reasonable man in the defendant's position would have relied on the expertise of Ford and Weber, more especially since there had been no previous fires from the same source. This is effectively what the defendants had done. However the Court of Appeal upheld the conclusions of Judge Holt that the defendants had been negligent in failing to examine or test and modify the ferrule and in failing to warn owners of the existence of the danger. This seems a very high standard of care indeed. The decision lends support to the view that the imposition of strict liability through Part 1 of the Consumer Protection Bill will have only a limited effect on the effective scope of liability.

Contempt of Court

C J MILLER, BA, LLM
Barrister, Professor of Law, University of Warwick

Compared with some previous years, 1986 saw only a small number of cases on contempt of court reported in the All England Law Reports. However the importance of the subject has been apparent in the background in a wide variety of areas, including those of journalists seeking to protect their sources of information (*Maxwell v Pressdram*, Times, 12 November 1986, now reported in [1987] 1 All ER 656), justices attempting to remain anonymous (*Felixstowe Justices, ex p Leigh*, Times, 8 October 1986, now reported in [1987] 1 All ER 551) and, regrettably, industrial disputes.

Contempt and libel proceedings

The decision of the Court of Appeal in *A-G v News Group Newspapers Ltd* [1986] 2 All ER 833 raised a number of interesting issues both as to the relationship between libel and contempt and as to the scope and interpretation of the Contempt of Court Act 1981. The background was the alleged activities of the cricketer, Ian Botham, during the MCC tour of New Zealand in 1984. According to the Mail on Sunday in an article published on 11 March 1984, England's premier all-rounder had not confined himself to such pursuits as card-playing as are traditionally associated with cricket tours. He had rather smoked marijuana in public places, possessed and supplied cocaine, and behaved in an unseemly manner during the test match at Christchurch. A further article of 8 April 1984 in the same newspaper repeated some of these allegations and added for good measure that in a hotel in Auckland he had encouraged two girls, whom he had never met previously, to have sex with him. Not surprisingly, the respective articles were followed by writs for libel. The newspaper pleaded justification in defence and the case was set down for trial no earlier than March 1987. Some two years later, on 6 April 1986, the defendant proprietors of another national newspaper, the News of the World, published a not dissimilar article linked to the then current tour of the West Indies. The main headline was: 'He snorted drugs on pitch. Botham Cocaine and Sex Scandal'. This was to be followed by a further article to be published on 13 April 1986 covering the same general ground as the earlier Mail on Sunday articles about the New Zealand tour in 1984. The matter having been referred to the Attorney-General, he applied for an injunction restraining publication of the intended article. This was granted by Leggatt J, who was satisfied that the publication would create a substantial risk of serious prejudice to the libel proceedings. The defendants appealed to the Court of Appeal which discharged the injunction for reasons which have a general importance to the development of the law of contempt.

One point of general interest addressed by the Court of Appeal is the relationship between the strict liability rule of contempt which exists to protect the fair trial of particular legal proceedings, and the rule in *Bonnard v Perryman* [1891] 2 Ch 269. Since the Mail on Sunday had entered a plea of justification, the prima facie position under *Bonnard v Perryman* was that the plaintiff, Ian Botham, could not have obtained an injunction restraining its repetition of the libel. Clearly, it would not be satisfactory if this important safeguard for press freedom could be readily circumvented by the simple expedient of seeking an injunction restraining the publication of the same material on the ground that it would constitute a contempt. Admittedly in the present case the application was against a different newspaper (the News of the World) which was seeking to resurrect an old story and the plaintiff was the Attorney-General. The involvement of the Attorney-General may be thought to provide a measure of protection. However the protection is less than complete, more especially as it has been held that s 7 of the Contempt of Court Act 1981 (requirement of consent of Attorney-General for institution of proceedings for a contempt of court under the strict liability rules) does not apply to applications for an injunction to prevent an anticipated contempt: see *Peacock v London Weekend Television* [1985] CA Transcript 723 and the judgment of Sir John Donaldson, MR (at 836) in the present case. It applies only where it is alleged that a contempt has already been committed. Hence if an individual plaintiff is to be prevented from claiming relief it will be by virtue of *Bonnard v Perryman*, rather than s 7. As against these considerations it should be said that, in spite of the well-known problems associated with 'gagging writs', defamation proceedings which are instituted genuinely are as deserving of the protection of the law of contempt as any other civil action. Indeed they probably need it more, since it is likely that a jury trial will be involved. Of course, the problem is to reconcile these competing considerations or, perhaps more realistically, to decide which shall prevail in which circumstances.

The approach of the Court of Appeal was, in effect, to require the rule in *Bonnard v Perryman* to give precedence to the 'strict liability rule' of contempt. This structured approach seems, with respect, to be sensible since, as Parker LJ observed at (p 843), to fail to grant relief would then be tantamount to licensing the commission of a criminal offence. The extent of protection for the press will then depend on the safeguards in the 1981 Act itself and in respect of the 'strict liability rule' these are not inconsiderable. For example, there is the requirement—satisfied in the present case—that the proceedings be 'active'. There is also the limited defence in s 4(1) of the Act for contemporary reports of legal proceedings and the qualification to liability in s 5 for publications which contribute to a discussion of matters of general public interest. In addition, s 6 of the Act expressly preserved any defence to a charge of contempt under the strict liability rule which would have been available at common law. It is at present unclear whether such additional defences, for which the Act does not make provision, exist, although it is of interest to note that Parker LJ expressed the view (at 843) that they did not.

In the present case the matter ultimately turned on the test of liability for contempt set out in s 2(2), which required that the publication create 'a substantial risk that the course of justice in the proceedings in question will be seriously impeded or prejudiced'. The judgments in the Court of Appeal adopt a robust approach in holding that the Attorney-General's application was premature. A period of ten to eleven months would pass before the trial and, in spite of the popular nature and large circulation of the newspaper, the statutory test was not satisfied. The general conclusion was supported by some further helpful, if familiar, analysis of the double test contained in s 2(2). For example, Sir John Donaldson accepted a submission that the requirement that the risk be 'substantial' meant that it be 'not minimal'. It was not necessary that it be 'weighty'. This accords with the view of Lord Diplock in A-G v English [1982] 2 All ER 903 at 919 (see also All ER Rev 1982, p 59). As Sir John also pointed out, the risk part of the test will usually be important in the context of the width of the publication. He continued (at 841):

> 'To declare in a speech at a public meeting in Cornwall that a man about to be tried in Durham is guilty of the offence charged and has many previous convictions for the same offence may well carry no substantial risk of affecting his trial, but, if it occurred, the prejudice would be most serious. By contast, a nationwide television broadcast at peak viewing time of some far more innocuous statement would certainly involve a substantial risk of having some effect on a trial anywhere in the country and the sole effective question would arise under the "seriousness" limb of the test. Proximity in time between the publication and the proceedings would probably have a greater bearing on the risk limb than on the seriousness limb, but could go to both.'

He later cited with apparent approval, as did Sir George Waller, the well-known statement of Lawton J in R v Kray (1969) 53 Cr App Rep 412 at 415, expressing the firm belief that juries were generally quite capable of concentrating on the evidence and disregarding other sources of enlightenment.

The overall conclusion of the Court of Appeal on this matter seems realistic. Depending on the evidence ultimately adduced, the jury in the libel proceedings may or may not have difficulty in determining the truth or otherwise of the allegations. It is difficult to accept that there could be a serious risk of the deliberations being affected by another article in a popular newspaper which had rehashed similar allegations almost a year (or more) before.

Substituted orders and civil contempt

The decision of the Court of Appeal in Linnett v Coles [1986] 3 All ER 652 considered two points of general importance in the law of civil contempt. The defendant, having failed to obey court orders calling for the production of documents, had been committed to Winson Green prison, Birmingham, 'to be there imprisoned until further order'. He was arrested under a bench warrant and lodged in prison whereupon the Official Solicitor appealed to the Court of Appeal on his behalf. The first and most simple issue was whether the committal order was unlawful on its face since it was for an indefinite term. Section 14(1) of the Contempt of Court Act 1981 requires a committal to be for a 'fixed term' and the Court of Appeal had little difficulty in concluding that this applied to civil as well as to criminal contempts. This view was supported by the County Courts (Penalties for

Contempt) Act 1983, an enactment which reversed the effect of the decision of the House of Lords in *Peart v Stewart* [1983] 1 All ER 859 (see All ER Rev 1983, p 107). It would also have been supported by references to the Phillimore Committee report on Contempt of Court (Cmnd 5794, 1974, para 172) which recommended that 'sine die committals should be abolished and that fixed terms should be imposed in all cases'. Although there were arguments for preserving the power to commit for an indefinite term in cases of civil contempt, especially for breaches of mandatory injunctions, there was never any serious doubt that it had not survived the 1981 Act. Hence the original order had to be quashed.

The second issue was whether, the order having been quashed, there was any power to substitute another valid order. It seems that the research of counsel had revealed that hitherto there have been unsuccessful attempts to remedy irregularities, for example under the 'slip rule', but that s 13(3) of the Administration of Justice Act 1960 had not been considered in this context. A possible reason for this is that the primary purpose of s 13 was to establish an avenue of appeal against a summary committal for criminal contempt. Nonetheless it clearly applies to civil contempt as well. Moreover, s 13(3) is drafted in wide terms, so that: 'The court to which an appeal is brought under this section may reverse or vary the order or decision of the court below, and make such other order as may be just...' In a decision of considerable importance the Court of Appeal unanimously held that a substitute order could be made under this sub-section, although it was not necessary to do so in the present case.

In view of the constant stream of cases in which the Court of Appeal has found it necessary to quash orders where an irregularity has appeared on their face, it is curious that s 13(3) has not previously been considered in this context. Its wording is, however, clear and there is no reason why its application should be confined to cases where the order is good on the face. No doubt the present decision will make inroads into what Lord Denning has called 'the fundamental principle that no man's liberty is to be taken away unless every requirement of the law has been strictly complied with': see *McIlraith v Grady* [1967] 3 All ER 625 at 627. Yet, as Dillon LJ pointed out (at 657), it is also important not to overlook the position of the party who has suffered from the contemnor's act, especially where domestic violence or matrimonial cases are involved. So far as the practical effect of the decision is concerned, much will depend on the willingness of the court to act under s 13(3). The present case suggests that a general willingness is appropriate. According to Lawton LJ (at 656–57):

> 'It will depend on the facts of each case whether justice requires a new [order] to be substituted. If there has been no unfairness or no material irregularity in the proceedings and nothing more than an irregularity in drawing up the committal order has occurred, I can see no reason why the irregularity should not be put right and the sentence varied, if necessary, so as to make it a just one.'

A just sentence could even be a longer one, although, as Lawton LJ recognised, the court 'should hesitate a long time before exercising its power to increase sentences'.

After *Linnett v Coles* there remains the possibility that a contemnor might seek to avoid the implications of s 13(3) of the 1960 act by applying for habeas corpus. The point was discussed by the Court of Appeal and the fairly clear message is that it is unlikely that such an application would succeed. Woolf LJ approached the point by suggesting (at 658) that it might amount to an abuse of the process of the court on the basis of the reasoning in *O'Reilly v Mackman* [1982] 3 All ER 1124, HL. Lawton LJ, having described the writ (at 656) as 'probably the most cherished sacred cow in the British constitution', noted that 'the law has never allowed it to graze in all legal pastures.' In particular, it was generally excluded where sentences had been passed by courts of competent jurisdiction. He then went on to equate a committal for civil contempt with such a case by saying that it was 'pertinent to remember that civil contempt of court is a common law misdemeanour which can be tried on indictment (which it never is nowadays) or summarily'. The authority cited for this proposition is *Balogh v Crown Court at St Albans* [1974] 3 All ER 283, a case of alleged criminal contempt. This suggestion that a civil contempt is a common law misdemeanour is in danger of becoming accepted through uncritical repetition. Certainly civil contempt attracts many of the safeguards usually associated with criminal proceedings. However this does not, of itself, make it a criminal offence. The better view, it is submitted, is the one associated with Sir John Donaldson in *Goad v AUEW (No 3)* [1973] ICR 108 at 111 that non compliance with an injunction, even as a matter of policy, is 'unlawful, but it is in no way criminal'.

Procedural requirements on breach of undertakings

Finally, the decision of the Court of Appeal in *Hussain v Hussain* [1986] 1 All ER 961 is of interest as pointing to some areas of distinction between a breach of an undertaking and a breach of a court order. The matter arose from divorce proceedings in the county court in which the husband had given an undertaking not to molest his wife. The undertaking had been recited in the formal order of the court, but this was not indorsed with a penal notice. Nor was the order served on the husband.

On a subsequent application to commit the husband for breach of the undertaking these points were quite properly taken in his defence. On appeal to the Court of Appeal Sir John Donaldson, MR stressed (at 963) that 'an undertaking to the court is as solemn, binding and effective as an order of the court in the like terms'. However the procedural requirements differed as between the two since CCR Ord 29, r 1, with its requirement inter alia of personal service, and the equivalent RSC Ord 45, r 5 had no direct application to committal for breach of an undertaking. The point is not simply a technical one. It reflects the obvious difference that since an undertaking is given rather than imposed the giver may be presumed to know of its contents. Moreover, the lack of a penal notice does not work injustice where the alleged contemnor understands the seriousness of any breach. This was true of the husband in the present case since he was an educated man who had been advised both by counsel and solicitors. Accordingly his appeal against a one month term of imprisonment was dismissed.

Contract

MICHAEL P F FURMSTON, TD, BCL, MA, LLM
Barrister, Professor of Law, University of Bristol

1986 was not a vintage year for contract cases. There was only one decision of the House of Lords and even this was not perhaps of the first importance. Nevertheless there were a number of interesting cases.

1. Terms of contract

Three cases concerning the problems arising in spelling out the terms of the contract in a professional relationship where much is left unsaid. Two of these, *Eyre v Measday* [1986] 1 All ER 488, and *Thake v Maurice* [1986] 1 All ER 497, raise very similar facts and issues and can conveniently be considered together. In the former case Mr and Mrs Eyre in 1978 had three children aged 16, 14 and 10. They did not wish to have any more children. Mrs Eyre was 35 years old and wished to stop using the Pill which she had been advised presented a significant risk of serious side effects if she continued its use. She did not wish to switch to any other form of contraception and her husband did not wish to have a vasectomy. She therefore decided to be sterilised and National Health Service sterilisations not being available in her part of the country went to see the defendant who was a consultant gynaecologist in Brighton. The defendant undertook to carry out a sterilisation by an operation called a laparoscopy which involved applying a clip to the fallopian tubes.

In April 1979 the plaintiff discovered to her surprise that she was pregnant and in October 1979 she gave birth to a boy. Although allegations that the operation was negligently carried out were originally made, these were by the time of the appeal fully abandoned. The plaintiff's case by then was that the defendant had contracted to make her sterile and that, although not negligent, he had failed to do so.

It was accepted that the defendant told the plaintiff and her husband that the operation was irreversible, that is, that it would not be possible if the plaintiff changed her mind about wishing to have further children to perform an operation to reverse the effect of sterilisation. It was also agreed that there was a small risk, said to be between two and six in every thousand, that a pregnancy would follow after such an operation. It was agreed that the defendant had not explicitly drawn this risk to the attention of the plaintiff and her husband. The judge found that there was no sterilisation technique available which gave a 100% guarantee of success.

Mrs Eyre contended that the affect of the consultation with the defendant prior to the operation amounted to a binding contractual undertaking by him that the operation would make her irreversibly sterile. It was accepted by counsel for the defendant that the plaintiff and her husband did indeed believe that the operation was 100% certain to make her sterile. On the other hand there was no doubt that the defendant and all competent gynaecologists knew perfectly well that there was a small risk of pregnancy even after a carefully conducted operation of this kind. The Court of Appeal affirming French J, held that the defendant had not contractually undertaken that the operation would make the plaintiff sterile. It is worth emphasising that in this case the plaintiff presented the argument in terms of what was to be implied into the contract. The Court of Appeal had no doubt that it would readily be implied that the defendant had undertaken to take reasonable care but was equally clear that an attempt to imply a term that the operation was guaranteed to be successful would not pass the *Moorcock* or officious bystander tests.

In *Thake v Maurice* a differently constituted Court of Appeal had to consider the correctness of the judgment of Peter Pain J (discussed All ER Rev 1984, p 73). It will be remembered that in this case Mr and Mrs Thake had five children and again wished to have no more. In this case National Health Service sterilisations were available but the waiting list was very long and the Thakes could not afford to have a private sterilisation. It was therefore decided that Mr Thake should have a vasectomy. After the defendant had carried out the operation Mrs Thake became pregnant, but because she did not suspect that she might be pregnant the opportunity for an abortion passed before it became apparent that the vasectomy had not been effective.

In this case also it was agreed that the defendant had warned the husband and wife that the operation was irreversible, that is that they would not effectively be able to change their minds to decide once more to have children. It was also clear that doctors knew that re-canalisation, that is a spontaneous reformation of the canal through which the sperms pass, might take place. Although this was disputed, the trial judge held and the Court of Appeal agreed that the defendant had not explicitly warned the Thakes of the possibility of re-canalisation. The Thakes' argument was that although the vasectomy had been carefully carried out, the defendant was either in breach of contract because he had undertaken that the vasectomy would definitely make Mr Thake sterile, or was negligent in having failed adequately to warn them of this possibility. Peter Pain J had held for the plaintiffs on the contract point and Kerr LJ agreed. The majority of the Court of Appeal however (Neill and Nourse LJJ) took a different view on the contract point. Both Peter Pain J and Kerr LJ took the view that the effect of the consultation with the defendant with its emphasis on irreversibility was to amount to an express undertaking that the operation was guaranteed to make Mr Thake sterile. At first sight it seems puzzling that there could be different views over the express terms of the contract when there was no difference of view between the four judges who considered the case as to what was said during the consultation. The solution seems to lie in the application of the objective test of agreement. All four judges agreed that Mr and Mrs Thake left the consultation thinking that the operation would definitely make Mr Thake sterile; equally all four judges agreed that Mr Maurice never intended to give a guarantee that the operation could not possibly fail. The key appears to be to ask what a reasonable person in the position of the plaintiffs would have believed the defendant was undertaking. This depends very largely on what knowledge one should ascribe to the reasonable man in this position. Clearly one should not assume that the reasonable man knows that vasectomies sometimes spontaneously re-canalise since this would be to attribute to him the critical piece of knowledge at stake. However the majority took the view that it was reasonable to attribute to the reasonable man the knowledge 'that in medical science all things, or nearly all things, are uncertain [since] that knowledge is part of the general experience of mankind'.

However, the whole of the court was agreed in holding for the plaintiffs on an alternative theory, that Mr Maurice was negligent in having failed to warn the Thakes of the possibility that Mr Thake might spontaneously become fertile. If he had warned them of this then they would have been alert to the possibility and would have had the possibility of an abortion because they would have discovered at a much earlier stage that Mrs Thake was in fact pregnant. Of course a claim in negligence required the court to consider whether a reasonable doctor in the position of the defendant would have given such a warning. In fact no independent professional evidence was led by either side but the defendant, who had contended in his own evidence that he had given such a warning, was readily persuaded in cross-examination to agree that such a warning was necessary and this was treated as adequate evidence of the professional standard.

In *Sim v Rotherham Metropolitan Borough Council* [1986] 3 All ER 387 Scott J had to consider, in the context of the recent and bitter teachers strike, what were the contractual obligations of a teacher in respect of cover for colleagues who were absent. A number of cases were tried together but the relevant facts were substantially the same. In each case the plaintiff was a secondary school teacher who had refused to cover for an absent colleague and whose employer had made a deduction from his pay by way of set-off (this remedial question is discussed below in p 92). Each of the teachers was employed under a contract which incorporated conditions set out in a booklet entitled 'Conditions of Service of School Teachers in England and Wales'. Although this booklet ran to over 60 pages there was no explicit statement of exactly what teachers had to do and indeed condition 11 stated *'Definition of the Teachers' Day, Duties and Holiday Entitlement.* There are no existing national collective agreements on these matters beyond that affecting the school midday break which is set out in Appendix VII'.

There was uncontradicted evidence that secondary school teachers did not teach all the timetable periods at the school and that these untimetabled periods were commonly used for the preparation of classes or marking. There was further uncontradicted evidence that in practice all schools had arrangements under which if a teacher was absent for a day someone on behalf of the headteacher would arrange for another teacher to supervise (and if possible teach) the relevant classes. This was commonly done, for instance, by putting up a notice in the staff common room at the beginning of the day. All local authorities had arrangements to reinforce this system by providing supply teachers where the absence lasted more than a few days.

In each of the cases the plaintiffs on the instructions of their unions refused a direction to cover for an absent colleague. The argument of the plaintiffs was that providing cover was voluntary and was not part of the contractual obligations of a teacher. (There are of course a whole range of

activities such as staff meetings, parents meetings, clubs and activities after
school or in the lunch hour, which teachers have habitually carried out in
the past and which might similarly present problems as to whether there
was a contractual obligation to carry them out. These questions were not
specifically at issue in this case though obviously the decision will have
important implications when they come before the courts).

The argument put forward by the plaintiffs and their union attaches great
weight to what is explicitly stated in the contract. However Scott J cogently
pointed out that 'a contract for employment of a professional in a
professional capacity would not normally be expected to detail the
professional obligations expected of the employee under the employment
contract'. It would of course be extremely difficult to write a contract which
covered all the obligations of a professional by a way of express terms. It
seems to follow therefore, that as the judge held 'school teachers have
professional obligations towards the pupils in their schools. Their
contractual duties must include at least the duty to discharge those
obligations'.

Of course there is plenty of scope for argument as to exactly where the
line is to be drawn in respect of such professional obligations. Nevertheless
the unions do not seem to have chosen to fight on the most suitable ground
since it is clear that teachers will sometimes be absent and that it is
extremely undesirable to leave classes unsupervised full of energetic and
high spirited teenagers such as are likely to be found in a secondary school.
It is also extremely unsatisfactory that such children should be sent home
because there is no teacher available to take one of their classes. This leads
very strongly to the conclusion that some system of cover for absent
colleagues needs to be implied if the administration of the school is to run
smoothly.

2 Undue influence, economic duress, inequality of bargaining power

In both the cases which arose this year a loan transaction was attacked by the
borrower not on the grounds of undue influence directly applied by the
lender, but on the theory that undue influence by an intermediary should be
treated as undue influence by the lender. In both cases the intermediary was
the person who actually stood to gain from the transaction; in one case the
husband and in the other case the son of the borrower. This type of factual
situation obviously raises very difficult issues and it is not surprising that
differently constituted Courts of Appeal took the view that the cases fell on
different sides of the line. In *Kingsnorth Trust Ltd v Bell* [1986] 1 All ER 423,
a husband wished to borrow £18,000 in order to expand the activities of a
partnership which he ran in conjunction with his son and the son's wife.
One of the securities offered for the loan was a second mortgage on the
matrimonial home in which the wife had a beneficial interest. The lenders
were a Bristol firm who engaged Bristol solicitors to prepare documents to
carry out the transaction. The Bristol solicitors sent the documents to the
husband's solicitors in Carlisle and asked them to act as their agents for the
completion of the documents.

The husband's solicitors gave the documents to the husband who undertook to get his wife to complete them. The husband told the wife lies about the purpose of the transaction and concealed from her its true purpose. It was accepted that the wife (who was the second wife) would not have agreed to charging the matrimonial home to support a business venture involving the son by the first marriage. The Court of Appeal held that the effect of this way of handling the transaction was that the plaintiffs had in effect made the husband their agent for the purpose of getting the wife to sign the charge documents and that they were therefore effected by his fraud and undue influence. At first sight it seems hard on the plaintiffs who had done no more than entrust the transaction to a competent and respectable firm of solicitors that the result should follow. It was explained by Dillon LJ on the grounds that there were only two possible correct analyses of the situation. One was that the effect of the Bristol solicitors asking the Carlisle solicitors to act as their agents was to make the Carlisle solicitors sub-agents of the plaintiffs so that the plaintiffs became bound by the conduct of the partner in the Carlisle firm allowing the husband to take the documents away for signature by the wife. The alternative theory was that the Bristol solicitors were sending the documents to the Carlisle solicitors who were to act as agents for the husband. This equally produced an unacceptable result since this would have amounted to the plaintiffs agents leaving it to the husband's agent to procure the wife's signature. In practice this means that as a rule the plaintiffs or their Bristol solicitors should have communicated directly with the wife and probably that they should have taken steps to ensure that she had independent advice.

In *Coldunell Ltd v Gallon* [1986] 1 All ER 429 the plaintiff's lenders had in fact attempted to communicate directly with the defendant but apparently without success. In this case a son in his fifties wishes to borrow some £20,000 as a short-term loan in connection with his business. He persuaded his elderly parents to help him. A proposal was made to the plaintiffs that they should lend £20,000 to the father, everyone's expectation being that he would then lend the money to the son. The loan was to be secured by a charge on the house where the parents lived which was owned by the father. The managing director of the plaintiffs said that they would require a first charge on the house and would charge interest at 20%. He looked at the outside of the house and formed the view that it would be adequate security for a short-term loan of this amount. The paperwork was entrusted to the plaintiff's solicitors. The senior partner of that firm prepared a form of charge for execution by the father and a form of consent for execution by the mother. The letter to the mother required her signature to be witnessed by a solicitor and advised her that she should get independent advice as to the effect of the charge. The covering letter to the father in connection with the charge contained similar advice.

Precisely what happened to these letters was the subject of disputed evidence. The senior partner of the plaintiff's solicitors gave evidence that these letters had been prepared on his instructions. The father and mother gave evidence that they had not received them and that the charge and consent documents which they had signed had been shown to them for the first time by the son who had brought a solicitor with him who had spent a few moments explaining the documents to the mother before they were signed. (This solicitor was not a partner or employee in the plaintiff's solicitors firm). The most probable hypothesis was that the son had succeeded in intercepting the letters either at the office of the plaintiff's solicitors or at his parents' home. On this basis the Court of Appeal held that the trial judge's finding that the plaintiff's solicitors had entrusted the task of getting the documents signed to the son could not be sustained. If the son was not the agent of the plaintiffs then of course his undoubted dishonesty towards his parents could not be attributed to the plaintiffs. On this analysis it followed that the transaction could not be set aside.

There is a further difficulty which occurs to the present writer but which does not appear to have been urged before the courts. It is fairly clear that the intention of all the parties, both the plaintiffs, the son and the father and mother, was that the father would borrow the money from the plaintiffs and then lend it to the son. In fact what happened however, after the completion of all the paperwork, was that the plaintiff's solicitors gave to the son a cheque for £19,658.75 (that is £20,000 less their charges) made out in favour of the father. The son then forged an endorsement in his father's name in favour of a company with which the son was connected and the money disappeared from sight. Since the endorsement by the father was held to be a forgery and was therefore a nullity, it is a little difficult to see why the father was treated as ever having had the money. It does not have appeared to have occurred to the defendants to argue that they did not have to repay because they had never borrowed the money.

3 Agency

Clearly the two previous cases are of considerable interest on the general question of whether or not one person acts as an agent for another. A third case of agency is *Armagas Ltd v Mundogas SA* [1986] 2 All ER 385 in which the House of Lords affirmed the decision of the Court of Appeal (discussed 1985 All ER Rev 101). It may be remembered that in this case the respondents Mundogas owned a ship and there were negotiations about a possible sale of the ship to Armagas for $5,750,000. Armagas were only willing to buy the ship if they could immediately charter it back to Mundogas for three years at $350,000 a month. Armagas employed for the negotiations a broker who stood to earn a very substantial commission by way of a share in the ship if the transaction went through. He realised that Mundogas were not willing to charter the ship back for three years and corruptly persuaded Mundogas's chartering manager to enter into a three year charter. The chartering manager had neither actual nor apparent authority to enter into such a transaction, but he explicitly told Armagas that he had been given authority to enter into this particular three year charter. Simultaneously Mundogas were told that the ship had been chartered back for a year. The broker and the chartering manager hoped that chartering rates would remain above $350,000 for at least another two years so that the charter could be renewed for further periods of a year and neither Armagas or Mundogas would ever be any the wiser. In fact the chartering market collapsed, Mundogas refused to renew at the end of the first year and Armagas then brought an action for wrongful termination of the three year charter. Armagas argued that the chartering manager had apparent authority to enter into the transaction because of his explicit statement to Armagas that he had such authority. The House of Lords held that this line of reasoning was clearly wrong. Although it was theoretically possible that an agent who was known to have no authority to enter into tranactions of a particular kind might have ostensible authority to enter into a particular transaction of the same kind, such apparent authority could only arise from some conduct of the principal which held the agent out as having this authority. The agent could not by alleging that he had authority invest ostensible authority in himself.

The House of Lords also held that Mundogas were not vicariously liable in tort for the fraudulent misrepresentations made by the chartering agent.

4 Discharge

Although *Re Charge Card Services Ltd* [1986] 3 All ER 289 is primarily a case for the chapter on commercial law, it is worth noting here as an example where a creditor can correctly be held to have agreed to accept an alternative form of payment in absolute discharge of the debtor's initial obligations. Briefly the case concerns a chargecard scheme under which cardholders could obtain petrol from garages by signing a sales voucher completed by the garage. Obviously the initial purchase of the petrol would normally create a debt between the garage and customer and equally the garage by accepting payment by card would be looking primarily to the card company for payment. The question presented by the case is whether when the card company goes into liquidation the garage can then look to the original customer for payment. Millett J held that in such circumstances the reasonable inference was that the garage took the card in absolute discharge of the customer's obligations and thereafter looked only to the card company for payment.

5 Contributory negligence

1985 saw two first instance decisions on the applicability of the defence of contributory negligence to actions for breach of contract. 1986 saw another such decision in the judgment of Hobhouse J in *Forsikringsaktieselskapet Vesta v Butcher* [1986] 2 All ER 488. The main point in this case was an interesting and difficult point on the proper law of contracts of insurance and reinsurance which will be found discussed in the chapter on Conflict of Laws. It is not necessary therefore to examine the facts here in any detail. Hobhouse J identified three different categories of case where the applicability of the 1945 Act to claims brought in contract could arise. These were:

'1.   Where the defendant's liability arises from some contractual provision which does not depend on negligence on the part of the defendant.
2.   Where the defendant's liability arises from a contractual obligation which is expressed in terms of taking care (or its equivalent) but does not correspond to a common law duty to take care which would exist in the given case independently of contract.
3.   Where the defendant's liability in contract is the same as his liability in the tort of negligence independently of the existence of any contract.'

The judge observed that the border between categories 2 and 3 would move from time to time as the scope of liability in tort expanded or contracted. The decision in *Basildon DC v J E Lesser (Properties) Ltd* [1985] 1 All ER 20 (discussed All ER Rev 1985, p 97) fell into category 1. The decision in *A B Marintrans v Comet Shipping Co Ltd* [1985] 3 All ER 442 (discussed All ER Rev 1985, p 97) was he thought an example of either category 1 or category 2. He recognised however that the reasoning used by Neill LJ to decide that case was equally applicable to category 3 cases. Hobhouse J thought however that it was clear that category 3 cases should be treated differently. There was no doubt that in a category 3 case the plaintiff was entitled to sue in tort and that if he did sue in tort the defendant would have a defence of contributory negligence available to him. In the circumstances the fact that the plaintiff could also choose to sue in contract did not justify a different result unless the contract expressly provided for a different result. In other words apportionment under the Contributory Negligence Act should be the normal incident of such a contract unless it were an express or implied term of the contract that apportionment was not to be a feature of it. Hobhouse J came to this conclusion recognising that it differed from the analysis of Neill LJ but fortified by the fact that in many category 3 cases the point had been treated as so obvious as not to require comment and that the decision of the Court of Appeal in *Sayers v Harlow UDC* [1958] 2 All ER 342 was a binding decision on apportionment in such a case.

6 Remedies

In *Sim v Rotherham Metropolitan Borough Council* [1986] 3 All ER 387, the facts of which have already been discussed, the plaintiffs argued that even if they had broken their contract by refusing to cover for their colleagues so that the defendants were entitled to damages, the defendants were not entitled to deduct those damages by way of set-off but should have paid the plaintiff's wages in full and then brought an action for damages.

At first sight this seems a rather arid question once it is agreed that the damages are due. In fact it illustrates the overwhelming importance in the English system of remedial questions. The amount of the deduction made by the defendants varied but was usually of the order of between £2 and £3. It is obvious that, except as a test action in order to ventilate questions of principle, it was very unlikely that an education authority would actually sue a teacher for a sum of damages as small as £3. Conversely in ordinary circumstances a teacher would be equally, if not more, reluctant to start an action against his employer for a sum of that kind. The ability to set off the claim therefore would be of enormous tactical advantage. It is important to note that the amount of the damages deducted was not disputed as being a reasonably correct estimate of the plaintiff educational authority's loss. Obviously there might have been cases in which the educational authority suffered no loss at all, for example, because another member of staff who was not a union member or belonged to a different union had been willing to take on the cover responsibility. In such a case the plaintiff would have broken his contract but the defendant would have suffered no loss. Scott J rejected any notion that the education authority would be entitled to make a deduction from the teacher's pay because he had broken the contract if that had not caused a loss or to make a deduction which exceeded the amount of the loss. Theories put forward by some of the authorities that it was possible to arrive at a correct amount of deduction by proportionate comparisons of the amount of time not worked to the length of the working week were rejected. This point is of great practical importance since in an employment contract it will in practice very often be the case that the employer will find it difficult to show any quantifiable loss flowing from the breach of contract. After a full and careful analysis Scott J rejected the argument that equitable set off was not applicable to employment contracts.

There has been considerable academic literature in recent years suggesting that the courts should take a wider view of the applicability of specific performance as a remedy on the grounds that there are many instances in which careful analysis shows that damages do not adequately compensate the plaintiff. In this context the decision of Mervyn Davies J in *Posner v Scott-Lewis* [1986] 3 All ER 513 may be regarded as a not insignificant straw in the wind. In this case the plaintiffs were tenants in a block of residential flats in London of which the defendants were the landlords. One of the landlord's covenants in the leases was 'to employ (so far as in the lessor's power lies) a resident porter for the following purposes ...' The plaintiff sought specific performance of this covenant. The defendant's affidavits alleged that they were not in breach of the covenants since they employed a non-resident porter who carried out all the duties which the resident porter was required by the covenant to do. The judge had little difficulty in dismissing this argument since it was a central part of the obligation to provde a resident porter that he would be present continuously with obvious advantages in terms of access to the block of flats by delivery men and 24 hour availability of portering services. The facts of the case are of course highly reminiscent of the well-known decision in *Ryan v Mutual Tontine Westminster Chambers Assoc* [1893] 1 Ch 116 where the Court of Appeal refused to grant specific performance of a contract between a landlord and a tenant by which the landlord undertook to employ a porter to perform certain services for the benefit of the tenant on the grounds that specific performance would require 'constant superintendence by the Court'. Mervyn Davies J was satisfied that this reason at least for the decision could not be supported in view of the critical comments of the House of Lords in *Shiloh Spinners Ltd v Harding* [1973] AC 691 and the cautionary words of Megarry J in *C H Giles & Co Ltd v Maurice* [1972] 1 All ER 960 at 969–70 and Megarry V-C in *Tito v Waddell (No 2)* [1977] 3 All ER 129 at 307–8. It was quite clear in the present case that damages would not be an adequate remedy since no sum of money would enable the plaintiffs to go out on the market and buy themselves a resident porter. The judge could see no difficulty in defining sufficiently what had to be done in order to comply with the order of the court or in securing such compliance. Certainly if one were to balance the hardship to the defendant in granting specific performance with the hardship to the plaintiffs in being deprived of the resident porter the balance of the hardship would seem to lie in favour of the plaintiffs.

7 Illegality

There were no fewer than six cases involving problems of illegality in 1986 making it clearly the topic of the year. Of these, *Phoenix General Insurance Co of Greece SA v Halvanon Insurance Co Ltd* [1986] 1 All ER 908 raises again the questions posed in *Bedford Insurance Co Ltd v Instituto De Resseguros Do Brasil* [1984] 3 All ER 766 and *Stewart v Oriental Fire & Marine Insurance Co Ltd* [1984] 3 All ER 777 (discussed at All ER Rev 1984, p 79) as to the effects of carrying on business under the Insurance Companies Act 1974 without authorisation. The defendants had reinsured certain insurance contracts into which the plaintiffs had entered. For present purposes the central question was whether the defendants could rely on the defence that the insurance policies written by the plaintiffs were illegal as policies they were not authorised to issue. This was put either by saying that the plaintiffs had committed a criminal offence by writing the policies and were therefore seeking to benefit from their own crime or, alternatively, that the plaintiffs themselves were not liable under these insurance policies and therefore had suffered no loss which they could claim under the reinsurance contracts.

The plaintiffs carried on insurance business in London. Under the 1974 Act they were authorised for 'marine, aviation and transport insurance business'. Under the original categories employed by the 1974 Act business written by the plaintiffs fell within the authorised categories but new categories were substituted by regulations issued in 1977 which were complex and difficult to understand. For present purposes it is sufficient to say that the effects of the 1977 changes was that the plaintiffs by carrying on writing the same risks as they had written under the 1974 Act were now writing unauthorised risks and it was these unauthorised risks which were the subject of the present litigation. It was clear therefore that the plaintiffs were committing a criminal offence by writing the relevant policies. (The plaintiffs may or may not have appreciated this. In view of the complexity of the categorisation it was by no means impossible that they did not realise it. This was quite irrelevant to their criminal liability since liability was clearly strict and not dependent on proof of mens rea.)

Hobhouse J had little difficulty in concluding that if the plaintiffs were committing a criminal offence by writing the policies, then the policies which were written were consequently illegal. It was true that the Insurance Companies Act 1974 did not explicitly say that individual contracts of insurance were illegal; it said that the writing of relevant insurance business was forbidden. However since the insurance business could only be written by making individual policies for insurance it necessarily followed that the insurance company was forbidden from issuing such policies since writing the policies was an inevitable and necessary and not an incidental or collateral result of the carrying on of the business. In this respect therefore Hobhouse J had no difficulty in preferring the view of Parker J in the *Bedford* case to that of Leggatt J in the *Stewart* case.

What are the effects of this decision as to the legality of the policies? For this purpose it seems necessary to distinguish between the effects of the original insurance contract and of the reinsurance contract. As far as the reinsurance contract was concerned it is difficult to see how the plaintiffs could be entitled to reinsure a policy which they had been forbidden by statute to write. Hobhouse J had little difficulty in concluding that such an argument could not be sustained, agreeing in this result with Parker J in the *Bedford* case.

Much more difficulty surrounds the question of the original insurance contract. It is clear that this cannot be enforced by the insurer. What is the position of the insured who in normal circumstances would have no idea that the insurer is not authorised to carry on the relevant business? Since the purpose of the insurance scheme of authorisation under the Insurance Companies Act is to protect the insured, it seems paradoxical to say that the effect of the Act is that although he has paid his premiums he is not entitled to be compensated against his loss. (Presumably he could recover the premiums on the grounds that he was not in pari delicto with the insurer but this is hardly adequate compensation.) In this respect Hobhouse J agreed with Leggatt J in *Stewart* that the insured under the original contract of insurance was not prevented from enforcing it. This is clearly what one would wish the position to be but it is not at all clear how one can correctly reach this result once it has been held that the original contract of insurance is one which is expressly prohibited by statute. Such classic cases as *Re Mahmoud and Ispahani* [1921] 2 KB 716 show that if a contract is prohibited by statute it cannot be enforced by either party, even though one party had no means of knowing facts which were relevant to the categorisation of the contract as prohibited. One possible avenue of escape here is the argument that in some circumstances the guilty party has warranted in a separate contract that facts exist which make the contract legal, see *Strongman (1945) Ltd v Sincock* [1955] 2 QB 525.

Very similar issues were raised by the decision in *SCF Finance Co Ltd v Masri (No 2)* [1986] 1 All ER 40. In this case the plaintiffs had been handling transactions on behalf of the defendant in commodity and financial futures. During the period between April 1983 and early 1984 the defendants had lost some $1.7 million through these transactions. About half of this sum had been paid by him to the plaintiffs and the plaintiffs claimed the balance as monies which they had expended on behalf of the defendant. The defendant raised a number of defences and indeed counterclaimed in respect of these transactions. For present purposes the critical argument was the allegation that the plaintiffs were carrying on a deposit-taking business within the meaning of s 1(2) of the Banking Act 1975. There was no doubt that the plaintiffs had in effect extended credit to the defendant by trading on his behalf in American futures markets without having been put fully in funds to do so. The plaintiff operated a money account and called on the defendant to make payments as his debit balance ran up. The defendant made a significant number of payments, though usually not as large as were called for. One of the plaintiff's main arguments was that the way in which the business was operated did not amount to deposit taking at all. (It appears that although the defendants' account was very seldom in credit, other customers trading in the same way would have accounts which were in credit. The plaintiffs settled their debts with brokers on a day to day basis. Accounts produced by the plaintiffs showed that at the end of each month the plaintiffs always held more of their own funds in credit than the aggregate monies owed to their trading clients who were in credit.)

Logically the solution to the problems presented by the case might be thought to depend on deciding first whether the plaintiffs were accepting deposits without being authorised to do so and secondly, what was the legal effect of so doing? However Leggatt J thought that in the circumstances it was easier to decide the case by holding that even if the plaintiffs were in breach of s 1 of the Banking Act by taking unauthorised deposits then they could rely on s 1(8) of the Act which provides 'the fact that the deposit is taken in contravention of this Section should not affect any civil liability arising in respect of the deposit or the money deposited.' Leggatt J thought that the scheme of the Act was to protect depositors. This protection of depositors, did not require protection of the defendant since the defendant's losses in no way were the result of his having made deposits but were the result of his having speculated unsuccessfully in commodity futures.

In *Thackwell v Barclays Bank plc* [1986] 1 All ER 676, the plaintiff who owned a gold mine wished to raise money to exploit it. He entered into a complex and dishonest scheme with S a director of R Ltd to raise money by means of a bogus hire purchase arrangement. The scheme was that the plaintiff would invoice AJ Ltd for £44,227 in respect of two items supposedly sold by the plaintiff to AJ Ltd. (One of the items did not exist and the other was overvalued.) AJ Ltd then sold these items as well as other items to R Ltd who raised £80,000 by means of a hire purchase agreement from a finance company. The finance company issued a cheque for £80,000 to AJ Ltd and a director of AJ Ltd took the cheque to a branch of the defendant bank. While he was there he met S who later handed to the manager two cheques drawn on AJ Ltd's account, one made payable to S himself, and the other made payable to the plaintiff for £44,227 but apparently endorsed by the plaintiff. S told the manager to pay this latter cheque into R Ltd's account. In fact S had forged the endorsement of the plaintiff on the cheque and if the manager had compared the two cheques he would have seen that the handwriting on them was the same and that one of the endorsements was clearly a forgery.

The plaintiff brought an action against the bank alleging negligence and conversion. This obviously raises familiar issues under s 4 of the Cheques Act 1957 which are discussed in the chapter on Commercial Law, pp 28–31 above. However, the bank also raised as a separate defence the argument that in any case the plaintiff was debarred from bringing an action because he was party to a fraudulent refinancing scheme and that this was the reason for the issuing of the cheque to the plaintiff in the first place.

Counsel for the plaintiff relied on the familiar argument that it was not necessary for the plaintiff to rely on any illegal transaction in order to succeed. (It should be noted that counsel for the plaintiff was simultaneously arguing on the facts that the plaintiff was innocent of any participation in the fraudulent refinancing scheme, a contention which was not accepted by the judge.) The argument was that the plaintiff's cause of action was the conversion of cheque drawn in his favour by AJ Ltd. He contended that in order to succeed the plaintiff did not need to go into the history of previous transactions which had led AJ Ltd to issue a cheque in the plaintiff's favour. Hutchison J had little difficulty in rejecting this argument. Once it was held that the plaintiff was implicated in the scheme it followed necessarily that public policy should debar him from recovering the proceeds. (The present case was not of course an action in contract against the bank but virtually all the relevant cases are contract cases and it therefore seems appropriate to note the case here.)

Another ingenious and dishonest scheme to raise money came before the Court of Appeal in *Mansouri v Singh* [1986] 2 All ER 619. In this case the plaintiff was an Iranian National who wished to get substantial assets out of Iran which he could not do because of Iranian exchange control regulations. He therefore arranged with the defendant who was a travel agent operating in England to buy airline tickets in Iran and forward them to the defendant in England to be exchanged for sterling at double the normal rate of exchange. The advantage of this scheme was that under international travel arrangements airline tickets can be converted in exchange for cash anywhere in the world. As part of the proceeds of this scheme the defendant issued a cheque for £33,334 in favour of the plaintiff but stopped the cheque before it was paid. The plaintiff sued on the cheque. The defendant argued that the underlying transaction behind the cheque was contrary to the Bretton Woods Agreement Order in Council (1946). The plaintiff argued that the cheque was a wholly autonomous transaction and that he could sue on it irrespective of the transaction which laid behind it. (In fact the case was remitted to the trial judge for further trial of the Bretton Woods issues. However the court considered the above argument first since if correct it would have meant that it was unnecessary to decide whether the agreement was in fact contrary to the Bretton Woods Order in Council.) The Court of Appeal effectively regarded this point as being covered by the decision of the House of Lords in *United City Merchants (Investments) Ltd v Royal Bank of Canada* [1982] 2 All ER 720, [1983] AC 168 in which it was held that a letter of credit raised in relation to a sale transaction which had disguised foreign exchange evasion purposes could not be enforced. It is of course well established that letters of credit like cheques are usually autonomous but it seems clear that this argument must yield to the more powerful arguments of policy.

Two cases shed light on the doctrine of restraint of trade. In *Kerr v Morris* [1986] 3 All ER 217, the parties were general medical practitioners carrying on practice in partnership within the National Health Service. The partnership agreement contained a provision by which a partner could be compelled to retire from the partnership if given 12 months' notice by all the other partners and a further provision providing that for a period of two years following his expulsion from the partnership the former partner was not entitled to practice within a radius of two miles from the place where the partnership practice was operating at the time when he ceased to be a partner.

Difficulties broke out within the partnership and the three plaintiffs gave an appropriate notice to the defendant. The defendant bought a property a few doors away from the partnership surgery with a view to setting up practice there as soon as the 12 months' notice expired. The plaintiffs sought an interlocutory injunction to restrain the defendant from opening a practice. Of course in respect of other professional practices such as solicitors questions would arise as to whether the restriction was reasonable in relation to time and geographical area. On facts such as these in such a case it would be very likely that the court would grant an interlocutory injunction on balance of convenience grounds. However, the defendant argued that in respect of general medical practices the situation was different in that any post termination of partnership provision was void since it restrained patients from going to a particular practitioner, and/or on the grounds that since the partners could no longer sell the goodwill of a National Health Service partnership they had no interest which they were entitled to protect. Both these arguments were rejected by the Court of Appeal. It was thought that there was nothing inherently inconsistent with the scheme of the National Health Service in permitting contracts in which, subject to the general law on restraint of trade, a doctor agreed not to practice in a particular area. National Health Service patients had no right to the services of a particular doctor at a particular place. On the second argument, although it was true that sales of the goodwill had been barred this did not affect the fact that the goodwill was still a valuable asset of the partnership and that therefore the partners were entitled to make reasonable agreements designed to protect the value of the goodwill.

Faccenda Chicken Ltd v Fowler [1986] 1 All ER 617 was not strictly speaking a restraint of trade case since there was no express covenant. Nevertheless the facts of the case are of considerable interest since they raise difficult questions as to the borderline between what is implicit in a master and servant relationship and what a master may legitimately require by express provision. In this case the plaintiff company was engaged in the business of marketing fresh chickens. It employed Mr Fowler in 1973 as its sales manager and he developed a method of selling the chickens from refrigerated vans which went out each day to a planned series of retail outlets. This produced a very significant expansion of this side of the plaintiff's business. In November 1980 Mr Fowler left the plaintiff's business and in May 1981 he set up his own business in competition with the plaintiff selling fresh chickens from refrigerated vans. He advertised for staff and a substantial number of employees left the plaintiff's and went to work for him. The plaintiffs brought an action claiming damages in breach of the contract of employment in using the plaintiff's sales information. Since there was no express covenant, the question for the Court of Appeal was what was implicit in the employment relationship in the present case. It was clearly stated than an employee owes a former employer a less wide duty than is owed by an existing employee. Nevertheless it would clearly be a breach of contract for any existing employee to supply a competitor with lists of his employer's customers, or indeed to run a private business in his spare time, which competed with the employer using this information. Not all such confidential information however was entitled to protection against use by a former employee. The Court of Appeal thought that such confidential information could be used by an employee unless the information was classed as a trade secret or was so confidential that it required the same protection as trade secrets. It is perhaps worthwhile drawing attention here to the explicit statement at 626 where the court rejected the suggestion:

'that an employer can protect the use of information . . . even though it does not include either a trade secret or its equivalent by means of a restrictive covenant . . . a restrictive covenant will not be enforced unless the protection sought is reasonably necessary to protect a trade secret or to prevent some personal influence over customers being abused in order to entice them away.'

In deciding whether the information was a trade secret or equivalent to a trade secret, the court thought it necessary to have regard to such questions as the status of the employee (ie was he regularly handling confidential information), the nature of the information itself, whether the employer had stressed the confidentiality of the information to the employee and whether the relevant information could easily be isolated from non-confidential information, which was part of the same package of information. Applying these tests, the court was clear that the sales information possessed by the defendants did not fall in to the category of a trade secret.

Criminal Law, Criminal Procedure and Sentencing

G J BENNETT, MA
Barrister, Lecturer in Law, University of Leeds

BRIAN HOGAN, LLB
Barrister, Professor of Common Law, University of Leeds

CRIMINAL LAW

General principles

1 Duress

The law relating to duress has developed apace in recent years and very much in favour of its expansion. Cases like *R v Kray* (1969) 53 Cr App Rep 125, *R v Hudson* [1971] 2 All ER 244, *DPP for Northern Ireland v Lynch* [1975] 1 All ER 913 may be said to have taken the larger view but the brake was applied (in so far as the Privy Council decision can apply the brake) in *Abbott v The Queen* [1976] 3 All ER 140 where it was held that duress was not available to the principal (perpetrator) in murder. The judges have been by no means unanimous on the proper development of the defence as the powerful dissents in *Lynch* and *Abbott* show. And the argument is not yet over as *R v Howe and another* [1986] 1 All ER 833 shows.

Two appeals were involved, that of Howe and Bannister in the one and that of Burke and Clarkson in the other. The common features were that Howe, Bannister and Burke were principals in killings and were charged with murder. Each claimed that he had participated in the killing only because of a threat that he would be killed if he did not. In both cases the trial judge declined to put the defence of duress to the jury on the grounds that it was not a defence to a principal in murder. All three were convicted of murder.

The Court of Appeal dismissed all three appeals. It was held that *Lynch* went no further than holding that duress was a defence to a secondary party (aider and abettor) in murder and that *Abbott* reinforced the view that it was not available to a principal.

Dealing with the matter quite shortly Lord Lane CJ delivered his judgment with evident passion. He could see that there were illogicalities in denying the defence to the perpetrator while extending it to the secondary party but thought that the preferable way to resolve that anomaly was not to extend it to the perpetrator but to deny it to both. At all events this was not the time to extend the defence when acts of terrorism are commonplace. His Lordship thought that if duress were to be at all allowed as a defence to murder it should, on analogy with provocation, merely reduce the crime to manslaughter so that account could be taken of it in sentencing.

So in this matter the Lord Chief Justice has firmly nailed his colours to the mast. He thinks the law has gone far enough already if not too far and his fears seem to be fuelled by his belief that the defence is easy to raise and that it may be difficult for the prosecution to disprove beyond reasonable doubt when the facts are ordinarily known only to the defendant himself. But this may be equally true of a defence of accident or of self-defence and no one seriously suggests that these should be no more than a matter of mitigation; and such arguments apply with equal validity to duress as a defence to all crimes and not merely to murder. Once the principle is accepted that a man has a defence to a charge of crime where, owing to threats of death or serious personal injury, neither he nor a person of reasonable firmness could fairly be expected to do otherwise, it is indefensible to stop short in the one case where the crime is murder and the defendant is a principal in it.

Inevitably the issue in *Howe* has been certified for the House of Lords. Quite which way they will go is anyone's guess. Once more the law is up for grabs.

2   Parties to crime

In the second of the cases taken together in *Howe and another* there was a further point of sufficient importance that it too was certified. Apart from raising duress, which was denied him, Burke claimed that when it came to shooting the victim the gun had gone off accidentally and that as the killing was unintentional it amounted to no more than manslaughter. Counsel for Burke's co-defendant, Clarkson, also argued that the trial judge was wrong to withdraw Burke's defence of duress because, had it been successful, not only would Burke have been acquitted but so too Clarkson. This must be one of the boldest arguments advanced in a criminal case since 1189. With more plausibility counsel argued that if Burke could properly be convicted only of manslaughter then Clarkson's guilt could rise no higher than manslaughter. With more plausibility because the proposition is supported by the Court of Appeal's decision in *R v Richards* [1973] 3 All ER 1088 where it was held that where the principals were convicted of the less serious offence of malicious wounding, a secondary party could not be convicted of the more serious offence of wounding with intent to cause grievous bodily harm though the actus reus of the more serious offence was committed and the defendant had the relevant mens rea.

The Court of Appeal, while it felt obliged to follow *Richards,* thought it incorrectly decided and has, in effect, invited the House of Lords to overrule it. As Lord Lane said, it would seem absurd (with respect there is no 'seems' about it) that if A hands a gun to D telling D that it is loaded only with a blank which D is to fire at and scare X, that while D would commit manslaughter, A should escape a conviction for murder though he knew the gun to be loaded with a live round and intended X's death. This time the House of Lords must inevitably agree. If they do not then your reviewers undertake to print a full apology in capital letters in the 1987 Review.

3   Force in prevention of crime

By s 3(1) of the Criminal Law Act 1967 a person may use 'such force as is reasonable in the circumstances in the prevention of crime, or in effecting or assisting in the lawful arrest of offenders.' This section is normally invoked to justify conduct which would otherwise constitute an offence against the person such as an assault, but there is no reason in principle why it may not be invoked to justify what would amount to some other offence such as an offence of damage to property. In s 3(1) 'force' is not expressly confined to force as applied to the person and there is nothing to suggest that it should be implicitly so confined. The terms of s 3(1) are broad and were surely meant to justify any conduct, provided it be reasonable in the circumstances, done in the prevention of crime.

In *R v Renouf* [1986] 2 All ER 449 the defendant, lawfully entitled to arrest X who had driven off after an attack on the defendant, told his wife to telephone the police and then set off in pursuit in his own car. Initially the defendant's idea was merely to keep track of X so that the police could arrest him but, fearing that X might escape altogether, he executed a manoeuvre to force X's car off the road and bring him to a stop. In respect of this manoeuvre he was charged with, and convicted of, reckless driving contrary to s 2 of the Road Traffic Act 1972, the trial judge declining to allow the jury to consider a defence under s 3(1) of the Criminal Law Act.

The Crown sought to support the conviction on the ground that the manoeuvre created an obvious and serious risk to the occupants of the car which the defendant, as he admitted, had decided to take. His driving was thus reckless and there was no place for the s 3(1) defence since the offence under s 2 was not qualified by any such provision as 'without lawful excuse'. The Court of Appeal rejected the Crown's argument and quashed the conviction. The court clearly saw s 3(1) as being of general application. It was certainly not disposed to confine its application only to the use of force but not to reckless acts immediately preceding the application of the force.

The decision seems an eminently sensible one. The Crown's submission seems to have been based on the assumption that a person is reckless if he knowingly takes a risk. But there is more to recklessness than that: recklessness is the taking of an unreasonable risk. Whether the risk taken is unreasonable will depend on the circumstances; it may be unreasonable to risk serious bodily harm to bring a shoplifter to book but not a dangerous gunman. Since reckless driving involves the taking of an unreasonable risk it was most assuredly relevant to consider the action in the terms of s 3(1). It would certainly be odd if force directly applied to the person of a suspect who took to his heels would be justified but not force indirectly applied to a suspect who takes to his car.

4 Attempts

Practitioners, being the sensible down-to-earth sort of people that they are, have much less reverence for the problem of impossibility in attempts than have the academics. After all its not every day of the week that a client is charged with attempting to handle stolen goods which were not stolen; or with attempting to deal with a controlled drug which was not a controlled drug; or with attempting to have intercourse with a girl under 16 who was not under 16. Put in these starkly simplistic terms it must be clear, even to the hypothetical first year law student, that there is no actus reus, nor could there be, of any offence known to law and throughout the history of the criminal law that has been fatal to a charge of crime.

But no longer so, it seems. Though in *Anderton v Ryan* [1985] 2 All ER 355; All ER Rev 1985, p 104, the House of Lords held that there could be no attempt to handle stolen goods where the goods were not stolen, the House decided less than a year later in *R v Shivpuri* [1986] 2 All ER 334 that there could be a conviction for attempting to deal with a controlled drug though the substance dealt in was not a controlled drug at all. *Anderton v Ryan* was sent packing.

Sighs of relief all round. The Criminal Attempts Act 1981 had been given its intended effect (there can be no doubt about that) and that Royal Scot of academic argument—impossibility in attempts—had been consigned not to an honourable place in the National Railway Museum but to a derelict siding, there to rust away. But there is around the place the odd, eccentric, conservationist who goes to that derelict siding to apply an oily rag to the machinery and to keep polished the brass controls.

The trouble with *Shivpuri* is that it assumes that the Criminal Attempts Act has somehow ordained that a missing ingredient in the actus reus can be provided by mens rea. Lord Bridge, delivering the principal speech in *Shivpuri*, thought that he and other members of the House in *Anderton v Ryan* had gone astray in describing Mrs Ryan's conduct in purchasing a non-stolen video recorder as 'objectively innocent'. The mistake was to categorise the purchase of a non-stolen article as 'innocent' without regard to Mrs Ryan's belief that it was stolen. But, with respect, Lord Bridge was barking up a tree in an entirely different part of the forest. The proof of an actus reus has nothing whatever to do with the defendant's state of mind, nor has it anything to do with the so-called innocence of the act. Assume, for instance, that X is driving a vehicle when he has consumed alcohol to an extent that he is twice, or thrice, over the legal limit and is in such a condition that he is a patent danger to other users of the road. Assume he is breathalysed with a perfectly reliable device that has not been approved by the Secretary of State, or that the test is administered by a constable not in uniform. Such provisions may seem remote from the gravamen of the offence and certainly X is no less dangerous because the device was not approved or because the constable was not in uniform. But even the hypothetical first year law student knows that X cannot be convicted of the offence of driving with an excessive blood-alcohol concentration. X has driven with an excessive blood-alcohol concentration (and there is no way that can be said to be 'innocent') but there is more to the offence than that. Parliament, rightly or wrongly, has added a few bits and pieces to the actus reus which have nothing to do with the gravamen of the offence. There is, however, no escaping them if the offence is to be proved. But the requirement goes to the wall if an attempt is charged for now it is enough that the motorist *believed* the device had been approved or *thought* that the constable was in uniform.

And here's another funny thing. The Law Commission whose fond child, with some unwanted plastic surgery, the Criminal Attempts Act was, had thought that prosecutions would be unlikely in the 'extreme and exceptional' cases that the Act, if applied in accordance with their intentions, would lead. Lord Bridge pointed out that *Anderton v Ryan* had itself falsified the Law Commission's prognosis but he nevertheless thought it would hold good for other cases, particularly that of the 'young man having sexual intercourse with a girl over 16, mistakenly believing her to be under that age . . .' But Lord Bridge's young man intends (no need to rely on strict liability here) to commit a serious offence. Why should he not be convicted of the attempt? How does his offence differ from that of the man who mistakenly intends to deal in cannabis or cocaine? What if he is not a 'young' man? What age does he have to be before a prosecution for an attempt is thought appropriate?

It may be said, however, that the House of Lords, having changed its mind once, is unlikely ever to change it again. So we can confidently say we have heard the last of this. Perhaps.

But this is not the end of the *Shivpuri* saga. The substantive offence, of being *knowingly* concerned in harbouring goods the import of which is prohibited, arose under s 170(1)(b) of the Customs and Excise Management Act which in Sch 1 provides for different penalties according to whether the drug is class A or B (in which case the maximum punishment is 14 years' imprisonment) or class C (in which case the maximum punishment is 5 years' imprisonment). Counsel for Shivpuri argued (relying on *R v Courtie* [1984] 1 All ER 740; All ER Rev 1984, p 115) that there were three distinct offences each with different ingredients. So fas as mens rea was concerned, he submitted, it had to be proved that the defendant knew of the importation of goods in the appropriate category and thus the trial judge had misdirected the jury in saying that it mattered not whether Shivpuri believed the substance to be herion (Class A) or cannabis (Class B) or some other prohibited drug.

Lord Bridge approached this problem in what might be called, for want of a beter expression, a commonsense way. An educated layman could identify some of the drugs listed but by no means all. 'If a man were accused of being knowingly concerned in the importation of mytheldesorphine (Class A),' he said, 'what would a jury make of his defence that he believed it to be methylphenidate (Class B) or methaqualone (Class C)?'

Had the offence been under the Misuse of Drugs Act 1971 the answer would be quite simple. It would seem that the framers of that legislation had anticipated just this sort of problem and met it in s 28 by providing that the accused is not entitled to an acquittal by reason only that he is mistaken as to which particular controlled drug he possesses. There is no equivalent provision in the Customs and Excise Management Act 1979. Why not? The answer according to Lord Bridge was that *R v Hussain* [1969] 2 All ER 1117 had decided under the predecessor to s 170 of the 1979 Act (Customs & Excise Act 1952, s 304) that the offence was committed whenever the defendant was knowingly concerned in the importation of something which he knew to be prohibited though he did not know into precisely which prohibited class it fell. The framers of the 1979 Act must have assumed, he said, that *Hussain* was good law, making it unnecessary to have in the the 1979 Act a provision such as s 28 in the Misuse of Drugs Act 1971. '(T)he decision in *R v Hussain*', concluded Lord Bridge, 'has effectively been adopted and indorsed by the legislature and thus remains good law.

This, with respect, is a pretty bold exercise in statutory interpretation. The framers of the 1979 Act may for all we know (and we don't) have assumed that *Hussain* was correctly decided but does such an 'assumption' (nowhere stated or even hinted at in the legislation) give to that decision legislative effect? This is a novel principle and stands in marked contrast to the words, known to every hypothetical first year law student, of Lord Herschell in *Bank of England v Vagliano Bros* [1891] AC 107:

> 'The proper course is, in the first instance, to examine the language of the statute and to ask what is its natural meaning uninfluenced by any considerations derived from the previous state of the law, and not to start with inquiring how the law previously stood, and then, assuming it was probably intended to leave it unaltered, to see if the words of the enactment will bear an interpretation in conformity with this view.'

Moreover, though s 304 of the 1952 Act is the predecessor of s 170 of the 1979 Act, they are hardly in pari materia. Section 304 probably created only one offence punishable in all cases (save for cases where some other statute created a different penalty) by a maximum of two years' imprisonment. Section 170 together with Sch 1 of the 1979 Act sharply distinguishes between importing Class A and B drugs as against importing Class C drugs as the vast disparity in punishment shows. The logic which says that the mens rea in relation to the lesser will suffice for the more serious might just as well be applied to saying that the mens rea of an assault will do for murder since both involve hurt to the person.

This has gone on long enough, but another lick of paint. Quite how someone can *knowingly* deal (or attempt to *knowingly* deal) in a prohibited substance which is not a prohibited substance is nowhere convincingly explained. X imports sheep thinking that they are horses. Are we really to say that he *knowingly* imports horses? Does it make more sense to say that he knowingly attempts to import horses? When Parliament uses the formula, as it has, of 'knowing or believing' are we now to read this as 'believing or believing'? Of course if the formula is used in legislation post *Shivpuri* we will be able to say that since Parliament will have assumed the correctness of *Shivpuri,* 'knowing' means 'believing'.

5   Conspiracy

Conspiracy continues to spawn difficulties and it can come as no surprise that yet another case, *R v Cooke* [1986] 2 All ER 985, reached the House of Lords in the period under review. *R v Ayres* [1984] 1 All ER 619; All ER Rev 1984, p 98 had (apparently) set the law on a definite footing by holding that the offences of statutory conspiracy and common law conspiracy are mutually exclusive; hence if the agreement is to commit a crime involving fraud (theft, deception etc) it must be charged as a statutory conspiracy and only where the agreement, if carried out, would not necessarily amount to a crime is a common law conspiracy to be charged.

This stark dichotomy posed considerable practical problems (see All ER Rev 1985, pp 104, 112) so the House was asked for further guidance in *Cooke.* The defendant, a British Rail steward, had agreed with others to take their own refreshments on board with a view to selling them to passengers and pocketing the proceeds. On the face of it, this was a case where the defendant was guilty of a statutory conspiracy (going equipped to cheat contrary to s 25 of the Theft Act 1968 or of false accounting contrary to s 17 of that Act) but the defendant was charged only with a common law conspiracy to defraud and of that he was convicted. Following *Ayres* the Court of Appeal quashed the conviction but then certified the question whether common law conspiracy could be charged where the evidence showed that there was such a conspiracy to defraud one victim (ie British Rail) and in addition disclosed a statutory conspiracy to defraud a different victim (ie the passenger buying the substituted food).

The House of Lords answered the question in the affirmative and in so doing held that the stark alternatives offered in *Ayres* were by no means so stark as they seemed. It was never meant to be the law, it was explained, that a common law conspiracy could not be charged simply because the carrying out of the agreement necessarily involved the commission of some statutory crime if, over and above the commission of the statutory crime, there is a substantial element of fraudulent conduct which would not if done by one person amount to a crime. It seems to follow, therefore, that if the substance of the offence is a common law conspiracy to defraud X the fact that the conspiracy will necessarily but incidentally involve statutory crimes (eg taking a motor vehicle, falsifying accounts) it is still permissible to include a count for common law conspiracy. It would further seem that the case for adding the common law charge is even stronger when its victim is X (in this case British Rail) when the statutory offence is committed against Y (in this case the passenger).

There were thus ample grounds for allowing the Crown's appeal but the House indicated that they would have allowed the appeal on the narrower ground that there was no evidence that the statutory offences under ss 25 and 17 would necessarily have been committed. As for the s 25 offence the House was not prepared to assume (though the Court of Appeal in *R v Doukas* [1978] 1 All ER 1061 seems to have assumed this) that even upright citizens necessarily refuse to take and pay for refreshments where they know the buffet car staff are on the fiddle. A surprising conclusion? In the ordinary run of case this must be a matter of inference tested by reference to the hypothetical reasonable and upright customer. Perhaps the answer will depend on whether the train is a pullman or a soccer special. And as for the s 17 offence the employer's accounts were not rendered false by an employee's failure to record the sales of the employee's own property.

This re-interpretation of *Ayres* will meet some of the difficulties but, as the House conceded, by no means all. Lord Bridge was not prepared to say, for instance, how *R v Tonner* [1985] 1 All ER 807; All ER Rev 1985, p 104 would have been decided according to the newly articulated criteria. The real remedy lay in legislation.

Offences against the person

1 Intention and murder

In All ER Rev 1985, p 134, it was observed (without any pretense to prescience) that the House of Lords' decisions in *R v Maloney* [1985] 1 All ER 1025; All ER Rev 1985, p 108, and *R v Hancock & Shankland* [1986] 1 All ER 641; All ER Rev 1985, pp 108, 134, were not the final word on the meaning of intention in the criminal law in general and in murder in particular. The Court of Appeal returned to the matter in *R v Nedrick* [1986] 3 All ER 1.

The case was strikingly similar to that of *R v Hyam* [1974] 2 All ER 41. The defendant had a grudge against a woman and, as he claimed with an intention only to frighten her, he poured paraffin through the letter box of her house and set fire to it. The house was burned down and one of the woman's children died of asphyxiation and burns.

The trial judge (the trial took place before the House of Lords had offered its views in *Maloney* and *Hancock*) directed the jury along the *Hyam* lines. The defendant was guilty of murder not only if he intended to kill or cause serious bodily harm but also if in setting fire to the house 'he knew it was highly probable that the act would result in serious bodily injury to somebody inside the house, even though he did not desire it.'

The Court of Appeal substituted a conviction for manslaughter for the one to murder. It was clear that neither *Maloney* nor *Hancock* equated foresight of probability or high probability with intention. This, with respect, was clearly right. *Maloney* and *Hancock* may have left certain things unclear but they left it clear that the *Hyam* direction was inadequate.

The court might have left it at that but Lord Lane CJ thought it prudent to add a word or three. He reiterated that in the ordinary run of case no difficulty was likely to be encountered with intention but added that there would be cases, of which the instant case was an example, where further directions might need to be given. Having regard to *Maloney* and *Hancock* Lord Lane thought that in such cases the jury might find it helpful to ask themselves (i) how probable was the consequence? and (ii) did the defendant foresee that consequence? If the defendant did not foresee that consequence or did but considered that the risk of it occurring was slight then it would be easy for the jury to conclude that the consequence was not intended. 'On the other hand', said Lord Lane:

> 'if the jury are satisfied that at the material time the defendant recognised that death or serious bodily harm would be virtually certain (barring some unforeseen intervention) to result from his voluntary act, then that is a fact from which they may find it easy to infer that he intended to kill or do serious bodily harm, even though he may not have had any desire to achieve that result ... Where the charge is murder and in the rare cases where the simple direction is not enough, the jury should be directed that they are not entitled to infer the necessary intention unless they feel sure that death or serious bodily harm was a virtual certainty (barring some unforeseen intervention) as a result of the defendant's actions and that the defendant appreciated that such was the case.'

This is a brave effort on Lord Lane's part to equip the trial judge with a direction which will provide for the 'rare' case (such cases are by no means as rare as 'rare') consistently with what was said by the House in *Maloney* and *Hancock*. But does not such a direction take us back to the quicksand of probability theory (All ER Rev 1985, p 110) that must be avoided if any meaningful line is to be drawn between intention and recklessness? Foresight of a 75% probability is not enough but foresight of virtual (or moral) certainty is enough. Yet does probability theory, assuming any jury can calculate the odds, say, of killing the inmates of a house by setting fire to it, have any bearing on the issue of intention other than that the jury will be more inclined to believe (strictly, left in doubt as to) the defendant's claim that he did not intend a consequence which experience shows to be unlikely than it will believe his claim that he did not intend the consequence which experience shows to be very likely? But to jump from these inferences of common sense to the conclusion that the defendant intends a consequence that he foresees as virtually certain (ie very highly probable) is as non-sensical as to say that the defendant cannot be found to intend a consequence that is virtually certain not to, or even cannot, occur. In *R v White* [1910] 2 KB 124 the defendant administered to his mother a dose of cyanide which was much too small to have killed her but this did not vitiate the jury's finding that he intended to kill her. By parity of reasoning a defendant does not intend a consequence simply because he foresees it as highly probable, very highly probable or virtually certain. The so-called 'rare' case (difficult rather than rare) occurs where the defendant does not desire the consequence. In such cases it is necessary to do no more than explain to the jury that intention and desire are not always the same and that a man who knows or believes that a particular consequence will follow from his actions may properly be said to intend that consequence even though he would much prefer (or want or hope) that it will not happen.

2 Damage to property endangering life

In *R v Steer* [1986] 3 All ER 311 the defendant had a number of disagreements with his business partner which provoked considerable ill-feeling. So much so that the defendant went round to the partner's house and when the partner and his wife appeared at a bedroom window in response to his ring on the doorbell, he loosed off a few shots at them with an automatic rifle. The bullets smashed the bedroom window (the defendant pleaded guilty to a charge of criminal damage in respect of that) but since the lives of the partner and his wife were obviously endangered the defendant faced a further charge of damaging property being reckless whether life would be endangered contrary to s 1(2) of the Criminal Damage Act. He was convicted on this count, the trial judge rejecting a submission that he had no case to answer because it was not by the damaging of the property (the window) that life was endangered.

The Court of Appeal quashed the conviction, holding that s 1(2) required that life be endangered *by* the damaging of the property. It was not enough that life was endangered by something done by the defendant nor that what the defendant does causes damage to property at the same time. The endangerment of life must be caused by the damaging of the property.

With respect the decision seems entirely right. To take a simple example. Suppose that X, bent on endangering Y's life by severing the brake cable on Y's car, forces and damages the lock to Y's garage. X has now damaged property (the lock) with the necessary intent but there is as yet no completed offence because it is not the damaging of the lock, that endangers life. While in *Steer* the damaging of the window was contemporaneous with the endangerment, the damaging of the window no more endangers life than the damaging of the garage lock.

Steer points up what might be thought to be an oddity which is that it is not an offence recklessly to endanger life unless it takes the form of endangerment by damaging property. Had the defendant in *Steer* intended to kill he would have been guilty of murder if he succeeded or attempt if he did not. Had he recklessly killed he would have been guilty of manslaughter but this time if he misses he commits no offence more serious than common assault.

Offences against property

1 Theft

Credit cards and cheque cards spawn so many frauds that it may be wondered whether, as an alternative to using traditional charges which may involve difficult issues of ownership and causation, it might not be better to make an offence of their dishonest use. *R v Navvabi* [1986] 3 All ER 102 seems to make the point and others beside. The defendant had been convicted of a hatful of charges involving fraud. One of these concerned the obtaining of gambling chips in return for cheques supported by a banker's card, the defendant well knowing that he had insufficient funds in the bank to meet the cheques. In respect of these transactions the defendant was charged with, and convicted of, theft, the argument being that each time he delivered a cheque he appropriated the amount specified on the cheque from the bank.

This was not an argument which found favour with the Court of Appeal which quashed the conviction. Appropriation may be a wide ranging concept but the argument that each time the defendant passed a cheque for £50 or £100 he appropriated (ie assumed the right of an owner in respect of) £50 or £100 of the bank's general assets was held to be misconceived. The transaction gave the payee a right to payment from the bank but did not amount to any appropriation of money in the bank.

In *AG's Reference (No 1 of 1985)* [1986] 2 All ER 219 the Court of Appeal was troubled by a problem that seems to have been last raised over one hundred years ago in *R v Cullum* (1873) LR 2 CCR 28. Cullum, older heads who were paying attention to their teachers may recall, was the captain of a barge owned by Mr Smeed. Mr Smeed had ordered Captain Cullum to take a load of bricks to London and to bring back the barge empty but the bold captain loaded up a cargo of manure on his way back and pocketed the £4 he received as freight. It was held that Cullum could not be convicted of stealing (embezzling, in those distant days) because, and though Cullum had dishonestly used his employer's chattel to make a profit for himself, the employer never became the owner of the money paid as freight. The employer could have sued Cullum for the *amount* of money paid as freight because Cullum had unjustly enriched himself at his employer's expense, but the employer had no claim on the £4 in specie.

It is not enough for theft, and sometimes we all need reminding of this, that someone is on the fiddle. To steal, property *belonging to another* must be appropriated. In *AG's Reference (No 1 of 1985)* the defendant was engaged on his employer's premises to sell only goods supplied by his employer but he made a few dishonest pounds on the side by selling at those premises goods supplied by a third party. Was he guilty of stealing the money he dishonestly made?

The Court of Appeal held not. The profit dishonestly made by the defendant did not belong to his employer for in law the employer never had possession or control of it nor did he acquire a *proprietary* right or interest in it by his employee's dishonest use of the employer's premises or name. The prosecution relied on s 5(3) of the Theft Act 1968 which provides:

> 'Where a person receives property from or on account of another, and is under an obligation to the other to retain and deal with that property or its proceeds in a particular way the property or proceeds shall be regarded (as against him) as belonging to the other.'

But the point was, as it was in *Cullum*, that cheating is not the same as theft. The employer was no doubt entitled to recover by civil action the secret profit made by his employee but when the customers paid their money across the counter for the goods supplied by the third party the employer had no proprietary right to '*that* property or its proceeds'. As Blackburn J pointed out in *Cullum* the owner of the barge had no contract with the freighterer on which he could sue or be sued. So the employer in this case had no contract with the customers in respect of the goods supplied by the third party. The employer had personal remedies he could pursue against his employee but he had acquired no proprietary interest in the money paid to his employee by the customers.

2 Forgery

By s 3 of the Forgery and Counterfeiting Act 1981:

> 'It is an offence for a person to use an instrument which is, and which he knows to be, false, with the intention of inducing somebody to accept it as genuine, and by reason of so accepting it to do or not to do some act to his own or another's prejudice.'

The section makes it clear beyond a peradventure that the defendant must know that the instrument is false and intend another person to accept it as genuine. The issue in *R v Tobierre* [1986] 1 All ER 346 was whether it must be proved that the defendant additionally intended the other to act to his prejudice.

The defendant had claimed and had been paid child benefit by signing his wife's name in the allowance book. He thus knew that he had caused the Secretary of State to accept a false instrument as genuine but he claimed that he did not intend the Secretary to act to his prejudice in that he believed he was fully entitled to the payments. The trial judge appears to have directed the jury that it was enough that the defendant intended a false instrument to be accepted as genuine and did not, or did not adequately, explain that it must be proved that he must also intend the other to act to his prejudice. The resulting conviction was inevitably quashed. Any other conclusion would have produced the astonishing result that no mens rea is required as to a fundamental aspect of a serious crime.

Miscellaneous offences

1 Controlled drugs

In *R v Maginnis* [1986] 2 All ER 110 the Court of Appeal declined to follow its earlier decision in *R v Delgado* [1984] 1 All ER 449; All ER Rev 1984, p 103 concerning the meaning of supplying a controlled drug contrary to s 5(3) of the Misuse of Drugs Act 1971. The cases are factually essentially the same in that in both a third party left controlled drugs with the defendant which the defendant intended to return to the third party at a later stage. In *Delgado* it was held that 'supply' was to be given its ordinary meaning and extended to a transfer of control from one person to another. In *Maginnis*, however, the court thought there was more to 'supply' than that: it connoted a transfer of control for the benefit of the recipient and a restoration of control by a bailee to his bailor was insufficient to constitute a supply. As the court said, where a shoe mender or cloakroom attendant restores the shoes or the coat to a bailor these would not be thought of as a 'supply' of the shoes or the coat to the bailor. Fair enough, perhaps, but there is the difference that the bailor of controlled drugs, unlike the bailor of the shoes or the coat, cannot enforce the return of the drugs. Leave to appeal to the House of Lords has been granted.

To a charge of possessing a controlled drug (cannabis) contrary to s 5(2) of the Misuse of Drugs Act, the defendant in *R v Martindale* [1986] 3 All ER 25 admitted that he had knowingly come into possession of the drug some two years previously, had placed it in his wallet but sometime later had forgotten all about it. The trial judge and the Court of Appeal were at one in holding that his lapse of memory did not constitute a defence. Possession cannot, as it were, come and go according to the state of the possessor's memory from time to time. No doubt if it had been his gold watch that he had forgotten about, the defendant would hardly have denied possession of that had someone stolen it.

2   Public order

And now, as they say, for something completely different. In *Masterton v Holden* [1986] 3 All ER 39 two lovers were seen at a bus stop kissing and cuddling and fondling one another and, as is so often the case with lovers, they appeared to be entirely oblivious to the presence of other persons in the vicinity. Nothing so far to excite more than a passing glance and still less to occasion a breach of the peace—except that the lovers were both men. This did excite more than a passing glance. Two couples happened by and one of the men called out, 'You filthy sods. How dare you in front of our girls?' They were arrested and charged with 'insulting . . . behaviour . . . whereby a breach of the peace may be occasioned' contrary to s 54(13) of the Metropolitan Police Act 1839.

We all know from *Brutus v Cozens* [1972] 2 All ER 1297 that 'insulting' is an ordinary English word and its interpretation is to be determined by the trier of fact. The magistrates in this case found the behaviour insulting and the Divisional Court agreed. The court thought that while the behaviour might be better categorised as offensive or disgusting (which was not an offence) it could be properly described as insulting, the insult being the implication that other people would find such conduct in a public street acceptable. The magistrates were thus entitled to conclude as a matter of fact that the behaviour was insulting.

But would the magistrates equally have been entitled to conclude 'as a matter of fact' that the behaviour was not insulting? The exegisis to which 'insulting' was subjected by the Divisional Court suggests that the meaning of this ordinary word is no mere matter of fact. It is clearly undesirable that the same behaviour should in one case be held to be insulting and criminal while in another the contrary is held. But this is a conclusion of which *Brutus v Cozens* apparently admits.

The defendants' counsel also took the point that the insulting behaviour should be directed at another person and there was no evidence of that here since the defendants were unaware of other persons in the vicinity. While there is authority for saying that all that needs to be intended is the behaviour, the court appears not to have favoured so strict a construction of the offence. The conduct had taken place in London's Oxford Street at 1.55 am and the magistrates were entitled to conclude that the defendants would have known that other persons would likely be present. This makes sense. The defendants might have been oblivious, or indifferent to, the presence of others but they could hardly have been unaware of them.

CRIMINAL PROCEDURE

Bail

Flights of judicial fancy are, perhaps not surprisingly, comparatively rare in the field of criminal procedure but the peculiar genius of Watkins LJ in *Schiavo v Anderton* [1986] 3 All ER 10 positively glows with originality. This emphatic and briskly argued judgment nevertheless puts one more in mind of Oscar Wilde's definition of genius as an infinite capacity for causing pain than of any panacea for the anxious magistrates' clerk.

The defendant had failed to surrender to bail in June 1983, preferring instead to take a two year sojourn in Southern Spain. The justices accordingly issued a bench warrant for his arrest pursuant to s 7(1) of the Bail Act 1976 and he was duly arrested on his return to England. In July 1985 he pleaded guilty before the magistrates to the offence of failing to surrender to bail under s 6(1) of the 1976 Act and was thereupon commited to the Crown Court for sentence. At this hearing the defendant argued that he should be allowed to change his plea to not guilty since the magistrates had no jurisdiction to try the offence. It was, so it was contended, a summary offence and an information had not been laid within six months from the time when the offence was committed as required by s 127 of the Magistrates' Courts Act 1980 Act. As a result, the case was remitted to the stipendiary magistrate. He concluded that the defendant could properly be found guilty on the grounds either that the offence of failure to surrender to bail under s 6(1) of the 1976 Act was an indictable offence to which s 127 of the 1980 Act did not therefore apply or that in effect an information had been laid in June 1983 when the magistrates were asked to issue a warrant under s 7(1) of the 1976 Act. The stipendiary thereupon committed him yet again to the Crown Court for sentence, and so the matter eventually came before the Divisional Court.

Watkins LJ rejected both of the stipendiary's findings. On the issue of whether the s 7(1) proceedings constituted the laying of an information he concluded:

'For present purposes what is important is that it must actually be what it seems to be, namely an information designed for the purpose of initiating criminal proceedings. In other words, a deliberate act which commences in the conventional sense a prosecution which ultimately will have the effect of bringing an offence and offender before the court. In this case it was a mere incident in the history of the affair that a warrant was applied for and issued...'

The consideration of this point was in any event rendered superfluous by the judge's conclusion that the offence created by s 6 was not a conventional criminal offence but rather an anomalous provision, having no ancestry earlier than the 1976 Act itself, which partook more of the nature of a contempt. Just as it was the invariable practice for judges in the Crown Court to deal with contempt during the trial of their own motion, why should the magistrates deal with breaches of s 6 of the 1976 Act differently?

Watkins LJ accordingly laid down the following guidelines for the 'proper construction' of s 6 of the 1976 Act:

'(1) the magistrates' court and the Crown Court each require separately a power to punish for the offence of absconding; (2) the offence is not subject to the general rule that trial be commenced by information; (3) the initiation of the simple procedure for trial by the court's own motion and not by formal charge, as seems to have happened here, is the only proper way to proceed; (4) it is not one of those offences triable on indictment or either way; (5) it is an offence only triable in the court at which proceedings are to be heard in respect of which bail has been granted; (6) it is expected that the trial of the offence will take place immediately following the disposal of the offence in respect of which bail was granted.'

Doubtless there are advantages in freeing a magistrates' court from the complexities of more formal process in such cases, but the bold assertion that proceeding of its own motion is the only proper way to deal with the s 6 offence seems to go rather further than is necessary. A charge under s 6 of the 1976 Act, unlike some forms of contempt, may lead to a specific criminal conviction which, for example, is sufficient to activate a suspended sentence, *R v Tyson* (1978) 68 Cr App R 314. The implied analogy to the law of contempt may therefore do less than justice to the seriousness of an offence under the 1976 Act. Watkins LJ also expressly rejects the suggestion by Roskill LJ in *R v Harbax Singh* [1979] 1 All ER 524 at 527 that a judge might consider it more appropriate to remit a case to the magistrates where there is a dispute, rather than dealing with it himself. A further consequence of the decision is that it seems to represent a blow against the tripartite classification of offences clearly envisaged by the Criminal Law Act 1977. One possible exception to this scheme was noted in an earlier Review in the case of *R v Harrow JJ, ex p Osaseri* [1985] 3 All ER 185; All ER Rev 1985, p 124. The present case appears to be an even clearer example.

A further practical difficulty arising out of the decision is the issue of how such proceedings are to be conducted. It would hardly seem appropriate that the magistrates' clerk should take on the role of something like a prosecutor. How could this be easily squared with the responsibility to safeguard the interests of, as is not unknown in the magistrates' courts, the unrepresented defendant (see Gibson, (1986) JP 150, 212)? In *R v Gateshead Justices, ex p Usher and another* [1981] Crim LR 491, a decision of the Divisional Court apparently overlooked by the court in the present case, Ormrod LJ appeared to regard it as 'perfectly ludicrous' that the magistrates' clerk should take on the role of prosecutor in a s 6 offence.

It was presumably some awareness of the theoretical and practical difficulties outlined which subsequently led to the issue of a Practice Note [1987] 1 All ER 128 with a view to, as the Lord Chief Justice put it with an uncharacteristic expression of understatement, 'clarifying any misunderstandings' as to the effect of the decision. The Note, whilst of course confirming the tenor of the judgment of Watkins LJ, makes clear that the court should proceed by its own motion only following an express invitation to do so by the prosecutor. It is the prosecutor who will then conduct the case and call the evidence. By contrast, when there is a failure to answer to bail granted by a police officer there is not thought to be the same compelling justification for the court to act on its own motion for defiance of an order. Accordingly in such cases, whether it is a failure to surrender to custody at a court or police station, proceedings should be initiated by charging the accused or the laying of an information.

Crown Court

1 Appeal

In *R v Crown at Croydon, ex p Clair* [1986] 2 All ER 716 the defendant was one of three persons convicted by the magistrates' court of assaulting a police officer in the execution of his duty. All three appealed to the Crown Court but at the beginning of the hearing counsel for Clair made an application to the court that the appeal might be heard so far as he was concerned in his absence. The reason for this was that he had just been successful in obtaining a job and did not want to jeopardise it by informing his employers of the conviction and then seeking time off to attend the appeal. The judge, however, refused the application and counsel accordingly felt he had no option but to withdraw the appeal. At the end of the appeal the two other appellants had their convictions quashed on a ground that applied equally to Clair, who thereupon sought an order from the Divisional Court of certiorari and mandamus to direct the Crown Court to hear his appeal. The Divisional Court granted the application. The defendant was not on bail or in custody and, being represented by counsel, was deemed not to be absent. The position was just the same as in the Criminal Division of the Court of Appeal where appellants do not always choose to attend the hearing of their appeal. A further difficulty, however, arose as to the effect of counsel's withdrawal of the applicant's appeal. Once an appeal has been abandoned the Crown Court is functus officio and it is well established that such an abandonment can only be disregarded if it can be treated as a nullity. An abandonment deliberately made on a mistaken view of the law cannot be so treated, as the Court of Appeal established after an exhaustive review of the authorities in *R v Medway* [1976] 1 All ER

527. If the Court of Appeal considers that the abandonment will cause injustice to an appellant, the proper course, at least in the case of trial on indictment, is to invite the Secretary of State to make a reference under s 17 of the Criminal Appeal Act 1968. This apparently formidable problem was circumvented by adopting a somewhat ingenious approach suggested by Clair's counsel. Once, he said, the Crown Court judge had refused to hear the appeal (which was tantamount to saying that it would be dismissed) there was nothing to abandon because you cannot abandon what no longer exists. In any event, Croom-Johnson LJ seemed to regard the abandonment under the circumstances of this case as at least 'tantamount to a nullity'. This is a difficult concept which seems to owe its genesis to the need in this case not to perpetrate an obvious injustice upon the defendant. Whilst sympathising with the court's dilemma, the case at least raises the possibility that some summary equivalent of s 17 of the Criminal Appeal Act should be considered to relieve the court from resorting to some rather subtle subterfuges. There may after all be other circumstances when such a reference would be appropriate, especially in view of the decision in *R v Foster* [1984] 2 All ER 679; All ER 1984, p 113 which makes clear that even a free pardon only removes the effects of the conviction, not the conviction itself.

2 Change of plea

The Divisional Court in *R v Plymouth JJ and another, ex p Hart* [1986] 2 All ER 452 has clarified the proper procedure to be adopted when an appeal is made to the Crown Court on the basis that a guilty plea before the magistrates was equivocal. What lay behind this application was the apparent conflict between the two decisions of the court in *R v Rochdale JJ, ex p Allwork* [1981] 3 All ER 434 and *R v Plymouth JJ, ex p Whitton* (1980) 71 Cr App R 322.

The defendant, who was not legally represented, had pleaded guilty before the magistrates to a breathalyser offence under s 6 of the Road Traffic Act 1972. Notwithstanding his plea he subsequently sought leave from the Crown Court to appeal out of time and at this hearing produced a letter, which he claimed had been read out at the hearing there, which effectively disclosed a defence under s 6(2) of the 1972 Act. Finding that a prima facie case of equivocal plea had been made out the Crown Court adjourned the hearing and asked for affidavit evidence from the chairman of the bench and the court clerk setting out the full circumstances of the defendant's conviction, and particularly details of whether the letter had indeed been read out before the magistrates. The clerk to the justices made enquiries of the magistrates and court clerk involved and expressed the view that the plea had been made unequivocally. Accordingly, relying on the authority of the *Whitton* case, the clerk took the view that the magistrates' court was functus officio the matter and that the Crown Court had no jurisdiction to proceed further. The Crown Court, having decided on such evidence as was available to it that this was an equivocal plea, preferred to follow the *Allwork* case and ordered the case to be remitted to the justices for rehearing on the basis of a plea of not guilty. This unseemly impasse was ultimately resolved by the Divisional Court in favour of the Crown Court, its jurisdiction stemming from the terms of what is now s 48 of the Supreme Court Act 1981. The Crown Court, it was stated, had to satisfy itself that the plea was equivocal before the case could be remitted to the magistrates. Obviously the court would need to have evidence as to what happened at the hearing before the magistrates and this should normally be provided by affidavits from the chairman of the bench or the clerk or possibly both. If a dispute were to arise as to whether a proper inquiry was made at the Crown Court, that was a matter which could only be resolved by the Divisional Court, although it was thought that this was unlikely to be necessary if the suggested procedure was adopted. It was also suggested that, without denying his right to apply directly to the Divisional Court to have the issue of plea decided, it would normally be more expeditious and less costly to have the issue of plea resolved in accordance with this suggested procedure in the Crown Court.

3 Judicial review

Since the decision in *R v Preston Crown Court, ex p Fraser* [1984] Crim LR 624 there had been clear authority that the Divisional Court has no power to review an order of the Crown Court that a count should lie on the file and not be proceeded with without the leave of that court or the Court of Appeal. Even though the reasoning of Ackner LJ in that case had been overtaken by Lord Bridge's disapproval in *Smalley v Crown Court at Warwick* [1985] 1 All ER 769, it comes as no great surprise that the same result was achieved in the very similar circumstances of *R v Central Criminal Court, ex p Raymond* [1986] 2 All ER 379. The basis of the defendant's objection to the trial judge's decision not to proceed with various other counts which would not, even if they had resulted in a guilty verdict, have added to the length of the extended sentence to which he had already been sentenced, was that it was unfair that the prosecution should be able to pick and choose which indictments the defendant had to face. The Divisional Court based its rejection of the application on the terms of s 29(3) of the Supreme Court Act 1981 which gives the High Court jurisdiction over the Crown Court, 'other than its jurisdiction in matters relating to trial on indictment.' Woolf LJ took the view that the judge's decision fell within the terms of this exception. It was analogous to the decision to adjourn a case, albeit an adjournment which may never result in a trial, and this decision was a matter upon which the trial judge should have the final word.

This decision is doubtless a welcome clarification of the law relating to what is an everyday procedure in the Crown Court. Unfortunately previous decisions by the courts on the proper ambit of s 29(3) of the 1981 Act have not led to such conclusive results. In *R v Crown Court at Cardiff, ex p Jones and others* [1973] 3 All ER 1027, it was held that an order of the Crown Court that an acquitted defendant who has been legally aided should make a contribution to his costs was a matter 'relating to trial on indictment' which was not open to judicial review. In *R v Smith* [1974] 1 All ER 651 the Court of Appeal expressed the obiter opinion that the same was true of an order that a solicitor personally pay the costs thrown away by the adjournment of a trial. Unfortunately, the authority of these cases is uncertain in the light of *Smalley v Crown Court of Warwick and others* [1985]

1 All ER 769. The House of Lords decided that an order estreating the recognisance of a surety for bail was not a matter within the terms of s 29(3) of the 1981 Act and was therefore open to judicial review. Lord Bridge went on, however, expressly to doubt the correctness of the decisions both in *Jones* and *Smith*. For this reason alone, it seems likely that there is scope for further litigation in this area. Most recently, the Divisional Court in *R v Crown Court at Maidstone, ex p Gill* [1987] 1 All ER 129 had to consider the effect of a forfeiture order made under s 27 of the Misuse of Drugs Act 1971.

The trial judge in this case, having sentenced the defendant, made an order at a subsequent hearing for the forfeiture of two cars at least one of which had been used by the defendant in the course of supplying drugs. Both cars were in fact owned by the defendant's father who was not a party to the son's offences. It was accordingly held that the order did not come within the terms of s 29(3) of the 1981 Act and was therefore open to judicial review. Clearly the order in this case did not affect the conduct of the trial which, as far as the defendant was concerned had been concluded with his plea of guilty and sentencing. No doubt it would have been otherwise if the forfeiture order had been made against the defendant himself at the time of sentencing.

4 Variation of sentence

On the powers of the Crown Court to vary a sentence from a magistrates' court, see *Dutta v Westcott* [1986] 3 All ER 381 under Sentencing at p 121, below.

Jury

The institution of the English jury has received its fair share of government and public attention throughout 1986. First there was the *Report of the Fraud Trials Committee* (HMSO, 1986), better known as the Roskill Report, which recommended the restriction of the right to jury trial in certain cases of fraud. This was followed by the government's White Paper *Criminal Justice: Plans for Legislation* (Cmnd 9658 of 1986) which raised the distinct, indeed likely, possibility that there will be legislation to reduce or abolish the right of peremptory challenge. The two cases which reached the All England Reports, on the other hand, were more concerned with the sort of problems that might arise in any trial by jury.

The decision of the Court of Appeal in *R v Spencer* [1985] 1 All ER 673, which was discussed in All ER Rev 1985, p 126, was reversed by the House of Lords [1986] 2 All ER 928. Again much of the discussion in their Lordship's was taken up with the issue of corroboration (see p 158, below). On the jury issue the House of Lords simply took a different view of what inferences could fairly be drawn from the facts. Whereas the Court of Appeal did not consider that there was any realistic chance that the jurors who had not been discharged had been biased or prejudiced by their contact with the discharged juror, Lord Hailsham felt less confident that one could properly speculate as to what did or didn't take place in the jury room. As Lord Ackner put it, he felt a 'lurking doubt that justice may not have been done.' Such cases are always likely to turn to a large extent on their own peculiar facts, and the facts in this case were perhaps marginal. One can hardly, however, criticise the House of Lords for adopting an approach which is a supposed cornerstone of the English Law, that of giving the accused the benefit of any doubt.

The Privy council was less troubled by doubt in *Nanan v The State* [1986] 3 All ER 248. The accused had been charged with the murder of his wife which, under the law of Trinidad and Tobago, required a unanimous verdict to secure a conviction. When the jury came to give their verdict the foreman was asked, in the presence of the rest of the jury, if they had come to a unanimous verdict, and if so, whether they found the defendant guilty or not guilty. Both questions were loudly and clearly answered in the affirmative. The next day the foreman informed the authorities that he had not understood the meaning of the word 'unanimous' and that the jury had in fact been divided eight to four on the issue of guilt.

The defendant's appeal based upon this supposed irregularity sank without trace beneath a heavy weight of authority. Lord Goff, giving the opinion of the Board, concluded that where a verdict has been given in the sight and hearing of the entire jury without any expression of dissent, the court will not later receive evidence from a member of the jury that he did not in fact agree with the verdict or that his apparent agreement was based upon a misapprehension. The two policy reasons justifying this view could be summed up first in the principle of interest rei publicae ut finis sit litium, and secondly in the need to protect jurors from pressure to reveal their deliberations or to alter their view.

The presumption of assent which arises in these circumstances is likely to be a difficult burden to displace. Even so the Board was anxious to make clear that exceptional cases might arise where this could be done. An example of such a case was provided by *Ras Behari Lal v R* [1933] All ER 723 where the juror because of his insufficient knowledge of English was unable to follow the proceedings. No invasion of the privacy of the jury room was there held to be involved in receiving evidence, either from another juror or anyone else, that a juror was not competent and not therefore qualified to give an assent. Such cases must, one would think, be comparatively rare.

Magistrates

1 Bail

See *Schiavo v Anderton* [1986] 3 All ER 10 and [1987] 1 All ER 128, above p 112.

2 Civil liability

The long and unhappy saga of Mr Solanke seems finally to have come to an end. In *R v Waltham Forest JJ, ex p Solanke* [1986] 2 All ER 981 the Court of Appeal affirmed the decision of Woolf J, [1985] 3 All ER 727 which is discussed in All ER Rev 1985, p 128. The brief judgment of the Master of the Rolls confirms that an act done by a magistrate outside or in excess of jurisdiction can nevertheless be regarded as having been done 'in execution of his office as a justice' within the meaning of s 52 of the Justices of the Peace Act 1979. The result is that the magistrates, at least, are protected from civil liability by the limitation of damages in such cases to the sum of 1p.

3 Road traffic

On special reasons for not disqualifying, see *Chatters v Burke* [1986] 3 All ER 168, p 124, below.

4 Service of documents

It is not unusual for counsel to have documents, of varying degrees of helpfulness, pressed into his hands in the course of proceedings. That care is now needed in their receipt is shown by the Divisional Court's decision in *Penman v Parker* [1986] 2 All ER 862. As part of a prosecution for driving with an excess blood alcohol level it was necessary to serve an analyst's and doctor's certificate made admissible by the terms of s 10 of the Road Traffic Act 1972. The difficulty arose because instead of the documents being served on the defendant they were handed to counsel at a hearing in the magistrates court. He physically accepted them, placed them with the other papers in the case and then apparently thought no more about them. At the eventual hearing the point was taken on behalf of the defendant that the documents had never been properly served upon the defendant, which in turn required consideration of the question of counsel's authority to accept service in such circumstances. Obviously this is a matter of some importance having regard to the frequency with which counsel may well find himself on his own when appearing before magistrates.

Curiously enough although there was authority for the proposition that service could be effected through the agency of solicitors or even the defendant's wife, the point had not previously arisen in relation to counsel. Nevertheless on the anology of the earlier cases the court decided that counsel did have authority to accept service in the circumstances and indeed had done so in this case. Having said this, the court also made it clear that they had taken into account the conditions which often prevail in the magistrate's courts and that the authority of counsel to accept service is generally much more limited than that which is possessed by solicitors. This point was reinforced by the observation that counsel is not bound to accept service of documents. The obiter view was expressed that it would be perfectly proper for counsel to make clear that he was not prepared to accept service on behalf of his client and to suggest that any service should take place upon the client himself or his solicitors.

5 Summary trial

Last year's All England prize for the best procedural own-goal of the season had to be awarded to *R v Holinshead* [1985] 2 All ER 769; All ER Rev 1985, p 118. Whilst it has to be conceded that it is not really in the same league, the air of futility that hovers around the decision in *R v Newham Juvenile Court, ex p F (a minor)* [1986] 3 All ER 17 at least makes it a contender for this year's competition. The defendant in this case, who was aged 16, appeared before the magistrates charged with robbery and firearm offences. The magistrates exercised their discretion under s 24(1) of the Magistrate's Courts Act 1980 in favour of summary trial rather than a committal for trial on indictment. Subsequently, having failed to surrender to bail and after allegedly committing further offences, the defendant found himself before a differently constituted bench some weeks later. This bench apparently considering the same evidence took the view that the summary trial was not appropriate, having regard to the gravity of the circumstances, and purported to reverse the earlier decision of the magistrates and commit the defendant to the Crown Court for trial. The defendant sought an order to quash this decision and so restore the original order for summary trial.

The Divisional Court acceded to the defendant's application. Although a decision by magistrates under s 24(1) of the 1980 Act was reversible at any time up to the beginning of summary trial or committal proceedings if there had been a change of circumstances since the original decision was made, or if existing circumstances of which it had been unaware were drawn to its attention, a decision reached after proper inquiry could not be reversed later simply by reconsidering the same material. In the view of Stephen Brown LJ the whole scheme of the 1980 Act suggested that this was not a statutory power which the magistrates possessed. Similar considerations, it was stated by McCullough J, applied to the decision to go back on a determination in favour of trial on indictment and decide instead upon summary trial.

What is somewhat curious about the case is the Divisional Court's obvious sympathy for the view taken by the second bench of magistrates. There almost certainly was fresh evidence which the magistrates could have relied upon to justify a reversal of the earlier decision, but unfortunately they appeared not to have explicitly relied upon such evidence. What is more, it is perfectly clear that once the magistrates had commenced summary trial they would be empowered under the terms of s 25(6) of the 1980 Act to discontinue the trial and proceed as examining magistrates. One cannot resist the suspicion that that is exactly what the magistrates were likely to do and that the Divisional Court fully appreciated this. Would it not have been more sensible to recognise the reality of the situation? Although it is not referred to in the judgment, Stephen Brown LJ had dealt with a similar situation in *R v Southend JJ, ex p Wood,* (1986) Times, 8 March, which turned upon the construction of s 25(2) of the 1980 Act. In that case also the view was taken that, since the court had not begun to try the information, it was not possible, at least under s 25(2) of the Act to change their decision in favour of summary trial and order trial on indictment instead. Are both decisions victories for form over substance?

6 Legal aid

The meaning of the phrase 'date fixed for... trial' within the terms of reg 6E (2)(c) of the Legal Aid in Criminal Proceedings (General) Regulations 1968 received an authoritative clarification in *R v Bury Magistrates, ex p N (a minor)* [1986] 3 All ER 789. The Divisional Court held that this meant not the date of the defendant's first appearance in court after being charged, because no one except the court had prior power to fix the date for trial or inquiry, but rather whatever date the court itself fixed on the occasion of that first appearance. The judgment of Watkins LJ revealed an unfortunate disparity between different courts in the interpretation of the regulations which meant that some defendants might have been incorrectly informed that, since there was less than 21 days before their first appearance, they were not in a position to apply to a criminal legal aid committee for a review of a refusal by the magistrates to grant legal aid. It was also clear, however, that many courts had approached the matter correctly even before this decision following the consideration of this issue by a committee of the Law Society and the Justices Clerks' Committee in 1984.

Compensation

The Court of Appeal in *R v Criminal Injuries Compensation Board, ex p Warner and others* [1986] 2 All ER 478 affirmed the Divisional Court's decision, reported in [1985] 2 All ER 1069 and discussed in All ER Rev 1985, p 132, that suicide by jumping onto a railway line in the path of an oncoming train was not a 'crime of violence' which could be compensated under the Board's scheme. Lawton LJ, giving the judgment of the court, reached his conclusion in a rather different way to the Divisional Court. Rather than construing the guidelines of the Board as if it were a statute or a technical definition, the proper approach was said to depend upon whether a reasonable and literate man would consider he ought to be compensated under the scheme. Looking at the nature of the crime rather than its consequences, the facts in the present case did not disclose a 'crime of violence.'

What Lawton LJ said about not approaching the guidelines as if they were a statute may well soon be overtaken by events. Part V of the Criminal Justice Bill currently before Parliament places the Criminal Injuries Compensation Scheme for the first time on a formal statutory footing. The impetus for this reform has been aided by the adoption of the European Convention on the Compensation of Victims of Violent Crimes (see Cmnd 9167, HMSO) and the Interdepartmental Working Party, *Criminal Injuries Compensation: a statutory scheme* (HMSO, 1986). It is a little early to speculate what eventual form this Bill will take, but a definition of crime of violence is contained in cl 74.

SENTENCING

Appeal to Crown Court

The tactical considerations in a defendant's appeal to the Crown Court were highlighted in the significant case of *Dutta v Westcott* [1986] 3 All ER 381. The defendant had been convicted of a number of motoring offences, some of which carried penalty points. The magistrates had not imposed any penalty points because of s 19(1) of the Transport Act 1981, which was considered in All ER Rev 1983, p 152, makes clear that this sanction cannot be combined with disqualification and in this case the defendant had been disqualified for driving without insurance. The defendant's appeal to the Crown Court was successful and the conviction on this charge was quashed. What the Crown Court then proceeded to do was to impose penalty points in relation to the other offences notwithstanding that the grounds of appeal had been based solely upon the conviction for driving without insurance. This in turn led to the consideration of s 48 of the Supreme Court Act 1981 which undoubtedly does give the Crown Court power to vary or increase the sentence, at least in regard to 'the decision which is the subject of the appeal.'

The Divisional Court, in a rather bold construction of the section, came to the conclusion that the Crown Court had acted quite correctly. 'The decision' included all the sentences imposed by the magistrates on that occasion and was not limited to the decision specifically appealed against. Any other approach could clearly have led to anomalies in sentencing and the Divisional Court took into account the fact that the Crown Court rehears an appeal from the magistrates de novo and with a fresh view of the matter. The effect of the decision, therefore, is to make clear that the Crown Court has a power similar to that explicitly given to the Criminal Division of the Court of Appeal by s 11(2) of the Criminal Appeal Act 1968.

Bankruptcy, fines and imprisonment

The facts in *R v Garner and others* [1986] 1 All ER 78 were concerned with fraud on an enormous scale and the consequent inter-relationship of fines, imprisonment and criminal bankruptcy orders. There was the further difficulty that, having regard to the sums involved, the maximum terms of imprisonment imposed by statute were relatively short and the effect of non-payment of fines correspondingly large in terms of the 'global' sentence. The Court of Appeal laid down a number of guidelines in balancing these various considerations.

Whether the motive is punishment or confiscation, it is wrong to impose a fine if a defendant is unable to pay it. Normally, if the sentencer considers the term of imprisonment adequate, a punitive fine is not appropriate. Exceptionally, if even the maximum permitted sentence is thought to be inadequate, a positive fine could properly be added. On the other hand, there is nothing wrong in adding a fine if the defendant had made a profit from his wrongdoing and it is wrong to look at the imprisonment to be served in default as additional punishment. It is rather a means of coercing the offender into surrendering the profit of his wrongdoing. The court did, however, regard the limit of one year's imprisonment in default of payment as in some cases totally inadequate. As regards a criminal bankruptcy order, it should only be in rare cases that such an order is made in addition to a fine, such as when it is completely clear that even after the fine has been paid there will be ample funds to satisfy the creditor. To do otherwise would effectively be to give priority to the fine over compensation.

The main significance of this decision is the context of several other cases which have considered the same issue is that it apparently rejects the principle of what one might call the 'global' sentence which appeared first in *R v Savundranayagam and Walker* [1968] 3 All ER 439. The shortcomings of that approach have been commented upon by Professor Thomas in *Principles of Sentencing* (2nd edn, 1979) p 324, particularly in relation to the fact that by discounting the primary sentence of imprisonment to allow for the possibility that the default term might be activated the offender was effectively given a chance to buy his way out of a part of his sentence, provided he did indeed have the necessary funds. Although the decision is to be welcomed as a careful consideration of the issue in which several unreported decisions are discussed, this area still seems to be left in a state of some confusion. There now seem to be two streams of authority on an important matter of general principle. One branch, flowing from *Savundranayagam*, supports the 'global' approach; the other, exemplified in the present case, does not. As Professor Thomas points out in [1986] Crim LR 68 this situation 'gives rise to fundamental issues as to the status of decisions of the Court on sentencing matters.'

In the course of his judgment Hodgson J drew attention to the shortcomings of English law in not providing proper means for estimating the extent of a defendant's gains from his wrongdoing and then confiscating them. Since this decision the Drug Trafficking Offences Act 1986 has been implemented with its draconian powers to order forfeiture at least in relation to the profits of the drugs trade. More generally cll 46–70 of the current Criminal Justice Bill set out detailed provisions for the confiscation of an offender's property when the gains from the criminal enterprise being dealt with exceed £10,000. If enacted, these provisions may go some way to filling the lacuna identified by the court.

Forfeiture

The decision of the Court of Appeal in *R v Slater* [1986] 3 All ER 786 regarding forfeiture has now been overtaken by the provisions of the Drug Trafficking Act 1986. In so far as the decision may have any wider significance, this too is likely to be subject to provisions in the current Criminal Justice Bill, cll 46–70.

Guidance for sentences

Rape

In *R v Billam* [1986] 1 All ER 985 the Court of Appeal has laid down important and relatively detailed guidelines on the proper sentence in cases of rape. Although they cannot be said to show any particularly new departures from the approved practice of the past, they are quite clearly a response to the finding that many sentences in recent times have tended in the court's view towards the lenient.

The starting point for rape by an adult is said to be five years. If two or more men are involved or there is a burglarious element this increases to eight years. A person convicted after a campaign of rape may face a sentence of fifteen years. Where there is an element of perversion or psychopathy suggesting a continuing source of danger for women, life will be the appropriate sentence. The court listed eight aggravating features which would increase the sentence, as for example use of a weapon, a criminal record for similar offences or the age of the victim. Because of the stress of giving evidence in such cases a plea of guilty 'perhaps more so than in other cases' will lead to a reduction, but what has been sometimes called the 'contributory negligence' of the victim is explicitly stated not to be a mitigating factor. The court adverted to the fact that about one third of those convicted of rape are under twenty one and so fall within the scope of the Criminal Justice Act 1982, s 1. Generally speaking most offences of rape are 'so serious that a non-custodial sentence cannot be justified.' The appropriate sentence would therefore normally be of youth custody, following the terms suggested for adult offenders, but with some reduction to allow for the factor of youth. In the case of a juvenile the magistrates' court should never accept jurisdiction but instead commit to the Crown Court to ensure that the appropriate sentencing powers are available.

The task of a sentencer even after these helpful guidelines is unenviable. A recent illustration is the so-called Ealing Vicarage rape which has excited widespread media criticism of the court's leniency. A moment's reflection shows that Leonard J's sentences were impeccably correct in their global effect when considered in relation to the Court of Appeal's guidelines. One common misunderstanding of these guidelines, at least in some parts of the media, is that the so-called starting points represent minimum sentences. This is incorrect. It is explicitly stated that they represent the starting point in a contested trial. If, therefore, one takes a discount of one third for a plea of guilty the normal sentence for an unaggravated case on a plea will be in the region of three and a half years.

Special reasons for not disqualifying

In *Chatters v Burke* [1986] 3 All ER 168 the Divisional Court suggested criteria to be taken into account when magistrates are invited to consider special reasons for not disqualifying a driver pursuant to a conviction for driving with excess alcohol contrary to s 6(1) of the Road Traffic Act 1972. The court suggested seven matters which should be considered: (1) how far the vehicle was in fact driven; (2) in what manner it was driven; (3) the state of the vehicle; (4) the driver's intention to drive any further; (5) the prevailing road and traffic conditions; (6) the danger of contact with other road users; (7) the reason for the vehicle being driven at all. Of these seven matters, Taylor J expressed the opinion that item (6) was the most important, and the case clarifies certain earlier authorities in making the point that the distance driven is of itself not a sufficient determinant whether special reasons should be found or not. On the other hand, as the facts of the present case showed, the shortness of the distance driven may well be relevant in assessing the impact of the other factors.

Employment Law

IAN SMITH, MA, LLB
Barrister, Dean of the School of Law, University of East Anglia

After the spate of case law in 1985 concerning trade union law, largely due to the miners' strike, the reported cases in 1986 have concerned principally individual employment law. They have been numerous, 16 in all though with the last three being continuations of cases considered last year. Three cases show the continued importance of the contract of employment, one having been central to the teachers' dispute and the other two concerning the doctrine of frustration (through imprisonment and illness). Two Court of Appeal cases on continuity of employment (crucial to most statutory employment rights) cover, in one case, problems of sporadic employment and, in the other (at last), the proper construction to be placed on the continuity provisions in the Transfer of Undertakings Regulations. The House of Lords produced two significant decisions on the law of unfair dismissal, one of which raised the question of the relevance of procedural lapses after the date of dismissal, with the other possibly having far-reaching consequences on the lingering 'fact or law' controversy, so vital when appealing from a tribunal decision. The ECJ have also been busy this year, with three cases on the equal treatment directive, the first two of which led to statutory amendments by the Sex Discrimination Act 1986. Discrimination law was also affected by two Court of Appeal decisions on the coverage of the Sex Discrimination Act 1975. Finally, the sole reported case on trade union law raised obscure points on union *de*-amalgamation, not directly covered by the relevant legislation on union amalgamation.

Contracts of employment—content and remedies

As part of industrial action during the teachers' dispute the plaintiff teachers refused to cover for absent colleagues and at the end of the month in question the defendant employers deducted appropriate amounts from their pay. The plaintiffs brought actions to recover the amounts deducted and the matter came before Scott J in the Chancery Division in *Sim v Rotherham Metropolitan Borough Council* [1986] 3 All ER 387. The question of cover arrangements was not expressly covered by the teachers' contracts of employment, and so two questions arose for decision: (i) was there an implied contractual duty to cover for absent colleagues; (ii) if there was (and the teachers were in breach of it) had their employers the right to deduct amounts in respect of the contractual breach, by way of equitable set-off? In a newsworthy judgment on the facts on the first point, Scott J held that in the circumstances providing cover was an implied obligation in a teacher's professional contract, so that the plaintiffs were in breach. However, the second point was of more legal significance, if less newsworthy, for the plaintiffs argued that the doctrine of equitable set-off should not apply to contracts of employment—they accepted that (*if* they were in breach) they could be sued for damages (as in *NCB v Galley* [1958] 1 All ER 91), but argued that an employer has no right simply to deduct from wages, especially as any such right could undermine established disciplinary procedures. However, Scott J decided against them on this point too— equitable set-off does apply to contracts of employment, as to other forms of contract law and on the facts here the employers' actions were lawful; the decision follows that of Park J in *Royle v Trafford Borough Council* [1984] IRLR 184 and could be important in any case of 'guerilla' action, withdrawal of goodwill or other industrial action falling short of a strike *provided* the employer can show breach of a properly contractual obligation.

Contracts of employment—frustration by illness or imprisonment

Where an employee has lost his employment through long-term illness or imprisonment, he may (if he has accumulated the qualifying two years' service) claim unfair dismissal; this is certainly legally possible, even if in practice he may well lose on the facts. However, if either of these factors is held to have *frustrated* his contract of employment, that will rob him of the right in law to bring his case since there is then no 'dismissal' and, in a rare exercise of logic, you cannot be unfairly dismissed if you have not been dismissed. Thus, a finding of frustration drives a coach and pair through any statutory rights dependent on having been dismissed. Not surprisingly therefore, there have been attempts to banish the doctrine from employment law, either directly (as in the decision of Bristow J in *Harman v Flexible Lamps Ltd* [1980] IRLR 418 in the case of illness) or indirectly by tightly circumscribing its possible ambit (as in the judgment of Waite J in *F C Shepherd & Co Ltd v Jerrom* [1985] IRLR 275). However, although such an approach may be strongly supportable on policy reasons, it did require a rather creative judicial approach towards the problems raised and in two decisions this year the Court of Appeal have restored orthodoxy to this area.

In *Notcutt v Universal Equipment Co Ltd* [1986] 3 All ER 582 the employee's employment was terminated after he had a heart attack, his doctor having told the employers that he probably would not work again. The contract of employment did not give a right to sick pay, but he had been given notice by his employers and he claimed that by virtue of the Employment Protection (Consolidation) Act 1978, Sch 3, para 3 he was entitled by law to sick pay during the notice period. The employers refused to pay it, so he sued for it in the county court. However, the judge accepted the employers' argument that the illness had in fact already frustrated the contract, even before any purported notice had been given. On appeal, the Court of Appeal upheld the judge's decision; in the first reported case before them directly on the point, they held that the doctrine of frustration *can* apply to contracts of employment (even where they may be terminated by the employer by relatively short notice in any event) and that it can arise in a case of major illness. The orthodox contractual test in *Davis Contractors Ltd v Fareham Urban District Council* [1956] 2 All ER 145, HL was applied and the views of Bristow J in *Harman v Flexible Lamps Ltd* disapproved. It will be noticed that this case in fact concerned a common law claim for money owed, but there is no reason why the decision should not apply in a statutory action before an industrial tribunal.

The facts of *F C Shepherd & Co Ltd v Jerrom* [1986] 3 All ER 589 concerned the other principal area for frustration claims—the sentencing of the employee to an immediate term of imprisonment. Here, to dismiss may well be fair on the facts anyway, as a dismissal for 'some other substantial reason' (Employment Protection (Consolidation) Act 1978, s 57(1)(b); *Kingston v British Railways Board* [1984] IRLR 147, CA), but the question again arises as to whether the employer can go further and stop an unfair dismissal claim dead in its tracks by pleading frustration. As stated above, when this case was in the EAT Waite J gave a judgment that materially diminished the possibility of such a defence being successful. The facts were that the employee, an apprentice plumber, was sentenced to Borstal for offences of violence; when released, his employers refused to take him back and defended his unfair dismissal action on the ground that the sentence had frustrated the contract. The tribunal disagreed (awarding him £7,090 compensation) and on appeal the EAT upheld their decision, on the basis that as the relevant apprenticeship contract contained provisions covering this type of misconduct it was not the sort of unforeseen event that could in law produce frustration. As many contracts of employment will contain such provisions, this reasoning could have made frustration difficult to establish in imprisonment cases. However, on further appeal the Court of Appeal disapproved this reasoning. They held that frustration of a contract of employment can arise from imprisonment (thus impliedly overruling an earlier EAT case to the contrary, *Norris v Southampton City Council* [1982] IRLR 141) and that on the facts that had happened here; the employee lost his compensation (a fact that was not as widely reported in the newspapers as the original award by the tribunal had been, in terms such as 'Borstal thug gets £7,000 from employer'). One major problem had to be resolved—was not the frustrating event self-induced by the employee and, if so, should that not rule out frustration (see, in general contract law, *Paal Wilson & Co A/S v Partenreederei Hannah Blumenthal* [1983] 1 All ER 34, HL)? This problem was solved in two ways—Balcombe LJ accepted Lord Denning MR's view in *Hare v Murphy Brothers Ltd* [1974] 3 All ER 940, CA, that the frustrating event was actually the imposition of the sentence, not the misconduct by the employee, but Lawton and Mustill LJJ took a more fundamental approach—that, properly understood, the requirement that neither party be at fault only meant that neither party could *rely* on his *own* misconduct to establish a defence of frustration. As the employer was relying on the *employee's* fault here, that requirement was satisfied and frustration could succeed; to hold otherwise would be to allow the party at fault (the employee) to benefit from his own misdeeds by using them to defeat an otherwise sound defence.

Continuity of employment—irregular employment

Establishing continuity of employment may be vital in establishing any statutory employment right where a claim is subject to completion of a qualifying period of employment (a redundancy or unfair dismissal claim, for example, normally requiring service with the employer for two years or more). The Employment Protection (Consolidation) Act 1978, Sch 13, para 9 contains special provisions safeguarding continuity through certain employment hiccoughs. Paragraph 9(1)(b) preserves it through 'temporary cessations of work', but the application of this delphic phrase to an intermittent employment pattern (as opposed to the odd lay-off in otherwise normal employment) had to be considered by the Court of Appeal in *Flack v Kodak Ltd* [1986] 2 All ER 1003. The applicants had worked for the employers over a number of years in the photo-finishing department, but this employment had been seasonal and sporadic; they were taken on when demand was high and dismissed when it fell off. When the department was closed down, they claimed redundancy payments but they could only succeed if their employment could be deemed to have been continuous under para 9(1)(b). The tribunal held against them; they did so by taking a mathematical approach to whether the cessations were 'temporary', comparing each gap in employment as a percentage of the periods in work before and after it. They felt constrained to apply this approach by dicta by Lord Diplock in *Ford v Warwickshire CC* [1983] 1 All ER 753, HL and, applying it, they found in the case of all of the applicants that there were gaps during the last few years of employment which mathematically could not be described as 'temporary', so that continuity was broken in each case. However, the EAT allowed their appeal and that decision was upheld by the Court of Appeal who held that the tribunal were *not* bound to take a mathematical approach—it is true that the relationship between time in work and time out of it is an important factor (possibly decisive), but they held that a tribunal may properly look at *all* the circumstances of the employment when deciding whether a gap is temporary; moreover, although the requirement in redundancy law is for continuous employment for the two years before the date of the redundancy and that it is gaps during that period that will disqualify, a tribunal may still look at the *whole* period of employment to assess the significance of any gaps. The Court of Appeal have thus sanctioned a wider enquiry, with more discretion to the tribunal and reaffirmed that, while *Ford's* case is important in the case of successive fixed term contracts with gaps between them, the leading case on the construction of para 9(1)(b) generally remains the previous decision of the House of Lords in *Fitzgerald v Hall Russell & Co Ltd* [1969] 3 All ER 1140. The case was remitted to the industrial tribunal for reconsideration.

Continuity of employment—transfer of undertaking

The troublesome continuity of employment provisions of the Transfer of Undertakings (Protection of Employment) Regulations 1981 have finally received an authoritative pronouncement from the Court of Appeal in *Secretary of State for Employment v Spence* [1986] 3 All ER 616, though perhaps not with the result that may have been expected. Regulation 5 effects the automatic transfer of a contract of employment to the transferee employer (in a case to which the regulations apply, ie a 'relevant transfer') where the employee was employed by the transferor employer 'immediately before' the transfer. It was held in several EAT decisions (principally *Alphafield Ltd v Barratt* [1984] 3 All ER 795) that this phrase assumed that there could be a gap of sorts between the transferor employer dismissing the employee and the transfer but the regulation might still apply (the gap in *Alphafield* of two days having been held permissible). This clearly has important repercussions on who pays redundancy payments when the employee is not kept on. Regulation 5 was meant to be a protective measure for the employee, but the first thing to notice about *Spence* is that it was a topsy-turvey case in which the employees were arguing that the regulation did *not* apply. The facts were that Co A was about to cease trading and on the day in question dismissed the employees at 11 am; however, at 2 pm the business was in fact bought by Co B which the following day re-employed the employees. The latter wished to 'cash in' their accrued redundancy rights against Co A (actually against the Secretary of State for Employment under the Employment Protection (Consolidation) Act 1978, s 106, since Co A was insolvent) and so argued that their continuity was *broken* by the transfer. To succeed they had to show that reg 5 did not apply, which would only be the case if they were *not* employed immediately before the transfer. On the previous case authority they would have lost, since a gap of only three hours would surely have been permissible. However, the Court of Appeal overruled the previous authorities (particularly *Alphafield*) and held that 'immediately before' meant at the time of the transfer so that no gap is permissible (even of three hours on the same day)—the contract of employment must subsist at the moment of transfer. Clearly this decision was in favour of these particular employees, given their particular desire on the facts, but it does not need great imagination to envisage cases in which this decision could materially lessen the protection of employees faced with the announcement of a transfer and who *do* want reg 5 to apply. Equally, the case helps the transferee employer who wishes to take over the business without the existing workforce since he does not have to insist (as he had to under the now overruled earlier cases) that the transferor dismiss the workforce *well* before the transfer in order to be sure of avoiding the effects of the regulation. As the Court of Appeal points out, however, this narrower approach is fully in line with the view of the ECJ on the interpretation of Council Directive 77/187/EEC in pursuance of which the Regulations were passed (see in particular *Wendelboe v L J Music Ap S: case 19/83* [1986] 1 CMLR 476, ECJ).

Unfair dismissal—the relevance of internal procedures

Under modern employment practices and contracts of employment a dismissed employee may well have internal remedies available, as well as the external remedy of complaint to an industrial tribunal; these remedies will frequently involve an appeal against the decision to dismiss to a higher level of management (and sometimes a further appeal, eg to ACAS arranged arbitration). Given the low level of reinstatement through tribunals, such internal procedures may well be preferable to an employee wishing to retain his job. However, if an internal appeal is unsuccessful, or is procedurally irregular, the employee may wish to claim unfair dismissal—what then is to be the relationship between the internal and external remedies? In particular, can the proceedings on internal appeal be taken into account when a tribunal is deciding on the fairness of the dismissal under the Employment Protection (Consolidation) Act 1978, s 57(3)? The problem here has always been the decision of the House of Lords in *W Devis & Sons Ltd v Atkins* [1977] 3 All ER 40 that a tribunal must look at the facts as known to the employer at the date of dismissal, not at facts coming to light later. That case concerned after-acquired evidence of other misconduct, but its reasoning could cause problems with internal appeals—procedures containing them will often work on the basis of an effective dismissal followed later by an appeal hearing; if that is the case, it could be argued on a strict reading of *Devis* that the proceedings at the appeal are inadmissible since they post-date the actual dismissal. A series of EAT decisions had attempted to avoid such a narrow approach and the House of Lords have now set the matter straight in *West Midlands Co-operative Society v Tipton* [1986] 1 All ER 513. The employee was dismissed, after warnings, for absenteeism; ostensibly the dismissal at that point may have been fair. However, his contract of employment gave him a right to appeal to the chief executive office but the latter, in breach of contract, refused to entertain such an appeal. Could that render the dismissal unfair under s 57(3)? The Court of Appeal ([1985] ICR 444) had held that it could not—evidence of the failure to allow the appeal might be admissible for the limited purpose of casting light on something that had happened prior to the dismissal, but otherwise the employee's claim was defeated by *Devis*. However, the House of Lords reversed that decision and restored the original decision of the tribunal in favour of the employee. They took the wider view (approving the previous EAT decisions) that in reality an appeal procedure is an integral part of a dismissal process; to ignore it would be artificial and so on that approach to consider the proceedings at appeal (or, as here, the improper withholding of an appeal) does *not* compromise the rule in *Devis* which, properly understood, remains good law. Lord Bridge put it thus (at 521):

> 'A dismissal is unfair if the employer unreasonably treats his real reason as a sufficient reason to dismiss the employee, either when he makes his original decision to dismiss or when he maintains that decision at the conclusion of an internal appeal. By the same token, a dismissal may be held to be unfair when the employer has refused to entertain an appeal to which the employee was contractually entitled and thereby denied to the employee the opportunity of showing that, in all the circumstances, the employer's real reason for dismissing him could not reasonably be treated as sufficient. There may, of course, be cases where, on the undisputed facts, the dismissal was inevitable, as for example where a trusted employee, before dismissal, was charged with, and had pleaded guilty to, a serious offence of dishonesty committed in the course of his employment. In such a case the employer could reasonably refuse to entertain a domestic appeal on the ground that it could not affect the outcome. It has never been suggested, however, that this was such a case.'

This decision is a welcome clarification of a longstanding problem. However, one subsidiary problem remains for the employee, concerning timing. In the course of his speech, Lord Bridge approved the principle in *J Sainsbury Ltd v Savage* [1981] ICR 1 EAT, that if an internal appeal fails the employee remains dismissed *as from the original date of dismissal*; this is most material in that the three month time limit for bringing a claim of unfair dismissal then flows from *that* date (not the later date of the hearing) and it was held in *Palmer v Southend-on-Sea Borough Council* [1984] 1 All ER 945,

CA (see All ER Rev 1984, p 128) that waiting for the result of an internal appeal will *not* normally be a good ground for inviting the tribunal to extend the time limit. Nothing in *Tipton* casts doubt on that decision and so tactically the dismissed employee should still be advised to put his application in to the tribunal within three months of the original dismissal and then to apply (if necessary) to the tribunal for a postponement pending the outcome of the internal appeal.

Unfair dismissal—questions of fact and law

Important cases not infrequently arise from odd facts; in employment law the minister of religion could become the equivalent of the beloved gastropod of the law of tort. In *Davies v Presbyterian Church of Wales* [1986] 1 All ER 705 the House of Lords had to decide whether a pastor of the Presbyterian Church of Wales was an 'employee' who could therefore claim unfair dismissal when he was dismissed from his pastorate. They held that he was not. The case is of course important on its facts and contains interesting discussion on the position in law of ministers of religion, but it may seem a million miles from everyday employment law. However, it contains one facet that could be of extreme importance—Lord Templeman's speech, giving the House's unanimous decision, proceeds on the basis that the question to be decided (was there or was there not here a contract of employment?) was a *question of law*, and as such fully reviewable by the higher courts on appeal. To the non-specialist in industrial law that may not exactly appear earth-shattering, but to the cognoscenti it immediately appears to be out of line with the approach taken fairly uniformly throughout this decade by the Court of Appeal and the EAT. That approach has been to categorise almost all issues as questions of fact in order to reduce the number of appeals from tribunals (which can only be on points of law) and to counter what has been perceived as overlegalism in the tribunals and in employment law generally. The examples of this are legion (see Smith & Wood, *Industrial Law* (3rd edn, 1986) pp 224–232, 'The attack on legalism') and, to take the facts of the instant case, the Court of Appeal held in *O'Kelly v Trusthouse Forte plc* [1983] 3 All ER 456 and *Nethermere (St Neots) Ltd v Gardiner* [1984] ICR 612 that whether a particular contract was one of employment or for services was a matter of fact. The result of such an approach is that the tribunal's decision on the facts can only be appealed against if it is *perverse* (see the general rules laid down in *Edwards v Bairstow* [1956] AC 14, HL). Not surprisingly, therefore, the applicant in *Davies* who had won his case before the tribunal argued that it was not open to the appellate courts to reverse that decision on the facts as to his employed status, unless the tribunal's decision was so wrong as to be perverse. However that argument was roundly disapproved by Lord Templeman who said (at 709):

> 'On behalf of the appellant it was first submitted, on the authority of *Edwards v Bairstow* [above], that the decision of the industrial tribunal that the appellant was employed under a contract of service was not susceptible to reversal by an appellate court because the tribunal instructed itself correctly as to the law, took into account all relevant circumstances and reached a conclusion that was reasonable. In my opinion this submission confuses fact and law. The decision

in *Edwards v Bairstow* has nothing to do with this case. An appeal from the industrial tribunal is expressly conferred by statute on a question of law. The question to be determined is a question of law, namely whether on the true construction of the book of rules a pastor of the Church is employed and is under a contract of service. If the industrial tribunal erred in deciding that question, the decision must be reversed . . .'

This passage is so clearly different from the approach in cases such as *O'Kelly* and *Nethermere* (neither of which is cited in the speech) that it raises the question whether the decision may mark a major change of direction in the continuing 'fact or law' controversy. Watch this space.

Sex discrimination—excluded employments

The reports for 1986 contain two decisions of the Court of Appeal on limitations on the coverage of the employment-related provisions of the Sex Discrimination Act 1985. The first, *Gunning v Mirror Group Newspaper Ltd* [1986] 1 All ER 385, concerns the very meaning of 'employment'. One factor that marks off discrimination law from other areas of employment protection law is that it adopts a wide definition of employment—s 82(1) of the 1975 Act defines it as not just working under a contract of employment but also under 'a contract personally to execute any work or labour', thus including some who in other contexts would be considered independent contractors and so outside legal protection (eg in the areas of redundancy and unfair dismissal). The facts of this case show, however, that even this wider definition has its limits. The applicant was a woman who was not permitted by a newspaper company to take over an area distributorship from her father; she complained of unlawful sexual discrimination but the question arose whether this sort of distributorship came within the extended definition of employment. The Court of Appeal held that even where some personal work was involved the tribunal must still consider (a) whether there was some obligation by one contracting party to execute personally any work or labour *and* (b) whether that was the *dominant purpose* of the contract. They held on the facts that limb (b) was not satisfied here and so the applicant's claim failed since she was not within the scope of the Act.

In the second case, *Houghton v Olau Line (UK) Ltd* [1986] 2 All ER 47, the applicant was clearly employed and so generally within the scope of the Act, but she fell foul of one of the specific exclusions. Section 6(2) renders it unlawful to discriminate (by dismissal) against a woman 'employed . . . at an establishment in Great Britain'; s 10(1) then states that 'employment is to be regarded as being at an establishment in Great Britain unless the employee does his work wholly or mainly outside Great Britain', with exceptions for those employed on ships or aircraft registered here. The applicant was dismissed from her employment with an English company, working on a German-registered ferry plying between Sheerness and Flushing; she claimed that her dismissal was an act of illegal sex discrimination, but her claim failed because on the facts she worked 'wholly or mainly outside Great Britain', on a foreign-registered ship.

Sex discrimination—the EEC dimension

Three decisions of the ECJ concerning sex discrimination and the Equal Treatment Directive (Council Directive 76/207/EEC) are reported in this year's volumes. The first two raised questions of retirement provisions and the third a point relating to the national security exception. The most widely reported in the press was *Marshall v Southampton and South West Hampshire Area Health Authority (Teaching)* [1986] 2 All ER 584, which has led to a major legislative change. Miss Marshall was compulsorily retired at the age of 62 from a job in which men were allowed to work to 65. Her claim of sex discrimination under domestic law was defeated by the Sex Discrimination Act 1975, s 6(4) which allows such discrimination in relation to death or retirement. The question then arose whether she could claim under the directive instead. This claim succeeded before the ECJ which held that the principle of equal treatment was so important that it was to be applied strictly; moreover, the provision in the subsequent directive on social security (Council Directive 79/7/EEC, on which see *Burton v British Railways Board* [1982] 3 All ER 537) allowing states to retain differential *pension* ages was held not to defeat her claim. One of several points established or reinforced by the case is thus that, contrary to the layman's understanding, retirement ages and pension ages are *not* necessarily the same thing—see, to like effect, the second reported case (decided at the same time) of *Roberts v Tate & Lyle Industries Ltd* [1986] 2 All ER 602 where it was held that there was in fact no discrimination where men and women were offered early pensions at the same age of 55 (even though the employer *could* lawfully have discriminated in the women's favour) and also the subsequent decision of the ECJ (on a reference from Holland) in *Beets-Proper v F Van Lanschot Bankiers NV* [1986] ICR 706. *Marshall* and *Roberts* also contain important constitutional points of EEC Law which are considered at pp 136 et seq, below; however, it is important to note that because of the adoption by the ECJ of the principle that EEC directives can only have 'vertical' direct effect, the right established in *Marshall* for a woman not to be compulsorily retired at an earlier age than a man in the same employment only applied to women employed in the public sector. However, the greater importance of the case was that it gave the political impetus to the enactment of such a right for all employees; this has now come about under the Sex Discrimination Act 1986, s 2 and 3 which will (from a date still to be appointed by order at the time of writing) amend both the 'death or retirement' exception in the Sex Discrimination Act 1975 and the 'past normal retirement age' exclusion in unfair dismissal law contained in the Employment Protection (Consolidation) Act 1978, s 64(1)(b). Thus, the dismissal of a woman employee merely because she has reached retirement age will become potentially discriminatory and unfair if a man in the same job is permitted to retire at a later age; in practice this means that a woman may demand to work past a pension age that is earlier than that for a man, which is what Miss Marshall wanted in the first place.

The third ECJ case reported is *Johnston v Chief Constable of the Royal Ulster Constabulary* [1986] 3 All ER 135. The applicant was a female member of the RUC Reserve whose employment was discontinued in 1980 because she was not able to undertake ordinary police duties; this was because of a new policy that women would not be trained in the use of firearms or carry them. Her claim of sex discrimination to an industrial tribunal was defeated art 53 of the Sex Discrimination Order (NI) 1976 which excludes action taken 'for the purposes of safeguarding national security or of protecting public safety or public order' and provides that a certificate from the Secretary of State to that effect is to be conclusive evidence. Such a certificate had been issued in the applicant's case and so the Chief Constable argued that her claim was ruled out. However, she sought to circumvent that by basing her claim also on the equal treatment provisions of Directive 76/207. The point was referred to the ECJ which, in an important decision on the general effect of the directive, held that the general rights contained in it could *not* be excluded by national provisions such as those contained in art 53. Any exclusion of those rights therefore has to fall also within the terms of the directive itself, particularly art 2(2) which applies where 'the sex of the worker constitutes a determining factor' (that being for the national courts to decide, not the ECJ). Further, they held that art 2(2) which refers to exclusions 'for the protection of women' is to be construed narrowly as referring only to matters concerned with pregnancy and motherhood. As well as being an important statement on the application of the directive and its exclusions, this case must also cast doubt on the Sex Discrimination Act 1975, s 52 which contains a similar certification procedure (though restricted to matters of national security)—this otherwise cast-iron exclusion may now be amenable to challenge in any case where an applicant may rely on the directive instead of the Act; in such a case, the exclusion would have to come within s 52 *and* the provisions of art 2(2) of the directive.

Trade union law—the problems of divorce

The procedures to be adopted in the case of an amalgamation by two or more trade unions are covered in some detail in the Trade Union (Amalgamations, etc) Act 1964. However, that Act does *not* govern *de*-amalgamations and the problems that can arise are seen in *Burnley Nelson Rossendale and District Textile Workers' Union v Amalgamated Textile Workers Union* [1986] 1 All ER 885. The plaintiff union had joined the defendant federated union, retaining much autonomy; the defendant union's rules did not govern the question of secession from it. When the plaintiff union decided to secede the question arose as to whether it was entitled to part of the defendant union's funds. Failing agreement, the plaintiff union sought the determination of the court. However, Tudor Price J in the Queen's Bench Division held that he could not make such a determination—a court may be asked to interpret a union's rules and in doing so may take a broad and liberal approach but (showing considerable judicial restraint) he held that that does not mean that a court can go further and infer rules that do not exist—to do so would be 'an unjustified intervention into the affairs of the union' (at 890). The only similar case on secession, *Keys v Boulter (No 2)* [1972] 2 All ER 303, where Megarry J wound up a registered trade union under the court's inherent jurisdiction, did not apply here, since in that case the contending parties had already reached agreement on dissolving the federated union. Thus, the question of succession could show up a legal lacuna where it is not covered by union rules; unions thinking of a marriage would do well therefore to decide in advance what is to happen to the property in the event of a later divorce.

Postscript—the continuing story

Finally, three cases were reported this year which are continuations of sagas considered in last year's Review. In *Faccenda Chicken Ltd v Fowler* [1986] 1 All ER 617, the Court of Appeal upheld the decision of Goulding J (All ER Rev 1985, p 142) in this case on the protection of trade secrets; their decision contains a useful resume of the law on this difficult subject, and in particular it reaffirms that the implied duty of confidentiality on an *ex*-employee is narrower than that on an existing employee, especially in the area of information short of actual trade secrets which becomes part of the employee's general working knowledge—that will not be protectable (even with the aid of a putative restraint of trade clause) once the employment ceases.

In *Thomas v University of Bradford* [1986] 1 All ER 217 the Court of Appeal affirmed the decision of Whitford J (All ER Rev 1985, p 143) that a university visitor's exclusive jurisdiction did not extend to alleged breaches of contract of employment, so that a dismissed lecturer was free to bring such proceedings in the ordinary courts.

Finally, the decision of the Divisional Court in *Sealand Petroleum Co Ltd v Barratt* [1986] 2 All ER 360 follows on from that in *Bristow v City Petroleum Ltd* [1985] 3 All ER 463, Div Ct (All ER Rev 1985, p 141). In the latter case it was held that the antique and partial provisions of the Truck Acts could not help a petrol station cashier who had had deductions made from his wages in respect of till deficiencies since they were not 'fines'. In *Sealand*, however, that case was distinguished on the basis that here the nature of the deduction on the facts was more of a financial penalty (ie a 'fine') than genuine provision for the recovery of compensation for losses. The line between the two cases is clearly a thin one, but the important point is that now both of them are of historical interest only—since 1 January 1987 the Truck legislation has been repleaded by Part I of the Wages Act 1986 and replaced by provisions on deductions generally that apply to all kinds of workers, with specific provisions giving extra protection to workers in retail employment who may only have up to ten per cent of a wage payment deducted in respect of cash or stock deficiencies; the troublesome distinction between a fine and recovery of compensation has now disappeared, though doubtless the new legislation will throw up its own horrors of interpretation in good time.

European Community Law

CHRISTOPHER GREENWOOD, MA, LLB
Barrister, Fellow of Magdalene College, Cambridge

Community legal order

Directives: direct effect

The decision of the Court of Justice in Case 152/84 *Marshall v Southampton and South West Hampshire Area Health Authority (Teaching)* [1986] 2 All ER 584 has settled a long dispute concerning the extent to which directives are capable of having direct effect, ie of creating rights and duties which must be enforced by the national courts. The draftsmen of the EEC Treaty, of course, did not intend directives to have any kind of direct effect. Article 189 of the EEC Treaty provides that: 'A directive shall be binding, as to the result to be achieved, upon each Member State to which it is addressed, but shall leave to the national authorities the choice of form and methods.'

What was envisaged was that national courts would apply the national measures by which the State concerned chose to give effect to the directive, rather than the directive itself. If the State failed in its obligation to give effect to the directive, the Commission could institute enforcement proceedings against the State.

Nevertheless, in Case 41/74 *Van Duyn v Home Office* [1975] 3 All ER 190, the Court of Justice, spurred on by the dismal record of Member States in failing to implement Community directives, ruled that where a Member State had failed to implement a directive, an individual could rely upon the terms of the directive against the State once the deadline for implementation had passed. The court thus gave directives a limited form of direct effect: so long as the provisions of a directive met the normal criteria for direct effect, they could confer rights upon individuals or companies against the State. The court left open, however, the question whether directives might also be capable of 'horizontal' direct effect, ie of imposing duties, as well as rights, upon individuals which might be enforced against them by other individuals in litigation with which the State was not concerned. This question is of considerable practical importance in two situations: first where a State has completely failed to implement a directive by the date required and, secondly, where a State has adopted implementing measures which do not properly implement the directive.

In *Marshall* the court answered this question by stating that 'a directive may not of itself impose obligations on an individual and . . . a provision of a directive may not be relied upon as such against an individual' (at 600). This categorical rejection of the notion that directives might have horizontal direct effect is surprising since the court had gone out of its way not to address this question in numerous cases and need not have dealt with it in *Marshall*, since both the Court of Justice and the Court of Appeal (which had made the reference) found that the area health authority was an arm of the State. Moreover, the judgment contains only the most cursory review of the arguments for and against horizontal direct effect, the court apparently being content to adopt the reasoning of Advocate General Sir Gordon Slynn.

The court's refusal to accord directives horizontal direct effect has attracted much criticism (see, eg N Foster (1986) 11 EL Rev 222). The court seems to have accepted the Advocate General's submission that to accord directives horizontal direct effect would be to distort the entire scheme of art 189. However, since directives were not intended to have any kind of direct effect, the scheme of art 189 had already been distorted in *Van Duyn*. By limiting the direct effect of directives as it did, the court in *Marshall* created a largely artificial distinction between the rights of employees in the private and public sectors. Determining whether a particular body is an arm of the State or not is also likely to create problems. If an area health authority is an arm of the state for these purposes, what about a nationalised industry or a university which receives most of its funds from the government? In addition, since Member States continue to drag their feet in implementing directives, it can be argued that the best way to ensure that directives are uniformly observed throughout the Community is by allowing individuals to rely upon them in as many situations as possible.

Nevertheless, the court was probably right to take the stand that it did. It was intolerable that so important a question as whether directives could impose obligations upon individuals should have remained in doubt and the Advocate General deserves congratulations for getting the court to grasp this nettle at last. While the court's departure from its activist tradition will disappoint many, it needs to be remembered that the decision that directives could have even the limited direct effect recognised in *Van Duyn* led to a revolt by courts in France and West Germany. An extension of this direct effect to cases not involving the State would probably have encountered further resistance in the national courts. Moreover, the distinction between the public and private sectors may act as a spur to States to implement directives properly in the first place. In the important field of directives on employment matters the effect of *Marshall* is to place the public sector employer (and thus the government) in a worse position than the private employer, a consideration which may encourage governments to take remedial action. Finally, a decision in favour of horizontal direct effect might well have aroused opposition in the national parliaments to the provisions of the Single European Act, the ratification of which was then being debated, since the Act will increase the powers of the Community to issue directives and enlarge the scope for majority voting.

The decision in *Marshall* does not mean that, in a case between two private parties, the provisions of a directive cannot be of any significance. The directive cannot itself be the source of rights or duties in such a case but where a State has enacted national legislation purporting to give effect to a directive, the 'national courts are required to interpret their national law in the light of the wording and the purpose of the directive' (Case 14/83 *Von Colson and Kamman v Land Nordrhein-Westfalen* [1984] ECR 1891). Similarly, in Case 222/84 *Johnston v Chief Constable of the Royal Ulster Constabulary* [1986] 3 All ER 135 (below, p145), the court held that an industrial tribunal in Northern Ireland was under a duty in Community law to interpret delegated legislation adopted to give effect to Directive 76/207 in the light of the Directive and so as to give proper effect to the provisions of the

Direetive. Advocate General Darmon was even more explicit about the duties of the national court. Referring to the decision in Case 106/77 *Amministrazione delle Finanze dello Stato v Simmenthal Spa* [1978] ECR 629, he maintained that it was the duty of the national court to give full effect to the relevant rule of Community law whatever the national legislation might say. While *Johnston*, like *Marshall*, was an action against an arm of the State, the importance of the directive as an aid to the interpretation of national legislation in cases between private parties was stressed in Case 262/84 *Beets-Proper v Van Lamschot Bankiers NV* (not yet reported). It seems that in a case against the State, the national court's duty is to give priority to a directly effective provision in a directive, whereas in a case between private parties the directive is only an aid to interpretation. However, the difference may be more apparent than real where national legislation which purports to give effect to the directive has been enacted.

Judicial review: principle of proportionality

In the course of a long line of decisions concerning the interpretation and validity of Community acts, the Court of Justice has developed a series of general principles of Community law against which the validity of the act in question is measured. One of these principles is the principle of proportionality, the essence of which is that a penalty or a restriction on the exercise of a Community freedom may be imposed for a legitimate purpose but must not be disproportionate to the end sought to be achieved. This principle has formed the basis for many of the court's decisions in matters relating to the common agricultural policy. Its importance is illustrated by one of the rare cases concerning the policy to arise in the English courts, Case 181/84 *R v Intervention Board for Agricultural Produce, ex p E D & F Man (Sugar) Ltd* [1986] 2 All ER 115.

To export sugar from the EEC it is necessary to obtain a licence from one of the national boards which administer the common agricultural policy. At the relevant time, the governing principles were set out in Council Regulation 1785/81 and the procedures to be followed were established by Commission Regulation 1880/83. It was first necessary to make an offer to export. If the Board accepted the offer, the offeror then had four days in which to apply for an export licence and five days from the grant of the licence in which to export the sugar. The offeror had to deposit a security at the time of making the offer and art 6(3) of Commission Regulation 1880/83 provided that the security was automatically forfeit if he failed either to apply for the licence or to export the sugar within the time limits. Man Sugar were three hours late in applying for an export licence, due to the absence from work of the employee responsible for sending the application, and the Board forfeited their security of £1,670,370 which, as Advocate General Mancini pointed out, was equivalent to three years profit for the firm. Man challenged this decision in the High Court which referred to the Court of Justice a question about the validity of art 6(3) of Regulation 1880/83.

Applying the principle of proportionality, the court had no difficulty in finding that art 6(3) was invalid insofar as it required the automatic imposition of the same draconian penalty for a minor breach of the obligation to apply for a licence as for failure to export the sugar within the time allowed. The primary obligation was to export the sugar. The obligation to apply for a licence was in the nature of an administrative formality (the United Kingdom had actually suggested to the court that it could be dispensed with altogether) and the penalty imposed upon Man was therefore wildly excessive.

For the application of the principle of proportionality in a different context, see below, p 146.

National remedies for violations of community law: competition

In *Cutsforth and others v Mansfield Inns Ltd* [1986] 1 All ER 577, Sir Neil Lawson reiterated that remedies are available in the English courts for breaches of certain provisions of Community law (see also All ER Rev 1983, pp 190–2 and All ER Rev 1985, pp 152–4). The plaintiffs complained that the defendants, on becoming the landlords of a chain of public houses, had included in the tenancy agreements for those houses a condition that amusement machines were only to be obtained from suppliers nominated by the defendants with the result that the plaintiffs, who had previously supplied amusement machines to all but one of the public houses, were required to remove their machines. The plaintiffs alleged that there had been violations of art 86 (abuse of dominant position) and 85 (restrictive agreements between undertakings) of the EEC Treaty.

The court held that the plaintiffs had failed to raise a serious question with regard to art 86, since the defendants, although an important brewery in the north of England, did not occupy a dominant position within a substantial part of the common market. There were, however, serious questions to be tried with regard to art 85. The effect of the tenancy agreements was to restrict competition and, taking the tenancy agreements as a whole, there was a potential effect upon trade between Member States, so that the requirements of art 85(1) appeared to have been satisfied. In addition, it was questionable to what extent the defendants could rely upon the block exemption for beer supply agreements in Commission Regulation 1984/83, since the Commission had expressed the view that the practice of insisting upon nominated suppliers for amusement machines fell outside the scope of the exemption. Since damages would not provide an adequate remedy, the court granted an interim injunction restraining the defendants from requiring their tenants not to continue their contractual arrangements with the plaintiffs.

Free movement of goods

Restrictions imposed on gounds of public morality

Despite its reputation in the Rumpole stories as a byword for boredom, the Uxbridge Magistrates' Court has its moments. One such was when it ordered the forefeiture as obscene articles of some life-size rubber dolls which Conegate Ltd had attempted to import from West Germany. Although the papers which accompanied them referred to the dolls as 'window display models', some of their features, together with the fact that they were described on the packaging as 'love love' dolls or 'Miss World specials', suggested that they were intended for more exotic use. Conegate challenged the forefeiture order made under s 42 of the Customs Consolidation Act 1876 as a violation of the prohibition on quantitative restrictions on imports from other Member States laid down by art 30 of the EEC Treaty. The United Kingdom sought to justify the prohibition by relying on art 36 which permits restrictions justified, inter alia, on grounds of public morality, so long as they do not 'constitute a means of arbitrary discrimination or a disguised restriction on trade between Member States'. The United Kingdom also relied upon Case 34/39 *R v Henn and Darby* [1980] 2 All ER 166, in which the Court of Justice had, in effect, accepted the legality of a ban imposed under the same legislation on imports of obscene books and films.

In Case 121/85 *Conegate Ltd v Customs and Excise Commissioners* [1986] 2 All ER 688, the Court of Justice rejected the United Kingdom arguments and distinguished *Henn and Darby*. The court accepted that it was for each State to determine its own standards of public morality—there was no Community concept of public morality—even though that would mean that some States imposed more restrictive measures than did others. However, as a derogation from a fundamental Community right, art 36 had to be strictly construed and the court held that considerations of public morality would not justify a ban on the import of goods unless the State took serious measures to prohibit the manufacture and marketing of the same goods within its territory. Although the United Kingdom described the attitude of English, Scottish and Northern Irish law towards goods of the kind in issue as one of uncompromising hostility, there was no prohibition on their manufacture in the United Kingdom and, in England and Northern Ireland, only limited restrictions upon marketing. These measures, the court implied, and Kennedy J subsequently accepted, fell far short of what was necessary if the United Kingdom was to justify a complete prohibition on imports of the goods.

Although the court's decision raised many hackles in Britain, the criticism of it is misconceived. The court did not challenge the United Kingdom's characterisation of the dolls as obscene or deny that the United Kingdom had the right, under art 36, to ban their import on grounds of public morality. The court accepted that it was for each Member State to determine its own standards of public morality. We are not asked to suffer a Community concept of 'Euro-morals'. What the court did object to was the different standards adopted in respect of imports and domestic products. If the dolls so offended British notions of morality that their import had to be prohibited, surely their manufacture and marketing in the United Kingdom should have been prohibited as well. The fact that dolls of this kind were not, in fact, being manufactured in the United Kingdom, was immaterial. To justify the ban on imports, the United Kingdom needed to take serious and effective measures against potential manufacture in the United Kingdom. The court's earlier decision in *Henn and Darby* was distinguished because the items in question in that case were subject to substantial prohibitions within the United Kingdom.

The decision follows closely the earlier decision in Cases 115 and 116/81 *Adoui and Cornauille v Belgian State* [1982] ECR 1665, in which the court had held that Belgium could not justify the exclusion or deportation of nationals of other Community States for activities (in that case prostitution) which it was perfectly lawful for Belgian nationals to undertake. The decisions in *Adoui* and *Conegate* show that the court is not prepared to accept double standards in which people or goods crossing a frontier are subject to far more stringent restrictions on grounds of public morality or public policy than apply within the territory concerned. While this attitude may be inconvenient to governments (and may, incidentally, show that Case 41/74 *Van Duyn v Home Office* [1975] 3 All ER 190 would be decided differently today), it makes good sense. It is, after all, the nature of the goods or the activity that is objectionable, not their origin or the nationality of the parties.

Two other features of the decision require brief comment. First, the court accepted that in a State which, like the United Kingdom, contained more than one jurisdiction, it was not necessary that the law relating to the marketing and manufacture of obscene goods should be the same in each jurisdiction. However, taken as a whole, the various laws had to impose restrictions commensurate with those imposed on imports. Secondly, the High Court, in making the reference to the Court of Justice, asked whether the ban on imports of the dolls might be justified by reference to art 234 of the EEC Treaty on the grounds that the United Kingdom was required by the Geneva Convention for the Suppression of Traffic in Obscene Publications 1923, and the Universal Postal Convention to adopt such a ban. At the hearing all parties accepted that these treaties were not, in fact, relevant to the case but the court used the opportunity to reiterate that art 234 preserved only the rights and obligations arising from treaties with non-Community states concluded before the entry into force of the EEC Treaty (or, in the case of the United Kingdom, the Act of Accession) in relations between a Member State and a non-Community country. It could not be invoked to justify departures from the EEC Treaty in trade between two Member States.

Common commercial policy: oil exports to Israel

Case 174/84 *Bulk Oil (Zug) AG v Sun International Ltd and Another (No 2)* [1986] 2 All ER 744 contains a number of interesting observations regarding the operation of the common commercial policy on exports to non-Community countries and the division of power between the Community and the Member States. The case arose out of a contract for the sale of North Sea oil by Sun International to Bulk Oil. The contract contained a clause which provided: 'Destination free but always in line with the exporting country's government policy. United Kingdom government policy, at present, does not allow delivery to South Africa.'

In January 1979 the United Kingdom government had adopted a policy which limited the export of North Sea oil to members of the EEC or the International Energy Agency and other States with which there was an 'existing pattern of trade'. One of the States excluded by this policy was Israel. When it became apparent that Bulk intended to deliver the contract oil to Israel, Sun's supplier (BP) refused to load Bulk's ship. In arbitration proceedings Bulk claimed damages for non-delivery, arguing that the United Kingdom policy, which had never been given formal legal force, was contrary to EEC law. The arbitrator rejected this argument and awarded damages to Sun. The High Court made a reference to the Court of Justice (see [1984] 1 All ER 386 and All ER Rev 1984, p 144).

Bulk's first argument was that the ban effectively imposed by the United Kingdom on oil exports to Israel was contrary to the EEC–Israel Agreement of 11 May 1975 (OJ 1975 L 136, p 1). The weakness in this argument was that, although the Agreement prohibited customs duties on both imports and exports between the EEC and Israel, it expressly prohibited quantitative restrictions (into which category the British oil policy would fall) only in relation to imports from Israel to the EEC and thus appeared to leave EEC States free to restrict exports to Israel. However, Bulk argued that a prohibition on quantitative restrictions on exports was implicit in the agreement, because art 11 provided that 'the agreement shall not preclude prohibitions or restrictions on imports, exports or goods in transit' which were justified on certain grounds. Alternatively, Bulk maintained that the British oil policy contravened art 25 of the Agreement prohibiting 'measures likely to jeopardise the attainment of the objectives of the Agreement'.

This argument was rejected by the court and Advocate General Sir Gordon Slynn. Both took the view that the omission of an express prohibition of quantitative restrictions on exports was deliberate and an implied prohibition could not be deduced from art 11, the terms of which were based on art 36 of the EEC Treaty and the purpose of which was to justify, not prohibit, restrictions. Sir Gordon Slynn thought that the reference to exports in art 11 was probably inadvertent. Since restrictions on exports were not prohibited by the Agreement, they could not be said to jeopardise the attainment of its objectives and thus violate art 25.

The court and the Advocate General also dismissed Bulk's second argument, that, since export policy was a matter of exclusive Community competence, a Member State no longer had the right to impose unilateral restrictions on exports to non-community countries. The court accepted that the common commercial policy created under the provisions of art 113 of the EEC Treaty meant that export controls fell within the exclusive powers of the Community, so that national measures were permissible only if specifically authorised by the Community. In the case of crude oil, however, that authorisation had been given by art 10 of Council Regulation 2603/69, a provision which was held to be within the margin of appreciation enjoyed by the Council in implementing the common commercial policy and to apply not only to restrictions already in existence in 1969 but also to new restrictions like those introduced by the United Kingdom.

Two subsidiary arguments advanced by Bulk were given short shrift. There was no breach of art 34 of the EEC Treaty merely because the United Kingdom policy also restricted exports to other Member States where re-export to a State like Israel was envisaged. There was no intention to provide an advantage for the United Kingdom's production or domestic market inherent in the policy nor was there any specific effect on trade between Member States. Similarly, the argument that there was a breach of art 85 of the Treaty because the policy required a destination clause to be inserted in all contracts for sale of North Sea oil was rejected because the policy did not restrict or distort competition within the common market.

The court was, however, of the view that the United Kingdom had been under a legal obligation to notify the other Member States and the Commission before adopting the 1979 policy. Since this matter was not raised in any of the High Court's questions and the Court of Justice considered that it did not have the full facts, the decision does not expressly state that the United Kingdom had failed to discharge this obligation. Nevertheless, the implication is there. The United Kingdom had notified the other Member States by informing the Committee of Permanent Representatives (COREPER) but there appears to have been no formal notification to the Commission in advance of the adoption of the policy. The court's decision was based upon two Council decisions dating from 1961–2 concerning the transitional phase which the court held had subsequently been reaffirmed insofar as the duty of notification was concerned. The Advocate General had taken a different view. He thought that the decisions had ceased to have effect and that any duty of notification was a matter of comity only. The court and the Advocate General agreed, however, that even if there had been a breach of the duty, that did not confer rights upon private parties.

The decision is conservative in its general tone. Given the activist record of the Court of Justice, one cannot help feeling that it could have found that the EEC–Israel Agreement impliedly prohibited national restrictions on exports had it wanted to do so. Nevertheless, the court's view is a realistic as well as a restrained one. To deny Member States a measure of discretion regarding the export of so strategically significant a product as oil would be a highly undesirable move at a time when the Community does not have a common foreign policy. While greater co-operation in this sphere is an important goal on the road to greater European union, it is not one of the goals that the court should seek to achieve through its jurisprudence. Progress here must come through the political institutions. By reiterating the principle that the Community must authorise national measures regarding exports the court has gone as far as is prudent.

Sex discrimination

Retirement and pensions

The extensive Community law prohibition on sex discrimination in matters of employment is subject to one major exception. Daunted by the difficulty and the expense of introducing a common pensionable age in those States (including the United Kingdom) where men and women become eligible for a state pension at different ages, the Council of Ministers agreed to exclude this kind of discrimination from the scope of the general prohibition. Article 7 of Council Directive 79/7 thus permits the adoption of different ages for men and women 'for the purposes of granting old age and retirement pensions and the possible consequences thereof for other benefits'. Two recent cases have clarified the scope of this provision but suggest that it is becoming increasingly untenable.

Case 152/84 *Marshall v Southampton and South West Hampshire Area Health Authority (Teaching)* [1986] 2 All ER 584 shows that art 7 does not permit the adoption of different ages of compulsory retirement for men and women. The authority required its employees to retire on becoming eligible for a State pension, so that female employees had to retire at 60 whereas their male counterparts could continue working until they were 65. Miss Marshall's challenge to this policy failed under English law, because the Sex Discrimination Act 1975 s 6(4) permitted discrimination in relation to 'provision for retirement'. The Court of Justice held, however, that the authority's policy was contrary to the principle of equal treatment in working conditions contained in Council Directive 76/207.

The issue in Case 151/84 *Roberts v Tate and Lyle Industries Ltd* [1986] 2 All ER 602 was rather different. When the employer closed one of its factories and made the staff redundant, it initially offered all employees within five years of the pensionable age under the company's pension scheme an early pension in lieu of redundancy. Since women became eligible for a company pension at 60 and men at 65, this offer meant that female employees of 55 and over and male employees of 60 and over could opt for an early pension. Male employees complained that this scheme discriminated against them and the company then offered an early pension on identical terms to all employees over the age of 55. Miss Roberts, who was 53, complained that the new scheme was discriminatory because men received a pension ten years before they would normally have become entitled to it whereas women obtained their pensions only five years early. This argument stands the principle of non-discrimination on its head and received short shrift from the Commission, the Advocate General and the court. Although the case could have been disposed of on the ground that Directive 76/207 did not have direct effect against a private employer (see above, p 136, the court made clear that the action would not have succeeded anyway. While Directive 79/7 permitted the adoption of different pensionable ages in respect of a State pension scheme, it did not apply to the benefits granted by an employer on redundancy.

In both cases the court made clear that art 7 of Directive 79/7 provided for derogation from a fundamental principle of Community law—equal treatment in relation to working conditions—and must therefore be strictly construed. In *Marshall* this approach meant drawing a distinction between the pensionable age, at which a person becomes eligible for a State pension, and the retirement age, at which an employer requires his employees to retire. The cost and difficulty of altering the pensionable age may justify discrimination, at least for a transitional period, in that respect but since there is no reason to suppose that women lose their faculties earlier than men or are more difficult to employ in their early sixties, no similar justification exists for maintaining discrimination in the age of retirement. Similarly, as the Advocate General pointed out in *Roberts*, to have held that Tate and Lyle's decision to treat men and women equally in relation to early retirement was discriminatory, because the early retirement scheme should have reflected the discrimination already built in to the main pension scheme, 'would have the effect of extending a discrimination which is currently tolerated in respect of retirement pensions but which clearly the Community is working, albeit slowly, to eliminate' (at 607).

While these two decisions are welcome, they are not without difficulty. In particular, two problems are likely to emerge. First, the distinction between the pensionable age (in which discrimination is permitted) and the retirement age) (in which it is not) is far from easy to apply, as may be seen from a comparison of *Marshall* and *Roberts* with the decision in Case 19/81 *Burton v British Railways Board* [1982] 3 All ER 537. In *Burton* a male employee objected that female employees had been allowed to take early retirement under a voluntary scheme at the age of 55, whereas men did not become eligible for the scheme until they were 60. In other words, his complaint was similar to that of the male employees in *Roberts* regarding the company's original offer. The Court of Justice held that Mr Burton had not been the object of discrimination. This decision can be reconciled with *Marshall* and *Roberts* but the task is not an easy one. *Burton* concerned access to pensions and retirement benefits, whereas *Marshall* was about the right to remain at work. The decision in *Roberts* can be read as limited to a finding that different pensionable ages, while permissible, are not compulsory. Nevertheless, there are hints in *Roberts* that the original offer to the workforce might have been contrary to Community law, so that the continued authority of *Burton* must be open to question. Even if *Burton* remains good law, the picture is far from satisfactory. All three decisions concern the common problem of provision for retirement so that it makes no sense at all to allow discrimination in one case but not in the others.

Secondly, there are indications in *Roberts*, particularly in the opinion of Advocate General Slynn, that it may be contrary to Community law to maintain different pensionable ages in private pension schemes. Directive 79/7 deals with social security and State schemes and the Court has held in *Marshall* and *Roberts* that art 7 of the Directive is to be strictly construed. There have also been signs in the judgment in Case 170/84 *Bilka-Kaufhaus Gmbh v Weber von Hartz* [1986] 2 CMLR 701 and a number of other cases that the court may take a stricter view in respect of private pension schemes operated by the employer on the grounds that the pensions in these cases constitute 'pay' and thus fall within the prohibition on discrimination in art 119 of the EEC Treaty. Given the complicated relationship between State and private pensions in the United Kingdom, it could cause chaos if they were to be governed by different rules regarding discrimination in the pensionable age. These difficulties are the price which must be paid if the four Member States which still maintain different pensionable ages (Belgium, Greece, Italy and the United Kingdom) are not prepared to grasp the nettle of introducing a common pensionable age into their State schemes.

Justification for discrimination: police officers

Case 222/84 *Johnston v Chief Constable of the Royal Ulster Constabulary* [1986] 3 All ER 135 dealt with the controversial question of policing in Northern Ireland. Although the Royal Ulster Constabulary ('RUC') employed both male and female officers, after the start of the terrorist campaign in 1970 it was decided that women officers would not normally carry firearms or be assigned to duties where it was necessary for officers to be armed. In 1980 the Chief Constable decided that, since it had become necessary for officers to be armed for general police duties, women officers would no longer be assigned to those duties and the contracts of women officers serving in the RUC Reserve would not be renewed, because they would no longer be needed. Mrs Johnston maintained that the decision not to renew her contract after six years in the RUC Reserve constituted unlawful discrimination. The Chief Constable admitted that the policy was discriminatory but maintained that it was lawful under art 53 of the Sex Discrimination (Northern Ireland) Order 1976 as 'an act done for the purpose of safeguarding national security or protecting public safety order'. The Secretary of State granted a certificate to that effect which, under the Order, the industrial tribunal was obliged to treat as conclusive.

The Court of Justice held that it was incompatible with the provisions of Council Directive 76/207 for a Member State to purport to exclude a national court's powers of judicial review by requiring the court to treat as conclusive the Secretary of State's certificate. The 1976 Order was intended to give effect to the Directive, art 6 of which required that Member States provide effective judicial remedies for individuals who complained that they had been the object of discrimination in breach of the Directive. In addition, it was a general principle of Community law and notions of human rights that the application of a fundamental Community right, such as the right to equal treatment in employment, should be subject to judicial control. While it was possible that the discrimination practised in this case was justifiable under the directive on grounds relating to the protection of public safety, the national authorities were not entitled to arrogate to themselves the right to determine that question by excluding it from the courts.

The court rejected the United Kingdom's argument that there was a general principle of Community law, manifested in the public policy and national security exceptions contained in numerous provisions of the Treaties, that the Treaties and Community legislation did not restrict the powers of the States to take whatever action they deemed necessary on grounds of public order and safety. Although Community law contained certain specific exceptions for measures taken on these grounds, a general exception would make these specific provisions superfluous. The court also rejected the argument that the RUC policy could be justified under art 2(3) of the Directive as a measure for the protection of women. That provision related only to the protection of a woman's biological condition or her special relationship with her child. It could not, in Advocate General Darmon's words, be invoked to justify restricting the rights of women on account of a supposed need for protection derived from cultural or political considerations. There was no evidence that the biological condition of women police officers placed them in greater danger in Northern Ireland.

On the other hand, the court was prepared to accept that the RUC's action might be justified under art 2(2) of the Directive on the grounds that policing in Northern Ireland involved activities 'for which, by reason of their nature or the context in which they are carried out, the sex of the worker constitutes a determining factor'. The court held that the context in which the RUC operated might be such that 'the carrying of firearms by policewomen might create additional risks of their being assassinated and might therefore be contrary to the requirements of public safety' (at 158). It was for the industrial tribunal to determine whether this was in fact the case. However, the court emphasised that the tribunal also had to take into account the principle of proportionality: that any derogation from the principle of equal treatment had to be no more than was strictly necessary to achieve the legitimate objective of protecting public safety. In this context, the tribunal would have to consider whether Mrs Johnston and other RUC Reserve policewomen could not have been allocated to other duties.

The importance of the decision is twofold. First, like the decision in *Marshall* (above), it makes clear that an individual employed by the State can rely upon the provisions of Directive 76/207 whatever national law may say. Even a person claiming against a private employer, who cannot therefore, rely upon the direct effect of the Directive (above, p 136), can invoke the Directive as an aid to the interpretation of national legislation. Secondly, while the court seemed prepared to accept that the initial decision not to arm policewomen and therefore not to allocate them to duties where it was necessary that officers be armed might be compatible with the Directive, it was clearly hinting that the later decision to dispense with the services of RUC Reserve policewomen altogether might violate the principle of proportionality. The final word on this matter rests with the industrial tribunal.

For further comment on the decisions in *Marshall, Roberts* and *Johnston,* see the chapter on Employment Law, pp 133 et seq above.

Social security: invalid care allowance

Case 150/85 *Drake v Chief Adjudication Officer* [1986] 3 All ER 65 breaks no new legal ground but has had a significant practical impact within the British social security system. Mrs Drake gave up her job to care for her severely disabled mother. She contended that the decision to refuse her an invalid care allowance, on the ground that s 37(3)(a)(i) of the Social Security Act 1975 provided that this allowance was not payable to a married woman living with her husband, was contrary to Council Directive 79/7 which sought to establish the principle of equal treatment in the sphere of social security. Since the invalid care allowance was payable to a married man living with his wife who gave up his job to look after a disabled relative, it was not contested that the scheme was discriminatory. The Chief Adjudication Officer argued, however, that, because the invalid care allowance was paid to the person caring for the invalid and not to the invalid herself, it fell outside the scope of art 3(1) of the Directive, which applied only to schemes which 'provide protection against the following risks:— . . . invalidity'.

The Court of Justice did not accept this argument. Mrs Drake was a member of the working population who had given up her job because of invalidity. The fact that it was her mother, rather than herself, who was disabled was immaterial. The court pointed out that other Member States frequently paid an allowance to the disabled person to enable that person to pay for assistance. The fact that the United Kingdom chose to pay an allowance direct to the caring relative instead could not remove the allowance from the scope of the Directive. The decision shows once again that the Court of Justice is far readier to look at the substance, rather than the form, of national legislation than English courts have proved to be when confronted with matters like social security legislation. The decision is so self-evidently right it is regrettable that the United Kingdom ever chose to contest the point.

Evidence

ADRIAN A S ZUCKERMAN, LLM, MA
Fellow of University College, Oxford

The burden of proof in criminal cases

The principle concerning the burden of proof was set out by Viscount Sankey LC in *Woolmington v DPP* [1935] AC 462 at 481–2:

> 'Throughout the web of the English Criminal Law one golden thread is always to be seen, that it is the duty of the prosecution to prove the prisoner's guilty subject . . . to the defence of insanity and subject also to any statutory exception. If, at the end of and on the whole of the case, there is a reasonable doubt, created by the evidence given by either the prosecution or the prisoner, as to whether the prisoner killed the deceased with malicious intention, the prosecution has not made out the case and the prisoner is entitled to an acquittal. No matter what the charge or where the trial, the principle that the prosecution must prove the guilt of the prisoner is part of the common law of England and no attempt to whittle it down can be entertained.'

Thereafter it was assumed that there were only two exceptions to this cardinal rule: the exception concerning insanity and statutory exceptions. In 1974 *R v Edwards* [1974] 2 All ER 1085 undermined this assumption. It was held there that the common law recognised a further exception to the golden rule. This exception was limited to statutory offences which prohibit the doing of an act save in specified circumstances or by persons of specified classes or with specified qualifications or with the licence or permission of specified authorities. In such cases it is for the accused to prove that he comes within the exemptions, exceptions, provisos and the like. In other words, the court decided that s 81 of the Magistrates' Courts Act 1952, now s 101 of the Magistrates' Courts Act 1980, represented the common law. This section provides:

> '. . . if the Information or Complaint . . . shall negative any Exemption, Exception, Proviso, or Condition in the Statute on which the same shall be framed, it shall not be necessary for the Prosecutor or complainant in that behalf to prove such Negative, but the Defendant may prove the Affirmative thereof in his Defence, if he would have the Advantage of the Same.'

What was disturbing about the *Edwards* rule was the fact that the burden of proof could be thrown on the accused merely because the draftsman of the legislation in question happened to adopt a certain grammatical form. Fortunately, the *Edwards* rule suffered from an inherent flaw: there is no distinction of substance between an element forming part of the definition of the offence and an element forming an exemption, exception or proviso to such definition. Substantively, there is no difference between a provision saying: 'It is forbidden for any person to drive without a driving licence', and a provision saying: 'It is forbidden for any person to drive, except where such person has a driving licence'. In the absence of a distinction of substance the rule enunciated in *Edwards* could depend on a distinction of grammar. Like all grammatical rules, however, such a rule must stand up to the test of usage. That is to say, it would have to be adopted by both the legislature and the court for the purpose of allocating the burden of proof. However, this was not the case, as I argued in 'The third exception to the *Woolmington* rule', (1976) 92 LQR 402. Since the *Edwards* ruling is supported by neither a substantive distinction nor by grammatical usage it can never amount to a rule.

The House of Lords has accepted now that there was no third exception to the *Woolmington* rule. The accused in *R v Hunt* [1986] 1 All ER 184 was charged with unlawful possession of a controlled drug, morphine, contrary to s 5(2) of the Misuse of Drugs Act 1971. Under the Misuse of Drugs Regulations 1973, preparations containing 0.2 per cent or less morphine were exempted from the prohibition. At the trial the prosecution proved that the substance found in the accused's possession contained morphine but it did not prove its proportion in the preparation. Arguing that the prosecution bore the burden of proving that morphine exceeded 0.2 per cent, the accused pleaded no case to answer and when his argument and plea were rejected he pleaded guilty.

The Court of Appeal dismissed the accused's appeal holding that once the prosecution has proved that the accused possessed morphine it was for him to prove that the substance contained no more than 0.2 per cent morphine. On appeal to the House of Lords (opinions being delivered on December 4 1986, reported in [1987] 1 All ER 1) two issues were dealt with. First, in what circumstances does the burden of proof lie on an accused? Secondly, when the accused bears the burden of proof, does he bear merely an evidential burden or does he also carry the burden of persuasion?

On the first issue the House decided that *Edwards* did not amount to a rule of exception. It merely provided a guide to statutory interpretation which could be used as a first step in construction but which did not conclusively determine the allocation of the burden; per Lord Griffiths [1987] 1 All ER at 11. Inevitably, the House of Lords also decided that s 101 of the Magistrates' Courts Act 1980 fulfills a similar function and does not represent a rule of exception any more than *Edwards* does. This aspect of the decision is enormously important because it cuts down the scope for departures, in both summary proceedings and trial on indictment, from the rule that the burden in criminal cases is on the prosecution. It would no longer automatically follow that the burden rests on the accused merely because the statute creating the offence happens to use the word 'exemption', 'exception', 'proviso' or the like.

The question which had to be answered next concerned the principle governing statutory construction. Counsel for the accused sought to limit the statutory exceptions to provisions that expressly, and not just by implication, impose the burden on the accused. He relied, in addition to the above statement in *Woolmington*, on the dictum in *Mancini v DPP* [1941] 3 All ER 272 at 279 where Viscount Simon LC referred to *Woolmington* and said: 'the rule is of general application in all charges under the criminal law. (The only exceptions arise, as explained in *Woolmington's* case, in the defence of insanity and in offences where the onus of proof is specially dealt with by statute.)' Reliance was also placed on a dictum to similar effect in *Jayesena v R* [1970] 1 All ER 219 at 221.

However, none of these dicta address themselves directly to the issue under discussion and they cannot withstand competing considerations with direct bearing on the subject. First, numerous cases have already interpreted non-express statutory provisions as imposing the burden on the accused outside the confines suggested by counsel for Hunt. Secondly, had the House decided that the common law recognised no statutory exceptions other than express ones, the burden in trials on indictment would have been at variance with that dictated by s 101 for summary proceeding. This might not have been objectionable if the jurisdiction of magistrates and of the Crown Court was mutually exclusive. In fact many serious offences, of which possession of prohibited drugs is one, are triable both summarily and on indictment. Consequently, had counsel's argument been accepted, as Lord Griffiths explained, the 'law would have developed on absurd lines if in respect of the same offence the burden of proof . . . differed according to whether the case was heard by magistrates or on indictment' [1987] 1 All ER at 9.

Having concluded that a statute may impose the burden on the accused by implication, and not only by express provision, the House of Lords had to consider how a court should decide whether there was such implication within any given statute. To appreciate the importance of this issue one has to turn now to the second issue that was considered.

This issue was concerned with the nature of the burden that the accused has to discharge when the proof rests on him. Counsel for the accused contended that, insanity apart, whenever the burden rests on the accused he bears only an evidential burden. Namely, he has only to adduce sufficient evidence from which a reasonable jury might infer the relevant facts and at the end of the day it is the prosecution who must prove, beyond reasonable doubt, that the accused did not come within the exemption. This is consonant with the principle that an accused must be acquitted unless the prosecution has proved beyond reasonable doubt all the elements of the offence. A negative fact, such as the absence of a licence, is a condition for liability whether or not it is expressed in terms of an 'exemption', 'exception' or 'proviso'. Consequently, to hold that the jury must convict even where they are in doubt about whether the accused possessed, for instance, a licence, is contrary to the principle I have just mentioned. Unfortunately, although the principle is clear, authority does not unequivocally support it; see my discussion in (1976) 92 LQR at 422.

The House of Lords has decided that when the accused does bear the burden of proof in relation to certain facts: he bears a burden of persuading the jury, on the balance of probabilities, of the existence of such facts. It would have been better to have decided that, short of a direct and unambiguous statutory provision to that effect, the burden of persuasion always rests on the prosecution. Such a ruling would not only have been consistent with principle but would also have placed the decision concerning the benefit of reasonable doubt fairly and squarely on parliament. It would have obliged parliament to state so clearly and publicly if it wished to legislate that a person may be convicted of an offence despite the fact that one of its elements has not been proved by the prosecution. As it is the courts have saddled themselves with the responsibility of deciding, albeit as a matter of statutory interpretation, when the burden of persuasion rests on the accused.

The House of Lords was conscious of the responsibility it had undertaken and articulated a number of guidelines for the future. Lord Griffiths explained that, while a court interpreting a statute should consider the various practical ramifications of the interpretation one way or the other, the most important consideration was the ease with which the accused could prove his innocence. 'Parliament', he said, 'can never lightly be taken to have intended to impose an onerous duty on a defendant to prove his innocence in a criminal case, and a court should be very slow to draw such inference from the language of the statute' ([1987] 1 All ER at 11). It seems that Lord Ackner too was alive to the need for restraint when he described the placing of the burden on the accused as 'necessary implication' from the words of the statute; see ibid at 15, 19. Indeed, this restraint may be observed in the decision arrived at by the House of Lords in the present case: the House insisted that the burden of proving the proportion of morphine in the preparation rested on the prosecution throughout, allowed the appeal and quashed the conviction.

Three important points emerge from the decision under consideration. First, the House of Lords has clearly renaged on the *Edwards* theory, according to which the burden could be imposed on the accused merely because the draftsman had casually adopted a certain grammatical form and without any deliberation about the wisdom of such outcome. Secondly, the House of Lords has now insisted that any imposition of the burden on the accused must be adequately justified. Thirdly, we have the assurance of the House that, short of an express command by the legislature, an accused will not be saddled with an onerous burden to prove his innocence.

The speeches in the House make quite clear that the imposition of the burden on the accused will in future be justified, broadly speaking, only where the statute prohibits an act generally but goes on to allow it to be performed by specified classes of persons or by persons with special permits. The practical effect of the imposition of the burden on the accused to show that he belongs to the designated class, such as the medical profession, or that he has the necessary permit or licence, would be very limited. Suppose that an activity is prohibited in the absence of a licence to engage in it and that the burden of proving the absence of a licence rests entirely on the prosecution. To discharge its burden, it would ordinarily be sufficient for the prosecution to give evidence that the accused was asked to produce his licence and declined to do so. If the accused then fails to come forward with a licence or with a credible explanation for its absence, the prosecution will have gone a long way to discharging its burden of persuasion on this point. Consequently, to say that it is upon the accused, rather than the prosecution, to prove licence does not make much practical difference. The accused would have to do the same as he would have had to do, had the burden rested on the prosecution: to produce his licence or a credible explanation for its absence. If it turns out, therefore, that *Hunt* has confined the imposition of the burden on the accused to such situations, the golden thread will have been strengthened.

Proof of non-intoxication

Under s 25 of and Sch 8 to the Transport Act 1981 the proportion of alcohol in a specimen of breath provided by the accused may be proved by the production of results obtained by a device called Intoximeter 3000. Such results create a presumption about the proportion of alcohol in the accused's blood. In *Hughes v McConnell* [1986] 1 All ER 268 the Divisional Court considered the means by which such presumption may be rebutted.

The evidence before the magistrates was as follows. The police noticed the accused's car swerving several times. They stopped him and got the impression that he was drunk. The accused then underwent a breath test with Alcotest 80 which showed positive. He was arrested and taken to the police station where, at about midnight, he underwent another breath test with Intoximeter 3000 which produced the results that were subsequently proved at his trial. The prosecution expert testified that the proportion indicated by the test could only have been produced by the consumption of five and a half to six and a half pints of beer, or their equivalent, that a person with the proportion of alcohol indicated in the results would be in a stupor and that he would not be sober before 9 am and possibly 1 pm. On the accused's side the evidence was, first, that he had only drunk one and a half pints of beer that evening. Secondly, that before he was released at 3.40 am he underwent another test with the Alcotest 80 which showed negative and, thirdly, that on being released he appeared sober and was even able to drive normally. The Alcotest 80, it should be noted, is used only for screening and its results carry no special legal weight.

The magistrates, having found the accused's evidence convincing, were left in a reasonable doubt about the correctness of the results of the Intoximeter 3000 and acquitted. On appeal, the Divisional Court held that the justices were not entitled to take into account the factors canvassed by the accused as rebutting the correctness of the result and directed the justices to convict. To hold that a person must be convicted even where the trier of fact is not convinced of his guilt is an extreme conclusion which, one assumes, a court of justice will reach only on the most compelling grounds. Yet the only ground for the decision that appears in the report is the statement of Watkins LJ ([1986] 1 All ER at 271):

> '. . . I perceive very considerable danger arising from a failure to recognise that a device of this kind [Intoximeter 3000], which is properly approved, can only be shown to be defective by evidence which goes directly to the defective nature of the instrument itself.'

If Watkins LJ statement of the law is accepted, the results of Intoximeter tests will in effect amount to an irrebuttable presumption. There will be no practical way that an accused can prove, by direct evidence, that the machine was defective. The accused has no access to the machine and the police, it emerged, make a practice of refusing to provide accused persons with the machine's maintenance record (remarkably, the court voiced no criticism of this practice). While his Lordship accepted that it was practically impossible for the accused to challenge the accuracy of the machine with which he was tested, he consoled himself with the fact that suspects could insist on blood or urine tests following the Intoximeter test. It is difficult, though, to see how this evidence will amount to 'direct evidence of [the] imperfection' of the Intoximeter device any more than the evidence of a test by Alcotest 80 or the other circumstantial evidence offered by the accused in the instant case. There is no statutory authority nor common sense support for the conclusion that 'the only way in which the ineffectiveness on the Intoximeter 3000 could have been attacked here was by direct evidence of imperfection' (ibid at 272).

His Lordship did not spell out what the dangers of a different ruling might be but one can speculate. If evidence of consumption of drink by the accused and evidence of his sober behaviour were admissible, the risk is that the courts would be swamped by defence witnesses called to testify on these matters. Much of this testimony, one may assume, would be biased or misleading and would create much confusion and delay in the administration of justice. These fears are very real but the path chosen by the court to prevent abuses is questionable. It is one thing to say that accused persons are not entitled to unlimited opportunities of sewing confusion and causing delay, it is quite another to hold that an accused may not adduce evidence capable of proving his innocence. It is true that by adopting the latter course one necessarily achieves the former, but one does so at a disproportionate cost to the principle that the innocent should not be punished.

A far better solution would be to hold that oral evidence of consumption is on the whole of negligible value and that rebuttal of the presumption created by the Intoximeter results could only be justified where oral evidence is corroborated by some other independent evidence, such as the Alcotest 80 result in the present case. To prevent litigants from wasting time and creating confusion, the justices could make substantial costs awards and, possibly, impose heavier sentences. Alternatively, if a system of irrebuttable presumption is to operate, then it must be shown to be full proof. This could be achieved by insisting on a combination of an Intoximeter test and a blood or urine test. The solution chosen by the court in the present case is contrary to principle and should not be allowed to subsist in a criminal justice system which prides itself on its protection of the innocent.

Section 1(f)(ii) of the Criminal Evidence Act 1898

Under s 1(f)(ii) of the Criminal Evidence Act 1898 an accused giving evidence on his own behalf may be cross-examined on his criminal record if he has given evidence of his own good character or if he has attacked the character of the prosecution's witnesses. Although its wording is not obscure the section continues to be troublesome. The fact that the Lord Chief Justice feels obligated to recant a three year old decision is a fair measure of the trouble. In *R v Watts* [1983] 1 All ER 101 the accused, a man of low intelligence, was charged with indecent assault on a woman. The victim did not identify him. He was arrested because he had a record for indecent assaults and lived near the scene of the crime. The evidence against him consisted of a confession which the accused denied having made. His denial was held by the trial judge to have involved the imputation that the police had fabricated his confession and the accused was cross-examined on his record for indecent assaults on very young girls. In his summing up the trial judge told the jury:

'The fact that a person has committed an offence on a previous occasion does not make him any more or less likely to be guilty of committing an offence on a subsequent occasion. It is not evidence. It was only allowed to be brought to your knowledge because of the serious allegations of misconduct which are made by the defendant . . . against the police.'

On this Lord Lane CJ commented ([1983] 1 All ER at 105):

'The jury in the present case was charged with deciding the guilt or innocence of a man against whom an allegation of indecent assault on a woman has been made. They were told that he had previous convictions for indecent assaults of a more serious kind on young girls. They were warned that such evidence was not to be taken as making it more likely that he was guilty of the offence charged, which it seems it plainly did, but only as affecting his credibility, which it almost certainly did not.'

In *Watts* the Lord Chief Justice went on to explain that while the trial judge's direction was 'sound in law', 'it would have been extremely difficult, if not practically impossible, for the jury to have done what the judge was suggesting', [1983] 1 All ER at 104. This is plain common sense, yet the Lord Chief Justice no longer feels able to say that this is also the law. In *R v Powell* [1986] 1 All ER 193 his Lordship said that in *Watts* the court had 'overlooked the "tit for tat" principle' and that too much attention had been paid to 'the question whether the previous offences did or did not involve dishonesty in the ordinary sense of the word' (at 198). He concludes in *Powell* that when the accused has been cross-examined on his previous convictions under s 1(f)(ii) the judge must instruct the jury 'that the previous convictions should not be taken as indications that the accused had committed the offence.' The question therefore arises: Is *Powell* sound law?

The accused in *Powell* was charged with living on the earnings of prostitution. Police witnesses testified that they observed prostitutes using the defendant's premises, paying him money and being assisted by him. The accused admitted that his premises had been used by prostitutes but contended that it was done without permission. For the rest, his defence was that the police fabricated the entire story and that he was a man of means who did not need to seek money in prostitution. The prosecution were allowed to put it to the accused that he had a number of previous convictions for similar offences. The Court of Appeal approved of this course, Lord Lane CJ saying ([1986] 1 All ER at 198):

'. . . if there is a real issue about the conduct of an important witness which the jury will have to settle in order to reach their verdict, the judge is entitled to let the jury know the previous convictions of the man who is making the attack. The fact that the defendant's convictions are not for offences of dishonesty, the fact that they are offences bearing a close resemblance to the offences charged, are matters for the judge to take into consideration when exercising his discretion, but they certainly do not oblige the judge to disallow the proposed cross-examination.'

If the previous offences are similar to the offence charged they will, in common sense, generally increase the probability that the accused committed the offence charged. This would suggest that *Powell* cannot be sound law.

Much of the trouble arises from the combined effect of two assumptions that lurk in the background: first, that there is a difference of principle between relevance to the issue and relevance to credibility and, secondly, that the function of the jury is to ascertain the objective facts and nothing else. The idea that, in theory, relevance to the issue is different from relevance to credibility is untenable as I tried to show in All ER Rev 1982, p 128, and at greater length in *Facts In Law*, ed Twining, (1983) p 145. But even if there is some such theoretical distinction it would be of no consequence when applied to the accused giving evidence in his own behalf. If the accused says he did not commit the offence charged, clearly this is evidence going to the issue since, if believed, it makes it more probable that he did not commit the offence. Since the accused's word carries a certain probability regarding the commission of the offence, anything that affects the weight of his word directly affects the probability of the commission of the offence. Consequently, to tell the jury that evidence which undermines the accused's credibility is not evidence that bears on the commission of the offence is misleading.

The assumption concerning the function of the jury is also far from self-evident (I discuss this in 'Law, fact or justice?' (1986) 66 Boston LR 487). It is assumed that the jury's task is merely to ascertain the objective facts and that it must neither concern itself with moral judgment nor decide questions of law. However, our system of criminal justice is not designated to secure pure objectivity. We do not have a jury in criminal trials because juries are preculiarly adept in ascertaining the objective truth. The jury system fulfills a different function: that of securing public support for the administration of justice; Devlin, *The Judge* (1981) p 127. The support of the public is obtained by making the ordinary standards of justice and morality the final arbiter of guilt or innocence; *Devlin*, p 141.

As s 1(f)(ii) acknowledges, the accused is allowed to call evidence of his own good character. The accused's good character could, and most probably does, influence the jury's deliberation in ways that have little to do with the objective facts. It could lead a jury to decide that in view of the accused's unblemished character they will run no risk of mistaken conclusion of guilt; they will therefore refrain from conviction even where no reasonable doubt remains. Or they could come to the conclusion that although the elements of the offence have been proved, they will not convict a particularly worthy person. The jury's freedom to acquit amounts to a legal recognition of their freedom to take just this kind of consideration into account. Consequently, when a trial judge instructs the jury to disregard the accused's criminal past, he is asking them to refrain from doing something which is both natural outside the law and permissible in court when the accused's merits, rather than demerits, are put on the scales.

The combined effect of the two assumptions I have been discussing is disastrous as far as combating prejudice is concerned. The first assumption instructs the jury to do the impossible and the second disables the courts from instructing juries on sensible ways of dealing with the accused's character, when the law itself recognises that character can have a moral influence on the verdict. Clearly, the central weakness of the present strategy is that it does not allow the trial judge to address the jury on the main problem that the jury is likely to face when it retires to consider its verdict. The problem is how to avoid the infliction of undue prejudice upon the accused when they know him to possess a criminal record. Both the judge and the jury have to face this problem, though at different stages of the trial. For the judge the question is how to contain the extent to which the accused's criminal antecedents is disclosed. For the jury it is how to limit the damage to the accused, once his antecedents have been disclosed.

The containment aspect arises in two situations under s 1(f)(ii): where the accused has given evidence of his good character and where he has made imputation on the prosecution's witnesses. In the former the problem is not difficult because it is basically up to the accused whether to keep the lid on his previous record or to let it come out. Where the accused has not put his character in issue but has made imputations, such as that the police fabricated his confession, the problem is far more difficult. On the one hand, it could be said that, since the prosecution has to convince the jury that its witnesses are telling the truth, their credibility should stand or fall by their own performance in the witness box and without any reference to the accused's past. On the other hand, it is impossible to ignore the fact that when one has to decide which of two persons is telling the truth, their relative moral worth is very important.

Our law is alive to both these aspects. Where the accused's defence is that the prosecution's witnesses have fabricated their evidence but he does not take the stand to say so on oath, the prosecution cannot, everything else being equal, call evidence of his criminal character. It is only when he takes the stand to put up his own word against theirs that the question arises. In *Selvey v DPP* [1968] 2 All ER 497 it was argued that s 1(f)(ii) allowed cross-examination of the accused on his criminal record only where imputations upon the prosecution's witnesses were gratuitous and not strictly necessary to his defence. The House of Lords was correct to dismiss the argument because the purpose of cross-examination is not to punish the accused for making unnecessary imputations but to help the jury reach a balanced judgment. The issue of the accused's character, however, arises only where there is direct competition between the accused's credibility and that of a prosecution witness and when the circumstances are such that one of them must be intentionally lying. There is no direct competition where the suggestion is that the witness is merely mistaken because the jury is not then limited to a choice between honesty and dishonesty. This point emerges from the section itself when it authorises cross-examination for casting imputations on the 'character' of witnesses for the prosecution and not merely contradicting them.

It does not follow that wherever the accused suggests that the prosecution witness is lying, the former should be exposed to cross-examination. The court should still ask itself how necessary is the competition of characters to the ends of justice. This is recognised in the existence of a discretion to disallow cross-examination within s 1(f)(ii) if the prejudicial effect of such examination is likely to exceed any probative gains. This formulation of the problem is not wholly satisfactory because it only captures one aspect of the judicial task. It addresses itself to the question of whether the contribution that the accused's record makes to resolving the competition of credibility is worth the trouble that its reception may cause. It does not, however, address itself to the more difficult and more common question: Is it just and proper to allow the trial to develop into a competition of characters?

It is clear that the courts are as concerned to grapple with the second problem even though they describe it in terms of the first. In *Watts,* for example, the real question was not whether the accused's previous offences undermined his credibility, but whether it was right that emphasis should be transferred from the strength of the prosecution's case to a contest to credibilities. The Lord Chief Justice rightly criticised the cross-examination of the accused because the circumstantial evidence was weak and the confession, which the accused denied making, may well have been unreliable in view of the accused's low intelligence. Judicial instinct is correct in allowing, generally, a full blown credibility contest only where there is a fundamental contradition between the prosecution and the defence and it is evident that one of the conflicting versions is caused by intentional mendacity. In *R v Burke* (1986) 82 Cr App R 156, for instance, the accused maintained that the police concocted the circumstantial evidence, planted drugs and invented a confession. It is inconceivable that, in such circumstances, the issue can be settled without going into the accused's antecedents. *Powell* too falls under this category because accused's defence was that the prosecution wove a tissue of lies to incriminate him (see also *R v Owen* (1986) 83 Cr App R 100).

Cases such as *Braithwaite,* considered in *R v Powell* [1986] 1 All ER 193, are on the border line. There two policemen gave evidence that they saw the accused jostle a woman in the street and steal her purse, whereupon they gave chase and apprehended the accused. The accused said that the policemen had not seen what they claimed. Cross-examination of the accused on offences similar to that charged then followed. The Court of Appeal disapproved and quashed the conviction. In *Powell* the Court of Appeal has now expressed misgivings about this judgment. The reason for the difference of opinion between the two panels of the Court of Appeal lies in the failure to distinguish between the two questions I have outlined above. If one only asks whether the previous offences affected the accuseds' denials, then the answer is clearly positive. But if one asks the further question of whether it is right in these circumstances to allow a full blown contest of credibility to arise, the answer is far from clear. If this distinction is articulated trial judges will be able to provide clearer reasons for the exercise of discretion and appellate jurisdiction would be better placed to assess the outcome.

So far I have discussed the steps taken to contain the disclosure of the accused's criminal record. But what is done for the accused when his record has had to be revealed? The answer is: very little. The courts fail to take adequate steps to couteract the prejudicial effect of the evidence. They tell juries that the accused's record is only relevant to credibility and not to guilt, which suggests that there is some special legal rule to be observed. By creating a conflict between the normal standards familiar to the jury and legal standards judges have made it unlikely that juries would defer to a legal standard which they do not understand in preference to a moral one which they do. Instead judges should bring into the open the inevitable moral conflict inherent in evidence of past criminal record and strive to persuade juries that the principles of criminal justice reflect their own moral perceptions. Only if juries understand that the need to try the accused solely for the offence charged represents a value which they themselves uphold will they be able to resist the temptation of convicting because of the accused's bad character. It is not suggested that the court could wipe out prejudice by some magic words. But trial judges could help the jury withstand the rush of animosity that a criminal record is bound to create in their minds.

Corroboration

In *R v Spencer* [1986] 2 All ER 928 the House of Lords has taken another step away from the stale technicalities that dominated the law of corroboration before the House's previous forays into this area in *DPP v Hester* [1972] 3 All ER 1056 and in *DPP v Kilbourne* [1973] 1 All ER 440. The accused, male nurses in an institution for the confinement of mentally disturbed prisoners, were charged with mistreatment of inmates. The case against them was entirely founded on the testimony of the complainants. In his summing up the trial judge warned the jury to approach the complainants' evidence with great care for three reasons: first, because the complainants were persons of bad character with criminal records, secondly, because they were mentally disturbed and, thirdly, because they had grudges against the accused and may well have conspired to give false testimony. Although the judge also emphasised the absence of independent corroboration the jury convicted. The accused appealed to the Court of Appeal on the ground that the judge had failed to use the word 'dangerous' in his direction. It was contended that the judge should have told the jury, as is the practice in relation to accomplices, that it was dangerous to convict on the uncorroborated evidence of these witnesses.

The Court of Appeal rejected this argument and dismissed the appeal, see [1985] 1 All ER 673 and All ER Rev 1985, p 164. The House of Lords endorsed the Court of Appeal's decision holding, in the words of Lord Ackner, that 'the obligation to warn the jury does not involve some legalistic ritual to be automatically recited by the judge', in the absence of which recital the conviction will be quashed: [1986] 2 All ER at 937. The duty of the judge was to suit his summing up to the circumstances of the case before him so as to appraise the jury of any special difficulties of which they should be aware when considering their verdict.

The present decision has gone some way towards arresting the scourge of formalism in that it establishes that even where a corroboration warning is required as a matter of a rule of practice, as in relation to accomplices and the complainants of sexual assaults, the warning need not use any special words, such as 'dangerous', so long as it is sufficient to impress the jury with the nature of the risk and its seriousness: [1986] 2 All ER at 937-8. (For an illustration of an insufficient warning see *R v Stewart* (1986) 83 Cr App R 327).

However, two sources of confusing formalism still remain. First, the House of Lords has not dismantled the existing categories of common law corroboration. This means that a warning, albeit informal, is necessary whenever the witness for the prosecution is a complainant of sexual assault, an accomplice or a child. Outside these categories the need for warning is governed by the question of whether there is some unusual risk of mistake or mendacity, in the circumstances of the case. Within these categories a warning is mandatory regardless of its practical necessity or, indeed, wisdom. A justification for this distinction, according to Lord Ackner, is that the unreliablity of witnesses in these categories is not obvious. This is an inadequate justification. Whether the danger of unreliability is obvious or not will depend on the circumstances of each case, and so should the judicial warning. Had this been the guiding principle, apparently safe convictions, such as the one in *R v Birchall* (1986) 82 Cr App R 208, would not have been quashed.

The second remaining source of formalism is the body of technical, and frequently counterproductive, rules about the nature corroboration which continue to apply to the categories of complainants of sexual assaults, accomplices and children. One such rule is that to be corroborative the evidence must implicate the accused in the commission of the crime. To count as corroboration it is not enough that a piece of evidence supports the witness' credibility, however convincingly and independently; see for instance *R v Donat* (1986) 82 Cr App R 173 at 178.

Another rule concerning the nature of corroboration was derived from the dictum of Lord Hailsham in *DPP v Kilbourne* [1973] 1 All ER at 452, where he said that corroboration 'can only be afforded to or by a witness who is otherwise to be believed'. Taken at face value this dictum was interpreted as meaning that 'the jury should be directed first to consider whether the complainant's evidence is . . . credible, if it is not no amount of corroboration will cure it, unless the tendered corroboration is sufficient by itself to establish guilt': *Turner v Blunden* [1986] 2 All ER 75 at 78. How judges could ever have subscribed to such spurious logic is difficult to understand. Happily, Lord Hailsham has seized the opportunity in *R v Spencer* [1986] 2 All ER at 931–2, to relieve us of this rule. He declared that in writing those words in *Kilbourne* he did not mean to differ from Lord Reid's view that when 'one is doubtful whether or not to believe a particular statement one naturally looks to see whether it fits in with other statements or circumstances relating to the particular matter; the better it fits in the more one is inclined to believe it' ([1973] 1 All ER at 456). It is hoped that judges will not continue to fell obliged, as did the Court of Appeal in *R v Donat* (1986) 82 Cr App R 173 at 177, to follow the now discredited interpretation of that dictum. There may continue to be situations where, once the complainant's evidence is disbelieved, the corroborative evidence may not be sufficient, on it own, to justify conviction. But we do not need to subscribe to a 'rule' in order to reach this conclusion (as did the Court of Appeal in *R v Rahmoun* (1986) 82 Cr App R 217; cf *R v Olaleye* (1986) 82 Cr App R 337).

There is a further aspect which the decision in *Spencer* leaves unresolved but which is bound to cause trouble unless addressed. In certain circumstances the witnesses for the prosecution are so inherently unreliable that no warning is able to remove a lingering doubt that the jury's verdict was unsafe. The present case came very close to creating such a doubt and sooner or later the courts will have to consider this aspect.

In conclusion, while *Spencer* has improved the rules of corroboration, there is still a way to go before English law reaches the Canadian stage of development under which in all cases the form of the warning and the nature of corroboration is governed by common sense rather than by rules of law: *Vetrovec v R* 136 DLR (3d) 89.

Legal professional privilege

For many decades judges and academic lawyers have been puzzling over the contradiction presented by the pair of cases: *Calcraft v Guest* [1898] 1 QB 759 and *Ashburton v Pape* [1913] 2 Ch 469. In both cases documents covered by legal professional privilege fell into the hands of an opponent in litigation. In the *Calcraft* case the issue was whether the opponent may adduce in evidence a copy of the original document. The Court of Appeal's answer was a clear 'Yes'. In support of this conclusion Lindley MR referred to Parke B judgment in *Lloyd v Mostyn* (1842) 10 M & W 478 where the latter said that a copy of an original would be admissible even where the copy was facilitated by the theft of the original. The factual background to the *Ashburton* was similar. This time, however, Ashburton, whose legal documents fell into the hands of his opponent, Pape, applied for an order that Pape return the documents to him and refrain from using them in the litigation. The Court of Appeal granted the required injunction.

Ever since this judgment it has been assumed that these results cannot be both correct. Either a copy of the original is admissible or it is not. If it is admissible in evidence, an injunction to restrain its use in evidence should not be granted. Alternatively, if it is inadmissible, an injunction to restrain its use in evidence would be redundant because the duty of the trial judge would be to exclude it even in the absence of an injunction. The Court of Appeal has now decided in *Goddard v Nationwide Building Society* [1986] 3 All ER 264 that, on the contrary, both cases are correct. It held that the courts are bound to protect confidentiality by injunctive relief as indicated in the *Ashburton* case. May LJ, explained (at 270):

> 'If a litigant has in his possession copies of documents to which legal professional privilege attaches, he may nevertheless use such copies as secondary evidence in his litigation: however, if he has not yet used the documents in that way, the mere fact that he intends to do so is no answer to a claim against him by the person in whom the privilege is vested for delivery up of the copies or to restrain him from disclosing or making any use of the information contained in them.'

To remove any doubt Nourse J added: 'The crucial point is that the party who desires the protection must seek it before the other party has adduced the confidential communication in evidence or otherwise relied on it at the trial.'

May LJ was quite frank in his assessment of this solution. He said: 'I confess that I do not find the decision in *Lord Ashburton v Pape* logically satisfactory, depending as it does on the order in which applications are made in litigation.'

There is a further reason for finding this solution unsatisfactory. To tell a litigant that in order to prevent his document, or a copy thereof, from being used in evidence he must seek an injunction in the High Court, rather than merely object to the evidence when it is adduced, is to put him to great and unnecessary expense. Untutored litigants, finding themselves in this situation, might be excused for coming to the conclusion that this law is designed for the benefit of the lawyers rather than the litigants.

In fact a solution to the *Calcraft-Ashburton* puzzle is within reach. It requires the drawing of a distinction between two legal doctrines that have become confused in this pair of cases. The first is the legal protection of confidentiality. May LJ was right in his view that the *Ashburton* case was concerned to protect confidence 'in the same way, for instance, as the courts protect the trade secrets of an employer against the unauthorised use of them by an employee' ([1986] 3 All ER at 268). The second doctrine is the doctrine of immunity from disclosure in evidence, of which legal professional privilege is an instance. It is axiomatic that the two doctrines do not completely overlap. A right to confidence does not, of itself, entail a right to withhold evidence from a court of law. Generally, the duty to disclose relevant evidence in court overrides confidence. For instance, I have a right to restrain unauthorised publication of my personal and intimate papers, but I have no shield from their production in court if they are needed for doing justice in civil or criminal proceedings. Privilege from disclosure in legal proceedings is, therefore, a separate doctrine. Under this doctrine certain communications are exempt from the legal process of obtaining evidence (ie from orders of discovery and from the duty of disclosure under subpoenas ad testificandum and duces tecum).

Our puzzle is caused by the fact that a document covered by legal professional privilege comes under both doctrines: it is confidential and it is immune from production. However, it must be borne in mind that even in respect of one and the same document confidence and immunity from production do not always go hand in hand. For instance, if litigation develops between the lawyer and his client, the lawyer will be prevented for using privileged documents not because he has no right to know their contents, which he naturally does, but because of the immunity. In the situation that arose in our famous pair of cases and in the case under consideration, a privileged document fell into the opponent's hands and he wished to adduce a copy in evidence. The fact that the document is confidential does not provide an independent ground for objection to production in evidence, any more than would my objection to testifying on the ground that I am asked to reveal my private and intimate affairs. Justification for excluding the evidence can come only from the doctrine of legal professional privilege.

Ashburton v Pape presents no obstacle to seeking a solution within the confines of legal professional privilege. First, it is far from clear what the case actually decided, as Tapper showed in (1972) 35 MLR 83. Secondly, it did not really address itself to the scope of legal professional privilege but concentrated on confidentiality which, as I have shown, is irrelevant to the evidential issue. Consequently that decision should not have prevented the Court of Appeal from considering the real question in the appeal: Does the rationale of the doctrine of legal professional privilege require that the contents of a document be immune from use in evidence when it has come to be known outside the lawyer–client relationship?

The privilege exists due to a combination of two reasons: first, to obtain justice in the courts the citizen needs legal advice and, secondly, he would be deterred from seeking such advice if the could not rest assured that whatever passes between himself and his lawyer will remain immune from the compulsory process of disclosure in evidence. Whether this rationale justifies a rule whereby privileged communications are excludable from evidence even when they have escaped the confines of the client–lawyer relationship is doubtful. It may be said that it is not really necessary to have such a rule in order to encourage the professional confidentiality.

Whatever decision the courts arrive at, however, they must make up their minds and not leave us in the litigious and expensive limbo created by our twin cases. Whether it is decided that the documents continue to be immune or, on the contrary, that they are admissible, there should be no need for injunctions. Moreover, if it is decided that immunity is lost once a document has been mistakenly revealed by the party's solicitor, it would be illogical, as Hoffmann J explained in *Re Briamore Manufacturing Ltd* [1986] 3 All ER 132, to hold that only a copy would be admissible but not the original. In such circumstances the privilege will have been lost for all purposes and the original should become admissible by compulsory process in the ordinary way.

Public interest immunity

Before 1968, to secure immunity from disclosure in evidence of a document a minister of the Crown had only to sign a certificate that the evidence in question belonged to a class which it was in the public interest to keep secret. Alternatively, the minister could sign a document to say that the contents of the document in question was such as to demand secrecy in the public interest. Since the minister did not need to justify his statement, claims were usually made for entire classes rather than individual documents. The invocation of Crown privilege had reached such extensive and unjustified proportions that the House of Lords in *Conway v Rimmer* [1968] 1 All ER 874 introduced a new principle for dealing with claims on public interest grounds (for a discussion of this development see *Crime, Proof and Punishment, Essays in Memory of Sir Rupert Cross*, ed C F H Tapper (1981) p 248). The new principle stated, first, that immunity could not be claimed by the state as a matter of right or of privilege but had to be sought from the court. Secondly, in deciding whether to accede to a request for immunity (whether from an organ of the state or anyone else) the court had to balance, on the one hand, the public interest in the documents remaining immune from production against, on the other hand, the general interests of the administration of justice and the specific interests of the party seeking disclosure.

The demands of the balancing exercise are considerable. On the one side of the equation the court has to place the public interest. This interest may be either in immunity for an entire class of information or in immunity for a specific document, regardless of class. A class interest arises in cases such as police informers, where the public interest lies in protecting all informers so as to promote law enforcement. In these situations the specific information sought may also happen to be sensitive in itself, but need not be so. In the class of police informers individual identities are of course also secret. By contrast, social welfare documents may not be individually of a sensitive nature but could be considered for immunity as a class, as in the case of *Gaskin v Liverpool City Council* [1980] 1 WLR 1549.

Either way, a claim for immunity has to be balanced against the general interest in the administration of justice (ie in the courts being seen to decide on all the evidence) and the interests of the individual litigant seeking disclosure to enforce his rights. It is an inescapable corollary of the balancing process that there cannot be an a priori answer to the question whether certain documents are immune from production; until the balancing exercise has been gone through one cannot tell. Disclosure of the same kind of evidence may be ordered in certain situations but not in others. This point is illustrated by *R v Rankine* [1986] 2 All ER 566. The issue in that case was whether policemen, testifying to having observed the accused selling drugs, were obliged to reveal the location of the secret observation post from which they watched the accused. The Court of Appeal held that there was a very weighty public interest in non-disclosure because disclosure might deter citizens from facilitating the police with observation posts. This consideration justified the withholding of the information. But the court emphasised that if the disclosure had been necessary in order to avoid miscarriage of justice, the court would not have hesitated in ordering it. It follows, therefore, that there is no such thing as immunity for ever.

Over the years the lack of attention paid to this aspect of *Conway v Rimmer* has caused a lot trouble and *Peach v Commissioner of Police of the Metropolis* [1986] 2 All ER 129 is a case in point. The administratix of the estate of Blair Peach, who was killed during a demonstration, sued the police on the grounds that the deceased was killed by a policeman. The police disclosed the existence of relevant documents, such as statements of witnesses, but claimed public interest immunity. They argued that the materials in question were produced for the purpose of an inquiry by the Police Complaints Board under s 49 of the Police Act 1964 and that documents falling into this class are immune from production according to *Neilson v Laugharne* [1981] 1 All ER 829. This argument is at odds with *Conway v Rimmer* for it was the essence of that decision that immunity is not a matter of a priori rule but of ad hoc balancing process. It is difficult to believe that in the *Neilson* case the Court of Appeal sought to modify the basis of public interest immunity, nor could it have done so in the face of a clear House of Lords authority. Sir Neil Lawson, whose decision was the subject of the appeal in the *Peach* case, was entirely right to decide that while he was bound by *Neilson v Laugharne* to hold that there was a public interest in protecting the confidentiality of documents produced for s 49 inquiries, he was not relieved of the need to balance this interest against the countervailing interests that presented themselves in the case before him.

To hold that the *Neilson* case created a class immunity would have very odd consequences. It would follow that if a court decides that the public interest is on the whole in favour of disclosure of a particular piece of evidence, future courts remain free to engage in the balancing exercise. But if a court decides that the public interest lies in the witholding of a certain piece of evidence, this decision creates a class immunity and the hands of future courts are tied forever and again. In holding that the decision in the *Neilson* case left no room for a balancing exercise in respect of documents created for a s 49 inquiry, the Court of Appeal in *Peach* must have been unaware of full implications of *Conway v Rimmer*. This oversight forced the court to engage in complicated analysis of whether the documents in question were really brought about for the purpose of a s 49 inquiry. Difficult questions had to be considered: When is an allegation against the police a 'complaint' for the purpose of s 49? Is it enough that the police believed that there had been a 'complaint' when in fact there is not one? Is it enough that the police believe that they are conducting a s 49 inquiry? What conditions have to be fulfilled for there to be a s 49 inquiry? These are difficult questions of a rather technical nature and of no bearing whatever on the substance of the issue in the case: Does the public interest demand the suppression of relevant evidence?

Another misconception, which emerged only incidentally, concerns waiver of immunity. Fox LJ remarked that it was accepted by the parties that the Police Commissioner could not waive public interest immunity. In one sense it is true. Since the Crown no longer has a privilege (ie a claim of right), there is nothing for it to waive. But it is not the case that the Commissioner's agreement to disclosure is immaterial. In every case the court must decide whether the public interest requires non-disclosure. The Commissioner's view that the public interest will not be harmed by disclosure will be as important a consideration to be placed in the balance, as would the Commissioner's view that the public interest demands secrecy (see my note in (1983) 99 LQR 14).

In other respects, however, the present case strengthens the *Conway v Rimmer* philosophy. Having decided that the documents were brought about only partly for a s 49 inquiry but predominantly for the general investigation of the deceased's death, the Court of Appeal felt free of the supposed shackles of *Neilson v Laugharne*. The court balanced the competing interests and decided that the claim for disclosure must win. Purchas LJ explained ([1986] 2 All ER at 144):

> 'Bearing in mind that after a period of some six years the fair trial of a civil action in which the evidence is given orally, based on recollection, the conduct of that trial would be seriously inhibited if contemporary statements were not available for the purpose either of refreshing the memory of the makers of those statements or for cross-examining them were they to testify to facts not supported by the contents of those statements.'

This is the correct approach and it should be applied in relation to every single claim. The fact that on a previous occasion a court decided that the balance was in favour of non-disclosure may provide valuable guidance but it should not alter the need for considering the competing interests afresh.

Note

Extradition

I M YEATS, BCL, MA
Barrister, Lecturer in Law, Queen Mary College, University of London

The government of the Federal Republic of Germany sought the surrender of Alan Rees to stand trial in Germany for his alleged involvement in the kidnapping of a German national in Bolivia. The fugitive advanced a number of arguments before the House of Lords (*Rees v Secretary of State for the Home Department* [1986] 2 All ER 321), of which the most interesting concerned the admissibility in the committal proceedings of evidence taken in Bolivia. Section 14 of the Extradition Act 1870 provides: 'Depositions or statements on oath, taken in a foreign state, ... may ... be received in evidence in proceedings under this Act.'

Did 'in a foreign state' mean 'any foreign state' or the 'foreign state seeking extradition'? There was no clear authority. Evidence taken in a third state was treated as admissible in *R v Governor of Brixton Prison, ex p Thompson* [1911] 2 KB 82, although there had been no argument on the point. On the other hand its inadmissibility was effectively conceded in *R v Governor of Pentonville Prison, ex p Singh* [1981] 3 All ER 23 and may have been implied in dicta of Lord Diplock in *Dowse v Government of Sweden* [1983] 2 All ER 123 at 126–7, [1983] 2 AC 464 at 470.

The House of Lords had been faced with a similar verbal uncertainty in *Tzu-Tsai Cheng v Governor of Pentonville Prison* [1973] 2 All ER 204, [1973] AC 931 and decided by a majority and after considering a variety of principles of statutory construction that the words 'offence of a political character' were impliedly limited to 'offence of a political character quoad the requesting state'. In *Rees* the House unanimously and with a similar variety of supporting principles held that the corresponding verbal limitation was not to be implied.

The statute on its face is not confined to evidence taken in the requesting state; by contrast other provisions in the 1870 Act do clearly refer to the requesting state where that limitation is intended (ss 11 and 17). Section 1 of the short-lived Act of 1886 expressly limited the power to: 'any Foreign State with which Her Majesty may have entered into, or may hereafter enter into, any Treaty for the Extradition of fugitive Offenders or Persons accused of Crimes.'

From this it was deduced that Parliament had consciously widened the concession in 1870. These considerations outweighed the resulting anomaly that evidence taken in a foreign state but not that taken in any part of Her Majesty's possessions would be admissible, since s 14 could not on any construction apply to the latter.

Wider considerations of parliamentary purpose tended to the same conclusion. The evidence taken in a third state might not be evidence tending to prove the identity of the fugitive or the commission of the offence, but might also, for instance, be evidence supporting an argument that the offence was of a political character, so that the wider construction might sometimes favour the fugitive. Although Parliament had provided (s 2) that an arrangement with a foreign state cannot be made until the Government has satisfied itself of the standards of justice in that country, there need be no such anxiety about standards of justice in the country in which the evidence was taken, since it is tendered only for the purposes of committal and the ultimate trial will take place according to the judicial system of the state seeking extradition. The House also held, in line with other decisions preventing the magistrate, where possible, from having to determine questions of foreign law (eg, *Government of Denmark v Nielsen* [1984] 2 All ER 81, [1984] AC 606) that he was concerned only with whether the evidence justified committal and not with whether it might in due course under German law be admissible at the trial. (In a very different context the Divisional Court in *R v Governor of Pentonville Prison, ex p Goets* [1986] 2 All ER 630 distinguished between the admissibility before the magistrate of photographs obviously from police files tendered to prove identity and the eventual admissibility of such photographs at the trial.)

The fugitive relied also on art XI of the Federal Republic of Germany (Extradition) Order 1960 (SI 1960/1375) which requires the State applied to to admit sworn depositions etc 'taken in the other State'. It was an identical article in the treaty with Norway that led to the concession in *ex p Singh* mentioned above without reference to s 14 of the Act. Section 2 of the 1870 Act provides that when the Act has been applied by Order in Council to a foreign State with which an arrangement has been concluded, the order may 'render the operation thereof subject to such conditions, exceptions and qualifications as may be deemed expedient'. The House of Lords declined to treat art XI as indirectly or by implication imposing a limitation on the application of s 14 to the arrangement with Germany.

The appellant also advanced a series of arguments relating to procedure. A requisition by a foreign state was held not to be spent once the Secretary of State had issued an order to the magistrate under s 7, so that the Secretary of State might validly issue a second order without there being a fresh requisition. The second order had been issued because there were difficulties as to the form and authentication of the original Bolivian evidence and Bolivian evidence free from such difficulties was received too late to be validly admitted in the proceedings arising out of the first order. The magistrate terminated those proceedings and ordered the discharge of Rees who was then immediately re-arrested on a warrant issued pursuant to the second order. This was further held not to be an abuse of process since it facilitated an earlier resolution of the issues in dispute by avoiding prolonged argument about the original Bolivian evidence. Further there was no infringement of art XII of the treaty with Germany. Although by that article the fugitive was entitled to be set at liberty within two months of his first remand in custody unless sufficient evidence to justify his extradition had by then been produced, this did not preclude his re-arrest under a fresh order any more than a decision by the magistrate to set at liberty prevented an ultimate decision to commit for extradition when fresh evidence had been presented.

The House also noted with apparent approval the agreement of counsel that the court but not the magistrate could in an appropriate case review the Secretary of State's discretion under s 7 of the Extradition Act.

Family Law

S M CRETNEY, DCL, FBA
Solicitor, Professor of Law, University of Bristol

The clean break–When does final mean final?

The decision of the House of Lords in *Livesey (formerly Jenkins) v Jenkins* [1985] 1 All ER 106 clarified the scope of the reciprocal duty which lies on a divorcing couple to disclose full details of financial and other matters relevant to the making of a consent order; but the case has many difficult implications the consequences of which will need some time to work out. The prophecy, made in All ER Rev 1985, p 177, that the reports would not have seen the last of the subject has now been fulfilled in the dramatic case of *Barder v Barder* [1986] 2 All ER 918, which once again highlights an underlying dilemma of the modern law.

It is a fundamental principle of all civilised legal systems that there should be an end to litigation, and this principle is particularly appropriate to matrimonial cases based on the 'clean break' intended to encourage divorced partners to put the past behind them and to begin a new life not overshadowed by the relationship which has broken down: *Minton v Minton* [1979] AC 593 at 608. Yet this principle must be made compatible with justice, 'so the law allows appeals; so the law, exceptionally, allows appeals out of time; so the law still more exceptionally, allows judgments to be attacked on the ground of fraud; so limitation periods may, exceptionally be extended': *The Ampthill Peerage Case* [1976] 2 All ER 411 at 418, per Lord Wilberforce. The question of where the line is to be drawn between, on the one hand, achieving finality and, on the other, avoiding manifest injustice is really the issue which it will ultimately fall to the House of Lords to decide.

In *Barder* on 20 February 1985 the divorce court had by consent made a clean break order in full and final settlement of all claims made or capable of being made by the wife: the husband was to transfer all his interest in the matrimonial home to the wife within 28 days. But on 25 March 1985 the wife killed her two children and committed suicide. She left a will leaving her property to her mother. The documents necessary to transfer the husband's interest had not been executed. Was he still obliged to comply with the court's order? Yes, said a majority of the Court of Appeal.

In matrimonial cases, many orders can be varied and variation is normally the appropriate procedure to give effect to changes of circumstance subsequent to the date of the original order. But it is the clear policy of the law that lump sum and property adjustment orders should not be capable of being varied; and indeed it would be wholly inconsistent with the clean break philosophy to allow such variation: 'each party takes a clean break order for better or for worse' ([1986] 2 All ER at 922). The demands of justice in relation to such orders are met by permitting appeals (within specified time limits or with leave) and actions to set the order aside on grounds the extent of which has not yet been finally settled—fraud, mistake and really significant non-disclosure certainly: *Robinson v Robinson* [1982] 2 All ER 699 at 700 as approved in *Livesey v Jenkins* per Lord Brandon of Oakbrook ([1985] 1 All ER at 117); undue influence unaccompanied by fraud or non-disclosure perhaps not: see *Tommey v Tommey* [1982] 3 All ER 385 but doubted by Lord Brandon in *Livesey v Jenkins* (above).

The underlying unity is that all the grounds on which setting aside has so far been accepted relate to matters existing at the time when the original order was made (see *Robinson* above). None of them existed—assuming that the wife then had no intention of ceasing to use the house as a family home—at the time when the order in *Barder* was made.

Are there, then, any circumstances in which an order can be set aside because of supervening events? Two possibilities have been canvassed in the case law. First, if there is a properly constituted appeal the court will take into account all the facts then known to it, and may in the result substitute a just order for what has become an unjust order: *Livesey v Jenkins* ([1985] 1 All ER at 119), explaining and justifying the decision in *Wells v Wells* [1980] CA Transcript 526. Secondly, it may be that if the order is still executory (as was the case in *Barder*) the court may refuse enforcement if in the circumstances then prevailing it would be inequitable to permit it: *Thwaite v Thwaite* [1981] 2 All ER 789 at 794 per Ormrod LJ.

The Court of Appeal in *Barder* spoke with three different voices. Dillon LJ would have given the husband leave to appeal out of time, and allowed the appeal on the ground that the whole basis on which the order had been made was falsified within little more than a month from the date of the order. Stephen Brown LJ attached importance to the fact that the court's jurisdiction in the suit ended on the wife's death. Even though the right to enforce the order against the husband survived for the benefit of her estate as a cause of action the mere fact that she had died did not make it inequitable to allow enforcement. Woolf LJ placed greater emphasis on the fact that the only way in which the order could be attacked was by granting the husband leave to appeal out of time, and such leave should only be granted in very special and exceptional circumstances. The stark dilemma has thus (for the time being) been settled in favour of the public interest in ending litigation; but this result has been achieved only at some cost in terms of justice to the husband. It is, of course, now well settled that the effect of a consent order derives from the order of the court rather than from the agreement between the parties: *de Lasala v de Lasala* [1979] 2 All ER 1146; but there may be those who would think contractual analogies (and particularly, perhaps, that of frustration) better capable of promoting justice in this area with little risk of opening the floodgates to endless questioning of concluded matters.

A clean break on variation?

The modern practice (so Balcombe J put it in *Harman v Glencross* [1986] 1 All ER 545 at 557) is to favour the so-called clean break 'wherever possible'; and the complex but clear provisions inserted into the Matrimonial Causes Act 1973 [s 25A] by the Matrimonial and Family Proceedings Act 1984 impose duties and confer on the court the powers which are necessary to give effect to this preference where in all the circumstances it would be appropriate to do so.

The rules governing variation of an existing periodical payments order have traditionally been governed by a code distinct from that which governs the making of the original order, and it is still the case that the court has no power to make a capital provision order on an application to vary a periodical payments order, and indeed it has effectively no power to vary capital provision orders: Matrimonial Causes Act 1973, s 31(5). But the court is now directed in variation proceedings, not only to give first consideration to children of the family, but also to consider whether in all the circumstances and after having regard to any change in circumstances since the making of the original order it would be appropriate to terminate any periodical payments order after a period sufficient to enable the maintained spouse to adjust 'without undue hardship': Matrimonial Causes Act 1973, s 31(7).

No doubt the reason why it was thought necessary to preserve the prohibition on ordering a capital payment on a variation application was to give the husband reasonable security in planning his financial affairs after divorce: it is one thing to put the whole of the spouses' assets at the court's discretion at the time of the divorce, but quite another to leave them forever subject to the possibility of further exercise of the court's extensive adjustive powers. Yet the lack of a power to order capital provision on a variation application makes it much less likely that the court will then be able to apply the clean break philosophy; for in the absence of such a power how can the wife be given adequate compensation for her income loss?

In *S v S* [1986] 3 All ER 566 the ex-wife of an immensely wealthy pop-star spent what she needed regardless of her means; she professed an ignorance of, and (as the judge found) took as little interest as possible in, the details of household budgeting. The husband tried to help by arranging for accountants to control and monitor her expenditure; but she found that control irksome, feeling that as the divorced spouse of so rich a man she ought to be wholly relieved of financial anxiety. She became increasingly resentful at what she considered to be the husband's meanness, and applied for periodical payments of £23,000 per annum (which had been a part of a complex divorce settlement) to be increased.

For his part, the husband sought to be freed of any further liability to make periodical payments on his paying the wife a lump sum of £120,000 (which would give her a total capital of some £420,000); but the wife was not prepared to accept what she regarded as a compulsory commutation of her right to periodical payments. The question was accordingly whether the court had jurisdiction to terminate the wife's periodical payments in exchange for the husband's payment of a capital sum. Waite J held that it would be consistent with the policy of the law to give the legislation a broad construction; and that the court did have such jurisdiction provided that it was satisfied that the result would be consistent with the statutory requirements relating to the welfare of children, and that it would enable the wife to adjust without undue hardship to the ending of her income payments.

Waite J held that to end the wife's periodical payments would be for the child's benefit since it would remove the sole remaining source of serious dispute between her parents; but that the appropriate figure for him to pay would be £400,000 (rather than the £120,000 he had offered). If the husband did not agree to this, the periodical payments would be increased to £70,000 per annum. The important point of law is that the court in effect has power in variation proceedings to impose a clean break solution on an unwilling wife although it has no power to impose such a solution on an unwilling husband.

Great expectations?

The court's powers on divorce extend to virtually all the spouses' economic worth with only limited exceptions—notably the right to future benefits under a pension scheme. In practice, of course, pension expectations are often a very significant proportion of the family's property, to such an extent that the woman's loss of entitlement to an index-linked widow's pension has been held prima facie to constitute grave financial hardship such as will justify the court in refusing a decree founded on the five-year separation 'fact': *Le Marchant v Le Marchant* [1977] 3 All ER 610 at 612. The courts have therefore tried to bring assets of this kind into account, and have used three main techniques.

First, if one party has a contingent or vested interest in property (albeit the interest is of uncertain value) the court may order that he or his personal representatives should pay to the other the whole or a specified fraction of the property when it falls into possession: see, for example, *Milne v Milne* (1981) 2 FLR 286, CA (half of capital sum receivable on retirement in ten years time or earlier death under supermarket manager's pension scheme to be transferred to wife if surviving). Secondly, the court may take the pension expectation into account as one of the 'financial resources which each of the parties ... has or is likely to have in the forseeable future' (Matrimonial Causes Act 1973, s 25(2)(a)): see *Richardson v Richardson* (1978) 9 Fam Law 86, CA (57 year-old civil servant entitled to capital sum on retirement at 60; wife's order for immediate lump sum, which could be paid out of husband's existing free capital, increased to take into account). Thirdly, the court may adjourn the application until such time as the sum in question becomes payable.

All these techniques were discussed by Wood J in *Roberts v Roberts* [1986] 2 All ER 483, where the wife of a warrant officer sought an order giving her a share of the terminal grant for which the husband would be eligible in six years' time. Wood J held, first, that an order that the husband pay a proportion of the grant if and when it was paid constituted a charge on the grant and was accordingly void under the express provisions of the Army Act 1955, s 203—provisions which appear to have been overlooked in *Priest v Priest* (1980) 1 FLR 189, where such an order was made. Secondly, it would be wrong to make an order for an immediate lump sum: the husband (unlike the husband in *Robinson*, above) had no free capital; and in any case it would be impossible to calculate an appropriate figure since the size of the terminal grant could not be realistically assessed. Finally, it is the policy of the law (see *Minton v Minton* [1979] 1 All ER 79) that parties should know where they stand as soon as possible. Hence, adjournments should not be granted to the uncertain future, but only for periods not exceeding some four to five years: see *Michael v Michael* [1986] 2 FLR 389, CA, and contrast *Davies v Davies* [1986] 1 FLR 497, CA.

The family versus the creditors

Family law has traditionally been concerned with the conflict of interest between the parties to a marriage; but increasingly the courts have had to resolve conflicts between the interests of the family or one of its members on the one hand and the interests of the creditors of another member of the family on the other. Many of these conflicts have arisen in the context of an assessment of the nature and extent of the beneficial interests of the family in the family home (see p 173, below); but *Harman v Glencross* [1986] 1 All ER 545 was a case in which the Court of Appeal had to strike a fair balance in the context of the court's jurisdiction to make orders for ancillary relief on divorce.

The wife filed a divorce petition. After she had been granted a decree nisi, one of the husband's creditors obtained judgment and a charging order absolute against the husband's interest in the matrimonial home. The court ordered that the charging order be subject to any order for ancillary relief; and in the ancillary relief proceedings ordered the husband to transfer his interest in the home to the wife. The creditor's appeal was dismissed.

It is impossible briefly to summarise all the issues which arise, but the following are amongst the more important. First, if a charging order has been made before the divorce petition has been filed, the wife will be left to her rights to resist sale on an application under the Law of Property Act 1925, s 30; but if the charging order is made after the petition the application to make it absolute should be heard by the divorce court at the same time as the ancillary relief application. Secondly, in such a case, the divorce court must seek to balance the interests of the wife and the creditor. This necessarily involves consideration of whether the interests of wife and creditor could be reconciled. (It might, for example, be right to make the order absolute if the enforcement of the order would still leave the wife with sufficient equity to rehouse herself and her children; but in other cases a *Mesher* order, preserving the wife's right of occupation for some time whilst still leaving an interest upon which the creditor's claim could bite, would be appropriate.) The balancing exercise involves consideration of all the circumstances: thus, the court should consider whether the creditor could effectively deprive the wife of her interest by making the husband bankrupt—in which case any transfer of property order would remain vulnerable to an application to set it aside as a settlement made at an undervalue: Matrimonial Causes Act 1973, s 39 and Insolvency Act 1986, s 341(1) and Sch 14, preserving the substance of Bankruptcy Act 1914, s 42(1). Moreover, the creditor should give evidence of how he would be affected by a failure to order sale. Finally, the balancing exercise is a matter for judicial discretion; and accordingly—perhaps a crucial point in this case—a decision by the judge of first instance as to how that discretion should be exercised will not normally be upset on appeal.

It remains to be seen how the court's balancing of the competing family and financial interests in charging order cases would now be influenced by analogy with the new guidelines contained in the 1986 insolvency legislation, which attempt to give some guidance on how the balance is to be struck on applications for the sale of a bankrupt's matrimonial home— broadly speaking requiring the court (and it is expressly provided that this means the bankruptcy court and not the divorce court) to assume that the interests of a bankrupt's creditors outweigh all other considerations (such as the needs of children) once a year has elapsed since the bankruptcy: Insolvency Act 1986, s 336(4), (5).

Divorce and the Revenue

Divorce is no doubt a disasterous affair for many of the 300,000 or more adults and 150,000 or more young children who are involved each year; but for some the financial consequences at least have been mitigated by various well-known tax-efficient devices. In particular, the divorced may do what it is the consistent policy of the law to disallow to the married: they may effectively split the income of the family unit to minimise the overall burden of taxation. In particular, a court order (albeit consensual) whereby one party is directed to make periodical payments to his infant and unmarried child effectively transfers the title to that income to the child for tax purposes. Since a child, however young, has the same entitlement to a personal relief (£2,335 per annum in 1985/6) as any other unmarried person the effect is that an affluent father can transfer that sum to the child at a net cost to himself of only £934—ie £2,335 less tax at the father's assumed marginal rate of 60 per cent.

It had become accepted that an order for payments to be made direct to the child's school in settlement of the fees would be effective in this way provided that the order used a formula approved by the Revenue: *Practice Direction (Minor: payments of school fees)* [1983] 2 All ER 679; and indeed the formula could effectively provide for automatic upward adjustment as the fees increased. A feature of the arrangement was that the child was required to enter into a contract with the school, which (it was assumed) was perfectly valid as a contract for the child's benefit; and it may be that such a provision was deemed essential in order to meet the objection that the payment was made to relieve the paying father of his own contractual obligation rather than a payment on the child's behalf.

Such an arrangement may have seemed artificial (and note the judgment of Lord Denning MR in *Mills v IRC* [1973] Ch 225 at 240), but it is worth pointing out that it achieved no more than could equally be done by an order for payments to the child direct. Under such an order, the payments would normally be paid to the custodial parent in her capacity as the child's legal guardian; so that one might say the direct payment scheme was only really necessary if the payer lacked confidence that the custodial parent would indeed meet the fees out of the child's income.

In any event, the scheme passed without any overt judicial objection until the decision of the Court of Appeal in *Sherdley v Sherdley* [1986] 2 All ER 202. The novelty of that case was that the application was by a father who himself had custody and care and control for an order against himself; and Wood J refused to make the order apparently following a policy adopted for some years by the judges of the Family Division. The father's appeal to the Court of Appeal failed for reasons more fully discussed in the article on

Taxation, p 293, below, but on appeal to the House of Lords, the traditional view that such orders can be made, was accepted (1987) Times 9 April.

In the context of family law it perhaps suffices to say that there seems to be little doubt that a spouse may properly seek an order against himself provided that he has good cause to do so: see *Peacock v Peacock* [1984] 1 All ER 1069 as applied in in *Simister v Simister* [1987] 1 All ER 233. The real question, therefore, becomes one of social policy—that is to say, whether it is right for tax relief to be available in these circumstances. The House of Lords some years ago decisively checked the burgeoning of a welfare-benefit planning approach: *Supplementary Benefits Commission v Jull* [1981] AC 1025; and there must be some concern that a consequence of *Sherdley* will be pressure for legislation to remove what have come to be accepted as legitimate methods of mitigating the financial consequences of divorce.

Property–The family outside marriage

It has been clear since the early 1970s that neither the common law nor equity have any special property regime for married couples: see *Pettitt v Pettitt* [1970] AC 777, HL, (particularly per Lord Upjohn at 813); *Gissing v Gissing* [1971] AC 886, HL. Paradoxically, this has made it easier for the law to develop rules governing the family property rights of the, apparently growing, number of persons who are not married to one another but have nonetheless lived in a relationship exhibiting many of the traditional incidents of marriage. This is because what is in issue is not the existence or non-existence of the status of marriage but rather the nature of the relationship between a couple and the inference as to their intentions which the court can derive therefrom.

In theory, therefore, there is no special law of family property; and the relevant case law is accordingly more fully dealt with in the chapter of this Review dealing with Land Law and Trusts, pp 186 et seq, below. But it is right to record here the main impact of some important decisions for family law.

The result of the year's cases from the point of view of those (usually women) whose claim is for some fair and equitable return for years of hard unremitting and unpaid participation in caring for a family—see for example in *Burns v Burns* [1984] Ch 317 where a woman had given up her job and, for close on 20 years, been an unmarried housewife with two children—has been from this perspective broadly favourable, but there have also been a number of adverse decisions.

The major step forward is represented by the Court of Appeal's decision in *Grant v Edwards* [1986] 2 All ER 426, where the parties and their children lived together for some years in a house bought in the man's name. The woman was nevertheless held to be entitled to a half share when the relationship broke down. The significance of the case is the emphasis given to the principle that the primary question is one of intention; and the fact that the court was prepared to find an intention to share from all the circumstances—in particular, the man's statement that his partner's name was not to go onto the title deeds because to do so might cause difficulties in her then pending divorce. Contributions towards the purchase of the house or the running of the household are thus relevant, at this stage, to the extent that they assist in ascertaining the parties' intentions; but the true significance of the making of contributions is as a means to the end of showing the parties' intentions, rather than (as is sometimes assumed) an end in itself.

However, the second aspect of *Grant v Edwards* perhaps marks one of the steps backward in the year under review. If proof of a common intention were of itself sufficient to justify the court in finding a beneficial interest, a legal owner who (as in *Layton v Martini* [1986] FLR 227) offered his partner a life of financial security would almost inevitably find a trust imposed on his legal interest for the partner's benefit. But to accept as sufficient the fact that the parties intended to share would infringe the principle that equity will not assist a volunteer; and the court in *Grant v Edwards* therefore took pains to emphasise that a person claiming a beneficial interest under the doctrines of implied resulting or constructive trust must also show that she acted on the intention to her detriment. This aspect of the matter reinforces the importance of contributions in money or money's worth in establishing a successful claim; such contributions may not only be cogent evidence of intention, but also serve to establish the necessary detrimental reliance on that intention.

In cases where the dispute is between the former partners, determination of their beneficial interests (if any) will normally be the end of the matter—and the Court of Appeal in *Goodman v Gallant* [1986] 1 All ER 311 has emphasised that if the conveyance or transfer purports to declare the nature and extent of the beneficial interests a court will not normally allow that declaration to be questioned. But the dispute may well involve a third party who has dealt with one of the partners: is he to be bound by an informally created beneficial interest? The (much criticised) decision of the Court of Appeal in *City of London Building Society v Flegg* [1986] 1 All ER 989 suggests that where the beneficiary is in actual occupation of registered land at the relevant time the fact that a dealing is effected by two or more trustee proprietors will not cause that interest to be overreached and converted into money.

In cases where the land is unregistered, the question whether the beneficiary's interest will bind a purchaser or mortgagee will usually depend solely on the question of notice. Thus, in *Kingsnorth Trust Ltd v Tizard* [1986] 2 All ER 54 the husband had told lenders that he was single, and the lenders' surveyor had seen no evidence of occupation of the house by the wife or any other female. But Judge John Finlay QC (sitting as a High Court judge) held that the lenders were bound by the wife's interest since a prearranged inspection on a Sunday afternoon did not constitute 'such . . . inspections . . . as ought reasonably to have been made.' (LPA 1925, s 199).

If lenders know of the existence of some occupier other than the borrower they will normally require that person to sign a waiver of the interest; but such a waiver will not be effective if (for example) the lender or his agent misrepresents its scope or effect—for example: 'it's just to be a short term bridging loan for the business', whereas in fact it was a long term loan for a new business: *Kingsnorth Trust Ltd v Bell* [1986] 1 All ER 423, CA. These cases often in practice turn on whether a husband borrower has been constituted the lender's agent: in *Bell* it was held that he had been; but in *Coldunell Ltd v Gallon* [1986] 1 All ER 429 he was not. In practice, lenders would do well to ensure that the occupier has independent advice.

Finally, it is important to remember that it is not only a property right in the sense in which that term was classically defined by Lord Wilberforce—'definable, identifiable by third parties, capable in its nature of assumption by third parties, and [with] some degree of permanence or stability': *National Provincial Bank Ltd v Ainsworth* [1965] AC 1175 at 1248—which may be important in disputes about family assets. *Maharaj v Chand* [1986] 3 All ER 107, PC, appears at first sight to involve only a somewhat exotic point about the interpretation of the Fiji Native Land Trust Act; but in reality it turns on the important point that the unmarried partner who has no legal or equitable interest in the family home may nevertheless be able to resist possession proceedings on the basis of a promissory estoppel founded on the defendant's representation that the building in question would be a permanent home for the defendant and her children.

Occupation rights

It may be that in England a housewife, whether married or unmarried, will rarely need to rely on promissory estoppel because of the existence of elaborate statutory protection which includes the Matrimonial Homes Act 1983 and the Domestic Violence and Matrimonial Proceedings Act 1976. However, as Lord Scarman pointed out in the leading case of *Richards v Richards* [1983] 2 All ER 807 at 818, HL, the legislation although sometimes described as a code is in fact a 'hotpotch of enactments of limited scope passed into law to meet specific situations or to strengthen the powers of specified courts.' Lord Scarman added that 'the sooner the range, scope, and effect of these powers are rationalized into a coherent and comprehensive body of statute law, the better'; but regrettably no such rationalisation has taken place. The fact that there are unsatisfactory gaps in the law, at least insofar as it affects the unmarried, is well demonstrated by the Court of Appeal's decision in *Ainsbury v Millington* [1986] 1 All ER 73.

Susan Ainsbury was a 17 year old who had lived with her boyfriend Derek and their baby daughter Samantha in a jointly tenanted council house. Whilst Derek was serving a prison sentence Susan married, and her husband moved into the house. Derek was released, and returned home. There was 'something of a row'; and Susan, Samantha, and Mr Ainsbury went to live in overcrowded and unsatisfactory conditions with Susan's mother. Susan applied under the Guardianship of Minors Acts 1971 to 1973 for an order requiring Derek to vacate the house, and permitting her and Samantha to return, together with her husband.

The Court of Appeal upheld the judge's decision that he had no power to make an ouster order under the Guardianship of Minors Act 1971; and, since one co-owner has no right to exclude the other, Susan had no legal right in support of which an ouster injunction could be granted under what is often called the inherent jurisdiction of the court (in fact now contained in the Supreme Court Act 1981, s 37).

The case—apart from raising interesting questions about the right of concurrent owners inter se in modern conditions—exposes a gap in the protection available to the unmarried housewife: Susan could not apply for an order under the Domestic Violence and Matrimonial Proceedings Act 1976 because, at the time of the incidents which gave rise to the application (and indeed for some considerable time before) she was not living with Derek 'in the same household as husband and wife': s 1(2). As Dillon LJ said (at 77) it is unsatisfactory 'that there should be various statutory codes covering applications for ouster orders and somewhat of a limbo position where the statutory codes are not applicable.'

Yet there are obvious difficulties in filling the gap: first, Susan was in effect applying for a property adjustment order in respect of the family home. But the court has no statutory power to make such an order; and the issue of the extent to which the law should equate marriage with extra-marital cohabitation, which inevitably arouses strong feelings, has never been comprehensively considered in this country. In any case, the decision might be seen as one better taken by the housing authority as part of its public law duties, but it is not at all clear, under the law as it now stands, that they would be able to obtain possession against Derek: see Housing Act 1985, s 84 and Sch 2.

Relevance of children's interests

Would the result have been any different if the court had had jurisdiction to make an order—for example, because at the relevant time Susan and Derek were living together—and was therefore in a position to exercise its discretion to grant an injunction? It is clear that Samantha's welfare would still not have been the paramount consideration: the principle enunciated by the House of Lords in *Richards* (above) must equally apply to the unmarried: cf *Spindlow v Spindlow* [1979] 1 All ER 169; and this cannot be avoided by issuing proceedings under the guardianship legislation. But in *Essex County Council v T* (1986) Times, 15 March the court held that it was perfectly proper first of all to deal with issues relating to the child's legal custody, necessarily applying the paramountcy principle; and then, in the light of that decision about the child's needs, to decide an application for ouster. The result may be that the interests of the child will in many cases remain dominant.

Children–adoption and custodianship

In deciding whether to dispense with parental agreement to adoption on the ground that agreement is being unreasonably witheld the court attaches considerable importance to the child's welfare. This is because, as Lord Hailsham put in *Re W (An Infant)* [1971] AC 682:

> '... the fact that a reasonable parent does pay regard to the welfare of his child must enter into the question of reasonableness as a relevant factor. It is relevant in all cases if and to the extent that a reasonable parent would take it into account. It is decisive in those cases where a reasonable parent must so regard it.'

In practice, this approach has perhaps led the courts to give greater weight than in the past to welfare as the crucial factor in dispensation cases; but it has been said that short of amending legislation there must be a limit to this shift: *Re H; Re W (Adoption: Parental Agreement)* (1982) 4 FLR 612 at 624, per Purchas LJ.

The fact that there is still a crucial distinction between adoption and other cases dealing with the custody of a child (in which the child's welfare is the paramount consideration) was firmly underlined by the Court of Appeal in *Re V (a minor) (adoption: consent)* [1986] 1 All ER 752. A mother had left her 21-month-old daughter with foster-parents, and at one time she had agreed that the foster-parents could adopt the child. However, she changed her mind; and by the time of the hearing (which took place when the child had been with the foster-parents for nearly three years) she believed that in the long term the right thing would be for the child to return to live with her and her two younger children. The President of the Family Division dispensed with the mother's agreement, but—apparently believing that access in the future would be in the child's interests—gave the mother liberty to apply to the court for directions for access to the child.

The Court of Appeal held that the President had been wrong. First, the purpose of making an adoption order is to transfer irrevocably the parental rights and duties from the birth parents to the adoptive parents; and to impose conditions giving the birth parent a continuing interest in the child is irreconcilable with that objective, and destructive of the security which the institution of adoption is intended to promote: see also (to the same effect) *Re GR (Adoption: Access)* [1985] FLR 643 and *Re C (A Minor) (Adoption Order: Condition)* [1986] 1 FLR 643. Secondly, it was not, in all the circumstances, unreasonable for the mother to wish to reunite her family, and her withholding of agreement to the permanent severance of all her legal links with her daughter could thus not properly be described as unreasonable. To some extent the case may underline the validity of the distinction drawn in *Re H; Re W* (above) between the situation in which the child has originally been placed for adoption (when agreeement will more readily be held to have been unreasonably witheld) and cases in which the initial placement was for fostering.

The adoption agency's role

It is possible to argue that the thrust of recent developments in the law is to shift the emphasis in child care decision making from social work agencies towards the courts; but the policy of the adoption legislation is clearly based on a close collaboration. In particular, the formal role of adoption agencies has been greatly extended by the Adoption Agencies Regulations 1983: such agencies must now comply with an elaborate code of procedure in an attempt to ensure that the best possible placement decisions are taken and the interests of all those concerned properly considered and protected. In *Re T (a minor) (adoption: parental consent)* [1986] 1 All ER 817 the agency did not comply with the prescribed formalities: in particular, they failed to notify the mother of decisions taken by the Adoption Panel, and they failed to notify her of the fact that her child had been formally placed for adoption. Perhaps fortunately the court held that these requirements were directory only; and the adoption order was upheld since there had been substantial compliance with the regulations and the mother had not in fact been prejudiced by the irregularities which had occurred.

When does a parent lose the right to retrieve his child?

In that respect, then, the result was as it would have been under the old law which attached less formal importance to the role of the adoption agency.

But in another respect the decision marks a significant change in the law. Although the birth parent has the right to withdraw his agreement to adoption at any time before the making of the order, the fact that such agreement has been given operates to deprive the parent of his legal right to remove the child from the prospective adopters: Adoption Act 1958, s 34(1), the wording of which was changed by Children Act 1975, s 29. It has been assumed by many, including the author of a DHSS guidance leaflet, that only a written agreement would have this drastic consequence; but the Court of Appeal found insufficient reason in the statutory language construed against the background of a new procedure for the giving of parental consent to limit the word 'agreement' in this way. The mother had therefore by orally agreeing that the child should be adopted lost her right to require the return of the child.

Custodianship or adoption?

The year under review was the first complete year in which the custodianship provisions of the Children Act 1975 were in force. Although none of the cases so far reported addresses directly the difficult issues involved in deciding if custodianship is to be preferred to adoption— whether in those circumstances (for example, of adoption applications by relatives) in which the legislation itself seems specifically to indicate some preference for custodianship or in the exercise of the court's general discretion (Children Act 1975, s 37(2)) to make a custodianship order if more appropriate. But *Re V (a minor) (adoption: consent)* (above) does give some indication of the circumstances in which custodianship may have a role. There the child had been with foster-parents for three years; but the court decided, for reasons already given, that the mother was not unreasonable in witholding her agreement to the adoption which she had at one stage favoured. The court therefore ordered that the child remain a ward in the care and control of the foster-parents. However, Oliver LJ indicated that if custodianship had then been available it might have been the right solution. Not only would custodianship provide a greater formality and a greater degree of permanence than the care and control order, but the 'more imposing title' might help to 'supply a psychological gap'.

A father's rights

The question of whether the child's birth parents should continue to have access is often in practice decisive of the issue whether the child should be adopted or not. If there is no access, the prospects of being able to re-establish a true family link in the future diminishes sharply; and the court is likely to regard such prospects as being of crucial importance in deciding whether or not parental agreement can be dispensed with: see *Re H; Re W (Adoption: Parental Agreement)* (1982) 4 FLR 614; *Re V (a minor) (adoption: consent)* [1986] 1 All ER 817. It would be difficult to exaggerate the gravity of this issue; but if the child's father is not married to the mother his position is also bedevilled by procedural complexities.

In *R v Oxford JJ, ex p D* [1986] 3 All ER 129 the father's relationship with the mother broke down, and their daughter was taken into care. The father's visits to the child were, after a time, stopped because they upset the child, but he was allowed to keep in touch by sending her letters and cards. However, the local authority ultimately decided to apply to free the child for adoption. The father then made a complaint to the magistrates seeking custody against the mother and access against both the mother and local authority. The question was whether the magistrates had any jurisdiction to hear the access application.

The question was of vital importance to the father because it was clear that there was no legal procedure (apart from making representations in any adoption or freeing proceedings) in which he could question a decision which would almost certainly effectively deprive him of any entitlement to see his daughter again: he could not seek access in wardship (*A v Liverpool City Council* [1981] 2 All ER 385); and he was not a parent for the purposes of either the Children and Young Person's Act 1969 or the Child Care Act 1980 (including the access order provisions specifically introduced into it in 1983). Waite J held that the magistrates did have jurisdiction to hear the application: the language of the Guardianship of Minors Act 1971 was sufficiently wide to cover an access application by the natural father notwithstanding the fact that the child was in local authority care. The judge was however careful to emphasise that the decision on jurisdiction did not indicate any view on the merits of the application.

There will no doubt be a strong feeling that a parent should not be put at risk of losing all contact with his child without having the opportunity of the issues being investigated by a court: yet it does seem strange that legislation which is clearly primarily directed to private law disputes between parents should be invoked to resolve what is essentially a public law dispute about the exercise of a local authority's statutory discretion. The oddity is all the greater since the wide-ranging access order provisions now incorporated in the 1980 Act are specifically directed to that public law issue, and Parliament chose in terms to exclude the natural father from the category of those entitled to invoke that procedure. It is to be hoped that the father's position will be clarified in the Family Law Reform Bill introduced by the Government at the end of the year to give effect to the Law Commission's proposals in relation to illegitimacy.

Proof of parentage

The Law Commission's proposals will involve the abolition of the affiliation procedure with its distinctive requirement (Affiliation Proceedings Act 1957, s 4) that no order can be made in a case where evidence is given by the mother unless that evidence is corroborated in some material particular by other evidence to the court's satisfaction. The actual decision in *Turner v Blunden* [1986] 2 All ER 75, to the effect that blood test evidence was nevertheless capable of constituting such corroboration although it did not by itself establish paternity but merely pointed to it, may thus be of only historical interest. But of course parentage will still remain a matter of great significance under the reformed law. A child whose parents are not married to each other will be able to seek support under the guardianship legislation in the same way as any other child but he will only succeed if parentage is established. This may often prove difficult; but the facts of *Taylor v Blunden* give some indication of the potential of blood test evidence in resolving disputes. The tests in that case indicated that if the defendant was not the child's father, only two other men in a random sample of 1,000 could be; and such material will clearly often be of value as an important factor in the totality of evidence on which a reliable finding can be based. Moreover, other scientific evidence ('genetic finger printing') may be even more valuable in establishing the truth.

Land Law and Trusts

P J CLARKE, BCL, MA
Barrister, Fellow of Jesus College, Oxford

This year, these two chapters have been amalgamated. Although there is a range of cases on individual points in both land law and trusts, a considerable number of this year's more important decisions concern both areas of law, involving trusts for sale—or bare trusts—affecting property held—or occupied—jointly.

1 The wife who occupies unregistered land

Since *Williams & Glyn's Bank Ltd v Boland* [1980] 2 All ER 408 it has been clear that a contributing co-occupier of registered land will have an overriding interest under the Land Registration Act 1925, s 70(1)(g) as a 'person in actual occupation'. No question of notice or reasonableness is involved: the fact of occupation plus a property right is what matters, unless the proviso to the paragraph is invoked. *Williams & Glyn's Bank Ltd v Boland*, however, gave no clue to the position in unregistered land, but it was generally assumed that a contributing co-occupier in unregistered land would have an equitable interest protected by the equitable doctrine of notice, now contained in the Law of Property Act 1925, s 199(1). *Kingsnorth Trust Ltd v Tizard* [1986] 2 All ER 54 (MP Thompson [1986] Conv 283) confirms this view, but in a way which places a higher burden on an investigating purchaser than might have been expected and which could be regarded as attempting to bring the position in unregistered land close to that in registered land, rather than applying the traditional equitable doctrine of notice in a novel situation. A husband (H) was sole legal owner of a house, in which his wife (W) had a half-share in equity. The marriage broke down, and W left the house to live nearby. There were twins, a boy and a girl, who, at the material time, were almost 15. H looked after the children, but if he was away from the house for the night (which happened not infrequently), W slept in the house in a spare room. Also, W came to the house on most days to provide the children with breakfast and to prepare them for school. In the evening she would give the children and herself an evening meal, leaving before H arrived home. H wished to raise money by mortgaging the house, and made application to Kingsnorth for finance, stating, untruthfully, that he was single. Kingsnorth, through a broker, arranged for a surveyor to inspect the property: it was agreed that any information the surveyor acquired or ought to have acquired would be imputed to Kingsnorth. The surveyor arranged with H to inspect the property on a Sunday afternoon, H having arranged with W that she would have the children for the day. The surveyor found evidence of occupation by H and by the twins, and thought that the spare room (where W in fact slept) was used for storage. H told the surveyor that he was separated and that his wife was living nearby. The surveyor, in evidence, indicated that he was suspicious, and was looking for evidence of female occupation though that of a girl-friend, rather than a wife. However, 'he drew the line . . . at opening cupboards and drawers' ([1986] 2 All ER at 61).

First, was W in occupation? In *Caunce v Caunce* [1969] 1 All ER 722 and *Bird v Syme-Thompson* [1978] 3 All ER 1027 it was held that the presence of an owner/mortgagor obviated the need to inquire of other co-occupiers whose interests appeared compatible with his; these decisions could not stand with *Williams & Glyn's Bank Ltd v Boland* [1980] 2 All ER 408. However, in the cases cited above, the wife's occupation was continuous: in *Kingsnorth Trust Ltd v Tizard* it was not. 'Physical presence' did not mean 'continuous and uninterrupted' presence; the fact that W was in the house for part of most days, that 'her life and activities were based on her presence' ([1986] 2 All ER at 59), and that she occasionally slept there, was sufficient. The case thus indicates a benevolent attitude towards 'occupation': moreover, if the element of regularity is important, it may well be that a person may be in occupation of more than one property. Thus, the wife who lives with her husband in their London flat during the week, and their Oxfordshire cottage at weekends would surely be in occupation of both. If one assumes, however, that the wife goes to London on Monday morning with her husband, and returns on Wednesday afternoon ostensibly to prepare the cottage for the weekend, but instead spends the period from each Wednesday evening to each Friday lunchtime with her lover in Berkshire, preparing joint meals, looking after his house, and sleeping with him, why is she not in occupation there as well? Her life and activities are surely based on her presence in all three houses. It may be argued that it will be unlikely that she will have 'contributed' to the Berkshire cottage sufficiently for her to acquire a property right, but that does not by itself refute or weaken the argument against occupation as such.

Second, the judge held that as the surveyor was looking for evidence of female occupation, this implied that he approached the inspection on the basis that H was not married. Once it emerged that H *was* married, the surveyor had a duty to convey the information to his principal, who, in turn, would then be on notice that further investigation was required. Moreover, even if the judge was wrong on this point, he considered that the reference in the report to the existence of 'Son and Daughter' was, by itself, sufficient to put the principal (the mortgagee) on notice that a wife existed.

The judge then concluded that 'the [further] inquiries which in these circumstances ought reasonably to have been made by the plaintiffs would . . . have been such as to have appraised them of the fact that [W] claimed a beneficial interest in the property' ([1986] 2 All ER at 62). Moreover, H had arranged matters so that the surveyor would not find W in the house, but the plaintiffs had constructive notice of sufficient facts to prevent them from claiming free of her interest. The judge declined to state what would amount to a reasonable inspection: it depended on all the circumstances ([1986] 2 All ER at 64).

There are two difficulties with this aspect of the judge's judgment. First, the concentration on the wife's occupation as a means of protecting rights rather than on the rights themselves may obscure the true issue. If W had property rights, these would be relevant to the value of the security that H could offer, and so the *rights* of W rather than her *occupation per se* would be of concern to a mortgagee. If W had contributed to the purchase price of property, but had left to reside permanently elsewhere she would manifestly not be in occupation, but would still have rights. In other words, a mortgagee is not—or should not be—concerned with whether a wife is in occupation, but rather with whether she has rights. A wife in occupation and a wife out of occupation may both have rights, and although occupation may provide notice of these rights, so might other circumstances. Concentration on occupation if the land is registered is understandable, because of the existence of the Land Registration Act 1925, s 70(1)(g), but is not, as such, relevant in the context of unregistered land.

Second, the approach contrasts, to some extent at least, with that adopted by the Court of Appeal in *Bristol and West Building Society v Henning* [1985] 2 All ER 606; All ER Rev 1985, pp 198–9. In that case, a co-occupier had notice of a prospective mortgagee; the onus of declaring her rights to that mortgagee was on the occupier—'a subtle reversal of the orthodox doctrine of notice'—(Welstead, [1985] CLJ at 355). In *Kingsnorth Trust Ltd v Tizard*, the wife did not have notice of the prospective mortgagee, and the approach of the court is considerably to strengthen the orthodox doctrine of notice, in that the onus, and a high onus at that, was on the mortgagee.

Third, and by way of contrast, the judge's analysis of 'reasonableness' may place too high a burden on a purchaser or mortgagee. Clearly, the vendor should be asked if anyone else occupies the house. It is probable that he should be asked if he is married (though Lord Wilberforce in *Williams and Glyn's Bank Ltd v Boland* [1980] 2 All ER 408 considered that the law should apply equally to all contributing co-occupiers, but cf *Northern Bank Ltd v Henry* [1981] IR 1 a case in which the Irish Court of Appeal made some extremely sensible observations about the whole problem of notice and the respective positions of a purchaser and an interest-holder). Any person whose existence is thus revealed should be asked—presumably if he can reasonably be found—what his or her rights are. Physical inspection of the property is necessary (cf *Hunt v Luck* [1902] 1 Ch 428). *Kingsnorth Trust Ltd v Tizard* is important in that it indicates that the timing and circumstances of the inquiries may matter. As indicated above, the judge did not articulate the details of what would be reasonable: but it is clear that a purchaser or mortgagee may have to be more astute to detect fraud than might have previously been expected. The vendor who says that he is away at work all week and watching his football team play away on Saturday, and who prefers a visit from a surveyor on a Sunday is equated with the scheming husband who packs his family off for the day to arrange a sale or mortgage in their absence. Moreover, even if the inquiries are made at a proper time, the question still remains as to what is reasonable. A purchaser or mortgagee who finds evidence of female occupation in a male-owned house may well not know whether this indicates the presence of a wife, a live-in mistress, a teenage daughter, a sister, a housekeeper or a guest and if the vendor answers inaccurately—but apparently reasonably—will the occupier's rights be lost? Surely a purchaser or mortgagee cannot be expected to ask questions of a guest—or someone who he is told is such? The law is in danger both of encouraging offensive conduct and yet of leaving rights undiscovered, and it is perturbing that such a common problem has still not received satisfactory judicial or statutory-resolution.

One final footnote to the case: if an agent makes inquiries which a court later holds are not sufficiently stringent, it would presumably follow that he can be sued in negligence—for surely reasonableness should not mean different things in different branches of the law?

2 The wife and the husband's creditors

The 1984 Review (All ER Rev 1984, pp 184-7) contained a discussion of three cases, *First National Securities v Hegerty* [1984] 1 All ER 139, affirmed [1984] 3 All ER 641, *Thames Guaranty v Campbell* [1984] 1 All ER 144, affirmed [1984] 2 All ER 585, and *Harman v Glencross* [1984] 2 All ER 577. These involved consideration of the increasingly common situation where the husband's judgment creditor and the wife are competing for the husband's interest in the matrimonial home. In *First National Securities Ltd v Hegerty*, the husband's judgment creditor was given protection, whereas in *Thames Guaranty v Campbell* and in *Harman v Glencross* he was not. In *Hegerty*, Stephenson LJ clearly regarded the order in *Harman v Glencross* as incorrect ([1984] 3 All ER at 648). The appeal in *Harman v Glencross* has now been heard ([1986] 1 All ER 545 (J Warburton [1986] Conv 218)), and the decision of Ewbank J upheld.

Mrs Glencross had filed a petition for divorce and sought, inter alia, a property adjustment order in relation to the matrimonial home. Mr Harman, a business creditor of Mr Glencross, obtained judgment against him for over £9,000, and obtained an order under the Charging Orders Act 1979, against his beneficial interest on the matrimonial home. The registrar (upheld by Ewbank J) ordered Mr Glencross' interest to be transferred to the wife, thus leaving the creditor with no property to which the charging order could attach. The Court of Appeal upheld the decision, and Balcombe LJ, in particular, took the opportunity to lay down some general guidelines which will be of considerable use in the future.

There is one preliminary point needing consideration. The Charging Orders Act 1979, s 3(5) speaks of 'a person interested in any property to which the order relates'. The property charged was, strictly speaking, not the matrimonial home, but the husband's share in it; Balcombe LJ, however, took the broad rather than the literal view and held that the order related to the house as well. Fox LJ did not accept this but reached the same result by a different route: 'interested in' was not a technical term of property law, and was wider than 'interest'.

The main point of principle, however, was the relative importance to be attached to the interests of the wife and to those of the husband's judgment creditors. Counsel for the judgment creditor attached great importance to statements in *First National Securities v Hegerty* by Stephenson LJ (with whose judgment O'Connor LJ concurred) which indicated that the court should not use its discretion under the Matrimonial Causes Act 1973 to override the rights of a judgment creditor, and that the rights of a creditor and the wife might best be considered in an application for an order under the Law of Property Act 1925, s 30 (see [1984] 3 All ER at 648). The Court of Appeal in *Harman v Glencross* viewed these passaged as obiter dicta. However, just because the court was not prepared automatically to subordinate the interests of the wife to those of a judgment creditor, so it would not automatically adopt the converse position. As Balcombe LJ said ([1986] 1 All ER at 554): 'Not all judgment creditors are faceless corporations ... I see no reason why, in a proper case, the judgment creditor should not be entitled to put in evidence of the hardship he would suffer if he were denied a charging order or if its enforcement were unduly postponed.'

Balcombe LJ then considered how the competing interests could be balanced: first, did the discretion given to the court under the Law of Property Act 1925, s 30 give the wife sufficient protection? The cases including, for example, *Re Lowrie* [1981] 3 All ER 353 seemed to prefer the creditors' interests (though cf *Re Holliday* [1980] 3 All ER 385, which may be regarded as a decision on its own facts, in which the husband may have deliberately—and tactically—made himself bankrupt). In any event, the Insolvency Act 1986, s 336 now clarifies the position. Second, the court might, in the exercise of its family jurisdiction, make a *Mesher v Mesher* ([1980] 1 All ER 126) order postponing sale: such orders, however, restricted to one property, were becoming less popular, both because they tied the wife to a house which may be inappropriate, and deferred the creditor's interest for a considerable period. (The variant of a *Mesher* order whereby the husband's interest would be transferred to another property would be useless as the wife would not be protected against the judgment creditor on sale even though she would be protected against the husband). Third, an order could be made transferring the husband's interest in the property to the wife. This, of course, would defeat the judgment creditors entirely, and might, in any event, fall foul of the Bankruptcy Act 1914, s 42(1) as a voluntary settlement which might be avoided by the trustee in bankruptcy (now see the Insolvency Act 1986, s 339).

He then considered how, in general, the courts should deal with similar problems in the future. First, where a judgment creditor has obtained a charging order nisi and has applied to have it made absolute before the wife has *started* (writer's italics) divorce proceedings, there is no reason for refusing the order. The wife is left to her rights under the Law of Property Act 1925, s 30 to protect her right of occupation. Second, if the wife petitions for divorce before the judgment creditor obtains a charging order nisi, the court should consider whether it is proper to make the charging order absolute even before the wife's application for ancillary relief is heard. Such an order will be made (as in *Llewellin v Llewellin* [1985] CA Bound Transcript 640) where, putting it simply, there is sufficient money to satisfy everybody. Third, (as will be the normal case), if the circumstances are insufficiently clear to make an immediate charging order absolute, the whole issue should be referred to the Family Division, which would consider all the circumstances of the case. It would be rare indeed that an outright transfer of the husband's share to the wife would be ordered, as this would deprive the judgment creditor's charging order of any effect. Fourth, if a charging order absolute has been made, it would require very special circumstances for the court to set aside the order: such a circumstance might be that the wife had not been heard on the original application.

Once again, the courts have been faced with the fundamentally insoluble problem of which of two parties shall suffer for the actions of a third.

Clearly, the wife cannot always triumph over the husband or vice versa, but the law as stated by the Court of Appeal seems now to encompass two different—and to some extent irreconcileable—propositions. First, if and when a case is considered by the Family Division, all the circumstances are to be taken into account: in other words, there is a wide, if not an infinite, discretion, to do what is just in the circumstances. Second, in deciding whether a case should be considered in this way at all, regard must be had to the times when the charging order was obtained and when the divorce petition was issued. In other words, the wife who thinks her husband has large debts and may be unable to meet them, must file a divorce petition first as a preventive measure: something that seems contrary to any sensible view of the matrimonial legislation. Moreover, a husband who sees a divorce coming and who wishes to make his wife's position as unpleasant as possible, will run up large debts, default in their payment, not oppose judgment and rely on the creditors moving swiftly under the Charging Orders Act 1979 to overtrump any potential claim by the wife to his (the husband's) property. *Qui prior est tempore, potior est jure* is a maxim well known to property lawyers; it now seems to be one with which family lawyers should become acquainted. Much, of course, will depend on how rigidly the guidelines offered by Balcombe LJ are followed. In this context, the upholding of Ewbank J's decision to confirm the validity of the charging order absolute, even though the divorce petition had been filed, indicates that the word 'guidelines' means what it says; it does not mean 'rules'.

Kingsnorth Trust Ltd v Bell [1986] 1 All ER 423 is an unusual variation of the increasingly common problem of a dispute between a creditor who has obtained a mortgage from the husband of 'his' property in which his wife has an interest, and the wife herself. The creditor asked the husband to obtain the wife's signature to a document, which he obtained by means of fraudulent misrepresentation. The Court of Appeal held that the husband was the creditor's agent, and therefore the creditor, as principal, was bound, by the fraudulent misrepresentation. The case is further considered in the article on Contract, p 88 above.

3 Trustees for sale and the rights of occupiers

The decision in *Williams & Glyn's Bank Ltd v Boland* [1980] 2 All ER 408 caused a great upset to conveyancers and others. Six years later, the decision in *City of London Building Society v Flegg* [1986] 1 All ER 989 (102 LQR 344, D J Hayton [1986] Conv 131 and 136 NLJ 208, C Harpum [1986] CLJ 202, R J Smith 49 MLR 519) has administered a shock that may be even greater: whereas *Boland* could be reconciled with principle and statute, *Flegg* (as the case will hereafter be called) cannot be so simply regarded. Perhaps the best thing about *Flegg* is that an appeal to the House of Lords is pending.

It will be remembered that in *Boland* a sole registered proprietor had mortgaged his house to a bank and then defaulted. The bank failed to secure vacant possession because the mortgagor's wife had an interest by way of a tenancy in common under an undisclosed statutory trust for sale which was protected by the Land Registaration Act 1925, s 70(1)(g). In *Flegg*, the facts were vitally different: *joint* proprietors held the property. The prophetically named 'Bleak House' was bought by Mr & Mrs Flegg, and their daughter and son in law, Mr & Mrs Maxwell-Brown, as a house in which they all intended to live. All contributed to the price, but notwithstanding their solicitor's advice, the Fleggs were not registered as co-proprietors, the names of the Maxwell-Browns alone appearing on the register. The conveyance to them contained an express trust for sale, regarding them (and them alone) as beneficial joint tenants, and also gave them full powers to mortgage the property. Indeed, a mortgage with the Hastings and Thanet Building Society was raised, with the full authorisation of both the Maxwell-Browns and the Fleggs. Later, the Maxwell-Browns moved out, leaving the Fleggs in sole occupation, and then further mortgaged the property to the City of London Building Society, who did not know about the Fleggs, and who, on default by the Maxwell-Browns, sought to obtain possession of the property. The Fleggs argued that they were entitled as equitable tenants in common to remain in the house and they were protected by the Land Registration Act 1925, s 70(1)(g).

The argument was accepted by Dillon LJ (with whom Kerr LJ and Sir George Waller concurred). Two reasons were given: first, it was irrelevant that the disposition was made by two registered proprietors; *Boland* applied just as much where there were two registered proprietors as where there was one. Second, if, as in *Flegg*, a tenant in common was in occupation, the Law of Property Act 1925, s 14 protected his rights against the overreaching provisions of the Act.

The first ground is surprising. With one exception (C Sydenham [1980] Conv 427), academic opinion supported the view that *Boland* only applied to a situation where there was one registered proprietor; an express concession to that effect had been made by counsel in the Court of Appeal (see [1979] Ch 312 at 341) and both leading counsel in the House of Lords made statements which seemed to assume this (see [1980] AC 487 at 488 at 501). The underlying assumption seems to have been that where there are two registered proprietors, and a restriction on the register, that the interests of beneficiaries are overreached.

Various points arise. First, whatever the position under the Land Registration Act, why was the mortgage to the City of London Building Society not valid? The conveyance granted express powers of mortgaging 'Bleak House' to the Maxwell-Browns; moreover, if there were not express restrictions of the mortgaging powers, the assumption would be that these powers were unfettered.

Second, the Court of Appeal seem to have found difficult in accepting the possibility of an overriding interest subsisting against some persons but not against others: this was 'impossible to fit in with the scheme of the Land Registration Act 1925' ([1986] 1 All ER at 995). This must surely be wrong: first, the date of the creation of an overriding interest will determine who it binds. Further, if any contributing occupier under a trust for sale with a single trustee consents to a mortgage, that mortgagee will take subject to the co-occupier's interest, whereas a later mortgagee who has not obtained the co-occupiers' consent to his mortgage will surely be subordinated to the co-occupier's interest; this follows from *Boland* itself. RJ Smith argues to the contrary (see 49 MLR at 523) but his argument, that a single owner holding as trustee for sale has no inherent power to mortgage so as to affect beneficiaries under a resulting trust seems contrary to the decision in *Boland* itself, even though the point does not appear to have been raised.

Third, the decision appears to make a nonsense of the doctrine of overreaching. Since *National Provincial Bank Ltd v Ainsworth* [1965] 2 All ER 472 extirpated the heresy of the deserted wife's equity being a property right and thus binding third parties, it has been clear that 'rights' under the Land Registration Act 1925, s 70(1)(g) means 'property rights', defined according to general principle. Therefore, if the rights in question are not property rights, they cannot be within the paragraph. Counsel's arguments to this end were dismissed as being 'inconsistent with the whole scheme of the Act' ([1986] 1 All ER at 995c). As Harpum points out, however, two of the main principles behind the scheme are the mirror principle and the curtain principle: the register reflects the title, and trusts are kept off the register and thus off the purchasers title. *Flegg* ignores both.

However, there may be some arguments in favour of Dillon LJ's position. In *Hodgson v Marks* [1970] 2 All ER 684, the Court of Appeal emphasised that if there were rights in existence held by an occupier, these rights would not be defeated by a proprietor apparently armed with the power to dispose of the property. Moreover, *Blacklocks v JB Developments (Godalming) Ltd* [1981] 3 All ER 392 can be read as providing an occupier, who has a right to rectify a deed so as to give him a proprietary interest, with an overriding interest. These points may not fully counter the objections above, but they may be of some interest in a wider context.

Dillon LJ's second reasoning depends on the Law of Property Act 1925, s 14. (In parenthesis, one may ask why, in a case on registered land, reference is being made to the Law of Property Act without cross-reference to the Land Registration Act):

> 'This Part of this Act [ie ss 1–39] shall not prejudicially affect the interest of any person in possession or in actual occupation of land to which he may be entitled in right of such possession or occupation.'

These are clearly wide words, relating as they do, to the whole of the provisons affecting trusts for sale; and yet they have been little litigated. It now seems clear that s 14 was originally intended to give occupiers with registrable interests under the Land Charges machinery an alternative means of protection. This was achieved in the Law of Property Act 1922 but the sections became misplaced in the 1925 consolidation (see 41 Conv (NS) 419). It may, moreover, have been a working out of the doctrine of *Hunt v Luck* [1902] 1 Ch 428. However, the section is clearly worded so as to 'overtrump' anything in the first part of the Law of Property Act 1925, including the overreaching provisions of s 2.

However, it should be noted that the doctrine of overreaching exists independently of statute. If, before 1925, there was a trust for sale, payment to two trustees would protect a purchaser unless there were something in the trust deed (for example a requirement of consultation or of consent) which put him on notice. If the purchaser knew of a breach of trust, matters would, of course, be different. Nothing in the 1925 Act seems to remove this pre-1926 doctrine; indeed, certain parts of it (eg Law of Property Act 1925 ss 27, 28(1)) seem positively to reinforce it.

Secondly, if s 14 means what Dillon LJ says it means, certain parts of the Law of Property Act are otiose; s 26(1), for instance, provides that if the consent of more than two persons is required to the execution of a trust for sale, the consent of any two is sufficient for the purchaser's purposes. 'If *Flegg* is correct, the consent of *all* occupying beneficiaries is needed. Further, s 26(3) provides that in a statutory trust for sale, the trustees must consult the beneficiaries, and give effect to their wishes (or, if there is a dispute, to the wishes of the majority by value, provided this is consistent with the general interest of the trust), but the purchaser need not be concerned to see that this is done. Again, if *Flegg* is correct, the trustees must consult all beneficiaries under both express and statutory trusts for sale and must respect the refusal of consent to sell by any single occupying beneficiary, no matter how small his interest, who wishes to remain; most important of all, the purchaser is affected if consent is not obtained.

Third, the rights of a tenant in common under a trust for sale are assumed to be as stated in the judgment in the Court of Appeal of Denning LJ in *Bull v Bull* [1955] 1 QB 234. There, the Court of Appeal thought that trustees for sale under a statutory trust could not evict an occupying beneficiary with a minority interest under the trust, without obtaining a court order under the Law of Property Act 1925, s 30. (Counsel seems to have conceded that express trusts for sale were similar here to statutory trusts: see [1955] 1 QB at 235.) This is contrary to the Law of Property Act, s 26(3); and Denning LJ's references to rights of possession before 1926 ignore the fact that legal tenancies in common can no longer exist. Moreover, Denning LJ was not concerned with the position of a third party; he was concerned with the rights of a beneficiary before sale. The trustees, however, could not give vacant possession. Finally, reference to the Law of Property Act 1925, s 30 cannot advance the argument: the section gives the court a discretion to exercise existing rights, not to create new ones.

One wistful thought: it is clear that the draftsmen left a lacuna in the co-ownership provisions of the Law of Property Act so far as the case of a single trustee for sale holding on trust for tenants-in-common is concerned. References in *Bull v Bull* to the Settled Land Act 1925, s 36(4) do not convince; moreover, Stamp J in *Caunce v Caunce* [1969] 1 All ER 722 seems to have assumed that the equitable doctrine of notice applied in such situations, the doctrine of overreaching thus not operating. Lord Denning MR appears to have favoured the idea of a bare trust rather than a trust for sale in this situation, when giving judgment in the Court of Appeal in *Boland* see [1979] 2 All ER 697 at 704. Such an approach would support the result in *Flegg*, but is difficult to reconcile with the approach of the House of Lords in *Boland* itself.

It may also be noted that it was agreed on all sides that the Fleggs had an interest in the property. This was so notwithstanding that there was an express declaration of trust: normally such a declaration is conclusive, see *Goodman v Gallant* [1986] 1 All ER 311, p 190, below. One must assume that the court was prepared to rectify the deed (cf *Pink v Lawrence* (1978) 36 P & CR 98) and *Blacklocks v JB Developments (Godalming) Ltd* [1981] 3 All ER 392 provides authority that the right to rectify may give occupiers a protectible property right.

Having considered some of the technical points in *Flegg*, some comments of a more general nature may be made. First, the duties of purchasers are now even higher: they must, in registered land, find out who all the occupiers are who have property interests, and obtain their consents, even though their vendors appear to be trustees for sale with clearly ascertained beneficiaries. Even in unregistered land, the duties are still high: 'reasonableness' may protect the purchaser from the undiscoverable occupier, but *Kingsnorth Trust Ltd v Tizard* [1986] 2 All ER 54, see p 181 above, indicates that high standards of diligence will be expected. Indeed, a would-be purchaser's best prospects of success may now be to attempt to repudiate the contract if the facts are not fully disclosed by the trustees as would-be vendors: they should disclose the interests of beneficiaries in possession, obtain their consent, and disclose the nature of the interests, even though they may be hidden behind trusts. Conveyancing, in short, has become even more hazardous.

It must be conceded, however, that *Flegg* is consistent with an ever-growing tendency, both in Parliament and the courts, to protect the rights of those presently in occupation of land. The Rent Acts, the Protection against Eviction Act, the Matrimonial Homes Act and the provisions of the Administration of Justice Acts protecting the mortgagor bear witness to Parliamentary concern. The growth of the deserted wife's equity (and its subsequent apotheosis in statute after the voices of infallibility in the House of Lords had held that it did not exist as a property right in *National Provincial Bank Ltd v Ainsworth* [1965] 2 All ER 472) was an early example of judicial creativity; similarly the 'purpose' doctrine, evolved in cases under the Law of Property Act 1925, s 30 such as *Bedson v Bedson* [1965] 3 All ER 307, the use of a constructive trust to protect the occupier in *Binions v Evans* [1972] 2 All ER 70, the assumption that a contractual licencee in occupation has a property right in *Midland Bank Ltd v Farmpride Hatcheries* (1980) 260 EG 493, and the use of equity to protect estoppel licences in cases such as *Pascoe v Turner* [1979] 2 All ER 945, all indicate a judicial willingness to allow apparently precarious rights to be protected. Even *Street v Mountford* [1985] 2 All ER 289 can be regarded in a similar light. Formalities have been subverted, and *Flegg* indicates that the subversion may now be reaching matters of principle. The result of the appeal to the House of Lords is eagerly awaited.

4 The sanctity of a declared trust

In *Cowcher v Cowcher* [1972] 1 All ER 943, Bagnall J emphasised that on a conveyance of property an express declaration of trust was advisable; this view was echoed by Griffiths LJ in *Bernard v Josephs* [1982] 3 All ER 162 (All ER Rev 1982, p 169). If, however, the declaration could be ignored, then the advice would be nugatory. *Goodman v Gallant* [1986] 1 All ER 311 (102 LQR 172, S Juss [1986] CLJ 205, JEM [1986] Conv 355) confirms that if there is a declaration of trust on the face of a conveyance, the courts will not normally be able to go behind it. The contrary view, based on Lord Denning MR's judgment in *Bedson v Bedson* [1965] 3 All ER 307 is now discredited. In *Goodman v Gallant*, Mrs Goodman and Mr Gallant purchased property as beneficial joint tenants. Mrs Goodman served notice to determine the equitable joint tenancy, and claimed three-quarters of the beneficial interest (the amount she would have received on a resulting trust basis). The Court of Appeal held that she was entitled to a half-share, this being the inevitable concomitant of severing an expressly declared equitable joint tenancy held by two people.

The decision is to be applauded on the simple ground that if the parties *expressly* declare their interests, the courts should not normally go behind the declaration. The courts had flirted with the contrary view in the 1960s, when it was thought that the Married Women's Property Act 1882, s 17 gave the courts power to vary property rights: see *Hine v Hine* [1962] 3 All ER 345, *Bedson v Bedson* [1965] 3 All ER 307. *Wilson v Wilson* [1963] 2 All ER 447, taking the contrary view, was upheld in *Pettit v Pettit* [1969] 2 All ER 385. The court's power to apply the doctrine of resulting trusts could only apply where there was no express trust (Law of Property Act, s 53) and would only be relevant where the statutory trusts had been imported under the Law of Property Act 1925, ss 34, 36.

It does not follow, however, that a plaintiff in the position of Mrs Goodman will be entirely without remedy. Buckley LJ stated in *Pink v Lawrence* (1977) 36 P & CR 98 at 101 that the document could be rescinded on the ground of fraud or mistake, or rectified so as to vary or delete the declaration of trust. Moreover, if rectification was available, an alternative and more direct relief might be available without actually going through the machinery of rectification. However, a high burden of proof is imposed on the claimant, and this may often make the remedy illusory: indeed, in *Goodman v Gallant* itself, Mrs Goodman did not believe she could successfully prove the mistake alleged ([1986] 1 All ER at 319b). A further possibility emerges from *Robinson v Robinson* (1976) 241 EG 153: if the purchasers have not executed the deed containing a declaration of trust, neither of them was estopped from going behind the declaration and adducing evidence as to circumstances which dictated how the beneficial interests should be determined. *Robinson v Robinson* was not considered in *Goodman v Gallant* and its status is not entirely clear. First, the purchasers would be relying on the deed for some purposes but not for others, which seems an odd stance for the court to accept. Second, whether purchasers execute a conveyance will depend on conveyancing matters unconnected with beneficial interests (though good conveyancing practice would always insist on trustees executing a document), and *Robinson v Robinson* gives a particular group of joint purchasers an apparent advantage. *Goodman v Gallant*, however, cannot be regarded as overruling *Robinson v Robinson* as the question 'when is there a declaration?' was not considered. Finally, if the solicitor, legal executive or licensed conveyancer who drafts the deed has either not taken proper instructions from his clients, or has not explained the significance of the deed to them, either of them may be able to sue him for negligence: cf *Walker v Hall* (1984) 5 FLR 126 at 129, per Dillon LJ. (This may be the 'alternative form of remedy' obliquely referred to in *Goodman v Gallant* [1986] 1 All ER at 320).

The Court of Appeal also took the opportunity to extirpate another possible heresy of Lord Denning. He had hinted in *Bedson v Bedson* and *Bernard v Josephs* that on severance of an equitable joint tenancy, an equitable tenancy in common in unequal shares could result. Such a result was impossible, because both of the nature of a joint tenancy, where the interest of each tenant is inevitably the same in extent, and of authority: *Leake v Bruzzi* [1974] 2 All ER 1196, *Pink v Lawrence* (1977) 36 P & CR 98. If parties wished, on severance, to have unequal shares, this could be spelt out by a trust in those terms; in the absence of such trust, the court could not interfere.

5 The informally created interest of the contributing cohabitant

Ever since the decisions of the House of Lords in *Pettitt v Pettitt* [1969] 2 All ER 385 and *Gissing v Gissing* [1970] 2 All ER 780 attempted to restrict the informal creation of rights in favour of wives and other co-occupiers, the courts have been faced by a range of claimants seeking the court's assistance to achieve what, in their eyes, is justice. The Denning Court of Appeal was generally sympathetic to such approaches: see eg *Cooke v Head* [1972] 2 All ER 38, *Eves v Eves* [1975] 3 All ER 768, and *Bernard v Josephs* [1982] 3 All ER 169, All ER Rev 1982, pp 169–73. However, *Burns v Burns* [1984] 1 All ER 244 (All ER Rev 1984, pp 167–69) seemed to return the law to the position as stated in *Pettitt* and *Gissing*. The most recent foray by the Court of Appeal in this area is *Grant v Edwards* [1986] 2 All ER 426 (DJ Hayton [1986] CLJ 394, J Warburton [1986] Conv 291). The judgments, particularly those of Mustill LJ and Sir Nicolas Browne-Wilkinson V-C, repay careful study, but the case may well engender uncertainty in an attempt to provide an equitable solution for every situation.

The facts were not unusual: Mr Edwards purchased a house in his name and that of his brother (who made no claim, and who played no part in the case); Mrs Grant lived with him, bore his children, and made substantial indirect contributions to the household expenses. Mr Edwards told Mrs Grant that her name would not be on the title because it might prejudice the matrimonial proceedings between herself and her husband. The house was partly destroyed by fire, and the insurance moneys not used for repair were placed into a joint account in the names of Mrs Grant and Mr Edwards. The relationship broke down, and Mrs Grant claimed a beneficial interest in the house: this claim was rejected by the trial judge, but the Court of Appeal held she was entitled to half the beneficial interest in the property. The reasoning was that, in the absence of direct contribution, Mrs Grant could establish a beneficial interest by establishing a constructive trust, which in turn depended on a common intention that she should have such an interest. This intention could be shown by direct evidence or by inference from actions, coupled with an acting to her detriment on the basis of the common intention, believing by so doing that she was acquiring an interest. On the facts, these requirements were fulfilled: first, the explanation by Mr Edwards as to why Mrs Grant's name was omitted was evidence of the intention; alternatively, the explanation stopped Mr Edwards from denying Mrs Grant's rights. Further, there was detriment because she had paid the financial contributions. Finally, the payment of the balance of the fire insurance moneys into a joint account, coupled with the other facts, was the best evidence of an intention to share the property or its proceeds.

Mustill LJ and Sir Nicolas Browne-Wilkinson V-C have taken the opportunity to lay down some useful general principles, and to summarise the law. Mustill LJ's general points may be summarised as follows, though the summary does not do justice to his language: (throughout A is the legal owner, and B is claiming an interest), (1) There is no law of family property, nor does the doing of work by B on A's property thereby confer a right on B. (2) The legal estate is in A; whether B has an interest depends on the general law of trusts. (3) Was there a bargain between A and B or a common intention at the time of acquisition? If yes, were there later acts by B that were detrimental and relied on the intention? This principle could also apply to acts after acquisition. 'The beneficial interests may change in the course of the relationship' [1986] 2 All ER at 435. (4) The event on acquisition may be (a) an express bargain, (b) an express but incomplete bargain, (c) an explicit promise by A, or (d) a common intention. (5) The court must decide whether the conduct is referable to the alleged bargain, promise or intention. (6) In (4a) above, it is a simple question whether the bargain has been complied with. (7) In (4b) and (4c) above, the position is similar. (8) In finding the terms of the arrangements in (b) and (d), the court must look at the true state of affairs; it must not impute an intention which did not exist. (9) The conduct of the parties may provide evidence of the bargain and/or intention or its precise terms. Great care is necessary here: examining later conduct to find an inference is different from examining it to find compliance with a bargain or intention proved in some other way.

Sir Nicolas Browne-Wilkinson V-C suggests that contributions made by the claimant may be relevant in four ways. First, as a means of showing an intention otherwise not able to be proved; second, as a corroboration of direct evidence; third, to show detriment in reliance on the common intention: fourth, to quantify the extent of the beneficial interest ([1986] 2 All ER at 437).

Both these statements of principle are helpful: there has been much loose talk about these matters in an attempt to do justice, and any clarification of the general issues is welcome. However, there are certain points that need emphasis and certain other matters that are still unclear.

First, the case *does* require proof of any intention: (a) the intention may be expressed (cf *Midland Bank plc v Dobson* [1986] 1 FLR 171); (b) it may be directly inferred from acts which make no sense unless the intention is present (eg the statements by Mr Edwards in the instant case and by the man in *Eves v Eves* that his mistress being under 21 (but over 18) could not hold the legal title); (c), and most problematically, it may be inferred from the acts of the parties. At least the concept of imputed (or imposed) intention is not regarded as relevant, though the line between inferred and imputed intention is easier to state than to draw.

Second, there is mention of 'bargain' and 'incomplete bargain'. It is presumed that the word 'bargain' was chosen rather than 'contract' to indicate a more flexible approach. Also, the requirement of intent to create legal relations may be difficult to prove. Moreover, an incomplete bargain is surely no bargain. To quote Mustill LJ's category (4b), the event happening on acquisition may be 'an express but incomplete bargain whereby the proprietor promises the claimant an interest in the property, on the basis that the claimant will do something in return. The parties do not themselves make explicit what the claimant is to do. The court therefore has to complete the bargain for them by means of implication'. Is this not imposing a bargain on the parties—something the court will normally refuse to do? A simple example shows this: if X agrees to sell Y ten tons of swedes in return for a promise by Y to do something, the contract would be void for uncertainty.

Third, notwithstanding the careful way in which the members of the Court of Appeal indicate that the evidence of contributions is relevant, their careful reasoning may lend a spurious air of certainty to what is often an incompletely planned and partially remembered situation. Further, the contribution and its circumstances may be intended by either party (if either intends anything at all) to have differing consequences.

Fourth, there is no consideration of the problems raised by formalities. Mustill LJ expressly notes that the beneficial interest may be created and may change without formality. Presumably the answer is that all the interests subsist under a constructive trust, and the provisions of the Law of Property Act 1925, s 53(2) provide a solution to all problems. Doubts were cast on this broad view in the context of resulting trusts in All ER Rev 1982, p 171; in particular, the changing of the size of the interest was considered to give rise to particular difficulties. The 'new model constructive trust' (cf *Lyus v Prowse Developments* [1982] 2 All ER 953, All ER Rev 1982, p 165) may overleap all these difficulties, but no formal justification is offered. Moreover, it is salutary to ask (as does Hayton [1986] CLJ at 397) why there was thought need for formality in situations such as this in the first place. Oral evidence—especially self-serving recollection—is often unsafe and the party who makes a good witness or the party who is perceived to have the merits on his or her side may easily be regarded as more important than what actually transpired. The complications inherent in the equitable doctrine of part performance provide a salutary warning to those who would use equity to subvert statutory formalities.

Fifth, detriment is said to be necessary. Although it is commonly to be found, a close reading of Lord Diplock's speech in *Gissing* [1976] AC 886 at 905 seems to indicate that the provision of detriment is an *example* of how an interest may be acquired, rather than a prerequisite for its acquisition. Certainly, cases such as *Eves v Eves* and *Burns v Burns* can be explained without the need for detriment. Moreover, *Greasley v Cooke* [1980] 3 All ER 710 cited by Sir Nicolas Browne-Wilkinson V-C (though in a different context) is a case on reliance, not detriment: see *Coombes v Smith* [1986] 1 WLR 808. In any event, it is difficult to see how the requirement imposes a burden on the claimant: if, as Nourse LJ indicates, incurring expenditure proves the detriment, the piece of evidence is satisfying two purposes: proof of the agreement and proof of detriment.

Sixth, Sir Nicolas Browne-Wilkinson V-C mentions the possibility of drawing an analogy with proprietary estoppel. There are clearly similarities, and it must be admitted that both the law of proprietary estoppel and the law of constrictive trusts are in a state of considerable uncertainty. Certainly, if the view of Oliver J in *Taylor Fashions Ltd v Liverpool Victoria Friendly Society* [1981] 1 All ER 897 at 918 that estoppel is based on 'unconscionability' were followed, there would be virtually infinite judicial discretion. This point, however, seems to have been raised neither in *Grant v Edwards* nor in *Coombes v Smith*.

Seventh, one important point was deliberately left open. After *Gissing v Gissing* it was unclear whether, in the absence of common intention, bargain, or direct contributions, a claimant could acquire an interest by indirect contributions, for example, to general household expenses. The Court of Appeal noted the problem but did not answer it.

The decision in *Grant v Edwards* was concerned with a dispute between a proprietor and a claimant as to rights over property. A purchaser, of course, is equally interested in such matters, both in registered land (*William & Glyns Bank Ltd v Boland* [1980] 2 All ER 408) and in unregistered land (*Kingsnorth Trust Ltd v Tizard* [1986] 2 All ER 53 (see p 181 above). *City of London Building Society v Flegg* [1986] 1 All ER 989 (see p 186 above) has further indicated the importance of what now appears to be a universal need to make inquiries. Hayton ([1986] CLJ at 398) makes an important point that the timing of the right may be crucial: what happens where the first detrimental act occurs between contract and completion? The Australian solution, adopted in *Muschinski v Dodds* (1986) 62 ALR 429, is to impose the constructive trust with effect from the date of the court order, thus protecting the claimant against the proprietor, but not against the third party.

Finally, *Grant v Edwards* was cited without comment, but with apparent approval, in *Maharaj v Chaud* [1986] 3 All ER 107 at 112.

6 Tenancies in common and business leases

Where property is held jointly, the legal estate being held by joint tenants, and there is no declaration of trust, how will equity require the beneficial interest to be held? There are clearly three situations where equity will presume that holders of the beneficial interests are tenants in common: purchasers who contributed unequally co-mortgagees, and partners. In *Malayan Credit Ltd v Jack Chia-MPH* [1986] 1 All ER 711 (JEM [1986] Conv 355) the Privy Council appear to have created a new category, though it will be argued that they have merely rediscovered a doctrine of respectable antiquity. The parties were granted a five-year lease of a floor of an office block in Singapore, the lease being silent as to how the property was beneficially owned. Before the lease had been granted, the parties had agreed that one would occupy 62% of the property, and the other the remainder. Liability for the rent and service charges was to be divided proportionately; these expenses and all others relating to the property were invoiced separately and proportionately to the parties, and paid by each of them. Disputes followed, and the defendant argued the property was held equally. Not surprisingly, the Privy Council rejected this argument. There were three possibilities: that the parties held in equity as joint tenants, that they held as tenants in common in unequal shares, or that they held as tenants in common in unequal shares. The Privy Council could see no difference between the acquisition for a lease by payment of a premium and the acquisition of a lease for a rack-rent: this seems entirely in accord with principle and with common sense. However their Lordships gave an example which may give rise to difficulty: after stating that where premises are held by legal joint tenants for their several business purposes, it would be improbable that they would intend to hold as joint tenants in equity (again, a proposition in accord with principle and common sense), Lord Brightman continues ([1986] 1 All ER at 714):

> 'Suppose that an accountant and an architect take a lease of premises containing four rooms, that the accountant uses two rooms, and that the architect uses two rooms. It is scarcely to be supposed that they intend that if, for example, the architect dies first . . . the beneficial interest is to survive to the architect.'

One is tempted to ask whether this is a true situation of co-ownership at all: do not the two professional men each separately occupy part of the premises?

As far as the issue of principle was concerned, it does appear that there was authority—not cited to the Privy Council—which can be regarded as supporting the view that leases taken jointly for business purposes should be held in equity on a tenancy in common. Thus, in *Lyster v Dolland* (1792) 1 Ves Jun 431, William and Thomas Lyster were joint tenants, and had mortgaged the premises. Lord Thurlow LC said:

> 'As to the moiety of William, they were joint lessees, but brought each of their quota of money upon the subject, and by the rules of equity in that case there is no survivorship . . . I allude to the case of a joint lease taken or a fee purchased to carry on a joint trade: the object being to carry on the trade, the Court thought, it would convert the joint property for the purposes of trade and making a common advantage.'

Similar statements are to be found in *Norway v Rowe* (1812) 19 Ves 143 at 157, referring to the decision of Lord Rosslyn in *Senhouse v Christian* (1795) 19 Beav 356n, and in *Jackson v Jackson* (1804) 7 Ves 591 at 596, both decisions of Lord Eldon LC. Certainly Sugden, *The Law of Vendors and Purchasers* (14th edn, 1862) pp 697-8 adopts a very general view:

> ' . . . dealings by the parties with the estate as tenants in common and other facts showing that they purchased as such may either establish the real nature of the purchase, or amount to the severance of the joint tenancy. But where the proportions of the money are not equal, *and this appears in the deed itself,* this makes them in the nature of partners . . . But in all cases of a joint undertaking or partnership, the survivor will in equity be a trustee for the representative of the deceased partner as to his share whether the purchase be in fee, or of a building lease, and money be laid out in erecting houses.'

Although the reference to a building lease may point to a premium being part at least of the consideration, there seems to have been an assumption that leasehold and freehold property should be treated similarly. It is always comforting to find authority, principle and common sense marching in step.

7 Licences

Maharaj v Chand [1986] 3 All ER 107 (Privy Council) is a case, in an unusual context, on the nature of an estoppel right over land. Under the Fiji Native Land Trust Act, a lessee is not allowed 'to deal with the land comprised in the lease' without the consent of the Native Land Trust Board. The Board had a policy of helping married people to obtain housing, and the plaintiff was granted a sub-lease of such land, stating in his application that he was married to the defendant, who was his de facto wife; he told her that he would use the house to provide a permanent home for them and for her two children. The plaintiff sought to evict the defendant, arguing, inter alia that she had no right to the property under the Act; the defendant relied on a promissory estoppel. The Privy Council took the view that the defendant had acquired a purely personal right against the plaintiff: the Land Court Board (who were not a party to the action) were concerned with dealing with *the land*, not with dealings inter partes which did not affect the Board. Later in their judgment, however, the Privy Council stated that, but for the Act, the defendant might have made a case for having acquired a property interest.

The Privy Council thus regarded a licence coupled with a promissory estoppel as not capable of binding third parties. This is in accord with the traditional view of licences, and differs from the view adumbrated by the Privy Council in *Plimmer v Wellington Corporation* (1884) 9 App Cas 699: see *Pennine Raceways v Kirklees Metropolitan Council* [1982] 3 All ER 628, All ER Rev 1982, p 173. It is noticeable that counsel did not advance the argument that estoppel is now a seamless garment, nor that estoppel licences are based on unconscionability. Likewise, he was not faced with facts such as those in *Pascoe v Turner* [1979] 2 All ER 945. The views of the Privy Council on these matters would have been interesting: as it is, the case presents a slightly tantalising glimpse into the subject of promissory estoppel, but no more.

8 Easements

The law of easements has always been susceptible to the need to adapt to changing social circumstances (as Lord St Leonards pointed out in *Dyce v Lady James Hay* (1852) 1 Macq 305 at 312–3) and the ever more intense development of urban areas and the expectation of increasingly improved working environments provide an area of conflict which tests the law's ability to react to these changes. In *Carr-Saunders v Dick McNeil Associates Ltd* [1986] 2 All ER 888, the plaintiff had, in 1968, purchased property in Covent Garden, the second floor of which was lit by three windows and a partially glazed door at the front and by two windows at the rear. The second floor was used first as an office, then opened up to provide one large room used as living accommodation and, finally, converted into six rooms, two of which each enjoyed use of a rear window. The defendants built two storeys on to the nearby premises and thus appreciably reduced the amount of light available. It was conceded by the defendants, that a right to light existed, but the basis on which the right existed and its quantum were not. First was the right to light one that applied to a building or to a room in it? Millett J followed the statements of Lord Davey in *Colls v Home and Colonial Stores* [1904] AC 179 at 202 and Maugham J in *Price v Hilditch* [1930] 1 Ch 500 at 508 to the effect that the right applied to a building, though Millett J seems to have treated 'the second floor' of the premises as being 'the building'. On the facts the internal arrangement was irrelevant, though the judge carefully stated that the extent of the right was not 'necessarily' to be determined by the arrangements that had been in existence. In particular, he did not have to consider the effect of major structural re-arrangements which had been in existence for a long period of time, although later in the judgment he indicated that it would be necessary to consider 'any other arrangement of that space which might reasonably be expected to be adopted in the future'. Although the point did not rise in the case, there might well be difficulties if the area were one where major developments and changes in use might take place—for example, industrialisation, the construction of high-rise office blocks, or gentrification. Millett J relied on a passage from Cockburn CJ's judgment in *Moore v Hall* (1878) 3 QBD 178 at 182): 'The matter to be considered is, whether there is any diminution of light for any purpose for which the dominant tenement may be reasonably considered available'. This statement is ambiguous, however; the phrase 'may be available' could relate to the present just as much as to the future.

Second, Millett J confirmed the rule that the relevant amount of light to be considered was not what had been removed, but what was left. This is entirely consistent with the statement of Harman LJ in *Hawker v Tomalin* (1969) 20 P & CR 550 at 552:

> 'It is always to be remembered that there is no property in light and that the question in light actions, is always, not how much the plaintiff has lost, but how much he will retain if the defendant's buildings be erected. If adequate light be left, the plaintiff has no right to complain.'

Millett J had considered the evidence, applying 'the conventional fifty-fifty rule, by which a room may be regarded as adequately lit for all ordinary purposes if 50 per cent or more of its area receives not less then one lumen of light at table level' ([1986] 2 All ER at 891). A lumen is defined as 'the amount of light received from 1/500th part of the sky on a dull, overcast day with fairly uniform diffusion of light'. Reflected light is not material: *Straight v Burn* (1869) LR 5 Ch App 163 at 166, per Gifford LJ. The fifty/fifty rule is recognised as a 'rule of thumb' (see *Ough v King* [1969] 3 All ER 859) not as a rule of law. It is recongised that there is inevitably uncertainty in determining the amount of light (see *Colls v Home and Colonial Stores, supra*, per Lords Davey and Lindley) and the evidence of witnesses and experts is thus vital. Millett J discounted, to some extent, the evidence of the lay witnesses, preferring that of experts. This contrasts with the attitude of judges in Ireland, who seem to prefer the evidence of the user of the premises to that of the expert: see the virulent judgment of Christian LJ in *Mackey v Scottish Widows Fund Life Association Society* (1877) IR 11 Eq 541 at 570 and the more moderate statement of Meredith J in *Smyth v Dublin Theatre Co Ltd* [1936] IR 692 that 'the evidence of experts is not as safe a guide as the evidence of those accustomed to use the room in question.'

The decision of Scott J in *Celsteel Ltd v Alton House Holdings Ltd* [1985] 2 All ER 562 was noted last year (All ER Rev 1985, pp 199–200); an appeal by the lessors on a procedural point was allowed by the Court of Appeal ([1986] 1 All ER 608), but the substance of Scott J's judgment (which has been the subject of a useful article by M P Thompson ([1986] Conv 31), was unaffected.

9 Mortgages

The Consumer Credit Act 1974 ss 137 to 141 provides for the re-opening of extortionate credit bargains. The sections, although dealing generally with the provision of credit, are applicable where a mortgage is involved; indeed s 138(4)(a) speaks specifically of 'security'. *Ketley (A) Ltd v Scott* [1981] ICR 241 showed the court taking a very limited view of what was an 'extortionate', and mortgagors who thought they might obtain relief more easily under the provisions of the legislation than under the general equitable rules relating to the reforming of mortgages were disappointed. This disappointment will be further enhanced by the decisions in *Davies v Directloans Ltd* [1986] 2 All ER 783 and in *Coldunell Ltd v Gallon* [1986] 1 All ER 429. In the former case, the judge emphasised that (i) the borrowers had obtained independent legal advice, (ii) they were under no greater pressure than was to be expected for house purchasers, (iii) the lenders were taking a greater risk because of the uncertain and insecure nature of the borrowers incomes, and (iv) that the rate charged (the true rate charged was 21.6 per cent, as against an equivalent rate charged by a building society of 16.95 per cent) was not grossly exorbitant. The judge emphasised that the Act provided a complete code in s 138(l) as to what 'extortionate' meant; it was wrong to equate the term with 'unconscionability' or to go outside the Act to ascertain its meaning. There might be an overalap between s 138(l) and the concept of 'moral reprehensibility' used by Browne-Wilkinson J in *Multiservice Bookbinding Ltd v Marden* [1978] 2 All ER 489, but there could be no incorporation of the test into the statute. *Coldunell Ltd v Gallon* is considered principally in the context of undue influence in the chapter on Contract (see p 89 above); but it contains one point of interest on the Consumer Credit Act. Under s 171(7), if the borrower alleges that the credit bargain is extortionate, the lender has the burden of showing that it is not ; this burden was effectively discharged, according to the Court of Appeal, by showing that the bargain was on its face a proper bargain, and that the lenders had behaved in the way that an ordinary commercial lender would be expected to act.

10 Contract and Conveyance

Attfield v DJ Plant Hire [1986] 3 All ER 273 raises an important point on the duties of a purchaser in possession under a contract of sale. P agreed to sell to D under a contract dated 13 September 1985 their leasehold interest in premises, together with goodwill, fixtures, fittings, trade equipment, and the stock in trade for a total of £29,000. The price was apportioned so that the leasehold interest was given a nil value. The contract incorporated the National Conditions of Sale (20th edn), which included the provision (cl 8) that if the purchaser were let into occupation of the property before completion, then, (inter alia) on seven days' notice given by the vendor, the purchaser would give up the property. The purchaser was let into possession on 12/13 August 1985 (ie before the contract) and notice to complete, properly given, expired on 31 October 1985. On that date, £7,500 of the £29,000 purchase price remained outstanding. P sought various remedies including payment into court by D of the moneys outstanding under the contract, or, in the alternaive, an order that the defendant forthwith relinquish possession, occupation or control of all assets that were the subject-matter of the contract.

The plaintiff sought a *Greenwood v Turner* ([1891] 2 Ch 114) order: this gave the defendant purchaser in possession the option either to pay the outstanding purchase price, or to relinquish possession to the vendors.

Scott J refused such an order, for three reasons: first, that it was inconsistent with clause 8 of the National Conditions; second, that a substantial part of the purchase-price had been paid; and third that, as the property agreed to be sold (being, in part, stock in trade) could not be returned to the vendor, such an order could not easily be applied. The second and third grounds do not call for further comment: as Scott J pointed out, the plaintiffs were not without other remedies which would adequately protect their position, especially as they held most of the purchase price and could seek specific performances or rescission. Therefore, if the working of a *Greenwood v Turner* order is discretionary, the discretion was sensibly exercised.

The first ground, however, is not so simple. Scott J noted that the point before him was not taken in two cases, where, on the facts, it could have been *Pearlberg v May* [1951] 1 All ER 1001, and *Maskell v Ivory* [1970] 1 All ER 488. However, in *Pearlberg v May* the Court of Appeal had considered the doctrine of *Greenwood v Turner* at some length. Three classes of cases were involved: first, where the purchaser had no contractual right to possession, where, if he had not paid the price he would be put to an election: it was unjust that he should have both the property and the purchase-money. Second, if a right to possession were granted under the contract, the availability of a remedy depended on whether the purchaser had ameliorated the property (in which case the vendor had better security and no order would be made) or whether the purchaser had lowered the value of the property, in which case the purchaser was required to pay the price (*Pope v Great Eastern Railway* (1866) LR 3 Eq 171). Third, there were cases where there was a conflict of law and equity, where the vendor sought to enforce his legal rights, but the purchaser obtained an injunction from a court of equity, although on certain conditions.

In *Attfield v DJ Plant Hire*, counsel for the vendor appears to have conceded that if the contract had in terms allowed the purchaser into possession, a *Greenwood v Turner* order could not have been obtained. In view of the second class of case in *Pearlberg v May*, this seems surprising, as the contracts in these cases appear to treat the principles underlying the grant of a *Greenwood v Turner* order as a rule of law rather than as a matter of discretion, and this is borne out by the treatment of the subject in *Williams' Vendor and Purchaser* (4th edn, 1936) pp 565-6).

This, moreover, casts some doubt on Scott J's view ([1986] 3 All ER at 277) that the court should, in this context, be slow to add rights and obligations to the parties' contract. Surely, if there is a rule of law that is relevant, the contract should be read subject to it. However, whatever is the history of the subject, Scott J's judgment has two merits: first, those who deal regularly with the National Conditions of Sale will be relieved to know that these conditions mean what they say and that additional remedies or liabilities are not involved; second, as stated earlier, on the facts of the case, the plaintiffs were well protected.

Celsteel Ltd v Alton House Holdings Ltd (No 2) [1986] 1 All ER 598 deals primarily with matters of Landlord and Tenant and is noted in the relevant chapter (p 210 below). However, one point of general interest to conveyancers emerges. Condition 14 of the National Conditions of Sale (20th edn) provide that property is sold subject to 'any rights of way and water, rights of common, and other rights, easements and latent liabilities *known* [writer's italics] to affect the property'. Counsel had argued that the vendor's knowledge for the purposes of this clause included constructive knowledge. This argument was rejected by Scott J the clause was based on the principle of caveat emptor, 'mitigated by a requirement of honest dealing'. A vendor has a duty to be honest with his purchaser, but no more.

The case *29 Equities Ltd v Bank Leumi (UK) Ltd* [1986] 2 All ER 873 contains two short points. A vendor wished to rescind a contract for the sale of a leasehold interest under condition 11(5) of the National Conditions of Sale. Knox J held that this right arose at the contractual date for completion; moreover, when a licence to asign was not available at the contractual date of completion, even though there was evidence that it would shortly be forthcoming, the vendor was entitled to rescind. The decision has since been reversed by the Court of Appeal ([1987] 1 All ER 108): the date when the issue fell to be considered was when the vendor purported to rescind and on that date it had to be decided in the light of common sense that the licence could not be obtained. On the facts, there was every indication that the licence could be obtained and therefore the purported rescission was ineffective.

11 Land Charges Act; cautions under the Land Registration Act

Hart v Emelkirk Ltd [1983] 3 All ER 15 recognised a new kind of receivership in leasehold property: the court, in the exercise of its power under the Supreme Court Act 1981, appointed a receiver to assist in the enforcement of covenants where the condition of the property demanded urgent attention.

In *Clayhope Properties Ltd v Evans* [1986] 2 All ER 795, the Court of Appeal held that such a receivership, in registered land was protectible, at the suit of a tenant, by means of a caution. Counsel for the landlord argued that the receivership did not create an interest in land (which was admitted), did not thus bind a purchaser, and was thus not properly registrable. Moreover, the Land Registration Act 1925, s 59(5) limited what is registrable under s 59(1) to writs and orders that, unless so protected, would be void as against a purchaser (cf Land Charges Act 1925, s 6, now Land Charges Act 1972, s 6; s 54 of the same Act spoke of 'any person interested in the land'. The Court rejected this view, attractive as it might seem from the point of view of the principles of general property law, because of the wide wording of the Land Charges Act, s 6, which spoke of 'Any order appointing a receiver . . . of . . . land'. Similarly, the court was not impressed with an argument based on an analogy with the Land Charges Act 1972, s 17(1), where the decisions in *Calgary and Edmonton Land Co Ltd v Dobinson* [1974] 1 All ER 484 and *Regan & Blackburn Ltd v Rogers* [1985] 2 All ER 180 (All ER Rev 1985, pp 202–3) had taken the view that a pending land action ('any action . . . relating to land or any interest in . . . land') meant an action claiming a proprietary right.

There is no doubt that the decision gives teeth to the receiver (or a tenant who hopes to benefit from the receiver's administration) appointed in circumstances such as *Hart v Emelkirk Ltd* and in *Clayhope Properties Ltd v Evans* itself. Further, the wide words of the Land Charges Act, s 6 seem to fit neatly the situation before the court. One is still left with the worry, however, that the framers of the legislation had not assumed that receivers would be apponted in such circumstances, their purpose, perhaps, having been rather to protect recognised proprietary interests. This would explain the pull between ordinary principles of property law on the one hand and the wording of statute and expediency on the other. The Nugee Report has indicated that the problems of tenants in blocks of flats such as those involved in *Clayhope Properties Ltd v Evans* may be considerable, and the Court of Appeal's decision ameliorates the tenant's difficulties. Whether the amelioration has been bought at the price of too great a sacrifice of principle remains to be seen.

12 Charity

The drafting of charitable bequests has long been known to be a matter which requires great care. The arbitrary and technical lines which divide the charitable from the non-charitable coupled with the rule that a gift that is part charitable and part non-charitable will fail may make the draftsman's task a demanding one. Certainly, since *Chichester Diocesan Fund and Board of Finance v Simpson* [1944] AC 341, coupling words such as 'benevolent' or 'philanthropic' as alternatives to 'charitable' has been known to lead to disaster. However, most draftsmen would think that use of the word 'and' might solve their problems. The decision of the Privy Council in *A-G of the Bahamas v Royal Trust Co* [1986] 3 All ER 423, however, indicates that this hope may be false. Here, the gift was 'for any purposes for and/or connected with the education and welfare of Bahamian children and young people'. Two points were agreed before the Board: first, that the law of charities was the same in the Bahamas as it is in England, and, second, that the word 'welfare' was too wide necessarily to fall within the scope of the charity. In view of the courts' stringent attitude to the construction of bequests this latter is understandable: it should be noted, however, that the Supplement to the Oxford English Dictionary lists amongst the definitions of 'welfare' the following: 'The maintenance of members of a group or community in a state of (especially physical and mental) well-being, especially as provided for and organised by legislation or social effort'.

The Board considered (i) that useful guidance was to be had from the judgment of Sargant J in *Re Eades* [1920] 2 Ch 353 (in which the phrase 'religious, charitable and philanthropic objects' was held not to constitute a valid charitable gift); (ii) the question was one of construction, and decisions on different (albeit similar) phrases were not helpful; (iii) 'welfare' was wider than 'education', and was therefore either otiose or had the effect of invalidating the gift. This last point seems to have been the decisive one and, as Lord Oliver said, it 'is not one which is susceptible of a great deal of elaboration'. However, three comments may be made. First, there was clearly an ambiguity in the document: why was the maxim *res magis valeat quam pereat* not applied, and the charitable purpose given the benefit of the doubt? Second, if the gift had been 'for purposes . . . connected with *both* [writer's italics] the education and welfare of Bahamian children', it is difficult to see how the result could have been the same. 'Education', being narrower (it is assumed) than 'welfare', would become the limiting word, and the gift would thus be valid. Finally (though this is now in hope rather than expectation), why cannot the courts construe 'and' as meaning 'both . . . and' and 'or' as meaning 'either . . . or'. Clarity would thus exist, albeit, it must be admitted, at the cost of some sophistication.

Brooks v Richardson [1986] 1 All ER 952 deals with two procedural points. The Royal Masonic Hospital was run by a charity (the Freemasons Hospital and Nursing Home); the constitution of this charity provided that donors to it of certain amounts would become Patrons, Vice-Patrons and Life Governors. Patrons and Vice-Patrons were automatically governors of the constitution, certain other individuals would be given the 'privileges' (cl 16) as if qualified as a Donor—ie as a Patron, Vice-Patron or a Life Governor. The plaintiff argued that the constitution both created a charitable trust and provided the basis of a contract between all the governors, which any one of them was entitled to enforce. Warner J rejected this argument: although the individual donors had paid money, they had not given consideration; they had acquired rights (or privileges see cl 16) to take part in the government of the charity, but no more. Warner J was referred, during argument, to the analogy of a members club, but 'the analogy . . . is, I think, imperfect, because the rights of a member of such a club are rights that he acquires for his benefit' ([1986] 1 All ER at 958). With respect, this approach may be too simplistic: it appears to adopt the distinction between inward-looking and outward-looking unincorporated associations which Brightman J had rejected in *Re Recher's Will Trusts* [1971] 3 All ER 401 as being unhelpful. The law relating to unincorporated associations is still in a state of development, and whereas there has been considerable amount of authority on the subject of non-charitable associations, there has been comparatively little about their charitable counterparts (though cf *Re Vernons Will Trusts* (1963) [1971] 3 All ER 1061 and *Re Finger's Will Trusts* [1971] 3 All ER 1051).

The constitution of the Freemasons Hospital and Nursing Home clearly created a trust, but since its governance was in the hands of individuals, it is unclear why a contract amongst such members could not subsist in tandem with the valid charitable trust. Contract and trust can co-exist (see, eg *Barclays Bank Ltd v Quistclase Investments Ltd* [1968] 3 All ER 651) and, a charitable trust could, conceivably, exist on a basis that the members should agree how it should be administered, subject always to the general law and, in particular, to the right of the Attorney-General to intervene. On the terms of the constitution, the references to 'donors' and to 'privileges' point away from such a conclusion, and so it is difficult to quibble with the result which Warner J reached: what is perturbing, however, is the apparently wholesale rejection of the analogy with unincorporated associations. On the facts, therefore, Warner J's findings that the proceedings were 'charity proceedings' within Charities Act 1960, s 28, (the authorisation of the Charity Commissioners being thus thus required before proceedings could be brought), and that the Attorney-General (as was normally the case in charity matters) should be a party to proceedings, seem totally unexceptionable.

13 Variation of trusts

1983 and 1985 have seen cases reported on the Variation of Trusts Act 1958 (see *Mason v Farbrother* [1983] 2 All ER 1078, All ER Rev 1983, p 378, *British Museum (Trustees) v AG* [1984] 1 All ER 337, All ER Rev 1984, p 308). 1986 saw a short, but important, decision on s 1(1)(a) and (b) of the Act. Section 1 provides that a court has jursidiction to approve a variation on behalf of:

> '(a) any person having, directly or indirectly, an interest, whether vested or contingent, under the trusts who by means of infancy or other incapacity is incapable of asserting, or
> (b) any person (whether ascertained or not) who may become entitled, directly or indirectly, to an interest under the trusts being at a future date or on the happening of a future event a person of any specified description or a member of any specified class of person, so however that this paragraph shall not include any person who would be of that description, or a member of the class, as the case may be, if the said event had happened at the date of the application to the court...'

This sub-paragraph seems designed to distinguish between those who are (if an assumption is made) present and ascertainable at the date of the action, and those who are not: the former can appear on their behalf, the latter cannot. This approach was adopted in *Re Suffert's Settlement* [1960] 3 All ER 561 and *Re Moncrieffe's Settlement Trusts* [1962] 3 All ER 838. In both the cases prospective next-of-kin were involved; in *Re Suffert* the next-of-kin (being immediate, depending only on *one* death,) could give consent themselves, whereas in *Re Moncrieffe* the next-of-kin (not being immediate, but depending on *two* deaths) could not. (The sub-paragraph, however is not easy to interpret: see Harris, *Variation of Trusts* (1975), pp 35 et seq).

In *Knocker v Youle* [1986] 2 All ER 914, income from a share of the trust fund was held for the settlor's daughter for life at 21, and on her death as she should appoint. In default of appointment, there was an accruer clause to another share of the trust fund settled on a son on similar trusts. If the trusts failed or determined, the property was to be held for, inter alia, the issue of the settlor's four sisters living at the date of such failure. In 1984, the issue were very numerous and some of them lived in Australia, and it was impracticable to obtain their consent. Warner J was asked, under the provisions of s 1(1), to approve a variation on behalf of such issue. He found two difficulties: first, many of the issue already had 'interests' under the trusts, albeit contingent interests. 'Interest' was clearly used in its technical sense, as the use of the phrase 'vested or contingent' in s 1(1)(a) showed. As they already had interests under s 1(1)(a), they were not persons 'who may become entitled' under s 1(1)(b).

Even if this difficulty could be overcome, Warner J considered that the issue were within the proviso to s 1(1)(b) rather than within the main body of the paragraph. There was only a single event to occur—or a single assumption to be made—before the class became ascertainable, and thus the case was similar to *Re Suffert* rather than to *Re Moncrieffe*. The second argument put forward was more complex: there was evidence that both brother and sister had both executed wills fully exercising their testamentary powers. Counsel argued that the event concerned in the proviso was the death of the survivor of the brother or sister on the date of issue of the originating summons and they would have therefore appointed all the property at that date. However, Warner J considered this did not reflect the true meaning of the proviso, which was 'designed to identify the presumptive *members* of the class at the date of the application to the court' [1986] 2 All ER 917 (writer's italics), rather than to consider whether at the date they would or would not have become entitled. In short, the proviso was concerned with existence, not entitlement. Counsel argued that the purpose of the Act was relevant in determining its construction, and the purpose was to obviate the need to join parties to applications under the Act where their interests were remote. Warner J noted, however, that 'remoteness' was not the test: what mattered (subject to the proviso) was whether the parties had—or might have—an interest.

14 Perpetuities

Re Drummond [1986] 3 All ER 45 (see P Luxton, [1986] Conv 427) is an example of the unyielding—and perhaps malevolent—way in which the unreformed law of perpetuities operates so as to defeat the perceived intentions of a settlor. A settlor in 1924 settled property on trust for himself for life, and then for such of his three daughters as were living at his death and attained 21 or married under that age and the issue of any daughter who might have predeceased him, such issue to take their parent's share equally amongst themselves on similar conditions. If a daughter died without a living child, her share was to be divided equally 'amongst such of the daughters as shall then be living and the issue of any of them who be then dead such issue taking their parent's share only on attaining the age of 21 or marrying under such age'. All three daughters survived the settlor, and in 1984, one died without issue. Was the daughter's share to be held on trust for the surviving two daughters, or was the trust affecting the share void for perpetuity? It was agreed on all sides that if 'issue' meant 'children and remoter issue' rather than 'children', then the gift must fail. The reasoning was as follows: (i) there must have been a possibility in 1984, however remote, of an interest resting outside the perpetuity period of level in being plus 21 years; (ii) the issue of a deceased daughter could only attain a vested interest at 21 or earlier marriage: such issue could be a grandchild (or even more remote descendant) of the daughter conceived after the daughter's death; therefore (iii) such grandchild or even more remote descendant might therefore attain a vested interest more than 20 years after the daughter's death and thus outside the perpetuity period. As always in the 'pre 1964' world of perpetuities, reality as it has occurred is ignored in favour of the theoretical possibility of the unlikeliest concatenation of circumstances presenting itself. Counsel, however, tried to avoid this seemingly inexorable logic in two ways. First, he argued that 'issue' meant 'children'. As the will was professionally drawn, and the words 'issue' and 'children' were both used, this was impossible to accept (cf *Re Hipwell* [1945] 2 All ER 476 at 478, per Lord Greene MR). Second, he argued that it might be possible to use the class-closing rules—or their absence—so as to prevent the rule against perpetuities from applying. The rule in *Andrews v Partington* (1791) 3 Bro CC 401 operates, as a rule of construction, to close a class when one member of the class became entitled and is used to resolve apparently contradictory intention in a settlement, ie whether property was to be distributed at a certain moment, or whether a whole class on issue was to benefit. *Andrews v Partington* normally operates benevolently, but in *Drummond* it would not do so, as the class might not close within the perpetuity period, unless the gift could be written down in some way. In *Re Cockle's Will Trusts* [1967] 1 All ER 391 and *Re Deeley's Settlement* [1973] 3 All ER 1127, where the gifts were, in essence, to X for life, and to his issue attaining 21, Stamp J and Goff J had respectively held (i) that the rule in *Andrews v Partington* was inappropriate where the class compared members of more than one generation, and (ii) that the gift could be saved by construing 'issue' as 'issue alive at X's death'. Mervyn Davies J in *Re Drummond* was unwilling to extend the benevolence in *Cockle* and *Deeley* to the case before him; the issue would only take directly if a daughter died without leaving a child; if there was a child, future generations would take at a later date—when (and if) the child in question failed to attain 21. In short, issue could not be restricted to issue alive at the daughter's death (which would have saved the gift), but had to include issue born after that death who would be alive at the death of the daughter's child.

The law revealed in *Re Drummond* seems arcane, and since the disposition antedates the 1925 legislation, this hardly seems surprising. The only consolation is that after 1964 the Perpetuities and Accumulations Act would allow the effect of a disposition to be governed both by the 'wait and see' provisions and by statutory class-closing rules.

Landlord and Tenant

PHILIP H PETTIT, MA
Barrister, Professor of Equity, University of Buckingham

Common law

International Drilling Fluids Ltd v Louisville Investments (Uxbridge) Ltd [1986]
1 All ER 321 is one of those useful cases where the Court of Appeal sets out
a series of propositions relating to a particular area of law—in this case the
grounds on which a landlord may be entitled to refuse his licence to the
assignment of a lease when, by the lease, such licence may not unreasonably
be withheld. The reasoning has since been applied, though with a different
result on the facts, in *Ponderosa International Development Inc v Pengap
Securities (Bristol) Ltd* [1986] 1 EGLR 66. Under the 30 year lease from 25
December 1971 the only permitted use was office use, and the tenant (the
first assignee) having vacated the premises in May 1984 sought the
landlord's licence to assign the lease to a company which wished to use the
buildings to provide serviced office accommodation. This use was within
the terms of the lease. The landlord by its solicitor refused to grant a licence,
the main ground being that 'the investment value of our clients' interest in
the property would be detrimentally affected by the proposed use'.

In his judgment, with which Mustill and Fox LJJ agreed, Balcombe LJ
deduced the following propositions from the authorities:

(i) The purpose of a covenant against assignment without the consent
of the landlord, such consent not to be unreasonably withheld, is to
protect the lessor from having his premises used or occupied in an
undesirable way, or by an undesirable tenant or assignee.

(ii) A landlord is not entitled to refuse his consent to an assignment on
grounds which have nothing whatever to do with the relationship
of landlord and tenant in regard to the subject matter of the lease.

(iii) The onus of proving that consent has been unreasonably withheld is
on the tenant.

(iv) It is not necessary for the landlord to prove that the conclusions
which led him to consent were justified, if they were conclusions
which might be reached by a reasonable man in the circumstances.

(v) It may be reasonable for the landlord to refuse his consent to an
assignment on the ground of the purpose for which the proposed
assignee intends to use the premises, even though that purpose is
not forbidden by the lease.

(vi) There is a divergence of authority on the question, in considering
whether the landlord's refusal of consent is reasonable, whether it is
permissible to have regard to the consequences to the tenant if
consent to the proposed assignment is withheld. Balcombe LJ went
on to say—and it is valuable to have Court of Appeal authority on
this point—that a proper reconciliation of the two streams of
authority can be achieved by saying that while a landlord need
usually only consider his own relevant interests, there may be cases

there is such a disproportion between the benefit to the landlord and the detriment to the tenant if the landlord withholds his consent to an assignment, that it is unreasonable for the landlord to refuse consent.

(vii) Subject to the above propositions, it is, in each case, a question of fact, depending on all the circumstances, whether the landlord's consent to an assignment is being unreasonably withheld.

At first instance the judge accepted that valuation evidence showed that reasonable professional men might take the view that, if the premises were put on the market, they might fetch less with the proposed assignee in occupation than if they had remained vacant for more than a year. However, he continued, there was no prospect of the premises being put on the market and accordingly there was no reasonable apprehension of damage to the landlord's property interest. Balcombe LJ held that the court should not interfere with this decision, and added that this was a case where it would be unreasonable for the landlord not to consider the detriment to the tenant if consent were refused.

Balcombe LJ further observed that the judge could, and should, have had regard to the fact that the proposed service office user was within the only form of user permitted by the lease. Where only one specific type of use is permitted it is not reasonable for the landlord to refuse consent to an assignment on the grounds of the proposed user (being within the only specific type of use), where the result will be that the property is left vacant and where the landlord is fully secured for the payment of rent. This was a further ground for affirming the first instance decision.

It should be noted that some words appear to have been omitted from p 327 of the report. In line g3 sense requires the insertion of words such as 'that he did not consider' following 'conclusion' and before 'that'.

It is surprising that the short point the court had to decide in *Field v Barkworth* [1986] 1 All ER 362 has apparently not previously come up for decision. A lease made on 13 December 1948 of premises comprising a farmhouse, three cottages, farm buildings and some 118 acres of agricultural land contained a covenant by the tenant: 'NOT to assign or underlet any part of the premises without the consent in writing of the landlord (such consent not to be unreasonably withheld).'

It will be observed that the covenant refers to '*any part* of the premises'. The tenant brought proceedings to ascertain whether an assignment or underletting by her of *the whole* of the demised premises required the consent in writing of the landlord. It was not in dispute that a covenant against assigment of the whole of the demised premises simpliciter would not prohibit the assigment of part only of those premises, and the tenant submitted that the case before the court was the converse of that. The tenant further submitted that a lease is to be construed strictly against the landlord and that a tenant's rights are not to be cut down except by clear words.

No doubt the draftsmen could have avoided the possibility of argument by using a common form provision such as 'the whole of the demised premises or any part thereof', but his failure to do so was of little assistance where the wording used was unambiguous and where in practice such a covenant is drafted in variant forms. Nicholls J took the view, it is submitted rightly, that the relevant words were clear and unambiguous:

'If after an assignment or underletting of the whole of the premises one asked the question "Has there been an assignment or underletting of any part of the premises?" the answer plainly would be Yes. The answer would be Yes because what had been assigned or underlet would be every part of the premises and this covenant against assignment or underletting of any part of the premises in my view plainly embraces the assignment or underletting of every part. As I see it, that is the beginning and end of this case' (at 364).

Surely nothing more needs to be said. The Court of Appeal said it was rightly decided in *Troop v Gibson* [1986] 1 EGLR 1.

Mancetter Developments Ltd v Garmanson Ltd [1986] 1 All ER 449 raised an interesting point on the law of waste, 'a somewhat archaic subject, now seldom mentioned', according to Dillon LJ, which led to some disagreements between the members of the Court of Appeal. The plaintiffs granted a 42 year lease from 24 June 1972 to Pilot Chemical Co Ltd, which put in various pipes which pierced the outside walls of the building and also put extractor fans in the outside walls. This was either done with the plaintiffs' consent, or any ground of objection was waived. It was agreed that the pipes and extractor fans were tenant's fixtures which Pilot would have been entitled to remove during the term of the lease.

Pilot got into financial difficulties and the receiver, in January 1978, agreed to transfer its assets, including the lease and trade fixtures, to Garmanson Ltd, a company formed for the purpose. The shares in Garmanson were transferred to another company of which the second defendant was managing director. He thereupon became the only active director until it too went into liquidation.

Garmanson took possession of the premises in February 1978, but left the premises and delivered up possession to the plaintiffs in October, having in the meantime removed the pipes and extractor fans. No attempt was made to fill in the holes made when these fixtures were installed. The exact status of Garmanson at the time of removal is somewhat obscure—the assignment of the lease by Pilot, for which the plaintiffs gave formal licence in September 1978, did not take place until March 1979. However the court did not need to decide the matter for it ruled that the plaintiffs were bound by the concession which the judge below supposed them to have made that Garmanson had the right to remove the tenant's fixtures, and assumed that the right was the same as that which Pilot had had.

Garmanson, being insolvent and in liquidation, the appeal was brought only by the second defendant, and the court had no hesitation in agreeing that if Garmanson was liable for waste the second defendant was personally liable because he directed and procured the acts causing the waste. The key question, therefore, was whether Garmanson was liable for waste.

Sir George Waller, dissenting, took the view that Pilot was guilty of waste when the holes were made, since what they had done was a 'spoil or destruction' to the building, but that Garmanson (and therefore the second defendant) did not commit an act of waste when it removed its own property without doing any further damage to the walls. With respect, the contrary view of Kerr LJ is to be preferred. The attachment of any fixture is likely to cause some 'damage' to the fabric of the building, but this does not constitute an act of waste unless it can be said to be so inconsistent with the terms of the lease as to constitute using the premises in an untenantlike manner.

The vital question according to the majority was whether removing the pipes and extractor fans without filling in the holes was an act of waste. The starting point is that fixtures become part of the realty and are irremovable by the tenant. From early times however the common law gave the tenant a right to remove tenant's fixtures. This right is independent of contract, though it may be confirmed or excluded by the terms of the lease. It is, however, subject to conditions. Thus, in general, it must be exercised before the lease expires (but see *New Zealand Government Property Corporation v HM & S Ltd* [1982] 1 All ER 624). Further, as Dillon LJ explained, it is a condition of the right of the tenant to remove tenant's fixtures that he makes good the damage. It was argued that the damage was limited to extra damage caused by the removal and did not require the filling up of the holes. Dillon LJ rejected this argument as contrary to common sense and his understanding of the concept of voluntary waste. A tenant who has chosen for his own convenience to instal tenant's fixtures though he is entitled to remove them cannot do so leaving the premises no longer wind and weather proof without becoming liable for waste. It may however be a different matter where it is a matter of mere decoration and does not affect the structure. And, as Kerr LJ pointed out, in most cases the matter will be covered by contractual stipulations: in cases where this is so it is doubtful whether an alternative claim in tort is permissible.

As Kerr LJ pointed out in *Manorlike Ltd v Le Vitas Travel Agency & Consultancy Services Ltd* [1986] 1 All ER 573 there have been many other cases of a highly technical nature on notices to quit. This was yet another. The question, according to Nourse LJ, was both short and exceedingly simple. It was whether a notice to quit 'within a period of three months from the date of service of this notice' was effective to determine a lease under whose terms the tenant was entitled to 'not less than three months' previous notice in writing expiring at any time'.

Notice was served on 22 May and it was not in dispute that a period of three months from that date expired at midnight on 22–23 August. The tenant contended that the requirement that he must leave 'within' three months meant that he must do so *before* midnight on 22–23 August and could not do so *at* midnight on that day. The court agreed in rejecting the contention on grounds both of language and of common sense. The precise meaning of a preposition such as 'within' depends on the context in which it is used. In the context of a period of time it was capable of meaning 'during' or 'before or at the expiry of' that period, and the tenant here would comply with the requirement by walking out of the door before, or on the stroke of midnight on 22–23 August. The notice was valid.

Celsteel Ltd v Alton House Holdings Ltd [1985] 2 All ER 562 discussed in All ER Rev 1985, pp 199, 200 under the title Land Law has been reversed in part by the Court of Appeal at [1986] 1 All ER 608. It needs to be mentioned briefly as an introduction to *Celsteel Ltd v Alton House Holdings Ltd (No 2)* [1986] 1 All ER 598. The first action before Scott J was a claim by the plaintiffs as the lessees of flats and garages at a block called Cavendish House that their rights of way over estate roads had been interfered with by a proposal by Mobil Oil Co Ltd, the second defendant, to erect a car wash on part of the road. The plaintiffs had been granted their leases by the predecessor in title to Alton House Holdings Ltd, the first defendant. Alton House had granted a 99 year lease to Mobil, under which a car wash was the authorised user.

The plaintiffs' claim succeeded and the judge granted an injunction not only against Mobil, but also against Alton House, on the ground that if the car wash had been constructed both Alton House and Mobil would have been joint tortfeasors in the interference with the right of way. There was no appeal against the substance of the judge's order, but Alton House appealed against the award of the injunction against them and the consequential order for costs. At a late stage the plaintiffs decided not to resist this appeal. However, Mobil, which had started contribution proceedings aganst Alton House, contested the appeal on the ground that if the injunction against Alton House was discharged they would have to bear the whole of the costs awarded to the plaintiffs.

Though in one sense the appeal was about costs, the court held that it was a perfectly genuine appeal against the substantive order. The injunction against Alton House was discharged because having granted the lease to Mobil they had no power themselves to do anything further towards the interference with the plaintiffs' rights by the erection of a car wash. There was no ground on which an injunction was necessary against them in relation to any future action. The question of costs was a little complicated. In the ordinary course the plaintiffs, as a result of the appeal, would have been ordered to pay the costs of Alton House against whom no substantive order was made at the end of the day. However, with the motive of defeating Mobil's claim for contribution, Alton House had disputed the plaintiffs' claim on the merits and lost on all the substantive matters in the action. In these circumstances it was held that the right order as against the plaintiffs was that there should be no order as to Alton House's costs. The effect of this was that Mobil would have to pay all the costs awarded to the plaintiffs.

The contribution proceedings had in fact already been determined some months earlier and are reported as *Celsteel Ltd v Alton House Holdings Ltd (No 2)*. In those proceedings Mobil claimed against Alton House that the injunction represented a breach of the covenant for quiet enjoyment in the lease granted to Mobil by Alton House. The covenant was that: '. . . the Tenant shall peaceably hold the demised premises for the term hereby granted without any interruption by the Landlord or any persons lawfully claiming through under or in trust for the Landlord.'

It will be remembered that the plaintiffs' leases were granted not by Alton House but by Alton House's predecessor in title. Alton House therefore argued that the plaintiffs were not persons 'claiming under' Alton House. Scott J was persuaded by this argument, observing that the covenant was in a qualified, limited form which did not amount to a guarantee of title. After citing *Woodfall, Hill and Redman* and *Halsbury* he expressed surprise at the absence of any clear judicial authority on the point. As already indicated he concluded that a qualified covenant for quiet enjoyment, such as the one before him, operates to protect the lessee against acts of the lessor or the acts of others done pursuant to rights granted or interests created by the lessor. Though there may be other categories of persons against whose acts the covenant protects the lessee, these do not include predecessors in title of the lessor and do not include the grantees of rights or interests created by predecessors in title of the lessor. Alton House thus succeeded on this ground of its defence.

Alton House had a second ground of defence, namely that it agreed to demise the premises to Mobil subject to the rights of way of the plaintiffs. That being so, it was contended, the exercise of those rights by the plaintiffs cannot be a breach of the covenant for quiet enjoyment. This defence was based on the terms of the option agreement leading to the grant of the lease. This agreement incorporated condition 14 of the National Conditions of Sale (20th edition) which was wide enough to cover the plaintiffs' rights. This defence failed, for incorporation of condition 14 was only possible in so far as the condition was not inconsistent with the express terms or conditions of the option agreement.

Mobil also put forward the contention, as an answer to the condition 14 defence, that even if it was incorporated into the option agreement, Alton House could not rely on it as in the lease itself the premises were not expressed to be demised subject to those rights. In the opinion of Scott J if by an agreement for sale the parties agree that the sale shall take effect subject to some particular incumbrance, it cannot be a breach of the vendor's covenant for quiet enjoyment that the particular incumbrance affects the property. The exercise by the incumbrancer of his rights cannot be a breach of the covenant. There is no need for the incumbrance in question to be specifically mentioned in the conveyance in order to bar the purchaser from suing on the covenant for quiet enjoyment for a breach constituted by exercise of the rights granted by the incumbrance. This last point was obiter since it had been held that condition 14 was not incorporated into the option agreement.

The result, of course, was that Mobil's contribution claim failed as Alton House succeeded on its first ground of defence.

Just as the Rent Acts have given rise to a number of cases in which the courts have been called upon to draw the line between a tenancy and a licence because a tenancy, including a tenancy at will, is a protected tenancy within the Acts while a licence is not, so Part II of the Landlord and Tenant Act 1954 has given rise to cases in which the task of the court has been to determine whether the tenant holds under a tenancy agreement or a periodic tenancy, in either of which cases he could claim to be protected under Part II of the 1954 Act, or whether he is merely a tenant at will, in which case it was undisputed that he would be unprotected by the Act. An addition to the list of such cases is *Cardiothoracic Institute v Shrewdcrest Ltd* [1986] 3 All ER 633. The facts were that on three occasions court orders had been made enabling the parties to enter into tenancy agreements which excluded the provisions of ss 24–28 of the 1954 Act, and therefore gave the tenant no security of tenure. The last agreement determined on 31 October 1983. As was well known to the parties, it is impossible to contract out of Part II, but on a joint application the court may authorise a tenancy which does not confer any security of tenure. In autumn 1983 negotiations began for a further tenancy and between the end of October 1983 and September 1985 a series of extensions was agreed, each subject to a condition that it should be the subject of a tenancy agreement approved by the court excluding the operation of ss 24–28. It was the intention of both parties that there should be no legally binding agreement between them until such order was obtained. Rent was tendered and accepted during the periods of these extensions.

Knox J in his judgment, since followed in *Niyazi Mehmet Uzun v Ramadan Ahmet* (27 June 1986, unreported) cited the observation of Scarman LJ in *Hagee (London) Ltd v A B Erikson & Larson (a Firm)* [1975] 3 All ER 234 at 237 to the effect that holding over and holding pending a negotiation are the classic circumstances in which a tenancy at will exists. He would clearly have found no difficulty in holding that it was a case of tenancy at will but for the giving and receiving of rent, the effect of which he carefully considered. He began by pointing out that the case just cited and *Bastow (dec'd) v Cox* (1847) 11 QB 122 are authorities for saying that the reservation and payment of rent does not prevent there being a tenancy at will, though those authorities are concerned with express tenancies at will. It is however clear that the giving and receiving of rent does not necessarily import the existence of a periodic tenancy. Reference was made to Lord Mansfield's statement in *Cheny (dec'd) v Batten* [1775–1802] All ER Rep 594 at 595: 'The question therefore is, *quo animo* the rent was received, and what the real intention of both parties was?' At one time the common law readily presumed an intention to create a periodic tenancy, but the fact that statutory protection is now the norm has become a significant factor in evaluating the parties' intention in paying and receiving rent. Knox J cited from Ormrod LJ's judgment in *Longrigg Burrough & Trounson v Smith* (1979) 251 EG 847 who said that the old presumption is unsound. 'The question now is a purely open question; it is simply: is it right and proper to infer from all the circumstances of the case, including the payments, that the parties had reached an agreement for a tenancy?' Knox J preferred not to express a view either on counsel for the tenant's argument that this dictum went further than necessary for the decision, or on counsel for the landlord's contention that the onus of proof to establish a periodic tenancy lies on the tenant.

The conclusion that the judge reached was that, taking into account the 1954 Act and the parties' knowledge of its operation, they did not intend to create a periodic tenancy pending the grant of a tenancy which they anticipated the court would approve under s 38(4). The payment and acceptance of rent was not a compelling reason for imputing such an intention, where, as was perfectly possible, they gave no serious thought to the legal repercussions of doing so.

Rent review clauses

Three cases reported successively are concerned with one particular problem that has arisen in connection with rent review clauses. They are *Datastream International Ltd v Oakeep Ltd* [1986] 1 All ER 966, decided by Warner J on 5 November 1985, *MFI Properties Ltd v BICC Group Pension Trust Ltd* [1986] 1 All ER 974, decided by Hoffman J on 31 January 1986, and *British Gas Corp v Universities' Superannuation Scheme Ltd* [1986] 1 All ER 978, decided by Browne-Wilkinson V-C on 6 February 1986. In each case the judge had the advantage of knowledge of the earlier case or cases in question.

The question that arose in each of these cases was whether or not a valuer, in fixing the new rent under a rent review clause, should take into account the fact that the lease in quesion contains provisions for further rent reviews in the future. A rent review clause usually provides for the new rent to be fixed by a valuer as being the rack rental which would be obtainable in the market at the review date if the demised premises were to be let on that date, and lays down a formula by which that rack rental is to be fixed. Such a formula commonly provides that the valuer is to assume a hypothetical letting of the premises on the open market on the terms of the actual lease but subject to certain artificial variations. A very common variation is that the valuer is to asssume that the hypothetical letting is on the terms of a lease containing the same provisions as the actual lease 'other than the amount of rent hereby reserved' *(Datastream)*, 'other than those relating to rent' *(MFI)*, 'other than as to the yearly rent' *(British Gas)*, or some other similar rent exclusion provision. The question then is whether the effect of the rent exclusion clause is to require the valuer to ignore the fact that the actual lease contains provisions for future rent review, on the footing that the rent review clause is itself a provision relating to rent. It was said that in the *British Gas* case disregard of future reviews might increase what would otherwise be the new rent by as much as 20 per cent.

Although, of course, decisions on construction depend upon the exact words used in the context of the particular lease, one can hope to find that there is an agreed approach to construction. As is pointed out particularly by Warner J (in the *Datastream* case) and Browne-Wilkinson V-C (in the *British Gas* case) this is not the position. There will normally be three possible constructions of a rent exclusion clause:
  (i) that it requires the valuer to ignore *all* provisions relating to rent in the lease,
 (ii) that it requires the valuer to ignore those provisions which relate to the quantification of rent, ie the rent payable immediately before the relevant review date *and* the provisions for future rent reviews,
(iii) that it requires the valuer to ignore only the rent actually payable before the review date, ie he must take into account the provisions for future reviews of the rent.

In the *British Gas* case Browne-Wilkinson V-C identified the different approaches to such a clause. On the one side, on which Browne-Wilkinson V-C himself fell, are Warner J (in the *Datastream* case), Hoffman J (in the *MFI* case, and, subsequently, in *Amax International Ltd v Custodian Holdings Ltd* (1986) 279 EG 759), and Vinelott J (in *Pearl Assurance plc v Shaw* (1984) 274 EG 490), who treat the literal construction and any intermediate construction as offending commercial common sense and give effect to the underlying commercial purpose by adopting construction (iii). On the other side are cases in which either the words are given their literal meaning (see *National Westminster Bank plc v Arthur Young McLelland Moores & Co* (1984) 273 EG 402), or the judge rejected the view that one should approach the construction of a rent review clause on the basis that it is intended to give effect to the normal commercial reason for including such a clause (see, eg, the *National Westminster* case).

Browne-Wilkinson V-C expressed his hope that the Court of Appeal would have an early opportunity to resolve the conflicting approaches. In view of the differences of opinion he felt free to choose what approach to follow and stated three propositions:
  (a) words in a rent exclusion provision which require *all* provisions as to rent to be disregarded produce a result so manifestly contrary to commercial common sense that they cannot be given literal effect;

(b) other clear words which require the rent review provision (as opposed to all provisions as to rent) to be disregarded must be given effect to, however wayward the result;

(c) subject to (b) in the absence of special circumstances it is proper to give effect to the underlying commercial purpose of a rent review clause and to construe the words so as to give effect to that purpose by requiring future rent reviews to be taken into account in fixing the open market rental under the hypothetical letting.

It would seem likely that these eminently sensible propositions will be affirmed if and when the point comes before the Court of Appeal.

The rent review clause in *Metrolands Investments Ltd v J H Dewhurst Ltd* [1986] 3 All ER 659 provided for an open market rent to be paid during the last seven years of a 21-year term which began on 19 February 1968. This rent was to be agreed between the landlord and the tenant and failing agreement by arbitration. There was a proviso to the effect that the decision of the arbitrators should be obtained before 19 August 1981 and that the rent should not in any event be less than £1,800 pa. There was also a break clause enabling the tenant to determine the lease on 18 February 1982 by notice in writing between 19 August 1981 and 18 November 1981. Neither landlord nor tenant made any attempt to operate the rent review procedure before 19 August 1981, nor did the tenant attempt to operate the break clause. Eventually on 2 December 1981 the landlords indicated that they wanted the rent to be reviewed. The tenants responded by claiming that the notice was too late and therefore invalid, and pointed out that it was now too late for it to operate the break clause.

Though the Court of Appeal reversed the decision of Peter Gibson J below, there was a large measure of agreement between them, not surprisingly since both courts were bound by the House of Lords decision in *United Scientific Holdings Ltd v Burnley B C* [1977] 2 All ER 62. This set what Slade LJ, giving the judgment of the court, called the initial starting point on the consideration of a rent review clause, namely that prima facie, and in the absence of sufficient contra-indications, it is not right to impute to the parties to a lease the intention that time is to be of the essence for the purpose of a rent review clause. However, as their Lordships recognised, in a case where a lease contains a break clause as well as a rent review clause and the timetables of the two clauses are closely interlocked, the interrelation of the two clauses is *likely* to suffice as a contra-indication sufficient to rebut the ordinary presumption; though everything must depend on the wording of the particular lease.

Peter Gibson J applying what he regarded as guidelines enunciated by the highest tribunal, took the view that the interrelation of the two clauses was a sufficient contra-indication and accordingly held that time was of the essence. The Court of Appeal agreed that there was the clearest possible interrelation between the timetable embodied in the rent review clause and that embodied in the break clause, yet held that in the context of the particular lease this was not a sufficient contra-indication to rebut the presumption that in the rent review clause time was not of the essence of the contract. It may be noted that the timetable in the break clause is treated quite differently. 'The tenant himself,' Slade LJ said, 'must on any footing be held strictly to the time limits laid down for the service of any notice by him to determine the lease.'

The main reason why the Court of Appeal took a different view to that taken by Peter Gibson J was that it regarded as of considerable importance a factor that Peter Gibson J had mentioned but treated as of little significance. This factor was that in the *Metrolands* case the event as to which time was said to be of the essence was the actual obtaining of the arbitrator's decision, something which was not within the landlord's full control. Even if the landlord had acted with all due diligence and promptness it might still have been the case that the decision of the arbitrator would not have been obtained by the specified date, 19 August 1981. Slade LJ cited as applicable a dictum of Viscount Dilhorne in the *United Scientific* case:

> 'It is most unlikely in these circumstances that the lessors, if they had been asked at the time the leases had been entered into to agree that time should be of the essence, would ever have agreed to that and I see no reason for imputing to them an intention which no reasonable landlord would have had.'

The second related reason given by the Court of Appeal was that any potential hardship to the tenant which might otherwise arise through tardy action by the landlord in initiating the review procedure could be eliminated, or at least substantially mitigated, by the tenant initiating such action himself. The point here was that the tenant, no less than the landlord, had the right to initiate a review.

It is, perhaps a trifle surprising that the court came to the *clear* conclusion that the intention to be attributed to the parties was that time should not be of the essence, if this is to be read as meaning that this was clearly the proper conclusion to reach. No doubt, as Slade LJ observed, 'the ultimate object of the court is construing clauses such as this... must be to ascertain the parties' intentions from the words they have used.' But there is a degree of artificiality involved. The parties are artificial legal persons and with respect it is submitted on such evidence as appears in the report that it is unlikely that the directors or other individuals who negotiated the lease or gave instructions to their solicitors adverted to the matter in question, or indeed that it was in the minds of their legal advisers—if it had been the clause would surely have been redrafted. Was it reasonable to assume, as the court said it was, that the tenants were aware of the risk inherent in the arbitrator failing to give his decision in due time and the 'obvious remedy' which lay in his hands? One wonders too whether the question to which it was said the court had to direct its mind was not somewhat oversimplified. It was put thus: 'is the proper intention to impute to the parties, from the words which they have used, the intention that the landlord shall lose his right to a review if the stipulated timetable is not strictly adhered to in the relevant respects?' This is almost a leading question and it is respectfully suggested should continue along the lines '... taking account of the fact that if the landlord retains his right the tenant may have to decide whether or not to determine the lease under the break clause without knowing what the revised rent is likely to be.' Had this question been put to each of the parties at the time the lease was executed they might well have given different answers. But there can, of course, only be one answer, ascertained as a question of construction of the words used in the light of admissible evidence of surrounding circumstances. Subject to possible review by the House of Lords, we now know what that answer is.

Business tenancies under Part II of the Landlord and Tenant Act 1984

In *Linden v Department of Health and Social Security* [1986] 1 All ER 691 Scott J was faced with some tricky questions of construction of the Landlord and Tenant Act 1954, Part II. The premises had been leased by the plaintiffs' predecessors in title to the Secretary of State for Social Services for 14 years from 24 June 1971. The question in issue was whether the Secretary of State was entitled to a new lease of the premises, which had been converted into a Hostel for Nurses and were managed by the Paddington and North Kensington Health Authority.

As is well known s 23 defines the tenancies to which Part II of the Act applies and expresses two criteria: (i) the property comprised in the tenancy must be or include premises occupied by the tenant; (ii) the premises must be occupied for the purposes of a business carried on by the tenant.

However, where the tenant is a government department there are special provisions in s 56. Sub-section (3) provides that Part II will apply to a tenancy held by or on behalf of a government department provided only that the property comprised therein is or includes premises occupied for any purposes of a government department. Sub-section (4) goes on to provide that sub-s (3): 'shall apply in relation to any premises provided by a Government department without any rent being payable to the department therefore as if the premises were occupied for the purposes of a Government department.'

Counsel for the defendant argued for a literal construction which, he submitted, covered the facts of the case. The Secretary of State, the tenant, provided the premises to the health authority rent free and thus the facts fell directly within the section. Scott J, however, was concerned by the very odd results he foresaw as flowing from their construction. 'If [t]his approach is right', he said, 'it would seem that every tenancy held by every government department would be entitled to the protection of Part II of the 1954 Act unless rent for the premises was being paid ... whether or not the premises were being occupied for any purpose of a government department and, perhaps, even if the premises were vacant.'

Scott J preferred to construe sub-ss (3) and (4) as dealing with the case where one government department has granted a tenancy to another government department rent free, in which case in his view Part II applies whether or not the premises are actually occupied for the purposes of a government department.

It is respectfully submitted that the argument of counsel for the defence may yet succeeed in a higher court. Though there may be difficulties one can see a certain logic in sub-ss (3) and (4). Sub-section (3) provides that Part II applies where there is a government department as tenant and the premises are occupied for any purposes of a government department. Sub-section (4) can be construed as deeming premises to be so occupied if the tenant department provides them rent free. Presumably it would be ultra vires for a government department to provide its premises rent free except in pursuance of its purposes.

Be that as it may, Scott J having decided that sub-s (4) did not apply had to consider whether the case was covered by sub-s (3). Under this sub-section the only criterion that had to be satisfied was that there should be someone in occupation of the premises whose occupation could be said to be for a purpose of a government department. The occupation of the health service employees was not such occupation—they occupied for ordinary personal residential purposes. However the judge found it just possible to hold that the health authority, as managers of the flats, was, for the purpose of sub-s (3) in occupation of the whole property. The judge thought the case a borderline one and noted in particular that one or more of the flats was usually vacant and under the control of the authority; that the authority had keys to all flats and visited them regularly; that the employees did not have exclusive possession; that not simply furniture but crockery and blankets were provided; and that the authority carried out full maintenance including decorating and quite trivial repairs.

Having held that the authority was in occupation, the next question was whether it was in occupation 'for any purposes of a government department'. The judge held that it was. The Secretary of State had power under s 87(1) of the National Health Service Act 1977 to acquire property 'to provide residential accommodation for persons employed for any of the purposes of this Act'. The exercise of these functions had been delegated to the authority and in pursuance thereof it was managing the premises in question. Its occupation was accordingly an occupation for a purpose of a government department.

This left a final question on the construction of s 23(3) which defines a holding as:

'... the property comprised in the tenancy, there being excluded any part thereof which is occupied neither by the tenant nor by a person employed by the tenant and so employed for the purposes of a business by reason of which the tenancy is one to which this Part of this Act applies.'

It was held that the authority, in acting on behalf of the Secretary of State in discharge of his statutory functions under the National Health Service Acts, was acting as agent for the Secretary of State. It followed that the authority's occupation of the premises is the occupation of the Secretary of State, the tenant, and that the persons employed by the authority in discharge of its delegated functions are, for the purposes of s 23(3), to be treated as the employees of the Secretary of State. The Secretary of State was accordingly entitled to claim a new lease of the whole of the premises.

Section 24A of the Landlord and Tenant Act 1954, introduced into the Act by the Law of Property Act 1969, enables the landlord to apply for the fixing of an interim rent for premises in respect of which there is an application for a new tenancy under Part II. Sub-section (2), as interpreted by *Stream Properties Ltd v Davis* [1972] 2 All ER 746, provides that the interim rent is payable from the date on which the landlord's proceedings for fixing an interim rent were commenced. The task for the court in *Thomas v Hammond-Lawrence* [1986] 2 All ER 214 was to ascertain the date of commencement.

The facts were that the landlord had served notice on the tenant determining the tenancy under s 25 and the tenant had made a normal application for a new tenancy. In the usual course the landlord served an answer on 27 May 1983 in which the landlord set out the grounds of his opposition to the grant of a new tenancy and, inter alia, applied for the determination of an interim rent under s 24A. However it was not until April 1985 that the landlord gave the tenant notice that he intended to apply to the county court judge on 10 July 1985 for an interim rent to be fixed. At the hearing the judge decided that the date on which proceedings were commenced was not the date of the answer (May 1983) but the date of the issue of the notice of the hearing in April 1985. The landlord now appealed against this decision.

The argument in support of the judge's decision was that CCR Ord 13, r 1 makes it mandatory to apply for an interim rent by summons and that therefore the issue of the summons in April 1985 was the date of commencement of the proceedings for the interim rent. The Court of Appeal rejected this submission and held that Ord 13, r 1 did not cover the whole ground. In the view of the court it was permissible for the landlord in his answer to the tenant's application for the grant of a new tenancy to put forward a claim for an interim rent as the landlord had done in the case before it and in such circumstances the date of the answer will be the date of commencement of the proceedings for the interim rent. This confirms the note to s 24A in the County Court Practice 1985 and is consistent with the practice form issued with the approval of the Lord Chancellor which includes in the form of answer an application for the determination of an interim rent.

Residential tenancies

Hewitt v Lewis [1986] 1 All ER 927, the only case under this heading, merits only a brief mention because situations which will be governed by it will soon cease to arise. It involved the construction of the Rent (Amendment) Act 1985 which was passed to reverse the decision in *Pocock v Steel* [1985] 1 All ER 434 which had held that on the true construction of Case 11 a landlord claiming to be the owner occupier had to have occupied the dwelling-house as his residence immediately before he let it to the statutory tenant. The amendment to Case 11 entitled a landlord to claim possession if he had occupied the dwelling-house as his residence at any time before the letting. Section 1(4) made it clear that the Act was intended to have some retrospective effect and the question in issue was whether it applied to a case on appeal where judgment had already been given against the landlord before the Act was passed, or, in other words, was it intended to apply to pending actions.

The court observed that the appeal was by way of rehearing and that the decision at first instance could not be said to have given the defendant anything in the nature of a vested right. It was held that the only realistic interpretation of the 1985 Act was that Parliament intended its retrospective effect to extend to pending actions. To construe it otherwise would cause expense and inconvenience to the landlord and would not significantly benefit the tenant, for it would immediately be open to the landlord to start a new action for possession in reliance on the new statute.

Agricultural holdings

In *Featherstone v Staples* [1986] 2 All ER 461 the plaintiffs had granted a lease to two brothers (the Staples) and Laughton Contracting Co Ltd, a company wholly owned by the plaintiffs, as joint tenants. The Staples and Laughton entered into a partnership agreement which provided, inter alia, that no partner could serve a counter-notice under s 24 without the consent of Laughton. The plaintiffs served a notice to quit on the Staples and Laughton and two days later Laughton gave the Staples notice of dissolution of the partnership. Some two weeks later the Staples, without Laughton's consent, served a counter-notice on the plaintiffs purported to be signed by the Staples 'on behalf of' the partnership which was described as 'tenant'. The issue in the action was whether the counter-notice was valid or void, in the light of the fact that only two of the three partner tenants had joined in giving the counter-notice, but that the third partner whose consent was not obtained was a company wholly owned by the landlords.

The relevant statutory provision was s 2 of the Agricultural Holdings (Notices to Quit) Act 1977 which provides in effect that where (a) notice to quit an agricultural holding is given to the tenant and (b) within a month the tenant serves an appropriate counter-notice, then the notice to quit shall not take effect unless the Agricultural Land Tribunal consents to its operation.

The other members of the court agreed with the judgment of Slade LJ who first dealt with the question whether some only of joint tenants could validly serve a counter-notice without the actual authority of the other joint tenants—it was not in dispute that if actual authority was given the counter-notice would be good.

After reciting the facts and setting out the relevant statutory provisions, Slade LJ discussed the cases. He began by giving the common law background as set out in *Leek and Moorlands Building Society v Clark* [1952] 2 All ER 492, namely that a periodic tenancy is to be continued into the next period only if all the holders of the joint tenancy so wish and that, if one does not, he is at liberty, on his own, to determine the tenancy. The substantial effect of a valid counter-notice is to achieve a renewal of the tenancy and if the legislature had the common law principles in mind when the Act was passed one might have expected it to contemplate that all the joint tenants must concur in an effective counter-notice. However the meaning of the phrase 'the tenant' in a statute depends on its context and in the context of some statutes has been construed as meaning 'the joint tenants or any one or more of them'. This was the case in *Howson v Buxton* [1928] All ER Rep 434, where however as was pointed out in *Jacobs v Chaudhuri* [1968] 2 All ER 124 the context was very special. The latter case was concerned with s 24 of the Landlord and Tenant Act 1954, and though there was much on the merits to be said in favour of the counter-notice given by one of two tenants the majority of the court held it to be invalid. The law was swiftly reversed by the Law of Property Act 1969 which introduced a new s 41A to the 1954 Act. Another case where tenant was given a generous construction was the Rent Act case of *Lloyd v Sadler* [1978] 2 All ER 529. However in the nearest case to the one before the court on the predecessor to s 2 of the 1977 Act, *Newman v Keedwell* (1977) 35 P & CR 393, Fox J held that tenant meant all of two or more joint tenants.

At first instance in *Featherstone v Staples* Nourse J felt able to distinguish *Newman v Keedwell* by holding that the word tenant in s 2 should be given a flexible meaning, so that, while in some cases it would fall to be read in a narrow sense, in others it could be read in a wider sense, bearing in mind the purpose of the section. He considered that in the circumstances of the case before him it should be construed in the wider sense so as to give security to those who need it.

Slade LJ was surely right to reject the flexible construction propounded by Nourse J and, with one possible qualification, to accept the view of Fox J in *Newman v Keedwell* that prima facie 'the tenant' means all the joint tenants in the case of a joint tenancy. The qualification which Slade LJ, without expressing a concluded view, suggested was that if the landlord himself (or perhaps a company controlled by him) was one of the joint tenants then his concurrence might not be necessary. This, Slade LJ said, would lead to a sensible and just result complying with the statutory objective.

The reason why Slade LJ did not need to come to a decision on the question of construction was that the counter-notice was to be treated as having been given with the authority of Laughton, even though that authority was not in fact given. The effect of the Partnership Act 1890 and the provisions of the partnership agreement would have given the Staples express authority to serve a counter-notice on behalf of the partnership but for the provision that no partner could serve a counter-notice without the consent of Laughton. Was this last provision valid? The House of Lords held in *Johnson v Moreton* [1978] 3 All ER 37 that a provision in a lease by which the tenant agreed not to serve a counter-notice would be void, and it was held that if A were to grant a tenancy to A, B and C under which A, B and C agreed with A as landlord not to serve a counter-notice without A's consent, that condition would be equally void. (At line h on 476 'enforceable' must be a misprint for 'unenforceable'). In the view of Slade L J it made no difference that in the case before him the relevant provision was contained not in the lease but in the partnership agreement. The right of the tenants other than the landlord to serve a counter-notice without the concurrence of the landlord joint tenant cannot be taken away by contract with the landlord whether or not this contract is contained in the lease or elsewhere.

Leasehold enfranchisement

In *Johnston v Duke of Westminster* [1986] 2 All ER 613 the question that had to be determined was the meaning of 'letting value' in s 4(1) of the Leasehold Reform Act 1967. Four underleases had been granted to separate tenants in 1948 each at a rent of £200 pa plus a premium of £1,250 or £1,500. Shortly before the underleases were due to expire the tenants applied to the court for orders then they were entitled to acquire the freeholds of their leases pursuant to the Act, the head lease having been previously surrendered to the freeholder.

The freeholders argued that the letting value was to be construed as the open market annual rent obtainable for the premises (let on the same terms) at the date of the grant of the tenancy, ie the rack rent. The evidence accepted by the trial judge was that this would have been less than £300 pa, his estimate being £200–£300 pa. On that basis the rent at the commencement of the tenancy exceeded two thirds of the letting value. The tenancy was not on that basis a tenancy at a low rent and the Act did not apply.

The tenants on the other hand contended that letting value is the total consideration that a landlord can obtain in the open market for the premises (let on the same terms) and included not only the rent but also any premium in so far as it is attributable to the granting of the tenancy rather than any collateral matters such as furniture, fittings etc. To ascertain the letting value the premium must first be decapitalised and expressed in annual terms and then added to the rent payable. The evidence here was that this would bring the letting value over £300 pa, and on that basis the rent of £200 pa would be less than two-thirds thereof and the Act would apply.

Lord Griffiths, with whose speech all the other Law Lords agreed, had no hesitation in saying that 'letting value' should be given the broad construction for which the tenants contended. 'Letting value' was to be construed as the best annual return obtainable in the open market for the grant of a long lease on the same terms whether this is achieved by letting at a rack rent or letting at a lower rent plus the payment of a premium. This construction, Lord Griffiths observed, was likely to make the calculation of letting value straightforward. Most cases to which the relevant provision applied, ie tenancies granted between the end of August 1939 and the beginning of April 1963, other than building leases, would involve both a rent and a premium, negotiated at arm's length between landlord and tenant. Normally the combination of rent and premium will be very strong prima facie evidence of the letting value and the only calculation required is to apply a mathematical formula based on actuarial principles to convert the premium into an annual sum. Exceptionally it may be possible though it would be difficult to show that this calculation would not reflect the true letting value. If this could be done the judge would have to determine the letting value on expert valuation evidence.

Lord Griffiths expressed considerable misgivings about the correctness of the formula adopted by the experts to express the premium in annual terms, as had the Court of Appeal, though being the agreed expert's evidence he did not think it appropriate to reopen it. It seems clear, however, that the formula used cannot be relied on in future. Lord Griffiths expressed the opinion that it should be done on a purely actuarial basis.

In conclusion it is worth noting Lord Griffiths' comment on *Gidlow-Jackson v Middlegate Properties Ltd* [1974] 1 All ER 830 where it was held that the letting value could not exceed the amount lawfully exigible under the Rent Acts and the court rejected the tenant's argument that the letting value should be assessed at the hypothetical annual rent obtainable in the absence of rent controls. In *Manson v Duke of Westminster* [1981] 2 All ER 40 Brandon LJ doubted the correctness of the decision and thought it should be reviewed by the House of Lords when a suitable case arose. Lord Griffiths said that the present case was not a suitable one and further said that he would not wish to encourage a challenge to *Gidlow-Jackson*.

Local authority housing–tenant's right to buy

The Housing Act 1980, as amended by the Housing and Building Control Act 1984, gives a council tenant, being a secure tenant, a right to buy his house in certain circumstances. The Act distinguishes between the right arising and being exercisable, and s 2(4) provides that the right 'cannot be exercised in any of the circumstances mentioned in Part II of. . . . Schedule [1]'. The first of the circumstances mentioned in Part II is in paragraph 1 which provides: 'the tenant is obliged to give up possession of the dwelling-house in pursuance of an order of the court, or will be so obliged at a date specified in such an order.'

In *Enfield London Borough Council v McKeon* [1986] 2 All ER 730 the facts were that the tenant served a notice under s 5 on the landlord in August claiming to exercise the right to buy and the landlord council served a notice on the tenant admitting the tenant's right in September. In November the landlord served a further notice on the tenant, as it was required to do so by s 10, containing the particulars required by the section, such as the proposed price. Between the service of these last two notices the landlord served a notice on the tenant indicating its intention to seek possession of the house on ground 13 of Sch 4 (accommodation more extensive than that reasonably required by the tenant), and it issued proceedings in the following January.

The tenant argued that she 'exercised' her right once and for all when she served her notice in August, and that this right was 'established' when the landlord served notice admitting the right to buy. Thereafter the landlord council became subject to a statutory obligation under s 16 to convey the house to her subject to the provisions of that section. Paragraph 1 of Part II of Sch 1, it was contended, had no relevance, because at the time when the tenant 'exercised' her right to buy there was no order for possession in existence.

The point on which the issue turned was when the tenant 'exercised' her right. The tenant's argument was good if, but only if, she was right in contending that there was a once and for all exercise of the right in August. The landlord's argument, however, that the 'exercise' of the tenant's right is a continuing process which begins when the tenant serves his notice claiming to exercise the right to buy and only ends when he finally pays the purchase price and takes his conveyance on completion, was accepted by the court. Accordingly if, as happened in this case, during the interim period before completion the court makes an order for possession, para 1 of Part II of Sch 1 will cause the tenant's right to buy to cease to be exercisable, and thus to be abrogated.

Slade LJ with whose judgment Eastham J agreed, came to the conclusion that the right is 'exercised' each and every time when the tenant takes any step towards the implementation of his right to purchase only after careful consideration. Three factors which weighed with him were: (1) the distinction drawn between a claim to exercise the right and the exercise of the right, (2) under s 16(11), where a tenant has claimed to exercise his right to buy, the tenancy continues until the appropriate grant is actually made to the tenant by way of completion, which may be two years or more later. Slade LJ did not think that the legislature could have contemplated that during this interim period the landlord would be deprived of his ordinary powers of management including the power to seek possession on one of the statutory grounds, (3) if the tenant's submission was well founded, a tenant could serve a s 5 notice after a possession action, instituted on good grounds, had proceeded almost to the point of the making of an order, with the purpose and effect of frustrating the order. This, Slade LJ thought, could not be right.

Practice and Procedure

ADRIAN A S ZUCKERMAN, LLM, MA
Fellow of University College, Oxford

Anton Piller orders, Mareva injunctions and related relief

The invention of Anton Piller orders and Mareva injunctions was met with universal approval. It was generally felt that the newly-devised procedures provided a much needed facility for doing justice to a plaintiff whose rights might otherwise be defeated by a ruthless and unscrupulous defendant. Now, however, we have good reasons for wondering whether our forebears were not the wiser for refraining from such inventions.

These procedures were never intended to become a staple litigation strategem. Referring to the Anton Piller order, one of its founding fathers said: 'The proposed order is at the extremity of this court's powers. Such orders, therefore, will rarely be made, and only when there is no alternative way for ensuring that justice is done to the plaintiff' (Ormrod LJ in *Anton Piller KG v Manufacturing Processes* [1976] 1 All ER 779 at 784). Despite this view, the extreme is now commonplace with the result that the ruthless and rich plaintiff has considerable scope for harassing his defendant and even forcing him out of business.

Scott J's powerful judgment in *Columbia Picture Industries v Robinson* [1986] 3 All ER 338 highlights the potential for abuse. The background was of the familiar kind. The plaintiffs, a number of film makers and distributors, suspected the defendant and his company (hereinafter 'the defendant'), who hired and sold pre-recorded video cassettes, of pirating their films. The plaintiffs issued a writ for breach of copyright against the defendant and almost simultaneously obtained, ex parte, an Anton Piller order directing the defendant to allow the plaintiffs' solicitors to enter, at any time between 8 am and 3 pm, the various premises where the defendant ran his business 'for the purpose of inspecting, photographing and looking for and removing into the Plaintiffs' Solicitors' custody' any illicit goods and any documents relating to such goods. The order stipulated that the solicitors were allowed to use up to five persons to carry out the search on the defendant's premises.

The order was executed by A E Hamlin & Co who, it emerged in the trial, had considerable experience in the Anton Piller field. The raid on the defendant's premises 'was a process that required to be and was planned with military precision', and was 'executed by some very experienced professionals', (at 354). These 'professionals' consisted of partners and employees of the above firm of solicitors. They ranged themselves, with police ready to attend, at three of the defendant's premises, in numbers not exceeding five at any one premise. They removed large quantities of tapes and documents and, as Scott J found ([1986] 3 All ER at 376):

> 'No attempt whatever was made by Hamlins, so far as I could tell from the evidence, to confine their seizures to material strictly covered by the order. They took everything as to which there was a question that they wished to investigate.'

The judge further found that no adequate receipts were given for what was taken, that Hamlins failed expeditiously to return the material which had been taken and that some of the material retained, far from being used in evidence, was irretrievably lost by Hamlins. His Lordship concluded that the retention 'for nearly three years was done by Hamlins without a shadow of right. It was . . . oppressive and in flagrant disregard of the defendants' rights' ([1986] 3 All ER at 376).

The removal and detention of the defendant's business records made it impossible for him to continue trading. On this score Scott J concluded (at 376–7):

> '. . . I was satisfied by the evidence in the case that the intention of the plaintiffs and Hamlins in applying for and obtaining the Anton Piller order was by that means summarily to close down the business of reproducing tapes being carried on from 8 Frederick Street [the defendant's premises]. They had, in my view, the expectation that the execution of the Anton Piller order would achieve that end. Hamlins' professional experience of the effect of executing Anton Piller orders in audio and video piracy cases justified that expectation. That intention was . . . an improper one. It represented an abuse of the Anton Piller procedure and it led . . . to an oppressive execution of the order.'

Perturbing as these violations of individual rights, in the name of the law, are, what is much more disturbing is the legal framework that has made them possible. The Anton Piller procedure has become very popular (Hamlins' themselves have executed 300 orders since 1974) and applications for orders seem invariably to succeed ([1986] 3 All ER at 369, 370). In their application for the order Hamlins failed to disclose material facts which would have militated against the granting of the order and which resulted in a 'misleading and unfair impression' being created regarding the nature of the defendant's activity ([1986] 3 All ER at 351). In the past courts emphasised the duty of solicitors and counsel to make full disclosure but Scott J was of the view that this obligation offered inadequate means for protecting defendants' rights even when solicitors act scrupulously and conscientiously.

A plaintiff's solicitors can only act on information supplied by their clients. Once they have satisfied themselves that their clients have a good case against the defendant they can only present the case in that light. The duty of counsel who appears in ex parte proceedings is to make full disclosure but not to put the case for the other side: *Amanuel v Alexandros Shipping Co* [1986] 1 All ER 278 at 282. No amount of talk about the solicitor's role as an officer of the court can alter the fact that a 'solicitor does not and cannot be expected to present the available evidence from the respondent's point of view': *Columbia Picture* case ([1986] 3 All ER at 370). Given our adversarial system, Scott J must surely be right when he says (at 375): 'I am doubtful whether it can really be the law that solicitors or counsel owe a duty to the court to have restraint as to the extent of the orders they seek'.

Another factor which is thought to provide a safeguard is the plaintiff's undertaking to compensate the defendant for any undue damage he suffers through the execution of an Anton Piller order. Scott J has now shown this to be a broken reed. The defendant was awarded a substantial damages but these were only in respect of his legal activities. A considerable part of the defendant's business was legitimate but it is doubtful whether the damages awarded fully compensated him for the permanent loss of this side of the business. Furthermore, as his Lordship explained (at 369–70), damages do not:

> 'meet the main objection to Anton Piller procedure. The main objection to the procedure is that the orders made produce for the respondents damaging and irreversible consequences without any hearing at which they can be heard. The respondents may lack the means or the strength of purpose to pursue the application for relief under the undertaking in damages. And even villains ought not to be deprived of their property by proceedings at which they cannot be heard.'

The present practice amounts to one of shooting first and compensating later if you hit the wrong person or the right person in the wrong spot. This is fundamentally at odds with the protection of rights in a democratic society. Clearly, the starting point must be that procedural safeguards should protect rights from being harmed in the first place and that compensation should only be an ancillary measure in the protective strategy. The law imposes strict limits on the right of the police to interfere with our freedoms. It does not encourage the police to do what is necessary for the apprehension of criminals and undertake to compensate the innocent if he is harmed in the process.

A flawed attitude to the defendants' rights pervades the area of these interlocutory ex parte remedies. In *Bayer AG v Winter* [1986] 1 All ER 733 the plaintiffs, a mighty multi-national company, suspected the defendants of distributing counterfeit insecticide and applied for an Anton Piller order to obtain from the defendant documents relating to the dealings in the insecticide. Fearing that the defendant might leave the country, they also applied for an order that the defendant deposit his passport with their solicitors and refrain from leaving the country until the Anton Piller order has been executed. The application came before Walton J who was unwilling to restrain the defendant's freedom of movement in the absence of authority. Fox and Ralph Gibson LJJ have now provided this authority. The former said (at 737):

> 'The position appears to be this: first . . . one asks what harm will this order do to him [the defendant]? If he says it will cause him some embarrassment or hardship he can apply to the High Court forthwith, on evidence, to ask that it be varied or, if necessary, discharged.'

This approach is the very cause of recent abuses. On general principle it is unjustified to interfere with a citizen's rights merely because this will benefit another citizen and will not do much harm to the former.

Another reason mentioned for issuing the order was that, when the plaintiffs' investigating agents interviewed the defendant, he refused to give details about his business. With due respect to the Court of Appeal, the defendant was entirely within his rights. A citizen is under no legal obligation to account for his actions even to the police. Why should his refusal to disclose his dealings to a private investigator be held against him and lead to the deprivation of his freedom? The Court of Appeal mentioned a further consideration: that the defendant had stated that he did not care where his merchandise came from as long as he could sell it. This factor, if proved, might well help the plaintiff to make out his case at the trial but it does not give him a right to impose on the defendant's freedom of action before the trial.

Prominent in its absence, however, was evidence showing that the defendant would abscond or destroy evidence if alerted of the action. There is in this respect a significant and undesirable relaxation of the requirements to be met before the issue of an Anton Piller order. In a case such as *Al Nahkel for Contracting and Trading Ltd v Lowe* [1986] 1 All ER 729, where the defendant was alleged to be in possession of money stolen from the plaintiffs and was about to board a flight out of the country, it might be justified to restrain his leaving the country by the newly revived writ of ne exeat regno. But this is a far cry from the circumstances of the *Bayer* case. In the latter it appeared 'doubtful' whether the defendant had a permanent residence in this country but doubt should certainly not be enough. The court should insist on compelling prima facie proof that he was about to leave the country.

Just as the authority to search the defendant's premises in *Columbia Picture Industries* gave rise to a dispute between the plaintiffs' solicitors and the defendant so has the authority to question the defendant given rise to a dispute between the plaintiffs' solicitors and the defendant in the *Bayer* litigation. In addition to an order for the handing over of documents, a Mareva injunction and an order restraining the movement of the defendant the Bayer conglomerate also obtained an order instructing the defendant to disclose his assets and to verify the information in an affidavit. Under the last order the plaintiffs' solicitors questioned the defendant personally and believing his answers to be unsatisfactory they applied to the High Court to have the defendant cross-examined and to further restrain his departure from the country: *Bayer AG v Winter (No 2)* [1986] 2 All ER 43. Counsel for the plaintiff was quite open about the purpose of this 'free-ranging' examination: to discover the whereabouts of the defendant's assets, the part he played in the alleged illegal transactions and the scope and details of these transactions. Scott J, before whom the application came, observed that the examination was intended to cover almost the whole area on which the defendant would be liable to cross-examination at the trial and refused to order such examination. It was wrong, in his view, to make an ex parte order on the basis that the defendant failed to satisfactorily answer the plaintiffs' questions without giving the defendant an opportunity to be heard; defendants are entitled not to have assumptions made against them in their absence. It was also wrong, he felt, to allow a free ranging examination before the plaintiffs have even served their statement of claim. Clearly, the judge was worried that the examination would be used as a vehicle for building up a claim. It is worthwhile quoting Scott J's conclusion ([1986] 2 All ER at 46–7):

> '. . . I find it very difficult to envisage any circumstances in which, as a matter of discretion, it would be right to make an order as is sought in the present case . . . Star chamber interrogatory procedure has formed no part of the judicial process in this country for several centuries. . . . The police, charged with the upholding of public law, cannot subject a citizen to cross-examination before a judge in order to discover the truth about the citizen's

misdeeds. How then, as a matter of discretion, can it be right in a civil case, in aid of rights which, however important, are merely private rights, to subject a citizen to such a cross-examination? A fortiori it cannot be right to do so in a case where the plaintiff seeking the cross-examination of the defendant is holding itself free to use the defendant's answers for the purpose of an application to commit him to prison for contempt.'

Needless to say, the application for further restraint on the defendant's freedom of movement was also rejected. Scott J observed that if the defendants wanted to take action in respect of alleged breaches of the orders by the defendant, the correct procedure was to seek his committal, in which case the hearing would be inter partes.

Dillon LJ also drew attention to the process by which plaintiffs' interests increasingly encroach upon those of defendants. In *Ashtiani v Kashi* [1986] 2 All ER 970 at 974 he said:

'. . . as applications for Mareva injunctions are almost invariably made ex parte in the first place, the form of order tends to be dictated by the form of draft minute order which the plaintiff's counsel has prepared. Not surprisingly, therefore, one finds the forms of order being progressively tightened up so as to be more and more beneficial to the plaintiff, and, conversely, more and more onerous to the defendant.'

The plaintiff brought an action against the defendant for money allegedly owed as a result of a business association between the parties. They obtained an ex parte order restraining the defendant from disposing of his assets within and without jurisdiction and ordering him to disclose the extent and location of all his assets within and without the jurisdiction. The defendant complied with the order, including disclosure of his bank accounts abroad, but applied for its discharge as far as the foreign assets were concerned. The order was discharged and the plaintiffs appealed. In the meantime the plaintiffs, having discovered the whereabouts of the defendant's assets abroad, made applications in foreign courts to have the defendant's foreign assets frozen in support of the English claim. The issue before the Court of Appeal was whether an order to restrain disposal of assets outside the jurisdiction and for discovery of such assets could be properly made.

The plaintiffs relied on an unreported case, *Bayer AG v Winter*, 19 March 1986, suggesting that Hoffmann J expressed himself strongly in favour of extending Mareva injunctions to foreign assets. Hoffmann J was quoted as saying that 'the underlying policy of the Mareva jurisdiction, to prevent a defendant from disposing of his assets in order to frustrate the execution of any judgment which the plaintiff may obtain, would suggest that this court should try to make its ultimate judgment effective by assisting the plaintiff to take steps to prevent the defendant from disposing of his assets in foreign jurisdictions as well.' However, reading the case in [1986] FSR 357 it is clear that these remarks were made in a different context and could not be advanced in support of the plaintiffs' argument.

Any discussion of the extent of the Mareva jurisdiction must take into account two important factors. First, since these injunctions are mostly granted ex parte they are necessarily made on very partial evidence which focuses on the plaintiff's interest. Secondly, an injunction can cause the defendant lasting and uncompensatable damage, as happened in *Columbia*

Picture Industries v Robinson [1986] 3 All ER 338 where the defendant's bank withdraw his overdraft facility which, in turn, contributed to his going out of business. Consequently the need for caution is as great, if not greater, when the issue concerns the extension of jurisdiction.

In the early occasions of Mareva injunctions there was a danger that a defendant with a foreign residence would remove his assets from England in order to place them beyond the reach of an eventual English judgment; eg *Nippon Yusen Kaisha v Karageorgis* [1975] 3 All ER 282. Subsequently the jurisdiction was extended to cases where there was a fear that the defendant would dissipate his assets within the jurisdiction. If the logic of the plaintiff's argument prevails and injunctions are available for restraining foreign assets there would be no reason for not bringing the circle full round by extending the jurisdiction to cases where all the defendant's assets, and not just some of them, are abroad (at present authority suggests that Mareva injunctions are not available in this situation: *Third Chandris Shipping Corpn v Unimarine SA, The Pythia etc* [1979] 2 All ER 972 at 984–5). There is a further consideration to be borne in mind. As a matter of general policy our law should encourage foreign institutions and individuals to do business in this country. A rule whereby their assets in any part of the world may be frozen as a consequence of contemplated litigation in this country would be a discouragement.

The Court of Appeal has decided in *Ashtiani* that it was unjustified to issue Mareva injunctions in respect of foreign assets and that in future they should not be granted. On its facts, the case involved a mere claim, but Dillon LJ left the door open for the possibility of an injunction where the plaintiff has a proprietary claim on specific assets or where he brings an action for tracing; [1986] 2 All ER at 976 (for discussion of the importance of the distinction between a mere claim for debt and a proprietary claim see All ER Rev 1982, p 214).

It was also decided that where there is no justification for restraining the disposal of foreign assets there is a no justification for ordering their disclosure. It remains, however, possible that such disclosure would be ordered where a defendant applies for discharge of an order relating to English assets and his overall means are relevant to the decision ([1986] 2 All ER 980). Dillon LJ added, however, that where a defendant is made to disclose foreign assets, the plaintiff should 'give an undertaking not to use any information disclosed without the consent of the defendant or the leave of the court' (at 978). Lastly, to bolster further the protection to defendants his Lordship advised that judges investigate, whether in ex parte or inter partes proceedings, the adequacy of the plaintiff's cross-undertaking in damages before making the order. By making the plaintiff provide some tangible security the courts will certainly help to redress the balance between the parties.

The Court of Appeal's ruling on discovery of foreign assets is sensible but it should not be taken to foreclose discovery of foreign assets in extreme cases. Where, for instance, the defendant is proved to be an international rogue who spreads his assets around the world for the express purpose of defeating any municipal judgment that may be given against him, the courts should not regard themselves bound by the *Ashtiani* decision. This case, it is submitted, does not purport to limit the courts' freedom of action in combating fraud.

Conclusion

One of the most disturbing aspects of recent cases is the evidence of the corrupting influence that the procedure has had. The solicitors in *Columbia Picture Industries*, for instance, adopted the habit of making defendants, upon whom they served an order, sign a form in which the defendant declared that he handed over the items seized 'willingly and without duress'. The solicitors then relied on the declaration in reply to the charge that they had seized unauthorised items. Scott J deprecated this practice saying that

> 'given the nature of Anton Piller orders and the circumstances of surprise and shock which almost always attend their execution, there is a very real danger in allowing the executing solicitors to go outside the terms of the order in reliance on an alleged consent on the part of the respondent' ([1986] 3 All ER at 356).

The Anton Piller procedure has brought solicitors into too close a contact with the contest between plaintiff and defendant. This makes it much more difficult for solicitors to maintain their relative detachment as officers of the court and far too easy for them to become identified with their clients' interests in an unhealthy and unseemly way. It is bad enough when the police adopt similar practices to those mentioned in the *Columbia Picture* case, but at least they do not fall into the category of officers of the court. Solicitors do, and their actions are bound to reflect ill on the administration of justice generally.

It is now a matter of urgency for the courts to redress a balance which has tilted so far against defendants that it is beginning to undermine the fairness of the civil process. To this end I venture a few suggestions.

1. The first thing to be done is to revert to a healthier starting point. If authority is needed, it is provided by Kerr LJ:

> 'It must always be remembered that if, or to the extent that, the grant of a Mareva injunction inflicts hardship on the defendant, his legitimate interests must prevail over those of the plaintiff, who seeks to obtain security for a claim which may appear to be well founded but which remains to be established at the trial' (*Nimemia Maritime Corpn v Trav Schiffahrtsgesellschaft mbH & Co KG* [1984] 1 All ER 398, 422).

This applies with equal force to Anton Piller applications. In an application for interlocutory relief the court should insist that plaintiffs come forward with positive proof of the seriousness of the dangers against which they seek to protect themselves at the defendant's expense. Any doubt in this regard should be resolved in favour of the defendant.

2. When an order has been obtained as a result of misleading information knowingly being given to the court, as in *Eastglen International Corpn v Monpare* (1986) 136 NLJ 1087, a new order should not be forthcoming even if the plaintiff then corrects the information. Such a rule would provide an effective incentive for plaintiffs to be careful and scrupulous. It is regrettable that the Court of Appeal has reversed Gatehouse J's decision in the last mentioned case and has decided that it would be unfair visit on the plaintiffs the sins of their former solicitors. As a reason for this view it was said that, if the plaintiffs suffered loss as a consequence of the removal of the order, they would probably have no remedy against the former solicitors; (1987) 137 NLJ 56. This reasoning might suggest that plaintiffs' interests come first and defendants' second, which is a pity.

3.   The duty of disclosure should become more specific. The courts should develop a list of categories of information to be disclosed when applications are made. For instance, plaintiffs must be made to disclose whether they have conveyed their suspicions to the defendant. Where, as in the *Columbia Picture Industries* and in the *Bayer* cases, the plaintiff has already interviewed the defendant through his agents there is no reason why he should not make him party to the application. (Indeed, in *Columbia Picture Industries v Robinson* the defendant had offered his assistance to the plaintiffs' agent and had shown him around his premises before the plaintiffs made their application, although this fact was suppressed in the application.) Similarly, the courts should always insist on being presented with evidence that the defendant would, if alerted, destroy evidence or dispose of assets.

4.   There is also scope to improve the monitoring of execution and notice should be taken of the guidelines proposed by Scott J, such as closer observance of the limits of orders and better documentation of what is seized ([1986] 3 All ER at 371–2).

5.   To avoid abuse the courts should strive, as far as possible, to see that a decent distance is maintained between the plaintiff's solicitors and the defendant. For instance, the former should not be authorised to interrogate the latter. As far as possible, Anton Piller orders should require defendants to hand over evidence rather than authorise the plaintiff's solicitors to rummage through the defendant's possessions.

6.   The time has arrived, much sooner than anyone would have predicted, to pause and ask ourselves the question raised by Scott J ([1986] 3 All ER at 369):

> 'What is to be said of the Anton Piller procedure which, on a regular and institutionalised basis, is depriving citizens of their property [and now of their freedom of movement] and closing down their businesses by orders made ex parte, on applications of which we know nothing and at which they cannot be heard, by orders which they are forced, on pain of committal, to obey, even if wrongly made?'

There is now quite a lot to be said against it. This question should not remain rhetorical but should figure in every single application in this form: What is so important about the vindication of the plaintiff's rights to justify interference with the defendant's rights of freedom and property merely on the plaintiff's say so?

7.   Much of the expansion of the jurisdiction may be attributed to inadequate dissemination of information within the judiciary. Since applications are heard in chambers, judges may remain ignorant for a long time about problems that have arisen in the exercise of the jurisdiction and are therefore unable to act in concert to solve them. It might be possible to improve the exchange of information amongst High Court judges.

Service outside the jurisdiction

Although the topics of service out of the jurisdiction under RSC Ord 11, r 1, and of forum non conveniens abound with authority the attention of the House of Lords is continually drawn to them. In *Spiliada Maritime Corp v Cansulex Ltd, The Spiliada* [1986] 3 All ER 843 the House of Lords made an attempt to clarify the law in a way that will enable trial judges to decide these issues without a nagging feeling that they are bound to get something wrong. Unlike some of its predecessors, the unanimous decision consists in one speech, that of Lord Goff. It is both brief, relative to the amount of previous authority on the subject, and lucid. The case is discussed in the article on Conflict of Laws, p 61 above. Here I should only like to draw the attention of to one point.

Lord Goff explained that the principles governing service out to the jurisdiction and those affecting the plea of forum non conveniens are the same. This ought now to result in the merging of two lengthy and convoluted lines of authority with a considerable gain in simplicity. The one remaining difference between the two topics concerned, basically, the burden of proof. When a plaintiff applies for permission to serve out of the jurisdiction he bears the burden of persuading the court that England is the appropriate forum for the trial of the action. By contrast, a defendant arguing that English proceeding should be stayed bears himself the burden of persuading the court that a foreign forum is more appropriate. (On related topics see: *Bank of Tokyo Ltd v Karoon* [1986] 3 All ER 468 CA; *Muduroglu Ltd v TC Ziraat Bankasi* [1986] 3 All ER 682 CA, discussed in the article on Conflict of Laws at p 60 above.)

An aspect of service out of jurisdiction under RSC Ord 11, r 1(1)(j), which was not touched upon by the House of Lords, troubled Webster J in *Amanuel v Alexander Shipping Co* [1986] 1 All ER 278. Before the issue of a writ, foreign shipowners, who were potential defendants, authorised agents within the jurisdiction to accept service. The plaintiffs served the agents accordingly and then applied for permission to join as defendant another foreign party: the charterers. The plaintiffs' application was made under r 1(1)(j) which provides: 'if an action begun by the writ being properly brought against a person duly served within the jurisdiction, a person out of the jurisdiction is a necessary or proper party thereto;'

The question arose whether the shipowners could be said to have been persons 'duly served within the jurisdiction'. Webster J decided that they were, following the Court of Appeal decision in *The Benarty* [1983] 1 Lloyds Rep 361. It was not disputed that had the shipowners agreed to accept service after the issue of the writ their acceptance would have amounted to voluntary submission to jurisdiction. It must therefore be right to conclude that a similar agreement before the issue of the writ has the same effect. Indeed, in the circumstances of the present case the pre-writ agreement was intended to achieve just that (in the event, however, judicial discretion was exercised against service out of the jurisdiction).

Deemed service

The issue of a writ at the request of a plaintiff stops the running of the limitation period. This does not necessarily mean that proceedings are now under way. Once the writ has been issued it is valid for service for twelve months: RSC Ord 6, r 8(1). Consequently, a plaintiff, who is not ready to proceed with his action but fears the expiration of the limitation period, will cause a writ to be issued (known as a 'protective' writ) and then delay its service to the defendant to give himself up to twelve months to prepare his case. Suppose now that the defendant has heard of the issue of the writ and, not wishing to have the uncertainty of the prospective action hanging over his head, he wants to bring matters to a head. Can he do so? When

addressed to Brandon J in *The Gniezno* [1967] 2 All ER 738 this question
received a positive and unqualified answer. His Lordship said (at 744):

> 'Looking at the matter as one of principle, it seems to me that a defendant
> ought to have a right to enter a voluntary appearance in this way so that in any
> case where an action is hanging over him he may take steps to have it
> dismissed. Under the present rules there is no obligation to serve a writ earlier
> than within twelve months ... In this way a defendant may have an action,
> the existence of which is known to him, hanging over him for a very
> considerable period. It seems to me desirable in principle that the defendant,
> faced with such a situation, should be able to obtain some finality.'

This decision was given when RSC Ord 10, r 1(3) provided:

> 'Where a writ is not duly served on a defendant but he enters an unconditional
> appearance in the action begun by the writ, the writ shall be deemed to have
> been duly served on him and to have been so served on the date on which he
> entered the appearance ...'

Ord 10 has since been amended and the corresponding provision is r 1(5):

> 'Subject to Order 12, rule 7, where a writ is not duly served on a defendant
> but he acknowledges service of it, the writ shall be deemed, unless the
> contrary is shown, to have been duly served on him and to have been served
> on the date on which he acknowledges services [sic]'

According to the Court of Appeal in *Abu Dhabi Helicopters Ltd v
International Aeradio plc* [1986] 1 All ER 395 the new rule has virtually
brought to an end the defendant's right to make an acknowledgment gratis,
as the right used to be called. In this case the plaintiffs' solicitors sent the
defendants' solicitors a copy of a writ stressing that they were doing so for
information only and not in order to serve it. The defendants' solicitors
replied by saying that 'we have entered a voluntary appearance to the Writ'
and invited the plaintiffs to serve a statement of claim. Evans J ruled that the
writ must be deemed to have been served. Dillon LJ gave two reasons for
overruling his decision. First, he thought that the reference in Ord 10, r 1(5)
to Ord 12, r 7 brought about a very considerable change in the practice
because its effect is that the acknowledgment of service does not amount to
a waiver of any irregularity in the writ or the service. Thus the defendant
may object to irregularities in the service even although he entered an
appearance ([1986] 1 All ER at 398–9). This is true but, with respect, it is
neither here nor there as far as acknowledgment *gratis* is concerned.

The second reason given by Dillon J concerned the words 'unless the
contrary is shown' in the new Ord 10, r 1(5). He felt that where, as in the
present case, it is shown that the writ has not been served then 'the contrary'
of service has been shown and the writ is not deemed to have been served
under r 1(5). He held that 'unless the contrary is shown' must be given its
ordinary meaning and that means that either the defendant or the plaintiff
can show that the writ has not been served in order to rebut the deemed
service.

There might have been some justification for this view had it been
possible to hold that the words in question had an ordinary meaning.
Unfortunately, whether or not they have any meaning at all, one thing is
clear: they do not have an ordinary meaning. If read literally r 1(5) affirms

and denies, at one and the same time, its central provision. The word 'contrary' clearly refers to the words 'to have been duly served'. In the 'ordinary' meaning the section therefore reads as follows: 'Where a writ is not duly served it shall be deemed to have been duly served unless it is shown not to have been duly served.' Dillon LJ's appeal to the ordinary meaning has resulted in throwing over an important right of defendants without solving the difficulty that the words 'unless the contrary is shown' pose. It is highly significant that it never occurred to the editors of the *White Book* that the new version of Ord 10, r 1(5) had the effect given to it in the present case: *The Supreme Court Practice 1985*, vol 1, para 10/1/13.

There is very little discussion in the Court of Appeal's judgment of the merits of the competing interpretations, except for one remark by Sir George Waller when he said ([1986] 1 All ER at 399): 'the law gives them [the plaintiffs] 12 months in which to serve the writ and I do not see any reason to restrict the construction of the words "unless the contrary is shown" so as to limit the benefit of those words to the defendants.' There is, however, an important reason of principle for restricting this freedom, as was explained in *The Gniezno* [1967] 2 All ER 738. This principle says that a defendant should have a right not to allow the possibility of litigation, which may or may not be pursued by the plaintiff, to hang over his head when he would prefer to know what the plaintiff proposes to do. If a plaintiff could obtain a writ shortly before the expiration of the limitation period and then delay its service for 12 months, this will in effect mean that every limitation period is extendable by one year at the discretion of the plaintiff. While this cannot have been the intention of the rules of practice, it is now the result of an 'ordinary meaning' interpretation which pays little attention to the principle as stake and which has blown over an important right of defendants.

By coincidence the very same words 'unless the contrary is shown' in a different section of Ord 10, r 1, also fell to be considered this year. Ord 10, r 1(3)(a) provides: 'the date of service shall, unless the contrary is shown, be deemed to be the seventh day . . . after the date on which the copy was sent to . . . the address in question;'

In *Hodgson v Hart District Council* [1986] 1 All ER 400 the plaintiffs sent a writ to the defendant shortly before the writ was due to expire. The seventh day after the sending of the writ fell after the date of expiry but the writ had actually been received by the defendant council before the expiry date. The defendant argued that according to r 1(3)(a) the writ must be deemed to have arrived on the seventh day irrespective of the true facts. The Court of Appeal rejected this argument holding that rule 1(3) merely creates a presumption which both parties are at liberty to rebut, and which the plaintiff in fact rebutted. This interpretation is unexceptionable since it conforms not only with 'ordinary meaning' but also with principle. The principle being that a party who has actually received an otherwise valid writ should not be allowed to claim that he has not received it.

Had the Court of Appeal considered this principle, even if only as a starting point, in *Austin Rover Group Ltd v Crouch Butler Savage Associates* [1986] 3 All ER 50, much confusion and doubt would have been avoided. The plaintiffs issued a writ against a partnership. Shortly before its 12 months of validity were up, they sent it by post to the partnership firm at the address at which the firm had been running its business before it moved to new premises. The Post Office re-addressed the letter and delivered it to the defendants' new premises, where it arrived and was seen by a partner well before the date of the writ's expiry. All the same, the defendants argued that there had not been due service. This wholly unmeritorious claim rested on the following argument. Service to partnerships is governed by Ord 81, r 3(1)(c) which requires that the writ be served 'by sending a copy of the writ by ordinary first-class post (as defined in Order 10, rule 1(2)) to the firm at the principal place of business of the partnership'. Since the writ was addressed to a place where the firm no longer carried its business, it was said, the service did not conform to the requirements of the rule. True, it was contended, Ord 10, r 1(2)(a) authorises posting 'to the defendant at his usual or last known address', but these words cannot be read into Ord 81, r 3(1)(c) which explicity refers to the 'principal place of business'.

Although the issue was fairly simple three separate judgments were delivered and the resolution of the appeal was by majority only. The intricate and highly technical arguments advanced by counsel were treated with almost an equal flair for technicality by their Lordships. Lloyd LJ said ([1986] 3 All ER at 60):

> 'I can understand it being said, "But here the writ arrived at the principal place of business and arrived in time, so what does it matter where it was sent?" I have much sympathy with that view. I dislike technicalities as much as anyone. But unfortunately the provisions relating to service by post have to be complied with. The fact that a writ has arrived does not mean that it has been properly sent. Suppose, for example, the document had been accidentally dropped on the way to the post, picked up by a stranger and delivered by hand. Nobody suggests, or could suggest, that that would have been good service. The document would not have been served personally and it would not have been sent by post.'

The view that the rules of service are purely technical is, presumably, founded on the belief that we need certainty in the service procedure and that certainty is more likely to be secured by technically precise adherence to the wording of the rules. I would, however, suggest that, far from promoting certainty, such a strategy undermines certainty by making the validity of service depend not on substance but on the latest twist which imaginative counsel is able to give to the words of the rules. A better strategy is to adhere to the principle which underlines the rule. This principle is stated in the opening section of Ord 10, r 1: '(1) A writ must be served personally on each defendant by the plaintiff or his agent.' The core requirement is, therefore, that the defendant receive, in person, the writ from the plaintiff so that he is made aware of the action against him and he is enabled to take the necessary steps to defend himself. Since it is often unnecessarily cumbersome or impractical for the plaintiff to physically deliver the writ into the defendant's hands the remainder of the Order creates rebuttable presumptions of service. The presumptions are useful but they are no more than presumptions. Where it is an undisputed fact, as in the present case, that the plaintiff intended to serve the writ and took steps to that end and, as a result, the writ found its way into the defendant's hands and mind, the principle of service has been satisfied.

Without disrepect, I should like to suggest that there would and should be proper service in the example postulated by Lloyd LJ. Indeed, there is nothing in the rules that forces a contrary conclusion. Ord 10, r 1(2) states that a 'writ ... may, instead of being served personally on' the defendant, 'be served ... (b) ... by inserting through the letter box a copy of the writ ... addressed to the defendant'. If I take my writ to the post office and but lose it on the way and a conscientious fellow citizen takes the trouble of putting it in the defendant's letter box he does so with my implied authority, as well as blessing, and the requirement of the rule has been fulfilled.

While not subscribing to the principle I have suggested, the majority, Lloyd LJ dissenting, held that there was valid service because the word 'sending' in Ord 81, r 3(1)(c) implied the entire process of dispatch, transmission and delivery and not just the initial dispatch. Consequently, the majority concluded, since the writ arrived at the defendants' principal place of business it was 'sent' there. While this result is entirely sensible, the narrow ground on which it was arrived at is likely to increase uncertainty and will in all probability lead to future litigation.

In view of comments made in this case about renewing expired writs after the limitation period, solicitors would be well advised to try to avoid having to have recourse to discretionary extension.

Dispensing with service

In an application by Westminster City Council to the Land Registry to register a charge against a building owned by the Iranian government and used as the Iranian embassy, before the cessation of diplomatic relations between Iran and the UK, the Iranian government raised an objection through its solicitors. The Chief Land Registrar referred the issue raised to the court. The council took out an originating summons but the solicitors acting for the Iranian government had no instructions to accept service. In the absence of diplomatic relations between the two countries the writ could not be served in accordance with the provisions of the State Immunity Act 1978, s 12(1) and the question was whether the service could be dispensed with. The relevant provision is RSC Ord 23, r 5—'(1) Where any party to a summons fails to attend on the first or any resumed hearing thereof, the Court may proceed in his absence if, having regard to the nature of the application, it thinks expedient to do so.' Peter Gibson J held in *Westminster City Council v Government of the Islamic Republic of Iran* [1986] 3 All ER 284 that a person 'fails to attend', for the purpose of the rule, only after he has been duly served. Since the Iranian government was not served, it did not 'fail to attend'. One would have thought that the purpose of the rule was to dispense with service where the defendant makes it impossible, by his own actions, to effect service. There were no doubt goods reasons of policy for not proceeding in the absence of the Iranian government in this case, but it would have been better to reach this result under the discretion conferred by r 5.

Discovery

Discovery in a foreign country

In All ER Rev 1985 I wrote: 'It emerges from *South Carolina Insurance Co v Assurantie Maatschappij 'de Zeven Provincien' NV* [1985] 2 All ER 1046 that the English courts are so jealous of their jurisdiction that they will forbid a party to proceedings in England to avail himself of better discovery facilities in another country.' I am happy to say that this is no longer the case. The House of Lords has now reversed the Court of Appeal's decision ([1986] 3 All ER 487). It has decided that a party availing himself of discovery facilities in another country is not invading his opponent's rights and he does not unconscionably interfere with the English court's control over its own procedures. Moreover, to the extent that the foreign discovery proceedings impose extra cost on the opponent, this is the opponent's own fault for not disclosing the evidence voluntarily.

Respect for foreign jurisdictions has found expression in another case: *MacKinnon v Donaldson Lufkin & Jenrette Securities Corp* [1986] 1 All ER 653. The plaintiff claimed to have been defrauded by a Bahamian company, which has since ceased to exist, of a large sum of money. The money was paid by the defendant into the Bahamian company's account with Citibank in New York. Citibank is an American Bank with a branch in London. The plaintiff obtained an order under the Bankers' Books Evidence Act 1879 ordering Citibank to allow the plaintiff to inspect entries in the bank's books which related to the defendants' account and which were kept in New York. He also obtained subpoenas ad testificandum and duces tecum to similar end. Citibank brought a motion to set aside the orders.

Hoffmann J gave two rulings. First, that the bank had a locus standi to bring a motion to set aside the orders without being joined as a party to the action. Secondly, and more importantly, his Lordship explained the distinction between the question regarding the jurisdiction to entertain an action and the question of making sovereign orders affecting other jurisdictions. While accepting that *Norwich Pharmacal Co v Customs and Excise Comrs* [1973] 2 All ER 943 provides authority for ordering a non-party to disclose information when he was involved, albeit innocently, in a tortious act against the plaintiff, Hoffmann J observed that case had no bearing on the question of the territorial limitations. An order to testify or to produce documents is, he observed, an exercise of sovereign authority. In exercising soverign authority it is incumbent on the state to practice restraint when its order might affect the sovereignty of other jurisdictions. Courts should not, he held, make an order 'requiring production by a non-party of documents outside the jurisdiction concerning business which it has transacted outside the jurisdiction'; [1986] 1 All ER at 659 (see also *Ashtiani v Kashi* [1986] 2 All ER 970 discussed above). He was all the more fortified in his conclusion by the fact that the plaintiff in the present case could apply to the American courts for the order they sought. He did, however, emphasise that there might be exceptional and pressing circumstances where an order of the kind sought by the present plaintiffs may be justified.

Disclosure of expert evidence

A novel point arose in *Shell Pensions Trust Ltd v Pell Frischmann & Partners* [1986] 2 All ER 911. The plaintiffs brought an action against the defendants, consulting engineers, alleging negligence in the construction of offices of which the plaintiffs were tenants. The official referee made an order under Ord 33 for disclosure of expert evidence before the trial. The defendants contended that such order can only be made with regard to independent expert witnesses and not with regard to a defendant proposing to give evidence from his own expertise. This argument was rejected by Judge John Newey QC who held that if the defendants were allowed to call one of their members to give expert evidence, not previously disclosed, this would necessitate adjournments and much waste of time. Yet such adjournments were the very thing that Ord 38 was designed to prevent. Consequently, he concluded, expert evidence to be given by the defendant himself was to be disclosed in the same way as would the report of any other expert.

Judgment

Variation of judgment after its delivery

The jurisdiction of a judge to reconsider his decision at any time before his order is drawn up or perfected has been confirmed in *Pittalis v Sherefettin* [1986] 2 All ER 227. Having given judgment in court, the county court judge changed his mind and the very next day notified the parties and gave them an opportunity to make representations. The Court of Appeal held that the judge was entitled to do so and commended him for giving the parties an opportunity to be heard.

Interest

A plaintiff sues defendants for damages. The defendants pay the plaintiff the sum claimed 'in full settlement', but the latter writes to say that he is accepting the payment as being only in respect of the principal and insists on interest. Can the plaintiff then pursue his claim and obtain interest? In *Edmunds v Lloyd Italico e L'Ancona Cia Di Assicuarazioni e Riassicurazioni SpA* [1986] 2 All ER 249 the Court of Appeal has given an affirmative answer to this question. The authority for awarding interest is to be found in s 35A of the Supreme Court Act 1981. Counsel for the defendants contended that s 35A did not confer the power to award interest on damages that have already been paid. Section 35A, sub-s 3(b) provides that where 'the defendant pays the whole debt to the plaintiff . . . the defendant shall be liable to pay the plaintiff simple interest . . . on . . . the debt for . . . the period between the date when the cause of action arose and the date of the payment.' The fact that the section makes specific provision for debt and not for damages should, on the plaintiff's argument, be taken to mean that interest is only payable in respect of the former but not the latter.

Sir John Donaldson MR rejected this argument, explaining that sub-s 3(a) was necessary because payment of a debt in full extinguishes the cause of action and if it were not for the sub-section the court would have no basis for giving judgment for interest. By contrast, payment of the full amount of damages claimed still leaves the court with power to give judgment on liability and to assess damages and interest, taking into account, of course, any payment made by the defendant. Since parliament clearly intended to empower the court to award interest there was nothing in sub-s 3(a) inconsistent with this intention.

Stay of execution

Schofield v Church Army [1986] 3 All ER 715 was concerned with a rather unusual situation. An industrial tribunal held that the respondent was unfairly dismissed by his employer, the appellant, and ordered the latter to pay the former compensation of £8,370. The respondent then obtained in the county court a garnishee order and the sum due was paid by the appellant into court. Meanwhile the appellant commenced an action in the High Court alleging that the respondent had stolen from his employers a sum of money exceeding the compensation due to him under the judgment of the industrial tribunal. Hence the appellants resisted the respondent's attempt to have payment out of court contending that the money should remain in court until judgment in the High Court action.

Under the County Court Rules, Ord 30, r 6 the county court has a discretion in the matter similar to that conferred on the High Court under RSC Ord 47, r 1. The question before the Court of Appeal concerned the proper exercise of the discretion. The judge below decided to order payment to the respondent because the appellants did not adduce sufficent evidence to persuade him that they had a strong chance of success in the High Court. In the Court of Appeal the appellant contended that the correct test to be applied to these circumstances was similar to that applicable under RSC Ord 14, r 3(2). Ord 14 applies to summary judgments and empowers the court to stay execution 'until after the trial of any counterclaim made or raised by the defendant'. Under this rule the practice is to order stay as long as the defendant's claim is not hopeless. The Court of Appeal held this test to be inappropriate to situations where a judgment has been obtained not summarily but after a full trial. At the same time the court felt that the test adopted by the judge below was too stringent.

According to Dillon LJ, once it is shown that there is a serious case to be tried on the counterclaim the question to be asked is: Why has this claim not been litigated? In the instant case the appellants had a perfectly good justification: the industrial tribunal had no jurisdiction to entertain their counterclaim. Since the appellant made it clear, when the tribunal gave its judgment, that he was proceeding with a counterclaim and has done so promptly it would be unjust, Dillon LJ concluded, that the money should be paid out to the respondent.

Two further decisions on execution should be noted. In *Bankers Trust Co v Galadari* [1986] 3 All ER 794 the Court of Appeal clarified the position regarding a fieri facias writ that has been set aside on appeal but subsequently restored on further appeal. It was decided that once the writ has been restored, its priority remains unaffected by it having been set aside. That is, its priority is determined by the date on which it was originally delivered to the sheriff for execution.

The other decision concerns execution of judgment upon the matrimonial home: see *Harman v Glencross* [1986] 1 All ER 545, discussed in the article on Family Law, p 171 above.

Costs

Security for costs

The Court of Appeal considered a novel question in *Taly NDC International NV v Terra Nova Insurance Co Ltd* [1986] 1 All ER 69: Has the court jurisdiction to order the plaintiff to give a security for costs to a third party (ie a party upon whom third party proceedings were served by the defendant)? Such orders are governed by Ord 23, r 1(1) which empowers the court to order the plaintiff to provide security upon the application of a defendant. Ord 23, r 1(3) requires references to plaintiff and defendant to 'be construed as references to the person (howsoever described in the record) who is in the position of plaintiff or defendant . . . in the proceedings in question . . .' The court held that since a plaintiff seeks no relief against a third party the latter cannot be said to be in the position of a defendant, unless he applied for, and was granted, leave to defend. Consequently a third party is not entitled to security. The fact that the plaintiff has made an interlocutory application against the third party makes no difference to this conclusion since the relative position of plaintiff and defendant is to be determined in relation to the proceedings as a whole.

Discretion in matters of costs

Section 51(1) of the Supreme Court Act 1981 provides:

> '. . . the costs of and incidental to all proceedings in the civil division of the Court of Appeal and the High Court . . . shall be in the discretion of the court, and the court shall have full power to determine by whom and to what extent the costs are to be paid.'

The House of Lords has held, in *The Vimeira* [1986] 2 All ER 409, that the discretion conferred by this section is not confined to ordering costs only against parties to the proceedings, thus overruling the Court of Appeal's decision, [1985] 3 All ER 641, discussed in All ER Rev 1985, p 233 (see also the new RSC Ord 4, r 9(2)).

The extent to which an appellate court will interfere with the trial judge's discretion in the matter of costs was considered in *Scherer v Counting Instruments Ltd* [1986] 2 All ER 529. The defendants applied to have the action against them dismissed for want of prosecution. The judge rejected their application but, nevertheless, ordered the plaintiff to pay the costs. In allowing an appeal against this decision the Court of Appeal held that the discretion in awarding costs had to be exercised according to established principles. These principles were, first, that the costs normally followed the event and, secondly, that consideration should be confined to circumstances leading to the litigation and its conduct. Where a judge departed from the normal rule in the absence of any special circumstances, he will be taken to have acted on extraneous grounds and his decision will be subject to appeal even in the absence of leave from the judge. Since in the present case there were no special circumstances, the judge's decision on costs was overruled. It should be noted that the principle that the costs should normally follow the event appears now in the new Ord 62, r 3.

In another decision the Court of Appeal has held that the fact that the judge has taken extraneous considerations into account in awarding costs is not necessarily fatal. If the extraneous considerations were not the overriding reason for his decision the court will refuse to interfere: *Smiths Ltd v Middleton (No 2)* [1986] 2 All ER 539.

Occasion for departure from the principle that the costs follow the event was provided by *Celsteel Ltd v Alton House Holdings Ltd* [1986] 1 All ER 608. The plaintiffs were lessees of flats. The freeholder, Alton House, granted a lease to Mobil Oil on another part of the estate for the purpose of building a car wash. The plaintiffs sought an injunction against Mobil and Alton House to prevent them from erecting the car wash on the ground that it would interfere with their right of way. The injunctions were granted and an order of costs was made against both Mobil and Alton House. On appeal it was decided that there was no ground for awarding an injunction against Alton House as they had no control over the proposed car project. However, the Court of Appeal refused to order the plaintiffs to pay Alton House's costs because the latter fought the plaintiffs' claim at the trial and lost on the substantive issue. The court decided not to make any order of costs as between the plaintiffs and Alton House. In view of the role played by Alton House one wonders whether it would not have been more appropriate to allow the plaintiffs their costs against Alton House as the trial judge had held.

The new bases of taxation

The most important development on costs this year consists in the promulgation of the new Ord 62. Under the old system there were five separate bases for taxing costs. The new rules provide only two bases: costs on a standard basis and costs on an indemnity basis. Thus Ord 62, r 3(4) provides:

> 'The amount of his costs which any party shall be entitled to recover is the amount allowed after taxation on the standard basis ... unless it appears to the Court to be appropriate to order costs to be taxed on the indemnity basis.'

The difference between the two bases is set out in Ord 62, r 12:

> '(1) On a taxation of costs on the standard basis there shall be allowed a reasonable amount in respect of all the costs reasonably incurred and any doubts which the taxing officer may have as to whether the costs were reasonably incurred or were reasonable in amount shall be resolved in favour of the paying party; ... (b) On a taxation on the indemnity basis all costs shall be allowed except insofar as they are of an unreasonable amount or have been unreasonably incurred and any doubts which the taxing officer may have ... shall be resolved in favour of the receiving party; ... (c) Where the Court makes an order for costs without indicating the basis of taxation or an order that costs be taxed on any basis other than the standard basis or the indemnity basis, the costs shall be taxed on the standards basis.'

In addition to the bases provided for by the old rules, the court also had discretion to award costs on any other basis it saw fit. Under the new rule no additional discretionary bases are allowed.

Old Ord 62 was most unsatisfactory. To quote Sir Robert Megarry V-C, the 'process of reading through the main body of the order, even without appendices, is one that brings to mind Oliver Cromwell's phrase, "an ungodly jumble". . . . and if one day there is to be a rewritten order, there will be little difficulty in achieving an improvement on the present drafting.' *EMI Records Ltd v Wallace Ltd* [1982] 2 All ER 980 at 983. The day has clearly come and, needless to say, Megarry V-C's prediction has been fulfilled. The present order is not only an improvement, it is a very considerable one. But even an improved order requires interpretation and the most obvious candidate for interpretation is, of course, the 'standard basis'.

Under the old indemnity basis a party recovered all the costs that he had incurred, provided of course that they were reasonable in nature and amount. Otherwise the successful litigant recovered, broadly speaking, roughly two thirds of his costs. Commenting on the two thirds practice in *Bartlett v Barclays Bank Trust Co Ltd* [1980] 2 All ER 92 at 98, Brightman LJ said—'Why this should be, I do not know, but the practice is well-established and I do not think that there is any sufficient reason to depart from that practice in the case before me.'

It may be thought unjust that a successful party, who has not been guilty of any procedural misconduct or delay, should be out of pocket. It was therefore contended before Knox J in *Bowen-Jones v Bowen-Jones* [1986] 3 All ER 163 that the passing of the new order should be seized upon to remove the injustice. On the assumption that the new 'standard basis' referred to the two thirds practice, it was suggested that it should now apply only where there was a genuine difference of opinion or of recollection and there was no deliberate attempt to keep the other party out of their money or to mislead the court. Knox J rejected the argument. He held that the standard basis was the successor of the former 'party and party' basis and of the 'common fund' basis and must be interpreted accordingly. It follows, therefore, that the two thirds practice will continue in the majority of cases while the indemnity basis will be confined to situations which would have qualified under the old practice for indemnity costs. Generally, these situations were confined to orders against contemnors.

Much confusion will be avoided if attention is focused on the new order rather than the old practice. Rule 12(1) says that under the standard basis 'there shall be allowed a reasonable amount in respect of all costs'. This means that the taxing officer approaches the assessment with the principle that he must award *only* a reasonable proportion of the costs incurred and not all of them. By contrast, rule 12(2) says that under the indemnity basis 'all costs shall be allowed'. Here the taxing officer approaches assessment with the assumption that *all* costs are recoverable, except when 'they are unreasonable in amount or have been unreasonably incurred.'

Brightman J's puzzlement notwithstanding, it is not difficult to imagine why the normal practice is that a successful party should only be awarded a reasonable proportion of the cost he has incurred rather than all of it. Legal charges vary enormously according to the scales adopted by individual firms of solicitors, the strategy pursued and counsel's fees. Justice does not require that the successful party should recoup his entire costs where he chose to avail himself of the most expensive legal services. If that were the case, the incentive to save would be diminished and the imbalance between rich and poor litigants would further increase. It is therefore sensible to empower the taxing officer to look at the successful party's costs and consider what a reasonable amount should be allowed in view of the prevailing scales, the course of the litigation and the like. A thrifty litigant may well receive his full cost, but only in exceptional circumstances should one start form a presumption of full recovery.

Having said that, attention should be drawn to a certain ambiguity in r 12(1). After stating that a 'reasonable amount' shall be allowed 'in respect of all costs reasonably incurred', it goes on to provide that 'any doubts which the taxing officer may have as to whether the costs were reasonably incurred or were reasonable in amount shall be resolved in favour of the paying party'. If it is the task of the taxing officer himself to determine the 'reasonable amount', how can he entertain doubt about it? If he concludes that an amount is reasonable, he cannot be in doubt. If he is in doubt, he cannot reach the conclusion that it is reasonable. However, rather than disturb the interpretation I have suggested, this part of the rule should be taken to mean that in estimating the reasonable amount the taxing officer should err in favour of the paying party.

In the Privy Council

Conflict of laws is not a subject one usually associates with orders of costs. Yet a question concerning the jurisdiction of courts of different countries to award costs in respect of the same litigation arose in *Tai Hing Cotton Mill Ltd v Liu Chong Hing Bank Ltd (No 2)* [1986] 1 All ER 897. The Privy Council held that, in appeals to the judicial committee, the Privy Council registrar was limited to the taxation of costs incurred in England while the Hong Kong registrar was limited to taxation of costs incurred in Hong Kong. It also held that while a party to an appeal before the Privy Council was entitled to be represented by counsel who represented him below, he was not entitled, if successful, to recover his counsel's travelling expenses. The reason given was that the successful party was not entitled to impose greater costs on his unsuccessful opponent than the latter would have incurred had the former been represented by local counsel. This reasoning illustrates the 'reasonable amount' principle that I have just discussed, but the wisdom of the conclusion is not beyond dispute. One should be conscious of the danger that this ruling might increase resentment abroad of the Privy Council's jurisdiction.

County court small claims arbitration

The small claims arbitration procedure was introduced in order to provide litigants pursuing humble claims, of up to £500, with easy access to our courts of justice. To that end the County Court Rules 1981 have devised a simple procedure, shorn of most of the formality and complexity that attends ordinary civil litigation. Generally speaking, the plaintiff need only fill in a form in order to institute proceedings. CCR Ord 19, r 5 provides:

'(3) Any hearing shall be informal and the strict rules of evidence shall not apply. (4) At the hearing the arbitrator may adopt any method of procedure which he may consider to be convenient and to afford a fair and equal opportunity to each party to present his case . . . '

Faithful to the spirit of this procedure, the county court judiciary has striven to make it simple and congenial for use by ordinary citizens. Thus, when the solicitor, representing the defendant in *Chilton v Saga Holidays plc* [1986] 1 All ER 841, proposed to cross-examine the plaintiff, suing in person for a failed holiday, the registrar ruled that the solicitor should suggest the questions to the registrar, who would then put them to the plaintiff. The defendant appealed to Judge Turner who found the registrar's ruling entirely sensible. The Court of Appeal has now reversed this ruling holding that a party who was represented by a solicitor or counsel in these arbitration proceedings had a right to use his representative to cross-examine the opponent even although the latter is not represented.

This decision is unfortunate. As I have explained, the purpose of the small claims arbitration is to open the doors of the court to the citizen who has a grievance but has not the resources, material or emotional, to institute a full blooded action. It is recognised that in the absence of an attractive and simple procedure in which the citizen can pursue his own claim many just complaints will go unsatisfied. In order not to deter ordinary untutored citizens, who feel foreboding at the very idea of contact with the law, the procedure has not only to be simple but it has also to inspire confidence. It was therefore eminently sensible of Mr Registrar Lusty to conclude that to give free reign to the cross-examination of the plaintiff by the defendants' solicitor would undermine confidence in the process. A simple litigant who is cross-examined by a sophisticated and experienced solicitor or counsel will clearly feel that the contest is unequal. And if he loses, however justly, he may well go away believing that his defeat was due to being manipulated by the solicitor during examination.

The rules themselves discourage legal representation by the provision that no costs are awardable in respect of such representation at the hearing. It is impractical to bar professional lawyers from the proceedings but, at the same time, it is desirable to curb their freedom to harm the confidence of the litigant who appears in person. The registrar and the judge proposed to do this through the exercise of discretion. What then were the reasons that the Court of Appeal found so compelling in overruling the courts below? First, Donaldson MR said that 'it would be an extremely odd situation if it were open to parties to be represented by those who have left the legal profession and not by those who are members of it.' ([1986] 1 All ER at 843–4). Surely, such an anomaly, and it is not necessary to investigate the probability of its occurrence, could be avoided by the exercise of discretion. Neither the registrar nor the judge were laying down an absolute rule in this respect.

Secondly, the Master of the Rolls held that the present procedure 'is basically an adversarial system, and it is fundamental to that each party shall be entitled to tender their own evidence, and that the other party shall be entitled to ask questions designed to probe the accuracy or otherwise . . . of the evidence that has been given.' Nothing in the registrar's ruling offended this principle. The defendant was not prevented from questioning the plaintiff's evidence, he was merely asked to put his questions through the registrar. Besides, there is nothing so sacred about the adversarial procedure that it should override the aim of giving the citizens easy access to the court.

Lastly, the Master of the Rolls felt that in situations such as the present one it was the duty of the registrar 'without entering the arena to a point where he is no longer able to act judicially, to make good any deficiencies in the advantage available to the unrepresented party' ([1986] 1 All ER at 844). The correct procedure, he considered, was for the registrar to pick up 'the unrepresented party's complaints' and put them to the other side. With due respect, this suggestion makes it much more likely that the registrar, in an attempt to correct the balance, will enter the arena as a champion of one party. The better course is, surely, for the registrar to ensure that the balance of advantage does not tilt in favour of one side in the first place, rather than try to rectify it once the balance has been thrown out.

It remains to be hoped that the rule committee will reconsider the situation and that, in doing so, it will draw on the experience of those who have administered the small claims arbitration system and who have intimate understanding of the needs of the untutored claimant.

Shipping

ROBERT P GRIME, BA, BCL
Professor of Law, University of Southampton

I Maritime claims in Reading

In 1886, Bowen LJ, in *Falke v Scottish Imperial Insurance Co* 34 Ch D 234, at
p 249, was able to declare roundly that: 'With regard to salvage... the
maritime law differs from the common law'. Whereas at common law
beneficial services rendered to the property of another create no liability to
reward the person rendering those services or even to make good his
expenditure, maritime law 'for the purposes of public policy and the
advantages of trade imposes in these cases a liability', reinforced by a
maritime lien over the maritime property benefited, to pay a just reward.
While in modern times it might be argued that the law of unjust enrichment
has advanced far enough to give a remedy to some at least of those good
neighbours who carry out 'terrene salvage', the law of salvage proper
applies only to maritime matters.

In *The Goring* [1986] 1 All ER 475, five gentlemen, members of the Island
Bohemian Club, were visiting their club premises on De Montford Island
which is just above Reading bridge in the River Thames when one of them
noticed the Goring, a small passenger vessel, apparently unmanned and
drifting down river towards a probable sticky end over Reading weir.
Using the club ferry boat the five of them eventually secured the Goring.
To press their claims for a just reward for this undeniably meritorious
service they issued a writ in rem in the Admiralty Court. So was their claim
to be considered as salvage, despite the fact that it was done in non-tidal
waters, far away from the seas 'where the great ships go'? Was it sufficient
that the Goring had received the benefit of successful, voluntary and
meritorious services and was undoubtedly a ship and therefore at least
arguably 'maritime property'? Or was Reading too far inland? After all, it
was as long ago as 1793 that Eyre CJ in *Nicholson v Chapman* 2 Hy Bl 254
had refused to apply the principles of salvage to 'goods upon the banks of a
navigable river' seemingly on the grounds that neither the property salved
nor the salvage operation was exposed to the 'storms, tempests and
accidents, far beyond the reach of human foresight to prevent', which he
regarded as inseparable risks of ocean navigation at that time, and which
justified the peculiar (and un-common-lawyerly) maritime notion of
salvage.

But the recognition of up-river salvage was only indirectly raised by *The
Goring*. The precise issue before the court was jurisdictional: the owners of
the Goring sought an order to set aside the writ on the ground either that
the Admiralty Court had no jurisdiction over salvage services rendered in
non-tidal waters or that the indorsement on the writ, containing the claim,
be struck out as scandalous, frivolous, vexatious or otherwise an abuse of
the process of the court: two ways of expressing the same view, that,

whatever the substantive law, a writ in rem might not issue in respect of non-tidal salvage. At first sight, such a point seems susceptible of an easy answer. The jurisdiction of the Admiralty Court is governed by s 20 of the Supreme Court Act 1981, para (j) of sub-s 2 of which includes 'any claim in the nature of salvage'. There was no doubt that those words should be interpreted unrestictedly as regards geographical limits to jurisdiction. The Admiralty Court had always taken jurisdiction 'in respect of salvage services occurring anywhere in the world'. Moreover, the legislative history supported a liberal approach: s 22(a) of the Supreme Court of Judicature (Consolidation) Act 1925, for example, conferred upon the Probate, Divorce and Admiralty Division jurisdiction over 'any claim in the nature of salvage for services rendered to a ship . . . whether rendered on the high seas or in the body of the county.'

The defendants offered what was perhaps the only answer available to them in those circumstances: that if a salvage reward was not payable as a matter of substantive maritime law in respect of services rendered in non-tidal waters, then the Admiralty Court could not by relying upon a geographically wide jurisdictional definition create a new cause of action. The plaintiff's claim could not properly be described as 'salvage'. Sheen J commented that the submission disclosed 'a confusion between the geographical limits of jurisdiction of the court and the cause of action' (a confusion which might possibly be described as an inevitable consequence of expressing jurisdictional rules partly in terms of particular substantive claims) and, after considering the desirability of encouraging salvage services in non-tidal waters as well as the absurdity of drawing distinctions between identically meritorious services rendered to burning vessels in tidal and in non-tidal anchorages, allowed the writ to stand.

At the outset of his judgment, Sheen J had noted the relative insignificance in economic terms of the case, since the service, although meritorious, did not involve high risks to the salvors and would not therefore have attracted a very high salvage reward: 'I cannot help thinking that the costs already incurred in this action may have exceeded the likely reward for the services in question.' It is, however, a matter of principle, and a not insignificant principle. Until Admiralty and Common Law march in step in the matter of entitlement to indemnity, recompense or reward for meritorious services rendered to property, a distinction will have to be made between salvage and other forms of unjust enrichment. *The Goring* tells us that salvage in non-tidal waters may be rewarded in Admiralty, but it does not tell us where in future the line will be drawn. If I can have a salvage reward for securing a pleasure-boat beneath Reading bridge, why not for protecting from the depredations of hooligans another pleasure-boat which happens to be on the back of a low-loader lorry *on* Reading bridge? There is already considerable authority on the issue, although most of it is ancient and often complicated by the possibility, much argued 200 years ago, of a common-law right to obtain at least compensation for work and labour for meritorious non-maritime 'salvage' services. Perhaps we must await further enlightenment from the Court of Appeal, whither *The Goring* is bound.

2 Wreck, salvage, abandonment and droits of Admiralty

1986 was the year for sunken transatlantic liners. Although the Titanic has appeared on our television screens, she has not yet appeared in our courts. The Lusitania, on the other hand, has. The Lusitania was torpedoed by a German U-boat on 7 May 1915. She sank in 315 feet of water some 11.8 miles south-south-west of the Head of Kinsale, a point which is and was outside the territorial sea of both Britain and Ireland. She contained some cargo and some personal property of her passengers.

As with the Titanic, the salvage of the vessel and its contents has long been the subject of debate, both practical and fantastic. The Lusitania, however, is an easier proposition than her film-star sister. Her precise position has been known for some years and both the depth of the water and the likely sea conditions have meant that salvage on her is a more realistic possibility than on the Titanic. Leaving to one side some rather mysterious work apparently carried out by naval personnel at a relatively early stage in the wreck's history, serious salvage operations began in 1982. They were moderately successful. The ship's bell and some 94 other assorted items were recovered. The question before the Admiralty Court in *Pierce v Bemis, The Lusitania* [1986] 1 All ER 1011 was whether those items belonged to those who had assisted in their recovery or whose interest derived from insurers ('the claimants') or the Department of Transport ('the crown'), the claimants having settled their differences *inter sese* before trial.

The case is almost as interesting for what it was not about then for its proper subjects. The proceedings concerned the 'contents' of the Lusitania, that is to say, the cargo and the personal property of the passengers. It did not concern the vessel itself, which for these purposes included 'hull, machinery, appurtenances, fixtures and fittings and the accoutrements, loose equipment, furniture or other goods owned at the time of the loss by the Cunard Steamship Co Ltd and used in her operation as a passenger liner.' A long list which could hardly avoid including the recovered ship's bell. The Lusitania herself, it was agreed 'between all parties', legally belonged to the successors of the war risk underwriters. Sheen J commented, clearly obiter, that the insurers had paid the owners in respect of the total loss of the ship and 'thereby acquired legal title to the ship'.

That is not, with respect, strictly accurate. It is, of course true that it is a condition precedent to a valid insurance claim for a total loss, whether actual or constructive, that there be an abandonment of the property insured to the underwriter (see per Brett LJ in *Kaltenbach v MacKenzie* (1878) LR 3 CP 467). Although at one time it was true to say that upon such abandonment the title to the property was automatically transferred to the underwriters, that rule could not easily survive the nineteenth century complexities of the registration of ships and formal instruments of transfer. If a ship could only be transferred by executing a bill of sale and amending the register, what possible effect on title might an informal abandonment to an underwriter, by notice or otherwise, have? Lord Truro in *Scottish Marine Insurance v Turner* (1853) 1 Macq HL Cas 334 at 342 thought that an *accepted* abandonment to underwriters of maritime property as a total loss operated as a binding contract formally to assign such property in the future, such assignment to be made effective as from the date of the notice of abandonment. However, when the Marine Insurance Act came to be passed in 1906, such subtlety was rendered unnecessary. The Act made it clear that what was by then the dominant view of the matter should be put beyond doubt. There is no automatic transfer even when an abandonment to the underwriters has been accepted by them: s 63 merely confers upon the insurer the right, where there is a valid abandonment, to take over the interest of the assured in the property. Section 79 provides for a similar entitlement to take over the property by way of subrogation upon payment of a claim.

It is, of course, quite possible that the London and Liverpool War Risks Association Ltd, 70 years ago, did take the necessary affirmative action to 'take over' the Lusitania either on abandonment or upon the settlement of the claim: but if they had, they would have been acting uncharacteristically. It is the almost invariable practice of marine underwriters not only not to take over the property but, in case of constructive total losses (not only more common in fact but much the preferred method of handling even those rare total losses which, like the Lusitania, seem unarguably actual) not even to accept a notice of abandonment from their assured, although the position of the latter is generally preserved by the use of the 'writ clause' whereby it is agreed that the assured is to be treated 'as if the writ had been issued' on the same day as the notice. Nor do underwriters usually take a direct interest in abandoned ships by way of subrogation on settlement of the claim.

Underwriters are not primarily in the business of shipowning and, in any case, a ship that is a constructive total loss is likely to prove also to be a *damnosa haereditas*. In the absence of further evidence, one cannot, of course, form a conclusion as to who owns the Lusitania. The issue was not before Sheen J in the case. But it is possible to examine the possibilities. If the underwriters did not 'take her over' (however that process might be effected) then she either remained the property of Cunard or, if effectively abandoned by her owners, she might possibly have become *res nullius*, available to the first occupier. There is no decision directly bearing on the issue and the dicta conflict (see the opinion of Bailhache J in *Boston Corpn v Fenwick and Co* (1923) 28 Comm Cas 367, and *contra* those of Greer LJ and Cohen LJ in the two cases of *Oceanic v Evans* (1934) 40 Comm Cas 108 and *Blane SS v Minister of Transport* [1951] 2 KB 965). Sheen J seemed to be of the opinion that the vessel had been effectively abandoned by Cunard: if that be so, it might be hard to avoid the *res nullius* conclusion.

If the case was not about abandonment under a contract of marine insurance, it was about the prerogative of droits of Admiralty. The right to 'wreck of the sea' is an ancient royal right. The Merchant Shipping Act 1894 which codified the common law in this as in many other areas, defines 'wreck' in s 510 as including 'jetsam, flotsam, lagan and derelict found in or on the shores of the sea or tidal water'. Since the contents of the Lusitania could not, by any definitional elasticity, be regarded as jetsam, flotsam or lagan, they could only be wreck if they were 'derelict'. The meaning of derelict is tranditionally accepted as property 'abandoned at sea by the master and crew without hope of recovery' (see per Sir William Scott in *The Aquila* (1798) 1 Ch Rob 37 at 41), an interpretation which takes us back once more to the vexed word 'abandon', used in so many confusingly different senses in maritime law and marine insurance. In *this* context it is clear that the subjective intentions of the master and crew when leaving the vessel are significant. In *Bradley v H Newsom Sons and Co* [1919] AC 16, [1918–19] All ER Rep 625, Viscount Haldane required for effective dereliction an 'act of volition' rather than an abandonment of the vessel under duress.

Bradley v H Newson and Co concerned a cargo of timber aboard the vessel *Jupiter*, which had been abandoned by master and crew after having been torpedoed by an enemy submarine. The House of Lords held that the cargo, then in the hands of the Receiver of Wreck, was not derelict and could be demanded by the consignees without further payment when it had been brought to land by salvors. That case might have seemed hard to distinguish on its facts, but Sheen J found it no problem ([1986] 1 All ER at 1015):

> 'Applying the same reasoning to the facts of this case, there can be no doubt that, when the master and crew and passengers abandoned the Lusitania, they did so in order to save their own lives and without any hope or intention of returning to her. If I had any doubt as to the state of mind of those who abandoned the ship shortly before she sank, the matter would be put beyond doubt by the fact that the Cunard Steamship Co claimed against and were paid by the underwriters on the basis of an actual total loss of their ship. The owners had abandoned their ship. So far as the owners of the contents are concerned, it is a necessary inference from the agreed facts and from the lapse of 67 years before any attempt was made to salve the contents that the owners of the contents abandoned their property.'

This passage bristles with difficulties. A ship and its contents may become derelict, and therefore 'wreck', but that says nothing as to ownership. It is hard to see how a shipowner may be deprived of his title to his ship merely because, say, in stress of weather the master has ordered 'abandon ship', still less that such circumstances should affect the rights of cargo-owners or passengers to their property. Such is recognised by the scheme of Wreck Receivership provided by the Merchant Shipping Acts. Wreck found in or about the shores of the country or brought ashore must, under penalty, be delivered to the Receiver. The Merchant Shipping Act 1894, s 521 expressly preserves the right of the 'owner of wreck' to estabish his claim before the Receiver and to take possession of his property upon paying 'salvage, fees and expenses due'. (This was the matter at issue in *Bradley v H Newsom*, where the House decided that, because the cargo of timber did not come within the definition of 'wreck', the consignees were entitled to take possession without making such payment: had it been wreck, they would have had to pay salvage, but in either case their title would have been unaffected.)

If dereliction cannot affect title, should conclusions as to title affect the decision on dereliction? As we have seen, Sheen J was of the opinion that title to the Lusitania was transferred to the underwriters at least by the time the claim for a total loss was settled by them. It is difficult to see how a maybe subsequent allocation of interests in consequence of an insurance claim could affect the characterisation of the Lusitania as derelict. Still less is it clear how a failure to assert rights of ownership by consignees of cargo or by passengers or their successors for the next 67 years should have that effect, or any other effect. The decisions, however, are clear. The contents of the Lusitania were at the time of the case derelict and therefore could be considered to be wreck. Sheen J seems also to be holding that the owners had effectively abandoned their title 'to the whole world' and caused their property to become *res nullius*, a conclusion not essential to the matter of droits of Admiralty which were raised by the case.

Sheen J further held that wreck might be 'wreck' although found upon the bed of the sea, neither afloat nor on shore, relying upon *HMS Thetis* (1835) 3 Hag Adm 228, *The Tubantia* [1924] P 78, [1924] All ER Rep 615 and *The Association and The Romney* [1970] 2 Ll Rep 59. The ground having thus been cleared, he approached the central question: did droits of Admiralty apply to wreck found outside territorial sea? The prerogative right to wreck, as we have seen, is a residual right: it may be asserted after the wreck has been held, unclaimed, for one year. The procedure involves the Receiver of Wreck. After a meticulous examination of the serpentine legislative history, Sheen J concluded that the Crown had an ancient right to unclaimed wreck found within the United Kingdom; that such a right might also have existed in respect of 'extra-territorial' unclaimed wreck and, if it had existed, may have been preserved by the provisions of the Merchant Shipping Act 1854; but the scheme of receivership established by the Merchant Shipping Act 1894 abrogated any such right by necessary implication, especially that of s 523 which defines Crown right as applying to wreck 'found in any part of Her Majesty's Dominions'; the extension by s 72 of the Merchant Shipping Act 1906 of the jurisdiction of Receivers of Wreck to extra-territorial wreck brought into the Kingdom did not extend (or revive) the residucal rights of the Crown. That, asserted Sheen J, constituted a lacuna.

If the Crown had no right, to whom did the contents belong? Sheen J had little difficulty in rejecting the surprisingly wide proposition of counsel for the Crown 'that there is no legal principle that the possessor of goods found outside territorial waters which are brought within the United Kingdom has a good title against all the world save the rightful owner'. Making passing reference to the venerable authority of *Armory v Delamirie* (1722) 1 Stra 505, [1558–1774] All ER Rep 121, he concluded ([1986] 1 All ER at 1023): 'If, as I have held, the Crown has no right to the property as a droit of Admiralty, there is not one with a better right to the property than the claimants'. How came such a right into existence? It can only be by occupancy, for salvage services in this century give only a right to a reward secured by a lien and no title. If by occupancy, then the property must be susceptible of occupation. It must have been abandoned to the whole world: the only mechanism for this operation offered is failure to organise salvage for 67 years. Which seems a startling proposition. Am I to lose my property because it seems too difficult or too expensive to organise rescue attempts? Yes, it would seem, if it is aboard ship.

3 Consignees against carriers in tort: *The Aliakmon* in the House of Lords

In All ER Rev 1985, pp 243, 244 we noted two decisions which represent the two most common maritime claims in negligence for purely pecuniary losses. In *Candlewood Navigation Corp v Mitsui OSK Lines, The Mineral Transporter, The Iberaki Maru* [1985] 2 All ER 935 the Privy Council decided that a time charterer of a negligently damaged ship had no claim. Only a plaintiff with a property interest in a ship could sue. In *Leigh and Sillavan Ltd v Aliakmon Shipping Co Ltd, The Aliakmon* [1985] 2 All ER 44, the Court of Appeal decided that a cargo receiver without title had no claim in tort for damage to the cargo. In this case, however, the court seemed prepared to journey some way along the route apparently mapped by Lord Wilberforce in *Anns v Merton London Borough* [1977] 2 All ER 492: for all members of the court there was sufficient 'proximity' for a prima facie duty of care, but for two (Sir John Donaldson MR and Oliver LJ) there were reasons of policy for not imposing a duty while for the third (Robert Goff LJ) the duty existed but had not been broken. The House of Lords has ([1986] 2 All ER 145) unanimously affirmed the decision of the Court of Appeal without adopting its reasoning.

Lord Brandon delivered the only substantial opinion. He set forth the issues with his customary clarity and dealt with them seriatim. The plaintiffs were purchasers on c & f terms who found themselves bound to pay for damaged goods but, owing to banking problems, holding a bill of lading subject to a reservation of a right of disposal by the sellers. The effect of that variation was that the buyers held the bill as agents for the sellers. They were therefore deprived of their title as 'holders in due course'. Had they acquired title, they would have had an action on the contract of carriage in virtue of s 1 of the Bills of Lading Act 1855. At first instance ([1983] 1 Ll Rep 203) Staughton J was able to interpret the facts to allow this conclusion, but his analysis commended itself neither to the Court of Appeal nor the House of Lords. Which left for Lord Brandon only the tort claim.

His Lordship's starting point was simply stated ([1986] 2 All ER at 149):

> 'My Lords, there is a long line of authority for a principle of law that, in order to enable a person to claim in negligence for loss caused to him by reason of loss of or damage to property, he must have had either the legal ownership of or a possessory title to the property concerned at the time when the loss or damage occurred, and it is not enough for him to have only had contractual rights in relation to such property which have been adversely affected by the loss of or damage to it.'

This proposition he supported by reference to a range of cases, beginning with *Cattle v Stockton Waterworks Co* (1875) LR 10 QB 453, [1874–80] All ER Rep 220, including *Konstantinidis v World Tanker Corp Inc, The World Harmony* [1965] 2 All ER 139, and finishing with *The Mineral Transporter*. In short, he asserted the principle in its traditional, it might be said its pre-*Anns*, form, applicable alike both to time charterers and to cargo-receivers, expressed as a general rule relating to all claims for damage to property. The only question that could be raised, therefore, was whether there might be an exception for cargo-receivers. Lord Brandon distinguished five arguments in favour of special treatment and rejected them all.

First, he could not distinguish cargo-receivers from time charters on the ground that the former were intended and expected to obtain title, nor, second, that the buyers had obtained any sort of equitable ownership sufficient to ground an action in tort. They had neither acquired one nor, if they had, would it have availed them.

The third, fourth and fifth grounds were all related. In essence they amounted to the proposition that the principles advanced by Lord Wilberforce in *Anns v Merton London Borough* had changed the law of negligence: that a duty existed wherever there was sufficient 'proximity', unless there were policy considerations for making an exception. Those principles had been applied by Lloyd J in *Schiffart und Kohlen GmbH v Chelsea Maritime Ltd, The Irene's Success* [1982] 1 All ER 218 (All ER Rev 1982, pp 254–6), where he had cast severe doubt on the then leading case of *Margarine Union GmbH v Cambay Prince Steamship Co Ltd, The Wear Breeze* [1967] 3 All ER 775, which doubts had been shared by Sheen J in *The Nea Tyhi* [1982] 1 Ll Rep 606 and by all the members of the Court of Appeal in the present case.

First, Lord Brandon Wilberforce's approach applicable only to 'a novel type of factual situation which was not analogous to any factual situation in which the existence of . . . a duty had already been held to exist' ([1986] 2 All ER at 153) and therefore of no application to circumstances where a duty had been held *not* to exist. *Anns* was for new developments: for old cases, old rules. He called in aid *The Mineral Transporter* and justified the position by reference inter alia to the 'floodgates' argument (rather severely handled in *Anns*), which, it will be recalled, concerns the risk, allegedly contained in economic loss cases, of allowing indeterminate liability to an indeterminate class of plaintiffs. On its face, the argument does seem less powerful in cases of cargo-receivers, where the potential plaintiffs are firmly predictable, than in ship-damage cases. Such was the view of Lloyd J in *Irene's Success*. Lord Brandon did not agree, adding a wedge to the floodgates ([1986] 2 All ER at 154): 'If an exception to the general rule be made in the field of carriage by sea, it would no doubt have to be extended to the field of carriage by land, and I do not think it possible to say that no undue increase in the scope of a person's liability for want of care would follow'.

Put shortly, *Anns* is to have no effect at sea. Only those with title or a similar interest can sue for damage to property: no special exception is to be made for cargo-receivers, any more than for time charterers. Lord Brandon was not convinced by the argument that the conclusion was irrational, nor was he seduced by Robert Goff LJ's somewhat subtle 'transferred loss' analysis (see [1985] 2 All ER 77). With respect it seems a pity that the overture played by Lord Wilberforce has not led on to Act 1 in shipping cases. It is hard to see why a clearly proximate cargo-receiver who cannot shift the loss to his seller may not sue the carrier responsible. If the answer is that liabilities in sea carriage are governed by international regimes such as the Hague Rules, dependent upon bills of lading, and a receiver ought not to be allowed to improve his position by *not* taking title under the bill, then it might have been clearer had that been given as the reason of 'compelling policy' for not imposing liability for negligence in circumstances of clear proximity.

See, also, the article on Tort p 309 below.

4 Charterer's indemnities

When a vessel is chartered unless the charterer wishes simply to fill it with his own goods for transportation to a foreign place of business of his, it will be necessary to issue bills of lading, either to evidence contracts of carriage effected by the charterer with others to fill the space he has bought, or to enable the negotiation of his own cargo to buyers before the ship reaches its destination. The legal regime of bills of lading requires that they be effective against the carrier—the shipowner—and to this end they will be presented to the ship's master for signature on the owner's behalf. The charterparty must thereforc address this question and provide both for the circumstances in which the charterer can expect the bills he presents to be signed and also for the proper allocation of responsibility as between owner and charterer of any consequential liabilities.

In a time charterparty the matter is approached relatively simply. An employment and indemnity clause (eg Baltime clause 9, NYPE clause 8) generally provides that the master shall sign bills presented and the charterers shall indemnify the owners for all consequences and liabilities that may arise from signing them. Voyage charters are slightly more complex. The Gencon form provides first an owners responsibility clause (clause 2) which essentially restricts the liability of the owners to (a) negligent stowage by 'owner's' stevedores, (b) personal want of due diligence in making the ship seaworthy and (c) personal default by owners or their managers. The bills of lading clause (clause 9) requires the master to sign bills but imposes on the charterer the obligation not to present bills inconsistent with the charter. The indemnity clause (clause 12) reads, in full: 'Indemnity for non-performance of this charterparty, proved damages not exceeding estimated amount of freight.'

In *Ben Shipping Co (Pte) Ltd v An Bord Bainne, The C Joyce* [1986] 2 All ER 177 the vessel was chartered under Gencon with certain variations. The bills of lading clause had been deleted and in its place a typed clause requiring all bills to be signed 'without delay' and further requiring that all bills include a clause paramount. The effect of a clause paramount is to import the Hague Rules. This was done. There was a cargo claim not in any way based upon any alleged fault for which the owners might be responsible under the owners responsibility clause. It was settled. The owners sought an indemnity from the charterers.

Bingham J in the Commercial Court had no doubt that the express indemnity clause had no appliction. He described it as 'somewhat anaemic', which might be thought charitable. Its meaning is not obvious, but it seemed clearly unfit for the task in hand. Could a wider indemnity clause be implied? Neither presumed intention nor business efficacy, the two usual vehicles for implication, was much help. The charterparty was perfectly workable as it stood and there was no evidence to be derived from its terms that the parties had intended a wide indemnity. The authorities did support the proposition that an indemnity might in some circumstances be derived from general principle, but Bingham J, having reviewed the authorities and incidentally placed heavy reliance upon the summing up of the case law by that great master of charterparty law, Scrutton LJ in *Dawson Line Ltd v AG Adler fur Chemische Industrie of Berlin* [1931] All ER Rep 546 at 549–550, concluded that an indemnity might be incorporated either as a consequence of a breach by the charterer or if the owner's complied with a particular request to sign bills. In this case the charterers were not in breach and the owners had merely carried out their contractual obligations. In this age, signing charterers' bills was so much a matter of ordinary commercial practice that Bingham J was not inclined to treat it, as he perceived the older authority seemed to, as a rather unusual concession made by the owners. Partly for those reasons, too, he was not prepared to regard the unamended clause 2 as 'bedrock', against which the typed replacement clauses should be interpreted. There was no justification for such a course of action. Nor, in that connection, was he prepared to read the palimpsest and make use of the deleted clause 9, with its requirement that the bills be consistent.

The final argument was based on estoppel. The owners, when faced with the cargo-claim, had invited the charterers to take over its management, alleging that, under clause 2, in the absence of their own personal default, etc, the liability was assigned to them. The charterers refused the chalice, rightly fearing poison. The owners claimed that they were thereby estopped from denying the fairness or validity of the settlement reached between owners and cargo interests. This Bingham J would not allow, contenting himself with remarking ([1986] 2 All ER at 187) that 'I do not think that any such principle can be clearly found in the authorities relied on'. The authorities were, it is true, rather ancient and quite unclear.

The *C Joyce* may not of itself be an important case. Perhaps it may be filed under two headings: (a) Sad Results of Typing New Clauses in Charterparties without Considering the Consequences; and (b) The Need for Care in the Use of Historical Argument in Shipping Cases.

5 Limitation, employment and multi-companies

The *Amoco Cadiz* litigation can perhaps stand as a gleaming example of what happens when principles of liability and limitation have to be applied to commercial operations utilising modern corporate structures with several interacting and often formally interconnected companies involved in the same operation. Who is liable? Who can limit? Whose fault is to be accounted 'actual fault' to defeat limitation? *McDermid v Nash Dredging and Reclamation Co Ltd* [1986] 2 All ER 676 is another example, albeit on a rather smaller scale.

Mr McDermid was at the time of the accident an 18-year-old deckhand employed by Nash. In the course of that employment he was directed to work in Sweden, in pursuance of a dredging contract negotiated with the Swedish government through Stevin Baggeren BV, Nash's Dutch parent company. In carrying out the contract, Nash made use of the tug Ina, owned by Stevin and commanded by Captain Sas, who was employed by Stevin. McDermid was directed to work aboard the Ina and through the proven negligence of Captain Sas, he lost his leg. Wisely fearing the difficulties of establishing liability against a Dutch company for an accident occurring in Swedish territorial waters, McDermid sued Nash, his English employer.

Were Nash liable? Three arguments were presented to Saughton J at first instance: that Nash had failed to provide proper supervision of McDermid;

that they had failed to establish a safe system of work; that they were vicariously liable for Captain Sas. The judge rejected the first two but held in favour of the plaintiff on the third: Captain Sas 'must be taken to be the servant of Nash'. In the Court of Appeal, Neill LJ, who gave the judgment of the court, was clearly unhappy with this approach. In particular he appears to have been very doubtful of the finding of fact that the system of work adopted aboard the tug by Captain Sas was not unsafe. After a stimulating review of the authorities, including the interesting *Wilsons and Clyde Coal Co Ltd v English* [1937] 3 All ER 628, with its near-strict 'mini-torts' of failing to provide a safe system of work, safe plant and materials, competent fellow employees and safe premises, so often regarded as dead, a casualty of the House of Lords in *Davie v New Merton Board Mills Ltd* [1959] 1 All ER 346, Neill LJ offered a synthesis. The court should 'look at all the circumstances in the light of the fact that it is the basic duty of the employer to take reasonable care so to conduct his operations as not to subject those employed by him to unnecessary risk' ([1986] 2 All ER at 685). His Lordship provided a checklist including all relationships between defendant, plaintiff and tortfeasor, degrees of control the difficulty of and the defendant's interest in the work done.

Perhaps the most important fact is the 'basic' duty to take care of the safety of employees mentioned above. Neill LJ spends a considerable space dealing with non-delegable personal duties of employers: a device which in the nineteenth century offered an escape route from the doctrine of common employment, and the only one clearly allowed for in the *fons et origo* of common employment, the judgment of Lord Abinger in *Priestley v Fowler* (1837) 3 M and W 1. Non-delegable duties may be old-fashioned and difficult, but their difficulties are nothing compared with the possible consequences of Staughton J's approach, which would have the user of a tug vicariously liable for the negligence of its master. Would the same have to apply were the tug chartered?

The limitation point was complicated but shorter. The Merchant Shipping (Liability of Shipowners and Others) Act 1958 conferred the benefit of limitation upon a 'master, member of the crew or . . . [person] in the course of his employment as a servant of the owners' as well as the 'owner . . . any charterer and any person interested in or in possession of the ship and, in particular, and manager or operator of the ship.' The aim of this clumsy mélange is clear, but there is one *casus omissus*: what if the 'master or crew' are not employed by anyone in the extended definition of 'shipowner'? Such persons are specifically included by the final phrase of s 3 (2) of the Act. On the facts of *McDermid v Nash Dredging and Reclamation Co Ltd* Nash was not a shipowner, nor yet a charterer or manager (*sed quaere* whether it was 'in possession' or an 'operator' of the Ina). It could only limit if Captain Sas was its 'servant'. Staughton J had found Nash liable vicariously for Captain Sas's negligence and he could not consistently hold that he was not Nash's servant for limitation purposes. The Court of Appeal, having rested the case on the non-delegable duty of Nash to provide for the safety of their employees, was not so constrained. No limitation was available. The decision is entirely justifiable, but in terms of the overall scheme of the Act it looks odd to hold a ship user liable for its negligent operation and not to allow limitation.

As a tailpiece, it might be noted that the 1976 Limitation Convention, brought into force in the UK in December 1986 in virtue of the Merchant Shipping Act 1979, if applied, would produce the same conclusion by a simpler route. 'Shipowners and salvors', as defined, may limit, and those for whom such may be legally responsible. 'Shipowner' includes 'charterer, manager and operator'.

See, also, the article on Tort, p 317 below.

Solicitors

BRIAN HARVEY, MA, LLM
Solicitor, Professor of Property Law, University of Birmingham

Introduction

1986 has not seen a plentitude of reported decisions in the All England Law
Reports on problems concerning solicitors. However, the one major case
discussed in this review does accurately reflect the stormy climate in which
the two branches of the legal profession in England and Wales and Ireland
find themselves working. The case is a somewhat spectacular one with
regard to the fame of the parties to the action. But it is also of the greatest
interest to lawyers since the Court of Appeal was required to analyse, in a
1986 perspective, the nature of the restriction of the right of audience in
High Court proceedings to barristers (with certain exceptions). In order to
complete the story it is proposed to discuss this case also in the context of
the debate between the Law Society's Contentious Business Committee and
the Senate of the Inns of Court and the Bar.

Right of audience in the High Court—Abse v Smith

In June 1982 Cyril Smith MP commented adversely in a radio interview on
the conduct of Mr Leo Abse MP and other Members of Parliament in
voting as they did at the time of the Falkland crisis. The word 'treason' was
mentioned. Mr Abse, together with 24 other Members of Parliament, sued
Mr Smith and Radio Trent for libel. By November 1984 the parties had
agreed that the matter could be settled by an explanation and apology in the
form of a statement in open court under RSC Ord 82, r 5(2).

Under this procedure a script is agreed of what it is intended to say in
open court for the approval of the judge. Mr Smith's solicitor prepared the
first draft of the agreed statement and this was approved by the other parties
with minor modifications. Counsel who had settled the defence also
approved the draft with one amendment. All parties then agreed the final
draft.

There was then a dispute as to the expense involved in reading out the
agreed statement in court. Mr Smith's solicitor enquired what counsel's fee
would be and the figure he was quoted he characterized as 'ridiculously
expensive'. Even the fee of the most junior member of the chambers was
one which was considered to be 'unnecssarily expensive'. Accordingly, Mr
Smith's solicitor (Mr Brett) sought leave of the court to appear himself and
to read the statement on behalf of Mr Smith. Leonard J decided that he must
hear argument in open court before reaching his conclusion. At this hearing
the judge refused the application on the grounds that he did not think that it
was within his power at that stage to alter the established practice of the
court, namely that there is no general discretion to allow persons other than
barristers to appear before the court. The judge emphasised, correctly, that
it was open to Mr Smith to read the statement himself.

Mr Smith then appealed to the Court of Appeal and the case became a matter of public interest. The issues were:
1. Was the trial judge mistaken in thinking that he had no discretion to permit a solicitor to appear on behalf of Mr Smith in these circumstances?
2. If he was so mistaken, should he have exercised that discretion in favour of granting permission and, on appeal, should the Court of Appeal now do so?
3. If the trial judge was right, has the Court of Appeal any greater discretion on appeal and, if so, how should it be exercised?
4. If neither he nor the Court of Appeal had any such discretion, had the judges generally, or the judges of the High Court and the judges of the Court of Appeal separately, in respect to their respective courts, any power to change the general practice of the court to grant audience only to litigants in person or to counsel?

Sir John Donaldson MR, giving the leading judgment, pointed out that both branches of the legal profession and the Lord Chancellor's Department were known to have under consideration the desirability of changes in the general practice of the courts and they needed to know what were the powers of the judiciary in this context.

The Master of the Rolls went on to conduct a brief survey of the features of all developed systems for the administration of justice. His conclusion was that in England and Wales the categories of those whom courts are prepared to hear as advocates for the litigants were defined by reference to the possession of particular professional qualifications. In many, and possibly most, other jurisdictions the criterion took the form of 'licensing' individual lawyers to practice in specified courts.

Why were these limitations introduced? Both Sir John Donaldson MR and May LJ (who delivered a short concurring judgment) were understandably anxious to stress that 'these limitations are not introduced in the interests of the lawyers concerned, but in the public interest' (per Sir John Donaldson MR at 353). Essentially the assumption of the court in this case was that by confining the general right of audience to barristers the following advantages in the conduct of litigation occur: 1. The contentions of the parties were presented in a concise and logical form; 2. This had the advantage that time would thereby be saved in reaching a decision; 3. Accordingly, other members of the public who needed to have their disputes resolved were more expeditiously dealt with; 4. In an extreme case the court might otherwise be led to reaching a wrong decision.

Both judges also stressed the importance of discipline and probity. Despite the potential for conflict between the interests of the client represented and the barrister's duty to the court, the administration of justice depended upon the judge's being able to assume that counsel is observing his duty to the court to assist it in reaching a proper decision.

If we may pause at this latter point, although never so stated the more cynical reader of the report thus far might assume that the judges would not have the same confidence in the probity of an advocate who happened to be a solicitor rather than a barrister, *assuming* that both had an equality of relevant skills. Since solicitors do have a joint right of audience in the lower courts including the county courts, any such influence would be an alarming one, but it is difficult to see how it can be avoided in the context of these remarks. It is perhaps a pity that this consideration was introduced. Sir John Donaldson MR's argument would have rested more strongly on the equally implicit assumption that, ceteris paribus, a barrister of standing is bound to have more experience of the actual conduct of High Court litigation than a solicitor of equal standing as matters stand at present.

After this somewhat debatable expression of where the public interest was seen to lie, flawed by unstated and questionable premises and making no mention of the public interest in the reduction of cost, the court reverted to rather safer ground in examining the authorities for the proposition that as a matter of established practice rights of audience in the High Court were limited, with exceptions, to barristers. The exceptions enumerated were:

1. Solicitors have a general right of audience in the High Court when sitting in chambers. They have a special right of audience in the High Court, including the Divisional Court, in bankruptcy matters and this has been extended to the hearing of matrimonial judgment summonses in open court in the Family Division of the High Court. This derived from statute.

2. It has been recognised in a number of cases, not least *Re Serjeants At Law* (1840) 6 Bing NC 187, 232, 235, 133 ER 74, 91, 93 that emergency situations could arise in which the court would have to permit others to plead and practice before it 'in order to prevent a failure in the administration of justice to the Queen's subjects, for which end all Courts of Justices were instituted' (see 6 Bing NC 235 at 238–239, 133 ER 93 at 94). Otherwise the proposition had to be accepted that it was not open to the Crown, by prerogative or executive act, to alter the usages and practices of the courts and to achieve changes thought undesirable by the judges themselves without an Act of Parliament. Numerous other cases were cited emphasising that the right of audience in other than exceptional circumstances in the High Court and above was confined to barristers. For instance, Byles J in *London Engineering and Iron Shipbuilding Co Ltd v Cowan* (1867) 16 LT 573 was untroubled by wider considerations of the public interest. He refused to allow the defendant's attorney to appear and consent to a verdict for the plaintiff for an agreed sum 'for the sake of members of the Bar'.

There was, however, one authority which was heavily relied on by counsel for Mr Smith. This was *Engineers' and Managers' Association v Advisory Conciliation and Arbitration Service (No 1)* [1979] 3 All ER 223 in which the Deputy General Secretary of a small trade union sought leave to intervene and personally to make representations on its behalf on a comparatively minor aspect which could affect it.

Lord Denning MR considered the new status of a trade union, namely a legal entity without being a body corporate, and referred to the statutory provisions governing rights of audience in the Employment Appeal Tribunal and the county court, both of which would have allowed Mr Hickling to be heard. He then stated ([1979] 3 All ER 223 at 225):

'I do not think that the 'High Court or the Court of Appeal should be in any different position . . . The general rule in the 'High Court and the Court of Appeal is that we only hear members of the Bar. But we do allow exceptions when the circumstances make it desirable. Take litigants in person. Sometimes we have heard a husband speaking for his wife: or a son speaking for his mother: and so forth. So also it seems to me that with this new thing, a trade union which is a legal entity but not a body corporate, we can ourselves decide whom we should allow to speak on its behalf. In the ordinary way I should have thought that a trade union as a legal entity, especially a large trade union with ample funds, on a complicated matter would think it right and proper to employ a solicitor to conduct the proceedings and instruct counsel to appear in the High Court to put its case on its behalf. While that is the general rule, it seems to me it can be subject to exceptions. If the court in its discretion thinks it right to make an exception, then it can do so.'

The other two judges in effect agreed with the proposition of Lord Denning MR. But in the present case Lord Denning's dicta were not pursued, having been made 'without further explanation'.

Having considered case law for authority the court looked in vain for useful guidance from primary or subordinate legislation. So far as subordinate legislation is concerned, RSC Ord 3, r 6 provides that any person may begin and carry on proceedings in the High Court by a solicitor or any person and that a body corporate may not begin or carry on proceedings otherwise than by a solicitor. RSC Ord 12, r 1 makes similar provision for defendants. No rule is concerned with appearances of advocates.

The court then briefly considered whether members of the Bar had a monopoly right which would be infringed by any extension of the rights of solicitors. This proportion was rejected (at 359–60):

'It would be surprising, to say the least, if the courts had allowed a right to arise which could fetter their inherent power to regulate their own practices in the interests of enabling them to act effectively within their jurisdiction. I do not therefore consider that the rights of audience at the Bar constitute any obstacle to extending the rights of audience of solicitors.'

The Court of Appeal then considered other arguments, also alleged to be based on the public interest, which, if the judge had a discretion, ought to persuade that judge to exercise it in this type of case in favour of hearing the solicitor. Briefly, in this particular case, departure from established practice was sought to be justifiable and indeed necessary for five reasons.

1.   A hearing was a formality involving no skills of advocacy whatsoever.
2.   The Royal Commission on Legal Services in its Report in 1979 (Cmnd 7648, vol 1, para 18.61, p 219) had stated

'where proceedings are formal or unopposed, we consider that they should be dealt with by the most economical means possible and that for this purpose the solicitor should have the appropriate right of audience—if, indeed, the matter cannot for any reason be dealt with by letter or telephone'.

3.   The Government in its response to the Report had stated that it accepted that a solicitor should have a right of audience to deal with certain formal matters in any court.
4.   The Senate of the Inns of Court and the Bar had responded similarly.
5.   The public interest required such an extension in the solicitors right of audience.

Sir John Donaldson MR confessed to some surprise that the views of the Government were prayed in aid of this application (at 360). 'It is fundamental that the courts are wholly independent of the executive . . . If the Government wishes to give effect to those views, it can only do so by persuading Parliament to legislate.' As to the views of the Royal Commission and of the Senate, in the end insofar as individual judges or the judges collectively had the power to alter the established practices of the court, they must be guided solely by their own view of what is required in the interests of the efficient and effective administration of justice.

Sir John Donaldson MR concluded that the trial judge had rightly approached the application of Mr Brett he heard as an advocate on the basis that he has been asked to exercise a general discretion to depart from the established practice of the High Court. This was in a situation in which there was no exceptional features. The learned judge wholly upheld that view. The public interest required that there should be known general practices and procedures in the High Court and that those should not be changed or departed from piecemeal by individual judges on the basis of their personal view of what those practices and procedures should be. The Court of Appeal could not in these circumstances intervene and his decision was affirmed.

In a short concurring judgment May LJ stressed that changes even in the treatment of unopposed applications made in open court should only be made after careful consideration to ensure that the public interest is indeed being served. The judge saw the public interest as being reflected in the following two principles:

1. Courts should retain the untramelled power of regulating their own proceedings unless they were already regulated by ancient usage or statute;
2.

> 'From the accumulated wisdom of the courts ... as well as from my own experience both as advocate and judge, I think that it is essential that those who act as advocates in our courts, particularly in the higher courts such as the Crown Court, the High Court and above, should be members of a profession or professions subject to a strict code of discipline and etiquette and who have been thoroughly trained and practised in the skills of advocacy, in the proper and expeditious conduct of litigation and in the law. One of the most important factors tending not only to the just, but also to the swift, determination of litigation, which is so desirable, is that those who act as advocates to the litigants concerned have been thoroughly trained and are indeed adequately experienced to do so' ([1986] 1 All ER at 361).

Both Sir John Donaldson MR and May LJ agreed that if changes were to be made it was 'for the judges collectively, as a collegiate body, to decide whether or not to modify established general practices and to promulgate such modifications by Practice Directions' (ibid).

Hot on the heels of this judgment of the Court of Appeal, which appears to be restrictive in its outlook, there appeared the following Practice Direction, [1986] 2 All ER 226:

> 'In addition to the cases in which solicitors already have rights of audience in the Supreme Court, and without prejudice to the discretion of a judge to allow a solicitor to represent his client in open court in an emergency, a solicitor may appear in the Supreme Court in formal or unopposed proceedings, that is to say those proceedings where (a) by reason of agreement between the parties there is unlikely to be any argument and (b) the court will not be called on to exercise a discretion.
>
> A solicitor may also represent his client in the Supreme Court when

judgment is delivered in open court following a hearing in chambers at which that solicitor conducted the case for his client.

> Hailsham of St Marylebone C
> Lane CJ
> John F Donaldson MR
> John Arnold P

9 May 1986.'

In fact the above Practice Direction does not weaken the thrust of the Court of Appeal's judgment in *Abse v Smith* [1986] 1 All ER 350. The Court of Appeal established the principle that important ad hoc changes in High Court practice should not be made at the discretion of an individual judge. The Practice Direction which was subsequently made reflected public disquiet, much publicised in the 'quality' press, of what was seen to be the unnecessary cost to litigants in having to employ counsel for this type of uncontroversial proceeding, albeit in the Supreme Court. Some seven years after the Royal Commission had advocated such a change, it was duly made. It is perhaps a pity that it took rather elaborate litigation to initiate this change.

As indicated in the Introduction above, *Abse v Smith* reflected a more publicised debate between the Law Society and the Bar concerning the whole structure of the legal profession. The judgment of the Master of the Rolls in *Abse v Smith* was prayed in aid by the draftsmen of the Response of the Bar to the document which precipitated the debate on structure. This was a discussion paper issued by the Law Society's Contentious Business Committee published early in 1986, leaked to the press and widely disseminated, and approved by the Council of the Law Society as a discussion document. This discussion paper must also be seen in the context of the setting up by the Bar and the Law Society of a Committee on the Future of the Legal Profession chaired by Lady Marre (with substantial lay representation) and the Lord Chancellor's own Civil Justice Review which is examining the arrangements for each of the main classes of civil business.

The Law Society's discussion paper proposed that:

1. There should continue to be two separate branches of the legal profession. There was a continuing need for a specialist power but it was envisaged that the Bar would be significantly smaller than its present size (some 5,500).

2. Entry to the Bar was proposed to be permitted only to those who have (a) passed a common vocational course, (something of an amalgam between the present Law Society and Bar examinations), (b) spent two years in articles; (c) spent a further two years in 'general practice'; and (d) qualified as a specialist by objective criteria including examinations where appropriate.

3. All lawyers, it was proposed, should have rights of audience in all courts but in higher courts rights of audience would be restricted to those (solicitors or barristers) who had gained the necessary qualifications to join specialist panels relevant to their particular interest.

4. All 'lawyers' should be eligible for appointment to any judicial office.

5. The public should have direct access to the Bar though this would in normal circumstances be after initial consultation with the lawyer.

6. The Bar should have a direct contractual relationship with a client in all cases.

7. Any firm of solicitors having to seek specialist help would seek it from another firm which had an appropriate specialist. This would be subject to a system of safeguards.

The Bar published a vigorous response to this set of proposals in June 1986, calling many of the proposals ill-thought out and self-contradictory. The Bar's response was designed to justify the continuing limitation of appointments to the judiciary almost entirely from practising barristers and defended the existing system of education and training at the Bar as being the most efficient one to produce specialist advocates. 'Distinguished lawyers from many common law countries have repeatedly praised the virtues of the English system after a critical comparison with their own'. It also pointed out that the facility for changing from solicitor to barrister existed and was not particularly difficult, but was little used. In 1985/86 only 29 applications for transfer were received and this figure may be higher than the number of transferors who actually practice as barristers.

It will be seen, then, that though the Court of Appeal in *Abse v Smith* were astute to avoid controversy in the way in which the reasons for that decision were formulated, the dispute is essentially a political one. The public interest cannot, with respect to the Court of Appeal, solely be regarded as the prerogative of the judiciary, even considered as a collegiate body. (Indeed, the Court of Appeal would probably reply that no such statement was intended). Debates in the Parliament of the United Kingdom do not suggest that the views of the judiciary, or of lawyers generally, are unquestiongly accepted by lay members of Parliament, particularly where there is a suspicion of self-serving and sectional interest. If predictions can be made it would seem to be a fairly safe bet that in the foreseeable future major changes in the education and training of both branches of the legal profession will be made. One does not have to look further than Northern Ireland to see a common system of vocational training for both barristers and solicitors. This in no way necessarily leads to fusion of the two branches but it does postpone the point at which a student has to take a decision and perhaps lead to potential lawyers making a better informed choice of vocation. A further prediction is that in the United Kingdom it seems unlikely, and is almost certainly undesirable, that there would be complete fusion of the profession. The Court of Appeal in *Abse v Smith* is correct, it is strongly suggested on the basis of Commonwealth experience, in suggesting that either de facto or de jure rights of audience in the superior courts in developed jurisdictions are likely to be limited to those most experienced and competent to conduct them. This proposition has the support in most jurisdictions of all the participants in the legal system. In those jurisdictions where the profession is fused (the majority within the Commonwealth) those specialising in office work do not have the time or inclination to do the necessary research which specialised advocacy involves and tend to envy the situation in England and Wales where the most experienced counsel is readily available to the most remote country solicitor. However, this does not justify an artificially bifurcated training system, outdated professional attitudes by one branch to the other and last, but by no means least importantly, a virtual monopoly of judicial appointments from members of the Bar. In this latter connection those responsible must recognise the fact that a very high proportion of the brightest law graduates are being recruited into the solicitors' profession, particularly by those large international firms practising in London or the larger provincial cities. This significant body of high calibre lawyers is at present outside the pool of those eligible for senior judicial appointment. It is not in the interests of the administration of justice that the public should be deprived of the services of this type of person in a judicial capacity where that person is otherwise suitable. Suitability could be enhanced by a more flexible and unified system of training, and perhaps also in the future, by a less elaborate system of civil procedure.

This debate will continue in 1987, the new General Council of the Bar (replacing the Bar Council and Senate) promising a more 'trade union role' in the face of challenges by solicitors and others to its interests.

Littaur v Steggles Palmer (a firm)

This case ([1986] 1 All ER 780) concerned a small point which is perhaps peripheral to the general subject of solicitors. It is nevertheless of some interest to them, not only because the Court of Appeal clarifies an important point as to costs but also because the facts were rather bizarre and involved the type of litigant whose activities could give cause for considerable concern to conscientious practitioners.

The appellant was a postage stamp dealer who had obtained overdraft facilities from a bank in excess of £1m. In June 1981 the bank issued a writ against Mr Littaur claiming over £1m and an Anton Piller order was granted to discover what stamps Mr Littaur then had in his possession. In July 1981 Robert Gough J granted to the bank a Mareva injunction restraining Mr Littaur from selling or disposing of certain stamps and requiring information as to stamp transactions. The stamps had in fact been removed from the jurisdiction and taken to Switzerland where they had been deposited in the left-luggage depot in Zurich railway station so as to be out of reach of the court.

Since Mr Littaur failed to provide this information, after an inter partes hearing an order was made committing Mr Littaur to prison for contempt of court. The order was suspended until 5.00 pm on 5 August. About mid-day on that day Mr Littaur revealed to his then solicitors the name of the purchaser of the stamps and departed abroad 'for a much needed holiday'. On his return he telephoned his solicitor and was informed that his message on 5 August last arrived too late and that he was therefore in contempt of court. After consulting several firms of solicitors he ultimately instructed the respondents to this appeal. Meanwhile the bank had obtained judgment in default and also the information that they required. They therefore took no steps to enforce the committal order.

Mr Lincoln, the partner in the respondent firm dealing with the matter, had made it clear to his client that he would act for him under a legal aid certificate (assuming one was granted) in relation to, and only in relation to, proceedings for purging Mr Littaur's contempt of court. A legal aid certificate was granted in July 1984 in relation to the contempt proceedings.

To reduce the complexities of this matter, suffice it to say that all parties understood that considerably more work than that concerned with the contempt proceedings was involved and that this work would be charged for privately and would not be paid for from the legal aid fund. But at the end of the day there was an outstanding balance of some £1,400 owed to the respondent firm of solicitors. Mr Littaur then instructed fresh solicitors in connection with the Mareva injunction who sought to obtain Mr Littaur's papers from Mr Lincoln. Mr Lincoln, however, claimed a lien on them. The new firm of solicitors contended that the purported lien was invalid by reason of a breach of reg 65 of the Legal Aid (General) Regulations 1980 (which restricts the payment for work done in 'any proceedings' in connection with which a legal aid certificate had been granted to such payments as may be made out of the legal aid fund). Furthermore, the new firm of solicitors argued that any money paid by or on behalf of Mr Littaur in respect of the work which had been done subsequent to the application to purge Mr Littaur's contempt should be repaid to Mr Littaur forthwith.

The Court of Appeal rejected this contention. The scope of the legal aid granted to Mr Littaur could easily be ascertained from the certificate itself. It was to take the appropriate proceedings to purge Mr Littaur's contempt of court for breach of the 1981 order in the proceedings brought against him by the bank. After that application had been dismissed, the certificate ceased to have any force. It had served its functions and that was the end of it. Yet it was submitted that it still remained in force since it had never been discharged (at 784, per Ackner LJ):

> 'To my mind, this suggests the falacious proposition that someone cannot be pronounced dead until it is established that he or she has been buried. The short answer, in my judgment, to this application is that no work for which Mr Littaur was charged was ever done during the currency of the certificate.'

Ackner LJ went on to emphasize that the phrase 'in connection with any proceedings' in reg 65 has a narrow meaning and refers specifically to the proceedings for which legal aid was granted even though those proceedings might only be incidental to the whole action. Accordingly the solicitor who represented the client in the contempt proceedings was not precluded from receiving payment from him for representing him in the main civil proceedings, or, if necessary, from claiming a lien on the papers pertaining to those civil proceedings.

This conclusion is, it is suggested with respect, completely consistent with common sense. Any contrary conclusion would have caused great difficulty to firms who would readily be accused of not acting in the public interest if they rigidly confined their activities to work covered by a legal aid certificate when it had clearly been agreed that other work would be paid for privately.

See, further, comments in the article on Practice and Procedure, p 231, above.

Statute Law

FRANCIS BENNION, MA (OXON)
Barrister, Research Associate of Oxford Centre for Socio-Legal Studies, member of the Law Faculty of Oxford University, former UK Parliamentary Counsel

Note

For the convenience of readers this article, like the corresponding article in the *All ER Annual Review 1985*, is arranged in conformity with the Code set out in the author's book *Statutory Interpretation* (Butterworths 1984), a reference to the relevant section of the Code being given after each heading.

Introductory

In the field of statute law, the year 1986 was noteworthy for the decision in *R v Horseferry Road Magistrates' Court, ex p Independent Broadcasting Authority* [1986] 2 All ER 666, which revolutionised the law of contempt of statute. The case, in which the present author appeared as counsel, is described in the note below related to Code s 13.

The year 1986 brought the usual crop of examples of widespread ignorance by the profession of the principles of statute law. This does much harm to the working of the law, and the implementation of the will of Parliament. The notes below respectively related to Code ss 13, 26, 125 (para (2) under the heading *Number*), 171, 174, 181, 190, 323 and 391 indicate ignorance or misunderstanding of statute law principles.

Mandatory and directory requirements (Code s 10)

The court will be more willing to hold that a statutory requirement is merely *directory* if any breach of the requirement is necessarily followed by an opportunity to exercise some judicial or official *discretion* in a way which can adequately compensate for that breach.

In *Re T (a minor) (adoption: parental consent)* [1986] 1 All ER 817 the Court of Appeal had to decide whether the notification requirements of the Adoption Agencies Regulations 1983, regs 11(2)(a) and 12(2)(f), are mandatory or merely directory. *Held* The requirements are directory only. Balcombe LJ said (at 827):

> 'If these regulations are treated, as I believe they should be, as directory, any breaches can still be taken into account at the hearing before the court for the making of the adoption order . . . Thus the rights of all parties concerned . . . can be properly and adequately protected at a stage where the court has a discretion . . .'

The offence of contempt of statute (Code s 13)

The important decision of the Divisional Court in *R v Horseferry Road Magistrates' Court, ex p Independent Broadcasting Authority* [1986] 2 All ER 666 ('the IBA Case') revolutionised the law relating to contempt of statute. Section 13 of the Code, which sets out this common law offence, runs as follows:

'Except where criminal sanctions are expressly laid down by the legislation in question, it is taken to be the legislator's intention, *unless the contrary intention appears*, that contravention of an enactment shall constitute the offence known as contempt of statute. For this at common law the offender, on conviction on indictment, is liable, subject to any other enactment, to imprisonment for such term as the court thinks fit, or a fine of any amount, or both.' (Italics added).

The significance of the IBA Case concerns the italicised phrase. Previously it was to be construed in the ordinary way, that is by gathering the legislative intention from any passages expressly bearing on the question and from the overall tenor of the enactment. Now, in the light of the IBA Case, the following sentence spelling out the meaning of the italicised phrase in this context needs to be added:

In considering for the purposes of the foregoing provision whether the contrary intention appears, the court is required to have regard, among other relevant considerations, to the following questions: (1) is the statutory duty mandatory or prohibitory? (2) is the enactment ancient or modern? (3) is there any other means (such as an application for judicial review) of enforcing the statutory duty?

The IBA Case turned on whether a breach of the Broadcasting Act 1981, s 4(3), which requires the IBA to satisfy themselves that their television programmes do not include subliminal images, constitutes the offence of contempt of statute. If it does, then the Divisional Court was required to allow the criminal proceedings instituted by Mr Norris McWhirter for an alleged breach of s 4(3) to continue. If it does not, then the IBA were entitled to succeed in their application for certiorari and prohibition to put a stop to the criminal proceedings.

In granting the IBA's application, the Divisional Court advanced the following reasons for holding that in a provision such as s 4(3) the contrary intention does indeed appear, thus displacing the presumption that contempt of statute applies.

1.   When Parliament intends to create an offence then nowadays it almost always says so in express terms.

2.   Breach of a statutory duty is more likely to amount to the common law offence of contempt of statute where the duty is prohibitory (ie where the doing of certain acts is *forbidden*) than where it is mandatory (positively *requiring* something to be done).

3.   Where breach of a statutory requirement can be dealt with by some other remedy, such as judicial review, it is less likely that Parliament intended a penal sanction. The existence of the other remedy ensures that the enactment will not, without an imputed criminal sanction, be a mere *brutum fulmen*.

4.   It is extremely unlikely that Parliament intended to create a criminal offence where the statutory duty depends on subjective considerations, for example whether the person who is under the duty used his best endeavours.

The Divisional Court held that the doctrine of contempt of statute is a mere rule of construction. They were unimpressed by the argument that statutes are drafted with the doctrine in mind, and that when it is intended to be disapplied that is achieved expressly, as for example in the Consumer Credit Act 1974, s 170. Leave to appeal to the House of Lords was refused. Accordingly the Divisional Court's decision stands, at least for the present, as the leading authority.

Since the decision may be challenged in some future case it is worth pointing out that the reasoning employed is in a number of aspects unsatisfactory.

It is not, with respect, correct to say, as Lloyd LJ did in this case (at 674), that the doctrine of contempt of statute is merely a rule of construction. On the contrary, the doctrine is a manifestation of the substantive common law rule that *any unlawful act affecting the public is indictable in the absence of an enactment to the contrary*. The question of construction solely concerns the point of whether a relevant enactment is or is not to the contrary. In other words the interpreter must decide, by construction of the enactment laying down the statutory duty, whether or not Parliament intended to disapply a substantive common law rule.

Again, to assert that when Parliament intends to create an offence it says so in terms is to beg the very question the court had to decide. In fact, as the court were told, Parliamentary Counsel draft (or ought to draft) with the doctrine of contempt of statute in mind. Where it does not seem necessary or advisable to spell out the offence expressly (perhaps because it is highly unlikely the statutory duty will be contravened, or the person subjected to it is a 'dignified' unit of the Constitution) the draftsman falls back on the common law doctrine as a long stop. The courts should accept that this is so. A substantive doctrine of the common law can be abolished only by legislation. As respects contempt of statute, Parliament deliberately chose not to enact the clause in a Law Commission Bill that would have abolished it (the Bill, minus this clause, was enacted as the Criminal Law Act 1977). The Divisional Court were informed of this but chose to ignore it, Lloyd LJ merely saying (at 675) that he found he could attach no weight to this argument.

Futhermore, to draw a distinction in this connection between prohibitory and mandatory duties is, it is submitted, erroneous. A statutory duty is a statutory duty. The draftsman of s 4(3), instead of saying that the IBA must satisfy themselves that their programmes do not include subliminal images, might equally have prohibited the IBA from broadcasting such images. That is indeed what the draftsman of the provision imposing a corresponding duty on the BBC chose to do. The way such a duty is worded is nothing more than a draftsman's quirk.

Lastly, under present conditions the s 4(3) duty is not, as the court held in the IBA Case, subjective. The technology exists, as the court were informed, to monitor all programmes automatically to ensure that subliminal messages are not included. The necessary machines can be easily obtained, at little cost.

Dynamic processing of legislation (Code s 26)

Decisions arrived at per incuriam

A court decision as to the legal meaning of an enactment which is arrived at per incuriam is not a binding precedent, and therefore does not amount to dynamic processing of the enactment.

In *Linnett v Coles* [1986] 3 All ER 652 the Court of Appeal held that, in the face of the wide discretion given to the court by the Administration of Justice Act 1960, s 13, previous decisions where s 13 had not been drawn to the court's attention must be treated as decided per incuriam. Lawton LJ said (at 655): 'None of the cases in this court to which counsel for the Official Solicitor has invited our attention are binding on us because seemingly the court never considered what powers it had to make a suitable order under s 13 of the 1960 Act'. (As to this case see also the notes on p 281 below related to Code s 290 and s 313).

Delegated legislation: parliamentary control of (Code s 51)

Judicial review

Where the enabling Act provides for parliamentary control of a Minister's exercise of a power to make delegated legislation, this precludes judicial review 'unless the minister and the House must have misconstrued the statute or the minister has . . . deceived the House': *Nottinghamshire County Council v Secretary of State for the Environment* [1986] 1 All ER 199 at 204, per Lord Scarman. In this case the Secretary of State's guidance as to local authority expenditure limits, required to be laid down by him under the Local Government, Planning and Land Act 1980, s 60(7) and (8), was ordered by the Act to be laid before and approved by the House of Commons.

Delegated legislation: doctrine of ultra vires (Code s 58)

Residual powers

An enabling enactment frequently includes so-called 'sweeping-up words' intended to confer residual powers to complete those expressly spelt out.

The Customs and Excise Management Act 1979, s 93(1) empowers the Commissioners of Customs and Excise to make regulations to 'regulate the deposit, keeping, securing, and treatment of goods in and the removal of goods from warehouse'. Section 93(2) goes on to state that such regulations may include provisions of certain specified kinds, and ends 'and may contain *such incidental or supplementary provisions* as the Commissioners think necessary or expedient for the protection of the revenue' (emphasis added).

The italicised words are typical 'sweeping-up words'. The courts tend to regard such words as being strictly limited in scope, as was illustrated by *R v Customs and Excise Commissioners, ex p Hedges & Butler Ltd* [1986] 2 All ER 164. The Divisional Court relied on the dictum of Viscount Dilhorne LC in *Daymond v South West Water Authority* [1976] AC 609 at 644 that:

'... "supplementary" means ... something added to what is in the Act to fill in details or machinery for which the Act itself does not provide—supplementary in the sense that it is required to implement what was in the Act.'

They held that regulations made in purported exercise of the residual power were ultra vires as not merely filling in details but attempting to create a new and radically more extensive set of powers additional to those detailed in the enabling enactment.

Duty to consult

Where an enactment conferring power to make delegated legislation requires the delegate to consult interested persons before exercising the power, this duty is mandatory rather than directory. It requires (a) the communication of a genuine invitation to give advice, and (b) a genuine consideration of that advice when given: *R v Secretary of State for Social Services, ex p Association of Metropolitan Authorities* [1986] 1 All ER 164 (insufficient time given for consultation before making regulations under Social Security and Housing Benefits Act 1983 s 36(1)).

Failure to comply with conditions for making delegated legislation

The fact that the delegate has failed to comply strictly with the conditions laid down in the enabling Act for the making of delegated legislation does not mean that the purported delegated legislation is necessarily void. If it has been acted on for a substantial period and rendering it ineffective would give rise to inconvenience the court may, in its discretion, decline to revoke it or to declare it void: *R v Secretary of State for Social Services, ex p Association of Metropolitan Authorities* [1986] 1 All ER 164 (insufficient time given for consultation before making regulations under Social Security and Housing Benefits Act 1983 s 36(1)).

Finding of implications (legitimacy of) (Code s 109)

It is not legitimate to find a restrictive implication limiting wide words conferring a statutory discretion on the court, since the necessary restriction can be effected by treating the discretion as *incorrectly exercised* if applied too widely. In *Aiden Shipping Co Ltd v Interbulk Ltd* [1986] 2 All ER 409 the House of Lords considered the Supreme Court Act 1981, s 51(1). This states that costs shall be in the discretion of the court, which 'shall have full power to determine by whom and to what extent the costs are to be paid'. *Held* No implication should be found restricting the width of this discretion.

Rules of interpretation laid down by statute (Code s 125)

Contrary legislative intention

A contrary legislative intention displacing a statutory rule of construction relating to a particular term may be manifested by the enactment which uses the term spelling out, in a way different to the statutory rule, how the term is to be construed.

In *Austin Rover Group v Crouch Butler Savage Associates* [1986] 3 All ER 50 the statutory rule in question was laid down by the Interpretation Act 1978, s 7. This states that, unless the contrary intention appears, service by post of a letter is deemed for the purposes of any Act to be effected by 'properly addressing', pre-paying and posting the letter. The Court of Appeal accepted that the Interpretation Act 1978 is applied to RSC Ord 10, r 1(2). Nevertheless the court held that r 1(2) displays a 'contrary intention' as respects the term 'properly addressing' in s 7. This is because r 1(2) describes in detail how a letter should be addressed, namely by putting on it 'the usual or last-known address' of the intended recipient.

Number

(1)   The simple phrase in the Interpretation Act 1978, s 6(c) 'words in the singular include the plural' disguises a number of difficulties. One of these is illustrated by the Agricultural Holdings (Notices to Quit) Act 1977, s 2(1)(b), which refers to a counter-notice given by 'the tenant'. What is the effect of this where there is a joint tenancy and not all the tenants join in giving the counter-notice? Does s 6(c) convert the reference into 'all the joint tenants' or into 'all or any of the joint tenants'? In *Featherstone v Staples* [1986] 2 All ER 461 the Court of Appeal held with some difficulty that the former meaning was correct. (On this point see further Bennion *Statute Law* (2nd edn, 1983) pp 194–195).

(2)   In *R v Secretary of State for the Environment, ex p Hillingdon LBC* [1986] 1 All ER 810 (affd [1986] 2 All ER 273) the Divisional Court held that 'committee' as used in the Local Government Act 1972, s 101(1)(a) was intended to have its modern meaning of a group of two or more persons, and not its former meaning of a person to whom any function is committed. This meant that the chairman of a local authority planning committee could not by himself constitute a 'committee' within the meaning of s 101(1)(a). The judgments below and on appeal do not mention the Interpretation Act 1978, s 6(c), under which, unless the contrary intention appears, words in the plural are to be taken as including the singular. This appears therefore to be yet another instance of s 6(c) being overlooked (for a previous example see All ER Rev 1985, p 258). It can scarcely be argued that Parliament's choice of a plural term in settling the wording of s 101(1)(a) indicates a 'contrary intention' since this would deprive s 6(c) of any effect. (As to this case see also the note on p 288 below related to Code s 370).

Potency of the term defined

An example of how the ordinary meaning of a term to which a special statutory definition is attached may sway the court in construing the definition is furnished by *A-G's Reference (No 1 of 1985)* [1986] 2 All ER 219. The prosecution alleged that the conduct of a salaried manager of a tied public house in selling his own beer on the premises and pocketing the proceeds fell within the statutory definition of theft as partially set out in the Theft Act 1968, s 5. *Held* This was not the true construction of the section. Lord Lane CJ said (at 226): 'If something is so abstruse and so far from the understanding of ordinary people as to what constitutes stealing, it should not amount to stealing'.

Powers and duties exercisable from time to time

The case of *R v Ealing LBC, ex p McBain* [1986] 1 All ER 13 concerned the duty of a housing authority under s 4(5) of the Housing (Homeless Persons) Act 1977. This says that where the authority are satisfied that an applicant is homeless and has a priority need their duty 'is to secure that accommodation becomes available for his occupation'.

When she had one child the applicant had unreasonably refused an offer of accommodation. A year later, by which time she had a second child, the applicant was refused accommodation on the ground of her earlier refusal. However by this time the accommodation previously offered would have been unsuitable because of the addition to the household. *Held* By virtue of the Interpretation Act 1978, s 12(1), which provides that where an Act imposes a duty it is implied, unless the contrary intention appears, that the duty is to be performed from time to time as occasion requires, the authority were in view of the changed circumstances under a fresh duty to house the applicant, and could not rely on her earlier refusal.

Service by post: presumed time of delivery

In the Interpretation Act 1978, s 7 (service deemed to be effected at the time at which letter would be delivered in the ordinary course of post, unless the contrary is proved) the phrase 'unless the contrary is proved' means 'unless the contrary is proved by evidence to the satisfaction of the court'. There is no room for any implication that such evidence can be adduced only by the defendant. See *Hodgson v Hart District Council* [1986] 1 All ER 400; *Abu Dhabi Helicopters Ltd v International Aeradio plc* [1986] 1 All ER 395.

Principles of interpretation derived from legal policy: the nature of legal policy (Code s 126)

Legal policy is an aspect of public policy. The court ought not to enunciate a new head of public policy in an area where Parliament has demonstrated its willingness to intervene when considered necessary.

In *Re Brightlife Ltd* [1986] 3 All ER 673 Hoffmann J was asked to declare that to allow parties to determine by agreement between them that a floating charge would become crystallised if the chargor ceased trading was an innovation which was contrary to public policy. Declining to do so, Hoffmann J said (at 680–681):

> 'The public interest requires the balancing of the advantages to the economy of facilitating the borrowing of money against the possibility of injustice to unsecured creditors. These arguments for and against the floating charge are matters for Parliament rather than the courts and have been the subject of public debate in and out of Parliament for more than a century. Parliament has responded [in various ways]. The limited and pragmatic interventions by the legislature make it in my judgment wholly inappropriate for the courts to impose additional restrictive rules on the ground of public policy. It is

certainly not for a judge of first instance to proclaim a new head of public policy which no appellate court has even hinted at before.'

Presumption that ancillary rules of law apply (Code s 144)

Development of applied rules

The court will not merely treat an existing rule of law as intended to apply in the construction of an enactment, but will if necessary go further and modify or develop the rule as it applies to that enactment.

The House of Lords did this in *British Leyland Motor Corp Ltd v Armstrong Patents Co Ltd* [1986] 1 All ER 850. The plaintiffs alleged that in copying parts of their vehicles, and marketing the copies as spare parts, the defendants were guilty of breaches of design copyright under the Copyright Act 1956, s 3. *Held* Parliament could not be taken to intend that the copyright should apply so as to enable the plaintiffs to deny purchasers of their cars the right to have them repaired by use of spare parts. In arriving at this result the House of Lords applied and modified the real property principle whereby a person is not to be permitted to derogate from his grant. (As to this case see also the note on p 280 below related to Code s 248).

Need for updating construction (Code s 146)

In *Pierce v Bemis* [1986] 1 All ER 1011 at 1019 Sheen J held that because of changes since its passing 'it is now necessary to disregard some part of the language of [the Merchant Shipping Act 1894]'.

Construction of Act or other instrument as a whole (Code s 149)

Effect of specific on general provision

Draftsmen who wish to make clear that a specific provision is not intended to modify the meaning of a wider general provision often preface the former with the formula 'without prejudice to the generality of [the general provision] . . .' Sometimes the words 'the generality of' are omitted, but the intended effect is the same. This formula has its dangers, since often courts find themselves mentally unable to disregard the special provision when construing the wider one: see, eg, *R v Akan* [1973] QB 491, followed in *R v Secretary of State for the Home Department, ex p Thornton* [1986] 2 All ER 641.

Every word to be given meaning

The Consumer Credit Act 1974, s 138 allows relief to be given where a credit bargain is 'grossly exorbitant'. In *Davies v Directloans Ltd* [1986] 2 All ER 783 at 794 the judge, Edward Nugee QC, expressed doubt whether the word 'grossly' added anything. He cited the well-known remark of Lord Cranworth (then Rolfe B) in *Wilson v Brett* (1843) 11 M & W 113 at 115–116 that he 'could see no difference between negligence and gross negligence— that was the same thing, with the addition of a vituperative epithet'. Mr Nugee did not advert to the established principle of construction requiring every work of an enactment to be given meaning. This particularly applies in a modern Act, where the draftsman must be taken to have inserted each word after due consideration. Here the addition of 'grossly' is clearly intended to tilt the balance away from any watered-down interpretation of the term 'exorbitant'.

Interpretation of broad terms (Code s 150)

Narrowing of term by implication

An implied intention that an unqualified broad term shall be construed as if a narrowing provision had accompanied it will not be found where the absence of such a provision is explicable only on the ground that it was not intended.

In *Puhlhofer v Hillingdon LBC* [1986] 1 All ER 467 the House of Lords declined to treat the term 'accommodation' in the Housing (Homeless Persons) Act 1977, ss 1 and 4 as qualified by an implied epithet such as 'appropriate' or 'reasonable'. If Parliament had intended such a narrowing of the meaning of 'accommodation' it would surely have said so. Moreover such a narrowing ran contrary to features of the Act. The Act did not increase the stock of housing available to authorities governed by it, and was not intended to enable persons to jump the queue of those whose names were on the waiting list for housing.

Textual amendment (Code s 171)

Rule in A-G v Lamplough

The rule in *A-G v Lamplough* (1878) 3 Ex D 214 requires that where some only of the words of an enactment have been repealed the remaining unaltered words must be given the same meaning they had before, unless the contrary intention appears from the amending Act.

The view that this rule no longer applies in the case of modern Acts gains support from the decision of the Divisional Court in *Wood v Commissioner of Police of the Metropolis* [1986] 2 All ER 570, though admittedly the rule was not mentioned in the judgments. Referring to the Vagrancy Act 1824, s 4, Nolan J said (at 574):

> 'The original wording of the part of s 4 under which the appellant was charged was:
>
> "... every person having in his or her custody or possession any picklock, key, crow, jack, bit, or other implement, with intent ... to break into any dwelling house, warehouse, coach house, stable or outbuilding or being armed with any gun, pistol [etc]".'

> The words between "every person" and "being armed" might have supported the proposition that this part of the section was concerned only with itinerant offenders, but those words were repealed by s 33(3) of and Pt I of Sch 3 to the Theft Act 1968. Consequently in the present case, as in *Ford v Falcone* [1971] 2 All ER 1138, there is nothing in the language of the present section in its amended form to prevent it from applying to those occupying or present on private property'.

(As to this case see also the note on p 281 below related to Code s 255 and the note on p 288 below related to Code ss 378–385).

Amendment of Act by delegated legislation (Code s 174)

The delusion that it is constitutionally improper for delegated legislation to amend Acts of Parliament persists. The damage it can do is shown by the following dictum of Donaldson MR in *Aden Refinery Co Ltd v Ugland Management Co* [1986] 3 All ER 737 at 739:

> 'With some prescience [the Commercial Court Committee in its 1978 Report on Arbitration (Cmnd 7284)] foresaw that there would be a need for successive amendments to the law of arbitration ... Accordingly, the committee recommended the establishment of an "Arbitration Rules Committee" with a view to relieving Parliament of the need frequently to consider amendments to the current Arbitration Acts. Unfortunately this recommendation was rejected on the grounds that it was constitutionally improper for subordinate legislation to be used to amend primary legislation. If this is indeed a constitutional principle, the presence of the Hallmarking Act 1973 on the statute book is somewhat surprising ... An analogous power in [the Arbitration Act 1979] might have obviated the need for a great deal of judicial effort, regarded by some as more legislative than adjudicative, and the idea of a specialist body with legislative powers seems worth reviving'.

Generalia specialibus non derogant (Code s 181)

In *Roberts v Roberts* [1986] 2 All ER 483 the principle *generalia specialibus non derogant* was in effect applied, though it is not specifically referred to in the judgment. In matrimonial proceedings an order had been made requiring the husband, an army non-commissioned officer, to pay the wife as a lump sum one quarter of his terminal gratuity, if and when received. The order was made under the Matrimonial Causes Act 1973, s 25(1)(a), which enables a financial provision order to be made having regard to 'the income, earning capacity, property and other financial resources which each of the parties to the marriage has or is likely to have in the foreseeable future'. Allowing an appeal by the husband, Wood J held that this general provision was subject to an earlier provision contained in the Army Act 1955, s 203 which prohibits a court from making any order restraining a person from receiving his army gratuity in full.

The case illustrates the frequency with which points are decided by the courts in apparent ignorance of relevant principles of statutory interpretation. There was in fact a possible argument for saying that s 203 does not apply in such a case as this, since it is not within the mischief aimed at by that section.

Retrospective operation: general presumption against (Code s 190)

Nature of retrospectivity

In applying the principles relating to retrospectivity it is important correctly to analyse whether or not the relevant application of the enactment in question would truly be retrospective. Confusion often arises on this score. In particular an application is not retrospective where the enactment is applied at a time after its commencement to a state of affairs subsisting at that time, even though that state of affairs came into existence before commencement.

This was overlooked by Sheldon J in *Chebaro v Chebaro* [1986] 2 All ER 897. The case concerned the application of the Matrimonial and Family Proceedings Act 1984, s 12(1), which provides that, where a marriage has been dissolved or annulled, or parties to a marriage have been legally separated, by proceedings in an overseas country, either party may apply for financial relief under the Act. This provision came into force on 16 September 1985. In *Chebaro* the parties' marriage had been dissolved in Lebanon on 16 April 1985.

Section 12(1) sets out a qualifying condition, namely that the marriage *has been dissolved etc*. On the ordinary meaning of this phrase, the question whether it has been dissolved etc before or after the commencement of s 12(1) is immaterial. All that matters is that the condition is satisfied at the time the application for financial relief is made. To treat s 12(1) as applying to the parties in *Chebaro* was not therefore to apply it retrospectively.

Nevertheless Sheldon J treated such an application of s 12(1) as retrospective. This involved him in a lengthy (but strictly unnecessary) examination of the authorities relating to retrospectivity. He concluded that these authorities did not require him to dismiss the application for financial relief, and that s 12(1) was applicable. This process would have been avoided if, as is submitted was the correct analysis, the case had been treated as not in truth involving retrospectivity.

Contrary intention

Where an amending enactment is expressed to be retrospective it will apply to pending actions, including appeals from decisions taken before the passing of the amending Act.

In *Hewitt v Lewis* [1986] 1 All ER 927 the Court of Appeal heard an appeal from a county court decision given before the coming into effect of the Rent (Amendment) Act 1985. The Act was passed to reverse the decision in *Pocock v Steel* [1985] 1 All ER 434; All ER Rev 1985, p 262 as to the legal meaning of the Rent Act 1977, Sch 15, Pt II Case 11. By s 1(4) of the 1985 Act this change of law was stated to apply to tenancies granted and notices given before, as well as after, the commencement of the 1985 Act. *Held* The change applied for the purposes of the instant appeal. Fox LJ said (at 930) 'I can see no reason why Parliament, having acted so speedily, should be taken as intending to force on the landlord a new action on an issue which more easily could be determined in the existing proceedings'.

This is in conformity with the principle, explained in Code s 332, that courts frown on attempts to construe an enactment in such a way as to frustrate or stultify legal proceedings under the Act. The courts are also reluctant to require litigants to embark on futile or unnecessary legal proceedings (see Code p 702).

Application of Act: foreigners and foreign matters within the territory (Code s 222)

Sovereign immunity

The existence of sovereign immunity may render compliance with a statutory requirement impracticable. In such a case the requirement is necessarily subject to an implied exception.

In *Westminster City Council v Government of the Islamic Republic of Iran* [1986] 3 All ER 284 the plaintiffs sought to serve on the defendants under the State Immunity Act 1978, s 12 an originating summons whereby the High Court would be empowered to resolve the question whether the plaintiffs could register a local land charge against the defendants under the Land Charges Act 1975, s 1(1)(a). The State Immunity Act 1978, s 12 required the originating summons to be served by being transmitted through the Foreign and Commonwealth Office to the Iranian Ministry of Foreign Affairs. It was not possible to do this because there was no British diplomatic representation in Iran and the Swedish embassy, which was looking after British interests there, declined to act. *Held* In the unavoidable absence of prior service of the summons on the defendants the court could not rule on the question which had been referred to it.

Drafting error

The common failure of draftsmen to provide adequately for the application of an enactment in relation to foreign elements, and the consequent need for the court to grope for a solution, is exemplified by *Re Collens (deceased)* [1986] 1 All ER 611, where Sir Nicolas Browne-Wilkinson V-C said:

'The truth of the matter is that the draftsman of [the Administration of Estates Act 1925] did not have in mind circumstances such as arise in the present case and one has to do one's best on the basis of the words he has used'.

The case concerned the application of the words in s 46 of the Act conferring a statutory legacy in cases of intestacy where part only of the estate fell to be administered under English law. *Held* In relation to the remaining part of the estate the literal meaning of s 46 must be modified by the court, since Parliament could not be taken to have intended the section to create a charge on assests the succession to which is regulated by a foreign law.

Application of Act: foreigners and foreign matters outside the territory (Code s 223)

Submission to the jurisdiction

The fact that a person has a presence within the territory does not mean that he is to be taken to have submitted to the jurisdiction of the territorial court where the subject-matter is wholly foreign.

In *MacKinnon v Donaldson Lufkin & Jenrette Securities Corp* [1986] 1 All ER 653 the plaintiff in an action before the High Court obtained against Citibank, a bank registered under United States law, a subpoena, and an order under the Bankers' Books Evidence Act 1879, s 7, in respect of a customer of Citibank which was a Bahamian company and relating to matters wholly outside the area of the High Court's territorial jurisdiction. Both the order and the subpoena were addressed to and served on Citibank at its London branch.

Held The order and subpoena would be discharged as beyond the jurisdiction of the court. Hoffmann J distinguished between the court's jurisdiction over persons and its jurisdiction over the subject-matter of an action. While the existence of the London branch office gave jurisdiction to bring Citibank before the court, it did not enable the court to make the orders sought, which were in respect of a wholly foreign subject-matter.

Application of Act: Britons and British matters outside the territory (Code s 224)

As Hoffmann J said in *MacKinnon v Donaldson Lufkin & Jenrette Securities Corp* [1986] 1 All ER 653 at 660: 'International law generally recognises the right of a state to regulate the conduct of its own nationals even outside its jurisdiction, provided that this does not involve disobedience to the local law'. (As to this case see further the note above related to Code s 223.)

Enacting history: amendments to Bill (Code s 239)

In *Pierce v Bemis* [1986] 1 All ER 1011 at 1017 Sheen J allowed counsel to cite, and himself cited in his judgment, extensive details as to the parliamentary proceedings on the Bill which became the Merchant Shipping Act 1906, including details as to how the clause that became the Merchant Shipping Act 1906, s 72 was added to the Bill during its passage through the House of Commons.

Enacting history: to ascertain the mischief (Code s 248)

In *British Leyland Motor Corp Ltd v Armstrong Patents Co Ltd* [1986] 1 All ER 850 the House of Lords allowed detailed argument relating to the Gregory Report (Report of the Copyright Committee (1952) Cmd 8662), upon which the Copyright Act 1956 was based. The argument was permitted to go beyond merely ascertaining the mischief, and touched on the intended legal effect of certain of the Act's provisions. It led to Lord Templeman saying (at 871): 'Thus s 9(8) of the Copyright Act 1956 was defective to achieve the intended purpose ...' On this Lord Edmund-Davies commented (at 853):

> 'My Lords, I have to say respectfully that I do not know what Parliament intended to do. Assume, as one reasonably may, that the Gregory Report was available to the legislators in 1956, and one will still have no knowledge of how far they intended to implement any of its recommendations when legislating as expansively as they did. We may think that they could, and should, have done better, but that is by the way.'

(As to this case see also the note on p 275 above related to Code s 144.)

Post-enacting history: delegated legislation made under Act (Code s 254)

In *Pharmaceutical Society of Great Britain v Storkwain Ltd* [1986] 2 All ER 635 the House of Lords used the language of the Medicines (Prescriptions Only)

Order 1980 as an aid in the construction of the enactment under which it was made, namely the Medicines Act 1968, s 58. Lord Goff of Chieveley said (at 639):

> 'It is unnecessary, in the present case, to consider whether the relevant articles of the order may be taken into account in construing s 58 of the 1958 Act: it is enough, for present purposes, that I am able to draw support from the fact that the ministers, in making the order, plainly did not read s 58 as subject to the implication proposed by counsel for the appellants.'

Post-enacting history: later Acts (Code s 255)

Where a term is used without definition in one Act, but is defined in another Act which is in pari materia with the first Act (ie deals with the same subject matter), the definition may be treated as applicable to the use of the term in the first Act.

This may be done even where the definition is contained in a later Act. Thus in *Wood v Commr of Police of the Metropolis* [1986] 2 All ER 570 the Divisional Court construed the undefined term 'offensive weapon' in the Vagrancy Act 1824, s 4 in the light of the definition of that term laid down for different though related purposes by the Prevention of Crime Act 1953, s 1(4). (As to this case see also the note on p 276 above related to Code s 171 and the note on p 288 below related to Code ss 378–385.)

Principle against doubtful penalisation: physical restraint of the person (Code s 290)

Habeas corpus

In *Linnett v Coles* [1986] 3 All ER 652 at 657 Dillon LJ said that the dictum by Lord Denning MR in *McIlwraith v Grady* [1968] 1 QB 468 at 477 that 'the fundamental principle that no man's liberty is to be taken away unless every requirement of the law has been strictly complied with' had been applied in relation to committals for contempt 'so rigorously as to lead to results, in some cases, that tend to make the court's own process appear ridiculous'. The Court of Appeal held that, in the face of the wide discretion given to the court by the Administration of Justice Act 1960, s 13(3), it could not support Lord Denning's dictum in *Cinderby v Cinderby* (1978) SJ 436 that where a committal is not in proper form the court cannot correct the slip. (As to this case see also the note on p 271 above related to Code s 26 and below related to Code s 313.)

Nature of purposive construction (Code s 313)

Purposive construction and judicial discretion

It is the duty of the court to exercise any discretion vested in it by an enactment in such a way as to further the purpose of the legislature in passing the enactment, and so as not to hinder that purpose. The same principle applies as respects furthering the purpose of related enactments, or indeed the law generally.

RSC Ord 6, r 8(2) confers a discretion to renew the validity of an expired writ. The Limitation Act 1980, s 11 provides that an action for damages for negligence in respect of personal injury shall not be brought after the expiry of a period of three years. In *Wilkinson v Ancliff (BLT) Ltd* [1986] 3 All ER 427 the Court of Appeal held that the discretion to renew a writ which has expired at the end of 12 months from the date of its issue should not be so exercised as to deprive a defendant of a reasonably arguable case that the limitation period had expired.

Slade LJ said (pp 435–436):

> 'If the court grants an application for renewal of a writ in a case where the application for renewal has not been made until after the 12-month period, and with it the validity of the writ, have expired, it is granting the applicant a substantial indulgence. If, on the other hand, the effect of such an order is to deprive the defendant of a limitation defence, it is depriving him of a defence which Parliament . . . intended he should have as of absolute right, for reasons of public policy . . . With these points in mind, it seems to me that, in the absence of special circumstances, it cannot be an appropriate exercise of the court's discretion to grant an indulgence of this nature . . .'

In *Linnett v Coles* [1986] 3 All ER 652 at 657 the Court of Appeal held that, in the face of the wide discretion given to the court by the Administration of Justice Act 1960, s 13, it could not support Lord Denning's dictum in *Cinderby v Cinderby* (1978) SJ 436 that where a committal is not in proper form the court cannot correct the slip. Lawton LJ said (at 655):

> 'I accept, of course, that judges must be vigilant concerning the liberty of the subject; but, if Parliament gives them discretionary powers, as s 13 of the 1960 Act seems to do, it is not competent for them to refuse to exercise those powers. It would be a misuse of powers for a judge to say: "I know Parliament has given me a discretion to vary orders in contempt appeals and make just ones, but I'm never going to use [it] . . ."'

(As to this case see also the note on p 271 above related to Code s 26 and the note on p 281 above related to Code s 290).

Judicial acceptance of legislator's purpose (Code s 318)

As to the duty of the court to comply loyally with a wish or intention clearly evinced by Parliament see the note on p 284 below concerning *R v Secretary of State for Social Services, ex p Connolly* [1986] 1 All ER 998 and related to Code s 335.

Construction against 'absurdity': avoiding an anomalous or illogical result (Code s 323)

Remedy not available in like cases

In *Coltman v Bibby Tankers Ltd* [1986] 2 All ER 65 Sheen J had to decide whether the definition of 'equipment' in the Employer's Liability (Defective Equipment) Act 1969, s 1(3) included a ship. The somewhat ill-drafted definition states that the term 'includes any plant and machinery, vehicles, aircraft and clothing'. Despite the failure to mention ships, which might thus have been held to be excluded either under the rank principle (Code s 386) or the expressio unius principle (Code ss 388–394), neither of which were mentioned in the judgment, Sheen J held that ships should be treated as included since it would be anomalous for the Act to give a remedy to a worker injured by a defect in say an aircraft or train but not to one injured by a defect in a ship.

Evasion distinguished from avoidance (Code s 327)

Ramsay principle

The *Ramsay* principle, whereby the court sets its face against purely artificial tax-avoidance schemes, is not confined to revenue cases.

In *Sherdley v Sherdley* [1986] 2 All ER 202 the Court of Appeal held that the principle should also be applied by the Family Division. A divorced father having care and control of his young children, who were being privately educated, sought under the Matrimonial Causes Act 1973, s 23(1)(d) an order against himself requiring him to pay to each child periodical amounts equivalent to its school fees. The sole purpose was to avoid tax by rendering the sums in question income of the children instead of their father. *Held* Since the sole purpose of the application was tax avoidance the court below was right to exercise its discretion by deciding to refuse the order.

Implied application of decision-making rules of natural justice, etc (Code s 335)

Duty to give reasons

Where a tribunal gives reasons 'one must somehow be able to read from the reasons the issue to which the reasons are directed': *R v Mental Health Review Tribunal, ex p Pickering* [1986] 1 All ER 99 at 104, per Forbes J. In this case it was held that reasons given under the Mental Health Tribunal Rules 1983 r 23(2) did not clearly indicate whether they referred to the diagnostic issue or to the issue whether public safety required the patient's retention in hospital.

R v Secretary of State for the Home Department, ex p Swati [1986] 1 All ER 717 concerned the requirement of the Immigration Appeals (Notices) Regulations 1984, reg 4(1)(a) that written notice of a decision shall 'include a statement of the reasons for the decision'. The notice given by the immigration officer said 'I am not satisfied that you are genuinely seeking entry only for this limited period' (ie one week). It was argued that this mere assertion of dissatisfaction was inadequate. *Held* The statement was adequate, and the immigration officer was not required to go further and state in the statutory notice the reasons for her dissatisfaction. Parker LJ said (at 728): 'What counsel for Mr Swati is in effect seeking is not the reasons for the refusal but the reasons for the reasons for the refusal and for that the 1984 Regulations do not provide'.

In *R v Secretary of State for Social Services, ex p Connolly* [1986] 1 All ER 998 at 1006 Slade LJ said that there is no basic requirement of natural justice that reasons should always be given when a discretion is exercised by a tribunal such as a social security commissioner (cf *The Antaios* [1985] AC 191). The Court of Appeal held that, where Parliament has conferred on the tribunal an express exemption from giving reasons, courts should not exert pressure on the tribunal in an attempt to induce it to give reasons in certain cases. (As to this case see further the note on p 282 above related to Code s 318).

Implied application of rules of contract law (Code s 337)

Frustration

Even though to treat the doctrine of frustration as applying in relation to a contract may defeat the apparent legislative purpose as respects contracts of that type, the court will, unless the contrary intention appears, nevertheless treat the doctrine as intended by Parliament to apply.

In *Notcutt v Universal Equipment Co (London) Ltd* [1986] 3 All ER 582 the Court of Appeal held a contract of employment frustrated by the worker's suffering of a heart attack inducing permanent unfitness for work even though the effect was to deprive him of a statutory benefit. Dillon LJ, in considering whether the Employment Protection (Consolidation) Act 1978, Sch 3 applied to give the worker a right to sick pay during his period of notice, accepted (at 585) that in this case 'the argument of frustration is of course unashamedly put forward to avoid the provisions of the Act'.

Held The contract of employment had been frustrated by the worker's illness. This brought the contract to an end before the date of service of the notice purporting to terminate it, and therefore the Act's provisions regarding sick pay during a period of notice never operated. (As to the doctrine of frustration see also the note on *F C Shepherd & Co Ltd v Jerrom* [1986] 3 All ER 589 on p 286 below, related to Code s 354).

Implied application of rules of criminal law (Code s 340)

Defences

An enactment which forbids specified conduct in absolute terms is nevertheless qualified by the implied importation of rules laying down defences.

In *R v Renouf* [1986] 2 All ER 449 the defendant was convicted of contravening the Road Traffic Act 1972, s 2, which states: 'A person who drives a motor vehicle on a road recklessly shall be guilty of an offence'. His defence was that his conduct was excused by the Criminal Law Act 1967, s 3(1), which states: 'A person may use such force as is reasonable ... in effecting or assisting in the lawful arrest of offenders'. The trial judge refused to leave this defence to the jury.

Held The judge was wrong, and the defence should have been left to the jury. Lawton LJ said (at 451):

'This evidence had two facets: one was what the prosecution alleged to be the acts of recklessness; and the other was that these same acts amounted to the use of reasonable force for the purpose of assisting in the lawful arrest of offenders . . . In our judgment the alleged presence of these two facets . . . was capable of providing [the appellant] with a defence'.

Implied application of rules of jurisdiction, evidence and procedure (Code s 341)

The Scherer principle

The reluctance of the courts to countenance attempts to oust their jurisdiction is strikingly illustrated by a case decided in 1977 but not reported until 1986. In *Scherer v Counting Instruments Ltd* [1986] 2 All ER 529 the Court of Appeal considered the Supreme Court of Judicature (Consolidation) Act 1925, s 31(1)(h), re-enacted in the Supreme Court Act 1981, s 18(1)(f)), which states:

'. . . no appeal shall lie without the leave of the court or judge making the order, from an order of the High Court or any judge thereof made . . . as to costs only which by law are left in the discretion of the court'.

The court below, although dismissing applications by the defendants in two actions brought against them by the plaintiffs for dismissal of the actions for want of prosecution, ordered the costs of the unsuccessful applications to be borne by the plaintiffs. The plaintiffs appealed, not having obtained leave to do so from the judge making the order. *Held* Since there was no material before the judge on which he could properly make the order it would be discharged notwithstanding s 31(1)(h).

Commenting on this decision in *Aden Refinery Co Ltd v Ugland Management Co* [1986] 3 All ER 737 at 744 Donaldson MR said:

'Counsel for the charterers' whole argument is based on the curious, but well-established, view of the law which binds this court to hold that s 18(1)(f) of the Supreme Court Act 1981 . . . has no application, if this court is able to say that the judge in the court below did not really exercise his discretion at all or based the exercise of his discretion on an inadmissible reason. This is referred to by the cognoscenti as "the *Scherer* principle" . . .'

Right to cross-examine

Where a new statutory forensic system is laid down it is to be assumed that Parliament intended the normal procedures of adversarial justice to apply.

In *Chilton v Saga Holidays plc* [1986] 1 All ER 841 the Court of Appeal considered the form of County Court arbitration procedure laid down by CCR Ord 19, r 5(2), which provides that any hearing shall be informal, and authorises the arbitrator to adopt any method of procedure which he may consider convenient. The arbitrator refused to allow the solicitor appearing for Saga Holidays to cross-examine Mr Chilton, who was appearing in person.

Held To deny cross-examination was effectively to deprive Saga Holidays of the services of their solicitor, and the rule could not be taken as intending this. Donaldson MR said (at 844):

'... both courts and arbitrators in this country operate on an adversarial system of achieving justice. It is a system which can be modified by rules of court; it is a system which can be modified by agreement between the parties; but, in the absence of one or the other, it is basically an adversarial system, and it is fundamental to that that each party shall be entitled to tender their own evidence and that the other party shall be entitled to ask questions designed to probe the accuracy or otherwise, or the completeness or otherwise, of the evidence which has been given.'

Reliance on illegality (allegans suam turpitudinem non est audiendus) (Code s 345)

Where a plaintiff cannot succeed unless he relies on an act by him which contravened a statute or was otherwise illegal, his action will fail.

In *Phoenix General Insurance Co of Greece SA v Halvanon Insurance Co Ltd* [1986] 1 All ER 908 the plaintiffs had, in contravention of the Insurance Companies Act 1974, entered into certain reinsurance contracts. By virtue of s 11(1) of the Act (repealed by the Insurance Companies Act 1981, s 36(2) and Sch 5 Pt I) it was an offence for the plaintiffs to enter into each of these contracts. The plaintiffs sued the reinsurers under the contracts.

Held Entry into the reinsurance contracts constituted the very type of business against which the system of Government authorisation created by the Act for the benefit of insured persons was directed. Accordingly the plaintiffs could not succeed. Hobhouse J relied on the following dictum of Denning LJ in *Marles v Philip Trant & Sons Ltd (No 2)* [1954] 1 QB 29 at 38:

> 'So far as the cause of action itself is concerned, the principle is well settled that if the plaintiff requires any aid from an illegal transaction to establish his cause of action, then he shall not have any aid from the court'.

Hobhouse J (at 918) distinguished the reinsurance contracts in the instant case from transactions in relation to which contravention of a statute is merely casual, adventitious or collateral. He also held (ibid) that the original contracts of primary insurance could be enforced by the innocent insureds, since the ultimate intention of the statute was clearly to benefit and protect them.

Hearing both sides (audi alteram partem) (Code s 346)

Oral representations

The decision in *R v Diggines, ex p Rahmani* [1985] 1 All ER 1073; All ER Rev 1985, p 266 was affirmed by the House of Lords on other grounds, not relevant to the audi alteram partem rule.

Benefit from own wrong: nullus commodum capere potest de injuria sua propria (Code s 354)

In *F C Shepherd & Co Ltd v Jerrom* [1986] 3 All ER 589 the respondent, an apprentice under a four-year contract of apprenticeship, was sentenced to detention in Borstal, for a period between six months and two years, in respect of convictions for affray and conspiracy to assault. He was released after six months, whereupon the employers refused to take him back. He sought to argue that the apprenticeship contract had not been terminated under the doctrine of frustration because the frustration was self-induced, and that therefore he was entitled under the Employment Protection (Consolidation) Act 1978, s 72 to compensation for unfair dismissal.

Held The respondent was not entitled to rely on his own default in order to obtain compensation under the statute. Mustill LJ said (at 601) that to rule otherwise would infringe what Diplock LJ described in *Hong Kong Fir Shipping Co Ltd v Kawasaki Kisen Kaisha Ltd* [1962] 2 QB 26 at 66 as 'the fundamental legal and moral rule that a man should not be allowed to take advantage of his own wrong'.

Agency: qui facit per alium facit per se (Code s 356)

Act done to agent

It is provided by the Road Traffic Act 1972, s 10(5) that a document of a type there mentioned is admissible in evidence 'only if a copy of it has been served *on the accused* not later than seven days before the hearing' (emphasis added). In *Penman v Parker* [1986] 2 All ER 862 the question arose whether this requirement was satisfied where, in the absence of the accused and his solicitor, the copy was served in the courtroom on counsel acting for the accused in proceedings related to the offence in question.

Held Such a notice may be validly served on an authorised agent. While counsel, as compared to a solicitor, possesses only a limited authority to accept service of documents, and has discretion to refuse to accept such service, his acceptance of the copy in the present circumstances constituted a valid service of it on the accused. The case is authority for saying that in a provision such as s 10(5) the words 'or his authorised agent' are to be treated as present by implication following the reference to the person on whom a document is to be served.

Ordinary meaning of words (Code s 363)

Words with several ordinary meanings

In *Hall v Cotton* [1986] 3 All ER 332 the Divisional Court considered the meaning of the word *possession*, as used in the Firearms Act 1968, s 2(1). This renders it an offence for a person to have a shotgun in his possession without holding a certificate under the Act. The respondent C left his two shotguns with the respondent T while he went on holiday. T lacked a shotgun certificate, and the question was whether he had acquired possession of the shotguns.

Held The term *possession* must here be regarded as having two meanings, either of which was applicable. While C retained proprietorial possession of the shotguns, T acquired custodial possession and was therefore guilty. Stocker LJ cited (at 335) a dictum of Lord Parker CJ in *Towers & Co Ltd v Gray* [1961] 2 QB 351 at 361: 'The term "possession" is always giving trouble'.

Technical terms (Code s 365)

Where a term appears which has both an ordinary and a technical meaning, the court will, when determining in which sense it is used, be guided by whether or not it is accompanied by other related technical terms. In *Knocker v Youle* [1986] 2 All ER 914 the term under consideration was *interest*, as used in the Variation of Trusts Act 1958, s 1(1)(b). To counsel's invitation to construe the word loosely, as a layman might, Warner J replied (at 916) that it was clearly used in its technical legal sense, since otherwise 'the words "whether vested or contingent" in para (a) of s 1(1) would be out of place'.

Archaisms (Code s 370)

Where in a modern Act Parliament uses a term which has an archaic meaning and also a (different) modern meaning it will be presumed, in the absence of any indication to the contrary, that the modern meaning is intended.

In *R v Secretary of State for the Environment, ex p Hillingdon LBC* [1986] 1 All ER 810 (affd [1986] 2 All ER 273) Woolf J held that 'committee' as used in the Local Government Act 1972, s 101(1)(a) was intended to have its modern meaning of a group of two or more persons, and not its obsolete meaning of a person to whom any function is committed. (As to this case see also the note on p 273 above related to Code s 125).

Ejusdem generis principle (Code ss 378–385)

The Divisional Court applied the ejusdem generis principle in *Wood v Commr of Police of the Metropolis* [1986] 2 All ER 570. The appellant was convicted of being armed with an offensive weapon with intent to commit an arrestable offence, contrary to the Vagrancy Act 1824, s 4. This applies to 'every person ... being armed with any gun, pistol, hanger, cutlass, bludgeon, or other offensive weapon'. The appellant was armed with a piece of broken glass which had just accidentally fallen out of a panel in his front door.

Held Applying the ejusdem generis principle, the term 'offensive weapon' in this phrase was to be construed as confined to articles made or adapted for use for causing injury to the person. (As to this case see also the note on p 276 above related to Code s 171 and the note on p 281 above related to Code s 255).

Expressio unius principle: words of extension (Code s 391)

Without explicitly saying so, the Commercial Court applied the principle *expressio unius est exclusio alterius* in *Swiss Bank Corp v Brink's MAT Ltd* [1986] 2 All ER 188. The case concerned the Warsaw-Hague Convention, which is set out in the Carriage by Air Act 1961, Sch 1, and declared by s 1(1) of the Act to have the force of law in the United Kingdom. Although, as he said (p 189), starting off with an inclination to award interest on damages payable to the plaintiffs by virtue of the Convention, Bingham J reached an opposite conclusion. Article 24(1) of the Convention places a monetary limit on the damages that can be awarded, while art 22(4) states that this shall not preclude the award of costs. There is no mention of interest.

Held The statement in art 22(4) indicated that but for it costs would be within the limit imposed by art 24(1), and it must therefore be treated as an extending provision. Since there were no such words of extension in relation to interest it must be taken as intended to be excluded.

Implication where statutory condition only partly met (Code s 396)

Ultra vires acts

Where a public authority reaches a decision for two purposes, one only of which is within its statutory powers, the validity of the decision depends on whether the other purpose is one of the main purposes or is merely subsidiary.

In *R v Inner London Education Authority, ex p Westminster City Council* [1986] 1 All ER 19 the Inner London Education Authority ('ILEA') had resolved under s 142(2) of the Local Government Act 1972 (which authorises spending on the publication of information on matters relating to local government) to spend £651,000 on an advertising campaign designed not only to publish legitimate information but also (illegitimately) to promote ILEA's opposition to the Government's rate-capping policy. *Held* The illegitimate purpose was a main purpose of the decision, which was therefore invalid.

Public interest immunity

Public interest immunity attaches to statements made for the purposes of a complaint against the police under the Police Act 1964, s 49 (see Code pp 752–753). Where statements are made partly for these purposes and partly for other purposes in relation to which public interest immunity does not lie, the question whether such immunity attached depends on the *dominant* purpose for which the statements were made: *Peach v Commr of Police for the Metropolis* [1986] 2 All ER 129. In this case statements of witnesses to the incident in which Blair Peach was killed in a demonstration were taken (1) for purposes of s 49; (2) for purposes of the inquest into the death; and (3) for purposes of a possible prosecution. *Held* The s 49 inquiry was not the dominant purpose, and therefore public interest immunity did not lie.

Succession

C H SHERRIN, LLM, PHD
Barrister, Senior Lecturer in Law, University of Bristol

Intestate succession

Every first year law student knows that one of the primary aims of the 1925 legislation was the assimilation of the law of real and personal property. Nowhere is this objective more clearly illustrated than in the unification of the law of intestate succession and in the provision of a statutory code applicable to both real and personal property. But in one important respect this assimilation was not achieved and an anomalous dichotomy remains.

Where conflict of laws points arise, the intestate succession to immovable property is governed by the lex situs; whereas the intestate succession to movables is regulated by the law of the domicile. The illogicality of this perpetuated distinction and the anomalous consequences that it can produce has been illustrated, for example, in *Re Rea* [1902] 1 IR 451 and frequently criticised, for example, by Dr Morris (1969) 85 LQR 339. The recently reported case of *Re Collens(decd), Royal Bank of Canada (London) Ltd v Krogh* [1986] 1 All ER 611, reinforces these criticisms.

The deceased was domiciled in Trinidad and Tobago and his intestate estate consisted of property in that country, and in Barbados and the United Kingdom. The United Kingdom property included immovable property. He was survived by a widow and by several children from a previous marriage. Following legal proceedings in Trinidad and Tobago the widow accepted $1m under a deed of compromise in settlement of her rights over the estate in that country. She then claimed that she was entitled in addition to the statutory legacy of £5000 (the appropriate figure in respect of a death in February 1966) out of the deceased's English estate by virtue of s 46 of the Administration of Estates Act 1925. It was common ground that the succession to the English immovable estate was governed by English intestacy law, and it was thought that any argument that this had been affected by the 1925 legislation was untenable. The question was whether she could take both the share of the Trinidad and Tobago estate under the law of the domicile which regulated the movable property and in addition claim the statutory legacy under the English law of intestacy in relation to the English immovable property. It was held that she could. Section 46 of the 1925 Act which states that '... the residuary estate of the intestate (other than the personal chattels) shall stand charged with the payment of a fixed net sum ...' can only regulate the succession to the immovable property in this country. The section can only impose a charge for the statutory legacy on the proceeds of the English immovables; there is no way in which the section can be made to impose a charge on assets not devolving under English law, since such a charge is part of the English law of succession (per Browne-Wilkinson V-C at 616). Thus it was not possible to say that the charge on the English immovable estate had been satisfied out of the overseas assets of the deceased. In a sentence s 46 cannot operate to create a charge on assets the succession to which is regulated by a foreign law (ibid), and so the charge had remained unsatisfied and the widow was entitled to the statutory legacy. This seems to be an inevitable result on the law as it now stands, because even if 'the residuary estate of the intestate' meant all the property worldwide of the intestate wherever situated (which was a possible construction of ss 33 and 46 of the 1925 Act, urged on the court), Parliament could not have intended to create beneficial interests in assets which for the purposes of the law of succession did not fall to be regulated by English law. The conclusion of the court is consistent with the earlier authorities of *Re Rea, Rea v Rea* [1902] 1 IR 451 and with the Victorian decision of *Re Ralston* [1906] VLR 689.

The Vice-Chancellor reached this conclusion 'with some regret' and one shares his opinion that the law might be more satisfactorily expressed if the whole of the succession were governed by the law of the domicile. Perhaps the Law Commission will accept the judge's invitation to consider the matter with a view to reform.

See also, the article on Conflict of Laws, pp 69, 70, above.

Family provision

The only other case reported in 1986 on the law of succession is *Whyte v Ticehurst* [1986] 2 All ER 158, which decided in an unremarkable way a straightforward point on the Inheritance (Provision for Family and Dependants) Act 1975. A widow made a claim against her deceased husband's estate on the ground that his will did not make reasonable provison for her. Five months later the widow herself died and her personal representatives applied for leave to carry on the proceedings on behalf of the estate. Counsel accepted that a claim for ancilliary relief under the Matrimonial Causes Act 1973 would not subsist for or against the estate of a deceased spouse but it argued that different considerations applied in respect of a claim under the 1975 Act which is not limited (in the case of a spouse) to financial provision for maintenance. The 1975 Act enables orders to be made for the transfer or settlement of property not limited to maintenance. It was argued that such a claim could enure to the state under the provisions of the Law Reform (Miscellaneous Provisions) Act 1934—in effect that a distinction should be drawn between, on the one hand, a claim for maintenance personal to the survivor which would die with him, and on the other, a claim for financial relief beyond that which was required for maintenance (which would be open to the spouse but not to any other applicant) which would survive for the benefit of the estate.

The court was not so persuaded. Earlier authorities, for example, *Sugden v Sugden* [1957] 1 All ER 300, had suggested that claims for ancillary relief in matrimonial proceedings did not survive the death of the claimant. This is because it is only when the order for financial provision has been made that the cause of action in effect arises. The court recognised the changed basis of relief now available in the 1973 Act and in the 1975 Act but thought that the decision in *Wachtel v Wachtel* [1973] 1 All ER 113 did not suggest that the wide powers given to the court in the new matrimonial legislation fundamentally altered the nature of the claim for financial relief made by one party to the marriage against the other (per Booth J, at 162, 163). The principles stated by Lord Denning in *Sugden v Sugden* thus continued to apply and no enforceable right arose until the order was actually made.

Further the court thought that the right to claim under the 1975 Act arose from the relationship of the two parties to the marriage and was personal to the survivor. On the death of both parties to the marriage the claim ceased to exist unless an order had been made giving rise to an enforceable cause of action which could subsist for the benefit of one estate against another. That was not the case here, since the widow's death preceded the making of any order in respect of her claim. Accordingly the registar's order refusing leave to the personal representatives to continue the proceedings was upheld.

Taxation

JOHN TILEY, MA, BCL
Barrister, Fellow of Queens' College, Cambridge

This year has been a relatively quiet one but several difficult issues have arisen and *Furniss v Dawson* [1984] 1 All ER 530, [1984] STC 153 continues to lie in the background as a topic of lively interest.

Furniss v Dawson

It was inevitable that *Furniss v Dawson* would continue to feature, but only two cases stand out. The first is the decision of the House of Lords in *Reed (Inspector of Taxes) v Young* [1986] STC 285 in which the House dismissed the Revenue's appeal from the decision of the Court of Appeal ([1985] STC 25); this case stands out for the negative but important point that the Revenue made no effort to use *Furniss v Dawson* and did not even cite it. The case involved a scheme using a limited partnership; the partnership deed allocated 95 per cent of the profits or losses to the limited partners to be shared by them in proportion to the amount of capital they had provided; each limited partner was liable for the losses allocated to him; which were to be set off against their interests in the partnership, any excess losses to be carried forward to be set against future profits arising but no partner to be liable for losses in excess of the amount of capital contributed. The claim arose under TA 1970, s 168 allowing the taxpayer to set trading losses off against general income. The Revenue argued that the total amount claimed by way of loss could not be said to have been 'sustained' as it exceeded the taxpayer's maximum liability—the amount of capital at risk. The Revenue's argument was weakened by the fact that they were prepared to concede, and indeed had little choice but to concede, that the taxpayer would be entitled to use such losses under s 171, by setting them off against future profits of the trade. Lord Oliver, with whom all the other Law Lords concurred, treated the matter as a short one not susceptible of any great elaboration. The trading losses of the partnership were conceptually quite distinct from the debts and liabilities of the firm and from the assets to be used to meet them.

By failing to base any argument on *Furniss v Dawson* the Revenue show that they do not regard that case as enabling them to undo any transaction simply because there may be a tax advantage behind it; rather, it is a doctrine dealing with composite transactions entered into solely for the avoidance of tax. In this case if the partnership generated profits, any losses of the early years would reduce each partner's share. FA 1985, s 48 and Sch 2 now enacts the Revenue's position.

Furniss v Dawson was most emphatically cited in second case, the decision of the Court of Appeal in *Sherdley v Sherdley* [1986] 2 All ER 202, [1986] STC 266. This case involved an application by a parent who already had custody of his three children for an order that he should be made to pay school fees for the children; the steps to be taken in making such an order were clearly set out in a *Practice Direction* [1983] 2 All ER 679; the Revenue agreed with the principle—see SP 15/80; the purpose of the order was to enable him to obtain a deduction for the amounts to be paid; there was no purpose behind the order other than the obtaining of the tax advantage; it was clear that the father would go on paying for the children if no order were made.

In the Family Division Wood J had held that he had jurisdiction to make the order but declined to exercise it in view of the policy of the judges of the Division. That policy appears to have been not to do anything which would invite the Revenue to consider the reintroduction of aggregation of the income of parent and child, the judge saying that one reason why the Revenue had not taken such a step was the refusal of the judges to make orders on the application of the custodial parent. In the Court of Appeal Sir John Donaldson MR condemned such a policy of 'appeasing' the Revenue; however he reached the same conclusion—as did Kerr and Balcombe LJJ and held that the court had jurisdiction. However according to Sir John the order should not be made because the Revenue would be able to disregard it. Under the scheme the child made a contract with the school and the father would make payments to the school; the school's officer received the money in discharge of the child's liability for the fees. For Sir John the first defect in the scheme was that the child had no capacity to make the contract; this is controversial since it overlooks the statements of Viscount Dilhorne in *IRC v Mills* [1974] 1 All ER 722 at 728 that a child has contractual capacity; perhaps this case will resolve this problem. The second defect was that *Furniss v Dawson* would strike the scheme down; the 'reality' was that the father's liability to pay the fees was being discharged. Kerr LJ thought the scheme would be 'unlikely' to work and he and Balcombe LJ thought that the courts should not exercise their discretion to make an order where the only purpose was to obtain a tax advantage; Balcombe LJ seems to have thought that the school fees would work at a technical level.

The result of this case has been a considerable amount of confusion. This is attributable to two causes. The first is the divergent voices on the point of whether the school fees scheme would work and even greater discordance on why it would not work. Thus Balcombe LJ would have been willing to make an order if it would be the only way of enabling a child who had begun private education to complete it. The second is the lack of clarity as to whether the fate of the school fees scheme can be extended to other arrangements in this area such as where the order is to be for payments to a child by the custodial parent at the suit of that parent and even where such an order is sought against a non-custodial parent by the custodial parent. Sir John's insistence on invoking the concept of 'reality' is not helpful since this highly slippery concept is not defined. 'Reality' and 'Substance' are notions to be found in the American material but all too often they defy analysis and fail to indicate to courts the facts which are to be determinative of the issue raised. Letting these concepts loose in the UK law will prove to be a very expensive mistake; one hopes therefore that the House of Lords will adopt a more analytical approach.

Furniss v Dawson was mentioned in *Baylis (Inspector of Taxes) v Gregory*

[1986] 1 All ER 289, [1986] STC 22 where Vinelott J concluded on the facts that the transactions could not be said to have been preordained and thus fell outside the new approach. However the judge also said that there would be a potential double taxation point. This will prove to be a real problem for the judges if they continue to use the new approach in anything less than a full blooded way. Adjustment of the base cost of assets is simply going to have to be effected; this is the sort of things American tax judges do without thinking since it is obviously right and indeed part of the fundamental structure of US tax thinking; it is also a consequence of 'reality.'

'Reality' also surfaced in *Commissioner of Inland Revenue v Challenge Corporation Ltd* [1986] STC 548, which is a fascinating case from New Zealand on the application of their general anti-avoidance provision. The importance for UK tax lawyers is two-fold. First, Lord Templeman distinguished tax avoidance from tax mitigation, thus holding that matters of tax mitigation were outside the scope of the provision—but perhaps also indicating that they lay outside *Furniss v Dawson*. Assignments of income by covenant were treated as mitigation where the covenant was in favour of a child at university but as avoidance by the Duke of Westminster. The second is the disagreement between Lord Templeman and Lord Oliver on whether the general provision should apply where the legislation contained an anti-avoidance provision for the area which did not apply; this sort of argument may become familiar here—the terms in which the debate is conducted appear somewhat sterile.

EEC

Three cases with EEC aspects require mention. *C & E Comrs v Apple and Pear Development Council* [1986] STC 192 is a decision of the House of Lords referring to the European Court the interpretation of the word 'consideration' and, in particular, whether a compulsory levy would be included; it was clear that it would not be included on the basis of a traditional English definition. It is hard to overestimate the importance of this decision, along with its premise that the UK legislation should be interpreted in the light of the relevant EC Council directives. VAT legislation will have to be interpreted along European lines; a comment that applies with equal force to capital duty, as is shown by the decision of Warner J in *National Smokeless Fuels Ltd v IRC* [1986] STC 300.

Hurd v Jones (HM Inspector of Taxes) [1986] STC 127 is a long judgment of the CJEC. The short question was how the UK could tax salaries of teachers employed at 'European Schools?' The facts of the case may explain the bitterness of the recent UK teachers dispute. In addition to his basic salary, on which he agreed he was liable to UK tax, the taxpayer received a 'European Supplement' to bring his national salary up to a European level and a 'differential allowance' based on certain national tax computations. The court ruled that where the burden of such payments fell directly on the Comunity budget member states were prohibited from levying tax but this did not have the 'direct effect' necessary to enable the taxpayer to rely on it in dispute with the state.

Employment income

In *Hamblett v Godfrey (Inspector of Taxes)* [1986] 2 All ER 513, [1986] STC 213, Knox J had to decide whether a payment made to an employee at GCHQ in return for giving up her right to belong to a trade union and certain statutory rights under the employment protection legislation was taxable. The payment was made because it was not thought right to remove these rights without any recognition. One should also note—although the judge said it was immaterial—that the offer of payment was coupled with a statement that it was taxable. The Special Commissioners had held that the sum was not taxable but the judge held that it was, a decision since upheld by the Court of Appeal. The decision is based on general principles of Schedule E and the Revenue did not proceed with a charge under FA 1976, s 61.

Knox J began by accepting the Commissioner's finding of fact that the payment was not made in return for her services but would not accept their conclusion that a payment could not be an emolument unless it was in return for the performance of duties of the office and for no other purpose. A test which confined Schedule E to payments by way of remuneration would obviously be too narrow. The case may thus be seen as undermining the reasoning of Walton J in *Donnelly v Williamson* [1982] STC 88, 54 TC 636 (All ER Rev 1982, p 283). He then turned to consider a test based on *Hochstrasser v Mayes* [1960] AC and asked whether the payment was received 'from' the employment. After listing the various factors he concluded that the payment had to be from the employment since it did not appear to be from anything else. What seems to have weighed with the judge as much as anything was that the only rights given up were connected with the employment at GCHQ rather than with general liberties such as the freedom to practice as an accountant *(Pritchard v Arundale* [1971] 3 All ER 1011) or as an amateur sportsman *(Jarrold v Boustead* [1946] 3 All ER 76).

The case leaves a slightly sour taste. First, it must surely be possible for our appellate courts to come up with a test for determining when a payment is taxable and when it is not. As this case shows there are many tests, all of them difficult to apply (see the note by Macdonald in [1986] BTR 314). In this context one hopes that they will also examine the issue of when payments for varying contracts will be subjected to the same golden handshake rules that apply on complete termination. Secondly, one wonders at the relatively short list of cases cited; perhaps this is desirable but if this case goes to the House of Lords one must hope for a complete review. Thirdly, one is surprised to find that one of the cases which was cited in argument does not appear in the judgment. As the Crown's exercise of the prerogative had been effective to remove the taxpayer's rights, the case was analogous to *Holland v Geogehegan* [1972] 3 All ER 333, 48 TC 482, where payments to dustmen returning to work after a strike as compensation for giving up their rights to 'totting' were held taxable on the basis that they were simply made as part of the arrangements for future work.

Wilson v Alexander (Inspector of Taxes) [1986] STC 365 needs less space. It was an appeal by a taxpayer in person who was a higher paid employee and who wished to argue that he was not taxable in respect of the use of a company car under the pre-1976 rules or the 1976 rule in s 64 on the basis that use of a car was not money or money's worth. Harman J duly held that the effect of statutory provisions (TA 1970, ss 195 and 196 and FA 1976, s 64) was to override the general principle in *Tennant v Smith* [1892] AC 150, 3 TC 158. The judge did not have to explore the distinction between expenses incurred as owner and those incurred as user, a matter irrelevant to the 1976 rules for cars but relevant to other assets; this was because the expenses in issue were clearly user ones.

Bray (Inspector of Taxes) v Best [1986] STC 96 is of more general interest. It concerned a distribution of assets from a trust established for the benefit of employees. Had the distribution occurred during the employment *Brumby (Inspector of Taxes) v Milner* [1976] STC 534 would clearly have applied but here the distribution took place after the employment had ceased. Walton J held that this made no difference and that tax was due. Three points arise. The first is to consider whether there was any basis upon which the trustees could have made the distribution without the payments being treated as employment income of the recipients. Thus the judge in concluding that the payments were rewards for services (a test rejected as not conclusive in *Hamblett v Godfrey*) placed emphasis on the facts that everyone who was eligible got something, that the only common factor among them was the employment and that the trustes had regard to no other factor but fairness in distributing among the employees and no investigation of personal merits was entered into. Thus had the trustees decided to make the distribution on the basis of personal circumstances, the charge might have been avoided, although in the light of *Hamblett v Godfrey* it is hard to be dogmatic on this point. If this is so one wonders whether trustees ought to take full advice before making the distributions on the tax implications of what they are doing although this is not to suggest that it necessarily follows that they would be guilty of breach of trust if, in their discretion, they adopted a scheme of distribution which attracted income tax. Secondly, if the trustees had made the distributions on some other basis so that Schedule E was escaped, how would the payment have been taxed? As this was a final distribution on the winding up of a scheme it is likely that the sums would have been treated as capital receipts.

The third point is the most troublesome. This is to wonder why the fact that the payment was made after the employment had ceased should not have had the effect of distinguishing *Brumby v Milner*. For years one of the axioms of tax theory has been the doctrine of the source, a doctrine which manifests itself in the rule that the source of the payment must exist in the tax year for which the payment is income, and many schemes exist to exploit this rule in connection with the remittance basis of taxation. This case can be reconciled with this doctrine only by procrustean methods. One way is to say that the source of the payment was the trust and that the trust existed in the year of payment; when it is objected that this might make the payments income under Schedule D Case III but cannot make them income under Schedule E it could be answered that the trust has an employment 'feel' about it; yet this is surely nonsense, the more so if a distribution by the trustees on some other basis would not have been Schedule E income. Another way is to argue that whenever the payments are made they are to be treated as income of the years of employment; this is what Walton J did although not in answer to the problem of the doctrine of the source, which seems to have been overlooked completely. The judge seems to have wanted to spread the payments back in order to avoid the tax consequences of treating the entire payment as income of the year of receipt but this seems to be an inadequate reason and his suggestions as to how to make the allocation to the different years simply underline that inadequacy. If the case goes on appeal we must hope for a more thorough examination of the timing rules under Schedule E.

A timing problem arose in the Privy Council case of *Board of Inland Revenue v Suite* [1986] 2 All ER 577, [1986] STC 292, an appeal from Trinidad and Tobago. A teacher had been suspended on half pay and—five years later—reinstated on terms which included full pay for the period of suspension. The court, dismissing the Revenue's appeal, held that the payments were income of the years for which they had been earned and so attributed them to the five years.

Lastly in this section we have *Platten (Inspector of Taxes) v Brown* [1986] STC 514 dealing with the now repealed provisions in FA 1977, Sch 7, para 2 allowing a 25% deduction for payments for duties performed outside the UK where there are 30 'qualifying days' in the year. Hoffmann J held that the rule as to qualifying days was simply a threshhold condition and therefore the reduction was available for days which were not qualifying days but on which the taxpayer worked abroad. He also held that the allocation of the year's payment to days worked abroad should be on a fraction of 365ths; he rejected the taxpayers' argument that the denominator of the fraction should be the number of days actually worked (261).

Business income

The first two cases concern the scope of Schedule D Case I. In *Marson (Inspector of Taxes) v Morton* [1986] STC 463 Browne-Wilkinson V-C held that he could not interfere with the conclusion of the Commissioners that a gain was not income. The facts are, to say the least, close to inviting reversal. The subject matter was land, the land produced no income, the taxpayers intended to sell within a year or two and actually sold after only three months and almost one half of the purchase price was raised by loan. Two matters stand out; one is that the taxpayers seem to have been extraordinarily relaxed about the whole thing—the case reads as if they had some money lying around and left it to their agent to do something with it by way of investment—and the second is the statement of the General Commissioners that the Crown now had the alternative of taxing the gain to CGT. Browne-Wilkinson V-C held that one could not infer from this an incorrect willingness on the part of the Commissioners to depart from the old cases. Mention of old cases requires one to welcome the mention of *Jones v Leeming* [1930] AC 415 which was cited but one is still mildly surprised at the result.

The second case on the scope of D I is the decision of the Privy Council in the Malaysian appeal of *Lim Foo Yong Sdn Bhd v Comptroller General of Inland Revenue* [1986] STC 255. The taxpayer company had developed a hotel site; a sale and leaseback of the property was followed by a reconstruction of the group to raise capital for the business by the sale of shares to the public. Was the profit arising on the leaseback or on the reconstruction or on the sale of the shares capital or income? Lord Oliver speaking for the Council gave an emphatic decision in favour of capital. This case stresses once again the importance of each case resulting on its own facts—although here the Privy Council decision reversed that of the Commissioners.

Torbell Ivestments Ltd and others v Williams [1986] STC 397 is a useful decision on the scope of trading, with the taxpayer here arguing in favour of trade so as to establish group relief. Harman J concluded that the transactions were entered into with a view (remote but genuine) to profit and so reversed the Commissioners. The case concerned the transfer of some loans from a banking subsidiary to the taxpayer. He then considered a Revenue argument that as the purpose of the transfer was to disembarrass the banking subsidiary the cost to the taxpayer of taking over the loans—the price paid to the bank—was not deductible. This met a strong reaction. In so far as the Inspector tried to show that there would be neither profit nor loss to the taxpayer on this basis, Harman J described the view as 'accounting rubbish.' If, as he thought, this would mean a tax on the gain with no allowance for the cost, the conclusion was one from which he revolted as a judge of the court. Having concluded that these were trading transactions, he thought that the costs of acquisition had to be allowed a trading expense—even though the loans did not feature in the accounts as trading stock.

MacKinlay (Inspector of Taxes) v Arthur Young McClelland Moores and Co [1986] STC 491 also deals with deduction of expenses. If a sole trader moves house so that he can take up business in another part of the country he cannot deduct his costs of removal as a business expense. If he works for a large company and the company pays the expense, the company can claim the deduction and, perhaps anomalously, the Revenue will not usually treat the payment as a taxable emolument. What happens if the person moving is a partner in a large firm? The firm's claim to deduct failed. The large partnership was the same as the sole trader. What surprises one about this case—and perhaps it is symptomatic of much that is wrong with modern tax practice—is that the judgment is so long. There is one short point—how should a partnership be taxed? As this has been settled for many years the only basis for argument is that some partnerships are so big that they ought to be treated as companies. This argument should be rejected on the ground that it would present the court with the unnecessary and difficult task of deciding when a partnership was big enough to be treated in this way. The taxpayers having opted to practice as partners instead of incorporating (a point that loses some of its force as there were other reasons why these partners could not incorporate) they should take the consequences of their chosen form. One hopes the higher courts will be similarly simple.

Southern Pacific Insurance Co (Fiji) Ltd v Commr of Inland Revenue [1986] STC 178, a Privy Council appeal from Fiji, is a short example of the application of the decision of the House of Lords in *Southern Railway of Peru Ltd v Owen* [1957] AC 334. In calculating the profits of an insurance business for a period sums could be deducted for accidents which occurred in a relevant year even though not reported until later as there was a rational basis for the figure and the appellate court was not entitled to ignore it.

Trusts

In *Stevenson (Inspector of Taxes) v Wishart and others* [1986] STC 74 Knox J had to consider whether sums paid out in the exercise of a power of appointment over capital to meet medical and nursing home expenses of a beneficiary were income of the beneficiary. The sums appointed were substantial (£109,000); no income was accumulated as it was all distributed to charity. At no point did the beneficiary have any power over the payments so as to divert them to another purpose. The Revenue's argument in essence was that recurrent sums paid for benefit of individual were income. After reviewing the line of cases beginning with *Brodies Trustees v IRC* (1933) 17 TC 432 Knox J held that they did not apply here as the power exercised was a power over capital and, although the beneficiary was a discretionary object of a power over income, there was nothing in the settlement to link these payments to any income interest of hers. He added that the fact that the money was used for an income purpose cannot make it income. This conclusion made it unnecessary to consider the argument whether the payments, if they had been of an income nature, fell within FA 1973, s 17(1) even though they were not made to the beneficiary but for her; however he did note that such a result was indicated by the dictum of Vinelott J in *IRC v Berrill* [1981] STC 784 at 798. The case offers considerable scope—and responsibility—for trustees in exercising their discretions.

Cholmondley v IRC [1986] STC 384 is important for two reasons. The first is that the scheme to use the device of a temporary protective trust to extract property from trust without CTT failed. Trustees appointed property on protective trusts for M for life with remainder to M's eldest son in tail male; as M was already tenant for life this would cause no charge to CTT. The following day they exercised a power of advancement in the protective trust in favour of the eldest son and argued that this brought about a 'failure or determination' of the protective trust and so came within FA 1975, Sch 5 para 18. Scott J held that para 18 required one to disregard the failure of the protective trust 'as such' but not the removal of trust property from the protective trust. This seems abundantly right although one does notice the phrase 'as such' yet again.

The second reason for noting the case is the way in which Scott J rebelled at the thought of having to give effect to the documents as if they were entirely separate; as he put it 'there never was any intention that [the property] should be held for [M] on protective trusts for his life.' One assumes that this is a tax rule only, in which case it is of interest as showing a robust post-*Furniss v Dawson* approach without invoking the Brightman doctrine in that case, but it would be of interest to know how Scott J would have thought M's estate should have been taxed had he died half way through the plan.

Capital Gains Tax

once again this has been a very active area of litigation. Some issues have been fairly small such as that in *Moore v Thompson (Inspector of Taxes)* [1986] STC 170; when is a caravan a dwelling house which is the taxpayer's only or main residence for CGTA 1979, s 101? The evidence showed that the taxpayer and his family had sometimes spent time at the caravan using it as their residence but other places had also been available to them as residences; Millett J treated this as a question of fact to be determined by the Commissioners. This case will be of practical interest as a companion to *Frost v Feltham* [1981] STC 115 where the issue was the deductibility of interest.

Passant v Jackson (Inspector of Taxes) [1986] STC 164 is a decision of the Court of Appeal dismissing the taxpayer's appeal from the decision of Vinelott J commented upon in last year's review (All ER Rev 1985, p 287); the issue concerned the purchase of assets in residue and the appeal was dealt with on a short point of property law, that a residuary legatee obtains no interest in any asset in the estate until administration is complete. Slade LJ agreed with Vinelott J that the taxpayer's claim was devoid of merit as he was seeking a double deduction; he also referred, without apology or hesitation, to the 'true nature' of the transaction.

Magnavox Electronics Co Ltd (in liquidation) v Hall [1986] STC 561 is another—and brief—Court of Appeal decision dismissing a taxpayer's appeal this time from the then Nicholls J ([1985] STC 260); this too was commented upon last year (see All ER Rev 1985, p 290). The short point was whether the taxpayer could claim that a disposal had taken place 'under' a contract so as to take advantage of the rule in CGTA 1979, s 27 timing the disposal at the date of the contract. The facts against the taxpayer were so overwhelming that the court did not have to explore what appears to be a very difficult question; just how much variation of a contract can take place before the eventual disposal takes place under the variation rather than the original contract? This issue is by no means a one way street for the Revenue since taxpayers who have made a contract to sell in March might wish to take advantage of some new provision announced in the Budget. In considering this problem one should note the decision of Harman J in *IRC v Mobil North Sea Ltd* [1986] STC 45. The issue was whether expenditure under contracts made in 1981 could be said to be incurred 'in pursuance of' an agreement entered into before 1981 because there was a general contractual framework between the parties made in 1979; the judge said that it could not.

Monarch Assurance Co Ltd v Special Commissioners [1986] STC 311 is a short case dealing with the construction of an administration provision—Taxes Management Act 1970, s 20(3) and (4). Could gains arising from the assignment of options to acquire shares in a company be said to be gains derived from the business of that company? Hoffmann J rejected the Revenue argument that the section applied whenever the gain arose from the relationship between the taxpayer and the company and insisted on some degree of economic nexus between the gains and the assets of the business. He observed that as the section required the leave of a Commissioner before the notice was issued it was not necessary to adopt an artificially narrow construction .

Chaney v Watkins (Inspector of Taxes) [1986] STC 89 is a tantalising case. A vendor had agreed to pay a sum to a protected tenant to obtain vacant possession; the Revenue accepted that such a sum would have been deductible. However the agreement was varied to oblige landlord to provide rent free accommodation in lieu. It was clear that as the sum had not been paid it could not be deducted but could the cost of the obligation? Nicholls J said that it could. One issue was whether CGTA 1979, s 32(1)(b) which requires that the expenditure be reflected in the asset at the time of disposal means to refer to the time of the contract or the time of the conveyance. The Crown argued for the date of conveyance while the taxpayer agreed that not all post contract events could be ignored; as so much had been agreed between the parties these matters were not explored in depth—later cases will clearly have to address the point. On these facts Nicholls J did not feel able to quantify the value of the obligation at the sum originally agreed and remitted the issue to the Commissioners.

Kirby v Thorn EMI plc [1986] STC 200 is an intricate case on CGTA 1979, s 20 which governs capital sums derived from assets notwithstanding that no asset is acquired. Company A sold subsidiaries to company B and covenanted not to compete with the subsidiaries for a period of five years; a large sum was received in return for the covenant. Was the sum a chargeable gain? Knox J, agreeing with the Commissioners, held that it was not. The covenant itself was not an asset which existed at the time of the disposal as it only came into being at that time; this distinction between creation and disposition is familiar in other areas of the law, eg Law of Property Act 1925, s 53(1)(c). He then identified the source of the payment not as A's shareholding in its subsidiaries but as A's ability to control those subsidiaries. The whole structure of the tax required the disposal of an asset and this ability to control was too nebulous to be an asset. This area is an extremely difficult one and one hopes that the case will go higher. In issue, amongst other things, is the correct tax treatment of a whole range of payments that escape income tax on the ground that they are capital payments; can such things escape capital gains tax also on the ground that they cannot be tied to specific 'assets?' In principle the answer is that they can but this case demands a closer analysis of what is meant by an asset, a matter which has lain dormant at the highest levels since *O'Brien v Benson's Hosiery Holdings Ltd* [1979] STC 735.

Powlson v Welbeck Securities Ltd [1986] STC 423 is another decision on sums derived from assets, here compensation for the release of an option to participate in a property development. The sums was held taxable; the right to participate was an asset and the rule stating the abandonment of an option was not the disposal of an asset was not meant to create an exception to s 20; a sums received in return for the abandonment was therefore taxable.

Westcott v Woolcombers Ltd [1986] STC 182 is a complicated and surprising case involving a group of companies. Co A acquired control of three companies, X, Y, Z. A transferred the holdings to B in return for shares in B. Later B sold the shares to C, the taxpayer, for £x; a short time later X, Y, Z were liquidated and C received £x on the distribution. The price originally paid by A was around £2x; Could C take over A's base cost and so claim an allowable loss? Hoffmann J held that it could as the policy of the provisions for transfers within groups (Taxes Act 1970, s 273) was one of tax neutrality. The Revenue's argument was that while s 273 clearly applied to the disposal of an asset within the group, the provisions dealing with corporate reorganisations directed equally clearly that the share exchange within CGTA 1979, s 85 was *not* a disposal (s 78). The decision sits oddly

with the approach of the House of Lords in *IRC v Burmah Oil* [1982] STC
30 where the House held that the same provisions prevented there being an
'acquisition' and there is a clear contrast with the meticulous exercise of
statutory construction in that case and the broader policy-based approach of
Hoffmann J in this case; this must all be seen as part of the new approach
and it is no surprise to find the judge citing Lord Wilberforce's dictum that
capital gains tax was created to operate in the real world. This case raises
issues too complex to investigate further here but readers are referred to the
trenchant criticisms in [1986] BTR 117, especially the point that the effect of
the decision appears to be to reduce the scope of TA 1970, s 279, a provision
which was not cited to the court. By next year we may have a Court of
Appeal decision to comment on.

Corporations

This section begins with two cases on the interpretation of the word 'may.'
In *Collard v Mining and Industrial Holdings Ltd* [1986] STC 230 Walton J had
to interpret FA 1972, s 100(6) which provides that where any ACT is
available for set off the company 'may' allocate that ACT to such of its
income for that period as it thinks fit. The company had foreign income on
which it was entitled to double taxation relief and UK income. It had paid a
dividend and therefore had ACT available; the ACT would more than
offset its corporation tax liability on its UK profits. The company argued
that it did not have to exercise the power of allocation at all and therefore
the procedure would be to determine first its income, then the corporation
tax, then deduct the double taxation relief and then set off the ACT against
the CT; the result in this case would be that no corporation tax would be
payable. The Revenue argued first that s 100(6) imposed a duty on the
company to allocate the ACT in some way and that the double tax relief
should be used after the ACT. What was at issue was some £250,000 in tax.
Both Revenue points failed. Walton J observed that the result contended for
by the Revenue would have been monstrously unjust and should not be
reached if by any reasonable construction a different result could be reached.
One should note that s 100(6) has now been amended by FA 1986, s 49 for
later years.

Among the reasons used by Walton J were that the word 'may' was
preceded in the section by the word 'shall' and so a contrast of meaning
might be inferred and that if there were a duty to exercise the power it
would presumably be open to the Revenue to exercise it in default by the
taxpayer and the legislation contained no guidance as to how this was to be
done. These points occur also in *R v H M Inspector of Taxes, ex p Lansing
Bagnall Ltd* [1986] STC 117 and 453 where Peter Gibson J and the Court of
Appeal had to consider FA 1972, Sch 16 par 3(1) under which annual
payments to charity by a close company 'may' be apportioned to the
participators. The Inspector said she had no discretion in the matter and that
she had to make the apportionment; the matter came before the courts by
way of judicial review. Both courts said 'may' means 'may' not 'must' and
that there was a discretion in the matter; after all a company might make a
donation to a charity of which the individual participator disapproved
violently. The Revenue had argued that their duty to be fair between

taxpayers was best carried out by applying the provision mechanically but this was rejected by the courts on the ground that the object of the legislation was not to penalise participants but to see that they did not, by reasons of their position as such (that phrase again), obtain an unfair advantage over others. Balcombe and Parker LJJ added that it would be appropriate for the Inspector to consider matters such as the size of the company, its turnover, the number of employees and the level of donations made by non-close companies of similar scope.

Lastly one should note the VAT decision of Kennedy J in *C & E Comr v J Boardmans (1980) Ltd* [1986] STC 10 that the Commissioners were being unreasonable in withholding the standard method of reckoning gross takings from a company formed to take over the business of an old company which had used an optional method. It was accepted that if the business had remained with the old company the optional method would have been continued and the judge had to decide whether he should treat the new company as separate from the old or, as a matter of commercial reality, a continuation of the old. He opted for the former.

International

There are no startling developments but a few reminders of basic principles and one long judgment on double tax relief. In addition to the four cases mentioned here one should note *Platten v Brown* (p 298, above) and *Collard v Mining and Industrial Holdings Ltd* (p 303, above).

Aspin v Estill (Inspector of Taxes) [1986] STC 323 was an appeal by a taxpayer in person; the appeal concerned the UK tax treatment of a retirement benefit to which he was entitled from the US Federal Department of Health Education and Welfare as a result of contributions he had made while employed in the USA. Mervyn Davies J held that the payments were taxable under Schedule D Case V but subject to the 10% deduction allowed under FA 1974, s 22. He held that the income was income from a foreign possession not being income consisting of emoluments from any office or employment, a conclusion which makes a nice contrast with *Bray v Best*. Quite what the taxpayer argued in court is unclear but before the Commissioners he had contended that the payment was not taxable as it was a social security retirement benefit; it is hard to see why this should make any difference unless he was trying to come within the terms of what is now concession A 24. As the judge said, the taxpayer's main complaint seems to have been that on his arrival in the UK he was advised that no tax would be chargeable; acting in reliance on this he had purchased property here and forefeited a right to return to the USA. No findings on this aspect were made by the Commissioners as they were not relevant to the issue directly before them. Although the judge gave the parties time to reach a compromise none proved possible; no order was made for costs. This aspect of the case show the need for a proper system of formal rulings in the UK; however present funding of the Inland Revenue appears to make such a system quite impossible.

I R C v Brackett [1986] STC 521 is a short case showing the use of TA 1970, s 478 to counteract the tax advantages of an offshore service company. The company was a Jersey company, the taxpayer was its only employee and his consultancy services its only trade. Hoffmann J held that by entering into the contract of employment with the company the taxpayer had created rights vested in the company and that there was therefore a transfer of assets within the terms of the wide definition of both 'assets' and 'transfer' in the TA 1970, s 478(8)(b). He also held that the taxpayer had power to enjoy the income of the company under subs 5(c) and, probably, (b). He then held that there was evidence to support the conclusion that the company was trading in the UK and therefore that the taxpayer was accountable for its tax under TMA s 79. In the days of the 'new approach' one might have expected a broad argument that the court should disregard the company as a step inserted solely for tax avoidance purposes; however this was not done.

Sun Life Assurance Co of Canada v Pearson [1986] STC 335 is a long case on the use of double tax relief by insurance companies in which the Court of Appeal upheld the decision of Vinelott J [1984] STC 461 on all matters and refused leave to appeal to the House of Lords. The case is chiefly of interest as showing the ways in which the principles of tax law apply to insurance companies and the lengths to which Parliament can go in altering those rules without those changes amounting to a breach of the double tax treaty. There was a subsidiary issue about when contracts of insurance were made 'through' the London office.

Lastly one should note R v Special Commissioner, ex p R W Forsyth Ltd [1986] STC 565 which reminds one that taxation is a matter of UK law rather than English or Scots law and it was held that the jurisdiction of a Special Commissioner extends throughout the UK; it followed from this that an English court 'probably' had jurisdiction to entertain an application for judicial review of a decision by a Special Commissioner sitting in London even though that decision related to only one matter in a case which in all other respects was dealt with in Scotland.

VAT

In addition to the important decision in C & E Comrs v Apple and Pear Development Council there have been other cases of interest. Whitechapel Art Gallery v C & E Comrs [1986] STC 156 is yet another decision on the problem of apportionment of input tax where there are both business and non-business activities. Kennedy J held that the predominant activity of the taxpayer, the free display of works of art, was a non-business one and not incidental to other business activity; hence the input tax would have to be apportioned. Grunwick Processing Laboratories Ltd v C & E Comrs [1986] STC 441 is an interesting case on the facts but ultimately turns on the burden of proof placed on the taxpayer to challenge an assessment—on balance of probabilities.

C & E Comrs v International Language Centres Ltd [1986] STC 279 is a short case holding that the Commissioners have the power to require the payment of VAT which has been collected by the taxpayer by direct action and are not confined to the assessment procedure; this parallel method is confined to sums which the taxpayer shows on his returns and so is rarely used.

C & E Comrs v Dearwood Ltd [1986] STC 327 is a decision of more general interest; it concerns the interpretation of the expression 'transfer of a business as a going concern' to a new company. The issue was whether test required that the new company could or would carry on the business. Deciding in favour of the taxpayer, McCowan J held that it was sufficient that the company could do so; the intention of the new company to change the business was irrelevant.

Re T H Knitwear (Wholesale) Ltd [1986] STC 572 is an interesting and important case concerning liquidations. The taxpayer company had gone into liquidation. Its debts included sums due to suppliers in respect of (i) the price (ii) VAT. In the liquidation proceedings the suppliers claimed only element (i); they recovered (ii) from the commissioners direct under the bad debt relief rules in FA 1978 (now VAT Act 1983, s 22). It was agreed that if they had obtained that relief but then proved for the whole of (i) and (ii) they would have had to account to the commissioners for the sum recovered. The liquidation proved totally succesful and the liquidator was left with the funds to be distributed to the contributories; the commissioners sought to recoup from this fund the tax they had to refund to the suppliers on the ground that they had succeeded to the suppliers' rights to charge VAT to the company; they failed. This case seems destined to go higher as it is most important and raises question of general law on subrogation and other grounds of restitution; it also deals with the role of a liquidator.

General

In *R v Mavji* [1986] STC 508 the Court of Appeal Criminal Division held that there was a common law criminal offence of cheating the public revenue despite the existence of a series of statutory offences carrying maximum terms of imprisonment; this case seems destined for the Lords.

EMI Records v Spillane [1986] 2 All ER 1016, [1986] STC 374 concerns the status of documents held under an *Anton Piller* order and, in particular, whether Customs and Excise officers could demand them. Browne-Wilkinson V-C held that a solicitor holding documents seized from another person holds them to the order of the court and is therefore not obliged to hand them over—on the facts however any obligation to the court had expired and, as the solicitor now held them to the sole order of that person, he could be made to hand them over. The judge made similar remarks about documents obtained under a court order for discovery. The court is clearly anxious to protect the judicial process and to do as little as possible to inhibit persons from producing documents relevant to the litigation in hand.

R v I R C, ex p J Rothschild Holdings plc [1986] STC 410 is an exceptional case in which the court ordered the Revenue to produce documents in judicial review proceedings brought by the taxpayer. The documents related to the Revenue's practice under FA 1973, Sch 19 and review was sought partly on the basis that the taxpayers had been given a telephone assurance that there was such a practice; the taxpayers argued that they came within it. Discovery was ordered because it would assist in showing the likelihood of the taxpayers' case. This does not open the door to discovery of Revenue practice for any taxpayer anxious to dispute his tax liability.

Lastly *John v James* [1986] STC 352, a case which becomes more glamorous as Elton John v Dick James. The issue was the amount the defendant should pay by way of damages for breach of contract in having accounted to the plaintiff for a sums less than was due to him and the extent to which deductions should be made on account of tax. The defendants argued that there should be a deduction on account of the tax they had to pay on the profits; this failed on what may be taken to be the facts, Nicholls J observing that he strongly suspected that the payments he was going to order would be deductible by the defendants. This may have been plausible in this case but clearly stores up trouble for later cases. The defendants argued that there should be a deduction on account of the tax the plaintiff would have to pay, as decided by the House of Lords in *British Transport Commission v Gourley* [1955] 3 All ER 796. This too failed but largely on practical grounds; deciding whether the plaintiff would have been free from tax would have involved investigations in too many countries. This conclusion is disappointing since the court thus avoided deep issues of timing; if the plaintiff received these sums now and they related to years of assessment more than six year earlier would they be income of the year of receipt or the year in which they arose?

Administration

There is the usual large crop of cases on administration; some raise points of interest. In *Honig and another v Sarsfield (Inspector of Taxes)* [1986] STC 246 the Court of Appeal upheld the lower court's decision that an assessment is made when it is entered in the Inspector's books and not when it is received by the taxpayer. In *Bye (Inspector of Taxes) v Coren* [1986] STC 393 the same court held that alternative assessments to income tax and capital gains tax were valid with the result that the Inspector could still proceed with the income tax assessment even after the capital gains assessment had become final through not being appealed against.

In *Baylis (Inspector of Taxes) v Gregory* [1986] 1 All ER 289, [1986] STC 22, Vinelott J applied TMA 1970, s 114 to correct the year stated on assessment—as no one had been misled he held that the court could correct the error but added that there was no statutory power by which an inspector could unilaterally alter the assessment once it had been made. *Aikman v White* [1986] STC 1 considered the issue whether there could be a 'failure' to send a return when the taxpayer had sent a form back by post but it had not reached the other end. It was held that there was no such failure on the facts because this was the method required by the C & E and therefore delivery to the Post Office was delivery to an agent of the Commissioners; the wider aspects of the problem remained unexplored although there are dicta to the effect that delivery to the Post Office would not normally be sufficient.

There are several cases on penalties. In *Khan v First East Brixton Comrs* [1986] STC 331 Harman J pointed out that the High Court has the power to reconsider the penalties on an appeal and is not concerned simply with whether the Commissioners' decision is unreasonable; he went on to hold that it was open to Commissioners to award penalties even though there were losses available to be set off against the income in respect of which penalties were sought. However in *Lear v Leek General Commissioners* [1986]

STC 542 Vinelott J said that the court would only interfere if the sums imposed were plainly disproportionate.

Lastly there have been many applications for judicial review, mostly unsuccessful. So the courts have held that judicial review is not appropriate for matters which can be dealt with by appeal or even by remission to the Commissioners—*R v Brentford General Commrs, ex p Chan and others* [1986] STC 65; however they have held that matters of unfairness of procedure are usually the province of judicial review rather than appeal *Brittain v Gibbs (Inspector of Taxes)* [1986] STC 418. One is therefore intrigued by the decision of Nolan J granting leave to apply for judicial review in *R v H M Inspector of Taxes, ex p Kissane and another* [1986] 2 All ER 37, [1986] STC 152. The judge, in a case where it was arguable that the inspector had acted irrationally in making the assessments, treated as relevant the fact that the taxpayer could recover costs in judicial review but not in an appeal.

Tort

B A HEPPLE, MA, LLB
Barrister, Professor of English Law, University College, University of London

Negligence

Economic loss

The most important decision reported in 1986 was that in *Leigh & Sillivan Ltd v Aliakmon Shipping Co Ltd, The Aliakmon* [1986] 2 All ER 145. The House of Lords has restored doctrinal certainty in an area characterised by doubt and confusion since *Junior Books Ltd v Veitchi Co Ltd* [1982] 3 All ER 201; All ER Rev 1982, pp 302–5. However, the leading speech, by Lord Brandon, is marked by an unneccessarily reactionary approach to the general question as to when a duty of care arises.

The highest court dismissed an appeal from the decision of the Court of Appeal [1985] 2 All ER 44; see All ER Rev 1985, pp 294–97. In the only speech, Lord Brandon (with whom Lords Keith, Brightman, Griffiths and Ackner agreed), held that the buyer who under a cif or c+f contract had accepted the risk of damage to the goods, was prevented by his lack of ownership or possessory title from suing the shipowner in negligence for damage occurring to the goods in the course of carriage. This result was predictable in view of the decision of the Judicial Committee of the Privy Council, in a judgment delivered before *The Aliakmon* came on for hearing, in *Candlewood Navigation Corp Ltd v Mitsui OSK Lines Ltd, The Mineral Transporter, The Ibaraki Maru* [1985] 2 All ER 935, All ER Rev 1985, pp 294–97, that a person who is not the owner or in possession of a chattel may not sue in negligence for economic loss.

In view of the Privy Council's decision, counsel did not seek to question this general principle. Instead he argued that an exception should be made for cif or c+f contracts. Such an exception would have required the House to overrule the decision of Roskill J (as he was then) in *Margarine Union Gmbh v Cambay Prince Steamship Co Ltd, The Wear Breeze* [1967] 3 All ER 775. Lord Brandon rejected all the grounds for this argument. First, the fact that a buyer under a cif or c+f contract was the prospective legal owner of the goods was not a material distinction from the other non-recovery cases in which the plaintiffs were not persons who had contracted to buy the property. Secondly, even if an equitable property in goods could be created or passed under the contract of sale (of which Lord Brandon at 151 was 'extremely doubtful') an equitable owner not in possession has no right to sue without joining the legal owner as a party to the action.

Thirdly, there was nothing in what Lord Wilberforce said in *Anns v Merton London Borough* [1977] 2 All ER 492 at 498–99, about the role of policy in negativing a prima facie duty of care, which would compel a departure from the line of authority against recovery. The need for certainty of the law 'of the utmost importance, especially but by no means only, in commercial matters', the danger of opening the 'floodgates' of unlimited liability to an indefinite number of persons (for example, in the carriage of goods by land), and the difficulties of equating any duty of care in tort to the buyer to the 'intricate blend of responsibilities and liabilities' under the Hague Rules incorporated in the shipper's contract, all pointed towards non-liability (on the latter point, however, see M Clarke [1986] CLJ 383).

Fourthly, there was no deficiency in the law because the buyers could have protected themselves when they agreed to a variation in the original contract of sale, by negotiating for the sellers to exercise the right to sue the shipowners for their account or to assign the right to sue to them.

Finally, Lord Brandon rejected Robert Goff LJ's 'principle of transferred loss' (on which see All ER Rev 1985, pp 296–97) as being contrary to and inconsistent with authority.

It is Lord Brandon's preoccupation with 'authority', and his treatment of Lord Wilberforce's dictum in the *Anns* case, that is the reactionary aspect of his reasoning. In 1982, in *Paterson Zochonis & Co Ltd v Merfarken Packaging Ltd*, only now reported in [1986] 3 All ER 522 at 539, Robert Goff LJ said that Lord Wilberforce's speech (which had been foreshadowed by more tentative remarks by Lord Reid in 1970) 'marked the coming of the age of law of negligence'. This was because it recognised that when new cases come before the court the inquiry was 'no longer whether the duty of care should be extended to the new situation'; it was rather, whether given reasonable foresight of damage to the plaintiff, there were any policy reasons for negativing or limiting the prima facie duty of care. At that time, in 1982, Robert Goff LJ thought that *Junior Books* had, in this respect, removed the difference between damage arising from physical loss and that from purely economic loss. Lord Brandon (at 153) first rejects the universality of Lord Wilberforce's approach (as foreshadowed two years ago by Lord Keith, see All ER Rev 1984, pp 292–94, and last year by Oliver LJ, see All ER Rev 1985, p 296), and then limits its applicability to 'a novel type of factual situation which was not analogous to any factual situation in which the existence of such a duty had already been held to exist'. Lord Brandon was as 'faint-hearted' (at 157) in relation to the duty of care as he was to the supposed 'principle of transferred loss'. As to the latter, Professor Markesinis [1986] CLJ 384 at 386 has pointed out that it offered a 'plausible reconciliation of the multitude of recent and confusing decisions on economic loss'.

He was even less bold about the possibilities opened up by *Junior Books*. This is not surprising since he was the dissenting Law Lord in that case. The only other member of the House in *Junior Books* to hear the present appeal was Lord Keith, and it will be recalled that he, too, dissented in part from Lords Fraser, Roskill and Russell. Lord Roskill's remarks in *Junior Books* about qualifying a duty of care in tort by reference to the terms of a contact to which the defendant is not a party were dismissed by Lord Brandon as obiter dictum and as not resting 'on any convincing legal basis' (at 155). The broader principle of 'detrimental reliance' which Lord Roskill formulated received no mention at all. The conclusion to be drawn from this (and the fact that the ratio of the majority in *Junior Books* has not affected the result is a single reported decision) is that *Junior Books* is now authority only for the proposition that the owner of a building may sue in negligence from a nominated sub-contractor for loss of profits and other economic loss caused by the need to take the building out of use to repair it, even though there is no imminent danger to health and safety (ie the reasons given by Lord Keith in *Junior Books*).

Lord Brandon's restrictive approach to the development of principle and the role of policy was unnecessary to the decision, which plainly can be justified on the policy grounds referred to by Lord Brandon himself. The need for a central mechanism to avoid imposing crushing liability on the defendant is self-evident. This mistake is to seek that control in a single rigid rule, such as that which bars recovery by the non-owner of chattels. A more plausible framework for decision-making is needed. The key factor in cases like *The Aliakmon* is that the parties are in what Harris and Veljanovsksi call an 'exchange relationship' ('Liability for Economic Loss in Tort', chapter 3 in *The Law of Tort* ed M Furmston, (1986) Duckworth). The voluntary contractual arrangements of the parties reflect what they regard as the optimal allocation of risks. It was open to the buyer in this case to seek to modify the agreement but he did not do so. Pearce and Tomkin (1986) 136 N LJ 1169 argue that 'it appears perverse to hold that a person who has suffered no loss [ie the seller] may recover substantial damages, while the person on whom that loss has fallen [the buyer] can recover nothing'. But this ignores the fact that the allocation of risks was voluntarily assumed, and it was open to them (all businessmen) to renegotiate their agreements.

A rigid rule that a person who is neither owner nor in possession of goods can never sue is incapable of achieving the objectives of the parties in all situations (eg the commodity trader who gets part of a bulk cargo), although it coincided with a satisfactory result in the present case. Lord Wilberforce's two-stage approach in *Anns* had the merit of flexibility, concentrating judicial minds on policy reasons for negativing or restricting liability. Among the policy factors relevant in this case, as in other cases where the parties have deliberately structured their contractual relationship so as to avoid direct liability inter se, is what Sir John Donaldson MR called the 'economic balance' between them. Lord Brandon's rule-orientated approach, on the other hand, is reminiscent of the pre-1932 categorisations of negligence rules and of the shackled judicial reasoning before Wilberforce's emancipation.

Professor Edward Griew, in the correspondence columns of (1986) 136 N LJ 1201, has added a provocative footnote to *The Aliakmon*. He suggests that s 3 of the Latent Damage Act 1986 may, by a sidewind, have given a consignee of goods a non-contractual cause of action against a carrier in respect of damage negligently caused to the goods by the carrier and occurring before the consignee obtains ownership. That result can be reached by a literal interpretation of the new Act, ignoring the sidenote to s 3 which refers to 'latent damage'. It seems unlikely that the courts would ignore the purpose of the 1986 Act in this way.

This case is also discussed in the article on Shipping, p 253, above.

Liability for acts of third parties

As already indicated, the Wilberforce approach was applied by the Court of Appeal in *Paterson Zochonis & Co Ltd v Merfarken Packaging Ltd* [1986] 3 All ER 522 (judgment delivered 29 October 1982). The question was whether a duty of care was owed by printers whose products (ie packaging and labels) had enabled a third party to infringe the plaintiff's copyright. Had Lord Brandon's precedent-based approach then been in vogue, the Court of

Appeal might simply have answered the question by reference to Lord Sumner's well-known statement in *Weld-Blundell v Stephens* [1920] AC 956 at 986 that 'in general (apart from special contracts and relations and the maxim *respondeat superior*), even though A is in fault, he is not responsible for injury to C which B, a stranger to him, deliberately chooses to do'. Instead the court treated earlier decisions as inconclusive, and examined the policy issues. This led to the conclusion on the pleaded facts that there did not exist, alongside the statutory duty not to infringe copyright, a parallel common law duty owed by a printer to prevent infringement. Oliver (at 531) and Fox LJJ (at 534) excluded any general duty of care of this kind, on the ground that, in the absence of knowledge of a dishonest purpose, it would impose an impossible burden on traders if they had to satisfy themselves that the goods they sold would not be used for some dishonest purpose which would damage others. Robert Goff LJ (at 539–43), on the other hand, took a far more expansive view of the duty of care. It was argued that 'it would be an admirable development if printers who negligently facilitate the commission of the tort of passing off were restrained' (at 539). The headnote (at 532) suggests that Robert Goff LJ found that there were 'special circumstances negativing' a duty of care. However, his judgment, while accepting that cases in which a printer may be held liable would be rare (at 543), was that there was no principle excluding liability. He found that the statement of claim disclosed no cause of action because the pleaded facts fell far short of establishing a breach of the standard of care in the circumstances (at 542). This judgment contains a useful statement of the principles relevant to liability for the acts of third parties (up to 1982), and several interesting examples on either side of the line.

Robert Goff LJ (at 541) pointed out that in these cases the problem may be analysed in terms of foreseeability, either at the stage of the breach of duty or at the stage of causation. Last year (All ER Rev 1985, p 302), a case relating to liability of a council for vandal damage was noted, in which the issue was regarded as one of causation. This year, in *King v Liverpool City Council* [1986] 3 All ER 544, the Court of Appeal preferred to deal with vandal damage as relating to duty rather than to causation (at 553). A council tenant's flat was flooded because vandals entered the vacant flat above hers and removed copper piping and other parts of the water system. She claimed damages from the council in negligence or nuisance alleging that they had been negligent in failing to secure the vacant flat. The trial judge made the crucial finding of fact that 'it is not possible for effective steps to be taken in a situation like this which could defeat the activities of vandals'. The Court of Appeal held that there was 'no duty'. The leading judgment of Purchas LJ cites earlier analogous authorities, but in effect allows the decision to turn on the trial judge's findings of fact. The present writer does not agree with Anthony Joslin (1986) 136 N LJ 543 at 546 that this finding was not necessary to support the ratio decidendi. The extensive quotations from Robert Goff LJ in *P Perl (Exporters) Ltd v Camden London BC* [1983] 3 All ER 161 at 171–72, and in *Paterson Zochonis & Co Ltd* (above), indicate that the ratio of this case is that there can be a duty in such circumstances, but only if the intervening act of the third party was likely to happen. On the facts this degree of foreseeability was not established. (cf *Ward v Cannock Chase DC* [1985] 3 All ER 537, All ER Rev 1985, pp 302–3).

Defective premises

Policy, or 'just and reasonable', considerations, played their part in *Investors in Industry Commercial Properties Ltd v South Bedfordshire District Council (Ellison & Partners (a firm) and other, third parties)* [1986] 1 All ER 787, CA. The point in issue was whether property developers could recover damages from the council which had been at fault in approving the design for defective foundations. (Proceedings by the developers against their structural engineers, who had been at fault, in designing the foundations, were discontinued because they were uninsured.) In determining the frontiers of *Anns*, in the light of *Peabody Donation Fund (Governors) v Sir Lindsay Parkinson* [1984] 3 All ER 529, HL, All ER Rev 1984, pp 292–94, Slade LJ, delivering the judgment of the Court of Appeal, felt 'bound to take into consideration whether it is just and reasonable' that a duty of care should exist. This led the court to decide that (1) the purpose of the council's supervisory powers is not to safeguard the building developer himself against economic loss incurred in the case of a building project 'or indeed anyone else against purely economic loss'; (2) the council will normally not owe a duty to the original building owner because it is incumbent on that owner to ensure that the building is erected in accordance with the building regulations; and (3) a fortiori the council owes no duty to the original building owner who has relied on professional advice of architects, engineers and contractors (at 805). In an obiter dictum the Court also suggested that the duty of care which the council owes to a subsequent occupier to take reasonable care to ensure that a building complies with the regulations is based on the need to prevent danger to the health or personal safety of the occupier and therefore the duty does not extend to a non-resident owner, even though he may be an 'occupier' for the other purposes such as under the Occupiers Liability Act (at 805).

The council had joined the architects as a third party, claiming an indemnity. Since the claim against the council failed this did not arise for decision by the Court of Appeal, but the opinion was expressed that an architect is normally not responsible for a specialist consultant appointed for a particular part of the work unless he ought to have been aware of and could reasonably have been expected to warn the client about a danger or problem arising in the course of the work allotted to the consultant (at 807–8). Leave to appeal was refused by the Appeal Committee of the House of Lords. The tide of authority which had been flowing against local authorities before *Peabody*, has now almost certainly been halted.

Wrongful birth

Attempts by parents to obtain damages for ineffective sterilisation on grounds of breach of an implied warranty by the defendant surgeon to render the plaintiff irreversibly sterile, failed in *Thake v Maurice* [1986] 1 All ER 497, CA (Neill and Nourse LJJ, Kerr LJ dissenting) reversing Peter Pain J on this point (see All ER Rev 1984, p 289), and in *Eyre v Measday* [1986] 1 All ER 488, CA. (See the chapter on Contract, p 85, above). However, in *Thake v Maurice*, the claim succeeded in what was for convenience referred to as 'contractual negligence', as well as negligence simpliciter, resulting from the duty of care owed by a surgeon to his patient. The Court of Appeal unanimously upheld Peter Pain J's finding that there had been a breach of the duty by reason of the surgeon's failure to warn of the 'slight risk' that the sterilisation operation might be ineffective. The judge was held to be entitled to reach this finding even without independent expert evidence as to whether failure to give such a warning fell below acceptable professional standards. Moreover, the causal link between the breach of duty and damage was established because the surgeon ought reasonably to have foreseen the risk of the female plaintiff not appreciating promptly that she had become pregnant.

As regards damages, Peter Pain J had held that the plaintiffs' claim for ante-natal pain and suffering should be offset by the happiness they had from the birth of a healthy child. The Court of Appeal allowed a cross-appeal on this point, and awarded an additional agreed sum of £1,500 for pain and suffering. Kerr LJ distinguished this from the head of damages for the 'time and trouble which needs to be devoted' to rearing the child which would be subject to an offset for the 'joy of the parents'. The justification for the distinction seems to be that there is a rough and ready judicial tariff for pain and suffering, but not yet for the non-pecuniary heads peculiar to wrongful conception cases (see generally, W V Horton Rogers (1985) 5 LS 296 at 309).

Proof of medical negligence

Wilsher v Essex Area Health Authority [1986] 3 All ER 801, CA, decides two important points. The first is that the law requires the trainee or learner doctor to be judged by the same standard as his or her more experienced colleagues. This was the decision of Mustill and Glidewell LJJ, but in a dissenting judgment Sir Nicolas Browne-Wilkinson V-C took the view that such a doctor would be liable only 'for acts or omissions which a careful doctor with his qualifications and experience would not have done or omitted' (at 833). The objective standard adopted by the majority relates the duty of care not to the individual but to the post which he or she occupies. Inexperience as such would be no defence, although (per Glidewell LJ) an inexperienced doctor might satisfy the standard of care by seeking the help and advice of his or her superior when necessary. The majority decision shows just how far the tort of negligence has departed from notions of personal fault (as with the learner driver: *Nettleship v Weston* [1971] 3 All ER 581, CA). This may be the position now in public hospitals, but in 'reliance' situations, for example where a medical student acts as a Good Samaritan, the learner would, presumably, be judged only by his or her professed standard of competence.

The second point decided by the Court of Appeal is that a plaintiff cannot shift the burden of proof on to the defendant doctor or the doctor's employer merely by showing that a step in the treatment which was designed to avert or minimise a risk had not been taken in the particular circumstances. This is retrograde because it means that the Court of Appeal disapproved Peter Pain J's attempt in *Clark v MacLennan* [1983] 1 All ER 416, All ER Rev 1983, p 337–38 (which he had followed as trial judge in the present case) to make the doctor justify his conduct once he was shown to have done an act involving an element of risk to the patient.

The problems relating to personal fault and the burden of proof would be avoided in cases such as this if, in future, practitioners were to formulate claims in the way suggested by the Vice-Chancellor and Glidewell LJ, directly against the health authority on grounds of a fault in the organisation (see below, vicarious liability). This would, as the Vice-Chancellor pointed out, raise awkward questions (eg is financial stringency an excuse for appointing inexperienced junior staff?) But, so long as Parliament fails to introduce an adequate system of no-fault compensation for medical accidents, the courts will have to be prepared to weigh the burden of precautions (eg more experienced staff) against the risks of injury.

Nuisance

A landlord is not not normally liable for nuisances created by his tenant. However, in *Tetley v Chitty* [1986] 1 All ER 663, McNeill J held the defendant council liable for the noise generated by the activities of a go-kart club on land belonging to the council. The council had granted the club a seven-year lease for the express purpose of developing the site as a go-kart track. The judge found that the noise was an 'ordinary and necessary consequence' or a 'natural and necessary consequence' of the authorised operations and so held that the landlords had given express, or at least implied consent to the nuisance on their land. This was a decision within well-established principles, as was the exercise of the judge's discretion to grant an injunction restraining the council from permitting the continuation of go-karting on the land on the ground that damages were a wholly insufficient remedy.

Libel

Those specialists who dance the 'artificial minuet' (as O'Connor LJ described it) of pleading in libel actions obtained guidance from two Court of Appeal decisions. In *Polly Peck (Holdings) plc v Trelford* [1986] 2 All ER 84, the Court dealt with some of the difficult problems which arise where a publication contains two distinct libels and the plaintiff selects one for complaint. It is well-established that the defendant is not entitled to assert the truth of the other by way of justification. One difficulty is to decide whether a defamatory statement is separate and distinct from other defamatory statements in the publication. The Court of Appeal indicated that a test is whether they have a 'common sting'. If they do, then the defendant is entitled to justify the sting and it is fortuitous that some or all of the facts so pleaded are culled from parts of the publication of which the plaintiff has chosen not to complain. Moreover, the defendant is entitled to look at the whole publication in order to aver that in their context the words bear a meaning different from that alleged by the plaintiff. The defendant is entitled to plead that in that meaning the words are true and to give particulars of the facts and matters on which he relies. These facts and matters too, may come from parts of the publication of which no complaint is made. These conclusions were at variance with dicta in the old case of

Brembridge v Latimer (1864) 4 New Rep 285, which was disapproved. Moreover, since the words in respect of which the action was brought did not contain 'two or more distinct charges against the plaintiff', s 5 of the Defamation Act 1952 did not apply.

In *Lucas-Box v News Group Newspapers Ltd* [1986] 1 All ER 177, the Court of Appeal disapproved the practice that a defendant does not state in his defence what he alleges is the natural and ordinary meaning of the words complained of. The case decides that a defendant who pleads justification must state the meaning which he seeks to justify. It follows from this case, and the *Polly Peck* case, that in future, where differences of meaning are put forward by the parties, the issue as to the possible meanings of the words will be confined to those pleaded. *Polly Peck* was applied by another division of the Court of Appeal in *Khashoggi v IPC Magazines Ltd* [1986] 3 All ER 577 (Sir John Donaldson MR and Slade LJ) when an interlocutory injunction was refused in a defamation action on the ground that the defendants might succeed in their plea of justification of the 'common sting' of inseparable allegations in the publication.

Damages for abuse of process

In *Speed Seal Products Ltd v Paddington* [1986] 1 All ER 91, the Court of Appeal reaffirmed that the cause of action for abuse of process, held to exist in *Grainger v Hill* (1838) 4 Bing NC 212, has not disappeared. An injunction was claimed in respect of an alleged disclosure of confidential information, and the defendants counterclaimed for damages on the grounds that the action was brought in bad faith for the ulterior motive of damaging the plaintiffs' business and not for the protection of any legitimate interest of the plaintiffs. Fox LJ (with whom Lloyd LJ and Sir George Waller agreed) held that the allegations pleaded in the counterclaim disclosed a good cause of action. Accordingly, the doubts expressed about this cause of action by Falconer J in *Digital Equipment Corporation v Darkcrest Ltd* [1984] Ch 512 at 523 have been laid to rest. As William Wells (1986) 102 LQR 9 at 11 points out, the action is likely to remain rare. However, it is useful as a counterclaim, although the damages recoverable may not be much more than the difference between party and party costs allowed on taxation and solicitor and client costs, unless exemplary damages are awarded.

Vicarious liability

Deceit

The House of Lords has affirmed the decision of the Court of Appeal (All ER Rev 1985, pp 306–7) in *Armagas Ltd v Mundogas SA, The Ocean Frost* [1986] 2 All ER 385, on similar grounds. The leading speech, by Lord Keith of Kinkel, like the judgments in the Court of Appeal, distinguishes vicarious liability for intentional wrongdoing by a 'servant' (sic), in particular dishonest conduct, from negligent or 'blundering' ways of carrying out the employer's work (at 391–92). The

> 'essential feature for creating liability of the employer is that the party contracting with the fraudulent servant should have altered his position to his

detriment in reliance on the belief that the servant's activities were within his
authority, or to put it another way, were part of his job, the belief having been
induced by the master's representations by way of words or conduct', (at
393).

Since the essence of employer's liability is now seen to be reliance by the
injured party on actual or ostensible authority, the dictum by Lord Denning
in *Navarro v Moregrand Ltd* [1951] 2 TLR 674 at 680, which suggested that
'course of employment' and 'ostensible authority' were not co-extensive,
can no longer be regarded as good law in the context of deceit.

Employer's liability for negligence of third party

Curiously, s 1 of the Employer's Liability (Defective Equipment) Act 1969,
defines 'equipment' so as to include 'any plant and machinery, vehicle,
aircraft and clothing' but makes no express mention of a 'ship'. In *Coltman v
Bibby Tankers Ltd, The Derbyshire* [1986] 2 All ER 65, Sheen J rejected a
contention that a 'ship' is simply a mariner's place of work and that the
'equipment' provided for seamen is the machinery on board ship. He
adopted a purposive interpretation of an Act which was designed to relieve
injured workers from the burden of suing the supplier or manufacturers of
defective equipment provided by the employer for purposes of his business,
and held that a 'ship' can be 'equipment'. (This decision has since been
overruled by the Court of Appeal.)

The plaintiff in *McDermid v Nash Dredging and Reclamation Co Ltd* [1986] 2
All ER 676, CA, was also a mariner, in this case an 18-year-old deckhand
whose left leg had to be amputated because of the negligence of the master
of a tug on which he was working. The tug was owned by the Dutch parent
company of the plaintiff's employer, an English company. He had agreed
to work on the tug in Swedish waters promising in writing that he would
comply with the lawful directions of the company's representatives. In
English law, by which the matter was governed, the Dutch company
would have been vicariously liable to the plaintiff for the negligence of their
employee, the tug master. But there were a number of practical difficulties
in the way of suing the Dutch company (on which see B Barrett (1986) 49
MLR 781 at 782), so the plaintiff's claim for damages was against his
employer, the English company. Staughton J ingeniously found that the tug
master was the 'servant' of the English company because the latter had
made him their 'foreman' through whom orders would reach the plaintiff.
He upheld the plaintiff's claim but decided that since the tug master was
their 'servant' the defendants were entitled to limit their liability (ie so as to
exclude future loss, pain and suffering and loss of amenity) under merchant
shipping legislation. The Court of Appeal agreed that the English company
was liable but on the different ground that the tug master was the 'agent or
delegate' of the employers to perform their duty to the plaintiff to take
reasonable care so to conduct their operations as not to subject him to
unnecessary risk. Since, on this analysis, the tug master was not their
'servant' they were not entitled to limit their liability under the Merchant
Shipping Acts.

Is *McDermid* an example of vicarious liability for the acts of an 'agent or
delegate' or of a 'personal non-delegable' duty of the employer? Neill LJ

recognised that this is a 'rather uneasy division' and that the 'legacy of the doctrine of common employment remains' (at 685). Unfortunately, Neill LJ's reasoning perpetuates this legacy and the confusion by treating the liability in this situation as a 'vicarious' one for the negligence of a 'delegate' *because* that negligence is in the eyes of the law the employer's own negligence (at 683). What the Court of Appeal was attempting to say is that the employer owes a duty higher than that ordinarily imposed by the tort of negligence. This itself contains a fallacy because the duty of care always springs from the facts of a particular status or relationship rather than a generalised duty which is the same in all situations. In the context of the employment relationship a contractual approach was favoured by Lord Wright in the famous case of *Wilson & Clyde Coal Co Ltd v English* [1938] AC 57. One could say that the duty is in effect a warranty by the employer to ensure that reasonable care is taken. (See generally, D Fleming [1986] CLJ 387).

Another and perhaps more fruitful approach, would be to make the employer's undertaking (and here the 'employers' were associated companies) *directly* and not vicariously responsible for the organisational fault of failing to provide a safe system of work and competent staff. This organisational approach to liability for negligence has since been approved, in the context of the liability of a health authority, by Sir Nicolas Browne-Wilkinson V-C and Glidewell LJ in *Wilsher v Essex Area Health Authority* [1986] 3 All ER 801, CA.

Damages

Exemplary or punitive damages

In *Rookes v Barnard* [1964] AC 1129 at 1225-26 Lord Devlin stated that one of the categories in which exemplary damages may be awarded is 'oppressive, arbitrary or unconstitutional action by servants of the government'. In *Holden v Chief Constable of Lancashire* [1986] 3 All ER 836, CA, the plaintiff, who was thought by the police to be acting suspiciously was unlawfully arrested and detained in a holding cell at a police station for 20 minutes. There was no oppressive behaviour and no aggravating circumstances. The judge withdrew the question of exemplary damages from the jury, who awarded the plaintiff £5. On appeal, a new trial was ordered. This was because the judge had misdirected the jury in two ways. First, he had suggested that if the police officers had made a simple mistake something less than 'ample compensation' should be awarded. Secondly, he had been wrong to limit exemplary damages to cases of oppressive behaviour or where aggravating circumstances such as malice were present. Wrongful arrest could fall with Lord Devlin's category, but the judge would be right to ask the jury to consider the absence of aggravating features and that the plaintiff had induced the arrest by 'trailing his coat'. Purchas LJ suggested that a police officer does not commit an unconstitutional act which calls for exemplary damages the moment he acts without authority. This case is a reminder of the doubtful utility of Lord Devlin's categories, and of the danger that they may be literally applied rather than asserting the overall principle of teaching the wrongdoer and others that 'tort does not pay'.

Aggravated damages

In theory, aggravated damages are quite distinct from exemplary damages because they are supposed to compensate for the distress and injured feelings caused by the way in which the defendant acted towards the plaintiff. The paltry sums of £6,750 and £10,250 respectively awarded to the victims of rape and serious sexual assaults in *W v Meah* and *D v Meah* [1986] 1 All ER 935, were justified by Woolf J (as he then was) on the ground that aggravated damages must be 'moderate' (at 942). The same judge's dislike of these damages was taken one stage further in *Kralj v McGrath* [1986] 1 All ER 54, when he refused to award them at all in respect of admitted medical negligence involving treatment by an obstetrician which was described by expert opinion as 'horrific' and 'wholly unacceptable' and which must have caused excruciating pain, and resulted in the death of one of the plaintiff's twin babies. The general damages of £10,500 did, however, take account of distress which would have made it more difficult for the plaintiff to overcome the consequences of the treatment and her unnecessary suffering, as well as her nervous shock at learning what had happened to her child and for grief at the loss of the child which made it more difficult for her to recover from her own injuries.

There is, of course, a paradox in the very idea of 'aggravated damages' because it implies damages aggravated beyond the amount required for compensation. Damages for injured feelings are now awarded in actions for breach of contract and there seems to be no reason why they should not be available in tort. It would be better for the law to develop in the direction favoured by Woolf J than to extend the category of 'aggravated damages' which is not only confusing but also operates without the restraints imposed on exemplary damages.

Damages for personal injuries and death

The case of *Meah v McCreamer (No 2)*, criticised in All ER Rev 1985, pp 309–10, is now reported in [1986] 1 All ER 943.

In April 1985, the Court of Appeal laid down as a guideline, an award of £75,000 for pain, suffering and loss of amenity for a typical case of tetraplegia: *Housecroft v Burnett* [1986] 1 All ER 332. The dead hand of pre-1978 awards was also removed in this case. O'Connor LJ (at 338) indicated that more recent awards are a better guide, for the purpose of updating the level of awards, because they are net of sums assessed separately which compensate for loss of amenity in part. Another issue discussed in this case is the award in respect of nursing care provided by a relative. O'Connor LJ (at 343) disapproved Lord Denning's dictum in *Cunningham v Harrison* [1973] QB 942 at 952 that such an award is held on trust for the relative. The award is to the plaintiff and the Court has to decide whether the amount is sufficient to enable the plaintiff to make reasonable recompense to the relative. Where the agreement to pay the relative is made for the purpose of trying to increase the award it is to be regarded as a sham. On the other hand, where the relative has given up gainful employment to look after the plaintiff the Court should award sufficient to ensure that the plaintiff does not lose thereby.

When damages are calculated on the basis of loss of earnings, should the earnings include or exclude the amount of any contribution to a compulsory contribution pension scheme which the plaintiff would have had to make if he had received those earnings? The proceedings to determine this question in *Dews v National Coal Board* [1986] 2 All ER 769, CA, were part of a wider dispute between the National Union of Mineworkers and the National Coal Board about lost pension rights (the plaintiff himself had 'lost' only £55 in contributions). The Court of Appeal held that the amount of lost contributions was to be excluded from the computation of damages. Sir John Donaldson MR reached this conclusion on the ground that only disposable income could be included in the calculation of damages for loss of earnings and compulsory contributions payable in a pension scheme under the contract of employment were not part of the employee's disposable income. Parker and Woolf LJJ, on the other hand, reasoned that the pension contributions were different in kind from wages received, being payments to secure future benefits and therefore were not lost if for any reason they were not paid. They were all agreed, however, that any resulting diminution in pension rights might be recoverable. The reasoning of the majority seems preferable to that of the Master of the Rolls because it avoids the unreasonable consequence (adverted to by Lord Reid in *Parry v Cleaver* [1970] AC 1 at 14) of making the contributions deductible where it is a term of the contract but not deductible where it is a voluntary contribution.

The decision does, however, leave open a number of conundrums. For example, what is the position of other contributions (eg to a charity or trade union) which the employee is contractually bound to make? And what about insurance premiums? Presumably, the correct approach now would be to compensate for any reduction in the value of the benefit, but not to give any credit for contributions or premiums not payable as a result of the accident (see Woolf LJ at 782).

Section 2(1) of the Law Reform (Personal Injuries) Act 1948, requires certain deductions to be made in respect of national insurance benefits 'against any loss of earnings or profits which has accrued or probably will accrue to the injured person from the injuries'. In *Foster v Tyne and Wear County Council* [1986] 1 All ER 567, the Court of Appeal, held that this provision applies in cases where the damages are assessed on the basis of loss of earning capacity as distinct from loss of future earnings. It has often been said that there is no real distinction between these two heads of damage, and that 'hardship in the labour market' can be subsumed under 'loss of prospective earnings'. The Court did not decide on the dispute about the juristic character of these heads of damages, but was content to say that the case fell within s 2(1) because 'without a prospective loss of earnings there would not, normally, at any rate, by any loss of earning capacity'.

Town and Country Planning

PAUL B FAIREST, MA, LLM
Professor of Law, University of Hull

Only two cases concerning Town and Country Planning appear in the 1986 All England Law Reports. Neither is concerned with fundamental planning issues, such as the definition of 'development', or the validity of planning conditions. Both cases, however, show some interesting features concerning enforcement law and practice.

Injunctions in support of the planning process

When can a local planning authority have recourse to injunctive remedies to restrain breaches of planning control? This was the issue in *Runnymede Borough Council v Ball and others* [1986] 1 All ER 629. Part V of the Town and Country Planning Act 1971 contains a detailed code for the enforcement of planning control. To what extent must a local planning authority exhaust its criminal remedies under this part of the Act before subjecting an offending developer to the more drastic penalties of the civil law, especially punishment for contempt of court?

Section 222 of the Local Government Act 1972 allows a local authority which considers it 'expedient for the promotion or protection of the interests of inhabitants of their area ... to institute [civil proceedings] in their own name'. The section thus dispenses with the previous need (in most cases) to obtain the Attorney-General's *fiat* to a relator action, which had acted as a filter to prevent inappropriate applications (see Sir Roger Ormrod at 639). The judiciary is properly concerned to see that this power is not misused, but the Court of Appeal was of opinion that the trial judge in the instant case had unduly restricted the ambit of injunctive relief, when he refused the council's application for this remedy.

The case concerned the activities of Ball, a landowner at Egham, in Surrey, within the Green Belt, who had begun to develop his land as a gipsy site. The co-defendants, who were equitable co-owners, were caravan-owners who proposed to occupy sites on the land. The first defendant's activities first came to the attention of the plaintiff council in September 1984. He was duly served with several enforcement notices (which he substantially disregarded) and three stop notices (which were also ignored). A summons was served on Mr Stevens (who appears in the narrative at various times as a bulldozer-driver and a shoveller of ballast) in respect of certain offences under the stop-notices. Before the date on which this summons was returnable, the council decided on more drastic action, and interlocutory injunctions were obtained from Vinelott J, together with an undertaking from the first defendant. Shortly thereafter, the council applied to His Honour Judge Blackett-Ord VC (sitting as a judge of the High Court in the Chancery Division) on a substantive motion for an injunction. The judge decided, as a matter of law, that the council did not bring itself within the principles justifying the exceptional grant of an injunction when statute provided for a criminal penalty for infringement of the law.

The council's appeal to the Court of Appeal was successful, and the injunctions were granted. In the view of the Court of Appeal, the trial judge had misdirected himself on the law, in holding that injunctive relief was only available in such cases where there was 'inadequacy of penalties' or 'deliberate and flagrant flouting of the law'.

On the facts of Balls's case, it could hardly be alleged that the penalties were inadequate, since the Town and Country Planning Act allows substantial fines to be imposed. It was thus quite different from the situation which had been considered by the House of Lords in *Stoke-on-Trent City Council v B & Q Retail Ltd* [1984] 2 All ER 332, a 'Sunday-trading' case, where the maximum fine on conviction has been judicially described as 'chicken feed'.

Sir Roger Ormrod was prepared to find, on the facts, that there had been a 'deliberate and flagrant flouting of the law'. He thought, however, that to require such conduct as a necessary condition for the grant of injunctive relief was mistaken. The notion that such conduct was essential was, in his view, a misunderstanding of certain remarks of Oliver J and Bridge LJ in *Stafford BC v Elkenford Ltd* [1977] 2 All ER 519. Although the 'deliberate and flagrant flouting of the law' test had formed the basis of Lord Fraser's speech in the *B & Q* case, it was not the ratio of the decision of the House of Lords, which the Court of Appeal believed to be found in Lord Templeman's speech, which was less restrictive.

What, then, is required? Clearly, something 'more than infringement' is required. Purchas LJ was unwilling to restrict the right to injunctive relief to any 'particular class or classes of infringement' and was prepared to leave the matter to the 'facts of the particular case' (at 637h). The key to his judgment may lie in the fact that, in the absence of injunctive relief, the defendants might have been able to present the local council with a fait accompli (at 636).

The basis of the decision may also be that in the circumstances of the case the Town and Country Planning Act enforcement procedure would simply be too slow. The possibilities for appeal against enforcement notices are, rightly, considerable; in criminal proceedings for breach of a stop notice, the validity of the stop notice itself can be challenged (see *R v Jenner* [1983] 2 All ER 46, noted in All ER Rev 1983, p 349). Given the importance to the public of the preservation of the Green Belt near London, the circumstances of the case were sufficient to justify recourse to civil remedies without first exhausting the processes of the criminal law (per Fox LJ at 634). A further discussion of the issues involved in this case will be found in an excellent note in the Cambridge Law Journal by Stephen Tromans (see [1986] CLJ 374–7). He contrasts the approach of the Court of Appeal in the instant case, where it seems to be assumed that special circumstances must exist to justify the grant of injunctive relief, with the approach to the Attorney-General's applications for relief, where the assumption seems to have been that relief should only be refused in exceptional circumstances.

Demolition of listed buildings—mens rea

Section 55 of the Town and Country Planning Act makes it an offence to 'execute . . . any works for the demolition of a listed building or for its alteration or extension', save where such works are authorised. Is this a strict liability offence, or is it necessary for the prosecution to show that the defendant knew that the building was a 'listed building'? This was the issue which came before the Queen's Bench Divisional Court (Watkins LJ and Sir Roger Ormrod) in *R v Wells Street Metropolitan Stipendiary Magistrate and another, ex p Westminster City Council* [1986] 3 All ER 4. The Divisional Court held the offence to be one of strict liability.

The case sounds like a bizarre example of misunderstood instructions. One Brian Martin, of a firm rejoicing in the unlikely title of Amazing Grates, was found removing various articles including chimney pieces, panelled doors, and staircase balustrading from a building in Wimpole Street, London. The building in question was a Grade II listed building. Martin, with a colleague called Hopkins (who has since left the country for the Antipodes) had been instructed by the Wimpole Street Clinic Ltd, the head lessees of the premises, to 'remove everything of value'. This was being done because the premises had stood empty for some time, and security had been compromised when 'the Fire Brigade smashed virtually every door' when attending a fire. The misunderstanding lay in the assumption that the Wimpole Street Clinic wanted fixtures and fittings removed, as well as the furniture left on the premises.

The council laid informations alleging a breach of s 55(1) of the Act against Hopkins, Martin, and Livesey (a director of Wimpole Street Clinic Ltd). Hopkins went down under, and Livesey was discharged because the magistrate took the view that there was no evidence that he caused the alterations to the listed buildings. Hence, only Martin was left; since there was no evidence that Martin knew the building was listed, and since (in his view) the s 55(1) offence required proof of mens rea, the magistrate acquitted Martin.

The council appealed to the Divisional Court, seeking a declaration that the s 55(1) offence was one of strict liability, and orders of certiorari and mandamus against the magistrate.

The issue was thus the simple one of the nature of the offence under s 55(1). Was it a crime of strict liability, as Westminster City Council contended, or an offence involving mens rea, as Martin contended?

Curiously, this exact point had never previously come up for decision, although the offence of tree destruction (in s 102 of the Act) had been held to be strict (see *Maidstone BC v Mortimer* [1980] 3 All ER 552.) Tree destruction, though, is less heavily punishable. The s 55(1) offence is punishable by imprisonment (see s 55(5)). This might have been a factor which would lead to an assumption that mens rea was required, since it is generally thought that the level of punishment is a factor which a court should take into account in deciding whether an offence is strict. It is however, recognised that offences punishable by imprisonment may be strict liability offences, as for example under the Hallmarking Act 1973 (see *Chilvers v Rayner* [1984] 1 All ER 843; for matters affecting the environment, see *Alphacell Ltd v Woodward* [1972] AC 824).

The Divisional Court accepted the test enunciated by Lord Scarman in the opinion of the Privy Council in *Gammon (Hong Kong) Ltd v Attorney-General of Hong Kong* [1984] 2 All ER 503. This test consists of five propositions:

> '(1) there is a presumption of law that mens rea is required before a person can be guilty of a criminal offence; (2) the presumption is particularly strong where the offence is "truly criminal" in character; (3) the presumption applies to statutory offences, and can be displaced only if this is clearly or by necessary implication the effect of the statute; (4) the only situation in which the presumption can be displaced is where the statute is concerned with an issue of social concern, and public safety is such an issue; (5) even where a statute is concerned with such an issue, the presumption of mens rea stands unless it can also be shown that the creation of strict liability will be effective to promote the objects of the statute by encouraging greater vigilance to prevent the commission of the prohibited act.' ([1984] 2 All ER at 508)

The Divisional Court was clearly prepared to regard the preservation of listed buildings as 'an issue of social concern', so as to bring the offence within the fourth test in Lord Scarman's list. A finding that the offence was one of strict liability would be effective to promote the objects of the statute by encouraging greater vigilance to prevent breaches. The fear of oppressive proceedings was dismissed by reference to that hoary old chestnut, the 'discretion to prosecute . . .'

Accordingly, in the result, the decision of the magistrate was quashed, and the matter was remitted to him to decide whether the evidence was sufficient to commit Martin for trial.